THE BEST

Robert F. Strauss

2005 THE BEST

UNIQUE NEW STATISTICS THAT COMPARE AND RANK THE BEST BATTERS IN BASEBALL HISTORY

Robert F. Strauss

FIRST EDITION

Beaver's Pond Press, Inc.
Edina, Minnesota

Total Offensive Production (TOP)™, Total Net Bases (TNB)™, Total Run Production (TRP)™, Total Base Average (TBA)™ and Run Production Average (RPA)™ are service marks of SportStats LLC, and cannot be used without its permission. Application for registration of these marks has been filed with the U.S. Patent and Trademark Office.

Babe Ruth & Ted Williams cover photos used with permission from the National Baseball Hall of Fame library, Cooperstown, NY. All rights reserved.

Mickey Mantle cover photo used with permission
from the George Brace Photo Collection. All rights reserved.

Barry Bonds cover photo by Don Smith, used with permission
from Getty Images. All rights reserved.

Cover and interior design by Mori Studio

ISBN 13: 978-1-59298-095-6
ISBN 10: 1-59298-095-3

Library of Congress Catalog Number: 2005920134

Printed in the United States of America

Preview Edition: February 2005
First Printing: March 2005

09 08 07 06 05   5 4 3 2 1

Beaver's Pond Press, Inc.

7104 Ohms Lane, Suite 216
Edina, MN 55439–2129
(952) 829-8818
www.beaverspondpress.com

to order, visit www.BookHouseFulfillment.com
or call 1-800-901-3480. Reseller discounts available.

This book is dedicated to my sons

Alex and David Strauss

The future belongs to those who will participate in its creation.

To my wife

Marcy Sangor Strauss

You are loved

CONTENTS

APPENDICES

ACKNOWLEDGEMENTS

This book is the product of years of thought and research. It is also the product of many minds that helped me formulate and complete a book of this magnitude.

Years ago, when my boys were in Little League, I was looking for new statistics that would better reflect how they had performed. Discussion with coaches and parents led to simple numbers that were the basis for the new statistics in this book. They are on the plaques that adorn one of my son's walls.

Starting in 2001, I began to write this book and compute the total offensive production statistics for players in the Hall of Fame and the greatest players of the day from sources too numerous to mention. I was spurred on in this endeavor by my sons, Alex and David, and my wife, Marcy. Each has taken the time to review and edit this book in turn, and to challenge my assumptions. Each has added great value to this project. Alex is responsible for a change to one statistical formula that makes it more accurate and comparable between baseball's eras. David is responsible for a substantial portion of the cover design. And Marcy has been a constant source of editorial comment, marketing assistance and much needed encouragement. My thanks to Marcy, Alex and David is beyond measure. I love you all.

I would also like to thank a number of members of Halsey Hall, Minnesota, Chapter of SABR (Society for American Baseball Research) who have reviewed this book, critiqued its statistics, and assisted in bringing this book to market. In particular, Tom Tuttle, Bob Tholkes and anonymous reviewers have helped me immensely. You have my deepest appreciation.

Finally, I would like to thank Milt Adams and all the people at Beaver Pond Press, Mori Studio and Book House Fulfillment for helping an amateur bring his first book to press. I hope the results are what you envisioned.

—Robert F. Strauss
February 16, 2005

INTRODUCTION

I have always had a fascination with baseball statistics. Checking the numbers associated with baseball and its players, particularly batting statistics, was and remains a ritual. How are my favorite players doing? Who hit the most home runs? Who is leading for the batting championship? Who has the most RBIs? Equally important in this analysis of statistics is the question of who should have won the MVP award? Who really was the best player of the year, or the decade, or in all of baseball history? That wonder does not subside with age.

With age, however, comes insight. The great players remembered from my youth were not always the best players, even when compared with their peers. Statistics can be misleading, and I have always wanted to know who really was the best. As I have compared the statistics of many great players, several types of questions have haunted me:

1. Are the recent great seasons of Barry Bonds, Alex Rodriguez, Sammy Sosa or Todd Helton as amazing as those of Willie Mays, Mickey Mantle or Hank Aaron, or even those of Babe Ruth, Lou Gehrig or Jimmy Foxx?

2. Would the lifetime achievements of Ted Williams, Hank Greenberg and Joe DiMaggio have been on a par with the greats like Aaron or Ruth if they had not lost prime baseball years to WWII and the Korean Conflict?

3. Can you compare the shortened career of Mickey Mantle or Lou Gehrig to the long careers of Ty Cobb or Hank Aaron?

4. How do the fabulous career of Sam Thompson, Ed Delahanty, Dan Brouthers and others in the 1880's and 1890's compare with those of Ty Cobb and Honus Wagner of the dead ball era, or Rogers Hornsby and Al Simmons of the 1920's and 1930's, or Frank Robinson and Duke Snider of the 1950's and 1960's?

5. How do players of the pumped up 90's and today compare to the greats of all of these eras, and have we entered a new golden age of baseball?

To address these questions, I needed first to determine the criteria on which to judge great offensive baseball players. I needed to determine what statistics should be used to measure the greatness of players from any age: to objectively determine who is **The Best**. I have therefore compiled four new statistics, factual and accurate, on which to rate batters throughout modern baseball history. These statistics, and the ratings of each player based on them, have then been combined into a single offensive production statistic upon which players of any era can be rated and ranked.

With these statistics in hand, this book answers one of the great questions haunting baseball history. It determines the basis on which we should measure baseball players. This book then compiles the statistics of the greatest baseball players of the last 120 years, compares them, and rates them by their batting records. To do this is much more than comparing lifetime statistics. Statistics of any sort can distort and deceive. The statistics used today are each deficient in one or more ways. This book determines the correct way to use the actual numbers of each player to determine batting prowess, and uses them to rank the greatest players against each other for overall hitting greatness.

CHAPTER 1

Looking for the Greatest Offensive Players

It is difficult to measure the offensive greatness of any player based on his statistics. It is even more difficult to measure the greatness of a player from other perspectives.

Defensive capability has its own statistics and its own limitations. How were errors scored from decade to decade? Where do the limitations of one fielder result in a hit, whereas a better fielder might get a glove on the ball and be charged with an error? Great defense at a key position such as shortstop or catcher may yield more benefit to a team than at third base; and the center fielder may be more beneficial to his team from a defensive perspective than the right fielder.

Additional strengths of a player as a team leader, or team clown, can greatly benefit the right team at the right time. Training new recruits to be better players, helping a teammate through a slump, or adding emotion and passion to the game all improve the performance of a team and help show the worth of a player. Three runs-batted-in (RBIs) in the seventh inning of an unimportant game when the team is down by 10 runs count the same as three RBIs in the first inning of a key game, or in the bottom of the ninth when down by two. They actually are not. Statistics can never take the place of human judgment in defining the real worth of a player to a team. Yet, statistics are the primary measurement upon which we must judge baseball players. Everything else is so subjective as to make true comparison of players impossible.

The measurement of defensive and/or leadership skills in combination with batting prowess in this book would be counter-productive. The statistical analysis I recommend to judge hitters will be controversial. To add other, subjective, determinations would only muddle the analysis, and avoid discussion on the statistical qualities that should be considered in rating hitters. As a result, this book will only look at the ability of a batter to help his team, as that team is situated, with his bat.

In looking for the greatest offensive players of the game, we need to understand what is truly important. Home runs are important. Batting average is important. Walks are important. But each statistic is, by its nature, only one piece of the puzzle.

Baseball is a team sport, and the results of individual statistics, to be truly important, must result in the greatest benefit to the team.

The ability of a player to help his team to win games (whether the team is good or bad) is the most important talent a player can have. The ability of a team to win is dependent upon the ability of its batters to create runs. Yet any true comparison must recognize the advantages a great team gives to a good player. A player should not be judged better solely because of a single number, say scoring 180 runs in a season, when he has three batters behind him who batted .350 and who each hit 50 home runs that year. An individual player's greatness must be measured by statistics that take all factors into account to the greatest extent possible. To explore and determine the best statistics, we must first determine the benefits and limitations of the current statistics used in baseball.

Baseball, more than any other sport, is known for its statistics. Today, we keep statistics on everything, including how a batter hits at night on artificial turf against right handed pitchers throwing curveballs low and away on a 2 and 1 count. Statistics may be interesting, and may be useful (i.e. in pitching to him at night with a 2:1 count). However, if statistics are to be used to rate and rank players, they must show more than simply how a player performed. They must give the best possible indication of how that player would perform for another team under different circumstances. Most of the key statistics used in baseball today fail to fully take these criteria into account. If the key element of great batters is their ability to participate in the creation of runs for their team, then the statistics of today fail to do this. A short analysis of current statistics and their limitations is illustrative.

1. **Batting Average.** The batting average (BA) predicts how many hits a batter will get for each given number of official at-bats. In determining the total value of a batter to his team, however, it fails to take several key elements of the game into account. A player with a .400 batting average, but only 300 at-bats for the season, may not be as productive as a batter hitting .350 over 600 at bats. And yet a player may hit .350 over 600 at-bats, but yield only 50 runs and 50 RBIs. Such production is unworthy of a great hitter, and the batting average fails to measure the success of that average to the team.

2. **Runs Batted In.** Runs-Batted-In (RBIs) generally indicates how well a player can hit with runners on base, and how well he can hit for extra bases, allowing runners to score from first or second base. Home run hitters, of course, get a RBI for the run they score. All this is important, but it only records one portion of the ability of a batter to create runs. Runs scored is the other category. This statistic further fails to account for the frequency of the RBIs. 150 RBIs in 400 at-bats shows a better ball player than 150 RBIs

in 600 at-bats. The number is also limited because of the effect teammates have on attaining it. Lou Gehrig achieved a tremendous number of RBIs in part because of the fact that he batted behind Babe Ruth and an illustrious Yankee team for many years. RBIs is therefore both an incomplete statistic and one that fails to consider the relative frequency of this achievement

3. **Runs.** Runs scored as a statistic has the same benefits and drawbacks as RBIs. Combining Runs and RBIs into a single statistic resolves the first objective, and should be a more complete statistic than the components individually. This combined number constitutes the first new statistic recommended by this book, the **Total Run Production**™ or **TRP** of a player. Of course, the ability to score the most Runs in the fewest chances needs to be measured and factored into any comparison of great hitters. The new **Run Production Average**™ or **RPA** statistic of this book computes that ability.

4. **Slugging Average.** The slugging average (SLG) takes into account the batting average and extra bases hit by a player, resulting in an average of the "total bases" of a batter over his official at-bats. Among the generally accepted statistics of today, slugging average is perhaps the most reliable in predicting offensive batting success. As an average, however, this statistic fails to take the daily participation of a player into account (one of the same faults as the batting average). A .700 slugging average over 300 at-bats is usually not as productive for the team over a season as the same average over 600 at-bats. As with the batting average, the slugging average further fails to take total batting opportunities into account. A player with a .600 slugging average over 500 at-bats with 100 walks may be substantially better for his team than a player with a .600 slugging average over 550 at-bats with only 50 walks. Assuming a .300 BA, the first player would have been on base 35 times more than the second. Slugging average also fails to take into account the Runs and RBIs created by the bases gained. Walking with the bases loaded may be better than a triple with the bases empty.

5. **On Base Percentage.** The on-base percentage (OBP) measures the ability of a player to reach base, primarily by hit or walk, over the total number of official plate appearances of the batter. This recognizes that the batter has not made an out, allowing other players on his team to score

him or others he may have advanced. This statistic, however, treats a walk as equivalent to a home run. One could have an OBP of .400 averaging 3 double plays and 2 walks every 5 plate appearances. Another player could have the same OBP for hitting 40 home runs in 100 at bats, and a third for batting .250 without power and walking 120 times over 600 plate appearances during the season. And as with all averages (including BA and SLG), the OBP fails to determine the benefit of that average to the team. There is no ability to tell how many Runs or RBIs that OBP has created.

6. **OBP + SLG.** Some modern analysts include a statistic adding the OBP and SLG for a single number that is to take all offensive numbers into account. This particular number, however, fails in several respects. In particular, it includes hits and at-bats twice while including walks, HBP (hit-by-pitch) and their plate appearances only once. This type of statistic, including all bases earned by a batter over all plate appearances, gives us some insight into the statistics that are important and should be used. I have therefore compiled statistics recognizing **Total Net Bases**™ or **TNB** and a **Total Base Average**™ or **TBA** to recognize all bases obtained by a player and their frequency to allow for the true comparison of offensive production between batters.

In the search for statistics that will allow for the meaningful comparative measurement of hitters, we need to go beyond current statistics to a set of numbers that will meet the following criteria:

1. The statistics must recognize the productivity of the player in both Runs and RBIs. This number, however, cannot be used as the exclusive statistic because of the help or hindrance teammates might give, and the need to understand the frequency of such run productivity.

2. The statistics must recognize both the power of the batter and his ability to get on base, truly crediting a player for all bases achieved and lost. Bases achieved by walks, hit-by-pitch, and stolen bases should be included while bases lost to being caught stealing should be subtracted. Again, this number cannot be the exclusive measure of a player because of the need to recognize the ability of a player to produce Runs and RBIs.

3. The statistics must take into account all batting opportunities of a player, recognizing that a player should be available to help his team as frequently as possible (hopefully for the entire season), and that getting on base,

whether by a hit or a walk, adds to the opportunities afforded the team to score. Those batting opportunities of the team should include HBP (being hit by a pitch) and SF (sacrifice flies), both currently being used in determining official plate appearances, and opportunities lost by grounding into a double play (GDP) which is not.

4. The statistics must allow for a reasonable comparison between players of different eras, even though complete statistics may not be available. It must be noted that differences in baseball rules may also limit comparability. While such comparisons may not be perfect, they should allow the relative ranking of all players.

If the purpose of a batter, for the benefit of his team, is to assist in creating runs, then the most meaningful statistic for comparative purposes would appear to be the total number of Runs scored and Runs-Batted-In (RBI) by a player, his **Total Run Production (TRP)**™. This statistic combines the two critical categories of run creation into a single number that easily allows for the comparison of players for any season or career.

As noted in Chapter 2, the Total Run Production of a player may not reflect the total worth of that batter because of the number of chances given to that player, (i.e. his total number of batting opportunities in a season or the total seasons played in a career). To compensate for this limitation, an additional statistic to be used should be the average number of Runs scored and RBIs by a player per batting opportunity; the player's **Run Production Average (RPA)**™. Excluding other factors, this one statistic should predict the number of runs a player can produce for a team over any given period of time.

Either of these statistics, the TRP or RPA, may be inflated or reduced because of the quality of the teammates with which the batter plays. A mediocre player on a great team may well compile more Runs and RBIs than a great player on a poor team, in total or on average. As a result, we must also use statistics that are predictive of run production, but based solely on the skills of the player.

Batting average, slugging average and on-base percentage are all indicators of run production. As noted in Chapter 2, however, each of these statistics is flawed in some way. More important, each reports only one portion of a total picture. A higher on-base percentage predicts the scoring of more Runs. A higher slugging average predicts greater Runs-Batted-In. Combining these statistics in a meaningful way is the best method to register the total ability of a player to produce the most runs for his team. The **Total Base Average (TBA)**™ of a player, showing the average total net bases produced by a batter per batting opportunity should be the best measure of this combined ability to produce Runs and RBIs. This is substantially more accurate than the OBP+SLG because it includes all net bases and factors them on an equal basis (OBP+SLG does not).

The RPA and the TBA, as statistical averages, have an additional limitation in failing to show the total period over which the average was computed. A player with few batting opportunities may look good on the basis of his Run Production Average, but fail to help his team due to the lack of adequate total runs produced. A similar result may occur with a high TBA. As a result, the **Total Net Bases (TNB)**™ of a player must be used to show the ability of a player to create Runs and RBIs for any team under any circumstance over a season or a career.

While every piece of information is useful, no one statistic is perfect. A combination of these improved statistics must be used to rate and rank offensive baseball players. The equal weighting of these four statistics—Total Run Production (TRP), Run Production Average (RPA), Total Net Bases (TNB) and Total Base Average (TBA)—should be used to compile a complete measure of a player's hitting capability. To be the best, a batter must position himself to produce runs through his total combined net bases, actually create the largest number of runs, and perform each of these feats at a prodigious rate per batting opportunity. In ranking batters in this book, each of these four statistics is rated against the highest total for any player in that category and given a 25% weight. The total of these ratings is then used to compute the rating of each player in a single statistic: **Total Offensive Production (TOP)**™. The statistics are defined as follows:

Total Run Production (TRP)™. The total of all Runs scored by the player plus all Runs-Batted-In by the player for the period over which the statistic is determined (i.e., a season, 5 year period or career).

Run Production Average (RPA)™. This average is the Total Run Production (TRP) of a player divided by his total batting opportunities (defined below).

Total Net Bases (TNB)™. This is a single number combining total bases as used for the determination of a player's slugging average (single =1, double =2, triple =3, and home run=4) plus the bases used for a player's on-base-percentage (walks, times hit by a pitch (HBP) and sacrifice flys (SF). To these numbers must be added the other bases created by a player and those reduced by the player. Total Net Bases therefore also adds a base for each stolen base and reduces the total for each time the player is caught stealing.

Total Base Average (TBA)™. This average is the Total Net Bases (TNB) of a player divided by his total batting opportunities (defined below).

Batting Opportunities. This is the same as plate appearances used today for computing a player's on-base-percentage, but adding one batting opportunity for each at-bat lost to the team due to hitting into a double play. It therefore includes (i) official at-bats; (ii) walks, HBP and SF (included in official plate appearances); and (iii) one additional batting opportunity for each time the player grounds into a double play (GDP).

Total Offensive Production (TOP)™. This is a combination of the relative ratings for the four individual statistics (TRP, RPA, TNB and TBA). Each player is ranked with all others for the same category and given a relative rating for that statistic based on the highest number in that category. The highest rating for a player in each category would be 100.00, and each player with a lesser statistic would be given a rating based upon his percentage of that number. If, for instance, the highest TRP for a season was 360, that player would have a 100.00 TRP rating. A player with a TRP of 270 would have a TRP rating of 75.00 (270/360). The combination of these four ratings is the TOP Rating of the player, adjusted to produce a 100.00 for the highest player and lower ratings for all others. By combining the best statistics available, statistics that cover all factors for batting prowess, the Total Offensive Production (TOP) of a player should allow each player to be judged against his peers on a fair and equal basis.

The rules of baseball, both written and unwritten, affect the ability of players of each era to be compared to those of other eras. To understand this, some of the changes to key baseball rules over time are summarized here:

Bats: The baseball bat was allowed to have one flat side and be 2½ inches in diameter from 1885–1892. The bat was required to be round and increased to 2¾ inches in diameter from 1895–present.

Strikes: Foul ball caught on bounce is no longer an out since 1883

3 strikes for a strikeout through 1886

4 strikes for a strikeout in 1887 (first called strike not counted)

3 strikes for a strikeout 1888-present

Strike first counted on foul bunt 1894

Strike first counted on foul tip 1895

Strike first counted on foul ball 1901 (National League)

Strike first counted on foul ball 1903 (American League)

Bunt on third strike is an out 1909–present

Strike Zone: Strike zone from top of shoulder to bottom of knee 1887–1949

Strike zone from armpits to top of knee 1950–1962

Strike zone from top of shoulder to bottom of knee 1963–1968

Strike zone from armpits to top of knee 1969–1987

Strike zone from mid-point between top of shoulder and top of uniform pants to the bottom of knees 1988–1995

Strike zone from mid-point between top of shoulder and top of uniform pants to the top of knees 1995–present

Balls & Walks: 8 balls for a walk 1880–1881

7 balls for a walk 1882–1883

6 balls for a walk 1884–1885

5 balls for a walk 1886–1888

4 balls for a walk 1889–present

Base on balls not recorded as a hit or at bat from 1888–present
Hit-by-pitch does not gain base if on hand or forearm 1892-1896. Current hit-by-pitch rule was adopted in 1897

Baseballs: Spitball and unorthodox ("freak pitch") deliveries banned beginning in 1920 (Each team was allowed 2 players 'grandfathered' in for career.)

17 spitball pitchers were named in 1921 for career. The last legal spitball pitcher retired in 1935.)

New, clean ball substituted regularly 1919, fully adopted in 1920

Pitchers not allowed to scuff ball before pitch, 1919-present

Pitchers not allowed to carry substances to doctor the ball since 1975

Pitches: Pitcher's arm not allowed above hip through 1883

Pitcher's arm not allowed above shoulder 1884-1886

Batters able to call for high or low pitch through 1886

Overhand pitching anywhere in the strike zone 1887-present

Pitcher's mound: 45 feet from the plate through 1878

50 feet from the plate 1879–1892

60 feet 6 inches from the plate 1893–present

Rubber introduced (vs. pitcher's box) 1893

Mound limited to 15 inches above field 1904–1968

Mound limited to 10 inches above the filed 1969–present

Stolen Bases: Stolen base counted for taking extra base on hit (i.e. taking second from first on a single) 1886–1897

Frivolous ninth inning uncontested steals discarded since 1920

Official Statistics: Stolen bases became an official statistic in 1887.

Strikeouts were not kept in the NL from 1897–1909

Strikeouts were not kept in the AL from 1901–1912

Runs-Batted-In was not an official statistic until 1920

Times caught stealing were not kept until about 1912, and irregularly until 1920

GDP (grounding into a double play) has been tracked since 1939

Sacrifice fly rules have changed from time to time, and were not kept until around 1954

Other Rules: Unlimited substitutions end 1891

Ground rule double for hit over fence less than 210 feet in 1888 (235 feet in 1892) (250 feet in 1926)

Infield fly rule adopted 1895

Sacrifice fly rule adopted 1908, but changed several times since

Home plate becomes five sided from a 12 inch square 1900
Minimum home run distance of 250 feet adopted 1925

Minimum home run distance of 325 feet adopted 1959

Players required to remove gloves and equipment from field 1954

Designated hitter rule for American League started 1973

Balls leaving the park are fair (home run) or foul based on when last seen by the umpire until 1931, when the determination is to be made at the spot the ball leaves the field

Conclusions:

1. Because of the huge differences in many rules, including the distance to the plate, the bat, walks, strikeouts, and the type of pitching allowed, no statistics before the mid-1880's are comparable to those for players after that date. Establishing the mound 60' 6" from a rubber to the mound and eliminating the flat bat make 1893 the year baseball and its statistics became truly comparable. Unfortunately, many great players have careers spanning the 1880's through the early nineteenth century. It is difficult to

determine what should be left out of their career statistics. I have included players and statistics from the 1880's and early 1890's in this book, and rated them on the same basis as modern players. While this is not accurate, to leave them out would be unfair as well. Every fan must individually judge of how these 19th century batters should be compared with players of the 20th and 21st centuries.

2. The change in the nature of the baseball pitching in 1919 and 1920 created the power hitter. This was the end of the dead ball era. The elimination of scuffed balls, spitball pitches and similar practices allowed the pitched ball to be seen and hit. The use of a more tightly wound and better built ball, and a ball that was substituted regularly, resulted in the batter hitting a solid (rather than a soggy) ball, created home runs and a different type of baseball than had existed before. The ball has been 'juiced' at times since, but the statistics of players in the dead ball era through 1919 will always be much different from those that came after that time. It is the right of every baseball fan to determine what might have been if Joe Jackson or Honus Wagner had played in the 1920's and 1930's.

3. Statistics on times caught stealing, grounding into a double play and sacrifice flies were not kept at all until the 1910's (caught stealing), around 1940 (GDP), and 1954 (sacrifice flies). Earlier statistics may be inaccurate or non-existent. These statistical changes give a small advantage to older players by failing to reduce their total bases or increase their batting opportunities for these items.

4. Statistics for players in the 1880's and 1890's have been recomputed in recent years with differences between statistical services. They should be viewed with caution. In addition, the lack of RBIs as an official statistic until 1920 means that the numbers given for players before that date are unofficial, and can vary from source to source.

Sources: *National Baseball Hall of Fame, The Baseball Encyclopedia*, Macmillan Publishing, 1974, *Jim Evans Official Baseball Rules Annotated*, 2004, *Baseball-Almanac.com*, 2004

Hank Aaron hit 755 lifetime home runs. Pete Rose had 4,256 lifetime hits. Both are amazing records, but not necessarily the results you would first look for in the star player you would want for this season. Roy Campanella was a great catcher, whose statistics for 1951, 1953 and 1955 were among the best in baseball and earned him three MVP awards. Yet, would he be the player of choice for his team in 1952, 1954 or 1956? In 1961, Roger Maris had an unbelievable year, combining for 274 Runs and RBIs along with 61 home runs, both league leading totals. That same year, a young Norm Cash batted a league leading .361 with a league leading 193 hits, combining for 251 Runs and a .662 Slugging Average. But neither player came close to those numbers in their playing years before or after.

With the recent $250 million 10 year contract for Alex Rodriguez, the importance of being a great player over a period of ten consecutive years must be recognized. A great player, perhaps the greatest player, is one who can do all things very well for at least 10 consecutive years. To look at **Total Offensive Production** for a ten consecutive year period (or perhaps a 5 consecutive year period) helps to equalize players who may have had poor starts or finishes to their careers. Comparing equivalent periods of time should help avoid debates such as the lost productivity of pitching years on Babe Ruth, the injury years of Mickey Mantle and the war years of Ted Williams when compared to the long and full careers of Ty Cobb, Hank Aaron and Eddie Murray.

Unfortunately, injury has limited the ability of many, perhaps most, great players to have ten consecutive excellent years. Even the best players have had bad seasons. Babe Ruth had abdominal surgery, a divorce and suspension in 1925, missing over 50 games. Hank Greenberg had a broken wrist in 1936, playing only 12 games. George Sisler missed all of the 1923 season due to illness. A broken foot and bad knees limited Mickey Mantle to only 65 games in 1963. More recently, Ken Griffey, Jr., Frank Thomas, Juan Gonzalez, and Manny Ramirez have all missed parts of seasons due to injuries. Those batters who have had the luxury of health and skill for ten consecutive prime years of play will have better TOP ratings and rankings for this period than other players who were not so lucky. No exceptions have been made except for years missed on account of military service.

For the players noted above and others, ten consecutive years may not tell the whole story. Measuring hitters over 5 consecutive years provides a similar, if shorter, comparison of great players in their prime.

Career statistics for any player are comparable when averages are used, but become skewed when total bases, RBIs or home runs are recorded. 2,295 runs scored by Rickey Henderson in 13,488 batting opportunities is less impressive that 1,888 runs scored by Lou Gehrig when it is realized that this was accomplished in only 9,557 batting opportunities. Measuring players based upon an equal number of batting opportunities allows for the true comparison of their skills rather than their longevity. All great players' careers are therefore rated and ranked on an equalized basis of 10,000 batting opportunities (and 10,000 official at-bats as an alternative). Their TOP ratings may surprise you.

Based upon the statistics available through 2004, many of today's best ball players rank among the elites of the game. 13 of the 50 best players, when compared for their best 10 consecutive year TOP statistical ratings, belong to active players, as do 15 of the 50 best 5 consecutive year TOP ratings. In lifetime statistics adjusted to 10,000 batting opportunities, 15 of the top 50 TOP ratings belong to active players. Here. however, it must be noted that the great players of today may not fare as well in the long run. It is generally recognized that the greatest years of a player are his early years, and those at the end of a career tend to reduce his averages. The excellence of a Manny Ramirez, Alex Rodriguez, or even a Barry Bonds will tend to diminish at the end of an illustrious career. The new careers of Todd Helton, Albert Pujols, and Vladimir Guerrero have yet to be fully tested at all, and should be considered glimpses at what might be.

As a lover of statistics, I also felt it was important to compare players for their best single season efforts, their best five consecutive year efforts, and their best ten consecutive years as well as over their full careers—actual and adjusted. Each is worthy of review, and each will allow fans to continue the debate of who is really **The Best**. So let us see what the numbers say about our heroes and the greatness of baseball legends.

Players' careers are usually measured by career totals. But these statistics provide an unfair advantage to players who have reached milestone plateaus such as 3000 hits or 500 home runs through longevity alone. Looking at total career numbers, one might assume that Hank Aaron or Rickey Henderson would be near the top. In reality, the last few years of a player's career do little that shows the greatness of the player in his prime. To truly compare the ability of baseball's best players, we need to determine how they would do in similar circumstances. This requires that the **Total Offensive Production (TOP)**™ of a player must be determined over an equal period.

Because total batting opportunities shows the total use of team resources (its opportunities to score) by a player, players are most comparable when analyzed over the same number of batting opportunities. In this manner, players who have had long careers are not favored when looking for the best projection for an average season or a clutch situation. While adjusting the number of batting opportunities or at-bats will not change the averages of a player (his **Run Production Average (RPA)**™ or **Total Base Average (TBA)**™), it will dramatically change the **Total Run Production (TRP)**™ and **Total Net Bases (TNB)**™ for that player. On this basis, using our key statistics and ratings, the TOP career statistics have been compiled for the greatest players in baseball history using three alternative computations:

1. TOP statistics, ratings and rankings based on 10,000 career batting opportunities. This uses actual career statistics and makes them proportional to 10,000 batting opportunities, giving each player an equal number of team chances at the plate.

2. TOP statistics, ratings and rankings based on 10,000 career at-bats. This uses actual career statistics and makes them proportional to 10,000 official at-bats, giving each player an equal number of chances to hit.

3. TOP statistics, ratings and rankings based on actual career statistics

It may be surprising that the players from the 1950's and 1960's fare relatively poorly in rating on the basis of equal batting opportunities or at-bats. Those players from the 1970's and 1980's barely rank at all for their lifetime comparative TOP statistics. It appears that the greats of baseball's golden age and those of the modern age (some too young to convince me of their staying power) are the real producers of runs, power and performance for their teams. A few players from the 1880's and 1890's also rank high on the charts, although their numbers may not be comparable to the players of later years.

The statistical table included in this chapter provides some of the current statistical information (BA, OBP and SLG) in addition to the actual TOP statistics for each player for each of the four key TOP statistics: Total Run Production, Run Production Average, Total Net Bases and Total Base Average. These TOP statistics are then compiled into the TOP Rating and Ranking of each player.

The summary of career and adjusted career statistics for each of the greatest 125 players is set forth in Appendix A (adjusted to 10,000 batting opportunities), Appendix B (adjusted to 10,000 official at-bats) and Appendix C (actual career); listed both in accordance with TOP ratings and alphabetically. The full year-by-year career statistics and analysis for each player from which the key TOP statistics are computed are set forth in Appendix G.

★ ★ ★ *The Best Careers—Three Ways* ★ ★ ★

	The top players as ranked for their careers in each category****:		
	TOP Career Ranking Based on 10,000 Batting Opportunities	TOP Career Ranking based on 10,000 Official At-Bats	TOP Career Ranking Based on Actual Career Totals
1.	Babe Ruth	Babe Ruth	Babe Ruth
2.	Lou Gehrig	Lou Gehrig	Barry Bonds**
3.	Ted Williams*	Ted Williams*	Lou Gehrig
4.	Jimmie Foxx*	Barry Bonds**	Hank Aaron
5.	Hank Greenberg*	Jimmie Foxx*	Ty Cobb
6.	Barry Bonds**	Hank Greenberg*	Ted Williams*
7.	Joe DiMaggio*	Mark McGwire	Jimmie Foxx*
8.	Sam Thompson***	Manny Ramirez**	Willie Mays*
9.	Dan Brouthers***	Joe DiMaggio*	Stan Musial*
10.	Ed Delahanty***	Dan Brouthers***	Mel Ott
11.	Manny Ramirez**	Jim Thome**	Cap Anson***
12.	Hack Wilson	Billy Hamilton***	Frank Robinson
13.	Rogers Hornsby	Frank Thomas**	Rickey Henderson
14.	Hugh Duffy***	Mickey Mantle	Mickey Mantle
15.	Alex Rodriguez**	Ed Delahanty***	Tris Speaker
16.	Mark McGwire	Hack Wilson	Rogers Hornsby
17.	Billy Hamilton***	Sam Thompson***	Honus Wagner
18.	Harry Stovey***	Alex Rodriguez**	Carl Yastrzemski
19.	Larry Walker**	Rogers Hornsby	Rafael Palmiero**
20.	Jim Thome**	Larry Walker**	Al Simmons*
21.	Mickey Mantle	Mel Ott	Ed Delahanty***
22.	Ty Cobb	Jeff Bagwell**	Joe DiMaggio*
23.	Johnny Mize*	Hugh Duffy***	Eddie Murray
24.	Al Simmons*	Charlie Keller***	Mike Schmidt
25.	Mel Ott	Ralph Kiner	Jeff Bagwell**
26.	Frank Thomas**	Johnny Mize*	Dave Winfield

     *   Player missed time for service in WWI, WWII or Korea

    **   Active in 2004. Statistics through 2004 season

   ***   Played in 1880's and 1890's

 **** Excludes players with less than 10 seasons of play (Included in the statistical charts here and in Appendices A, B & C)

Career Adjusted to 10,000 Batting Opportunities Listed by Total Offensive Production Ranking

Rank	Player	Years	Adjustment to 10,000 BO	AVG	OBP	SLG	Total Offensive Production Statistics				Rating
							TRP	RPA	TNB	TBA	
1	Ruth, Babe	1914-1935	0.951928	.342	.474	.690	4,176	.418	7,523	.752	100.00
2	Gehrig, Lou	1923-1938	1.046353	.340	.447	.632	4,063	.406	6,922	.692	94.65
3	Williams, Ted*	1939-1960	1.001703	.344	.482	.634	3,643	.364	6,963	.696	89.90
4	Foxx, Jimmie*	1925-1944	1.034340	.325	.428	.609	3,799	.380	6,658	.666	89.74
5	Greenberg, Hank*	1930-1947	1.632120	.313	.412	.605	3,798	.380	6,597	.660	89.32
6	Bonds, Barry **	1986-2004	0.853097	.300	.443	.611	3,338	.334	7,094	.709	87.12
7	DiMaggio, Joe*	1936-1951	1.284192	.325	.398	.579	3,759	.376	6,171	.617	86.01
8	Pujols, Albert**	2001-2004	3.568873	.333	.413	.624	3,583	.358	6,470	.647	85.90
9	Thompson, Sam	1885-1906	1.534448	.336	.388	.502	3,925	.393	5,771	.577	85.35
10	Brouthers, Dan	1879-1904	1.303781	.349	.429	.526	3,654	.365	6,188	.619	84.88
11	Delahanty, Ed	1888-1903	1.200768	.346	.412	.503	3,674	.367	6,105	.610	84.57
12	Helton, Todd**	1997-2004	2.043318	.339	.432	.616	3,408	.341	6,543	.654	84.29
13	Ramirez, Manny**	1993-2004	1.485443	.316	.411	.599	3,471	.347	6,362	.636	83.85
14	Wilson, Hack	1923-1934	1.828488	.307	.395	.545	3,560	.356	6,096	.610	83.14
15	Hornsby, Rogers	1915-1937	1.079680	.358	.434	.577	3,415	.342	6,337	.634	83.00
16	Duffy, Hugh	1888-1906	1.300390	.330	.390	.453	3,702	.370	5,796	.580	82.85
17	Rodriguez, Alex**	1994-2004	1.539172	.305	.381	.574	3,412	.341	6,284	.628	82.62
18	McGwire, Mark	1986-2001	1.281394	.263	.394	.588	3,307	.331	6,452	.645	82.48
19	Hamilton, Billy	1888-1901	1.326612	.344	.455	.430	3,220	.322	6,504	.650	81.78
20	Stovey, Harry	1880-1893	1.451800	.295	.366	.466	3,484	.348	5,938	.594	81.18
21	Walker, Larry **	1989-2004	1.282051	.314	.401	.568	3,267	.327	6,282	.628	80.86
22	Thome, Jim**	1991-2004	1.400756	.284	.410	.569	3,205	.320	6,329	.633	80.43
23	Mantle, Mickey	1951-1968	0.999001	.298	.421	.557	3,183	.318	6,368	.637	80.43
24	Cobb, Ty	1905-1928	0.782963	.367	.433	.513	3,274	.327	6,172	.617	80.22
25	Mize, Johnny*	1936-1953	1.342102	.312	.397	.562	3,295	.329	6,115	.611	80.09
26	Simmons, Al*	1924-1944	1.060333	.334	.380	.535	3,535	.354	5,676	.568	80.05
27	Ott, Mel	1926-1947	0.884173	.304	.414	.533	3,288	.329	6,101	.610	79.92
28	Berkman, Lance**	1999-2004	3.036745	.303	.416	.563	3,192	.319	6,265	.626	79.85
29	Thomas, Frank **	1990-2004	1.154068	.308	.429	.567	3,170	.317	6,252	.625	79.51
30	Griffey, Ken **	1989-2004	1.156337	.292	.377	.560	3,196	.320	6,126	.613	79.19
31	Guerrero, Vladimir**	1996-2004	1.983733	.325	.390	.589	3,160	.316	6,213	.621	79.13
32	Kelly, King	1878-1892	1.542258	.313	.372	.444	3,561	.356	5,489	.549	79.12
33	Averill, Earl	1929-1941	1.395284	.318	.395	.534	3,332	.333	5,874	.587	78.93
34	Klein, Chuck	1928-1944	1.397819	.320	.379	.543	3,311	.331	5,890	.589	78.80
35	Delgado, Carlos**	1993-2004	1.636393	.282	.392	.556	3,186	.319	6,115	.612	78.79
36	Bagwell, Jeff**	1991-2004	1.049869	.297	.408	.542	3,166	.317	6,099	.610	78.44
37	Anson, Cap	1871-1897	0.886918	.342	.401	.455	3,605	.361	5,291	.529	78.33
38	Gonzalez, Juan **	1989-2004	1.363512	.295	.343	.561	3,361	.336	5,729	.573	78.32
39	Keller, Charlie*	1939-1952	2.157963	.286	.410	.518	3,205	.320	5,995	.599	78.21
40	Belle, Albert	1989-2000	1.457301	.295	.369	.564	3,225	.323	5,953	.595	78.18
41	Williams, Ken*	1915-1929	1.832845	.319	.393	.530	3,250	.325	5,904	.590	78.14
42	Conner, Roger	1880-1897	1.130327	.325	.404	.491	3,311	.331	5,792	.579	78.13
43	Mays, Willie*	1951-1973	0.785546	.302	.384	.557	3,115	.311	6,134	.613	78.06
44	Kiner, Ralph	1946-1956	1.569120	.279	.398	.548	3,116	.312	6,131	.613	78.06
45	O'Neill, Tip	1883-1892	2.096436	.334	.399	.464	3,432	.343	5,501	.550	77.65
46	Kelley, Joe	1891-1908	1.252662	.321	.405	.454	3,271	.327	5,766	.577	77.48
47	Heilmann, Harry	1914-1932	1.151676	.342	.410	.520	3,259	.326	5,755	.575	77.27
48	Sosa, Sammy**	1989-2004	1.089799	.277	.348	.545	3,175	.317	5,890	.589	77.16
49	Aaron, Hank	1954-1976	0.701902	.305	.374	.555	3,138	.314	5,936	.594	77.03

Rank	Player	Years	Adjustment to 10,000 BO	AVG	OBP	SLG	Total Offensive Production Statistics				Rating
							TRP	RPA	TNB	TBA	
50	Musial, Stan*	1941-1963	0.773994	.331	.417	.559	3,019	.302	6,060	.606	76.41
51	Giambi, Jason**	1995-2004	1.695778	.297	.411	.540	3,044	.304	5,993	.599	76.27
52	Jones, Chipper**	1993-2004	1.474709	.304	.401	.537	3,059	.306	5,962	.596	76.25
53	Hafey, Chick	1924-1937	1.977066	.317	.372	.526	3,183	.318	5,735	.574	76.23
54	Piazza, Mike**	1992-2004	1.485001	.315	.385	.562	3,113	.311	5,861	.586	76.22
55	Jennings, Hughie	1891-1918	1.826150	.314	.393	.408	3,340	.334	5,447	.545	76.19
56	Snider, Duke	1947-1964	1.197461	.295	.380	.540	3,104	.310	5,869	.587	76.17
57	Garciaparra, Nomar**	1996-2004	2.168727	.322	.370	.549	3,138	.314	5,788	.579	76.04
58	Schmidt, Mike	1972-1989	0.980200	.267	.380	.527	3,040	.304	5,952	.595	75.95
59	Trosky, Hal*	1933-1946	1.734605	.302	.371	.522	3,204	.320	5,651	.565	75.92
60	Robinson, Frank	1956-1976	0.833681	.294	.389	.537	3,035	.304	5,934	.593	75.78
61	Goslin, Goose	1921-1938	1.035090	.316	.387	.500	3,200	.320	5,606	.561	75.58
62	Sheffield, Gary**	1988-2004	1.124986	.298	.400	.528	2,992	.299	5,938	.594	75.29
63	Canseco, Jose	1985-2001	1.203949	.266	.353	.515	3,122	.312	5,698	.570	75.25
64	Herman, Babe	1926-1945	1.618909	.324	.383	.532	3,042	.304	5,836	.584	75.21
65	Jackson, Joe	1908-1920	1.798885	.356	.423	.517	2,983	.298	5,929	.593	75.12
66	Johnson, Robert	1933-1945	1.231375	.296	.393	.506	3,106	.311	5,704	.570	75.09
67	Wagner, Honus	1897-1917	0.868508	.329	.392	.469	3,015	.302	5,796	.580	74.63
68	Allen, Dick	1963-1977	1.340662	.292	.378	.534	2,974	.297	5,859	.586	74.54
69	Gehringer, Charlie	1924-1941	0.987849	.320	.404	.480	3,162	.316	5,518	.552	74.53
70	Meusel, Bob	1920-1930	1.703287	.309	.356	.497	3,224	.322	5,374	.537	74.32
71	Bottomley, Jim	1922-1937	1.217878	.310	.369	.500	3,165	.317	5,465	.546	74.22
72	Speaker, Tris	1907-1928	0.856238	.345	.428	.501	2,920	.292	5,903	.590	74.19
73	Terry, Bill	1923-1936	1.426127	.341	.393	.506	3,135	.313	5,488	.549	74.00
74	Ordonez, Magglio**	1997-2004	2.304147	.307	.364	.525	3,058	.306	5,551	.555	73.67
75	Stargell, Willie	1962-1982	1.091703	.282	.360	.529	2,986	.299	5,683	.568	73.52
76	Vaughn, Mo	1991-2003	1.527884	.293	.383	.523	2,941	.294	5,713	.571	73.18
77	Matthews, Eddie	1952-1968	0.981547	.271	.376	.509	2,907	.291	5,740	.574	72.96
78	Medwick, Joe	1932-1948	1.204674	.324	.362	.505	3,109	.311	5,246	.525	72.10
79	Campanella, Roy	1948-1957	2.028809	.276	.360	.500	3,009	.301	5,421	.542	72.05
80	Killebrew, Harmon	1954-1975	0.992654	.256	.376	.509	2,846	.285	5,709	.571	72.02
81	Lajoie, Nap	1896-1916	0.976658	.339	.381	.466	3,033	.303	5,368	.537	71.98
82	Robinson, Jackie	1947-1956	1.720874	.311	.409	.474	2,893	.289	5,619	.562	71.98
83	Martinez, Edgar**	1987-2004	1.129688	.312	.418	.515	2,802	.280	5,772	.577	71.90
84	Dickey, Bill*	1928-1946	1.416832	.313	.382	.486	3,031	.303	5,353	.535	71.86
85	McCovey, Willie	1959-1980	1.014507	.270	.374	.515	2,824	.282	5,719	.572	71.82
86	Palmiero, Rafael**	1986-2004	0.845237	.289	.372	.517	2,866	.287	5,640	.564	71.79
87	Cravath, Gavy	1908-1920	2.202643	.287	.380	.478	2,850	.285	5,634	.563	71.57
88	Berra, Yogi	1946-1965	1.176747	.285	.348	.482	3,065	.307	5,178	.518	71.11
89	York, Rudy	1934-1948	1.460067	.275	.362	.483	2,961	.296	5,347	.535	70.99
90	Williams, Bernie**	1991-2004	1.215362	.301	.388	.488	2,893	.289	5,436	.544	70.76
91	McGriff, Fred **	1986-2004	0.961723	.284	.377	.509	2,788	.279	5,613	.561	70.68
92	Burkett, Jesse	1890-1905	1.053408	.342	.419	.451	2,802	.280	5,559	.556	70.49
93	Jackson, Reggie	1967-1987	0.863036	.262	.356	.490	2,807	.281	5,540	.554	70.43
94	Bichette, Dante	1988-2001	1.423285	.299	.336	.499	2,953	.295	5,206	.521	69.96
95	Galarraga, Andres**	1985-2004	1.099626	.288	.347	.499	2,881	.288	5,329	.533	69.91
96	Henderson, Rickey	1979-2003	0.741400	.279	.401	.419	2,528	.253	5,892	.589	69.43
97	Collins, Eddie	1906-1930	0.867227	.333	.424	.429	2,706	.271	5,565	.556	69.38
98	Fielder, Cecil	1985-1998	1.637197	.255	.345	.482	2,868	.287	5,265	.527	69.34

Rank	Player	Years	Adjustment to 10,000 BO	AVG	OBP	SLG	Total Offensive Production Statistics				Rating
							TRP	RPA	TNB	TBA	
99	Maris, Roger	1957-1968	1.692334	.260	.345	.476	2,838	.284	5,299	.530	69.20
100	Rice, Jim	1974-1989	1.067464	.298	.352	.502	2,882	.288	5,217	.522	69.18
101	Kluszewski, Ted	1947-1961	1.512859	.298	.353	.498	2,838	.284	5,259	.526	68.93
102	Cepeda, Orlando	1958-1974	1.122460	.297	.350	.499	2,802	.280	5,288	.529	68.69
103	Crawford, Sam	1899-1917	0.965065	.309	.362	.453	2,815	.282	5,262	.526	68.67
104	Sisler, George	1915-1930	1.138045	.340	.379	.468	2,798	.280	5,279	.528	68.59
105	Traynor, Pie	1920-1937	1.233198	.320	.362	.435	3,029	.303	4,814	.481	68.26
106	Waner, Paul	1927-1945	0.933271	.333	.404	.474	2,740	.274	5,330	.533	68.23
107	Banks, Ernie	1953-1971	0.945269	.274	.330	.500	2,780	.278	5,233	.523	68.06
108	Jeter, Derek**	1995-2004	1.583281	.315	.385	.463	2,739	.274	5,306	.531	68.06
109	Williams, Billy	1959-1976	0.933620	.290	.361	.492	2,693	.269	5,348	.535	67.79
110	Winfield, Dave	1973-1995	0.790014	.283	.353	.475	2,767	.277	5,205	.521	67.72
111	Bench, Johnny	1967-1983	1.128796	.267	.342	.476	2,785	.278	5,169	.517	67.69
112	Kaline, Al	1953-1974	0.845809	.297	.376	.480	2,711	.271	5,280	.528	67.55
113	Brett, George	1973-1993	0.845094	.305	.369	.487	2,686	.269	5,305	.530	67.41
114	Foster, George	1969-1986	1.249219	.274	.338	.480	2,780	.278	5,132	.513	67.39
115	Keeler, Willie	1892-1910	1.084952	.345	.391	.419	2,745	.274	5,130	.513	66.96
116	Howard, Frank	1958-1973	1.321353	.273	.352	.498	2,620	.262	5,350	.535	66.93
117	Dawson, Andre	1976-1996	0.912242	.279	.323	.482	2,704	.270	5,192	.519	66.88
118	Murray, Eddie	1977-1997	0.761557	.287	.359	.476	2,699	.270	5,190	.519	66.81
119	Murphy, Dale	1976-1993	1.081900	.265	.346	.469	2,665	.266	5,236	.524	66.71
120	Morgan, Joe	1963-1984	0.878503	.271	.392	.427	2,445	.244	5,617	.562	66.60
121	Yastrzemski, Carl	1961-1983	0.699252	.285	.379	.462	2,559	.256	5,228	.523	65.39
122	Parker, Dave	1973-1991	0.962279	.290	.339	.471	2,661	.266	4,989	.499	65.02
123	Mattingly, Don	1982-1995	1.265983	.307	.358	.471	2,666	.267	4,956	.496	64.86
124	Perez, Tony	1964-1986	0.899281	.279	.341	.463	2,629	.263	4,960	.496	64.45
125	Clemente, Roberto	1955-1972	0.956846	.317	.359	.475	2,604	.260	4,961	.496	64.15
126	Ripkin, Cal, Jr.	1981-2001	0.756258	.276	.340	.447	2,527	.253	4,810	.481	62.23
127	Rose, Pete	1963-1986	0.622975	.303	.375	.409	2,167	.217	4,656	.466	56.89

Career Adjusted to 10,000 Batting Opportunities Listed by Total Offensive Production Ranking

* Player missed time for military service

** Active player. Statistics through 2004 season

TOP ranking for players with less than 70% rating is based upon comparison to listed players only.

Career Adjusted to 10,000 Batting Opportunities Listed by Total Offensive Production Ranking

Rank	Player	Years	Adjustment to 10,000 AB	AVG	OBP	SLG	Total Offensive Production Statistics				Rating
							TRP	RPA	TNB	TBA	
1	Ruth, Babe	1914-1935	1.190618	.342	.474	.690	5,223	.418	9,409	.752	100.00
2	Gehrig, Lou	1923-1938	1.249844	.340	.447	.632	4,853	.406	8,268	.692	92.52
3	Williams, Ted*	1939-1960	1.297690	.344	.482	.634	4,720	.364	9,020	.696	91.50
4	Bonds, Barry **	1986-2004	1.099143	.300	.443	.611	4,301	.334	9,140	.709	88.43
5	Foxx, Jimmie*	1925-1944	1.229407	.325	.428	.609	4,516	.380	7,914	.666	87.51
6	Greenberg, Hank*	1930-1947	1.925669	.313	.412	.605	4,481	.380	7,784	.660	86.79
7	Pujols, Albert**	2001-2004	4.231909	.333	.413	.624	4,249	.358	7,672	.647	83.67
8	Helton, Todd**	1997-2004	2.468526	.339	.432	.616	4,118	.341	7,904	.654	82.85
9	McGwire, Mark	1986-2001	1.616292	.263	.394	.588	4,172	.331	8,138	.645	82.83
10	Ramirez, Manny**	1993-2004	1.794688	.316	.411	.599	4,194	.347	7,687	.636	82.42
11	DiMaggio, Joe*	1936-1951	1.466061	.325	.398	.579	4,291	.376	7,044	.617	82.26
12	Brouthers, Dan	1879-1904	1.486989	.349	.429	.526	4,168	.365	7,057	.619	81.14
13	Thome, Jim**	1991-2004	1.746420	.284	.410	.569	3,996	.320	7,890	.633	80.31
14	Hamilton, Billy	1888-1901	1.596934	.344	.455	.430	3,876	.322	7,830	.650	80.24
15	Thomas, Frank **	1990-2004	1.459641	.308	.429	.567	4,010	.317	7,907	.625	79.95
16	Mantle, Mickey	1951-1968	1.234263	.298	.421	.557	3,932	.318	7,867	.637	79.94
17	Delahanty, Ed	1888-1903	1.334579	.346	.412	.503	4,084	.367	6,785	.610	79.86
18	Wilson, Hack	1923-1934	2.100840	.307	.395	.545	4,090	.356	7,004	.610	79.76
19	Thompson, Sam	1885-1906	1.665556	.336	.388	.502	4,260	.393	6,264	.577	79.71
20	Rodriguez, Alex**	1994-2004	1.788909	.305	.381	.574	3,966	.341	7,304	.628	79.70
21	Hornsby, Rogers	1915-1937	1.223541	.358	.434	.577	3,870	.342	7,181	.634	79.10
22	Berkman, Lance**	1999-2004	3.727171	.303	.416	.563	3,917	.319	7,689	.626	79.10
23	Walker, Larry **	1989-2004	1.516990	.314	.401	.568	3,865	.327	7,433	.628	78.68
24	Ott, Mel	1926-1947	1.057530	.304	.414	.533	3,933	.329	7,297	.610	78.17
25	Bagwell, Jeff**	1991-2004	1.299207	.297	.408	.542	3,918	.317	7,547	.610	78.03
26	Delgado, Carlos**	1993-2004	1.996805	.282	.392	.556	3,888	.319	7,462	.612	77.83
27	Duffy, Hugh	1888-1906	1.428776	.330	.390	.453	4,068	.370	6,368	.580	77.81
28	Keller, Charlie*	1939-1952	2.638522	.286	.410	.518	3,918	.320	7,330	.599	77.33
29	Kiner, Ralph	1946-1956	1.921230	.279	.398	.548	3,816	.312	7,506	.613	77.23
30	Mize, Johnny*	1936-1953	1.552072	.312	.397	.562	3,810	.329	7,071	.611	77.07
31	Stovey, Harry	1880-1893	1.614466	.295	.366	.466	3,875	.348	6,603	.594	76.68
32	Griffey, Ken **	1989-2004	1.355197	.292	.377	.560	3,746	.320	7,180	.613	76.68
33	Guerrero, Vladimir**	1996-2004	2.285714	.325	.390	.589	3,641	.316	7,159	.621	76.01
34	Cobb, Ty	1905-1928	0.874967	.367	.433	.513	3,659	.327	6,897	.617	75.95
35	Giambi, Jason**	1995-2004	2.102165	.297	.411	.540	3,773	.304	7,429	.599	75.94
36	Belle, Albert	1989-2000	1.708526	.295	.369	.564	3,781	.323	6,979	.595	75.73
37	Mays, Willie*	1951-1973	0.919033	.302	.384	.557	3,644	.311	7,176	.613	75.53
38	Averill, Earl	1929-1941	1.574059	.318	.395	.534	3,759	.333	6,627	.587	75.06
39	Schmidt, Mike	1972-1989	1.197318	.267	.380	.527	3,713	.304	7,270	.595	75.06
40	Jones, Chipper**	1993-2004	1.780627	.304	.401	.537	3,693	.306	7,199	.596	74.93
41	Simmons, Al*	1924-1944	1.141162	.334	.380	.535	3,805	.354	6,109	.568	74.46
42	Conner, Roger	1880-1897	1.280902	.325	.404	.491	3,752	.331	6,563	.579	74.46
43	Sheffield, Gary**	1988-2004	1.369488	.298	.400	.528	3,643	.299	7,228	.594	74.29
44	Robinson, Frank	1956-1976	0.999400	.294	.389	.537	3,639	.304	7,114	.593	74.21
45	Gonzalez, Juan **	1989-2004	1.525553	.295	.343	.561	3,760	.336	6,410	.573	74.19
46	Kelly, King	1878-1892	1.688619	.313	.372	.444	3,899	.356	6,010	.549	74.19
47	Musial, Stan*	1941-1963	0.911411	.331	.417	.559	3,555	.302	7,135	.606	74.18
48	Klein, Chuck	1928-1944	1.541782	.320	.379	.543	3,652	.331	6,497	.589	74.14
49	Williams, Ken*	1915-1929	2.056767	.319	.393	.530	3,647	.325	6,625	.590	74.13

★ ★ ★ **THE BEST** ★ ★ ★

Career Adjusted to 10,000 Batting Opportunities Listed by Total Offensive Production Ranking

Rank	Player	Years	Adjustment to 10,000 AB	AVG	OBP	SLG	TRP	RPA	TNB	TBA	Rating
50	Kelley, Joe	1891-1908	1.430411	.321	.405	.454	3,735	.327	6,584	.577	74.11
51	Aaron, Hank	1954-1976	0.808800	.305	.374	.555	3,616	.314	6,840	.594	73.99
52	Sosa, Sammy**	1989-2004	1.246727	.277	.348	.545	3,632	.317	6,739	.589	73.86
53	Snider, Duke	1947-1964	1.396453	.295	.380	.540	3,620	.310	6,844	.587	73.59
54	Anson, Cap	1871-1897	0.974659	.342	.401	.455	3,962	.361	5,815	.529	73.58
55	Piazza, Mike**	1992-2004	1.722653	.315	.385	.562	3,611	.311	6,799	.586	73.46
56	O'Neill, Tip	1883-1892	2.322880	.334	.399	.464	3,803	.343	6,095	.550	73.22
57	Heilmann, Harry	1914-1932	1.284192	.342	.410	.520	3,634	.326	6,417	.575	73.08
58	Canseco, Jose	1985-2001	1.417033	.266	.353	.515	3,674	.312	6,707	.570	73.03
59	Johnson, Robert	1933-1945	1.445087	.296	.393	.506	3,645	.311	6,694	.570	72.77
60	Jennings, Hughie	1891-1918	2.065262	.314	.393	.408	3,777	.334	6,161	.545	72.55
61	Allen, Dick	1963-1977	1.579280	.292	.378	.534	3,503	.297	6,901	.586	72.37
62	Garciaparra, Nomar**	1996-2004	2.419550	.322	.370	.549	3,501	.314	6,458	.579	71.94
63	Trosky, Hal*	1933-1946	1.937609	.302	.371	.522	3,579	.320	6,313	.565	71.86
64	Killebrew, Harmon	1954-1975	1.227446	.256	.376	.509	3,519	.285	7,059	.571	71.61
65	Goslin, Goose	1921-1938	1.155268022	.316	.387	.500	3,572	.320	6,257	.561	71.51
66	Hafey, Chick	1924-1937	2.162162	.317	.372	.526	3,481	.318	6,272	.574	71.44
67	Gehringer, Charlie	1924-1941	1.128668	.320	.404	.480	3,613	.316	6,305	.552	71.31
68	Matthews, Eddie	1952-1968	1.171372	.271	.376	.509	3,470	.291	6,850	.574	71.29
69	Martinez, Edgar**	1987-2004	1.386386	.312	.418	.515	3,438	.280	7,083	.577	71.23
70	Vaughn, Mo	1991-2003	1.807664	.293	.383	.523	3,480	.294	6,759	.571	71.20
71	Jackson, Joe	1908-1920	2.007629	.356	.423	.517	3,329	.298	6,617	.593	71.07
72	Speaker, Tris	1907-1928	0.980873	.345	.428	.501	3,345	.292	6,762	.590	71.07
73	Herman, Babe	1926-1945	1.784758	.324	.383	.532	3,354	.304	6,434	.584	70.75
74	Stargell, Willie	1962-1982	1.261511	.282	.360	.529	3,450	.299	6,567	.568	70.72
75	Ordonez, Magglio**	1997-2004	2.626740	.307	.364	.525	3,486	.306	6,328	.555	70.44
76	McCovey, Willie	1959-1980	1.219959	.270	.374	.515	3,396	.282	6,877	.572	70.44
77	Robinson, Jackie	1947-1956	2.050441	.311	.409	.474	3,447	.289	6,695	.562	70.27
78	Wagner, Honus	1897-1917	0.959049	.329	.392	.469	3,330	.302	6,401	.580	70.26
79	Campanella, Roy	1948-1957	2.378121	.276	.360	.500	3,527	.301	6,354	.542	69.79
80	Bottomley, Jim	1922-1937	1.338509	.310	.369	.500	3,479	.317	6,006	.546	69.72
81	Palmiero, Rafael**	1986-2004	0.989805	.289	.372	.517	3,356	.287	6,605	.564	69.51
82	Terry, Bill	1923-1936	1.555694	.341	.393	.506	3,419	.313	5,986	.549	69.27
83	Meusel, Bob	1920-1930	1.826484	.309	.356	.497	3,458	.322	5,763	.537	69.02
84	McGriff, Fred **	1986-2004	1.141944	.284	.377	.509	3,310	.279	6,664	.561	68.89
85	Henderson, Rickey	1979-2003	0.912326	.279	.401	.419	3,111	.253	7,250	.589	68.87
86	Williams, Bernie**	1991-2004	1.435956	.301	.388	.488	3,418	.289	6,423	.544	68.80
87	Cravath, Gavy	1908-1920	2.531005	.287	.380	.478	3,275	.285	6,474	.563	68.66
88	York, Rudy	1934-1948	1.697505	.275	.362	.483	3,443	.296	6,216	.535	68.49
89	Jackson, Reggie	1967-1987	1.013788	.262	.356	.490	3,298	.281	6,508	.554	68.29
90	Dickey, Bill*	1928-1946	1.587302	.313	.382	.486	3,395	.303	5,997	.535	68.11
91	Berra, Yogi	1946-1965	1.323627	.285	.348	.482	3,448	.307	5,824	.518	67.53
92	Fielder, Cecil	1985-1998	1.939112	.255	.345	.482	3,397	.287	6,236	.527	67.50
93	Medwick, Joe	1932-1948	1.309758	.324	.362	.505	3,380	.311	5,704	.525	67.38
94	Burkett, Jesse	1890-1905	1.192037	.342	.419	.451	3,171	.280	6,290	.556	67.14
95	Collins, Eddie	1906-1930	1.004924	.333	.424	.429	3,135	.271	6,449	.556	66.83
96	Lajoie, Nap	1896-1916	1.042862	.339	.381	.466	3,238	.303	5,732	.537	66.72
97	Maris, Roger	1957-1968	1.960400	.260	.345	.476	3,288	.284	6,138	.530	66.64
98	Galarraga, Andres**	1985-2004	1.235178	.288	.347	.499	3,236	.288	5,986	.533	66.35

★ ★ ★ The Best Careers—Three Ways ★ ★ ★

Rank	Player	Years	Adjustment to 10,000 AB	AVG	OBP	SLG	Total Offensive Production Statistics				Rating
							TRP	RPA	TNB	TBA	
99	Rice, Jim	1974-1989	1.215805	.298	.352	.502	3,283	.288	5,942	.522	66.09
100	Morgan, Joe	1963-1984	1.077935	.271	.392	.427	3,000	.244	6,892	.562	65.97
101	Bichette, Dante	1988-2001	1.567152	.299	.336	.499	3,252	.295	5,733	.521	65.78
102	Kaline, Al	1953-1974	0.988533	.297	.376	.480	3,168	.271	6,171	.528	65.34
103	Cepeda, Orlando	1958-1974	1.261511	.297	.350	.499	3,149	.280	5,943	.529	65.20
104	Jeter, Derek**	1995-2004	1.813894	.315	.385	.463	3,138	.274	6,078	.531	65.20
105	Kluszewski, Ted	1947-1961	1.686625	.298	.353	.498	3,164	.284	5,863	.526	65.19
106	Bench, Johnny	1967-1983	1.305824	.267	.342	.476	3,221	.278	5,979	.517	65.15
107	Waner, Paul	1927-1945	1.057194	.333	.404	.474	3,104	.274	6,038	.533	65.01
108	Winfield, Dave	1973-1995	0.908843	.283	.353	.475	3,183	.277	5,988	.521	65.00
109	Williams, Billy	1959-1976	1.069519	.290	.361	.492	3,086	.269	6,126	.535	64.94
110	Howard, Frank	1958-1973	1.540595	.273	.352	.498	3,055	.262	6,238	.535	64.66
111	Banks, Ernie	1953-1971	1.061458	.274	.330	.500	3,122	.278	5,876	.523	64.59
112	Brett, George	1973-1993	0.966277	.305	.369	.487	3,071	.269	6,065	.530	64.52
113	Foster, George	1969-1986	1.423893	.274	.338	.480	3,168	.278	5,849	.513	64.40
114	Murray, Eddie	1977-1997	0.882145	.287	.359	.476	3,126	.270	6,012	.519	64.34
115	Murphy, Dale	1976-1993	1.256281	.265	.346	.469	3,094	.266	6,080	.524	64.32
116	Crawford, Sam	1899-1917	1.043950	.309	.362	.453	3,045	.282	5,692	.526	64.03
117	Yastrzemski, Carl	1961-1983	0.834168	.285	.379	.462	3,053	.256	6,236	.523	63.87
118	Sisler, George	1915-1930	1.209629	.340	.379	.468	2,974	.280	5,611	.528	63.44
119	Traynor, Pie	1920-1937	1.322926	.320	.362	.435	3,249	.303	5,165	.481	63.40
120	Dawson, Andre	1976-1996	1.007354	.279	.323	.482	2,986	.270	5,734	.519	62.97
121	Keeler, Willie	1892-1910	1.167679	.345	.391	.419	2,954	.274	5,521	.513	62.29
122	Mattingly, Don	1982-1995	1.427959	.307	.358	.471	3,007	.267	5,590	.496	61.68
123	Perez, Tony	1964-1986	1.022704	.279	.341	.463	2,990	.263	5,641	.496	61.53
124	Parker, Dave	1973-1991	1.068604	.290	.339	.471	2,955	.266	5,541	.499	61.37
125	Clemente, Roberto	1955-1972	1.057753	.317	.359	.475	2,878	.260	5,484	.496	60.42
126	Ripkin, Cal, Jr.	1981-2001	0.865726	.276	.340	.447	2,893	.253	5,506	.481	59.59
127	Rose, Pete	1963-1986	0.711592	.303	.375	.409	2,476	.217	5,318	.466	54.43

Career Adjusted to 10,000 Batting Opportunities Listed by Total Offensive Production Ranking

* Player missed time for military service

** Active player. Statistics through 2004 season

TOP ranking for players with less than 70% rating is based upon comparison to listed players only.

★ ★ ★ THE BEST ★ ★ ★

Actual Career Statistics Listed by Total Offensive Production Ranking

Rank	Player	Years	AVG	OBP	SLG	TRP	RPA	TNB	TBA	Rating
1	Ruth, Babe	1914-1935	.342	.474	.690	4,387	.418	7,903	.752	100.00
2	Bonds, Barry **	1986-2004	.300	.443	.611	3,913	.334	8,316	.709	91.96
3	Gehrig, Lou	1923-1938	.340	.447	.632	3,883	.406	6,615	.692	90.50
4	Aaron, Hank	1954-1976	.305	.374	.555	4,471	.314	8,457	.594	90.42
5	Cobb, Ty	1905-1928	.367	.433	.513	4,182	.327	7,883	.617	88.67
6	Williams, Ted*	1939-1960	.344	.482	.634	3,637	.364	6,951	.696	87.68
7	Foxx, Jimmie*	1925-1944	.325	.428	.609	3,673	.380	6,437	.666	86.25
8	Mays, Willie*	1951-1973	.302	.384	.557	3,965	.311	7,808	.613	86.10
9	Musial, Stan*	1941-1963	.331	.417	.559	3,900	.302	7,829	.606	84.95
10	Ott, Mel	1926-1947	.304	.414	.533	3,719	.329	6,900	.610	82.86
11	Anson, Cap	1871-1897	.342	.401	.455	4,065	.361	5,966	.529	81.24
12	Robinson, Frank	1956-1976	.294	.389	.537	3,641	.304	7,118	.593	81.00
13	Henderson, Rickey	1979-2003	.279	.401	.419	3,410	.253	7,947	.589	78.94
14	Mantle, Mickey	1951-1968	.298	.421	.557	3,186	.318	6,374	.637	78.53
15	Speaker, Tris	1907-1928	.345	.428	.501	3,410	.292	6,894	.590	78.19
16	Hornsby, Rogers	1915-1937	.358	.434	.577	3,163	.342	5,869	.634	78.18
17	Wagner, Honus	1897-1917	.329	.392	.469	3,472	.302	6,674	.580	78.10
18	Yastrzemski, Carl	1961-1983	.285	.379	.462	3,660	.256	7,476	.523	76.88
19	Palmiero, Rafael**	1986-2004	.289	.372	.517	3,391	.287	6,673	.564	76.19
20	Simmons, Al*	1924-1944	.334	.380	.535	3,334	.354	5,353	.568	76.09
21	Delahanty, Ed	1888-1903	.346	.412	.503	3,060	.367	5,084	.610	76.02
22	DiMaggio, Joe*	1936-1951	.325	.398	.579	2,927	.376	4,805	.617	75.16
23	Murray, Eddie	1977-1997	.287	.359	.476	3,544	.270	6,815	.519	74.95
24	Schmidt, Mike	1972-1989	.267	.380	.527	3,101	.304	6,072	.595	74.84
25	Bagwell, Jeff**	1991-2004	.297	.408	.542	3,016	.317	5,809	.610	74.84
26	Winfield, Dave	1973-1995	.283	.353	.475	3,502	.277	6,589	.521	74.49
27	Jackson, Reggie	1967-1987	.262	.356	.490	3,253	.281	6,419	.554	73.94
28	Brouthers, Dan	1879-1904	.349	.429	.526	2,803	.365	4,746	.619	73.70
29	Gehringer, Charlie	1924-1941	.320	.404	.480	3,201	.316	5,586	.552	73.22
30	Thomas, Frank **	1990-2004	.308	.429	.567	2,747	.317	5,417	.625	72.66
31	Collins, Eddie	1906-1930	.333	.424	.429	3,120	.271	6,417	.556	72.64
32	Goslin, Goose	1921-1938	.316	.387	.500	3,092	.320	5,416	.561	72.62
33	Sosa, Sammy**	1989-2004	.277	.348	.545	2,913	.317	5,405	.589	72.37
34	Conner, Roger	1880-1897	.325	.404	.491	2,929	.331	5,124	.579	72.11
35	McGwire, Mark	1986-2001	.263	.394	.588	2,581	.331	5,035	.645	72.07
36	Duffy, Hugh	1888-1906	.330	.390	.453	2,847	.370	4,457	.580	72.04
37	Matthews, Eddie	1952-1968	.271	.376	.509	2,962	.291	5,848	.574	71.84
38	Kaline, Al	1953-1974	.297	.376	.480	3,205	.271	6,243	.528	71.66
39	Brett, George	1973-1993	.305	.369	.487	3,178	.269	6,277	.530	71.54
40	Rose, Pete	1963-1986	.303	.375	.409	3,479	.217	7,474	.466	71.50
41	Greenberg, Hank*	1930-1947	.313	.412	.605	2,327	.380	4,042	.660	71.12
42	Lajoie, Nap	1896-1916	.339	.381	.466	3,105	.303	5,496	.537	71.10
43	Griffey, Ken **	1989-2004	.292	.377	.560	2,764	.320	5,298	.613	71.00
44	Heilmann, Harry	1914-1932	.342	.410	.520	2,830	.326	4,997	.575	70.72
45	Walker, Larry **	1989-2004	.314	.401	.568	2,548	.327	4,900	.628	70.65
46	Killebrew, Harmon	1954-1975	.256	.376	.509	2,867	.285	5,751	.571	70.53
47	Hamilton, Billy	1888-1901	.344	.455	.430	2,427	.322	4,903	.650	70.44
48	McGriff, Fred **	1986-2004	.284	.377	.509	2,899	.279	5,836	.561	70.28
49	Ripkin, Cal, Jr.	1981-2001	.276	.340	.447	3,342	.253	6,360	.481	70.08

Rank	Player	Years	AVG	OBP	SLG	Total Offensive Production Statistics				Rating
						TRP	RPA	TNB	TBA	
50	McCovey, Willie	1959-1980	.270	.374	.515	2,784	.282	5,637	.572	69.61
51	Sheffield, Gary**	1988-2004	.298	.400	.528	2,660	.299	5,278	.594	69.59
52	Thompson, Sam	1885-1906	.336	.388	.502	2,558	.393	3,761	.577	69.56
53	Morgan, Joe	1963-1984	.271	.392	.427	2,783	.244	6,394	.562	69.22
54	Ramirez, Manny**	1993-2004	.316	.411	.599	2,337	.347	4,283	.636	69.11
55	Stargell, Willie	1962-1982	.282	.360	.529	2,735	.299	5,206	.568	68.90
56	Waner, Paul	1927-1945	.333	.404	.474	2,936	.274	5,711	.533	68.87
57	Mize, Johnny*	1936-1953	.312	.397	.562	2,455	.329	4,556	.611	68.67
58	Snider, Duke	1947-1964	.295	.380	.540	2,592	.310	4,901	.587	68.51
59	Williams, Billy	1959-1976	.290	.361	.492	2,885	.269	5,728	.535	68.40
60	Kelley, Joe	1891-1908	.321	.405	.454	2,611	.327	4,603	.577	68.39
61	Banks, Ernie	1953-1971	.274	.330	.500	2,941	.278	5,536	.523	68.28
62	Dawson, Andre	1976-1996	.279	.323	.482	2,964	.270	5,692	.519	68.28
63	Crawford, Sam	1899-1917	.309	.362	.453	2,917	.282	5,452	.526	68.20
64	Thome, Jim**	1991-2004	.284	.410	.569	2,288	.320	4,518	.633	67.79
65	Canseco, Jose	1985-2001	.266	.353	.515	2,593	.312	4,733	.570	67.54
66	Stovey, Harry	1880-1893	.295	.366	.466	2,400	.348	4,090	.594	67.52
67	Rodriguez, Alex**	1994-2004	.305	.381	.574	2,217	.341	4,083	.628	67.19
68	Burkett, Jesse	1890-1905	.342	.419	.451	2,660	.280	5,277	.556	67.13
69	Gonzalez, Juan **	1989-2004	.295	.343	.561	2,465	.336	4,202	.573	66.77
70	Johnson, Robert	1933-1945	.296	.393	.506	2,522	.311	4,632	.570	66.75
71	Averill, Earl	1929-1941	.318	.395	.534	2,388	.333	4,210	.587	66.67
72	Klein, Chuck	1928-1944	.320	.379	.543	2,369	.331	4,214	.589	66.50
73	Martinez, Edgar**	1987-2004	.312	.418	.515	2,480	.280	5,109	.577	66.32
74	Bottomley, Jim	1922-1937	.310	.369	.500	2,599	.317	4,487	.546	66.30
75	Perez, Tony	1964-1986	.279	.341	.463	2,924	.263	5,516	.496	66.28
76	Rice, Jim	1974-1989	.298	.352	.502	2,700	.288	4,887	.522	65.51
77	Galarraga, Andres**	1985-2004	.288	.347	.499	2,620	.288	4,846	.533	65.31
78	Belle, Albert	1989-2000	.295	.369	.564	2,213	.323	4,085	.595	64.91
79	Medwick, Joe	1932-1948	.324	.362	.505	2,581	.311	4,355	.525	64.72
80	Parker, Dave	1973-1991	.290	.339	.471	2,765	.266	5,185	.499	64.66
81	Berra, Yogi	1946-1965	.285	.348	.482	2,605	.307	4,400	.518	64.49
82	Kelly, King	1878-1892	.313	.372	.444	2,309	.356	3,559	.549	64.35
83	Clemente, Roberto	1955-1972	.317	.359	.475	2,721	.260	5,185	.496	63.96
84	Allen, Dick	1963-1977	.292	.378	.534	2,218	.297	4,370	.586	63.94
85	Wilson, Hack	1923-1934	.307	.395	.545	1,947	.356	3,334	.610	63.65
86	Cepeda, Orlando	1958-1974	.297	.350	.499	2,496	.280	4,711	.529	63.57
87	Williams, Bernie**	1991-2004	.301	.388	.488	2,380	.289	4,473	.544	63.25
88	Sisler, George	1915-1930	.340	.379	.468	2,459	.280	4,639	.528	63.09
89	Kiner, Ralph	1946-1956	.279	.398	.548	1,986	.312	3,907	.613	63.01
90	Jones, Chipper**	1993-2004	.304	.401	.537	2,074	.306	4,043	.596	63.00
91	Keeler, Willie	1892-1910	.345	.391	.419	2,530	.274	4,728	.513	62.93
92	Piazza, Mike**	1992-2004	.315	.385	.562	2,096	.311	3,947	.586	62.82
93	Murphy, Dale	1976-1993	.265	.346	.469	2,463	.266	4,840	.524	62.76
94	Delgado, Carlos**	1993-2004	.282	.392	.556	1,947	.319	3,737	.612	62.65
95	Bench, Johnny	1967-1983	.267	.342	.476	2,467	.278	4,579	.517	62.49
96	Helton, Todd**	1997-2004	.339	.432	.616	1,668	.341	3,202	.654	62.25
97	Terry, Bill	1923-1936	.341	.393	.506	2,198	.313	3,848	.549	61.97
98	Traynor, Pie	1920-1937	.320	.362	.435	2,456	.303	3,904	.481	60.68

Actual Career Statistics Listed by Total Offensive Production Ranking

Rank	Player	Years	AVG	OBP	SLG	Total Offensive Production Statistics				Rating
						TRP	RPA	TNB	TBA	
99	Dickey, Bill*	1928-1946	.313	.382	.486	2,139	.303	3,778	.535	60.33
100	Herman, Babe	1926-1945	.324	.383	.532	1,879	.304	3,605	.584	60.03
101	Giambi, Jason**	1995-2004	.297	.411	.540	1,795	.304	3,534	.599	59.88
102	Williams, Ken*	1915-1929	.319	.393	.530	1,773	.325	3,221	.590	59.77
103	Vaughn, Mo	1991-2003	.293	.383	.523	1,925	.294	3,739	.571	59.67
104	Foster, George	1969-1986	.274	.338	.480	2,225	.278	4,108	.513	59.53
105	Trosky, Hal*	1933-1946	.302	.371	.522	1,847	.320	3,258	.565	59.17
106	Guerrero, Vladimir**	1996-2004	.325	.390	.589	1,593	.316	3,132	.621	58.97
107	York, Rudy	1934-1948	.275	.362	.483	2,028	.296	3,662	.535	58.90
108	Bichette, Dante	1988-2001	.299	.336	.499	2,075	.295	3,658	.521	58.63
109	Jennings, Hughie	1891-1918	.314	.393	.408	1,829	.334	2,983	.545	58.37
110	Meusel, Bob	1920-1930	.309	.356	.497	1,893	.322	3,155	.537	58.30
111	Jackson, Joe	1908-1920	.356	.423	.517	1,658	.298	3,296	.593	57.79
112	Howard, Frank	1958-1973	.273	.352	.498	1,983	.262	4,049	.535	57.74
113	Mattingly, Don	1982-1995	.307	.358	.471	2,106	.267	3,915	.496	56.98
114	O'Neill, Tip	1883-1892	.334	.399	.464	1,637	.343	2,624	.550	56.94
115	Hafey, Chick	1924-1937	.317	.372	.526	1,610	.318	2,901	.574	56.89
116	Keller, Charlie*	1939-1952	.286	.410	.518	1,485	.320	2,778	.599	56.82
117	Kluszewski, Ted	1947-1961	.298	.353	.498	1,876	.284	3,476	.526	56.42
118	Robinson, Jackie	1947-1956	.311	.409	.474	1,681	.289	3,265	.562	56.22
119	Garciaparra, Nomar**	1996-2004	.322	.370	.549	1,447	.314	2,669	.579	55.17
120	Fielder, Cecil	1985-1998	.255	.345	.482	1,752	.287	3,216	.527	55.13
121	Pujols, Albert**	2001-2004	.333	.413	.624	1,004	.358	1,813	.647	55.09
122	Jeter, Derek**	1995-2004	.315	.385	.463	1,730	.274	3,351	.531	54.76
123	Maris, Roger	1957-1968	.260	.345	.476	1,677	.284	3,131	.530	54.38
124	Campanella, Roy	1948-1957	.276	.360	.500	1,483	.301	2,672	.542	53.34
125	Berkman, Lance**	1999-2004	.303	.416	.563	1,051	.319	2,063	.626	53.02
126	Ordonez, Magglio**	1997-2004	.307	.364	.525	1,327	.306	2,409	.555	51.74
127	Cravath, Gavy	1908-1920	.287	.380	.478	1,294	.285	2,558	.563	51.67

Actual Career Statistics Listed by Total Offensive Production Ranking

* Player missed time for military service
** Active player. Statistics through 2004 season
TOP ranking for players with less than 70% rating is based upon comparison to listed players only.

Many players have had one or two great seasons in an otherwise mediocre career. Those seasons, though short in duration, deserve recognition. In this section I have included the TOP Ratings and Rankings of 380 of the best individual season efforts since 1884. Because of the rules in the late 1800's, some of the statistics of these early players are not comparable to those of modern players, but they are included for discussion as if fully comparable, with full TOP statistics and ratings in all categories.

I have tried to include all of perhaps the greatest 300 season totals in baseball history. However, 380 of the greatest individual seasons have been included in the Appendix to this chapter. For the remaining entries, I have included players, years and eras that might not otherwise have made the best of the best. Some the last 80 great seasons are presented to show the results of the best players in each decade, and help allow a better comparison of players between eras. This necessarily requires the exclusion of some excellent seasons. Primarily, the excluded seasons are by players who have even greater seasons included in this book. Also included are all players with a season total equal to or better than the following:

- Season Batting Average above .400
- Season Slugging Average above .700
- 50 or more Home Runs for the season
- 150 or more Runs scored in a season after 1900
- 150 or more Runs-Batted-In for a season

Based on individual seasons, there is little doubt about the greatest ball player. Babe Ruth has 8 of the top 22 seasons on record. Ruth and Lou Gehrig each have 4 of the top 12 seasons on record. Jimmie Foxx, Hank Greenberg and Rogers Hornsby are the only batters to have 2 or more championship seasons in the top 40. Barry Bonds ranks 8th for his great 2001 season, with Sammy Sosa and Mark McGwire as the only other modern players with a great individual season in the top 25. It may say something about the change in the nature of the game, but only Ted Williams has a season between 1938 and 1997 in the top 48 seasons on record. Mickey Mantle's great 1956 season ranks number 49. No season in the 1970's or 1980's ranks in the top 100

Below are the key statistics of each of these great seasons including their TRP, RPA, TNB and TBA. These are again compiled into the TOP Rating for each player's season. The complete statistics for each player for each of these seasons are in Appendix D. Appendix D-1 provides all statistics for each season listed according to their TOP Ranking; while Appendix D-2 lists the players in alphabetical order, numbering each season in order of their TOP Rating (and not chronologically).

★ ★ ★ The Best Single Seasons ★ ★ ★

The Greatest 300 Seasons & Others Listed by Total Offensive Production

Rank	Player	Player Season	Year	AVG	OBP	SLG	TRP	RPA	TNB	TBA	Rating
1	Ruth, Babe	1st	1921	.378	.512	.846	348	.505	610	.885	100.00
2	Ruth, Babe	2nd	1927	.356	.486	.772	322	.476	555	.820	92.55
3	Ruth, Babe	3rd	1920	.376	.532	.847	295	.483	541	.885	92.17
4	Gehrig, Lou	1st	1927	.373	.474	.765	324	.466	561	.806	92.08
5	Wilson, Hack	1st	1930	.356	.454	.723	337	.488	532	.770	91.86
6	Gehrig, Lou	2nd	1931	.341	.446	.662	347	.471	532	.723	90.49
7	Foxx, Jimmie*	1st	1932	.364	.469	.749	320	.456	550	.785	90.29
8	Bonds, Barry **	1st	2001	.328	.515	.863	266	.398	607	.907	89.35
9	Duffy, Hugh	1st	1894	.438	.500	.679	305	.503	482	.795	88.89
10	Gehrig, Lou	3rd	1930	.379	.473	.721	317	.463	521	.761	88.48
11	Gehrig, Lou	4th	1936	.354	.478	.696	319	.446	539	.753	88.34
12	Ruth, Babe	4th	1930	.359	.493	.732	303	.463	516	.788	88.00
13	Foxx, Jimmie*	2nd	1938	.349	.462	.704	314	.459	518	.757	87.87
14	Simmons, Al*	1st	1930	.381	.423	.708	317	.534	439	.739	87.84
15	Ruth, Babe	5th	1931	.373	.494	.700	312	.471	503	.760	87.75
16	Klein, Chuck	1st	1930	.386	.436	.687	328	.465	507	.718	87.60
17	Ruth, Babe	6th	1928	.323	.463	.709	305	.451	519	.768	87.17
18	Sosa, Sammy**	1st	2001	.328	.437	.737	306	.427	545	.760	86.95
19	Greenberg, Hank*	1st	1937	.337	.436	.668	320	.458	507	.725	86.89
20	Ruth, Babe	7th	1923	.393	.545	.764	282	.405	569	.818	86.77
21	O'Neill, Tip	1st	1887	.485	.531	.718	290	.466	492	.791	86.31
22	Ruth, Babe	8th	1926	.372	.516	.737	285	.444	514	.801	86.07
23	DiMaggio, Joe*	1st	1937	.346	.412	.673	318	.461	490	.710	85.75
24	McGwire, Mark	1st	1998	.299	.470	.752	277	.402	552	.801	85.09
25	Gehrig, Lou	5th	1934	.363	.465	.706	293	.425	524	.759	84.99
26	Hornsby, Rogers	1st	1922	.401	.459	.722	293	.425	521	.756	84.81
27	Hornsby, Rogers	2nd	1929	.380	.459	.679	305	.442	499	.723	84.64
28	Hornsby, Rogers	3rd	1925	.403	.489	.756	276	.469	468	.795	84.50
29	Williams, Ted*	1st	1949	.343	.490	.650	309	.411	532	.707	84.38
30	Thompson, Sam	1st	1895	.394	.432	.657	296	.520	410	.721	83.92
31	Greenberg, Hank*	2nd	1938	.315	.438	.683	290	.428	504	.743	83.64
32	Foxx, Jimmie*	3rd	1933	.356	.449	.703	288	.430	500	.746	83.50
33	Cobb, Ty	1st	1911	.420	.467	.621	274	.426	502	.781	83.35
34	Walker, Larry **	1st	1997	.366	.452	.720	273	.402	526	.775	82.96
35	Hamilton, Billy	1st	1894	.399	.516	.510	283	.408	519	.748	82.92
36	Gehrig, Lou	6th	1937	.351	.473	.643	297	.424	498	.711	82.84
37	Ruth, Babe	9th	1924	.378	.513	.739	264	.391	533	.790	82.49
38	Bonds, Barry **	2nd	2004	.362	.609	.812	230	.370	549	.883	82.27
39	Helton, Todd**	1st	2000	.372	.463	.698	285	.402	514	.725	81.94
40	Ramirez, Manny**	1st	1999	.333	.442	.663	296	.454	453	.695	81.83
41	Ruth, Babe	10th	1929	.345	.430	.697	275	.479	425	.740	81.61
42	Ott, Mel	1st	1929	.328	.449	.635	289	.435	471	.709	81.59
43	Kelley, Joe	1st	1894	.391	.501	.587	278	.448	457	.736	81.53
44	Klein, Chuck	2nd	1932	.348	.404	.646	289	.406	501	.705	81.33
45	Kelley, Joe	2nd	1895	.371	.462	.563	282	.472	428	.717	81.26
46	Bonds, Barry **	3rd	2002	.370	.582	.799	227	.369	536	.870	81.09
47	Herman, Babe	1st	1930	.393	.455	.678	273	.399	504	.737	80.84
48	Williams, Ted*	2nd	1941	.406	.553	.735	255	.414	483	.784	80.68
49	Mantle, Mickey	1st	1956	.353	.464	.705	262	.400	499	.762	80.57

The Greatest 300 Seasons & Others Listed by Total Offensive Production											
Rank	Player	Player Season	Year	AVG	OBP	SLG	Total Offensive Production Statistics				Rating
							TRP	RPA	TNB	TBA	
50	Helton, Todd**	2nd	2001	.336	.432	.685	278	.392	507	.715	80.38
51	Delahanty, Ed	1st	1893	.371	.426	.588	291	.451	439	.681	80.35
52	Williams, Ted*	3rd	1942	.356	.499	.648	278	.407	488	.714	80.29
53	Wilson, Hack	2nd	1929	.345	.425	.618	294	.450	438	.670	80.14
54	Williams, Ken*	1st	1922	.332	.413	.627	283	.425	465	.698	80.09
55	Thompson, Sam	2nd	1894	.404	.453	.666	256	.513	375	.752	80.06
56	Mantle, Mickey	2nd	1961	.317	.448	.687	260	.402	490	.757	80.01
57	Sosa, Sammy**	2nd	1998	.308	.377	.647	292	.394	499	.673	79.95
58	Greenberg, Hank*	3rd	1935	.328	.411	.628	291	.412	477	.676	79.93
59	Greenberg, Hank*	4th	1940	.340	.433	.670	279	.409	481	.705	79.91
60	McGwire, Mark	2nd	1999	.278	.424	.697	265	.394	498	.740	79.83
61	Gonzalez, Luis**	1st	2001	.325	.429	.688	270	.364	533	.718	79.63
62	Foxx, Jimmie*	4th	1930	.335	.429	.637	283	.432	451	.689	79.57
63	Browning, Pete	1st	1887	.402	.464	.547	255	.418	465	.762	79.51
64	Musial, Stan*	1st	1948	.376	.450	.702	266	.374	518	.729	79.48
65	Williams, Ted*	4th	1946	.342	.497	.667	265	.387	501	.732	79.45
66	Gehrig, Lou	7th	1932	.349	.451	.621	289	.409	474	.670	79.35
67	Gehrig, Lou	8th	1928	.374	.467	.648	281	.426	455	.689	79.32
68	Lajoie, Nap	1st	1901	.422	.459	.635	270	.466	409	.705	78.93
69	Jennings, Hughie	1st	1895	.386	.445	.515	284	.486	388	.664	78.93
70	Foxx, Jimmie*	5th	1936	.338	.440	.631	273	.395	484	.700	78.79
71	Trosky, Hal*	1st	1936	.343	.382	.644	286	.428	445	.666	78.73
72	Delahanty, Ed	2nd	1894	.400	.472	.561	280	.496	375	.665	78.59
73	Ruth, Babe	11th	1932	.341	.489	.661	257	.436	434	.737	78.52
74	Delahanty, Ed	3rd	1895	.399	.496	.599	254	.443	426	.743	78.48
75	Bonds, Barry **	4th	1993	.336	.458	.677	252	.368	510	.745	78.28
76	Bagwell, Jeff**	1st	2000	.310	.424	.615	284	.385	488	.661	78.17
77	Cuyler, Kiki	1st	1930	.355	.428	.547	289	.399	470	.649	78.13
78	Klein, Chuck	3rd	1929	.356	.407	.657	271	.404	464	.693	78.03
79	Thompson, Sam	3rd	1887	.406	.446	.589	284	.460	402	.652	77.91
80	Burks, Ellis	1st	1996	.344	.408	.639	270	.385	485	.692	77.90
81	Delahanty, Ed	4th	1896	.394	.469	.610	257	.446	416	.722	77.83
82	Kelley, Joe	3rd	1896	.370	.475	.535	247	.399	466	.753	77.79
83	Griffey, Ken **	1st	1997	.304	.382	.646	272	.380	488	.682	77.63
84	Stovey, Harry	1st	1889	.308	.393	.525	271	.427	433	.683	77.56
85	Bonds, Barry **	5th	1996	.308	.461	.615	251	.366	503	.734	77.55
86	Bagwell, Jeff**	2nd	1999	.304	.454	.591	269	.360	511	.684	77.49
87	Delahanty, Ed	5th	1899	.408	.464	.585	270	.427	432	.684	77.46
88	Williams, Ted*	5th	1939	.327	.436	.609	276	.404	454	.664	77.13
89	O'Doul, Lefty	1st	1929	.398	.465	.622	274	.382	479	.667	77.07
90	Belle, Albert	1st	1996	.311	.410	.623	272	.370	492	.669	76.98
91	Pujols, Albert**	1st	2003	.359	.439	.667	261	.374	487	.698	76.95
92	Foxx, Jimmie*	6th	1934	.334	.449	.653	250	.384	473	.727	76.85
93	Griffey, Ken **	2nd	1996	.303	.392	.628	265	.411	442	.686	76.83
94	Cash, Norm	1st	1961	.361	.487	.662	251	.366	493	.719	76.67
95	Gehrig, Lou	9th	1933	.334	.424	.605	277	.404	448	.653	76.66
96	Delgado, Carlos**	1st	2000	.344	.470	.664	252	.349	515	.712	76.66
97	Brouthers, Dan	1st	1887	.419	.488	.614	254	.393	461	.713	76.65
98	Simmons, Al*	2nd	1929	.365	.398	.642	271	.442	407	.664	76.64

★ ★ ★ The Best Single Seasons ★ ★ ★

The Greatest 300 Seasons & Others Listed by Total Offensive Production

Rank	Player	Player Season	Year	AVG	OBP	SLG	TRP	RPA	TNB	TBA	Rating
99	Mize, Johnny*	1st	1947	.302	.384	.614	275	.410	440	.657	76.60
100	Robinson, Frank	1st	1962	.342	.421	.624	270	.378	476	.667	76.48
101	Sisler, George	1st	1920	.407	.449	.632	259	.381	472	.695	76.46
102	Mays, Willie*	1st	1962	.304	.384	.615	271	.374	480	.662	76.38
103	Brouthers, Dan	2nd	1894	.345	.423	.553	265	.442	404	.673	76.32
104	Rodriguez, Alex**	1st	2001	.318	.399	.622	268	.358	499	.666	76.31
105	Maris, Roger	1st	1961	.269	.372	.620	274	.384	467	.654	76.31
106	Mays, Willie*	2nd	1955	.319	.400	.659	250	.367	485	.711	76.08
107	Rodriguez, Alex**	2nd	2002	.300	.392	.623	267	.361	491	.664	76.01
108	Bottomley, Jim	1st	1928	.325	.402	.628	259	.398	446	.686	75.93
109	Terry, Bill	1st	1930	.401	.452	.619	268	.388	458	.663	75.93
110	Belle, Albert	2nd	1998	.328	.399	.655	265	.367	483	.668	75.89
111	Snider, Duke	1st	1955	.309	.418	.628	262	.398	445	.676	75.82
112	Rodriguez, Alex**	3rd	2000	.316	.420	.606	266	.390	454	.666	75.80
113	Foster, George	1st	1977	.320	.382	.631	273	.387	456	.646	75.68
114	Bonds, Barry **	6th	2000	.306	.440	.688	235	.383	458	.747	75.67
115	Griffey, Ken **	3rd	1998	.284	.365	.611	266	.362	485	.661	75.64
116	Averill, Earl	1st	1931	.333	.404	.576	283	.404	435	.621	75.64
117	Hamilton, Billy	2nd	1895	.393	.494	.493	240	.387	453	.731	75.54
118	Speaker, Tris	1st	1923	.380	.469	.610	263	.392	448	.668	75.48
119	Kiner, Ralph	1st	1949	.310	.432	.658	243	.359	485	.716	75.35
120	Snider, Duke	2nd	1953	.336	.419	.627	258	.377	464	.677	75.32
121	Medwick, Joe	1st	1937	.374	.414	.641	265	.386	453	.659	75.31
122	Giambi, Jason**	1st	2000	.333	.476	.647	245	.364	478	.710	75.28
123	Rodriguez, Alex**	4th	1996	.358	.414	.631	264	.385	453	.660	75.22
124	Bagwell, Jeff**	3rd	1994	.368	.451	.750	220	.448	380	.774	75.15
125	Belle, Albert	3rd	1995	.317	.401	.690	247	.378	459	.703	75.10
126	Averill, Earl	2nd	1936	.378	.438	.627	262	.385	451	.663	75.09
127	Hornsby, Rogers	4th	1921	.397	.458	.639	257	.390	445	.675	75.03
128	Simmons, Al*	3rd	1932	.322	.368	.548	295	.411	417	.581	74.99
129	Pujols, Albert**	2nd	2004	.331	.415	.657	256	.359	480	.673	74.89
130	Williams, Ted*	6th	1948	.369	.497	.615	251	.387	446	.688	74.88
131	Anson, Cap	1st	1886	.371	.433	.542	264	.472	357	.639	74.77
132	Thomas, Frank **	1st	2000	.328	.436	.625	258	.358	479	.665	74.74
133	Brown, Tom	1st	1891	.321	.397	.469	249	.376	456	.688	74.57
134	Delgado, Carlos**	2nd	2003	.302	.426	.593	262	.367	466	.653	74.54
135	Williams, Ted*	7th	1947	.343	.499	.634	239	.340	498	.709	74.52
136	Galarraga, Andres**	1st	1996	.304	.357	.601	269	.386	443	.636	74.52
137	Foxx, Jimmie*	7th	1939	.360	.464	.694	235	.409	416	.723	74.46
138	Musial, Stan*	2nd	1949	.338	.438	.624	251	.342	494	.674	74.33
139	Mize, Johnny*	2nd	1940	.314	.404	.636	248	.367	462	.683	74.21
140	Sheffield, Gary**	1st	2003	.330	.419	.604	258	.372	456	.657	74.19
141	DiMaggio, Joe*	2nd	1941	.357	.440	.643	247	.394	430	.686	74.16
142	Hornsby, Rogers	5th	1927	.361	.448	.586	258	.392	432	.657	74.14
143	Bonds, Barry **	7th	2003	.341	.529	.749	201	.361	457	.820	74.12
144	DiMaggio, Joe*	3rd	1938	.324	.386	.581	269	.408	414	.627	74.11
145	McGwire, Mark	3rd	1996	.312	.467	.730	217	.386	433	.770	74.09
146	Clolavito, Rocky	1st	1961	.290	.402	.580	269	.374	452	.628	74.09
147	Snider, Duke	3rd	1954	.341	.423	.647	250	.362	466	.675	74.08

Rank	Player	Player Season	Year	AVG	OBP	SLG	Total Offensive Production Statistics				Rating
							TRP	RPA	TNB	TBA	
148	Bagwell, Jeff**	4th	1997	.286	.425	.592	244	.336	499	.686	74.05
149	Ott, Mel	2nd	1936	.328	.448	.588	255	.388	436	.663	74.04
150	Gonzalez, Juan **	1st	1998	.318	.366	.630	267	.388	435	.631	74.00
151	Rosen, Al	1st	1953	.336	.422	.613	260	.368	457	.646	73.88
152	Bonds, Barry **	8th	1998	.303	.438	.609	242	.340	490	.689	73.84
153	Cuyler, Kiki	2nd	1925	.357	.423	.598	246	.358	468	.680	73.78
154	Gehrig, Lou	10th	1929	.300	.433	.584	253	.371	452	.663	73.77
155	Kiner, Ralph	2nd	1947	.313	.417	.639	245	.362	462	.682	73.73
156	Sosa, Sammy**	3rd	1999	.288	.367	.635	255	.350	477	.654	73.72
157	Griffey, Ken **	4th	1999	.285	.384	.576	257	.360	464	.650	73.68
158	Foxx, Jimmie*	8th	1929	.354	.463	.625	241	.387	431	.693	73.65
159	Sheffield, Gary**	2nd	1996	.314	.465	.624	238	.343	483	.697	73.62
160	Kelly, King	1st	1886	.388	.483	.532	234	.438	376	.704	73.58
161	Helton, Todd**	3rd	2003	.358	.458	.630	252	.349	476	.659	73.56
162	Walker, Larry **	2nd	1999	.379	.458	.710	223	.425	387	.737	73.52
163	Duffy, Hugh	2nd	1893	.378	.432	.480	267	.454	359	.611	73.42
164	Williams, Billy	1st	1970	.322	.391	.586	266	.366	453	.623	73.41
165	Greenberg, Hank*	5th	1934	.339	.404	.600	257	.391	425	.646	73.40
166	Aaron, Hank	1st	1962	.323	.390	.618	255	.374	443	.651	73.37
167	Jackson, Reggie	1st	1969	.275	.411	.608	241	.352	469	.685	73.31
168	DiMaggio, Joe*	4th	1939	.381	.448	.671	234	.442	369	.698	73.30
169	DiMaggio, Joe*	5th	1948	.320	.396	.598	265	.385	430	.624	73.30
170	Matthews, Eddie	1st	1953	.302	.406	.627	245	.357	462	.673	73.25
171	Goslin, Goose	1st	1930	.308	.382	.601	253	.387	427	.653	73.21
172	Mantle, Mickey	3rd	1957	.365	.512	.665	215	.342	474	.755	73.13
173	Aaron, Hank	2nd	1963	.319	.391	.586	251	.346	474	.654	73.11
174	Foxx, Jimmie*	9th	1935	.346	.461	.636	233	.359	456	.703	73.03
175	Vaughn, Mo	1st	1996	.326	.420	.583	261	.339	481	.625	73.02
176	Morgan, Joe	1st	1976	.320	.444	.576	224	.373	438	.729	73.00
177	Walker, Larry **	3rd	2001	.350	.449	.662	230	.377	434	.711	73.00
178	Trosky, Hal*	2nd	1934	.330	.388	.598	259	.378	434	.634	72.98
179	Stovey, Harry	2nd	1890	.297	.404	.470	226	.399	409	.721	72.96
180	Sosa, Sammy**	4th	2000	.320	.406	.634	244	.340	479	.668	72.93
181	Giambi, Jason**	2nd	2001	.342	.477	.660	229	.333	487	.708	72.92
182	Killebrew, Harmon	1st	1969	.276	.427	.584	246	.339	480	.662	72.90
183	Jennings, Hughie	2nd	1896	.398	.469	.478	246	.415	393	.663	72.89
184	Lowe, Bobby	1st	1894	.346	.401	.520	273	.408	398	.595	72.85
185	Gehrig, Lou	11th	1935	.329	.466	.583	244	.363	450	.670	72.85
186	McGraw, John	1st	1894	.340	.451	.436	248	.403	405	.657	72.81
187	Kluszewski, Ted	1st	1954	.326	.407	.642	245	.365	447	.666	72.80
188	Kiner, Ralph	3rd	1951	.309	.452	.627	233	.343	473	.696	72.76
189	Ott, Mel	3rd	1932	.318	.424	.601	242	.361	450	.672	72.67
190	Jones, Chipper**	1st	1999	.319	.441	.633	226	.313	509	.706	72.64
191	Robinson, Frank	2nd	1966	.316	.410	.637	244	.347	467	.663	72.59
192	Alomar, Roberto**	1st	1999	.323	.422	.533	258	.371	437	.629	72.57
193	Cobb, Ty	2nd	1915	.369	.486	.487	243	.352	460	.666	72.54
194	Ruth, Babe	12th	1919	.322	.456	.657	217	.403	398	.738	72.52
195	Rice, Jim	1st	1978	.315	.370	.600	260	.342	471	.620	72.49
196	Sisler, George	2nd	1922	.420	.467	.594	239	.375	432	.677	72.49

The Greatest 300 Seasons & Others Listed by Total Offensive Production

Rank	Player	Player Season	Year	AVG	OBP	SLG	TRP	RPA	TNB	TBA	Rating
197	Conner, Roger	1st	1890	.372	.469	.572	237	.414	389	.679	72.46
198	Galarraga, Andres**	2nd	1997	.318	.389	.585	260	.377	429	.622	72.45
199	Wilson, Hack	3rd	1927	.318	.401	.579	248	.395	409	.651	72.43
200	Palmiero, Rafael**	1st	1999	.324	.420	.630	244	.356	454	.662	72.39
201	Ott, Mel	4th	1934	.326	.415	.591	254	.374	432	.635	72.36
202	Thome, Jim**	1st	2002	.304	.445	.677	219	.354	451	.730	72.33
203	Heilmann, Harry	1st	1923	.403	.481	.632	236	.391	411	.682	72.32
204	Martinez, Edgar**	1st	1995	.356	.479	.628	234	.360	446	.686	72.26
205	Stephens, Vern	1st	1949	.290	.391	.539	272	.373	430	.589	72.25
206	Thomas, Frank **	2nd	1996	.349	.459	.626	244	.362	444	.659	72.24
207	McCovey, Willie	1st	1969	.320	.453	.656	227	.358	447	.705	72.23
208	Thome, Jim**	2nd	1996	.311	.450	.612	238	.367	438	.675	72.23
209	Bagwell, Jeff**	5th	2001	.288	.397	.568	256	.347	461	.626	72.20
210	Robinson, Frank	3rd	1961	.323	.404	.611	241	.370	433	.665	72.13
211	Heilmann, Harry	2nd	1921	.394	.444	.606	253	.385	416	.633	72.11
212	Duffy, Hugh	3rd	1891	.341	.415	.477	234	.406	392	.681	72.06
213	Lynn, Fred	1st	1979	.333	.423	.637	238	.377	424	.672	72.06
214	Rodriguez, Alex**	5th	2003	.298	.396	.600	242	.331	480	.657	72.06
215	Speaker, Tris	2nd	1912	.383	.464	.567	226	.338	469	.702	72.05
216	Ott, Mel	5th	1930	.349	.458	.578	241	.385	415	.663	72.02
217	Gehringer, Charlie	1st	1936	.354	.431	.555	260	.357	446	.613	71.97
218	Bonds, Barry **	9th	1997	.291	.446	.585	224	.319	493	.701	71.95
219	Mays, Willie*	3rd	1961	.308	.393	.584	252	.374	426	.633	71.94
220	Latham, Artie	1st	1887	.316	.366	.413	246	.363	438	.647	71.87
221	Anderson, Brady**	1st	1996	.297	.396	.637	227	.328	480	.694	71.86
222	Campanella, Roy	1st	1953	.312	.395	.611	245	.406	390	.647	71.84
223	Conner, Roger	2nd	1889	.317	.426	.528	247	.418	378	.640	71.83
224	Conner, Roger	3rd	1887	.383	.464	.604	217	.345	456	.725	71.81
225	Williams, Ted*	8th	1940	.344	.442	.594	247	.367	432	.642	71.72
226	Hornsby, Rogers	6th	1924	.424	.507	.696	215	.343	457	.729	71.72
227	Bonds, Barry **	10th	1992	.311	.456	.624	212	.341	458	.738	71.71
228	Thomas, Frank **	3rd	1994	.353	.487	.729	207	.389	401	.754	71.70
229	Ramirez, Manny**	2nd	1998	.294	.377	.599	253	.372	426	.626	71.67
230	Duffy, Hugh	4th	1897	.341	.404	.478	260	.425	368	.601	71.62
231	Ramirez, Manny**	3rd	2000	.351	.457	.697	214	.396	395	.730	71.60
232	Simmons, Al*	4th	1931	.390	.444	.641	233	.414	379	.673	71.60
233	Mays, Willie*	4th	1954	.345	.411	.667	229	.351	448	.687	71.59
234	Musial, Stan*	3rd	1954	.330	.428	.607	246	.339	463	.639	71.53
235	Giambi, Jason**	3rd	2002	.314	.435	.598	242	.342	459	.649	71.51
236	Musial, Stan*	4th	1953	.337	.437	.609	240	.339	462	.653	71.42
237	Mays, Willie*	5th	1965	.317	.398	.645	230	.355	441	.682	71.42
238	Berkman, Lance**	1st	2001	.331	.430	.620	236	.339	461	.662	71.37
239	Burkett, Jesse	1st	1895	.423	.498	.542	232	.364	430	.675	71.34
240	Guerrero, Vladimir**	1st	2004	.337	.391	.598	250	.358	438	.627	71.32
241	Murphy, Dale	1st	1983	.302	.393	.540	252	.359	436	.621	71.29
242	Hafey, Chick	1st	1930	.336	.407	.652	215	.431	356	.713	71.26
243	Yastrzemski, Carl	1st	1967	.326	.418	.622	233	.341	457	.668	71.22
244	Canseco, Jose	1st	1988	.307	.391	.569	244	.339	459	.638	71.21
245	Thompson, Sam	4th	1893	.377	.432	.539	256	.401	388	.607	71.17

★ ★ ★ **THE BEST** ★ ★ ★

Rank	Player	Player Season	Year	AVG	OBP	SLG	TRP	RPA	TNB	TBA	Rating
							Total Offensive Production Statistics				
246	Aaron, Hank*	3rd	1959	.355	.401	.636	239	.336	463	.650	71.17
247	Banks, Ernie	1st	1958	.313	.366	.614	248	.357	435	.626	70.99
248	Rodriguez, Alex**	6th	1998	.310	.360	.560	247	.326	472	.624	70.93
249	Duffy, Hugh	5th	1890	.328	.391	.467	243	.373	416	.638	70.93
250	Aaron, Hank	4th	1957	.322	.378	.600	250	.363	426	.619	70.88
251	Gehringer, Charlie	2nd	1934	.356	.450	.517	261	.371	416	.592	70.87
252	DiMaggio, Joe*	6th	1936	.323	.352	.576	257	.386	399	.600	70.83
253	Thomas, Frank**	4th	1997	.347	.456	.611	235	.354	436	.657	70.80
254	Mays, Willie*	6th	1964	.296	.383	.607	232	.344	448	.664	70.79
255	Gonzalez, Juan**	2nd	1996	.314	.368	.643	233	.387	398	.661	70.77
256	Ordonez, Magglio**	1st	2002	.320	.381	.597	251	.372	414	.614	70.74
257	Stargell, Willie	1st	1973	.299	.392	.646	225	.366	420	.683	70.71
258	Mantle, Mickey	4th	1958	.304	.443	.592	224	.338	453	.683	70.69
259	Martinez, Edgar**	2nd	2000	.324	.423	.579	245	.361	426	.628	70.67
260	Bagwell, Jeff**	6th	1996	.315	.451	.570	231	.315	483	.658	70.64
261	Musial, Stan*	5th	1951	.355	.449	.614	232	.340	451	.660	70.63
262	Hafey, Chick	2nd	1929	.338	.394	.632	226	.401	381	.676	70.61
263	Thomas, Frank**	5th	1993	.317	.426	.607	234	.341	449	.655	70.60
264	Holmes, Tommy	1st	1945	.352	.420	.577	242	.336	456	.632	70.60
265	Stargell, Willie	2nd	1971	.295	.398	.628	229	.373	411	.669	70.58
266	Cepeda, Orlando	1st	1961	.311	.362	.609	247	.376	408	.621	70.56
267	Keeler, Willie	1st	1896	.392	.437	.502	236	.400	382	.647	70.56
268	Gehrig, Lou	12th	1926	.313	.420	.549	247	.364	421	.621	70.55
269	Yastrzemski, Carl	2nd	1970	.329	.452	.592	227	.320	474	.669	70.52
270	Heilmann, Harry	3rd	1927	.398	.475	.616	226	.390	391	.675	70.52
271	Averill, Earl	3rd	1934	.313	.414	.569	241	.344	445	.635	70.52
272	Klein, Chuck	4th	1931	.337	.398	.584	242	.370	414	.633	70.50
273	McCovey, Willie	2nd	1970	.289	.444	.612	224	.344	443	.680	70.49
274	Keeler, Willie	2nd	1894	.368	.424	.509	258	.396	384	.590	70.46
275	Davis, Tommy	1st	1962	.346	.374	.535	273	.377	403	.556	70.45
276	Thome, Jim**	3rd	2001	.291	.416	.624	225	.345	442	.677	70.44
277	Greenberg, Hank*	6th	1939	.312	.420	.622	224	.373	409	.681	70.44
278	Palmiero, Rafael**	2nd	1996	.289	.381	.546	252	.340	448	.605	70.42
279	Delgado, Carlos**	3rd	1999	.272	.377	.571	247	.357	428	.618	70.42
280	Burkett, Jesse	2nd	1893	.373	.485	.521	226	.386	394	.674	70.41
281	Rice, Jim	2nd	1979	.325	.381	.596	247	.351	435	.618	70.40
282	Thome, Jim**	4th	2003	.266	.385	.573	242	.344	443	.630	70.40
283	Medwick, Joe	2nd	1935	.353	.386	.576	258	.378	403	.590	70.37
284	Speaker, Tris	3rd	1920	.388	.483	.562	244	.373	409	.625	70.37
285	Ott, Mel	6th	1938	.311	.442	.583	232	.353	432	.657	70.35
286	Bottomley, Jim	2nd	1929	.314	.391	.568	245	.388	392	.621	70.34
287	Kelley, Joe	4th	1897	.390	.471	.517	231	.398	381	.657	70.33
288	Simmons, Al*	5th	1925	.384	.416	.596	251	.362	421	.607	70.31
289	Guerrero, Vladimir**	2nd	2000	.345	.410	.664	224	.341	444	.677	70.30
290	Hamilton, Billy	3rd	1889	.301	.412	.402	222	.351	432	.682	70.25
291	Ramirez, Manny**	4th	2004	.308	.397	.613	238	.350	434	.638	70.23
292	Cobb, Ty	3rd	1909	.377	.431	.517	223	.356	426	.679	70.23
293	Pujols, Albert**	3rd	2001	.329	.403	.610	242	.348	436	.626	70.17
294	Mantle, Mickey	5th	1955	.306	.431	.611	220	.344	439	.686	70.16

Rank	Player	Player Season	Year	AVG	OBP	SLG	Total Offensive Production Statistics				Rating
							TRP	RPA	TNB	TBA	
295	Jennings, Hughie	3rd	1894	.333	.408	.489	245	.431	347	.610	70.16
296	Mitchell, Kevin	1st	1989	.291	.388	.635	225	.348	434	.672	70.14
297	Piazza, Mike**	1st	1997	.362	.431	.638	228	.350	431	.662	70.05
298	Schmidt, Mike	1st	1980	.286	.380	.624	225	.342	440	.669	70.00
299	Keeler, Willie	3rd	1897	.432	.472	.544	221	.366	411	.680	69.97
300	York, Rudy	1st	1940	.316	.410	.583	239	.345	437	.631	69.97
301	Henderson, Rickey	1st	1985	.314	.419	.516	218	.329	454	.686	69.95
302	Bell, George	1st	1987	.308	.352	.605	245	.359	419	.614	69.89
303	Vaughn, Greg	1st	1998	.272	.363	.597	231	.346	433	.648	69.76
304	Keeler, Willie	4th	1895	.395	.445	.511	239	.391	382	.625	69.73
305	Robinson, Jackie	1st	1949	.342	.432	.528	246	.347	430	.606	69.61
306	Perez, Tony	1st	1970	.317	.401	.589	236	.339	438	.629	69.48
307	Fielder, Cecil	1st	1990	.277	.377	.592	236	.343	433	.629	69.46
308	Allen, Dick	1st	1966	.317	.396	.632	222	.365	406	.668	69.44
309	Bench, Johnny	1st	1970	.293	.345	.587	245	.359	412	.604	69.31
310	Castilla, Vinny**	1st	1998	.319	.362	.589	252	.350	422	.585	69.25
311	Cronin, Joe	1st	1930	.346	.422	.513	253	.381	385	.580	69.12
312	McGwire, Mark	4th	1997	.274	.393	.646	209	.314	462	.694	69.11
313	Jackson, Joe	1st	1911	.408	.468	.590	209	.329	442	.696	69.07
314	Yount, Robin	1st	1982	.331	.379	.578	243	.338	433	.602	68.97
315	Waner, Paul	1st	1927	.380	.437	.549	245	.357	410	.598	68.94
316	Beltre, Adrian**	1st	2004	.334	.388	.629	225	.335	436	.649	68.94
317	Mattingly, Don	1st	1985	.324	.371	.567	252	.341	428	.578	68.87
318	Jeter, Derek**	1st	1999	.349	.438	.552	236	.316	460	.615	68.87
319	Keller, Charlie*	1st	1941	.298	.416	.580	224	.365	399	.651	68.84
320	Belle, Albert	4th	1994	.357	.438	.714	191	.395	360	.744	68.79
321	Bichette, Dante	1st	1996	.313	.359	.531	255	.358	406	.570	68.79
322	Williams, Ted*	9th	1957	.388	.526	.731	183	.329	430	.772	68.77
323	Burkett, Jesse	3rd	1896	.410	.462	.540	231	.360	404	.630	68.74
324	Brett, George	1st	1980	.390	.454	.664	205	.390	366	.696	68.49
325	Meusel, Bob	1st	1921	.318	.356	.559	239	.377	381	.601	68.33
326	Johnson, Robert	1st	1939	.338	.440	.553	229	.350	410	.626	68.21
327	Martinez, Tino**	1st	1997	.296	.371	.577	237	.339	423	.604	68.20
328	Berger, Wally	1st	1930	.310	.375	.614	217	.354	402	.656	68.04
329	Killebrew, Harmon	2nd	1961	.288	.405	.606	216	.324	437	.655	67.97
330	Carew, Rod	1st	1977	.388	.449	.570	228	.326	433	.619	67.79
331	Olerud, John	1st	1993	.363	.473	.599	216	.313	449	.650	67.78
332	Crawford, Sam	1st	1911	.378	.438	.526	224	.353	400	.630	67.68
333	Wagner, Honus	1st	1908	.354	.415	.542	209	.333	420	.670	67.61
334	Williams, Bernie**	1st	2000	.307	.391	.566	229	.363	388	.615	67.61
335	Vaughan, Arky	1st	1935	.385	.491	.607	207	.340	411	.676	67.60
336	Appling, Luke	1st	1936	.388	.473	.508	239	.391	356	.583	67.45
337	McGraw, John	2nd	1899	.391	.547	.446	189	.352	389	.724	67.28
338	Parker, Dave	1st	1978	.334	.394	.585	219	.337	412	.634	67.17
339	Sheckard, Jimmy	1st	1901	.354	.407	.534	220	.364	381	.631	67.17
340	Dickey, Bill*	1st	1936	.362	.428	.617	206	.436	308	.653	67.15
341	Anson, Cap	2nd	1887	.421	.481	.571	209	.352	392	.661	67.11
342	Garciaparra, Nomar**	1st	1998	.323	.362	.584	233	.347	400	.595	67.08
343	Hartnett, Gabby	1st	1930	.339	.404	.630	206	.365	376	.667	66.99

The Greatest 300 Seasons & Others Listed by Total Offensive Production

Rank	Player	Player Season	Year	AVG	OBP	SLG	Total Offensive Production Statistics				Rating
							TRP	RPA	TNB	TBA	
344	Heath, Jeff	1st	1938	.343	.383	.602	216	.404	337	.630	66.90
345	Minoso, Minnie	1st	1954	.320	.411	.535	235	.341	404	.586	66.87
346	Kelly, King	2nd	1887	.394	.453	.547	182	.313	427	.735	66.80
347	Howard, Frank	1st	1969	.296	.402	.574	222	.304	448	.613	66.72
348	Torre, Joe	1st	1971	.363	.421	.555	234	.323	422	.583	66.60
349	Berra, Yogi	1st	1950	.322	.380	.533	240	.361	376	.566	66.48
350	Seymour, Cy	1st	1905	.377	.429	.559	216	.341	399	.629	66.46
351	Boggs, Wade	1st	1987	.363	.461	.588	213	.314	429	.632	66.28
352	Murray, Eddie	1st	1985	.297	.383	.523	235	.343	394	.575	66.24
353	Cobb, Ty	4th	1912	.410	.458	.586	202	.336	399	.664	66.19
354	Kingman, Dave	1st	1979	.288	.343	.613	212	.356	377	.633	66.06
355	Dawson, Andre	1st	1987	.287	.328	.568	227	.335	400	.591	65.97
356	Erstad, Darin**	1st	2000	.355	.409	.541	221	.293	451	.599	65.89
357	Sievers, Roy	1st	1957	.301	.388	.579	213	.320	414	.622	65.66
358	Winfield, Dave	1st	1979	.308	.395	.558	215	.309	426	.613	65.56
359	Kaline, Al	1st	1955	.340	.421	.546	223	.321	406	.585	65.10
360	Kelly, George	1st	1924	.324	.371	.531	227	.370	351	.572	65.03
361	Manush, Heinie	1st	1928	.378	.414	.575	210	.310	418	.617	65.03
362	Cravath, Gavy	1st	1913	.341	.407	.568	206	.353	366	.628	64.91
363	Ripkin, Cal, Jr.	1st	1991	.323	.374	.566	213	.289	431	.586	63.90
364	Collins, Eddie	1st	1912	.348	.450	.435	201	.312	400	.621	63.81
365	McGriff, Fred **	1st	1993	.291	.375	.549	212	.324	386	.590	63.74
366	Zimmerman, Heinie	1st	1912	.372	.418	.571	194	.323	385	.641	63.73
367	English, Woody	1st	1930	.335	.430	.511	211	.284	435	.585	63.62
368	Clemente, Roberto	1st	1966	.317	.360	.536	224	.319	390	.555	63.52
369	Puckett, Kirby	1st	1988	.356	.375	.545	230	.325	382	.540	63.50
370	Traynor, Pie	1st	1930	.366	.423	.509	209	.383	309	.566	62.42
371	Oliva, Tony	1st	1964	.323	.359	.557	203	.280	420	.580	62.12
372	Tucker, Tuck	1st	1894	.416	.456	.540	173	.475	219	.602	61.44
373	Carty, Rico	1st	1970	.366	.454	.584	185	.320	357	.617	61.07
374	Rose, Pete	1st	1969	.348	.428	.512	202	.273	411	.556	60.66
375	Wheat, Zack	1st	1922	.335	.388	.503	204	.313	357	.548	60.20
376	Gwynn, Tony	1st	1987	.370	.447	.511	173	.250	430	.622	60.09
377	Burkett, Jesse	4th	1899	.402	.467	.504	186	.292	377	.593	60.01
378	Suzuki, Ichiro**	1st	2001	.350	.381	.457	196	.266	396	.537	58.72
379	Dunlap, Fred	1st	1884	.412	.448	.621	160	.335	308	.644	58.69
380	Suzuki, Ichiro**	2nd	2004	.372	.414	.455	161	.210	398	.520	53.07

* Player missed time for military service
** Active player. Statistics through 2004 season
TOP ranking for players with less than 70% rating is based upon comparison to listed players only.

Selecting the best five consecutive years of most players is easy. For a few, there are substantial difficulties. Do you take the years with the best slugging average and on-base average, or the years with the most Runs and RBIs? In all cases, I have attempted to take the years that would result in the highest **TOP Rating** for the consecutive 5-year period as a whole. In a few cases, the use of consecutive years required dropping a great year because there were a few poor years (relatively) between the great years.

Loss of time due to military service (i.e. Ted Williams and Hank Greenberg) required the use of more than 5 years in a few instances. While only the best five consecutive years was used for any player, it should be noted that Babe Ruth and Lou Gehrig each had two completely separate great periods of five consecutive years, and that the second period for Ruth (1920-1924, most before Gehrig joined the Yankees) would have ranked second, while the second period for Gehrig (1933-1937) would have ranked fourth under the **TOP Rating** system. Other players like Barry Bonds, Ted Williams and Willie Mays also had excellent second 5 consecutive year periods.

As with the other sets of statistics, a summary list of the players and their 5 consecutive year totals is set forth here in order of the **TOP Rating**, listing their TRP, RPA, TNB and TBA. These are, of course, compiled into the single TOP Rating by which the players are ranked. Complete statistics compiled for each 5 consecutive year period is set forth in Appendix E. Appendix E-1 provides all statistics and ratings for players listed according to their TOP Ranking; while Appendix E-2 lists the players in alphabetical order.

Statistics for each year of the five consecutive years used in this computation are set forth in Appendix G.

The 21 players with the best 5 consecutive year performance:

1. Babe Ruth (1927-1931)
2. Lou Gehrig (1927-1931)
3. Jimmie Foxx (1932-1936)
4. Barry Bonds (2000-2004)**
5. Ted Williams (1941-1948)*
6. Chuck Klein (1929-1933)
7. Sammy Sosa (1998-2002)**
8. Ed Delahanty (1893-1897)
9. Rogers Hornsby (1921-1925)
10. Joe DiMaggio (1937-1941)
11. Hack Wilson (1926-1931)
12. Hank Greenberg (1937-1946)*
13. Joe Kelley (1894-1898)
14. Jeff Bagwell (1997-2001)**
15. Mark McGwire (1995-1999)
16. Todd Helton (2000-2004)**
17. Al Simmons (1928-1933)
18. Ken Griffey, Jr. (1996-2000)**
19. Alex Rodriguez (1999-2003)**
20. Hugh Duffy (1890-1894)
21. Mickey Mantle (1954-1958)

* Skips or consolidates war years in service
**Currently active player. Statistics through 2004 season.

★ ★ ★ *The Best 5 Consecutive Years* ★ ★ ★

5 Consecutive Year Statistics & Analysis Listed by Total Offensive Production Ranking

Rank	Player	Years	AVG	OBP	SLG	TRP	RPA	TNB	TBA	Rating
						Total Offensive Production Statistics				
1	Ruth, Babe	1927-1931	.351	.474	.722	1,517	.468	2,518	.776	100.00
N/R	Ruth, Babe	1920-1924	.370	.511	.777	1,382	.437	2,608	.825	98.45
2	Gehrig, Lou	1927-1931	.354	.458	.677	1,522	.440	2,521	.729	97.13
N/R	Gehrig, Lou	1933-1937	.346	.461	.648	1,430	.413	2,459	.710	92.89
3	Foxx, Jimmie*	1932-1936	.348	.454	.675	1,364	.406	2,463	.733	92.14
4	Bonds, Barry **	2000-2004	.339	.535	.781	1,159	.377	2,607	.847	92.07
5	Williams, Ted*	1942-1949	.351	.496	.643	1,342	.387	2,465	.711	90.07
6	Klein, Chuck	1929-1933	.359	.414	.636	1,351	.397	2,323	.682	88.46
7	Sosa, Sammy**	1998-2002	.306	.397	.649	1,327	.370	2,438	.680	87.69
8	Delahanty, Ed	1893-1897	.388	.460	.578	1,288	.436	2,029	.688	86.88
9	Hornsby, Rogers	1921-1925	.402	.474	.690	1,213	.398	2,211	.726	86.50
10	DiMaggio, Joe*	1937-1941	.350	.420	.638	1,294	.418	2,084	.674	86.09
11	Wilson, Hack	1926-1930	.331	.419	.612	1,294	.407	2,138	.673	86.02
12	Greenberg, Hank*	1937-1945	.323	.429	.645	1,244	.406	2,140	.698	85.89
13	Kelley, Joe	1893-1897	.367	.465	.538	1,234	.413	2,083	.697	85.51
14	Bagwell, Jeff**	1997-2001	.298	.425	.585	1,288	.355	2,388	.659	85.08
15	McGwire, Mark	1995-1999	.287	.438	.702	1,133	.375	2,261	.748	85.08
16	Helton, Todd**	2000-2004	.349	.450	.643	1,242	.354	2,396	.682	85.01
17	Simmons, Al*	1928-1932	.360	.404	.618	1,301	.436	1,932	.647	84.85
18	Griffey, Ken **	1996-2000	.290	.382	.604	1,278	.371	2,273	.660	84.65
19	Rodriguez, Alex**	1999-2003	.304	.394	.608	1,264	.363	2,293	.658	84.12
20	Duffy, Hugh	1890-1894	.356	.419	.500	1,255	.406	2,021	.654	83.52
21	Mantle, Mickey	1954-1958	.325	.451	.618	1,152	.356	2,255	.696	82.67
22	Ramirez, Manny**	1998-2002	.324	.424	.640	1,172	.386	2,047	.675	81.96
23	Kiner, Ralph	1947-1951	.294	.420	.609	1,178	.345	2,282	.669	81.92
24	Mays, Willie*	1961-1965	.308	.387	.606	1,203	.353	2,215	.650	81.56
25	Hamilton, Billy	1894-1898	.374	.486	.467	1,103	.359	2,145	.698	81.00
26	Musial, Stan*	1948-1952	.350	.441	.616	1,159	.334	2,296	.662	80.91
27	Aaron, Hank	1959-1963	.323	.383	.600	1,208	.348	2,213	.637	80.89
28	Belle, Albert	1994-1998	.314	.393	.626	1,181	.356	2,164	.651	80.85
29	Snider, Duke	1953-1957	.311	.407	.618	1,166	.353	2,174	.659	80.79
30	Jennings, Hughie	1894-1898	.359	.447	.470	1,208	.413	1,849	.632	80.73
31	Giambi, Jason**	1999-2003	.311	.444	.596	1,158	.333	2,287	.659	80.68
32	Thomas, Frank **	1993-1998	.334	.455	.631	1,133	.352	2,172	.675	80.67
33	Thompson, Sam	1892-1896	.355	.407	.543	1,224	.418	1,810	.618	80.46
34	Ott, Mel	1929-1933	.314	.418	.564	1,192	.372	2,048	.639	80.39
35	Delgado, Carlos**	1999-2003	.295	.418	.584	1,176	.338	2,242	.645	80.37
36	Cobb, Ty	1908-1912	.383	.436	.550	1,092	.356	2,097	.683	79.70
37	Stovey, Harry	1887-1891	.306	.392	.487	1,104	.364	2,049	.675	79.58
38	Gehringer, Charlie	1934-1938	.343	.434	.517	1,221	.353	2,053	.593	78.46
39	Walker, Larry **	1997-2001	.357	.445	.658	1,021	.374	1,925	.704	78.44
40	Thome, Jim**	1999-2003	.281	.413	.587	1,107	.335	2,153	.652	78.42
41	Heilmann, Harry	1921-1925	.379	.449	.587	1,125	.367	1,952	.636	77.95
42	Trosky, Hal*	1934-1938	.315	.372	.560	1,190	.358	1,990	.599	77.82
43	Medwick, Joe	1934-1938	.344	.380	.572	1,214	.360	1,977	.587	77.81
44	Burkett, Jesse	1893-1897	.391	.472	.519	1,105	.360	1,968	.641	77.59
45	Bottomley, Jim	1925-1929	.322	.391	.558	1,161	.355	1,994	.610	77.56
46	Guerrero, Vladimir**	1998-2002	.325	.391	.602	1,106	.319	2,200	.635	77.45
47	Brouthers, Dan	1887-1891	.360	.461	.518	1,094	.369	1,909	.644	77.39

5 Consecutive Year Statistics & Analysis Listed by Total Offensive Production Ranking

Rank	Player	Years	AVG	OBP	SLG	TRP	RPA	TNB	TBA	Rating
48	Williams, Ken*	1921-1925	.339	.421	.595	1,062	.373	1,869	.657	77.08
49	Jones, Chipper**	1998-2002	.320	.422	.578	1,090	.310	2,231	.635	76.98
50	Palmiero, Rafael**	1998-2002	.291	.393	.577	1,110	.318	2,186	.625	76.96
51	Terry, Bill	1928-1932	.360	.409	.555	1,163	.351	1,988	.600	76.96
52	Averill, Earl	1930-1934	.320	.395	.546	1,160	.345	2,010	.598	76.72
53	Robinson, Frank	1958-1962	.309	.395	.584	1,084	.336	2,042	.634	76.41
54	Gonzalez, Juan **	1995-1999	.311	.357	.613	1,099	.378	1,802	.619	76.14
55	Keeler, Willie	1894-1898	.393	.438	.495	1,124	.368	1,850	.606	76.07
56	Galarraga, Andres**	1994-1998	.305	.367	.577	1,110	.356	1,908	.612	75.91
57	Conner, Roger	1889-1893	.317	.428	.491	1,099	.367	1,843	.616	75.86
58	Mize, Johnny*	1936-1940	.339	.421	.611	1,032	.337	2,002	.654	75.80
59	Sheffield, Gary**	2000-2004	.312	.414	.575	1,074	.331	2,038	.628	75.75
60	Matthews, Eddie	1953-1957	.289	.400	.577	1,054	.326	2,065	.638	75.70
61	Lajoie, Nap	1897-1901	.366	.399	.546	1,071	.414	1,595	.616	75.50
62	Morgan, Joe	1973-1977	.303	.431	.508	988	.304	2,163	.666	75.24
63	O'Neill, Tip	1887-1891	.356	.424	.501	1,111	.364	1,825	.599	75.18
64	Martinez, Edgar**	1995-1999	.334	.455	.579	1,030	.312	2,111	.639	75.01
65	Schmidt, Mike	1979-1983	.275	.398	.576	1,025	.330	1,993	.641	74.82
66	Anson, Cap	1886-1890	.358	.440	.496	1,083	.367	1,790	.607	74.81
67	Banks, Ernie	1955-1959	.299	.361	.584	1,085	.326	2,018	.606	74.78
68	Sisler, George	1918-1922	.381	.426	.559	1,016	.341	1,913	.642	74.54
69	Johnson, Robert	1935-1939	.309	.408	.538	1,079	.337	1,939	.606	74.49
70	Hafey, Chick	1927-1931	.338	.398	.611	967	.386	1,667	.666	74.49
71	Waner, Paul	1926-1930	.359	.430	.537	1,078	.325	2,004	.605	74.44
72	Berkman, Lance**	2000-2004	.306	.420	.569	1,026	.322	2,011	.631	74.29
73	Herman, Babe	1929-1933	.342	.401	.574	1,025	.323	2,005	.631	74.22
74	Vaughn, Mo	1994-1998	.319	.408	.578	1,041	.323	2,002	.621	74.17
75	Goslin, Goose	1924-1928	.348	.413	.544	1,069	.345	1,877	.606	74.16
76	Williams, Bernie**	1996-2000	.324	.410	.551	1,075	.337	1,921	.602	74.11
77	Murphy, Dale	1983-1987	.290	.383	.536	1,067	.302	2,121	.599	73.94
78	Piazza, Mike**	1996-2000	.331	.401	.592	1,046	.335	1,917	.614	73.84
79	Wagner, Honus	1900-1904	.353	.415	.513	999	.344	1,853	.638	73.70
80	Bichette, Dante	1995-1999	.318	.355	.541	1,140	.341	1,868	.558	73.56
81	Ordonez, Magglio**	1999-2003	.312	.372	.546	1,100	.319	1,992	.578	73.52
82	McCovey, Willie	1966-1970	.295	.410	.587	982	.323	1,952	.641	73.30
83	Speaker, Tris	1920-1924	.371	.460	.565	1,004	.338	1,860	.627	73.18
84	Kelly, King	1884-1888	.348	.415	.504	986	.384	1,620	.631	73.14
85	Rice, Jim	1975-1979	.311	.360	.556	1,079	.311	1,987	.573	72.54
86	Stargell, Willie	1971-1975	.297	.389	.579	988	.335	1,837	.622	72.33
87	Kluszewski, Ted	1952-1956	.316	.383	.571	1,020	.323	1,895	.601	72.15
88	Foster, George	1976-1980	.297	.370	.550	1,035	.325	1,865	.585	71.71
89	Keller, Charlie*	1939-1943	.295	.416	.526	986	.328	1,832	.610	71.53
90	Yastrzemski, Carl	1966-1971	.297	.405	.529	992	.284	2,082	.597	71.28
91	Killebrew, Harmon	1960-1964	.267	.375	.558	981	.308	1,934	.608	71.27
92	Williams, Billy	1968-1972	.307	.372	.533	1,049	.298	1,995	.567	71.19
93	Henderson, Rickey	1982-1986	.285	.397	.450	916	.280	2,091	.639	71.16
94	Mattingly, Don	1984-1988	.332	.376	.541	1,073	.309	1,925	.554	71.08
95	Robinson, Jackie	1949-1953	.329	.430	.505	1,003	.314	1,891	.592	71.08
96	York, Rudy	1937-1941	.296	.390	.556	962	.350	1,675	.610	70.80

★ ★ ★ The Best 5 Consecutive Years ★ ★ ★

5 Consecutive Year Statistics & Analysis Listed by Total Offensive Production Ranking

Rank	Player	Years	AVG	OBP	SLG	Total Offensive Production Statistics				Rating
						TRP	RPA	TNB	TBA	
97	Cepeda, Orlando	1959-1963	.309	.354	.542	1,037	.316	1,861	.568	70.70
98	Collins, Eddie	1911-1915	.347	.451	.451	966	.310	1,877	.603	70.42
99	Dickey, Bill*	1935-1939	.317	.401	.545	963	.361	1,604	.601	70.40
100	Murray, Eddie	1981-1985	.304	.390	.530	1,000	.316	1,836	.580	70.16
101	Allen, Dick	1966-1970	.291	.381	.570	922	.326	1,757	.622	69.99
102	Jackson, Reggie	1973-1977	.279	.365	.522	972	.312	1,844	.592	69.94
103	Jeter, Derek**	1998-2002	.324	.398	.483	1,022	.286	1,995	.558	69.78
104	Canseco, Jose	1987-1991	.275	.355	.534	956	.325	1,742	.592	69.41
105	McGriff, Fred **	1990-1994	.294	.391	.547	939	.302	1,863	.600	69.30
106	Fielder, Cecil	1990-1994	.262	.352	.506	1,029	.312	1,809	.548	69.21
107	Maris, Roger	1958-1962	.263	.350	.517	984	.314	1,773	.567	68.81
108	Meusel, Bob	1921-1925	.312	.360	.521	986	.336	1,654	.563	68.72
109	Parker, Dave	1975-1979	.321	.377	.532	965	.294	1,878	.572	68.53
110	Bench, Johnny	1970-1974	.267	.347	.499	1,022	.303	1,817	.538	68.33
111	Berra, Yogi	1950-1954	.299	.364	.503	1,016	.327	1,674	.538	68.17
112	Winfield, Dave	1982-1986	.288	.349	.503	1,024	.308	1,775	.534	68.16
113	Crawford, Sam	1908-1912	.323	.373	.465	979	.310	1,734	.550	67.60
114	Kaline, Al	1955-1959	.318	.387	.515	969	.297	1,808	.554	67.56
115	Campanella, Roy	1949-1953	.296	.379	.543	919	.333	1,607	.582	67.56
116	Jackson, Joe	1911-1915	.368	.437	.532	858	.295	1,798	.619	67.52
117	Howard, Frank	1967-1971	.278	.374	.533	926	.273	1,949	.574	67.49
118	Garciaparra, Nomar**	1997-2001	.335	.385	.574	881	.324	1,639	.603	67.42
119	Brett, George	1979-1983	.328	.391	.557	882	.316	1,665	.596	66.99
120	Traynor, Pie	1927-1931	.338	.380	.461	1,009	.338	1,527	.512	66.40
121	Perez, Tony	1967-1971	.290	.350	.494	989	.286	1,813	.524	66.38
122	Ripkin, Cal, Jr.	1983-1987	.288	.356	.479	1,012	.274	1,883	.510	66.37
123	Cravath, Gavy	1913-1916	.298	.390	.500	879	.306	1,665	.580	65.91
124	Dawson, Andre	1979-1983	.296	.341	.507	907	.287	1,774	.562	65.91
125	Clemente, Roberto	1963-1967	.332	.376	.502	928	.276	1,779	.530	64.69
126	Rose, Pete	1965-1969	.322	.384	.466	872	.245	1,800	.506	61.49

* Consecutive excluding or consolidating years of military service
** Active player. Statistics through 2004 season
TOP ranking for players with less than 70% rating is based upon comparison to listed players only.

To be the best batter in baseball for a period of ten consecutive years is perhaps the consummate ability of a player to succeed. Some great baseball players have never had 10 good years, and their **TOP Rating** in this category reflects this. Other players, strong for 20 years, show less well when viewed over only a ten year period, where longevity does not improve statistics. For a few, injury or one relatively poor season has destroyed what might have been a monumental achievement over this time period.

As with the 5 consecutive year statistics, the best 10 consecutive seasons were selected for each player that resulted in the highest **TOP Rating**. Also as with the 5 year statistics, adjustments were made for military service. Of course, the ten year totals for each key statistic (TRP, RPA, TNB and TBA) are included. The full statistics, TOP statistics, ratings in each TOP statistic and overall TOP Rating for each player of the ten consecutive year period are set forth in Appendix F. Statistics for each year of the ten consecutive years used in these computations are set forth in Appendix G.

Players from the 1950's and 1960's do relatively well in this analysis, unlike in the analysis of career statistics. Perhaps there is more comparability of the hitters within each era of baseball than we are sometimes led to believe. It should be noted that some current players have only ten years of major league experience. Alex Rodriguez, for instance, has relatively low totals because he is required to include a season in which he played less than 50 games. The ten year **TOP Rating** for players like Rodriguez, Carlos Delgado, Manny Ramirez and others may well get much better over the next few years. As with the other sets of statistics, these players and their 10 consecutive year totals are set forth in order of the **TOP Ranking**.

The players with the best 10 consecutive season totals:

1. Babe Ruth (1920-1929)

2. Lou Gehrig (1927-1936)

3. Jimmie Foxx (1930-1939)

4. Ted Williams (1939-1951)*

5. Barry Bonds (1995-2004)**

6. Rogers Hornsby (1920-1929)

7. Ed Delahanty (1893-1902)

8. Joe DiMaggio (1936-1948)*

9. Mel Ott (1929-1938)

10. Jeff Bagwell (1994-2003)**

11. Mickey Mantle (1953-1962)

12. Willie Mays (1954-1963)

13. Stan Musial (1946-1955)

14. Al Simmons (1925-1934)

15. Hank Greenberg (1933-1946)*

16. Hugh Duffy (1889-1898)

17. Sammy Sosa (1994-2003)**

18. Manny Ramirez (1995-2004)**

19. Hank Aaron (1957-1966)

* Skips or consolidates war years in service
**Currently active player. Statistics through 2004 season.

★ ★ ★ *The Best 10 Consecutive Years* ★ ★ ★

Rank	Player	Years	AVG	OBP	SLG	Total Offensive Production Statistics				Rating
						TRP	RPA	TNB	TBA	
1	Ruth, Babe	1920-1929	.355	.488	.740	2,696	.438	4,875	.793	100.00
2	Gehrig, Lou	1927-1936	.350	.458	.660	2,944	.425	4,956	.715	99.29
3	Foxx, Jimmie*	1930-1939	.336	.440	.652	2,647	.405	4,623	.708	93.58
4	Williams, Ted*	1939-1951	.347	.484	.633	2,534	.387	4,574	.698	90.94
5	Bonds, Barry **	1995-2004	.315	.485	.684	2,263	.361	4,839	.773	90.89
6	Hornsby, Rogers	1920-1929	.382	.460	.637	2,348	.377	4,259	.684	86.68
7	Delahanty, Ed	1893-1902	.373	.445	.547	2,365	.397	3,903	.655	85.24
8	DiMaggio, Joe*	1936-1948	.330	.398	.589	2,423	.383	3,957	.625	84.21
9	Ott, Mel	1929-1938	.315	.421	.566	2,354	.360	4,166	.637	83.75
10	Bagwell, Jeff**	1994-2003	.301	.420	.574	2,315	.339	4,394	.643	83.55
11	Mantle, Mickey	1953-1962	.311	.438	.595	2,186	.351	4,227	.678	83.36
12	Mays, Willie*	1954-1963	.320	.393	.601	2,270	.334	4,431	.651	83.29
13	Musial, Stan*	1944-1954	.344	.435	.594	2,286	.328	4,468	.641	82.97
14	Simmons, Al*	1925-1934	.359	.403	.588	2,355	.392	3,728	.620	82.81
15	Greenberg, Hank*	1933-1946	.319	.412	.616	2,182	.390	3,742	.668	82.79
16	Duffy, Hugh	1889-1898	.340	.404	.467	2,372	.386	3,726	.606	82.11
17	Sosa, Sammy**	1995-2004	.286	.366	.588	2,279	.343	4,165	.627	81.79
18	Ramirez, Manny**	1995-2004	.320	.416	.607	2,216	.350	4,070	.643	81.64
19	Aaron, Hank	1957-1966	.319	.381	.577	2,302	.336	4,223	.616	81.45
20	Hamilton, Billy	1889-1898	.354	.464	.446	2,046	.342	4,077	.681	80.97
21	Thomas, Frank **	1991-2000	.320	.439	.581	2,196	.327	4,264	.635	80.86
22	Rodriguez, Alex**	1995-2004	.306	.383	.577	2,211	.343	4,066	.631	80.82
23	Griffey, Ken **	1991-2000	.299	.386	.590	2,140	.343	4,008	.642	80.23
24	Thome, Jim**	1995-2004	.288	.418	.585	2,092	.331	4,106	.649	79.84
25	Cobb, Ty	1908-1917	.380	.449	.536	1,988	.335	4,002	.675	79.46
26	Brouthers, Dan	1885-1894	.356	.448	.528	2,073	.372	3,570	.641	79.02
27	Thompson, Sam	1887-1896	.340	.394	.512	2,227	.398	3,310	.591	78.95
28	Averill, Earl	1929-1938	.323	.399	.542	2,223	.337	3,936	.596	78.71
29	Heilmann, Harry	1921-1930	.367	.439	.573	2,110	.360	3,664	.625	78.60
30	Mize, Johnny*	1936-1948	.324	.409	.588	2,056	.342	3,825	.636	78.29
31	Palmiero, Rafael**	1993-2002	.291	.382	.560	2,147	.317	4,125	.608	78.26
32	Robinson, Frank	1958-1967	.304	.395	.568	2,096	.325	4,009	.622	78.13
33	Klein, Chuck	1928-1937	.340	.396	.586	2,065	.358	3,623	.629	78.06
34	Kelley, Joe	1893-1902	.345	.432	.496	2,052	.366	3,536	.630	77.98
35	Belle, Albert	1991-2000	.298	.374	.571	2,150	.326	3,977	.603	77.87
36	Gehringer, Charlie	1929-1938	.333	.412	.507	2,247	.338	3,833	.576	77.82
37	Wagner, Honus	1899-1908	.353	.416	.512	1,992	.338	3,781	.642	77.48
38	Matthews, Eddie	1953-1962	.285	.392	.552	2,082	.316	4,039	.614	77.41
39	Schmidt, Mike	1974-1983	.269	.388	.548	2,042	.315	4,025	.622	77.18
40	Stovey, Harry	1883-1892	.301	.377	.479	2,012	.364	3,448	.623	76.81
41	Walker, Larry **	1993-2002	.331	.416	.613	1,866	.357	3,492	.668	76.80
42	Conner, Roger	1885-1894	.330	.424	.513	2,014	.351	3,564	.621	76.62
43	Snider, Duke	1949-1958	.306	.386	.564	2,046	.326	3,809	.607	76.22
44	Jones, Chipper**	1995-2004	.303	.400	.536	2,072	.306	4,039	.596	76.12
45	Goslin, Goose	1923-1932	.326	.397	.526	2,091	.329	3,734	.587	75.79
46	McGwire, Mark	1992-2001	.277	.424	.663	1,660	.362	3,277	.715	75.76
47	Kiner, Ralph	1947-1956	.279	.398	.548	1,986	.312	3,907	.613	75.59
48	Sheffield, Gary**	1995-2004	.305	.424	.558	1,923	.319	3,803	.630	75.48
49	Gonzalez, Juan **	1992-2001	.302	.350	.582	2,023	.351	3,408	.592	74.96

10 Consecutive Year Statistics & Analysis Listed by Total Offensive Production Ranking

Rank	Player	Years	AVG	OBP	SLG	Total Offensive Production Statistics				Rating
						TRP	RPA	TNB	TBA	
50	Burkett, Jesse	1892-1901	.371	.446	.485	2,001	.314	3,793	.595	74.70
51	Johnson, Robert	1933-1942	.298	.395	.520	2,037	.320	3,722	.585	74.67
52	Wilson, Hack	1924-1933	.310	.396	.553	1,893	.363	3,219	.617	74.34
53	Delgado, Carlos**	1995-2004	.284	.394	.560	1,906	.321	3,651	.614	74.13
54	Medwick, Joe	1933-1942	.329	.367	.529	2,141	.329	3,559	.547	74.01
55	Killebrew, Harmon	1961-1970	.266	.390	.547	1,922	.303	3,842	.606	73.96
56	Piazza, Mike**	1993-2002	.322	.389	.579	1,912	.328	3,499	.600	73.35
57	Waner, Paul	1927-1936	.349	.418	.512	2,005	.299	3,833	.571	73.26
58	Bottomley, Jim	1922-1931	.327	.390	.541	1,933	.350	3,252	.589	73.24
59	Martinez, Edgar**	1994-2003	.319	.435	.553	1,840	.307	3,687	.615	72.98
60	Anson, Cap	1884-1893	.333	.410	.467	2,000	.355	3,171	.562	72.77
61	Williams, Billy	1963-1972	.300	.366	.519	2,019	.283	3,963	.555	72.61
62	Lajoie, Nap	1897-1906	.363	.399	.528	1,843	.370	2,980	.599	72.52
63	Williams, Bernie**	1995-2004	.310	.398	.511	1,966	.306	3,630	.565	72.08
64	Henderson, Rickey	1982-1991	.289	.404	.452	1,711	.274	3,960	.634	71.95
65	Rice, Jim	1977-1986	.305	.360	.526	2,020	.299	3,668	.544	71.68
66	Speaker, Tris	1916-1925	.360	.448	.526	1,781	.306	3,520	.606	71.25
67	Giambi, Jason**	1995-2004	.297	.411	.540	1,795	.304	3,534	.599	71.12
68	Allen, Dick	1964-1973	.299	.387	.553	1,771	.303	3,536	.606	71.08
69	Keeler, Willie	1894-1903	.373	.416	.461	1,919	.318	3,386	.561	71.02
70	Terry, Bill	1926-1935	.348	.398	.516	1,927	.319	3,373	.559	71.00
71	Banks, Ernie	1955-1964	.282	.342	.538	1,909	.297	3,602	.561	70.81
72	Morgan, Joe	1969-1978	.280	.402	.453	1,760	.272	3,882	.600	70.75
73	Jackson, Reggie	1971-1980	.280	.366	.521	1,837	.302	3,537	.581	70.75
74	McGriff, Fred **	1988-1997	.287	.381	.523	1,851	.288	3,692	.574	70.63
75	Murray, Eddie	1978-1987	.298	.376	.506	1,910	.290	3,631	.552	70.27
76	Kelly, King	1882-1891	.320	.387	.462	1,754	.365	2,816	.586	70.20
77	Stargell, Willie	1965-1974	.286	.368	.545	1,775	.308	3,370	.585	69.87
78	McCovey, Willie	1962-1971	.283	.391	.557	1,691	.311	3,318	.610	69.80
79	Trosky, Hal*	1933-1944	.305	.373	.533	1,794	.331	3,123	.576	69.79
80	Winfield, Dave	1979-1988	.291	.362	.499	1,918	.297	3,493	.542	69.71
81	Williams, Ken*	1919-1928	.324	.399	.543	1,690	.336	3,039	.604	69.61
82	Murphy, Dale	1980-1989	.273	.361	.491	1,867	.280	3,680	.552	69.56
83	Herman, Babe	1926-1935	.328	.386	.539	1,729	.304	3,356	.590	69.33
84	York, Rudy	1937-1946	.281	.370	.496	1,871	.306	3,354	.548	69.29
85	Vaughn, Mo	1991-2000	.298	.387	.533	1,761	.300	3,407	.580	69.28
86	Kaline, Al	1955-1964	.310	.382	.507	1,819	.289	3,475	.552	68.62
87	Yastrzemski, Carl	1965-1974	.292	.399	.490	1,774	.270	3,674	.559	68.36
88	Berra, Yogi	1948-1957	.290	.355	.493	1,880	.322	3,096	.530	68.34
89	Brett, George	1979-1988	.316	.393	.535	1,698	.300	3,289	.582	68.20
90	Bichette, Dante	1991-2000	.305	.343	.512	1,851	.307	3,214	.534	68.02
91	Canseco, Jose	1986-1995	.270	.352	.516	1,718	.318	3,080	.570	67.93
92	Bench, Johnny	1969-1978	.269	.348	.493	1,825	.295	3,326	.538	67.78
93	Traynor, Pie	1922-1931	.324	.368	.449	1,951	.321	3,043	.500	67.70
94	Jackson, Joe	1911-1920	.357	.424	.519	1,623	.299	3,233	.595	67.59
95	Collins, Eddie	1909-1918	.329	.426	.424	1,666	.274	3,526	.580	67.54
96	Cepeda, Orlando	1958-1967	.309	.359	.528	1,744	.300	3,227	.555	67.39
97	Sisler, George	1918-1927	.351	.390	.499	1,722	.307	3,147	.561	67.38
98	Perez, Tony	1967-1976	.286	.350	.488	1,850	.281	3,429	.522	67.21

★ ★ ★ The Best 10 Consecutive Years ★ ★ ★

Rank	Player	Years	AVG	OBP	SLG	Total Offensive Production Statistics				Rating
						TRP	RPA	TNB	TBA	
99	Meusel, Bob	1920-1929	.311	.358	.500	1,769	.328	2,915	.540	67.12
100	Crawford, Sam	1905-1914	.316	.369	.460	1,786	.283	3,398	.538	67.08
101	Jennings, Hughie	1891-1900	.320	.400	.414	1,683	.351	2,672	.557	67.05
102	Galarraga, Andres**	1989-1998	.289	.347	.514	1,736	.305	3,122	.549	66.91
103	Foster, George	1975-1984	.283	.348	.500	1,789	.294	3,251	.534	66.86
104	Dickey, Bill*	1930-1939	.320	.389	.513	1,659	.332	2,810	.563	66.66
105	Robinson, Jackie	1947-1956	.311	.409	.474	1,681	.289	3,265	.562	66.64
106	Dawson, Andre	1979-1988	.286	.331	.496	1,749	.281	3,353	.539	66.50
107	Ripkin, Cal, Jr.	1983-1992	.279	.351	.458	1,873	.257	3,629	.497	66.20
108	Clemente, Roberto	1960-1969	.328	.375	.501	1,778	.279	3,354	.525	66.14
109	O'Neill, Tip	1883-1892	.334	.399	.464	1,637	.343	2,624	.550	65.72
110	Jeter, Derek**	1995-2004	.315	.385	.463	1,730	.274	3,351	.531	65.60
111	Mattingly, Don	1984-1993	.311	.359	.483	1,818	.275	3,336	.505	65.55
112	Howard, Frank	1962-1971	.276	.358	.511	1,636	.269	3,332	.549	65.02
113	Keller, Charlie*	1939-1949	.286	.410	.518	1,435	.319	2,698	.600	64.55
114	Kluszewski, Ted	1948-1957	.303	.357	.513	1,628	.295	2,980	.541	64.37
115	Hafey, Chick	1925-1934	.321	.376	.533	1,479	.321	2,678	.581	64.32
116	Rose, Pete	1969-1978	.315	.390	.438	1,701	.227	3,717	.496	63.39
117	Parker, Dave	1977-1986	.300	.351	.491	1,636	.279	3,060	.521	63.27
118	Maris, Roger	1957-1966	.260	.348	.490	1,488	.293	2,768	.544	62.01
119	Fielder, Cecil	1987-1996	.257	.348	.498	1,492	.298	2,708	.542	62.00
120	Campanella, Roy	1948-1957	.276	.360	.500	1,483	.301	2,672	.542	61.89

10 Consecutive Year Statistics & Analysis Listed by Total Offensive Production Ranking

* Consecutive excluding or consolidating years of military service
** Active player. Statistics through 2004 season
TOP ranking for players with less than 70% rating is based upon comparison to listed players only.

The **TOP Ratings** of the greatest hitters in baseball history create a few surprises, even for devotees of the game. Players such as Ed Delahanty, Al Simmons, Hank Greenberg, Mel Ott and Chuck Klein deserve more recognition as some of the greats of the game. Yet other excellent players fail to show the batting prowess we assign to them from legend.

Whatever period we may use to judge baseball's hitters, these new statistics give us the tools to measure batting greatness. Each of the **TOP** statistics: **Total Run Production (TRP)™, Run Production Average (RPA)™, Total Net Bases (TNB)™** and **Total Base Average (TBA)™**; allows us to rate and rank one aspect of true performance. Combining these simple and meaningful statistics into a single **TOP Rating** allows us to put into perspective the greatness of modern players and compare them with those of the 1920's and 1930's, as well as heroes of the 1950's and 1960's.

Each of Chapters 6 through 9 gives us the statistics that really matter in hitting. Each rating category, whether for a career or a season, brings to light lesser known heroes who have been relegated to second class citizenship by some baseball critics. Truly comparative **TOP Ratings** also recognize the greatness of some players, forgotten in today's more powerful game, who achieved marvelous things in the late 19th and early 20th centuries.

The **TOP** statistics—TRP, RPA, TNB and TBA—are real statistics based on the actual achievements of each player on the field for each period. The combined **Total Offensive Production (TOP)™** properly weights these statistics into a single measurable rating system that gives all of baseball's great players their rightful place in history. For some, it is a ranking among the pinnacle of the elite. For others, it is recognition that they were exceptional for their time, but only good when compared to even more magnificent hitters. We should all have teams with such 'average' players.

We cannot be certain of where today's baseball heroes will end their careers, or how some will fare over 5 or 10 consecutive years. Yet even for the purist, these new statistics should help prove that the game of today ranks with the game of yesterday in producing players of stature and ability.

Looking at the 21st Century

With the structure of the game today, players of the 21st century will create new records that demand our attention. Mark McGwire may be gone, but Barry Bonds is still amazing. Frank Thomas, Ken Griffey Jr, Larry Walker, Juan Gonzalez and Sammy Sosa appear to be winding down great careers, but Alex Rodriguez, Jeff Bagwell, Jim Thome and Manny Ramirez have a number of years left to add to their already large numbers. Younger players like Albert Pujols, Todd Helton, Carlos Delgado, Lance Berkman, and Vladimir Guerrero may surpass them all, as may players that are unheard of today. Baseball is a game of numbers, and the odds favor the future.

125 of the Greatest Players:

A-1
Players Listed by Total Offensive Production

A-2
Players Listed Alphabetically

(Rating and Ranking of Total Offensive Production Statistics in Chapter 6)

10,000 Batting Opportunities

Total Career Statistics Adjusted to 10,000 Batting Opportunities Listed by Total Offensive Production Ranking

Rank	Player	Years	Adjustment to 10,000 BO	G	AB	H	1B	2B	3B	HR	RUN	RBI	BB	SO
1	Ruth, Babe	1914-1935	0.951928	2,383	7,995	2,735	1,444	482	129	680	2,069	2,107	1,963	1,266
2	Gehrig, Lou	1923-1938	1.046353	2,264	8,372	2,847	1,602	559	171	516	1,976	2,087	1,579	827
3	Williams, Ted*	1939-1960	1.001703	2,296	7,719	2,659	1,540	526	71	522	1,801	1,842	2,024	710
4	Foxx, Jimmie*	1925-1944	1.034340	2,397	8,413	2,737	1,582	474	129	552	1,811	1,988	1,502	1,356
5	Greenberg, Hank*	1930-1947	1.632120	2,275	8,476	2,657	1,382	619	116	540	1,715	2,083	1,391	1,378
6	Bonds, Barry **	1986-2004	0.853097	2,317	7,761	2,329	1,183	480	66	600	1,766	1,572	1,964	1,218
7	DiMaggio, Joe*	1936-1951	1.284192	2,229	8,759	2,843	1,712	500	168	464	1,785	1,974	1,015	474
8	Pujols, Albert**	2001-2004	3.568879	2,245	8,433	2,809	1,531	675	32	571	1,784	1,799	1,085	996
9	Thompson, Sam	1885-1906	1.534448	2,156	9,213	3,093	2,176	500	224	193	1,932	1,993	691	347
10	Brouthers, Dan	1879-1904	1.303781	2,162	8,768	3,063	2,064	585	275	138	1,965	1,690	1,095	310
11	Delahanty, Ed	1888-1903	1.200768	2,191	8,997	3,114	2,163	612	217	121	1,916	1,758	890	293
12	Helton, Todd**	1997-2004	2.043318	2,319	8,277	2,803	1,575	670	45	513	1,700	1,708	1,363	1,107
13	Ramirez, Manny**	1993-2004	1.485443	2,280	8,277	2,614	1,448	566	21	579	1,585	1,887	1,298	1,827
14	Wilson, Hack	1923-1934	1.828488	2,465	8,704	2,671	1,616	486	123	446	1,616	1,944	1,232	1,304
15	Hornsby, Rogers	1915-1937	1.079680	2,439	8,824	3,163	2,072	584	182	325	1,705	1,710	1,121	733
16	Duffy, Hugh	1888-1906	1.300390	2,239	9,101	3,000	2,307	403	152	138	2,009	1,693	861	274
17	Rodriguez, Alex**	1994-2004	1.539172	2,201	8,604	2,627	1,528	476	37	586	1,725	1,687	984	1,733
18	McGwire, Mark	1986-2001	1.281394	2,401	7,928	2,084	1,006	323	8	747	1,495	1,812	1,688	2,045
19	Hamilton, Billy	1888-1901	1.326612	2,093	8,307	2,862	2,385	298	125	53	2,243	976	1,575	289
20	Stovey, Harry	1880-1893	1.451800	2,159	8,992	2,651	1,717	504	253	177	2,166	1,318	963	498
21	Walker, Larry **	1989-2004	1.282051	2,418	8,451	2,653	1,524	578	78	472	1,653	1,614	1,118	1,496
22	Thome, Jim**	1991-2004	1.400756	2,352	8,021	2,276	1,206	444	34	593	1,576	1,629	1,698	2,385
23	Mantle, Mickey	1951-1968	0.999001	2,399	8,094	2,413	1,462	344	72	535	1,675	1,507	1,733	1,711
24	Cobb, Ty	1905-1928	0.782963	2,375	8,948	3,281	2,390	567	233	92	1,758	1,517	978	280
25	Mize, Johnny*	1936-1953	1.342102	2,529	8,647	2,699	1,613	493	111	482	1,500	1,794	1,150	703
26	Simmons, Al*	1924-1944	1.060333	2,349	9,292	3,104	2,049	572	158	326	1,598	1,937	652	781
27	Ott, Mel	1926-1947	0.884173	2,414	8,361	2,543	1,596	431	64	452	1,644	1,645	1,510	792
28	Berkman, Lance**	1999-2004	3.036745	2,353	8,148	2,472	1,354	592	52	474	1,567	1,625	1,521	1,646
29	Thomas, Frank **	1990-2004	1.154068	2,222	7,907	2,439	1,410	512	13	503	1,510	1,661	1,673	1,309
30	Griffey, Ken **	1989-2004	1.156337	2,309	8,533	2,493	1,410	463	42	579	1,526	1,670	1,138	1,530
31	Guerrero, Vladimir**	1996-2004	1.983733	2,301	8,679	2,819	1,680	526	71	542	1,518	1,643	859	1,107
32	Kelly, King	1878-1892	1.542258	2,212	9,133	2,858	2,042	541	168	106	2,096	1,465	848	648
33	Averill, Earl	1929-1941	1.395284	2,327	8,864	2,817	1,747	560	179	332	1,708	1,624	1,080	723
34	Klein, Chuck	1928-1944	1.397819	2,450	9,066	2,902	1,823	556	103	419	1,633	1,679	840	728
35	Delgado, Carlos**	1993-2004	1.636393	2,329	8,195	2,312	1,183	561	18	550	1,455	1,731	1,353	2,032
36	Bagwell, Jeff**	1991-2004	1.049869	2,216	8,081	2,403	1,393	508	34	468	1,581	1,585	1,452	1,614
37	Anson, Cap	1871-1897	0.886918	2,217	9,100	3,108	2,374	517	130	86	1,764	1,841	872	268
38	Gonzalez, Juan **	1989-2004	1.363512	2,302	8,938	2,640	1,485	529	34	592	1,447	1,914	623	1,736
39	Keller, Charlie*	1939-1952	2.157963	2,525	8,179	2,341	1,420	358	155	408	1,565	1,640	1,692	1,077
40	Belle, Albert	1989-2000	1.457301	2,243	8,530	2,515	1,363	567	31	555	1,419	1,806	995	1,400
41	Williams, Ken*	1915-1929	1.832845	2,560	8,911	2,845	1,822	522	141	359	1,576	1,673	1,037	526
42	Conner, Roger	1880-1897	1.130327	2,246	8,824	2,865	1,968	485	257	156	1,816	1,494	1,133	508
43	Mays, Willie*	1951-1973	0.785546	2,350	8,548	2,579	1,540	411	110	518	1,620	1,495	1,149	1,199
44	Kiner, Ralph	1946-1956	1.569120	2,310	8,167	2,277	1,298	339	61	579	1,524	1,593	1,586	1,175
45	O'Neill, Tip	1883-1892	2.096436	2,210	9,025	3,010	2,243	465	193	109	1,845	1,587	883	306
46	Kelley, Joe	1891-1908	1.252662	2,299	8,757	2,812	2,052	442	237	81	1,775	1,496	1,140	200
47	Heilmann, Harry	1914-1932	1.151676	2,471	8,968	3,063	2,055	624	174	211	1,487	1,772	986	633
48	Sosa, Sammy**	1989-2004	1.089799	2,330	8,741	2,419	1,376	371	47	626	1,507	1,667	933	2,299
49	Aaron, Hank	1954-1976	0.701902	2,315	8,678	2,647	1,610	438	69	530	1,526	1,612	984	971
50	Musial, Stan*	1941-1963	0.773994	2,342	8,492	2,810	1,744	561	137	368	1,509	1,510	1,238	539

Total Career Statistics Adjusted to 10,000 Batting Opportunities Listed by Total Offensive Production Ranking

SB	CS	HBP	SF	GDP	AVG	OBP	SLG	Total Offensive Production Statistics				TRP Rating	RPA Rating	TNB Rating	TBA Rating	TOP Composite	
								TRP	RPA	TNB	TBA					TOP	Rating
117	111	40	-	2	.342	.474	.690	4,176	.418	7,523	.752	100.00	100.00	100.00	100.00	400.00	100.00
107	106	47	-	2	.340	.447	.632	4,063	.406	6,922	.692	97.29	97.29	92.01	92.01	378.59	94.65
24	17	39	20	197	.344	.482	.634	3,643	.364	6,963	.696	87.24	87.24	92.55	92.55	359.58	89.90
91	74	13	-	71	.325	.428	.609	3,799	.380	6,658	.666	90.97	90.97	88.50	88.50	358.95	89.74
95	42	26	-	108	.313	.412	.605	3,798	.380	6,597	.660	90.94	90.94	87.69	87.69	357.27	89.32
432	120	79	74	121	.300	.443	.611	3,338	.334	7,094	.709	79.93	79.93	94.30	94.30	348.47	87.12
39	12	59	-	167	.325	.398	.579	3,759	.376	6,171	.617	90.01	90.01	82.02	82.02	344.06	86.01
46	46	125	89	268	.333	.413	.624	3,583	.358	6,470	.647	85.80	85.80	86.01	86.01	343.62	85.90
362	-	97	-	-	.336	.388	.502	3,925	.393	5,771	.577	93.99	93.99	76.71	76.71	341.40	85.35
343	-	137	-	-	.349	.429	.526	3,654	.365	6,188	.619	87.51	87.51	82.25	82.25	339.52	84.88
578	-	113	-	-	.346	.412	.503	3,674	.367	6,105	.610	87.99	87.99	81.15	81.15	338.26	84.57
61	47	63	96	200	.339	.432	.616	3,408	.341	6,543	.654	81.61	81.61	86.97	86.97	337.16	84.29
49	45	100	89	236	.316	.411	.599	3,471	.347	6,362	.636	83.13	83.13	84.57	84.57	335.39	83.85
95	9	37	-	27	.307	.395	.545	3,560	.356	6,096	.610	85.25	85.25	81.03	81.03	332.56	83.14
146	69	52	3	-	.358	.434	.577	3,415	.342	6,337	.634	81.78	81.78	84.23	84.23	332.01	83.00
776	-	38	-	-	.330	.390	.453	3,702	.370	5,796	.580	88.65	88.65	77.04	77.04	331.39	82.85
316	77	126	89	197	.305	.381	.574	3,412	.341	6,284	.628	81.71	81.71	83.54	83.54	330.49	82.62
15	10	96	100	188	.263	.394	.588	3,307	.331	6,452	.645	79.20	79.20	85.76	85.76	329.91	82.48
1,243	-	118	-	-	.344	.455	.430	3,220	.322	6,504	.650	77.10	77.10	86.46	86.46	327.11	81.78
739	-	45	-	-	.295	.366	.466	3,484	.348	5,938	.594	83.43	83.43	78.93	78.93	324.73	81.18
292	96	165	81	185	.314	.401	.568	3,267	.327	6,282	.628	78.22	78.22	83.50	83.50	323.45	80.86
25	27	67	73	141	.284	.410	.569	3,205	.320	6,329	.633	76.74	76.74	84.12	84.12	321.73	80.43
153	38	13	47	113	.298	.421	.557	3,183	.318	6,368	.637	76.21	76.21	84.64	84.64	321.71	80.43
698	166	74	-	-	.367	.433	.513	3,274	.327	6,172	.617	78.41	78.41	82.04	82.04	320.90	80.22
38	3	70	-	133	.312	.397	.562	3,295	.329	6,115	.611	78.90	78.90	81.28	81.28	320.35	80.09
92	68	32	-	24	.334	.380	.535	3,535	.354	5,676	.568	84.65	84.65	75.45	75.45	320.20	80.05
79	2	57	-	73	.304	.414	.533	3,288	.329	6,101	.610	78.74	78.74	81.09	81.09	319.67	79.92
121	79	112	79	140	.303	.416	.563	3,192	.319	6,265	.626	76.43	76.43	83.27	83.27	319.40	79.85
37	27	82	122	216	.308	.429	.567	3,170	.317	6,252	.625	75.91	75.91	83.10	83.10	318.02	79.51
206	76	82	87	161	.292	.377	.560	3,196	.320	6,126	.613	76.67	76.67	81.71	81.71	316.76	79.19
274	147	115	67	280	.325	.390	.589	3,160	.316	6,213	.621	75.67	75.67	82.59	82.59	316.51	79.13
568	-	19	-	-	.313	.372	.444	3,561	.356	5,489	.549	85.27	85.27	72.96	72.96	316.47	79.12
98	80	46	-	10	.318	.395	.534	3,332	.333	5,874	.587	79.79	79.79	78.08	78.08	315.73	78.93
110	-	17	-	77	.320	.379	.543	3,311	.331	5,890	.589	79.29	79.29	78.30	78.30	315.19	78.80
15	11	200	100	152	.282	.392	.556	3,186	.319	6,115	.612	76.29	76.29	81.29	81.29	315.16	78.79
212	82	133	103	231	.297	.408	.542	3,166	.317	6,099	.610	75.82	75.82	81.07	81.07	313.78	78.44
262	14	28	-	-	.342	.401	.455	3,605	.361	5,291	.529	86.33	86.33	70.33	70.33	313.33	78.33
35	26	85	106	248	.295	.343	.561	3,361	.336	5,729	.573	80.48	80.48	76.16	76.16	313.28	78.32
97	50	22	-	108	.286	.410	.518	3,205	.320	5,995	.599	76.74	76.74	79.69	79.69	312.84	78.21
128	60	80	114	281	.295	.369	.564	3,225	.323	5,953	.595	77.23	77.23	79.13	79.13	312.71	78.18
282	194	51	-	-	.319	.393	.530	3,250	.325	5,904	.590	77.81	77.81	78.47	78.47	312.58	78.14
285	-	43	-	-	.325	.404	.491	3,311	.331	5,792	.579	79.28	79.28	76.99	76.99	312.53	78.13
266	81	35	71	197	.302	.384	.557	3,115	.311	6,134	.613	74.58	74.58	81.53	81.53	312.23	78.06
35	3	38	11	198	.279	.398	.548	3,116	.312	6,131	.613	74.62	74.62	81.49	81.49	312.22	78.06
338	-	92	-	-	.334	.399	.464	3,432	.343	5,501	.550	82.18	82.18	73.12	73.12	310.60	77.65
551	-	103	-	-	.321	.405	.454	3,271	.327	5,766	.577	78.32	78.32	76.64	76.64	309.93	77.48
129	74	46	-	-	.342	.410	.520	3,259	.326	5,755	.575	78.04	78.04	76.50	76.50	309.08	77.27
254	116	59	76	191	.277	.348	.545	3,175	.317	5,890	.589	76.02	76.02	78.30	78.30	308.63	77.16
168	51	22	85	230	.305	.374	.555	3,138	.314	5,936	.594	75.15	75.15	78.90	78.90	308.10	77.03
60	27	41	41	188	.331	.417	.559	3,019	.302	6,060	.606	72.28	72.28	80.55	80.55	305.66	76.41

10,000 Batting Opportunities

Total Career Statistics Adjusted to 10,000 Batting Opportunities Listed by Total Offensive Production Ranking

Rank	Player	Years	Adjustment to 10,000 BO	G	AB	H	1B	2B	3B	HR	RUN	RBI	BB	SO
51	Giambi, Jason**	1995-2004	1.695778	2,279	8,067	2,396	1,404	502	14	477	1,443	1,601	1,477	1,553
52	Jones, Chipper**	1993-2004	1.474709	2,274	8,282	2,514	1,538	479	40	457	1,526	1,532	1,382	1,293
53	Hafey, Chick	1924-1937	1.977066	2,537	9,144	2,898	1,767	674	132	324	1,536	1,647	735	943
54	Piazza, Mike**	1992-2004	1.485001	2,361	8,620	2,716	1,723	423	9	561	1,388	1,724	989	1,365
55	Jennings, Hughie	1891-1918	1.826150	2,305	8,842	2,776	2,171	411	161	33	1,806	1,534	634	214
56	Snider, Duke	1947-1964	1.197461	2,566	8,575	2,534	1,516	429	102	487	1,508	1,596	1,163	1,481
57	Garciaparra, Nomar**	1996-2004	2.168727	2,188	8,963	2,884	1,746	635	108	395	1,598	1,540	640	911
58	Schmidt, Mike	1972-1989	0.980200	2,356	8,187	2,190	1,195	400	58	537	1,476	1,563	1,477	1,846
59	Trosky, Hal*	1933-1946	1.734605	2,337	8,952	2,708	1,637	574	101	395	1,448	1,755	945	763
60	Robinson, Frank	1956-1976	0.833681	2,341	8,342	2,454	1,465	440	60	489	1,525	1,511	1,184	1,277
61	Goslin, Goose	1921-1938	1.035090	2,367	8,960	2,831	1,878	518	179	257	1,535	1,665	982	606
62	Sheffield, Gary**	1988-2004	1.124986	2,290	8,215	2,447	1,519	434	27	467	1,470	1,522	1,352	989
63	Canseco, Jose	1985-2001	1.203949	2,272	8,496	2,260	1,277	409	17	556	1,428	1,694	1,091	2,338
64	Herman, Babe	1926-1945	1.618909	2,513	9,071	2,943	1,826	646	178	293	1,428	1,614	842	895
65	Jackson, Joe	1908-1920	1.798885	2,393	8,960	3,188	2,236	552	302	97	1,570	1,412	934	284
66	Johnson, Robert	1933-1945	1.231375	2,294	8,521	2,526	1,566	488	117	355	1,526	1,580	1,324	1,048
67	Wagner, Honus	1897-1917	0.868508	2,421	9,056	2,979	2,107	565	219	88	1,511	1,504	836	284
68	Allen, Dick	1963-1977	1.340662	2,345	8,489	2,478	1,472	429	106	471	1,473	1,500	1,199	2,086
69	Gehringer, Charlie	1924-1941	0.987849	2,295	8,752	2,805	1,911	567	144	182	1,752	1,410	1,171	367
70	Meusel, Bob	1920-1930	1.703287	2,397	9,325	2,884	1,829	627	162	266	1,407	1,817	639	1,054
71	Bottomley, Jim	1922-1937	1.217878	2,425	9,099	2,817	1,800	566	184	267	1,433	1,732	809	720
72	Speaker, Tris	1907-1928	0.856238	2,388	8,729	3,010	2,040	679	191	100	1,611	1,309	1,182	188
73	Terry, Bill	1923-1936	1.426127	2,454	9,167	3,127	2,216	532	160	220	1,597	1,537	766	640
74	Ordonez, Magglio**	1997-2004	2.304147	2,306	8,772	2,689	1,671	553	35	431	1,438	1,620	767	993
75	Stargell, Willie	1962-1982	1.091703	2,576	8,654	2,437	1,396	462	60	519	1,305	1,681	1,023	2,114
76	Vaughn, Mo	1991-2003	1.527884	2,310	8,452	2,475	1,546	413	15	501	1,316	1,626	1,108	2,183
77	Matthews, Eddie	1952-1968	0.981547	2,347	8,379	2,272	1,352	347	71	503	1,481	1,426	1,417	1,460
78	Medwick, Joe	1932-1948	1.204674	2,390	9,198	2,977	1,943	651	136	247	1,443	1,666	526	664
79	Campanella, Roy	1948-1957	2.028809	2,465	8,531	2,355	1,467	361	37	491	1,272	1,737	1,081	1,016
80	Killebrew, Harmon	1954-1975	0.992654	2,417	8,087	2,071	1,190	288	24	569	1,274	1,572	1,548	1,687
81	Lajoie, Nap	1896-1916	0.976658	2,417	9,365	3,176	2,304	633	159	80	1,471	1,562	504	83
82	Robinson, Jackie	1947-1956	1.720874	2,378	8,393	2,612	1,814	470	93	236	1,630	1,263	1,273	501
83	Martinez, Edgar**	1987-2004	1.129688	2,322	8,148	2,538	1,592	581	17	349	1,377	1,425	1,449	1,358
84	Dickey, Bill*	1928-1946	1.416832	2,535	8,926	2,790	1,916	486	102	286	1,318	1,713	961	409
85	McCovey, Willie	1959-1980	1.014507	2,626	8,316	2,243	1,310	358	47	529	1,247	1,578	1,365	1,572
86	Palmiero, Rafael**	1986-2004	0.845237	2,300	8,539	2,470	1,488	483	32	466	1,366	1,500	1,107	1,103
87	Cravath, Gavy	1908-1920	2.202643	2,687	8,703	2,498	1,542	511	183	262	1,267	1,584	1,236	1,132
88	Berra, Yogi	1946-1965	1.176747	2,495	8,890	2,530	1,673	378	58	421	1,383	1,683	828	488
89	York, Rudy	1934-1948	1.460067	2,340	8,601	2,367	1,462	425	76	404	1,279	1,682	1,155	1,266
90	Williams, Bernie**	1991-2004	1.215362	2,193	8,464	2,549	1,676	487	66	320	1,517	1,376	1,195	1,319
91	McGriff, Fred **	1986-2004	0.961723	2,366	8,422	2,395	1,473	424	23	474	1,297	1,491	1,255	1,810
92	Burkett, Jesse	1890-1905	1.053408	2,172	8,837	3,025	2,421	331	195	79	1,799	1,003	1,084	242
93	Jackson, Reggie	1967-1987	0.863036	2,434	8,513	2,230	1,302	400	42	486	1,339	1,469	1,188	2,241
94	Bichette, Dante	1988-2001	1.423285	2,425	9,082	2,713	1,714	571	38	390	1,329	1,624	505	1,534
95	Galarraga, Andres**	1985-2004	1.099626	2,482	8,903	2,565	1,603	488	35	439	1,314	1,567	641	2,203
96	Henderson, Rickey	1979-2003	0.741400	2,284	8,126	2,265	1,618	378	49	220	1,702	827	1,624	1,256
97	Collins, Eddie	1906-1930	0.867227	2,451	8,630	2,874	2,291	380	162	41	1,578	1,127	1,303	248
98	Fielder, Cecil	1985-1998	1.637197	2,407	8,443	2,150	1,288	327	11	522	1,218	1,650	1,135	2,155
99	Maris, Roger	1957-1968	1.692334	2,476	8,633	2,242	1,376	330	71	465	1,398	1,440	1,103	1,240
100	Rice, Jim	1974-1989	1.067464	2,230	8,780	2,617	1,727	398	84	408	1,333	1,549	715	1,519

10,000 Batting Opportunities

Total Career Statistics Adjusted to 10,000 Batting Opportunities Listed by Total Offensive Production Ranking

SB	CS	HBP	SF	GDP	AVG	OBP	SLG	Total Offensive Production Statistics				TRP Rating	RPA Rating	TNB Rating	TBA Rating	TOP Composite	
								TRP	RPA	TNB	TBA					TOP	Rating
22	17	156	105	195	.297	.411	.540	3,044	.304	5,993	.599	72.89	72.89	79.66	79.66	305.10	76.27
174	59	21	94	221	.304	.401	.537	3,059	.306	5,962	.596	73.24	73.24	79.25	79.25	304.98	76.25
138	14	65	-	55	.317	.372	.526	3,183	.318	5,735	.574	76.22	76.22	76.24	76.24	304.92	76.23
25	30	36	59	296	.315	.385	.562	3,113	.311	5,861	.586	74.53	74.53	77.91	77.91	304.89	76.22
683	-	524	-	-	.314	.393	.408	3,340	.334	5,447	.545	79.98	79.98	72.41	72.41	304.78	76.19
119	66	25	38	199	.295	.380	.540	3,104	.310	5,869	.587	74.32	74.32	78.01	78.01	304.67	76.17
187	63	104	106	187	.322	.370	.549	3,138	.314	5,788	.579	75.15	75.15	76.94	76.94	304.17	76.04
171	90	77	106	153	.267	.380	.527	3,040	.304	5,952	.595	72.79	72.79	79.11	79.11	303.80	75.95
49	40	28	-	75	.302	.371	.522	3,204	.320	5,651	.565	76.72	76.72	75.12	75.12	303.68	75.92
170	64	165	85	224	.294	.389	.537	3,035	.304	5,934	.593	72.69	72.69	78.88	78.88	303.13	75.78
181	92	58	-	-	.316	.387	.500	3,200	.320	5,606	.561	76.64	76.64	74.52	74.52	302.31	75.58
231	105	124	108	201	.298	.400	.528	2,992	.299	5,938	.594	71.66	71.66	78.93	78.93	301.17	75.29
241	106	101	98	214	.266	.353	.515	3,122	.312	5,698	.570	74.75	74.75	75.74	75.74	301.00	75.25
152	-	18	-	70	.324	.383	.532	3,042	.304	5,836	.584	72.84	72.84	77.58	77.58	300.84	75.21
363	110	106	-	-	.356	.423	.517	2,983	.298	5,929	.593	71.42	71.42	78.81	78.81	300.46	75.12
118	79	30	-	126	.296	.393	.506	3,106	.311	5,704	.570	74.36	74.36	75.82	75.82	300.36	75.09
627	20	108	-	-	.329	.392	.469	3,015	.302	5,796	.580	72.21	72.21	77.05	77.05	298.51	74.63
178	70	21	71	220	.292	.378	.534	2,974	.297	5,859	.586	71.20	71.20	77.88	77.88	298.16	74.54
180	88	50	-	27	.320	.404	.480	3,162	.316	5,518	.552	75.72	75.72	73.35	73.35	298.14	74.53
242	174	36	-	-	.309	.356	.497	3,224	.322	5,374	.537	77.21	77.21	71.43	71.43	297.28	74.32
71	18	52	-	40	.310	.369	.500	3,165	.317	5,465	.546	75.79	75.79	72.64	72.64	296.87	74.22
372	110	88	-	-	.345	.428	.501	2,920	.292	5,903	.590	69.92	69.92	78.46	78.46	296.76	74.19
80	9	13	-	54	.341	.393	.506	3,135	.313	5,488	.549	75.06	75.06	72.95	72.95	296.01	74.00
189	88	78	81	302	.307	.364	.525	3,058	.306	5,551	.555	73.22	73.22	74.12	74.12	294.68	73.67
19	17	85	82	156	.282	.360	.529	2,986	.299	5,683	.568	71.50	71.50	75.55	75.55	294.09	73.52
46	28	165	69	206	.293	.383	.523	2,941	.294	5,713	.571	70.43	70.43	75.94	75.94	292.73	73.18
67	38	26	57	121	.271	.376	.509	2,907	.291	5,740	.574	69.62	69.62	76.30	76.30	291.84	72.96
51	2	31	-	245	.324	.362	.505	3,109	.311	5,246	.525	74.45	74.45	69.74	69.74	288.38	72.10
51	34	61	37	290	.276	.360	.500	3,009	.301	5,421	.542	72.05	72.05	72.06	72.06	288.21	72.05
19	18	48	76	241	.256	.376	.509	2,846	.285	5,709	.571	68.15	68.15	75.88	75.88	288.06	72.02
386	21	131	-	-	.339	.381	.466	3,033	.303	5,368	.537	72.62	72.62	71.35	71.35	287.93	71.98
339	93	124	15	194	.311	.409	.474	2,893	.289	5,619	.562	69.27	69.27	74.69	74.69	287.91	71.98
55	34	101	87	215	.312	.418	.515	2,802	.280	5,772	.577	67.09	67.09	76.72	76.72	287.61	71.90
51	41	44	-	69	.313	.382	.486	3,031	.303	5,353	.535	72.57	72.57	71.15	71.15	287.44	71.86
26	22	70	71	179	.270	.374	.515	2,824	.282	5,719	.572	67.63	67.63	76.02	76.02	287.30	71.82
80	34	72	94	188	.289	.372	.517	2,866	.287	5,640	.564	68.62	68.62	74.96	74.96	287.16	71.79
196	20	62	-	-	.287	.380	.478	2,850	.285	5,634	.563	68.25	68.25	74.89	74.89	286.29	71.57
35	31	58	52	172	.285	.348	.482	3,065	.307	5,178	.518	73.40	73.40	68.82	68.82	284.46	71.11
55	38	18	-	226	.275	.362	.483	2,961	.296	5,347	.535	70.90	70.90	71.07	71.07	283.95	70.99
175	103	44	63	235	.301	.388	.488	2,893	.289	5,436	.544	69.26	69.26	72.26	72.26	283.05	70.76
69	37	38	68	217	.284	.377	.509	2,788	.279	5,613	.561	66.76	66.76	74.61	74.61	282.73	70.68
413	-	79	-	-	.342	.419	.451	2,802	.280	5,559	.556	67.10	67.10	73.89	73.89	281.98	70.49
197	99	83	59	158	.262	.356	.490	2,807	.281	5,540	.554	67.23	67.23	73.64	73.64	281.73	70.43
216	104	58	104	250	.299	.336	.499	2,953	.295	5,206	.521	70.72	70.72	69.21	69.21	279.85	69.96
141	89	196	64	197	.288	.347	.499	2,881	.288	5,329	.533	68.99	68.99	70.83	70.83	279.64	69.91
1,042	248	73	50	128	.279	.401	.419	2,528	.253	5,892	.589	60.54	60.54	78.32	78.32	277.71	69.43
644	150	67	-	-	.333	.424	.429	2,706	.271	5,565	.556	64.79	64.79	73.97	73.97	277.53	69.38
3	10	70	75	277	.255	.345	.482	2,868	.287	5,265	.527	68.69	68.69	69.99	69.99	277.35	69.34
36	15	64	73	127	.260	.345	.476	2,838	.284	5,299	.530	67.96	67.96	70.43	70.43	276.78	69.20
62	36	68	100	336	.298	.352	.502	2,882	.288	5,217	.522	69.02	69.02	69.34	69.34	276.72	69.18

10,000 Batting Opportunities

10,000 Batting Opportunities

Total Career Statistics Adjusted to 10,000 Batting Opportunities Listed by Total Offensive Production Ranking

Rank	Player	Years	Adjustment to 10,000 BO	G	AB	H	1B	2B	3B	HR	RUN	RBI	BB	SO	
101	Kluszewski, Ted	1947-1961	1.512859	2,599	8,970	2,672	1,767	439	44	422	1,283	1,555	744	552	
102	Cepeda, Orlando	1958-1974	1.122460	2,384	8,898	2,639	1,715	468	30	425	1,270	1,532	660	1,312	
103	Crawford, Sam	1899-1917	0.965065	2,417	9,244	2,860	2,025	441	301	94	1,343	1,472	733	100	
104	Sisler, George	1915-1930	1.138045	2,339	9,408	3,200	2,414	484	187	116	1,461	1,337	537	372	
105	Traynor, Pie	1920-1937	1.233198	2,394	9,322	2,979	2,248	458	202	72	1,459	1,570	582	343	
106	Waner, Paul	1927-1945	0.933271	2,379	8,828	2,942	2,092	566	178	105	1,518	1,222	1,018	351	
107	Banks, Ernie	1953-1971	0.945269	2,390	8,905	2,442	1,488	385	85	484	1,234	1,546	721	1,168	
108	Jeter, Derek**	1995-2004	1.583281	2,163	8,729	2,745	1,993	448	66	237	1,642	1,097	885	1,539	
109	Williams, Billy	1959-1976	0.933620	2,323	8,729	2,531	1,646	405	82	398	1,316	1,377	976	977	
110	Winfield, Dave	1973-1995	0.790014	2,349	8,693	2,457	1,593	427	70	367	1,319	1,448	961	1,332	
111	Bench, Johnny	1967-1983	1.128796	2,436	8,644	2,312	1,416	430	27	439	1,232	1,553	1,006	1,443	
112	Kaline, Al	1953-1974	0.845809	2,396	8,556	2,543	1,721	421	63	337	1,372	1,339	1,080	863	
113	Brett, George	1973-1993	0.845094	2,288	8,746	2,665	1,720	562	116	268	1,338	1,348	926	767	
114	Foster, George	1969-1986	1.249219	2,470	8,773	2,405	1,528	384	59	435	1,232	1,548	832	1,773	
115	Keeler, Willie	1892-1910	1.084952	2,304	9,292	3,206	2,753	252	166	36	1,866	879	569	879	
116	Howard, Frank	1958-1973	1.321353	2,504	8,577	2,344	1,469	324	46	505	1,142	1,479	1,033	1,929	
117	Dawson, Andre	1976-1996	0.912242	2,396	9,056	2,531	1,583	459	89	400	1,253	1,451	537	1,377	
118	Murray, Eddie	1977-1997	0.761557	2,304	8,633	2,479	1,642	426	27	384	1,239	1,460	1,015	1,155	
119	Murphy, Dale	1976-1993	1.081900	2,359	8,612	2,284	1,432	379	42	431	1,295	1,370	1,067	1,891	
120	Morgan, Joe	1963-1984	0.878503	2,327	8,150	2,211	1,497	394	84	235	1,450	995	1,638	892	
121	Yastrzemski, Carl	1961-1983	0.699252	2,313	8,383	2,391	1,582	452	41	316	1,270	1,289	1,290	975	
122	Parker, Dave	1973-1991	0.962279	2,373	9,005	2,610	1,705	506	72	326	1,224	1,437	657	1,479	
123	Mattingly, Don	1982-1995	1.265983	2,260	8,866	2,726	1,860	560	25	281	1,275	1,391	744	562	
124	Perez, Tony	1964-1986	0.899281	2,497	8,793	2,457	1,591	454	71	341	1,144	1,486	832	1,679	
125	Clemente, Roberto	1955-1972	0.956846	2,328	9,046	2,871	2,061	421	159	230	1,355	1,249	594	1,177	
126	Ripkin, Cal, Jr.	1981-2001	0.756258	2,270	8,736	2,408	1,593	456	33	326	1,246	1,282	854	987	
127	Rose, Pete	1963-1986	0.622975	2,219	8,755	2,651	2,003	465	84	100	1,349	819	976	712	

* Player missed time for military service
** Active player. Statistics through 2004 season
TOP ranking for players with less than 70% rating is based upon comparison to listed players only.

Total Career Statistics Adjusted to 10,000 Batting Opportunities Listed by Total Offensive Production Ranking

SB	CS	HBP	SF	GDP	AVG	OBP	SLG	Total Offensive Production Statistics				TRP Rating	RPA Rating	TNB Rating	TBA Rating	TOP Composite	
								TRP	RPA	TNB	TBA					TOP	Rating
30	15	35	35	216	.298	.353	.498	2,838	.284	5,259	.526	67.96	67.96	69.90	69.90	275.72	68.93
159	90	114	83	245	.297	.350	.499	2,802	.280	5,288	.529	67.09	67.09	70.29	70.29	274.75	68.69
350	29	22	-	-	.309	.362	.453	2,815	.282	5,262	.526	67.41	67.41	69.94	69.94	274.70	68.67
427	145	55	-	-	.340	.379	.468	2,798	.280	5,279	.528	67.01	67.01	70.18	70.18	274.37	68.59
195	57	38	-	58	.320	.362	.435	3,029	.303	4,814	.481	72.53	72.53	64.00	64.00	273.04	68.26
97	1	35	-	119	.333	.404	.474	2,740	.274	5,330	.533	65.61	65.61	70.85	70.85	272.92	68.23
47	50	66	91	216	.274	.330	.500	2,780	.278	5,233	.523	66.57	66.57	69.56	69.56	272.26	68.06
318	82	146	47	193	.315	.385	.463	2,739	.274	5,306	.531	65.59	65.59	70.52	70.52	272.23	68.06
84	46	40	68	187	.290	.361	.492	2,693	.269	5,348	.535	64.50	64.50	71.08	71.08	271.17	67.79
176	76	20	75	252	.283	.353	.475	2,767	.277	5,205	.521	66.25	66.25	69.19	69.19	270.88	67.72
77	49	21	102	227	.267	.342	.476	2,785	.278	5,169	.517	66.68	66.68	68.71	68.71	270.78	67.69
118	68	47	88	229	.297	.376	.480	2,711	.271	5,280	.528	64.91	64.91	70.19	70.19	270.20	67.55
170	82	28	101	199	.305	.369	.487	2,686	.269	5,305	.530	64.31	64.31	70.51	70.51	269.65	67.41
64	39	65	85	245	.274	.338	.480	2,780	.278	5,132	.513	66.56	66.56	68.21	68.21	269.54	67.39
563	39	140	-	-	.345	.391	.419	2,745	.274	5,130	.513	65.73	65.73	68.19	68.19	267.83	66.96
11	12	44	57	289	.273	.352	.498	2,620	.262	5,350	.535	62.74	62.74	71.12	71.12	267.72	66.93
286	99	101	108	198	.279	.323	.482	2,704	.270	5,192	.519	64.75	64.75	69.02	69.02	267.53	66.88
84	33	14	97	241	.287	.359	.476	2,699	.270	5,190	.519	64.63	64.63	68.99	68.99	267.23	66.81
174	74	30	65	226	.265	.346	.469	2,665	.266	5,236	.524	63.81	63.81	69.60	69.60	266.83	66.71
605	142	35	84	92	.271	.392	.427	2,445	.244	5,617	.562	58.54	58.54	74.67	74.67	266.42	66.60
117	81	28	73	226	.285	.379	.462	2,559	.256	5,228	.523	61.28	61.28	69.49	69.49	261.54	65.39
148	109	54	83	201	.290	.339	.471	2,661	.266	4,989	.499	63.71	63.71	66.32	66.32	260.07	65.02
18	11	27	122	242	.307	.358	.471	2,666	.267	4,956	.496	63.84	63.84	65.88	65.88	259.45	64.86
44	30	39	95	241	.279	.341	.463	2,629	.263	4,960	.496	62.97	62.97	65.94	65.94	257.80	64.45
79	44	33	63	263	.317	.359	.475	2,604	.260	4,961	.496	62.34	62.34	65.95	65.95	256.58	64.15
27	29	50	96	265	.276	.340	.447	2,527	.253	4,810	.481	60.52	60.52	63.93	63.93	248.91	62.23
123	93	67	49	154	.303	.375	.409	2,167	.217	4,656	.466	51.90	51.90	61.89	61.89	227.58	56.89

10,000 Batting Opportunities

10,000 Batting Opportunities A - H

Total Career Statistics Adjusted to 10,000 Batting Opportunities Listed Alphabetically															
Rank	Player	Years	Adjustment to 10,000 BO	G	AB	H	1B	2B	3B	HR	RUN	RBI	BB	SO	
49	Aaron, Hank	1954-1976	0.701902	2,315	8,678	2,647	1,610	438	69	530	1,526	1,612	984	971	
68	Allen, Dick	1963-1977	1.340662	2,345	8,489	2,478	1,472	429	106	471	1,473	1,500	1,199	2,086	
37	Anson, Cap	1871-1897	0.886918	2,217	9,100	3,108	2,374	517	130	86	1,764	1,841	872	268	
33	Averill, Earl	1929-1941	1.395284	2,327	8,864	2,817	1,747	560	179	332	1,708	1,624	1,080	723	
36	Bagwell, Jeff**	1991-2004	1.049869	2,216	8,081	2,403	1,393	508	34	468	1,581	1,585	1,452	1,614	
107	Banks, Ernie	1953-1971	0.945269	2,390	8,905	2,442	1,488	385	85	484	1,234	1,546	721	1,168	
40	Belle, Albert	1989-2000	1.457301	2,243	8,530	2,515	1,363	567	31	555	1,419	1,806	995	1,400	
111	Bench, Johnny	1967-1983	1.128796	2,436	8,644	2,312	1,416	430	27	439	1,232	1,553	1,006	1,443	
28	Berkman, Lance**	1999-2004	3.036745	2,353	8,148	2,472	1,354	592	52	474	1,567	1,625	1,521	1,646	
88	Berra, Yogi	1946-1965	1.176747	2,495	8,890	2,530	1,673	378	58	421	1,383	1,683	828	488	
94	Bichette, Dante	1988-2001	1.423285	2,425	9,082	2,713	1,714	571	38	390	1,329	1,624	505	1,534	
6	Bonds, Barry **	1986-2004	0.853097	2,317	7,761	2,329	1,183	480	66	600	1,766	1,572	1,964	1,218	
71	Bottomley, Jim	1922-1937	1.217878	2,425	9,099	2,817	1,800	566	184	267	1,433	1,732	809	720	
113	Brett, George	1973-1993	0.845094	2,288	8,746	2,665	1,720	562	116	268	1,338	1,348	926	767	
10	Brouthers, Dan	1879-1904	1.303781	2,162	8,768	3,063	2,064	585	275	138	1,965	1,690	1,095	310	
92	Burkett, Jesse	1890-1905	1.053408	2,172	8,837	3,025	2,421	331	195	79	1,799	1,003	1,084	242	
79	Campanella, Roy	1948-1957	2.028809	2,465	8,531	2,355	1,467	361	37	491	1,272	1,737	1,081	1,016	
63	Canseco, Jose	1985-2001	1.203949	2,272	8,496	2,260	1,277	409	17	556	1,428	1,694	1,091	2,338	
102	Cepeda, Orlando	1958-1974	1.122460	2,384	8,898	2,639	1,715	468	30	425	1,270	1,532	660	1,312	
125	Clemente, Roberto	1955-1972	0.956846	2,328	9,046	2,871	2,061	421	159	230	1,355	1,249	594	1,177	
24	Cobb, Ty	1905-1928	0.782963	2,375	8,948	3,281	2,390	567	233	92	1,758	1,517	978	280	
97	Collins, Eddie	1906-1930	0.867227	2,451	8,630	2,874	2,291	380	162	41	1,578	1,127	1,303	248	
42	Conner, Roger	1880-1897	1.130327	2,246	8,824	2,865	1,968	485	257	156	1,816	1,494	1,133	508	
87	Cravath, Gavy	1908-1920	2.202643	2,687	8,703	2,498	1,542	511	183	262	1,267	1,584	1,236	1,132	
103	Crawford, Sam	1899-1917	0.965065	2,417	9,244	2,860	2,025	441	301	94	1,343	1,472	733	100	
117	Dawson, Andre	1976-1996	0.912242	2,396	9,056	2,531	1,583	459	89	400	1,253	1,451	537	1,377	
11	Delahanty, Ed	1888-1903	1.200768	2,191	8,997	3,114	2,163	612	217	121	1,916	1,758	890	293	
35	Delgado, Carlos**	1993-2004	1.636393	2,329	8,195	2,312	1,183	561	18	550	1,455	1,731	1,353	2,032	
84	Dickey, Bill*	1928-1946	1.416832	2,535	8,926	2,790	1,916	486	102	286	1,318	1,713	961	409	
7	DiMaggio, Joe*	1936-1951	1.284192	2,229	8,759	2,843	1,712	500	168	464	1,785	1,974	1,015	474	
16	Duffy, Hugh	1888-1906	1.300390	2,239	9,101	3,000	2,307	403	152	138	2,009	1,693	861	274	
98	Fielder, Cecil	1985-1998	1.637197	2,407	8,443	2,150	1,288	327	11	522	1,218	1,650	1,135	2,155	
114	Foster, George	1969-1986	1.249219	2,470	8,773	2,405	1,528	384	59	435	1,232	1,548	832	1,773	
4	Foxx, Jimmie*	1925-1944	1.034340	2,397	8,413	2,737	1,582	474	129	552	1,811	1,988	1,502	1,356	
95	Galarraga, Andres**	1985-2004	1.099626	2,482	8,903	2,565	1,603	488	35	439	1,314	1,567	641	2,203	
57	Garciaparra, Nomar**	1996-2004	2.168727	2,188	8,963	2,884	1,746	635	108	395	1,598	1,540	640	911	
2	Gehrig, Lou	1923-1938	1.046353	2,264	8,372	2,847	1,602	559	171	516	1,976	2,087	1,579	827	
69	Gehringer, Charlie	1924-1941	0.987849	2,295	8,752	2,805	1,911	567	144	182	1,752	1,410	1,171	367	
51	Giambi, Jason**	1995-2004	1.695778	2,279	8,067	2,396	1,404	502	14	477	1,443	1,601	1,477	1,553	
38	Gonzalez, Juan **	1989-2004	1.363512	2,302	8,938	2,640	1,485	529	34	592	1,447	1,914	623	1,736	
61	Goslin, Goose	1921-1938	1.035090	2,367	8,960	2,831	1,878	518	179	257	1,535	1,665	982	606	
5	Greenberg, Hank*	1930-1947	1.632120	2,275	8,476	2,657	1,382	619	116	540	1,715	2,083	1,391	1,378	
30	Griffey, Ken **	1989-2004	1.156337	2,309	8,533	2,493	1,410	463	42	579	1,526	1,670	1,138	1,530	
31	Guerrero, Vladimir**	1996-2004	1.983733	2,301	8,679	2,819	1,680	526	71	542	1,518	1,643	859	1,107	
53	Hafey, Chick	1924-1937	1.977066	2,537	9,144	2,898	1,767	674	132	324	1,536	1,647	735	943	
19	Hamilton, Billy	1888-1901	1.326612	2,093	8,307	2,862	2,385	298	125	53	2,243	976	1,575	289	
47	Heilmann, Harry	1914-1932	1.151676	2,471	8,968	3,063	2,055	624	174	211	1,487	1,772	986	633	
12	Helton, Todd**	1997-2004	2.043318	2,319	8,277	2,803	1,575	670	45	513	1,700	1,708	1,363	1,107	
96	Henderson, Rickey	1979-2003	0.741400	2,284	8,126	2,265	1,618	378	49	220	1,702	827	1,624	1,256	
64	Herman, Babe	1926-1945	1.618909	2,513	9,071	2,943	1,826	646	178	293	1,428	1,614	842	895	

Total Career Statistics Adjusted to 10,000 Batting Opportunities Listed Alphabetically

SB	CS	HBP	SF	GDP	AVG	OBP	SLG	Total Offensive Production Statistics				TRP Rating	RPA Rating	TNB Rating	TBA Rating	TOP Composite	
								TRP	RPA	TNB	TBA					TOP	Rating
168	51	22	85	230	.305	.374	.555	3,138	.314	5,936	.594	75.15	75.15	78.90	78.90	308.10	77.03
178	70	21	71	220	.292	.378	.534	2,974	.297	5,859	.586	71.20	71.20	77.88	77.88	298.16	74.54
262	14	28	-	-	.342	.401	.455	3,605	.361	5,291	.529	86.33	86.33	70.33	70.33	313.33	78.33
98	80	46	-	10	.318	.395	.534	3,332	.333	5,874	.587	79.79	79.79	78.08	78.08	315.73	78.93
212	82	133	103	231	.297	.408	.542	3,166	.317	6,099	.610	75.82	75.82	81.07	81.07	313.78	78.44
47	50	66	91	216	.274	.330	.500	2,780	.278	5,233	.523	66.57	66.57	69.56	69.56	272.26	68.06
128	60	80	114	281	.295	.369	.564	3,225	.323	5,953	.595	77.23	77.23	79.13	79.13	312.71	78.18
77	49	21	102	227	.267	.342	.476	2,785	.278	5,169	.517	66.68	66.68	68.71	68.71	270.78	67.69
121	79	112	79	140	.303	.416	.563	3,192	.319	6,265	.626	76.43	76.43	83.27	83.27	319.40	79.85
35	31	58	52	172	.285	.348	.482	3,065	.307	5,178	.518	73.40	73.40	68.82	68.82	284.46	71.11
216	104	58	104	250	.299	.336	.499	2,953	.295	5,206	.521	70.72	70.72	69.21	69.21	279.85	69.96
432	120	79	74	121	.300	.443	.611	3,338	.334	7,094	.709	79.93	79.93	94.30	94.30	348.47	87.12
71	18	52	-	40	.310	.369	.500	3,165	.317	5,465	.546	75.79	75.79	72.64	72.64	296.87	74.22
170	82	28	101	199	.305	.369	.487	2,686	.269	5,305	.530	64.31	64.31	70.51	70.51	269.65	67.41
343	-	137	-	-	.349	.429	.526	3,654	.365	6,188	.619	87.51	87.51	82.25	82.25	339.52	84.88
413	-	79	-	-	.342	.419	.451	2,802	.280	5,559	.556	67.10	67.10	73.89	73.89	281.98	70.49
51	34	61	37	290	.276	.360	.500	3,009	.301	5,421	.542	72.05	72.05	72.06	72.06	288.21	72.05
241	106	101	98	214	.266	.353	.515	3,122	.312	5,698	.570	74.75	74.75	75.74	75.74	301.00	75.25
159	90	114	83	245	.297	.350	.499	2,802	.280	5,288	.529	67.09	67.09	70.29	70.29	274.75	68.69
79	44	33	63	263	.317	.359	.475	2,604	.260	4,961	.496	62.34	62.34	65.95	65.95	256.58	64.15
698	166	74	-	-	.367	.433	.513	3,274	.327	6,172	.617	78.41	78.41	82.04	82.04	320.90	80.22
644	150	67	-	-	.333	.424	.429	2,706	.271	5,565	.556	64.79	64.79	73.97	73.97	277.53	69.38
285	-	43	-	-	.325	.404	.491	3,311	.331	5,792	.579	79.28	79.28	76.99	76.99	312.53	78.13
196	20	62	-	-	.287	.380	.478	2,850	.285	5,634	.563	68.25	68.25	74.89	74.89	286.29	71.57
350	29	22	-	-	.309	.362	.453	2,815	.282	5,262	.526	67.41	67.41	69.94	69.94	274.70	68.67
286	99	101	108	198	.279	.323	.482	2,704	.270	5,192	.519	64.75	64.75	69.02	69.02	267.53	66.88
578	-	113	-	-	.346	.412	.503	3,674	.367	6,105	.610	87.99	87.99	81.15	81.15	338.26	84.57
15	11	200	100	152	.282	.392	.556	3,186	.319	6,115	.612	76.29	76.29	81.29	81.29	315.16	78.79
51	41	44	-	69	.313	.382	.486	3,031	.303	5,353	.535	72.57	72.57	71.15	71.15	287.44	71.86
39	12	59	-	167	.325	.398	.579	3,759	.376	6,171	.617	90.01	90.01	82.02	82.02	344.06	86.01
776	-	38	-	-	.330	.390	.453	3,702	.370	5,796	.580	88.65	88.65	77.04	77.04	331.39	82.85
3	10	70	75	277	.255	.345	.482	2,868	.287	5,265	.527	68.69	68.69	69.99	69.99	277.35	69.34
64	39	65	85	245	.274	.338	.480	2,780	.278	5,132	.513	66.56	66.56	68.21	68.21	269.54	67.39
91	74	13	-	71	.325	.428	.609	3,799	.380	6,658	.666	90.97	90.97	88.50	88.50	358.95	89.74
141	89	196	64	197	.288	.347	.499	2,881	.288	5,329	.533	68.99	68.99	70.83	70.83	279.64	69.91
187	63	104	106	187	.322	.370	.549	3,138	.314	5,788	.579	75.15	75.15	76.94	76.94	304.17	76.04
107	106	47	-	2	.340	.447	.632	4,063	.406	6,922	.692	97.29	97.29	92.01	92.01	378.59	94.65
180	88	50	-	27	.320	.404	.480	3,162	.316	5,518	.552	75.72	75.72	73.35	73.35	298.14	74.53
22	17	156	105	195	.297	.411	.540	3,044	.304	5,993	.599	72.89	72.89	79.66	79.66	305.10	76.27
35	26	85	106	248	.295	.343	.561	3,361	.336	5,729	.573	80.48	80.48	76.16	76.16	313.28	78.32
181	92	58	-	-	.316	.387	.500	3,200	.320	5,606	.561	76.64	76.64	74.52	74.52	302.31	75.58
95	42	26	-	108	.313	.412	.605	3,798	.380	6,597	.660	90.94	90.94	87.69	87.69	357.27	89.32
206	76	82	87	161	.292	.377	.560	3,196	.320	6,126	.613	76.67	76.67	81.71	81.71	316.76	79.19
274	147	115	67	280	.325	.390	.589	3,160	.316	6,213	.621	75.67	75.67	82.59	82.59	316.51	79.13
138	14	65	-	55	.317	.372	.526	3,183	.318	5,735	.574	76.22	76.22	76.24	76.24	304.92	76.23
1,243	-	118	-	-	.344	.455	.430	3,220	.322	6,504	.650	77.10	77.10	86.46	86.46	327.11	81.78
129	74	46	-	-	.342	.410	.520	3,259	.326	5,755	.575	78.04	78.04	76.50	76.50	309.08	77.27
61	47	63	96	200	.339	.432	.616	3,408	.341	6,543	.654	81.61	81.61	86.97	86.97	337.16	84.29
1,042	248	73	50	128	.279	.401	.419	2,528	.253	5,892	.589	60.54	60.54	78.32	78.32	277.71	69.43
152	-	18	-	70	.324	.383	.532	3,042	.304	5,836	.584	72.84	72.84	77.58	77.58	300.84	75.21

10,000 Batting Opportunities   A - H

10,000 Batting Opportunities H - R

Total Career Statistics Adjusted to 10,000 Batting Opportunities Listed Alphabetically

Rank	Player	Years	Adjustment to 10,000 BO	G	AB	H	1B	2B	3B	HR	RUN	RBI	BB	SO
15	Hornsby, Rogers	1915-1937	1.079680	2,439	8,824	3,163	2,072	584	182	325	1,705	1,710	1,121	733
116	Howard, Frank	1958-1973	1.321353	2,504	8,577	2,344	1,469	324	46	505	1,142	1,479	1,033	1,929
65	Jackson, Joe	1908-1920	1.798885	2,393	8,960	3,188	2,236	552	302	97	1,570	1,412	934	284
93	Jackson, Reggie	1967-1987	0.863036	2,434	8,513	2,230	1,302	400	42	486	1,339	1,469	1,188	2,241
55	Jennings, Hughie	1891-1918	1.826150	2,305	8,842	2,776	2,171	411	161	33	1,806	1,534	634	214
108	Jeter, Derek**	1995-2004	1.583281	2,163	8,729	2,745	1,993	448	66	237	1,642	1,097	885	1,539
66	Johnson, Robert	1933-1945	1.231375	2,294	8,521	2,526	1,566	488	117	355	1,526	1,580	1,324	1,048
52	Jones, Chipper**	1993-2004	1.474709	2,274	8,282	2,514	1,538	479	40	457	1,526	1,532	1,382	1,293
112	Kaline, Al	1953-1974	0.845809	2,396	8,556	2,543	1,721	421	63	337	1,372	1,339	1,080	863
115	Keeler, Willie	1892-1910	1.084952	2,304	9,292	3,206	2,753	252	166	36	1,866	879	569	879
39	Keller, Charlie*	1939-1952	2.157963	2,525	8,179	2,341	1,420	358	155	408	1,565	1,640	1,692	1,077
46	Kelley, Joe	1891-1908	1.252662	2,299	8,757	2,812	2,052	442	237	81	1,775	1,496	1,140	200
32	Kelly, King	1878-1892	1.542258	2,212	9,133	2,858	2,042	541	168	106	2,096	1,465	848	648
80	Killebrew, Harmon	1954-1975	0.992654	2,417	8,087	2,071	1,190	288	24	569	1,274	1,572	1,548	1,687
44	Kiner, Ralph	1946-1956	1.569120	2,310	8,167	2,277	1,298	339	61	579	1,524	1,593	1,586	1,175
34	Klein, Chuck	1928-1944	1.397819	2,450	9,066	2,902	1,823	556	103	419	1,633	1,679	840	728
101	Kluszewski, Ted	1947-1961	1.512859	2,599	8,970	2,672	1,767	439	44	422	1,283	1,555	744	552
81	Lajoie, Nap	1896-1916	0.976658	2,417	9,365	3,176	2,304	633	159	80	1,471	1,562	504	83
23	Mantle, Mickey	1951-1968	0.999001	2,399	8,094	2,413	1,462	344	72	535	1,675	1,507	1,733	1,711
99	Maris, Roger	1957-1968	1.692334	2,476	8,633	2,242	1,376	330	71	465	1,398	1,440	1,103	1,240
83	Martinez, Edgar**	1987-2004	1.129688	2,322	8,148	2,538	1,592	581	17	349	1,377	1,425	1,449	1,358
77	Matthews, Eddie	1952-1968	0.981547	2,347	8,379	2,272	1,352	347	71	503	1,481	1,426	1,417	1,460
123	Mattingly, Don	1982-1995	1.265983	2,260	8,866	2,726	1,860	560	25	281	1,275	1,391	744	562
43	Mays, Willie*	1951-1973	0.785546	2,350	8,548	2,579	1,540	411	110	518	1,620	1,495	1,149	1,199
85	McCovey, Willie	1959-1980	1.014507	2,626	8,316	2,243	1,310	358	47	529	1,247	1,578	1,365	1,572
91	McGriff, Fred **	1986-2004	0.961723	2,366	8,422	2,395	1,473	424	23	474	1,297	1,491	1,255	1,810
18	McGwire, Mark	1986-2001	1.281394	2,401	7,928	2,084	1,006	323	8	747	1,495	1,812	1,688	2,045
78	Medwick, Joe	1932-1948	1.204674	2,390	9,198	2,977	1,943	651	136	247	1,443	1,666	526	664
70	Meusel, Bob	1920-1930	1.703287	2,397	9,325	2,884	1,829	627	162	266	1,407	1,817	639	1,054
25	Mize, Johnny*	1936-1953	1.342102	2,529	8,647	2,699	1,613	493	111	482	1,500	1,794	1,150	703
120	Morgan, Joe	1963-1984	0.878503	2,327	8,150	2,211	1,497	394	84	235	1,450	995	1,638	892
119	Murphy, Dale	1976-1993	1.081900	2,359	8,612	2,284	1,432	379	42	431	1,295	1,370	1,067	1,891
118	Murray, Eddie	1977-1997	0.761557	2,304	8,633	2,479	1,642	426	27	384	1,239	1,460	1,015	1,155
50	Musial, Stan*	1941-1963	0.773994	2,342	8,492	2,810	1,744	561	137	368	1,509	1,510	1,238	539
45	O'Neill, Tip	1883-1892	2.096436	2,210	9,025	3,010	2,243	465	193	109	1,845	1,587	883	306
74	Ordonez, Magglio**	1997-2004	2.304147	2,306	8,772	2,689	1,671	553	35	431	1,438	1,620	767	993
27	Ott, Mel	1926-1947	0.884173	2,414	8,361	2,543	1,596	431	64	452	1,644	1,645	1,510	792
86	Palmiero, Rafael**	1986-2004	0.845237	2,300	8,539	2,470	1,488	483	32	466	1,366	1,500	1,107	1,103
122	Parker, Dave	1973-1991	0.962279	2,373	9,005	2,610	1,705	506	72	326	1,224	1,437	657	1,479
124	Perez, Tony	1964-1986	0.899281	2,497	8,793	2,457	1,591	454	71	341	1,144	1,486	832	1,679
54	Piazza, Mike**	1992-2004	1.485001	2,361	8,620	2,716	1,723	423	9	561	1,388	1,724	989	1,365
8	Pujols, Albert**	2001-2004	3.568879	2,245	8,433	2,809	1,531	675	32	571	1,784	1,799	1,085	996
13	Ramirez, Manny**	1993-2004	1.485443	2,280	8,277	2,614	1,448	566	21	579	1,585	1,887	1,298	1,827
100	Rice, Jim	1974-1989	1.067464	2,230	8,780	2,617	1,727	398	84	408	1,333	1,549	715	1,519
126	Ripkin, Cal, Jr.	1981-2001	0.756258	2,270	8,736	2,408	1,593	456	33	326	1,246	1,282	854	987
60	Robinson, Frank	1956-1976	0.833681	2,341	8,342	2,454	1,465	440	60	489	1,525	1,511	1,184	1,277
82	Robinson, Jackie	1947-1956	1.720874	2,378	8,393	2,612	1,814	470	93	236	1,630	1,263	1,273	501
17	Rodriguez, Alex**	1994-2004	1.539172	2,201	8,604	2,627	1,528	476	37	586	1,725	1,687	984	1,733
127	Rose, Pete	1963-1986	0.622975	2,219	8,755	2,651	2,003	465	84	100	1,349	819	976	712
1	Ruth, Babe	1914-1935	0.951928	2,383	7,995	2,735	1,444	482	129	680	2,069	2,107	1,963	1,266

Total Career Statistics Adjusted to 10,000 Batting Opportunities Listed Alphabetically

SB	CS	HBP	SF	GDP	AVG	OBP	SLG	Total Offensive Production Statistics				TRP Rating	RPA Rating	TNB Rating	TBA Rating	TOP Composite	
								TRP	RPA	TNB	TBA					TOP	Rating
146	69	52	3	-	.358	.434	.577	3,415	.342	6,337	.634	81.78	81.78	84.23	84.23	332.01	83.00
11	12	44	57	289	.273	.352	.498	2,620	.262	5,350	.535	62.74	62.74	71.12	71.12	267.72	66.93
363	110	106	-	-	.356	.423	.517	2,983	.298	5,929	.593	71.42	71.42	78.81	78.81	300.46	75.12
197	99	83	59	158	.262	.356	.490	2,807	.281	5,540	.554	67.23	67.23	73.64	73.64	281.73	70.43
683	-	524	-	-	.314	.393	.408	3,340	.334	5,447	.545	79.98	79.98	72.41	72.41	304.78	76.19
318	82	146	47	193	.315	.385	.463	2,739	.274	5,306	.531	65.59	65.59	70.52	70.52	272.23	68.06
118	79	30	-	126	.296	.393	.506	3,106	.311	5,704	.570	74.36	74.36	75.82	75.82	300.36	75.09
174	59	21	94	221	.304	.401	.537	3,059	.306	5,962	.596	73.24	73.24	79.25	79.25	304.98	76.25
118	68	47	88	229	.297	.376	.480	2,711	.271	5,280	.528	64.91	64.91	70.19	70.19	270.20	67.55
563	39	140	-	-	.345	.391	.419	2,745	.274	5,130	.513	65.73	65.73	68.19	68.19	267.83	66.96
97	50	22	-	108	.286	.410	.518	3,205	.320	5,995	.599	76.74	76.74	79.69	79.69	312.84	78.21
551	-	103	-	-	.321	.405	.454	3,271	.327	5,766	.577	78.32	78.32	76.64	76.64	309.93	77.48
568	-	19	-	-	.313	.372	.444	3,561	.356	5,489	.549	85.27	85.27	72.96	72.96	316.47	79.12
19	18	48	76	241	.256	.376	.509	2,846	.285	5,709	.571	68.15	68.15	75.88	75.88	288.06	72.02
35	3	38	11	198	.279	.398	.548	3,116	.312	6,131	.613	74.62	74.62	81.49	81.49	312.22	78.06
110	-	17	-	77	.320	.379	.543	3,311	.331	5,890	.589	79.29	79.29	78.30	78.30	315.19	78.80
30	15	35	35	216	.298	.353	.498	2,838	.284	5,259	.526	67.96	67.96	69.90	69.90	275.72	68.93
386	21	131	-	-	.339	.381	.466	3,033	.303	5,368	.537	72.62	72.62	71.35	71.35	287.93	71.98
153	38	13	47	113	.298	.421	.557	3,183	.318	6,368	.637	76.21	76.21	84.64	84.64	321.71	80.43
36	15	64	73	127	.260	.345	.476	2,838	.284	5,299	.530	67.96	67.96	70.43	70.43	276.78	69.20
55	34	101	87	215	.312	.418	.515	2,802	.280	5,772	.577	67.09	67.09	76.72	76.72	287.61	71.90
67	38	26	57	121	.271	.376	.509	2,907	.291	5,740	.574	69.62	69.62	76.30	76.30	291.84	72.96
18	11	27	122	242	.307	.358	.471	2,666	.267	4,956	.496	63.84	63.84	65.88	65.88	259.45	64.86
266	81	35	71	197	.302	.384	.557	3,115	.311	6,134	.613	74.58	74.58	81.53	81.53	312.23	78.06
26	22	70	71	179	.270	.374	.515	2,824	.282	5,719	.572	67.63	67.63	76.02	76.02	287.30	71.82
69	37	38	68	217	.284	.377	.509	2,788	.279	5,613	.561	66.76	66.76	74.61	74.61	282.73	70.68
15	10	96	100	188	.263	.394	.588	3,307	.331	6,452	.645	79.20	79.20	85.76	85.76	329.91	82.48
51	2	31	-	245	.324	.362	.505	3,109	.311	5,246	.525	74.45	74.45	69.74	69.74	288.38	72.10
242	174	36	-	-	.309	.356	.497	3,224	.322	5,374	.537	77.21	77.21	71.43	71.43	297.28	74.32
38	3	70	-	133	.312	.397	.562	3,295	.329	6,115	.611	78.90	78.90	81.28	81.28	320.35	80.09
605	142	35	84	92	.271	.392	.427	2,445	.244	5,617	.562	58.54	58.54	74.67	74.67	266.42	66.60
174	74	30	65	226	.265	.346	.469	2,665	.266	5,236	.524	63.81	63.81	69.60	69.60	266.83	66.71
84	33	14	97	241	.287	.359	.476	2,699	.270	5,190	.519	64.63	64.63	68.99	68.99	267.23	66.81
60	27	41	41	188	.331	.417	.559	3,019	.302	6,060	.606	72.28	72.28	80.55	80.55	305.66	76.41
338	-	92	-	-	.334	.399	.464	3,432	.343	5,501	.550	82.18	82.18	73.12	73.12	310.60	77.65
189	88	78	81	302	.307	.364	.525	3,058	.306	5,551	.555	73.22	73.22	74.12	74.12	294.68	73.67
79	2	57	-	73	.304	.414	.533	3,288	.329	6,101	.610	78.74	78.74	81.09	81.09	319.67	79.92
80	34	72	94	188	.289	.372	.517	2,866	.287	5,640	.564	68.62	68.62	74.96	74.96	287.16	71.79
148	109	54	83	201	.290	.339	.471	2,661	.266	4,989	.499	63.71	63.71	66.32	66.32	260.07	65.02
44	30	39	95	241	.279	.341	.463	2,629	.263	4,960	.496	62.97	62.97	65.94	65.94	257.80	64.45
25	30	36	59	296	.315	.385	.562	3,113	.311	5,861	.586	74.53	74.53	77.91	77.91	304.89	76.22
46	46	125	89	268	.333	.413	.624	3,583	.358	6,470	.647	85.80	85.80	86.01	86.01	343.62	85.90
49	45	100	89	236	.316	.411	.599	3,471	.347	6,362	.636	83.13	83.13	84.57	84.57	335.39	83.85
62	36	68	100	336	.298	.352	.502	2,882	.288	5,217	.522	69.02	69.02	69.34	69.34	276.72	69.18
27	29	50	96	265	.276	.340	.447	2,527	.253	4,810	.481	60.52	60.52	63.93	63.93	248.91	62.23
170	64	165	85	224	.294	.389	.537	3,035	.304	5,934	.593	72.69	72.69	78.88	78.88	303.13	75.78
339	93	124	15	194	.311	.409	.474	2,893	.289	5,619	.562	69.27	69.27	74.69	74.69	287.91	71.98
316	77	126	89	197	.305	.381	.574	3,412	.341	6,284	.628	81.71	81.71	83.54	83.54	330.49	82.62
123	93	67	49	154	.303	.375	.409	2,167	.217	4,656	.466	51.90	51.90	61.89	61.89	227.58	56.89
117	111	40	-	2	.342	.474	.690	4,176	.418	7,523	.752	100.00	100.00	100.00	100.00	400.00	100.00

10,000 Batting Opportunities   H - R

10,000 Batting Opportunities S - Y

Rank	Player	Years	Adjustment to 10,000 BO	G	AB	H	1B	2B	3B	HR	RUN	RBI	BB	SO	
58	Schmidt, Mike	1972-1989	0.980200	2,356	8,187	2,190	1,195	400	58	537	1,476	1,563	1,477	1,846	
62	Sheffield, Gary**	1988-2004	1.124986	2,290	8,215	2,447	1,519	434	27	467	1,470	1,522	1,352	989	
26	Simmons, Al*	1924-1944	1.060333	2,349	9,292	3,104	2,049	572	158	326	1,598	1,937	652	781	
104	Sisler, George	1915-1930	1.138045	2,339	9,408	3,200	2,414	484	187	116	1,461	1,337	537	372	
56	Snider, Duke	1947-1964	1.197461	2,566	8,575	2,534	1,516	429	102	487	1,508	1,596	1,163	1,481	
48	Sosa, Sammy**	1989-2004	1.089799	2,330	8,741	2,419	1,376	371	47	626	1,507	1,667	933	2,299	
72	Speaker, Tris	1907-1928	0.856238	2,388	8,729	3,010	2,040	679	191	100	1,611	1,309	1,182	188	
75	Stargell, Willie	1962-1982	1.091703	2,576	8,654	2,437	1,396	462	60	519	1,305	1,681	1,023	2,114	
20	Stovey, Harry	1880-1893	1.451800	2,159	8,992	2,651	1,717	504	253	177	2,166	1,318	963	498	
73	Terry, Bill	1923-1936	1.426127	2,454	9,167	3,127	2,216	532	160	220	1,597	1,537	766	640	
29	Thomas, Frank **	1990-2004	1.154068	2,222	7,907	2,439	1,410	512	13	503	1,510	1,661	1,673	1,309	
22	Thome, Jim**	1991-2004	1.400756	2,352	8,021	2,276	1,206	444	34	593	1,576	1,629	1,698	2,385	
9	Thompson, Sam	1885-1906	1.534448	2,156	9,213	3,093	2,176	500	224	193	1,932	1,993	691	347	
105	Traynor, Pie	1920-1937	1.233198	2,394	9,322	2,979	2,248	458	202	72	1,459	1,570	582	343	
59	Trosky, Hal*	1933-1946	1.734605	2,337	8,952	2,708	1,637	574	101	395	1,448	1,755	945	763	
76	Vaughn, Mo	1991-2003	1.527884	2,310	8,452	2,475	1,546	413	15	501	1,316	1,626	1,108	2,183	
67	Wagner, Honus	1897-1917	0.868508	2,421	9,056	2,979	2,107	565	219	88	1,511	1,504	836	284	
21	Walker, Larry **	1989-2004	1.282051	2,418	8,451	2,653	1,524	578	78	472	1,653	1,614	1,118	1,496	
106	Waner, Paul	1927-1945	0.933271	2,379	8,828	2,942	2,092	566	178	105	1,518	1,222	1,018	351	
90	Williams, Bernie**	1991-2004	1.215362	2,193	8,464	2,549	1,676	487	66	320	1,517	1,376	1,195	1,319	
109	Williams, Billy	1959-1976	0.933620	2,323	8,729	2,531	1,646	405	82	398	1,316	1,377	976	977	
41	Williams, Ken*	1915-1929	1.832845	2,560	8,911	2,845	1,822	522	141	359	1,576	1,673	1,037	526	
3	Williams, Ted*	1939-1960	1.001703	2,296	7,719	2,659	1,540	526	71	522	1,801	1,842	2,024	710	
14	Wilson, Hack	1923-1934	1.828488	2,465	8,704	2,671	1,616	486	123	446	1,616	1,944	1,232	1,304	
110	Winfield, Dave	1973-1995	0.790014	2,349	8,693	2,457	1,593	427	70	367	1,319	1,448	961	1,332	
121	Yastrzemski, Carl	1961-1983	0.699252	2,313	8,383	2,391	1,582	452	41	316	1,270	1,289	1,290	975	
89	York, Rudy	1934-1948	1.460067	2,340	8,601	2,367	1,462	425	76	404	1,279	1,682	1,155	1,266	

Total Career Statistics Adjusted to 10,000 Batting Opportunities Listed Alphabetically

* Player missed time for military service
** Active player. Statistics through 2004 season
TOP ranking for players with less than 70% rating is based upon comparison to listed players only.

Total Career Statistics Adjusted to 10,000 Batting Opportunities Listed Alphabetically

SB	CS	HBP	SF	GDP	AVG	OBP	SLG	Total Offensive Production Statistics				TRP Rating	RPA Rating	TNB Rating	TBA Rating	TOP Composite	
								TRP	RPA	TNB	TBA					TOP	Rating
171	90	77	106	153	.267	.380	.527	3,040	.304	5,952	.595	72.79	72.79	79.11	79.11	303.80	75.95
231	105	124	108	201	.298	.400	.528	2,992	.299	5,938	.594	71.66	71.66	78.93	78.93	301.17	75.29
92	68	32	-	24	.334	.380	.535	3,535	.354	5,676	.568	84.65	84.65	75.45	75.45	320.20	80.05
427	145	55	-	-	.340	.379	.468	2,798	.280	5,279	.528	67.01	67.01	70.18	70.18	274.37	68.59
119	66	25	38	199	.295	.380	.540	3,104	.310	5,869	.587	74.32	74.32	78.01	78.01	304.67	76.17
254	116	59	76	191	.277	.348	.545	3,175	.317	5,890	.589	76.02	76.02	78.30	78.30	308.63	77.16
372	110	88	-	-	.345	.428	.501	2,920	.292	5,903	.590	69.92	69.92	78.46	78.46	296.76	74.19
19	17	85	82	156	.282	.360	.529	2,986	.299	5,683	.568	71.50	71.50	75.55	75.55	294.09	73.52
739	-	45	-	-	.295	.366	.466	3,484	.348	5,938	.594	83.43	83.43	78.93	78.93	324.73	81.18
80	9	13	-	54	.341	.393	.506	3,135	.313	5,488	.549	75.06	75.06	72.95	72.95	296.01	74.00
37	27	82	122	216	.308	.429	.567	3,170	.317	6,252	.625	75.91	75.91	83.10	83.10	318.02	79.51
25	27	67	73	141	.284	.410	.569	3,205	.320	6,329	.633	76.74	76.74	84.12	84.12	321.73	80.43
362	-	97	-	-	.336	.388	.502	3,925	.393	5,771	.577	93.99	93.99	76.71	76.71	341.40	85.35
195	57	38	-	58	.320	.362	.435	3,029	.303	4,814	.481	72.53	72.53	64.00	64.00	273.04	68.26
49	40	28	-	75	.302	.371	.522	3,204	.320	5,651	.565	76.72	76.72	75.12	75.12	303.68	75.92
46	28	165	69	206	.293	.383	.523	2,941	.294	5,713	.571	70.43	70.43	75.94	75.94	292.73	73.18
627	20	108	-	-	.329	.392	.469	3,015	.302	5,796	.580	72.21	72.21	77.05	77.05	298.51	74.63
292	96	165	81	185	.314	.401	.568	3,267	.327	6,282	.628	78.22	78.22	83.50	83.50	323.45	80.86
97	1	35	-	119	.333	.404	.474	2,740	.274	5,330	.533	65.61	65.61	70.85	70.85	272.92	68.23
175	103	44	63	235	.301	.388	.488	2,893	.289	5,436	.544	69.26	69.26	72.26	72.26	283.05	70.76
84	46	40	68	187	.290	.361	.492	2,693	.269	5,348	.535	64.50	64.50	71.08	71.08	271.17	67.79
282	194	51	-	-	.319	.393	.530	3,250	.325	5,904	.590	77.81	77.81	78.47	78.47	312.58	78.14
24	17	39	20	197	.344	.482	.634	3,643	.364	6,963	.696	87.24	87.24	92.55	92.55	359.58	89.90
95	9	37	-	27	.307	.395	.545	3,560	.356	6,096	.610	85.25	85.25	81.03	81.03	332.56	83.14
176	76	20	75	252	.283	.353	.475	2,767	.277	5,205	.521	66.25	66.25	69.19	69.19	270.88	67.72
117	81	28	73	226	.285	.379	.462	2,559	.256	5,228	.523	61.28	61.28	69.49	69.49	261.54	65.39
55	38	18	-	226	.275	.362	.483	2,961	.296	5,347	.535	70.90	70.90	71.07	71.07	283.95	70.99

10,000 Batting Opportunities S - Y

125 of the Greatest Players:

B-1
Players Listed by Total Offensive Production

B-2
Players Listed Alphabetically

(Rating and Ranking of Total Offensive Production Statistics in Chapter 6)

10,000 Official At-Bats

Total Career Statistics Adjusted to 10,000 Official At-Bats Listed by Total Offensive Production Rating

Rank	Player	Years	Adjustment to 10,000 AB	G	AB	H	1B	2B	3B	HR	RUN	RBI	BB	SO
1	Ruth, Babe	1914-1935	1.190618	2,980	10,000	3,421	1,806	602	162	850	2,588	2,635	2,455	1,584
2	Gehrig, Lou	1923-1938	1.249844	2,705	10,000	3,401	1,914	667	204	616	2,360	2,493	1,886	987
3	Williams, Ted*	1939-1960	1.297690	2,974	10,000	3,444	1,995	681	92	676	2,333	2,386	2,623	920
4	Bonds, Barry **	1986-2004	1.099143	2,985	10,000	3,001	1,525	619	85	773	2,275	2,026	2,530	1,570
5	Foxx, Jimmie*	1925-1944	1.229407	2,849	10,000	3,253	1,880	563	154	657	2,153	2,363	1,785	1,612
6	Greenberg, Hank*	1930-1947	1.925669	2,684	10,000	3,135	1,631	730	137	637	2,024	2,457	1,641	1,625
7	Pujols, Albert**	2001-2004	4.231909	2,662	10,000	3,331	1,815	800	38	677	2,116	2,133	1,287	1,181
8	Helton, Todd**	1997-2004	2.468526	2,802	10,000	3,387	1,903	810	54	620	2,054	2,064	1,647	1,338
9	McGwire, Mark	1986-2001	1.616292	3,029	10,000	2,628	1,269	407	10	942	1,886	2,285	2,129	2,580
10	Ramirez, Manny**	1993-2004	1.794688	2,755	10,000	3,159	1,750	684	25	700	1,915	2,279	1,569	2,207
11	DiMaggio, Joe*	1936-1951	1.466061	2,545	10,000	3,246	1,954	570	192	529	2,038	2,253	1,158	541
12	Brouthers, Dan	1879-1904	1.486989	2,465	10,000	3,493	2,354	668	314	158	2,241	1,927	1,249	354
13	Thome, Jim**	1991-2004	1.746420	2,932	10,000	2,838	1,504	554	42	739	1,965	2,031	2,117	2,974
14	Hamilton, Billy	1888-1901	1.596934	2,520	10,000	3,445	2,871	359	150	64	2,700	1,175	1,896	348
15	Thomas, Frank **	1990-2004	1.459641	2,810	10,000	3,084	1,784	648	16	636	1,909	2,100	2,116	1,655
16	Mantle, Mickey	1951-1968	1.234263	2,963	10,000	2,981	1,806	425	89	662	2,070	1,863	2,141	2,114
17	Delahanty, Ed	1888-1903	1.334579	2,436	10,000	3,461	2,404	681	242	135	2,130	1,954	989	326
18	Wilson, Hack	1923-1934	2.100840	2,832	10,000	3,069	1,857	559	141	513	1,857	2,233	1,416	1,498
19	Thompson, Sam	1885-1906	1.665556	2,340	10,000	3,358	2,362	543	243	210	2,097	2,164	750	376
20	Rodriguez, Alex**	1994-2004	1.788909	2,558	10,000	3,054	1,776	553	43	682	2,005	1,961	1,143	2,014
21	Hornsby, Rogers	1915-1937	1.223541	2,764	10,000	3,585	2,348	662	207	368	1,932	1,938	1,270	831
22	Berkman, Lance**	1999-2004	3.727171	2,889	10,000	3,034	1,662	727	63	581	1,923	1,994	1,867	2,020
23	Walker, Larry **	1989-2004	1.516990	2,861	10,000	3,139	1,804	684	93	558	1,955	1,910	1,323	1,770
24	Ott, Mel	1926-1947	1.057530	2,887	10,000	3,041	1,909	516	76	540	1,966	1,967	1,806	948
25	Bagwell, Jeff**	1991-2004	1.299207	2,743	10,000	2,974	1,724	629	42	579	1,957	1,962	1,797	1,997
26	Delgado, Carlos**	1993-2004	1.996805	2,841	10,000	2,821	1,444	685	22	671	1,775	2,113	1,651	2,480
27	Duffy, Hugh	1888-1906	1.428776	2,460	10,000	3,296	2,535	443	167	151	2,207	1,860	946	301
28	Keller, Charlie*	1939-1952	2.638522	3,087	10,000	2,863	1,736	438	190	499	1,913	2,005	2,069	1,317
29	Kiner, Ralph	1946-1956	1.921230	2,828	10,000	2,788	1,589	415	75	709	1,866	1,950	1,942	1,439
30	Mize, Johnny*	1936-1953	1.552072	2,924	10,000	3,121	1,866	570	129	557	1,735	2,075	1,330	813
31	Stovey, Harry	1880-1893	1.614466	2,401	10,000	2,948	1,910	560	281	197	2,409	1,466	1,070	554
32	Griffey, Ken **	1989-2004	1.355197	2,706	10,000	2,922	1,652	542	49	679	1,789	1,957	1,334	1,793
33	Guerrero, Vladimir**	1996-2004	2.285714	2,651	10,000	3,248	1,936	606	82	624	1,749	1,893	990	1,275
34	Cobb, Ty	1905-1928	0.874967	2,654	10,000	3,667	2,671	633	260	102	1,964	1,695	1,093	312
35	Giambi, Jason**	1995-2004	2.102165	2,825	10,000	2,970	1,741	622	17	591	1,789	1,984	1,831	1,926
36	Belle, Albert	1989-2000	1.708526	2,629	10,000	2,949	1,597	665	36	651	1,664	2,117	1,167	1,642
37	Mays, Willie*	1951-1973	0.919033	2,750	10,000	3,017	1,801	481	129	607	1,895	1,749	1,345	1,402
38	Averill, Earl	1929-1941	1.574059	2,626	10,000	3,178	1,971	631	201	375	1,927	1,832	1,218	815
39	Schmidt, Mike	1972-1969	1.197318	2,878	10,000	2,675	1,460	489	71	656	1,803	1,910	1,804	2,255
40	Jones, Chipper**	1993-2004	1.780627	2,746	10,000	3,036	1,857	579	48	552	1,843	1,850	1,668	1,562
41	Simmons, Al*	1924-1944	1.141162	2,528	10,000	3,340	2,205	615	170	350	1,720	2,085	702	841
42	Conner, Roger	1880-1897	1.280902	2,545	10,000	3,247	2,230	550	291	177	2,058	1,693	1,283	575
43	Sheffield, Gary**	1988-2004	1.369488	2,788	10,000	2,979	1,849	529	33	568	1,790	1,853	1,646	1,204
44	Robinson, Frank	1956-1976	0.999400	2,806	10,000	2,941	1,756	528	72	586	1,828	1,811	1,419	1,531
45	Gonzalez, Juan **	1989-2004	1.525553	2,575	10,000	2,953	1,661	592	38	662	1,619	2,142	697	1,942
46	Kelly, King	1878-1892	1.688619	2,421	10,000	3,129	2,236	593	184	117	2,295	1,604	929	709
47	Musial, Stan*	1941-1963	0.911411	2,758	10,000	3,308	2,053	661	161	433	1,776	1,778	1,457	634
48	Klein, Chuck	1928-1944	1.541782	2,703	10,000	3,201	2,010	614	114	463	1,801	1,852	927	803
49	Williams, Ken*	1915-1929	2.056767	2,873	10,000	3,192	2,044	586	158	403	1,769	1,878	1,164	590
50	Kelley, Joe	1891-1908	1.430411	2,625	10,000	3,211	2,343	505	270	93	2,027	1,708	1,302	229

Total Career Statistics Adjusted to 10,000 Official At-Bats Listed by Total Offensive Production Rating

SB	CS	HBP	SF	GDP	AVG	OBP	SLG	Total Offensive Production Statistics				TRP Rating	RPA Rating	TNB Rating	TBA Rating	TOP Composite	
								TRP	RPA	TNB	TBA					TOP	Rating
146	139	50	-	2	.342	.474	.690	5,223	.418	9,409	.752	100.00	100.00	100.00	100.00	400.00	100.00
127	126	56	-	2	.340	.447	.632	4,853	.406	8,268	.692	92.91	97.29	87.87	92.01	370.08	92.52
31	22	51	26	256	.344	.482	.634	4,720	.364	9,020	.696	90.36	87.24	95.86	92.55	366.02	91.50
556	155	102	96	156	.300	.443	.611	4,301	.334	9,140	.709	82.34	79.93	97.14	94.30	353.72	88.43
108	89	16	-	85	.325	.428	.609	4,516	.380	7,914	.666	86.45	90.97	84.10	88.50	350.03	87.51
112	50	31	-	127	.313	.412	.605	4,481	.380	7,914	.660	85.79	90.94	82.72	87.69	347.15	86.79
55	55	148	106	317	.333	.413	.624	4,249	.358	7,672	.647	81.34	85.80	81.54	86.01	334.69	83.67
74	57	77	116	242	.339	.432	.616	4,118	.341	7,904	.654	78.83	81.61	84.00	86.97	331.42	82.85
19	13	121	126	238	.263	.394	.588	4,172	.331	8,138	.645	79.87	79.20	86.49	85.76	331.31	82.83
59	54	120	108	285	.316	.411	.599	4,194	.347	7,687	.636	80.30	83.13	81.69	84.57	329.68	82.42
44	13	67	-	191	.325	.398	.579	4,291	.376	7,044	.617	82.16	90.01	74.87	82.02	329.05	82.26
391	-	156	-	-	.349	.429	.526	4,168	.365	7,057	.619	79.80	87.51	75.00	82.25	324.56	81.14
31	33	84	91	176	.284	.410	.569	3,996	.320	7,890	.633	76.50	76.74	83.86	84.12	321.22	80.31
1,496	-	142	-	-	.344	.455	.430	3,876	.322	7,830	.650	74.20	77.10	83.21	86.46	320.97	80.24
47	34	104	155	273	.308	.429	.567	4,010	.317	7,907	.625	76.77	75.91	84.03	83.10	319.81	79.95
189	47	16	58	139	.298	.421	.557	3,932	.318	7,867	.637	75.29	76.21	83.61	84.64	319.75	79.94
642	-	125	-	-	.346	.412	.503	4,084	.367	6,785	.610	78.19	87.99	72.11	81.15	319.43	79.86
109	11	42	-	32	.307	.395	.545	4,090	.356	7,004	.610	78.31	85.25	74.44	81.03	319.03	79.76
393	-	105	-	-	.336	.388	.502	4,260	.393	6,264	.577	81.57	93.99	66.57	76.71	318.84	79.71
367	89	147	104	229	.305	.381	.574	3,966	.341	7,304	.628	75.93	81.71	77.63	83.54	318.80	79.70
165	78	59	4	-	.358	.434	.577	3,870	.342	7,181	.634	74.09	81.78	76.32	84.23	316.41	79.10
149	97	138	97	171	.303	.416	.563	3,917	.319	7,689	.626	75.00	76.43	81.72	83.27	316.41	79.10
346	114	196	96	218	.314	.401	.568	3,865	.327	7,433	.628	74.00	78.22	79.00	83.50	314.73	78.68
94	2	68	-	87	.304	.414	.533	3,933	.329	7,297	.610	75.30	78.74	77.55	81.09	312.68	78.17
262	101	165	127	286	.297	.408	.542	3,918	.317	7,547	.610	75.02	75.82	80.21	81.07	312.11	78.03
18	14	244	122	186	.282	.392	.556	3,888	.319	7,462	.612	74.43	76.29	79.30	81.29	311.31	77.83
853	-	41	-	-	.330	.390	.453	4,068	.370	6,368	.580	77.88	88.65	67.68	77.04	311.25	77.81
119	61	26	-	132	.286	.410	.518	3,918	.320	7,330	.599	75.01	76.74	77.90	79.69	309.33	77.33
42	4	46	13	242	.279	.398	.548	3,816	.312	7,506	.613	73.05	74.62	79.77	81.49	308.93	77.23
43	3	81	-	154	.312	.397	.562	3,810	.329	7,071	.611	72.95	78.90	75.15	81.28	308.28	77.07
822	-	50	-	-	.295	.366	.466	3,875	.348	6,603	.594	74.18	83.43	70.18	78.93	306.72	76.68
241	89	96	102	188	.292	.377	.560	3,746	.320	7,180	.613	71.80	76.67	76.52	81.71	306.70	76.68
315	169	133	78	322	.325	.390	.589	3,641	.316	7,159	.621	69.71	75.67	76.08	82.59	304.05	76.01
780	185	82	-	-	.367	.433	.513	3,659	.327	6,897	.617	70.05	78.41	73.30	82.04	303.81	75.95
27	21	193	130	242	.297	.411	.540	3,773	.304	7,429	.599	72.24	72.89	78.95	79.66	303.74	75.94
150	70	94	133	330	.295	.369	.564	3,781	.323	6,979	.595	72.39	77.23	74.17	79.13	302.92	75.73
311	95	40	84	231	.302	.384	.557	3,644	.311	7,176	.613	69.76	74.58	76.26	81.53	302.14	75.53
110	90	52	-	11	.318	.395	.534	3,759	.333	6,627	.587	71.96	79.79	70.43	78.08	300.26	75.06
208	110	95	129	187	.267	.380	.527	3,713	.304	7,270	.595	71.08	72.79	77.26	79.11	300.25	75.06
210	71	25	114	267	.304	.401	.537	3,693	.306	7,199	.596	70.70	73.24	76.51	79.25	299.70	74.93
99	73	34	-	26	.334	.380	.535	3,805	.354	6,109	.568	72.84	84.65	64.92	75.45	297.86	74.46
323	-	49	-	-	.325	.404	.491	3,752	.331	6,563	.579	71.83	79.28	69.75	76.99	297.85	74.46
281	127	151	131	245	.298	.400	.528	3,643	.299	7,228	.594	69.74	71.66	76.82	78.93	297.14	74.29
204	77	198	102	269	.294	.389	.537	3,639	.304	7,114	.593	69.67	72.69	75.60	78.88	296.83	74.21
40	29	95	119	278	.295	.343	.561	3,760	.336	6,410	.573	72.00	80.48	68.13	76.16	296.76	74.19
621	-	20	-	-	.313	.372	.444	3,899	.356	6,010	.549	74.65	85.27	63.87	72.96	296.75	74.19
71	32	48	48	221	.331	.417	.559	3,555	.302	7,135	.606	68.05	72.28	75.83	80.55	296.71	74.18
122	-	19	-	85	.320	.379	.543	3,652	.331	6,497	.589	69.93	79.29	69.05	78.30	296.57	74.14
317	218	58	-	-	.319	.393	.530	3,647	.325	6,625	.590	69.82	77.81	70.41	78.47	296.51	74.13
629	-	117	-	-	.321	.405	.454	3,735	.327	6,584	.577	71.50	78.32	69.97	76.64	296.44	74.11

10,000 Official At-Bats

10,000 Official At-Bats

Rank	Player	Years	Adjustment to 10,000 AB	G	AB	H	1B	2B	3B	HR	RUN	RBI	BB	SO
51	Aaron, Hank	1954-1976	0.808800	2,667	10,000	3,050	1,855	505	79	611	1,758	1,858	1,134	1,119
52	Sosa, Sammy**	1989-2004	1.246727	2,666	10,000	2,768	1,575	424	54	716	1,724	1,907	1,067	2,631
53	Snider, Duke	1947-1964	1.396453	2,993	10,000	2,955	1,768	500	119	568	1,758	1,861	1,356	1,727
54	Anson, Cap	1871-1897	0.974659	2,437	10,000	3,415	2,609	568	143	95	1,939	2,023	958	294
55	Piazza, Mike**	1992-2004	1.722653	2,739	10,000	3,151	1,998	491	10	651	1,611	2,000	1,147	1,583
56	O'Neill, Tip	1883-1892	2.322880	2,448	10,000	3,336	2,485	516	214	121	2,044	1,758	978	339
57	Heilmann, Harry	1914-1932	1.284192	2,756	10,000	3,416	2,291	696	194	235	1,658	1,976	1,099	706
58	Canseco, Jose	1985-2001	1.417033	2,674	10,000	2,660	1,503	482	20	655	1,681	1,994	1,284	2,752
59	Johnson, Robert	1933-1945	1.445087	2,692	10,000	2,964	1,838	572	137	416	1,790	1,854	1,553	1,230
60	Jennings, Hughie	1891-1918	2.065262	2,606	10,000	3,139	2,456	465	182	37	2,043	1,735	717	242
61	Allen, Dick	1963-1977	1.579280	2,762	10,000	2,919	1,734	505	125	554	1,736	1,767	1,412	2,457
62	Garciaparra, Nomar**	1996-2004	2.419550	2,441	10,000	3,218	1,948	709	121	440	1,783	1,718	714	1,016
63	Trosky, Hal*	1933-1946	1.937609	2,610	10,000	3,025	1,829	641	112	442	1,618	1,961	1,056	853
64	Killebrew, Harmon	1954-1975	1.227446	2,989	10,000	2,560	1,472	356	29	703	1,575	1,944	1,914	2,085
65	Goslin, Goose	1921-1938	1.155268022	2,642	10,000	3,160	2,096	578	200	287	1,713	1,859	1,096	676
66	Hafey, Chick	1924-1937	2.162162	2,774	10,000	3,170	1,933	737	145	355	1,680	1,801	804	1,031
67	Gehringer, Charlie	1924-1941	1.128668	2,622	10,000	3,204	2,184	648	165	208	2,002	1,611	1,337	420
68	Matthews, Eddie	1952-1968	1.171372	2,801	10,000	2,712	1,613	415	84	600	1,768	1,702	1,691	1,742
69	Martinez, Edgar**	1987-2004	1.386386	2,849	10,000	3,115	1,953	713	21	428	1,690	1,748	1,779	1,666
70	Vaughn, Mo	1991-2003	1.807664	2,733	10,000	2,928	1,829	488	18	593	1,556	1,923	1,311	2,583
71	Jackson, Joe	1908-1920	2.007629	2,670	10,000	3,558	2,495	616	337	108	1,753	1,576	1,042	317
72	Speaker, Tris	1907-1928	0.980873	2,736	10,000	3,448	2,336	778	219	115	1,845	1,500	1,355	216
73	Herman, Babe	1926-1945	1.784758	2,770	10,000	3,245	2,013	712	196	323	1,574	1,779	928	987
74	Stargell, Willie	1962-1982	1.261511	2,977	10,000	2,816	1,613	534	69	599	1,508	1,943	1,182	2,442
75	Ordonez, Magglio**	1997-2004	2.626740	2,629	10,000	3,065	1,904	630	39	491	1,639	1,847	875	1,132
76	McCovey, Willie	1959-1980	1.219959	3,157	10,000	2,697	1,575	431	56	636	1,499	1,897	1,641	1,891
77	Robinson, Jackie	1947-1956	2.050441	2,834	10,000	3,113	2,161	560	111	281	1,942	1,505	1,517	597
78	Wagner, Honus	1897-1917	0.959049	2,673	10,000	3,290	2,327	624	242	97	1,669	1,661	924	314
79	Campanella, Roy	1948-1957	2.378121	2,889	10,000	2,761	1,719	423	43	576	1,491	2,036	1,268	1,191
80	Bottomley, Jim	1922-1937	1.338509	2,665	10,000	3,096	1,978	622	202	293	1,575	1,903	889	791
81	Palmiero, Rafael**	1986-2004	0.989805	2,693	10,000	2,892	1,743	566	38	545	1,600	1,757	1,297	1,292
82	Terry, Bill	1923-1936	1.555694	2,677	10,000	3,412	2,418	580	174	240	1,742	1,677	835	699
83	Meusel, Bob	1920-1930	1.826484	2,570	10,000	3,092	1,962	672	174	285	1,509	1,949	685	1,131
84	McGriff, Fred **	1986-2004	1.141944	2,809	10,000	2,843	1,749	504	27	563	1,540	1,770	1,490	2,149
85	Henderson, Rickey	1979-2003	0.912326	2,811	10,000	2,787	1,991	465	60	271	2,094	1,017	1,998	1,545
86	Williams, Bernie**	1991-2004	1.435956	2,590	10,000	3,011	1,980	576	78	378	1,792	1,626	1,412	1,558
87	Cravath, Gavy	1908-1920	2.531005	3,088	10,000	2,870	1,772	587	210	301	1,455	1,820	1,420	1,301
88	York, Rudy	1934-1948	1.697505	2,721	10,000	2,752	1,699	494	88	470	1,487	1,956	1,343	1,472
89	Jackson, Reggie	1967-1987	1.013788	2,859	10,000	2,620	1,530	469	50	571	1,572	1,725	1,395	2,633
90	Dickey, Bill*	1928-1946	1.587302	2,840	10,000	3,125	2,146	544	114	321	1,476	1,919	1,076	459
91	Berra, Yogi	1946-1965	1.323627	2,806	10,000	2,846	1,882	425	65	474	1,555	1,893	932	549
92	Fielder, Cecil	1985-1998	1.939112	2,850	10,000	2,546	1,526	388	14	619	1,443	1,955	1,344	2,552
93	Medwick, Joe	1932-1948	1.309758	2,599	10,000	3,236	2,113	707	148	269	1,569	1,811	572	722
94	Burkett, Jesse	1890-1905	1.192037	2,458	10,000	3,424	2,739	374	221	89	2,036	1,135	1,227	274
95	Collins, Eddie	1906-1930	1.004924	2,840	10,000	3,330	2,655	440	188	47	1,829	1,306	1,510	287
96	Lajoie, Nap	1896-1916	1.042862	2,581	10,000	3,391	2,460	676	170	86	1,571	1,668	538	89
97	Maris, Roger	1957-1968	1.960400	2,868	10,000	2,598	1,594	382	82	539	1,619	1,668	1,278	1,437
98	Galarraga, Andres**	1985-2004	1.235178	2,788	10,000	2,882	1,801	548	40	493	1,476	1,760	720	2,474
99	Rice, Jim	1974-1989	1.215805	2,540	10,000	2,981	1,967	453	96	464	1,519	1,764	815	1,730
100	Morgan, Joe	1963-1984	1.077935	2,855	10,000	2,713	1,837	484	103	289	1,779	1,221	2,010	1,094

Total Career Statistics Adjusted to 10,000 Official At-Bats Listed by Total Offensive Production Rating

SB	CS	HBP	SF	GDP	AVG	OBP	SLG	Total Offensive Production Statistics				TRP Rating	RPA Rating	TNB Rating	TBA Rating	TOP Composite	
								TRP	RPA	TNB	TBA					TOP	Rating
194	59	26	98	265	.305	.374	.555	3,616	.314	6,840	.594	69.23	75.15	72.69	78.90	295.98	73.99
290	132	67	87	218	.277	.348	.545	3,632	.317	6,739	.589	69.53	76.02	71.61	78.30	295.46	73.86
138	77	29	45	232	.295	.380	.540	3,620	.310	6,844	.587	69.30	74.32	72.74	78.01	294.37	73.59
288	16	31	-	-	.342	.401	.455	3,962	.361	5,815	.529	75.85	86.33	61.80	70.33	294.32	73.58
29	34	41	69	343	.315	.385	.562	3,611	.311	6,799	.586	69.13	74.53	72.26	77.91	293.83	73.46
374	-	102	-	-	.334	.399	.464	3,803	.343	6,095	.550	72.80	82.18	64.78	73.12	292.88	73.22
144	82	51	-	-	.342	.410	.520	3,634	.326	6,417	.575	69.58	78.04	68.20	76.50	292.32	73.08
283	125	119	115	252	.266	.353	.515	3,674	.312	6,707	.570	70.35	74.75	71.28	75.74	292.12	73.03
139	92	35	-	147	.296	.393	.506	3,645	.311	6,694	.570	69.77	74.36	71.14	75.82	291.09	72.77
772	-	593	-	-	.314	.393	.408	3,777	.334	6,161	.545	72.32	79.98	65.47	72.41	290.18	72.55
210	82	25	84	259	.292	.378	.534	3,503	.297	6,901	.586	67.06	71.20	73.35	77.88	289.49	72.37
208	70	116	119	208	.322	.370	.549	3,501	.314	6,458	.579	67.03	75.15	68.63	76.94	287.75	71.94
54	45	31	-	83	.302	.371	.522	3,579	.320	6,313	.565	68.52	76.72	67.09	75.12	287.44	71.86
23	22	59	95	298	.256	.376	.509	3,519	.285	7,059	.571	67.37	68.15	75.02	75.88	286.43	71.61
202	103	65	-	-	.316	.387	.500	3,572	.320	6,257	.561	68.39	76.64	66.50	74.52	286.04	71.51
151	15	71	-	61	.317	.372	.526	3,481	.318	6,272	.574	66.65	76.22	66.66	76.24	285.77	71.44
205	100	58	-	30	.320	.404	.480	3,613	.316	6,305	.552	69.17	75.72	67.00	73.35	285.24	71.31
80	46	30	68	144	.271	.376	.509	3,470	.291	6,850	.574	66.43	69.62	72.80	76.30	285.15	71.29
68	42	123	107	263	.312	.418	.515	3,438	.280	7,083	.577	65.83	67.09	75.28	76.72	284.91	71.23
54	33	195	81	244	.293	.383	.523	3,480	.294	6,759	.571	66.62	70.43	71.83	75.94	284.82	71.20
406	122	118	-	-	.356	.423	.517	3,329	.298	6,617	.593	63.73	71.42	70.32	78.81	284.28	71.07
426	127	101	-	-	.345	.428	.501	3,345	.292	6,762	.590	64.04	69.92	71.87	78.46	284.28	71.07
168	-	20	-	77	.324	.383	.532	3,354	.304	6,434	.584	64.20	72.84	68.38	77.58	283.00	70.75
21	20	98	95	180	.282	.360	.529	3,450	.299	6,567	.568	66.06	71.50	69.80	75.55	282.90	70.72
215	100	89	92	344	.307	.364	.525	3,486	.306	6,328	.555	66.81	73.22	67.63	74.12	281.78	70.44
32	27	84	85	215	.270	.374	.515	3,396	.282	6,877	.572	65.02	67.63	73.09	76.02	281.76	70.44
404	111	148	18	232	.311	.409	.474	3,447	.289	6,695	.562	65.99	69.27	71.15	74.69	281.09	70.27
692	22	119	-	-	.329	.392	.469	3,330	.302	6,401	.580	63.75	72.21	68.02	77.05	281.03	70.26
59	40	71	43	340	.276	.360	.500	3,527	.301	6,354	.542	67.52	72.05	67.53	72.06	279.16	69.79
78	20	58	-	44	.310	.369	.500	3,479	.317	6,006	.546	66.60	75.79	63.83	72.64	278.86	69.72
94	40	84	110	220	.289	.372	.517	3,356	.287	6,605	.564	64.26	68.62	70.20	74.96	278.04	69.51
87	9	14	-	59	.341	.393	.506	3,419	.313	5,986	.549	65.47	75.06	63.62	72.95	277.09	69.27
259	186	38	-	-	.309	.356	.497	3,458	.322	5,763	.537	66.20	77.21	61.24	71.43	276.08	69.02
82	43	45	81	258	.284	.377	.509	3,310	.279	6,664	.561	63.38	66.76	70.83	74.61	275.57	68.89
1,283	306	89	61	157	.279	.401	.419	3,111	.253	7,250	.589	59.56	60.54	77.05	78.32	275.47	68.87
207	122	52	75	277	.301	.388	.488	3,418	.289	6,423	.544	65.43	69.26	68.26	72.26	275.22	68.80
225	23	71	-	-	.287	.380	.478	3,275	.285	6,474	.563	62.70	68.25	68.81	74.89	274.65	68.66
65	44	20	-	263	.275	.362	.483	3,443	.296	6,216	.535	65.91	70.90	66.06	71.07	273.95	68.49
231	117	97	69	186	.262	.356	.490	3,298	.281	6,508	.554	63.14	67.23	69.16	73.64	273.16	68.29
57	46	49	-	78	.313	.382	.486	3,395	.303	5,997	.535	65.00	72.57	63.73	71.15	272.46	68.11
40	34	65	58	193	.285	.348	.482	3,448	.307	5,824	.518	66.01	73.40	61.89	68.82	270.14	67.53
4	12	83	89	328	.255	.345	.482	3,397	.287	6,236	.527	65.04	68.69	66.28	69.99	269.99	67.50
55	3	34	-	266	.324	.362	.505	3,380	.311	5,704	.525	64.72	74.45	60.62	69.74	269.53	67.38
467	-	89	-	-	.342	.419	.451	3,171	.280	6,290	.556	60.71	67.10	66.85	73.89	268.55	67.14
747	174	77	-	-	.333	.424	.429	3,135	.271	6,449	.556	60.03	64.79	68.53	73.97	267.32	66.83
412	22	140	-	-	.339	.381	.466	3,238	.303	5,732	.537	61.99	72.62	60.91	71.35	266.87	66.72
41	18	74	84	147	.260	.345	.476	3,288	.284	6,138	.530	62.94	67.96	65.23	70.43	266.57	66.64
158	100	220	72	221	.288	.347	.499	3,236	.288	5,986	.533	61.96	68.99	63.61	70.83	265.39	66.35
71	41	78	114	383	.298	.352	.502	3,283	.288	5,942	.522	62.85	69.02	63.15	69.34	264.35	66.09
743	175	43	103	113	.271	.392	.427	3,000	.244	6,892	.562	57.43	58.54	73.25	74.67	263.89	65.97

10,000 Official At-Bats

Rank	Player	Years	Adjustment to 10,000 AB	G	AB	H	1B	2B	3B	HR	RUN	RBI	BB	SO	
	Total Career Statistics Adjusted to 10,000 Official At-Bats Listed by Total Offensive Production Rating														
101	Bichette, Dante	1988-2001	1.567152	2,670	10,000	2,987	1,887	628	42	429	1,464	1,788	556	1,689	
102	Kaline, Al	1953-1974	0.988533	2,801	10,000	2,973	2,012	492	74	394	1,603	1,565	1,262	1,008	
103	Cepeda, Orlando	1958-1974	1.261511	2,679	10,000	2,966	1,928	526	34	478	1,427	1,722	742	1,475	
104	Jeter, Derek**	1995-2004	1.813894	2,478	10,000	3,145	2,284	513	76	272	1,881	1,257	1,014	1,763	
105	Kluszewski, Ted	1947-1961	1.686625	2,898	10,000	2,979	1,970	489	49	471	1,430	1,734	830	616	
106	Bench, Johnny	1967-1983	1.305824	2,818	10,000	2,674	1,638	498	31	508	1,425	1,797	1,163	1,669	
107	Waner, Paul	1927-1945	1.057194	2,695	10,000	3,332	2,370	641	202	119	1,720	1,384	1,153	398	
108	Winfield, Dave	1973-1995	0.908843	2,702	10,000	2,827	1,833	491	80	423	1,517	1,666	1,105	1,532	
109	Williams, Billy	1959-1976	1.069519	2,661	10,000	2,899	1,886	464	94	456	1,508	1,578	1,118	1,119	
110	Howard, Frank	1958-1973	1.540595	2,919	10,000	2,733	1,713	377	54	589	1,331	1,724	1,205	2,249	
111	Banks, Ernie	1953-1971	1.061458	2,683	10,000	2,742	1,671	432	96	543	1,385	1,737	810	1,312	
112	Brett, George	1973-1993	0.966277	2,616	10,000	3,048	1,966	643	132	306	1,530	1,541	1,059	877	
113	Foster, George	1969-1986	1.423893	2,815	10,000	2,741	1,741	437	67	496	1,404	1,764	948	2,021	
114	Murray, Eddie	1977-1997	0.882145	2,669	10,000	2,871	1,902	494	31	445	1,435	1,691	1,176	1,337	
115	Murphy, Dale	1976-1993	1.256281	2,739	10,000	2,652	1,663	440	49	500	1,504	1,590	1,239	2,196	
116	Crawford, Sam	1899-1917	1.043950	2,615	10,000	3,094	2,190	477	326	101	1,453	1,592	793	109	
117	Yastrzemski, Carl	1961-1983	0.834168	2,759	10,000	2,852	1,887	539	49	377	1,515	1,538	1,539	1,163	
118	Sisler, George	1915-1930	1.209629	2,486	10,000	3,401	2,566	514	198	123	1,553	1,421	571	396	
119	Traynor, Pie	1920-1937	1.322926	2,568	10,000	3,196	2,412	491	217	77	1,565	1,684	624	368	
120	Dawson, Andre	1976-1996	1.007354	2,646	10,000	2,794	1,748	507	99	441	1,383	1,603	593	1,520	
121	Keeler, Willie	1892-1910	1.167679	2,480	10,000	3,450	2,962	271	179	39	2,008	946	612	946	
122	Mattingly, Don	1982-1995	1.427959	2,549	10,000	3,074	2,098	631	29	317	1,438	1,569	840	634	
123	Perez, Tony	1964-1986	1.022704	2,840	10,000	2,794	1,809	516	81	388	1,301	1,690	946	1,909	
124	Parker, Dave	1973-1991	1.068604	2,635	10,000	2,898	1,894	562	80	362	1,359	1,595	730	1,642	
125	Clemente, Roberto	1955-1972	1.057753	2,574	10,000	3,173	2,278	465	176	254	1,498	1,380	657	1,301	
126	Ripkin, Cal, Jr.	1981-2001	0.865726	2,598	10,000	2,756	1,823	522	38	373	1,426	1,467	977	1,130	
127	Rose, Pete	1963-1986	0.711592	2,535	10,000	3,029	2,288	531	96	114	1,541	935	1,114	813	

* Player missed time for military service
** Active player. Statistics through 2004 season
TOP ranking for players with less than 70% rating is based upon comparison to listed players only.

Total Career Statistics Adjusted to 10,000 Official At-Bats Listed by Total Offensive Production Rating

SB	CS	HBP	SF	GDP	AVG	OBP	SLG	Total Offensive Production Statistics				TRP Rating	RPA Rating	TNB Rating	TBA Rating	TOP Composite	
								TRP	RPA	TNB	TBA					TOP	Rating
238	114	64	114	276	.299	.336	.499	3,252	.295	5,733	.521	62.26	70.72	60.92	69.21	263.11	65.78
137	79	54	103	268	.297	.376	.480	3,168	.271	6,171	.528	60.66	64.91	65.59	70.19	261.35	65.34
179	101	129	93	275	.297	.350	.499	3,149	.280	5,943	.529	60.28	67.09	63.16	70.29	260.82	65.20
365	94	167	54	221	.315	.385	.463	3,138	.274	6,078	.531	60.08	65.59	64.60	70.52	260.79	65.20
34	17	39	39	241	.298	.353	.498	3,164	.284	5,863	.526	60.58	67.96	62.31	69.90	260.75	65.19
89	56	25	118	262	.267	.342	.476	3,221	.278	5,979	.517	61.68	66.68	63.55	68.71	260.61	65.15
110	1	40	-	134	.333	.404	.474	3,104	.274	6,038	.533	59.43	65.61	64.17	70.85	260.05	65.01
203	87	23	86	290	.283	.353	.475	3,183	.277	5,988	.521	60.93	66.25	63.64	69.19	260.02	65.00
96	52	46	78	214	.290	.361	.492	3,086	.269	6,126	.535	59.07	64.50	65.11	71.08	259.76	64.94
12	14	51	66	337	.273	.352	.498	3,055	.262	6,238	.535	58.49	62.74	66.29	71.12	258.64	64.66
53	56	74	102	243	.274	.330	.500	3,122	.278	5,876	.523	59.77	66.57	62.45	69.56	258.35	64.59
194	94	32	116	227	.305	.369	.487	3,071	.269	6,065	.530	58.79	64.31	64.46	70.51	258.07	64.52
73	44	74	97	279	.274	.338	.480	3,168	.278	5,849	.513	60.66	66.56	62.16	68.21	257.59	64.40
97	38	16	113	279	.287	.359	.476	3,126	.270	6,012	.519	59.85	64.63	63.89	68.99	257.36	64.34
202	85	35	75	263	.265	.346	.469	3,094	.266	6,080	.524	59.24	63.81	64.62	69.60	257.27	64.32
379	31	24	-	-	.309	.362	.453	3,045	.282	5,692	.526	58.30	67.41	60.49	69.94	256.14	64.03
140	97	33	88	269	.285	.379	.462	3,053	.256	6,236	.523	58.45	61.28	66.28	69.49	255.50	63.87
454	154	58	-	-	.340	.379	.468	2,974	.280	5,611	.528	56.95	67.01	59.64	70.18	253.77	63.44
209	61	41	-	62	.320	.362	.435	3,249	.303	5,165	.481	62.20	72.53	54.89	64.00	253.61	63.40
316	110	112	119	219	.279	.323	.482	2,986	.270	5,734	.519	57.16	64.75	60.94	69.02	251.87	62.97
606	42	151	-	-	.345	.391	.419	2,954	.274	5,521	.513	56.56	65.73	58.67	68.19	249.15	62.29
20	13	30	137	273	.307	.358	.471	3,007	.267	5,590	.496	57.58	63.84	59.41	65.88	246.71	61.68
50	34	44	108	274	.279	.341	.463	2,990	.263	5,641	.496	57.25	62.97	59.95	65.94	246.11	61.53
165	121	60	92	223	.290	.339	.471	2,955	.266	5,541	.499	56.57	63.71	58.88	66.32	245.49	61.37
88	49	37	70	291	.317	.359	.475	2,878	.260	5,484	.496	55.10	62.34	58.29	65.95	241.68	60.42
31	34	57	110	303	.276	.340	.447	2,893	.253	5,506	.481	55.39	60.52	58.52	63.93	238.36	59.59
141	106	76	56	176	.303	.375	.409	2,476	.217	5,318	.466	47.40	51.90	56.52	61.89	217.71	54.43

10,000 Official At-Bats

10,000 Official At-Bats A-H

Rank	Player	Years	Adjustment to 10,000 AB	G	AB	H	1B	2B	3B	HR	RUN	RBI	BB	SO	
51	Aaron, Hank	1954-1976	0.808800	2,667	10,000	3,050	1,855	505	79	611	1,758	1,858	1,134	1,119	
61	Allen, Dick	1963-1977	1.579280	2,762	10,000	2,919	1,734	505	125	554	1,736	1,767	1,412	2,457	
54	Anson, Cap	1871-1897	0.974659	2,437	10,000	3,415	2,609	568	143	95	1,939	2,023	958	294	
38	Averill, Earl	1929-1941	1.574059	2,626	10,000	3,178	1,971	631	201	375	1,927	1,832	1,218	815	
25	Bagwell, Jeff**	1991-2004	1.299207	2,743	10,000	2,974	1,724	629	42	579	1,957	1,962	1,797	1,997	
111	Banks, Ernie	1953-1971	1.061458	2,683	10,000	2,742	1,671	432	96	543	1,385	1,737	810	1,312	
36	Belle, Albert	1989-2000	1.708526	2,629	10,000	2,949	1,597	665	36	651	1,664	2,117	1,167	1,642	
106	Bench, Johnny	1967-1983	1.305824	2,818	10,000	2,674	1,638	498	31	508	1,425	1,797	1,163	1,669	
22	Berkman, Lance**	1999-2004	3.727171	2,889	10,000	3,034	1,662	727	63	581	1,923	1,994	1,867	2,020	
91	Berra, Yogi	1946-1965	1.323627	2,806	10,000	2,846	1,882	425	65	474	1,555	1,893	932	549	
101	Bichette, Dante	1988-2001	1.567152	2,670	10,000	2,987	1,887	628	42	429	1,464	1,788	556	1,689	
4	Bonds, Barry **	1986-2004	1.099143	2,985	10,000	3,001	1,525	619	85	773	2,275	2,026	2,530	1,570	
80	Bottomley, Jim	1922-1937	1.338509	2,665	10,000	3,096	1,978	622	202	293	1,575	1,903	889	791	
112	Brett, George	1973-1993	0.966277	2,616	10,000	3,048	1,966	643	132	306	1,530	1,541	1,059	877	
12	Brouthers, Dan	1879-1904	1.486989	2,465	10,000	3,493	2,354	668	314	158	2,241	1,927	1,249	354	
94	Burkett, Jesse	1890-1905	1.192037	2,458	10,000	3,424	2,739	374	221	89	2,036	1,135	1,227	274	
79	Campanella, Roy	1948-1957	2.378121	2,889	10,000	2,761	1,719	423	43	576	1,491	2,036	1,268	1,191	
58	Canseco, Jose	1985-2001	1.417033	2,674	10,000	2,660	1,503	482	20	655	1,681	1,994	1,284	2,752	
103	Cepeda, Orlando	1958-1974	1.261511	2,679	10,000	2,966	1,928	526	34	478	1,427	1,722	742	1,475	
125	Clemente, Roberto	1955-1972	1.057753	2,574	10,000	3,173	2,278	465	176	254	1,498	1,380	657	1,301	
34	Cobb, Ty	1905-1928	0.874967	2,654	10,000	3,667	2,671	633	260	102	1,964	1,695	1,093	312	
95	Collins, Eddie	1906-1930	1.004924	2,840	10,000	3,330	2,655	440	188	47	1,829	1,306	1,510	287	
42	Conner, Roger	1880-1897	1.280902	2,545	10,000	3,247	2,230	550	291	177	2,058	1,693	1,283	575	
87	Cravath, Gavy	1908-1920	2.531005	3,088	10,000	2,870	1,772	587	210	301	1,455	1,820	1,420	1,301	
116	Crawford, Sam	1899-1917	1.043950	2,615	10,000	3,094	2,190	477	326	101	1,453	1,592	793	109	
120	Dawson, Andre	1976-1996	1.007354	2,646	10,000	2,794	1,748	507	99	441	1,383	1,603	593	1,520	
17	Delahanty, Ed	1888-1903	1.334579	2,436	10,000	3,461	2,404	681	242	135	2,130	1,954	989	326	
26	Delgado, Carlos**	1993-2004	1.996805	2,841	10,000	2,821	1,444	685	22	671	1,775	2,113	1,651	2,480	
90	Dickey, Bill*	1928-1946	1.587302	2,840	10,000	3,125	2,146	544	114	321	1,476	1,919	1,076	459	
11	DiMaggio, Joe*	1936-1951	1.466061	2,545	10,000	3,246	1,954	570	192	529	2,038	2,253	1,158	541	
27	Duffy, Hugh	1888-1906	1.428776	2,460	10,000	3,296	2,535	443	167	151	2,207	1,860	946	301	
92	Fielder, Cecil	1985-1998	1.939112	2,850	10,000	2,546	1,526	388	14	619	1,443	1,955	1,344	2,552	
113	Foster, George	1969-1986	1.423893	2,815	10,000	2,741	1,741	437	67	496	1,404	1,764	948	2,021	
5	Foxx, Jimmie*	1925-1944	1.229407	2,849	10,000	3,253	1,880	563	154	657	2,153	2,363	1,785	1,612	
98	Galarraga, Andres**	1985-2004	1.235178	2,788	10,000	2,882	1,801	548	40	493	1,476	1,760	720	2,474	
62	Garciaparra, Nomar**	1996-2004	2.419550	2,441	10,000	3,218	1,948	709	121	440	1,783	1,718	714	1,016	
2	Gehrig, Lou	1923-1938	1.249844	2,705	10,000	3,401	1,914	667	204	616	2,360	2,493	1,886	987	
67	Gehringer, Charlie	1924-1941	1.128668	2,622	10,000	3,204	2,184	648	165	208	2,002	1,611	1,337	420	
35	Giambi, Jason**	1995-2004	2.102165	2,825	10,000	2,970	1,741	622	17	591	1,789	1,984	1,831	1,926	
45	Gonzalez, Juan **	1989-2004	1.525553	2,575	10,000	2,953	1,661	592	38	662	1,619	2,142	697	1,942	
65	Goslin, Goose	1921-1938	1.155268022	2,642	10,000	3,160	2,096	578	200	287	1,713	1,859	1,096	676	
6	Greenberg, Hank*	1930-1947	1.925669	2,684	10,000	3,135	1,631	730	137	637	2,024	2,457	1,641	1,625	
32	Griffey, Ken **	1989-2004	1.355197	2,706	10,000	2,922	1,652	542	49	679	1,789	1,957	1,334	1,793	
33	Guerrero, Vladimir**	1996-2004	2.285714	2,651	10,000	3,248	1,936	606	82	624	1,749	1,893	990	1,275	
66	Hafey, Chick	1924-1937	2.162162	2,774	10,000	3,170	1,933	737	145	355	1,680	1,801	804	1,031	
14	Hamilton, Billy	1888-1901	1.596934	2,520	10,000	3,445	2,871	359	150	64	2,700	1,175	1,896	348	
57	Heilmann, Harry	1914-1932	1.284192	2,756	10,000	3,416	2,291	696	194	235	1,658	1,976	1,099	706	
8	Helton, Todd**	1997-2004	2.468526	2,802	10,000	3,387	1,903	810	54	620	2,054	2,064	1,647	1,338	
85	Henderson, Rickey	1979-2003	0.912326	2,811	10,000	2,787	1,991	465	60	271	2,094	1,017	1,998	1,545	
73	Herman, Babe	1926-1945	1.784758	2,770	10,000	3,245	2,013	712	196	323	1,574	1,779	928	987	

Total Career Statistics Adjusted to 10,000 Official At-Bats Listed Alphabetically

SB	CS	HBP	SF	GDP	AVG	OBP	SLG	Total Offensive Production Statistics				TRP Rating	RPA Rating	TNB Rating	TBA Rating	TOP Composite	
								TRP	RPA	TNB	TBA					TOP	Rating
194	59	26	98	265	.305	.374	.555	3,616	.314	6,840	.594	69.23	75.15	72.69	78.90	295.98	73.99
210	82	25	84	259	.292	.378	.534	3,503	.297	6,901	.586	67.06	71.20	73.35	77.88	289.49	72.37
288	16	31	-	-	.342	.401	.455	3,962	.361	5,815	.529	75.85	86.33	61.80	70.33	294.32	73.58
110	90	52	-	11	.318	.395	.534	3,759	.333	6,627	.587	71.96	79.79	70.43	78.08	300.26	75.06
262	101	165	127	286	.297	.408	.542	3,918	.317	7,547	.610	75.02	75.82	80.21	81.07	312.11	78.03
53	56	74	102	243	.274	.330	.500	3,122	.278	5,876	.523	59.77	66.57	62.45	69.56	258.35	64.59
150	70	94	133	330	.295	.369	.564	3,781	.323	6,979	.595	72.39	77.23	74.17	79.13	302.92	75.73
89	56	25	118	262	.267	.342	.476	3,221	.278	5,979	.517	61.68	66.68	63.55	68.71	260.61	65.15
149	97	138	97	171	.303	.416	.563	3,917	.319	7,689	.626	75.00	76.43	81.72	83.27	316.41	79.10
40	34	65	58	193	.285	.348	.482	3,448	.307	5,824	.518	66.01	73.40	61.89	68.82	270.14	67.53
238	114	64	114	276	.299	.336	.499	3,252	.295	5,733	.521	62.26	70.72	60.92	69.21	263.11	65.78
556	155	102	96	156	.300	.443	.611	4,301	.334	9,140	.709	82.34	79.93	97.14	94.30	353.72	88.43
78	20	58	-	44	.310	.369	.500	3,479	.317	6,006	.546	66.60	75.79	63.83	72.64	278.86	69.72
194	94	32	116	227	.305	.369	.487	3,071	.269	6,065	.530	58.79	64.31	64.46	70.51	258.07	64.52
391	-	156	-	-	.349	.429	.526	4,168	.365	7,057	.619	79.80	87.51	75.00	82.25	324.56	81.14
467	-	89	-	-	.342	.419	.451	3,171	.280	6,290	.556	60.71	67.10	66.85	73.89	268.55	67.14
59	40	71	43	340	.276	.360	.500	3,527	.301	6,354	.542	67.52	72.05	67.53	72.06	279.16	69.79
283	125	119	115	252	.266	.353	.515	3,674	.312	6,707	.570	70.35	74.75	71.28	75.74	292.12	73.03
179	101	129	93	275	.297	.350	.499	3,149	.280	5,943	.529	60.28	67.09	63.16	70.29	260.82	65.20
88	49	37	70	291	.317	.359	.475	2,878	.260	5,484	.496	55.10	62.34	58.29	65.95	241.68	60.42
780	185	82	-	-	.367	.433	.513	3,659	.327	6,897	.617	70.05	78.41	73.30	82.04	303.81	75.95
747	174	77	-	-	.333	.424	.429	3,135	.271	6,449	.556	60.03	64.79	68.53	73.97	267.32	66.83
323	-	49	-	-	.325	.404	.491	3,752	.331	6,563	.579	71.83	79.28	69.75	76.99	297.85	74.46
225	23	71	-	-	.287	.380	.478	3,275	.285	6,474	.563	62.70	68.25	68.81	74.89	274.65	68.66
379	31	24	-	-	.309	.362	.453	3,045	.282	5,692	.526	58.30	67.41	60.49	69.94	256.14	64.03
316	110	112	119	219	.279	.323	.482	2,986	.270	5,734	.519	57.16	64.75	60.94	69.02	251.87	62.97
642	-	125	-	-	.346	.412	.503	4,084	.367	6,785	.610	78.19	87.99	72.11	81.15	319.43	79.86
18	14	244	122	186	.282	.392	.556	3,888	.319	7,462	.612	74.43	76.29	79.30	81.29	311.31	77.83
57	46	49	-	78	.313	.382	.486	3,395	.303	5,997	.535	65.00	72.57	63.73	71.15	272.46	68.11
44	13	67	-	191	.325	.398	.579	4,291	.376	7,044	.617	82.16	90.01	74.87	82.02	329.05	82.26
853	-	41	-	-	.330	.390	.453	4,068	.370	6,368	.580	77.88	88.65	67.68	77.04	311.25	77.81
4	12	83	89	328	.255	.345	.482	3,397	.287	6,236	.527	65.04	68.69	66.28	69.99	269.99	67.50
73	44	74	97	279	.274	.338	.480	3,168	.278	5,849	.513	60.66	66.56	62.16	68.21	257.59	64.40
108	89	16	-	85	.325	.428	.609	4,516	.380	7,914	.666	86.45	90.97	84.10	88.50	350.03	87.51
158	100	220	72	221	.288	.347	.499	3,236	.288	5,986	.533	61.96	68.99	63.61	70.83	265.39	66.35
208	70	116	119	208	.322	.370	.549	3,501	.314	6,458	.579	67.03	75.15	68.63	76.94	287.75	71.94
127	126	56	-	2	.340	.447	.632	4,853	.406	8,268	.692	92.91	97.29	87.87	92.01	370.08	92.52
205	100	58	-	30	.320	.404	.480	3,613	.316	6,305	.552	69.17	75.72	67.00	73.35	285.24	71.31
27	21	193	130	242	.297	.411	.540	3,773	.304	7,429	.599	72.24	72.89	78.95	79.66	303.74	75.94
40	29	95	119	278	.295	.343	.561	3,760	.336	6,410	.573	72.00	80.48	68.13	76.16	296.76	74.19
202	103	65	-	-	.316	.387	.500	3,572	.320	6,257	.561	68.39	76.64	66.50	74.52	286.04	71.51
112	50	31	-	127	.313	.412	.605	4,481	.380	7,784	.660	85.79	90.94	82.72	87.69	347.15	86.79
241	89	96	102	188	.292	.377	.560	3,746	.320	7,180	.613	71.80	76.67	76.52	81.71	306.70	76.68
315	169	133	78	322	.325	.390	.589	3,641	.316	7,159	.621	69.71	75.67	76.08	82.59	304.05	76.01
151	15	71	-	61	.317	.372	.526	3,481	.318	6,272	.574	66.65	76.22	66.66	76.24	285.77	71.44
1,496	-	142	-	-	.344	.455	.430	3,876	.322	7,830	.650	74.20	77.10	83.21	86.46	320.97	80.24
144	82	51	-	-	.342	.410	.520	3,634	.326	6,417	.575	69.58	78.04	68.20	76.50	292.32	73.08
74	57	77	116	242	.339	.432	.616	4,118	.341	7,904	.654	78.83	81.61	84.00	86.97	331.42	82.85
1,283	306	89	61	157	.279	.401	.419	3,111	.253	7,250	.589	59.56	60.54	77.05	78.32	275.47	68.87
168	-	20	-	77	.324	.383	.532	3,354	.304	6,434	.584	64.20	72.84	68.38	77.58	283.00	70.75

10,000 Official At-Bats A-H

10,000 Official At-Bats H-R

Rank	Player	Years	Adjustment to 10,000 AB	G	AB	H	1B	2B	3B	HR	RUN	RBI	BB	SO
21	Hornsby, Rogers	1915-1937	1.223541	2,764	10,000	3,585	2,348	662	207	368	1,932	1,938	1,270	831
110	Howard, Frank	1958-1973	1.540595	2,919	10,000	2,733	1,713	377	54	589	1,331	1,724	1,205	2,249
71	Jackson, Joe	1908-1920	2.007629	2,670	10,000	3,558	2,495	616	337	108	1,753	1,576	1,042	317
89	Jackson, Reggie	1967-1987	1.013788	2,859	10,000	2,620	1,530	469	50	571	1,572	1,725	1,395	2,633
60	Jennings, Hughie	1891-1918	2.065262	2,606	10,000	3,139	2,456	465	182	37	2,043	1,735	717	242
104	Jeter, Derek**	1995-2004	1.813894	2,478	10,000	3,145	2,284	513	76	272	1,881	1,257	1,014	1,763
59	Johnson, Robert	1933-1945	1.445087	2,692	10,000	2,964	1,838	572	137	416	1,790	1,854	1,553	1,230
40	Jones, Chipper**	1993-2004	1.780627	2,746	10,000	3,036	1,857	579	48	552	1,843	1,850	1,668	1,562
102	Kaline, Al	1953-1974	0.988533	2,801	10,000	2,973	2,012	492	74	394	1,603	1,565	1,262	1,008
121	Keeler, Willie	1892-1910	1.167679	2,480	10,000	3,450	2,962	271	179	39	2,008	946	612	946
28	Keller, Charlie*	1939-1952	2.638522	3,087	10,000	2,863	1,736	438	190	499	1,913	2,005	2,069	1,317
50	Kelley, Joe	1891-1908	1.430411	2,625	10,000	3,211	2,343	505	270	93	2,027	1,708	1,302	229
46	Kelly, King	1878-1892	1.688619	2,421	10,000	3,129	2,236	593	184	117	2,295	1,604	929	709
64	Killebrew, Harmon	1954-1975	1.227446	2,989	10,000	2,560	1,472	356	29	703	1,575	1,944	1,914	2,085
29	Kiner, Ralph	1946-1956	1.921230	2,828	10,000	2,788	1,589	415	75	709	1,866	1,950	1,942	1,439
48	Klein, Chuck	1928-1944	1.541782	2,703	10,000	3,201	2,010	614	114	463	1,801	1,852	927	803
105	Kluszewski, Ted	1947-1961	1.686625	2,898	10,000	2,979	1,970	489	49	471	1,430	1,734	830	616
96	Lajoie, Nap	1896-1916	1.042862	2,581	10,000	3,391	2,460	676	170	86	1,571	1,668	538	89
16	Mantle, Mickey	1951-1968	1.234263	2,963	10,000	2,981	1,806	425	89	662	2,070	1,863	2,141	2,114
97	Maris, Roger	1957-1968	1.960400	2,868	10,000	2,598	1,594	382	82	539	1,619	1,668	1,278	1,437
69	Martinez, Edgar**	1987-2004	1.386386	2,849	10,000	3,115	1,953	713	21	428	1,690	1,748	1,779	1,666
68	Matthews, Eddie	1952-1968	1.171372	2,801	10,000	2,712	1,613	415	84	600	1,768	1,702	1,691	1,742
122	Mattingly, Don	1982-1995	1.427959	2,549	10,000	3,074	2,098	631	29	317	1,438	1,569	840	634
37	Mays, Willie*	1951-1973	0.919033	2,750	10,000	3,017	1,801	481	129	607	1,895	1,749	1,345	1,402
76	McCovey, Willie	1959-1980	1.219959	3,157	10,000	2,697	1,575	431	56	636	1,499	1,897	1,641	1,891
84	McGriff, Fred **	1986-2004	1.141944	2,809	10,000	2,843	1,749	504	27	563	1,540	1,770	1,490	2,149
9	McGwire, Mark	1986-2001	1.616292	3,029	10,000	2,628	1,269	407	10	942	1,886	2,285	2,129	2,580
93	Medwick, Joe	1932-1948	1.309758	2,599	10,000	3,236	2,113	707	148	269	1,569	1,811	572	722
83	Meusel, Bob	1920-1930	1.826484	2,570	10,000	3,092	1,962	672	174	285	1,509	1,949	685	1,131
30	Mize, Johnny*	1936-1953	1.552072	2,924	10,000	3,121	1,866	570	129	557	1,735	2,075	1,330	813
100	Morgan, Joe	1963-1984	1.077935	2,855	10,000	2,713	1,837	484	103	289	1,779	1,221	2,010	1,094
115	Murphy, Dale	1976-1993	1.256281	2,739	10,000	2,652	1,663	440	49	500	1,504	1,590	1,239	2,196
114	Murray, Eddie	1977-1997	0.882145	2,669	10,000	2,871	1,902	494	31	445	1,435	1,691	1,176	1,337
47	Musial, Stan*	1941-1963	0.911411	2,758	10,000	3,308	2,053	661	161	433	1,776	1,778	1,457	634
56	O'Neill, Tip	1883-1892	2.322880	2,448	10,000	3,336	2,485	516	214	121	2,044	1,758	978	339
75	Ordonez, Magglio**	1997-2004	2.626764	2,629	10,000	3,065	1,904	630	39	491	1,639	1,847	875	1,132
24	Ott, Mel	1926-1947	1.057530	2,887	10,000	3,041	1,909	516	76	540	1,966	1,967	1,806	948
81	Palmiero, Rafael**	1986-2004	0.989805	2,693	10,000	2,892	1,743	566	38	545	1,600	1,757	1,297	1,292
124	Parker, Dave	1973-1991	1.068604	2,635	10,000	2,898	1,894	562	80	362	1,359	1,595	730	1,642
123	Perez, Tony	1964-1986	1.022704	2,840	10,000	2,794	1,809	516	81	388	1,301	1,690	946	1,909
55	Piazza, Mike**	1992-2004	1.722653	2,739	10,000	3,151	1,998	491	10	651	1,611	2,000	1,147	1,583
7	Pujols, Albert**	2001-2004	4.231909	2,662	10,000	3,331	1,815	800	38	677	2,116	2,133	1,287	1,181
10	Ramirez, Manny**	1993-2004	1.794688	2,755	10,000	3,159	1,750	684	25	700	1,915	2,279	1,569	2,207
99	Rice, Jim	1974-1989	1.215805	2,540	10,000	2,981	1,967	453	96	464	1,519	1,764	815	1,730
126	Ripkin, Cal, Jr.	1981-2001	0.865726	2,598	10,000	2,756	1,823	522	38	373	1,426	1,467	977	1,130
44	Robinson, Frank	1956-1976	0.999400	2,806	10,000	2,941	1,756	528	72	586	1,828	1,811	1,419	1,531
77	Robinson, Jackie	1947-1956	2.050441	2,834	10,000	3,113	2,161	560	111	281	1,942	1,505	1,517	597
20	Rodriguez, Alex**	1994-2004	1.788909	2,558	10,000	3,054	1,776	553	43	682	2,005	1,961	1,143	2,014
127	Rose, Pete	1963-1986	0.711592	2,535	10,000	3,029	2,288	531	96	114	1,541	935	1,114	813
1	Ruth, Babe	1914-1935	1.190618	2,980	10,000	3,421	1,806	602	162	850	2,588	2,635	2,455	1,584

Total Career Statistics Adjusted to 10,000 Official At-Bats Listed Alphabetically

SB	CS	HBP	SF	GDP	AVG	OBP	SLG	Total Offensive Production Statistics				TRP Rating	RPA Rating	TNB Rating	TBA Rating	TOP Composite	
								TRP	RPA	TNB	TBA					TOP	Rating
165	78	59	4	-	.358	.434	.577	3,870	.342	7,181	.634	74.09	81.78	76.32	84.23	316.41	79.10
12	14	51	66	337	.273	.352	.498	3,055	.262	6,238	.535	58.49	62.74	66.29	71.12	258.64	64.66
406	122	118	-	-	.356	.423	.517	3,329	.298	6,617	.593	63.73	71.42	70.32	78.81	284.28	71.07
231	117	97	69	186	.262	.356	.490	3,298	.281	6,508	.554	63.14	67.23	69.16	73.64	273.16	68.29
772	-	593	-	-	.314	.393	.408	3,777	.334	6,161	.545	72.32	79.98	65.47	72.41	290.18	72.55
365	94	167	54	221	.315	.385	.463	3,138	.274	6,078	.531	60.08	65.59	64.60	70.52	260.79	65.20
139	92	35	-	147	.296	.393	.506	3,645	.311	6,694	.570	69.77	74.36	71.14	75.82	291.09	72.77
210	71	25	114	267	.304	.401	.537	3,693	.306	7,199	.596	70.70	73.24	76.51	79.25	299.70	74.93
137	79	54	103	268	.297	.376	.480	3,168	.271	6,171	.528	60.66	64.91	65.59	70.19	261.35	65.34
606	42	151	-	-	.345	.391	.419	2,954	.274	5,521	.513	56.56	65.73	58.67	68.19	249.15	62.29
119	61	26	-	132	.286	.410	.518	3,918	.320	7,330	.599	75.01	76.74	77.90	79.69	309.33	77.33
629	-	117	-	-	.321	.405	.454	3,735	.327	6,584	.577	71.50	78.32	69.97	76.64	296.44	74.11
621	-	20	-	-	.313	.372	.444	3,899	.356	6,010	.549	74.65	85.27	63.87	72.96	296.75	74.19
23	22	59	95	298	.256	.376	.509	3,519	.285	7,059	.571	67.37	68.15	75.02	75.88	286.43	71.61
42	4	46	13	242	.279	.398	.548	3,816	.312	7,506	.613	73.05	74.62	79.77	81.49	308.93	77.23
122	-	19	-	85	.320	.379	.543	3,652	.331	6,497	.589	69.93	79.29	69.05	78.30	296.57	74.14
34	17	39	39	241	.298	.353	.498	3,164	.284	5,863	.526	60.58	67.96	62.31	69.90	260.75	65.19
412	22	140	-	-	.339	.381	.466	3,238	.303	5,732	.537	61.99	72.62	60.91	71.35	266.87	66.72
189	47	16	58	139	.298	.421	.557	3,932	.318	7,867	.637	75.29	76.21	83.61	84.64	319.75	79.94
41	18	74	84	147	.260	.345	.476	3,288	.284	6,138	.530	62.94	67.96	65.23	70.43	266.57	66.64
68	42	123	107	263	.312	.418	.515	3,438	.280	7,083	.577	65.83	67.09	75.28	76.72	284.91	71.23
80	46	30	68	144	.271	.376	.509	3,470	.291	6,850	.574	66.43	69.62	72.80	76.30	285.15	71.29
20	13	30	137	273	.307	.358	.471	3,007	.267	5,590	.496	57.58	63.84	59.41	65.88	246.71	61.68
311	95	40	84	231	.302	.384	.557	3,644	.311	7,176	.613	69.76	74.58	76.26	81.53	302.14	75.53
32	27	84	85	215	.270	.374	.515	3,396	.282	6,877	.572	65.02	67.63	73.09	76.02	281.76	70.44
82	43	45	81	258	.284	.377	.509	3,310	.279	6,664	.561	63.38	66.76	70.83	74.61	275.57	68.89
19	13	121	126	238	.263	.394	.588	4,172	.331	8,138	.645	79.87	79.20	86.49	85.76	331.31	82.83
55	3	34	-	266	.324	.362	.505	3,380	.311	5,704	.525	64.72	74.45	60.62	69.74	269.53	67.38
259	186	38	-	-	.309	.356	.497	3,458	.322	5,763	.537	66.20	77.21	61.24	71.43	276.08	69.02
43	3	81	-	154	.312	.397	.562	3,810	.329	7,071	.611	72.95	78.90	75.15	81.28	308.28	77.07
743	175	43	103	113	.271	.392	.427	3,000	.244	6,892	.562	57.43	58.54	73.25	74.67	263.89	65.97
202	85	35	75	263	.265	.346	.469	3,094	.266	6,080	.524	59.24	63.81	64.62	69.60	257.27	64.32
97	38	16	113	279	.287	.359	.476	3,126	.270	6,012	.519	59.85	64.63	63.89	68.99	257.36	64.34
71	32	48	48	221	.331	.417	.559	3,555	.302	7,135	.606	68.05	72.28	75.83	80.55	296.71	74.18
374	-	102	-	-	.334	.399	.464	3,803	.343	6,095	.550	72.80	82.18	64.78	73.12	292.88	73.22
215	100	89	92	344	.307	.364	.525	3,486	.306	6,328	.555	66.81	73.22	67.63	74.12	281.78	70.44
94	2	68	-	87	.304	.414	.533	3,933	.329	7,297	.610	75.30	78.74	77.55	81.09	312.68	78.17
94	40	84	110	220	.289	.372	.517	3,356	.287	6,605	.564	64.26	68.62	70.20	74.96	278.04	69.51
165	121	60	92	223	.290	.339	.471	2,955	.266	5,541	.499	56.57	63.71	58.88	66.32	245.49	61.37
50	34	44	108	274	.279	.341	.463	2,990	.263	5,641	.496	57.25	62.97	59.95	65.94	246.11	61.53
29	34	41	69	343	.315	.385	.562	3,611	.311	6,799	.586	69.13	74.53	72.26	77.91	293.83	73.46
55	55	148	106	317	.333	.413	.624	4,249	.358	7,672	.647	81.34	85.80	81.54	86.01	334.69	83.67
59	54	120	108	285	.316	.411	.599	4,194	.347	7,687	.636	80.30	83.13	81.69	84.57	329.68	82.42
71	41	78	114	383	.298	.352	.502	3,283	.288	5,942	.522	62.85	69.02	63.15	69.34	264.35	66.09
31	34	57	110	303	.276	.340	.447	2,893	.253	5,506	.481	55.39	60.52	58.52	63.93	238.36	59.59
204	77	198	102	269	.294	.389	.537	3,639	.304	7,114	.593	69.67	72.69	75.60	78.88	296.83	74.21
404	111	148	18	232	.311	.409	.474	3,447	.289	6,695	.562	65.99	69.27	71.15	74.69	281.09	70.27
367	89	147	104	229	.305	.381	.574	3,966	.341	7,304	.628	75.93	81.71	77.63	83.54	318.80	79.70
141	106	76	56	176	.303	.375	.409	2,476	.217	5,318	.466	47.40	51.90	56.52	61.89	217.71	54.43
146	139	50	-	2	.342	.474	.690	5,223	.418	9,409	.752	100.00	100.00	100.00	100.00	400.00	100.00

10,000 Official At-Bats H-R

10,000 Official At-Bats S-Y

Rank	Player	Years	Adjustment to 10,000 AB	G	AB	H	1B	2B	3B	HR	RUN	RBI	BB	SO	
------	--------	-------	-------------------------	---	----	---	----	----	----	----	-----	-----	----	----	
			Total Career Statistics Adjusted to 10,000 Official At-Bats Listed Alphabetically												
39	Schmidt, Mike	1972-1989	1.197318	2,878	10,000	2,675	1,460	489	71	656	1,803	1,910	1,804	2,255	
43	Sheffield, Gary**	1988-2004	1.369488	2,788	10,000	2,979	1,849	529	33	568	1,790	1,853	1,646	1,204	
41	Simmons, Al*	1924-1944	1.141162	2,528	10,000	3,340	2,205	615	170	350	1,720	2,085	702	841	
118	Sisler, George	1915-1930	1.209629	2,486	10,000	3,401	2,566	514	198	123	1,553	1,421	571	396	
53	Snider, Duke	1947-1964	1.396453	2,993	10,000	2,955	1,768	500	119	568	1,758	1,861	1,356	1,727	
52	Sosa, Sammy**	1989-2004	1.246727	2,666	10,000	2,768	1,575	424	54	716	1,724	1,907	1,067	2,631	
72	Speaker, Tris	1907-1928	0.980873	2,736	10,000	3,448	2,336	778	219	115	1,845	1,500	1,355	216	
74	Stargell, Willie	1962-1982	1.261511	2,977	10,000	2,816	1,613	534	69	599	1,508	1,943	1,182	2,442	
31	Stovey, Harry	1880-1893	1.614466	2,401	10,000	2,948	1,910	560	281	197	2,409	1,466	1,070	554	
82	Terry, Bill	1923-1936	1.555694	2,677	10,000	3,412	2,418	580	174	240	1,742	1,677	835	699	
15	Thomas, Frank **	1990-2004	1.459641	2,810	10,000	3,084	1,784	648	16	636	1,909	2,100	2,116	1,655	
13	Thome, Jim**	1991-2004	1.746420	2,932	10,000	2,838	1,504	554	42	739	1,965	2,031	2,117	2,974	
19	Thompson, Sam	1885-1906	1.665556	2,340	10,000	3,358	2,362	543	243	210	2,097	2,164	750	376	
119	Traynor, Pie	1920-1937	1.322926	2,568	10,000	3,196	2,412	491	217	77	1,565	1,684	624	368	
63	Trosky, Hal*	1933-1946	1.937609	2,610	10,000	3,025	1,829	641	112	442	1,618	1,961	1,056	853	
70	Vaughn, Mo	1991-2003	1.807664	2,733	10,000	2,928	1,829	488	18	593	1,556	1,923	1,311	2,583	
78	Wagner, Honus	1897-1917	0.959049	2,673	10,000	3,290	2,327	624	242	97	1,669	1,661	924	314	
23	Walker, Larry **	1989-2004	1.516990	2,861	10,000	3,139	1,804	684	93	558	1,955	1,910	1,323	1,770	
107	Waner, Paul	1927-1945	1.057194	2,695	10,000	3,332	2,370	641	202	119	1,720	1,384	1,153	398	
86	Williams, Bernie**	1991-2004	1.435956	2,590	10,000	3,011	1,980	576	78	378	1,792	1,626	1,412	1,558	
109	Williams, Billy	1959-1976	1.069519	2,661	10,000	2,899	1,886	464	94	456	1,508	1,578	1,118	1,119	
49	Williams, Ken*	1915-1929	2.056767	2,873	10,000	3,192	2,044	586	158	403	1,769	1,878	1,164	590	
3	Williams, Ted*	1939-1960	1.297690	2,974	10,000	3,444	1,995	681	92	676	2,333	2,386	2,623	920	
18	Wilson, Hack	1923-1934	2.100840	2,832	10,000	3,069	1,857	559	141	513	1,857	2,233	1,416	1,498	
108	Winfield, Dave	1973-1995	0.908843	2,702	10,000	2,827	1,833	491	80	423	1,517	1,666	1,105	1,532	
117	Yastrzemski, Carl	1961-1983	0.834168	2,759	10,000	2,852	1,887	539	49	377	1,515	1,538	1,539	1,163	
88	York, Rudy	1934-1948	1.697505	2,721	10,000	2,752	1,699	494	88	470	1,487	1,956	1,343	1,472	

* Player missed time for military service
** Active player. Statistics through 2004 season
TOP ranking for players with less than 70% rating is based upon comparison to listed players only.

SB	CS	HBP	SF	GDP	AVG	OBP	SLG	Total Offensive Production Statistics				TRP Rating	RPA Rating	TNB Rating	TBA Rating	TOP Composite	
								TRP	RPA	TNB	TBA					TOP	Rating
208	110	95	129	187	.267	.380	.527	3,713	.304	7,270	.595	71.08	72.79	77.26	79.11	300.25	75.06
281	127	151	131	245	.298	.400	.528	3,643	.299	7,228	.594	69.74	71.66	76.82	78.93	297.14	74.29
99	73	34	-	26	.334	.380	.535	3,805	.354	6,109	.568	72.84	84.65	64.92	75.45	297.86	74.46
454	154	58	-	-	.340	.379	.468	2,974	.280	5,611	.528	56.95	67.01	59.64	70.18	253.77	63.44
138	77	29	45	232	.295	.380	.540	3,620	.310	6,844	.587	69.30	74.32	72.74	78.01	294.37	73.59
290	132	67	87	218	.277	.348	.545	3,632	.317	6,739	.589	69.53	76.02	71.61	78.30	295.46	73.86
426	127	101	-	-	.345	.428	.501	3,345	.292	6,762	.590	64.04	69.92	71.87	78.46	284.28	71.07
21	20	98	95	180	.282	.360	.529	3,450	.299	6,567	.568	66.06	71.50	69.80	75.55	282.90	70.72
822	-	50	-	-	.295	.366	.466	3,875	.348	6,603	.594	74.18	83.43	70.18	78.93	306.72	76.68
87	9	14	-	59	.341	.393	.506	3,419	.313	5,986	.549	65.47	75.06	63.62	72.95	277.09	69.27
47	34	104	155	273	.308	.429	.567	4,010	.317	7,907	.625	76.77	75.91	84.03	83.10	319.81	79.95
31	33	84	91	176	.284	.410	.569	3,996	.320	7,890	.633	76.50	76.74	83.86	84.12	321.22	80.31
393	-	105	-	-	.336	.388	.502	4,260	.393	6,264	.577	81.57	93.99	66.57	76.71	318.84	79.71
209	61	41	-	62	.320	.362	.435	3,249	.303	5,165	.481	62.20	72.53	54.89	64.00	253.61	63.40
54	45	31	-	83	.302	.371	.522	3,579	.320	6,313	.565	68.52	76.72	67.09	75.12	287.44	71.86
54	33	195	81	244	.293	.383	.523	3,480	.294	6,759	.571	66.62	70.43	71.83	75.94	284.82	71.20
692	22	119	-	-	.329	.392	.469	3,330	.302	6,401	.580	63.75	72.21	68.02	77.05	281.03	70.26
346	114	196	96	218	.314	.401	.568	3,865	.327	7,433	.628	74.00	78.22	79.00	83.50	314.73	78.68
110	1	40	-	134	.333	.404	.474	3,104	.274	6,038	.533	59.43	65.61	64.17	70.85	260.05	65.01
207	122	52	75	277	.301	.388	.488	3,418	.289	6,423	.544	65.43	69.26	68.26	72.26	275.22	68.80
96	52	46	78	214	.290	.361	.492	3,086	.269	6,126	.535	59.07	64.50	65.11	71.08	259.76	64.94
317	218	58	-	-	.319	.393	.530	3,647	.325	6,625	.590	69.82	77.81	70.41	78.47	296.51	74.13
31	22	51	26	256	.344	.482	.634	4,720	.364	9,020	.696	90.36	87.24	95.86	92.55	366.02	91.50
109	11	42	-	32	.307	.395	.545	4,090	.356	7,004	.610	78.31	85.25	74.44	81.03	319.03	79.76
203	87	23	86	290	.283	.353	.475	3,183	.277	5,988	.521	60.93	66.25	63.64	69.19	260.02	65.00
140	97	33	88	269	.285	.379	.462	3,053	.256	6,236	.523	58.45	61.28	66.28	69.49	255.50	63.87
65	44	20	-	263	.275	.362	.483	3,443	.296	6,216	.535	65.91	70.90	66.06	71.07	273.95	68.49

Total Career Statistics Adjusted to 10,000 Official At-Bats Listed Alphabetically

10,000 Official At-Bats S-Y

125 of the Greatest Players:

C-1
Players Listed by Total Offensive Production

C-2
Players Listed Alphabetically

(Rating and Ranking of Total Offensive Production Statistics in Chapter 6)

	Actual Career Statistics Listed by Total Offensive Production Ranking														
Rank	Player	Years	G	AB	H	1B	2B	3B	HR	RUN	RBI	BB	SO	SB	
1	Ruth, Babe	1914-1935	2,503	8,399	2,873	1,517	506	136	714	2,174	2,213	2,062	1,330	123	
2	Bonds, Barry **	1986-2004	2,716	9,098	2,730	1,387	563	77	703	2,070	1,843	2,302	1,428	506	
3	Gehrig, Lou	1923-1938	2,164	8,001	2,721	1,531	534	163	493	1,888	1,995	1,509	790	102	
4	Aaron, Hank	1954-1976	3,298	12,364	3,771	2,294	624	98	755	2,174	2,297	1,402	1,383	240	
5	Cobb, Ty	1905-1928	3,033	11,429	4,191	3,053	724	297	117	2,245	1,937	1,249	357	892	
6	Williams, Ted*	1939-1960	2,292	7,706	2,654	1,537	525	71	521	1,798	1,839	2,021	709	24	
7	Foxx, Jimmie*	1925-1944	2,317	8,134	2,646	1,529	458	125	534	1,751	1,922	1,452	1,311	88	
8	Mays, Willie*	1951-1973	2,992	10,881	3,283	1,960	523	140	660	2,062	1,903	1,463	1,526	338	
9	Musial, Stan*	1941-1963	3,026	10,972	3,630	2,253	725	177	475	1,949	1,951	1,599	696	78	
10	Ott, Mel	1926-1947	2,730	9,456	2,876	1,805	488	72	511	1,859	1,860	1,708	896	89	
11	Anson, Cap	1871-1897	2,500	10,260	3,504	2,677	583	147	97	1,989	2,076	983	302	295	
12	Robinson, Frank	1956-1976	2,808	10,006	2,943	1,757	528	72	586	1,829	1,812	1,420	1,532	204	
13	Henderson, Rickey	1979-2003	3,081	10,961	3,055	2,182	510	66	297	2,295	1,115	2,190	1,694	1,406	
14	Mantle, Mickey	1951-1968	2,401	8,102	2,415	1,463	344	72	536	1,677	1,509	1,735	1,713	153	
15	Speaker, Tris	1907-1928	2,789	10,195	3,515	2,382	793	223	117	1,881	1,529	1,381	220	434	
16	Hornsby, Rogers	1915-1937	2,259	8,173	2,930	1,919	541	169	301	1,579	1,584	1,038	679	135	
17	Wagner, Honus	1897-1917	2,787	10,427	3,430	2,426	651	252	101	1,740	1,732	963	327	722	
18	Yastrzemski, Carl	1961-1983	3,308	11,988	3,419	2,262	646	59	452	1,816	1,844	1,845	1,394	168	
19	Palmiero, Rafael**	1986-2004	2,721	10,103	2,922	1,761	572	38	551	1,616	1,775	1,310	1,305	95	
20	Simmons, Al*	1924-1944	2,215	8,763	2,927	1,932	539	149	307	1,507	1,827	615	737	87	
21	Delahanty, Ed	1888-1903	1,825	7,493	2,593	1,801	510	181	101	1,596	1,464	741	244	481	
22	DiMaggio, Joe*	1936-1951	1,736	6,821	2,214	1,333	389	131	361	1,390	1,537	790	369	30	
23	Murray, Eddie	1977-1997	3,026	11,336	3,255	2,156	560	35	504	1,627	1,917	1,333	1,516	110	
24	Schmidt, Mike	1972-1989	2,404	8,352	2,234	1,219	408	59	548	1,506	1,595	1,507	1,883	174	
25	Bagwell, Jeff**	1991-2004	2,111	7,697	2,289	1,327	484	32	446	1,506	1,510	1,383	1,537	202	
26	Winfield, Dave	1973-1995	2,973	11,003	3,110	2,017	540	88	465	1,669	1,833	1,216	1,686	223	
27	Jackson, Reggie	1967-1987	2,820	9,864	2,584	1,509	463	49	563	1,551	1,702	1,376	2,597	228	
28	Brouthers, Dan	1879-1904	1,658	6,725	2,349	1,583	449	211	106	1,507	1,296	840	238	263	
29	Gehringer, Charlie	1924-1941	2,323	8,860	2,839	1,935	574	146	184	1,774	1,427	1,185	372	182	
30	Thomas, Frank **	1990-2004	1,925	6,851	2,113	1,222	444	11	436	1,308	1,439	1,450	1,134	32	
31	Collins, Eddie	1906-1930	2,826	9,951	3,314	2,642	438	187	47	1,820	1,300	1,503	286	743	
32	Goslin, Goose	1921-1938	2,287	8,656	2,735	1,814	500	173	248	1,483	1,609	949	585	175	
33	Sosa, Sammy**	1989-2004	2,138	8,021	2,220	1,263	340	43	574	1,383	1,530	856	2,110	233	
34	Conner, Roger	1880-1897	1,987	7,807	2,535	1,741	429	227	138	1,607	1,322	1,002	449	252	
35	McGwire, Mark	1986-2001	1,874	6,187	1,626	785	252	6	583	1,167	1,414	1,317	1,596	12	
36	Duffy, Hugh	1888-1906	1,722	6,999	2,307	1,774	310	117	106	1,545	1,302	662	211	597	
37	Matthews, Eddie	1952-1968	2,391	8,537	2,315	1,377	354	72	512	1,509	1,453	1,444	1,487	68	
38	Kaline, Al	1953-1974	2,833	10,116	3,007	2,035	498	75	399	1,622	1,583	1,277	1,020	139	
39	Brett, George	1973-1993	2,707	10,349	3,154	2,035	665	137	317	1,583	1,595	1,096	908	201	
40	Rose, Pete	1963-1986	3,562	14,053	4,256	3,215	746	135	160	2,165	1,314	1,566	1,143	198	
41	Greenberg, Hank*	1930-1947	1,394	5,193	1,628	847	379	71	331	1,051	1,276	852	844	58	
42	Lajoie, Nap	1896-1916	2,475	9,589	3,252	2,359	648	163	82	1,506	1,599	516	85	395	
43	Griffey, Ken **	1989-2004	1,997	7,379	2,156	1,219	400	36	501	1,320	1,444	984	1,323	178	
44	Heilmann, Harry	1914-1932	2,146	7,787	2,660	1,784	542	151	183	1,291	1,539	856	550	112	
45	Walker, Larry **	1989-2004	1,886	6,592	2,069	1,189	451	61	368	1,289	1,259	872	1,167	228	
46	Killebrew, Harmon	1954-1975	2,435	8,147	2,086	1,199	290	24	573	1,283	1,584	1,559	1,699	19	
47	Hamilton, Billy	1888-1901	1,578	6,262	2,157	1,798	225	94	40	1,691	736	1,187	218	937	
48	McGriff, Fred **	1986-2004	2,460	8,757	2,490	1,532	441	24	493	1,349	1,550	1,305	1,882	72	
49	Ripkin, Cal, Jr.	1981-2001	3,001	11,551	3,184	2,106	603	44	431	1,647	1,695	1,129	1,305	36	
50	McCovey, Willie	1959-1980	2,588	8,197	2,211	1,291	353	46	521	1,229	1,555	1,345	1,550	26	

Actual Career Statistics Listed by Total Offensive Production Ranking

CS	HBP	SF	GDP	AVG	OBP	SLG	Total Offensive Production Statistics				TRP Rating	RPA Rating	TNB Rating	TBA Rating	TOP Composite	
							TRP	RPA	TNB	TBA					TOP	Rating
117	42	-	2	.342	.474	.690	4,387	.418	7,903	.752	98.12	100.00	93.45	100.00	391.57	100.00
141	93	87	142	.300	.443	.611	3,913	.334	8,316	.709	87.52	79.93	98.33	94.30	360.09	91.96
101	45	-	2	.340	.447	.632	3,883	.406	6,615	.692	86.85	97.29	78.22	92.01	354.36	90.50
73	32	121	328	.305	.374	.555	4,471	.314	8,457	.594	100.00	75.15	100.00	78.90	354.05	90.42
212	94	-	-	.367	.433	.513	4,182	.327	7,883	.617	93.54	78.41	93.21	82.04	347.20	88.67
17	39	20	197	.344	.482	.634	3,637	.364	6,951	.696	81.35	87.24	82.19	92.55	343.33	87.68
72	13	-	69	.325	.428	.609	3,673	.380	6,437	.666	82.15	90.97	76.11	88.50	337.74	86.25
103	44	91	251	.302	.384	.557	3,965	.311	7,808	.613	88.68	74.58	92.34	81.53	337.13	86.10
35	53	53	243	.331	.417	.559	3,900	.302	7,829	.606	87.23	72.28	92.57	80.55	332.63	84.95
2	64	-	82	.304	.414	.533	3,719	.329	6,900	.610	83.11	78.68	81.59	81.09	324.47	82.86
16	32	-	-	.342	.401	.455	4,065	.361	5,966	.529	90.92	86.33	70.55	70.33	318.13	81.24
77	198	102	269	.294	.389	.537	3,641	.304	7,118	.593	81.44	72.69	84.17	78.88	317.17	81.00
335	98	67	172	.279	.401	.419	3,410	.253	7,947	.589	76.27	60.54	93.97	78.32	309.10	78.94
38	13	47	113	.298	.421	.557	3,186	.318	6,374	.637	71.26	76.21	75.37	84.64	307.48	78.53
129	103	-	-	.345	.428	.501	3,410	.292	6,894	.590	76.27	69.92	81.52	78.46	306.17	78.19
64	48	3	-	.358	.434	.577	3,163	.342	5,869	.634	70.74	81.78	69.40	84.23	306.15	78.18
23	124	-	-	.329	.392	.469	3,472	.302	6,674	.580	77.66	72.21	78.92	77.05	305.83	78.10
116	40	105	323	.285	.379	.462	3,660	.256	7,476	.523	81.86	61.28	88.40	69.49	301.03	76.88
40	85	111	222	.289	.372	.517	3,391	.287	6,673	.564	75.84	68.62	78.91	74.96	298.33	76.19
64	30	-	23	.334	.380	.535	3,334	.354	5,353	.568	74.57	84.65	63.30	75.45	297.97	76.09
-	94	-	-	.346	.412	.503	3,060	.367	5,084	.610	68.44	87.99	60.12	81.15	297.69	76.02
9	46	-	130	.325	.398	.579	2,927	.376	4,805	.617	65.47	90.01	56.82	82.02	294.31	75.16
43	18	128	316	.287	.359	.476	3,544	.270	6,815	.519	79.27	64.63	80.58	68.99	293.47	74.95
92	79	108	156	.267	.380	.527	3,101	.304	6,072	.595	69.36	72.79	71.80	79.11	293.06	74.84
78	127	98	220	.297	.408	.542	3,016	.317	5,809	.610	67.46	75.82	68.69	81.07	293.03	74.84
96	25	95	319	.283	.353	.475	3,502	.277	6,589	.521	78.33	66.25	77.91	69.19	291.68	74.49
115	96	68	183	.262	.356	.490	3,253	.281	6,419	.554	72.76	67.23	75.90	73.64	289.52	73.94
-	105	-	-	.349	.429	.526	2,803	.365	4,746	.619	62.69	87.51	56.12	82.25	288.57	73.70
89	51	-	27	.320	.404	.480	3,201	.316	5,586	.552	71.59	75.72	66.05	73.35	286.71	73.22
23	71	106	187	.308	.429	.567	2,747	.317	5,417	.625	61.44	75.91	64.05	83.10	284.51	72.66
173	77	-	-	.333	.424	.429	3,120	.271	6,417	.556	69.78	64.79	75.88	73.97	284.42	72.64
89	56	-	-	.316	.387	.500	3,092	.320	5,416	.561	69.16	76.64	64.04	74.52	284.35	72.62
106	54	70	175	.277	.348	.545	2,913	.317	5,405	.589	65.15	76.02	63.91	78.30	283.38	72.37
-	38	-	-	.325	.404	.491	2,929	.331	5,124	.579	65.51	79.28	60.59	76.99	282.36	72.11
8	75	78	147	.263	.394	.588	2,581	.331	5,035	.645	57.73	79.20	59.54	85.76	282.22	72.07
-	29	-	-	.330	.390	.453	2,847	.370	4,457	.580	63.68	88.65	52.70	77.04	282.07	72.04
39	26	58	123	.271	.376	.509	2,962	.291	5,848	.574	66.25	69.62	69.15	76.30	281.32	71.84
80	55	104	271	.297	.376	.480	3,205	.271	6,243	.528	71.68	64.91	73.82	70.19	280.61	71.66
97	33	120	235	.305	.369	.487	3,178	.269	6,277	.530	71.08	64.31	74.22	70.51	280.13	71.54
149	107	79	247	.303	.375	.409	3,479	.217	7,474	.466	77.81	51.90	88.38	61.89	279.98	71.50
26	16	-	66	.313	.412	.605	2,327	.380	4,042	.660	52.05	90.94	47.79	87.69	278.48	71.12
21	134	-	-	.339	.381	.466	3,105	.303	5,496	.537	69.45	72.62	64.99	71.35	278.40	71.10
66	71	75	139	.292	.377	.560	2,764	.320	5,298	.613	59.38	76.67	60.27	81.71	278.03	71.00
64	40	-	-	.342	.410	.520	2,830	.326	4,997	.575	63.30	78.04	59.09	76.50	276.93	70.72
75	129	63	144	.314	.401	.568	2,548	.327	4,900	.628	56.99	78.22	57.94	83.50	276.66	70.65
18	48	77	243	.256	.376	.509	2,867	.285	5,751	.571	64.12	68.15	68.00	75.88	276.16	70.53
-	89	-	-	.344	.455	.430	2,427	.322	4,903	.650	54.28	77.10	57.98	86.46	275.82	70.44
38	39	71	226	.284	.377	.509	2,899	.279	5,836	.561	64.84	66.76	69.01	74.61	275.21	70.28
39	66	127	350	.276	.340	.447	3,342	.253	6,360	.481	74.75	60.52	75.20	63.93	274.41	70.08
22	69	70	176	.270	.374	.515	2,784	.282	5,637	.572	62.27	67.63	66.65	76.02	272.57	69.61

Actual Career Statistics

Actual Career Statistics Listed by Total Offensive Production Ranking

Rank	Player	Years	G	AB	H	1B	2B	3B	HR	RUN	RBI	BB	SO	SB	
51	Sheffield, Gary**	1988-2004	2,036	7,302	2,175	1,350	386	24	415	1,307	1,353	1,202	879	205	
52	Thompson, Sam	1885-1906	1,405	6,004	2,016	1,418	326	146	126	1,259	1,299	450	226	236	
53	Morgan, Joe	1963-1984	2,649	9,277	2,517	1,704	449	96	268	1,650	1,133	1,865	1,015	689	
54	Ramirez, Manny**	1993-2004	1,535	5,572	1,760	975	381	14	390	1,067	1,270	874	1,230	33	
55	Stargell, Willie	1962-1982	2,360	7,927	2,232	1,279	423	55	475	1,195	1,540	937	1,936	17	
56	Waner, Paul	1927-1945	2,549	9,459	3,152	2,242	606	191	113	1,627	1,309	1,091	376	104	
57	Mize, Johnny*	1936-1953	1,884	6,443	2,011	1,202	367	83	359	1,118	1,337	857	524	28	
58	Snider, Duke	1947-1964	2,143	7,161	2,116	1,266	358	85	407	1,259	1,333	971	1,237	99	
59	Williams, Billy	1959-1976	2,488	9,350	2,711	1,763	434	88	426	1,410	1,475	1,045	1,046	90	
60	Kelley, Joe	1891-1908	1,835	6,991	2,245	1,638	353	189	65	1,417	1,194	910	160	440	
61	Banks, Ernie	1953-1971	2,528	9,421	2,583	1,574	407	90	512	1,305	1,636	763	1,236	50	
62	Dawson, Andre	1976-1996	2,627	9,927	2,774	1,735	503	98	438	1,373	1,591	589	1,509	314	
63	Crawford, Sam	1899-1917	2,505	9,579	2,964	2,098	457	312	97	1,392	1,525	760	104	363	
64	Thome, Jim**	1991-2004	1,679	5,726	1,625	861	317	24	423	1,125	1,163	1,212	1,703	18	
65	Canseco, Jose	1985-2001	1,887	7,057	1,877	1,061	340	14	462	1,186	1,407	906	1,942	200	
66	Stovey, Harry	1880-1893	1,487	6,194	1,826	1,183	347	174	122	1,492	908	663	343	509	
67	Rodriguez, Alex**	1994-2004	1,430	5,590	1,707	993	309	24	381	1,121	1,096	639	1,126	205	
68	Burkett, Jesse	1890-1905	2,062	8,389	2,872	2,298	314	185	75	1,708	952	1,029	230	392	
69	Gonzalez, Juan **	1989-2004	1,688	6,555	1,936	1,089	388	25	434	1,061	1,404	457	1,273	26	
70	Johnson, Robert	1933-1945	1,863	6,920	2,051	1,272	396	95	288	1,239	1,283	1,075	851	96	
71	Averill, Earl	1929-1941	1,668	6,353	2,019	1,252	401	128	238	1,224	1,164	774	518	70	
72	Klein, Chuck	1928-1944	1,753	6,486	2,076	1,304	398	74	300	1,168	1,201	601	521	79	
73	Martinez, Edgar**	1987-2004	2,055	7,213	2,247	1,409	514	15	309	1,219	1,261	1,283	1,202	49	
74	Bottomley, Jim	1922-1937	1,991	7,471	2,313	1,478	465	151	219	1,177	1,422	664	591	58	
75	Perez, Tony	1964-1986	2,777	9,778	2,732	1,769	505	79	379	1,272	1,652	925	1,867	49	
76	Rice, Jim	1974-1989	2,089	8,225	2,452	1,618	373	79	382	1,249	1,451	670	1,423	58	
77	Galarraga, Andres**	1985-2004	2,257	8,096	2,333	1,458	444	32	399	1,195	1,425	583	2,003	128	
78	Belle, Albert	1989-2000	1,539	5,853	1,726	935	389	21	381	974	1,239	683	961	88	
79	Medwick, Joe	1932-1948	1,984	7,635	2,471	1,613	540	113	205	1,198	1,383	437	551	42	
80	Parker, Dave	1973-1991	2,466	9,358	2,712	1,772	526	75	339	1,272	1,493	683	1,537	154	
81	Berra, Yogi	1946-1965	2,120	7,555	2,150	1,422	321	49	358	1,175	1,430	704	415	30	
82	Kelly, King	1878-1892	1,434	5,922	1,853	1,324	351	109	69	1,359	950	550	420	368	
83	Clemente, Roberto	1955-1972	2,433	9,454	3,000	2,154	440	166	240	1,416	1,305	621	1,230	83	
84	Allen, Dick	1963-1977	1,749	6,332	1,848	1,098	320	79	351	1,099	1,119	894	1,556	133	
85	Wilson, Hack	1923-1934	1,348	4,760	1,461	884	266	67	244	884	1,063	674	713	52	
86	Cepeda, Orlando	1958-1974	2,124	7,927	2,351	1,528	417	27	379	1,131	1,365	588	1,169	142	
87	Williams, Bernie**	1991-2004	1,804	6,964	2,097	1,379	401	54	263	1,248	1,132	983	1,085	144	
88	Sisler, George	1915-1930	2,055	8,267	2,812	2,121	425	164	102	1,284	1,175	472	327	375	
89	Kiner, Ralph	1946-1956	1,472	5,205	1,451	827	216	39	369	971	1,015	1,011	749	22	
90	Jones, Chipper**	1993-2004	1,542	5,616	1,705	1,043	325	27	310	1,035	1,039	937	877	118	
91	Keeler, Willie	1892-1910	2,124	8,564	2,955	2,537	232	153	33	1,720	810	524	810	519	
92	Piazza, Mike**	1992-2004	1,590	5,805	1,829	1,160	285	6	378	935	1,161	666	919	17	
93	Murphy, Dale	1976-1993	2,180	7,960	2,111	1,324	350	39	398	1,197	1,266	986	1,748	161	
94	Delgado, Carlos**	1993-2004	1,423	5,008	1,413	723	343	11	336	889	1,058	827	1,242	9	
95	Bench, Johnny	1967-1983	2,158	7,658	2,048	1,254	381	24	389	1,091	1,376	891	1,278	68	
96	Helton, Todd**	1997-2004	1,135	4,051	1,372	771	328	22	251	832	836	667	542	30	
97	Terry, Bill	1923-1936	1,721	6,428	2,193	1,554	373	112	154	1,120	1,078	537	449	56	
98	Traynor, Pie	1920-1937	1,941	7,559	2,416	1,823	371	164	58	1,183	1,273	472	278	158	
99	Dickey, Bill*	1928-1946	1,789	6,300	1,969	1,352	343	72	202	930	1,209	678	289	36	
100	Herman, Babe	1926-1945	1,552	5,603	1,818	1,128	399	110	181	882	997	520	553	94	

Actual Career Statistics

Actual Career Statistics Listed by Total Offensive Production Ranking

CS	HBP	SF	GDP	AVG	OBP	SLG	Total Offensive Production Statistics				TRP Rating	RPA Rating	TNB Rating	TBA Rating	TOP Composite	
							TRP	RPA	TNB	TBA					TOP	Rating
93	110	96	179	.298	.400	.528	2,660	.299	5,278	.594	59.49	71.66	62.41	78.93	272.49	69.59
-	63	-	-	.336	.388	.502	2,558	.393	3,761	.577	57.21	93.99	44.47	76.71	272.39	69.56
162	40	96	105	.271	.392	.427	2,783	.244	6,394	.562	62.25	58.54	75.61	74.67	271.06	69.22
30	67	60	159	.316	.411	.599	2,337	.347	4,283	.636	52.27	83.13	50.64	84.57	270.61	69.11
16	78	75	143	.282	.360	.529	2,735	.299	5,206	.568	61.17	71.50	61.56	75.55	269.77	68.90
1	38	-	127	.333	.404	.474	2,936	.274	5,711	.533	65.67	65.61	67.53	70.85	269.66	68.87
2	52	-	99	.312	.397	.562	2,455	.329	4,556	.611	54.91	78.89	53.86	81.25	268.91	68.67
55	21	32	166	.295	.380	.540	2,592	.310	4,901	.587	57.97	74.32	57.95	78.01	268.26	68.51
49	43	73	200	.290	.361	.492	2,885	.269	5,728	.535	64.53	64.50	67.73	71.08	267.84	68.40
-	82	-	-	.321	.405	.454	2,611	.327	4,603	.577	58.40	78.32	54.43	76.64	267.79	68.39
53	70	96	229	.274	.330	.500	2,941	.278	5,536	.523	65.78	66.57	65.46	69.56	267.37	68.28
109	111	118	217	.279	.323	.482	2,964	.270	5,692	.519	66.29	64.75	67.31	69.02	267.37	68.28
30	23	-	-	.309	.362	.453	2,917	.282	5,452	.526	65.24	67.41	64.47	69.94	267.06	68.20
19	48	52	101	.284	.410	.569	2,288	.320	4,518	.633	51.17	76.74	53.42	84.12	265.46	67.79
88	84	81	178	.266	.353	.515	2,593	.312	4,733	.570	58.00	74.75	55.97	75.74	264.46	67.54
-	31	-	-	.295	.366	.466	2,400	.348	4,090	.594	53.68	83.43	48.36	78.93	264.40	67.52
50	82	58	128	.305	.381	.574	2,217	.341	4,083	.628	49.59	81.71	48.28	83.54	263.11	67.19
-	75	-	-	.342	.419	.451	2,660	.280	5,277	.556	59.49	67.10	62.40	73.89	262.88	67.13
19	62	78	182	.295	.343	.561	2,465	.336	4,202	.573	55.13	80.48	49.69	76.16	261.46	66.77
64	24	-	102	.296	.393	.506	2,522	.311	4,632	.570	56.41	74.36	54.77	75.82	261.36	66.75
57	33	-	7	.318	.395	.534	2,388	.333	4,210	.587	53.41	79.79	49.78	78.08	261.06	66.67
-	12	-	55	.320	.379	.543	2,369	.331	4,214	.589	52.99	79.29	49.83	78.30	260.41	66.50
30	89	77	190	.312	.418	.515	2,480	.280	5,109	.577	55.47	67.09	60.41	76.72	259.69	66.32
15	43	-	33	.310	.369	.500	2,599	.317	4,487	.546	58.13	75.79	53.06	72.64	259.62	66.30
33	43	106	268	.279	.341	.463	2,924	.263	5,516	.496	65.40	62.97	65.22	65.94	259.52	66.28
34	64	94	315	.298	.352	.502	2,700	.288	4,887	.522	60.39	69.02	57.79	69.34	256.53	65.51
81	178	58	179	.288	.347	.499	2,620	.288	4,846	.533	58.60	68.99	57.30	70.83	255.72	65.31
41	55	78	193	.295	.369	.564	2,213	.323	4,085	.595	49.50	77.23	48.30	79.13	254.16	64.91
2	26	-	203	.324	.362	.505	2,581	.311	4,355	.525	57.73	74.45	51.50	69.74	253.41	64.72
113	56	86	209	.290	.339	.471	2,765	.266	5,185	.499	61.84	63.71	61.31	66.32	253.19	64.66
26	49	44	146	.285	.348	.482	2,605	.307	4,400	.518	58.26	73.40	52.03	68.82	252.52	64.49
-	12	-	-	.313	.372	.444	2,309	.356	3,559	.549	51.64	85.27	42.08	72.96	251.96	64.35
46	35	66	275	.317	.359	.475	2,721	.260	5,185	.496	60.86	62.34	61.31	65.95	250.46	63.96
52	16	53	164	.292	.378	.534	2,218	.297	4,370	.586	49.61	71.20	51.67	77.88	250.36	63.94
5	20	-	15	.307	.395	.545	1,947	.356	3,334	.610	43.55	85.25	39.42	81.03	249.25	63.65
80	102	74	218	.297	.350	.499	2,496	.280	4,711	.529	55.83	67.09	55.71	70.29	248.91	63.57
85	36	52	193	.301	.388	.488	2,380	.289	4,473	.544	53.23	69.26	52.89	72.26	247.65	63.25
127	48	-	-	.340	.379	.468	2,459	.280	4,639	.528	55.00	67.01	54.85	70.18	247.04	63.09
2	24	7	126	.279	.398	.548	1,986	.312	3,907	.613	44.42	74.62	46.20	81.49	246.73	63.01
40	14	64	150	.304	.401	.537	2,074	.306	4,043	.596	46.39	73.24	47.81	79.25	246.69	63.00
36	129	-	-	.345	.391	.419	2,530	.274	4,728	.513	56.59	65.73	55.91	68.19	246.41	62.93
20	24	40	199	.315	.385	.562	2,096	.311	3,947	.586	46.88	74.53	46.67	77.91	245.99	62.82
68	28	60	209	.265	.346	.469	2,463	.266	4,840	.524	55.09	63.81	57.23	69.60	245.73	62.76
7	122	61	93	.282	.392	.556	1,947	.319	3,737	.612	43.55	76.29	44.19	81.29	245.31	62.65
43	19	90	201	.267	.342	.476	2,467	.278	4,579	.517	55.18	66.68	54.14	68.71	244.71	62.49
23	31	47	98	.339	.432	.616	1,668	.341	3,202	.654	37.31	81.61	37.86	86.97	243.75	62.25
6	9	-	38	.341	.393	.506	2,198	.313	3,848	.549	49.16	75.06	45.50	72.95	242.67	61.97
46	31	-	47	.320	.362	.435	2,456	.303	3,904	.481	54.93	72.53	46.16	64.00	237.62	60.68
29	31	-	49	.313	.382	.486	2,139	.303	3,778	.535	47.84	72.57	44.67	71.15	236.24	60.33
-	11	-	43	.324	.383	.532	1,879	.304	3,605	.584	42.03	72.84	42.63	77.58	235.07	60.03

Actual Career Statistics

Actual Career Statistics Listed by Total Offensive Production Ranking

Rank	Player	Years	G	AB	H	1B	2B	3B	HR	RUN	RBI	BB	SO	SB	
101	Giambi, Jason**	1995-2004	1,344	4,757	1,413	828	296	8	281	851	944	871	916	13	
102	Williams, Ken*	1915-1929	1,397	4,862	1,552	994	285	77	196	860	913	566	287	154	
103	Vaughn, Mo	1991-2003	1,512	5,532	1,620	1,012	270	10	328	861	1,064	725	1,429	30	
104	Foster, George	1969-1986	1,977	7,023	1,925	1,223	307	47	348	986	1,239	666	1,419	51	
105	Trosky, Hal*	1933-1946	1,347	5,161	1,561	944	331	58	228	835	1,012	545	440	28	
106	Guerrero, Vladimir**	1996-2004	1,160	4,375	1,421	847	265	36	273	765	828	433	558	138	
107	York, Rudy	1934-1948	1,603	5,891	1,621	1,001	291	52	277	876	1,152	791	867	38	
108	Bichette, Dante	1988-2001	1,704	6,381	1,906	1,204	401	27	274	934	1,141	355	1,078	152	
109	Jennings, Hughie	1891-1918	1,262	4,842	1,520	1,189	225	88	18	989	840	347	117	374	
110	Meusel, Bob	1920-1930	1,407	5,475	1,693	1,074	368	95	156	826	1,067	375	619	142	
111	Jackson, Joe	1908-1920	1,330	4,981	1,772	1,243	307	168	54	873	785	519	158	202	
112	Howard, Frank	1958-1973	1,895	6,491	1,774	1,112	245	35	382	864	1,119	782	1,460	8	
113	Mattingly, Don	1982-1995	1,785	7,003	2,153	1,469	442	20	222	1,007	1,099	588	444	14	
114	O'Neill, Tip	1883-1892	1,054	4,305	1,436	1,070	222	92	52	880	757	421	146	161	
115	Hafey, Chick	1924-1937	1,283	4,625	1,466	894	341	67	164	777	833	372	477	70	
116	Keller, Charlie*	1939-1952	1,170	3,790	1,085	658	166	72	189	725	760	784	499	45	
117	Kluszewski, Ted	1947-1961	1,718	5,929	1,766	1,168	290	29	279	848	1,028	492	365	20	
118	Robinson, Jackie	1947-1956	1,382	4,877	1,518	1,054	273	54	137	947	734	740	291	197	
119	Garciaparra, Nomar**	1996-2004	1,009	4,133	1,330	805	293	50	182	737	710	295	420	86	
120	Fielder, Cecil	1985-1998	1,470	5,157	1,313	787	200	7	319	744	1,008	693	1,316	2	
121	Pujols, Albert**	2001-2004	629	2,363	787	429	189	9	160	500	504	304	279	13	
122	Jeter, Derek**	1995-2004	1,366	5,513	1,734	1,259	283	42	150	1,037	693	559	972	201	
123	Maris, Roger	1957-1968	1,463	5,101	1,325	813	195	42	275	826	851	652	733	21	
124	Campanella, Roy	1948-1957	1,215	4,205	1,161	723	178	18	242	627	856	533	501	25	
125	Berkman, Lance**	1999-2004	775	2,683	814	446	195	17	156	516	535	501	542	40	
126	Ordonez, Magglio**	1997-2004	1,001	3,807	1,167	725	240	15	187	624	703	333	431	82	
127	Cravath, Gavy	1908-1920	1,220	3,951	1,134	700	232	83	119	575	719	561	514	89	

* Player missed time for military service
** Active player. Statistics through 2004 season
TOP ranking for players with less than 70% rating is based upon comparison to listed players only.

							Total Offensive Production Statistics				TRP Rating	RPA Rating	TNB Rating	TBA Rating	TOP Composite	
CS	HBP	SF	GDP	AVG	OBP	SLG	TRP	RPA	TNB	TBA					TOP	Rating
10	92	62	115	.297	.411	.540	1,795	.304	3,534	.599	40.15	72.89	41.79	79.66	234.48	59.88
106	28	-	-	.319	.393	.530	1,773	.325	3,221	.590	39.66	77.81	38.09	78.47	234.03	59.77
18	108	45	135	.293	.383	.523	1,925	.294	3,739	.571	43.06	70.43	44.21	75.94	233.63	59.67
31	52	68	196	.274	.338	.480	2,225	.278	4,108	.513	49.77	66.56	48.58	68.21	233.11	59.53
23	16	-	43	.302	.371	.522	1,847	.320	3,258	.565	41.31	76.72	38.52	75.12	231.67	59.17
74	58	34	141	.325	.390	.589	1,593	.316	3,132	.621	35.63	75.67	37.03	82.59	230.92	58.97
26	12	-	155	.275	.362	.483	2,028	.296	3,662	.535	45.36	70.90	43.30	71.07	230.64	58.90
73	41	73	176	.299	.336	.499	2,075	.295	3,658	.521	46.41	70.72	43.25	69.21	229.59	58.63
-	287	-	-	.314	.393	.408	1,829	.334	2,983	.545	40.91	79.98	35.27	72.41	228.57	58.37
102	21	-	-	.309	.356	.497	1,893	.322	3,155	.537	42.34	77.21	37.31	71.43	228.29	58.30
61	59	-	-	.356	.423	.517	1,658	.298	3,296	.593	37.08	71.42	38.97	78.81	226.29	57.79
9	33	43	219	.273	.352	.498	1,983	.262	4,049	.535	44.35	62.74	47.88	71.12	226.09	57.74
9	21	96	191	.307	.358	.471	2,106	.267	3,915	.496	47.10	63.84	46.29	65.88	223.12	56.98
-	44	-	-	.334	.399	.464	1,637	.343	2,624	.550	36.61	82.18	31.03	73.12	222.94	56.94
7	33	-	28	.317	.372	.526	1,610	.318	2,901	.574	36.01	76.22	34.30	76.24	222.77	56.89
23	10	-	50	.286	.410	.518	1,485	.320	2,778	.599	33.21	76.74	32.85	79.69	222.48	56.82
10	23	23	143	.298	.353	.498	1,876	.284	3,476	.526	41.96	67.96	41.10	69.90	220.92	56.42
54	72	9	113	.311	.409	.474	1,681	.289	3,265	.562	37.60	69.27	38.61	74.69	220.16	56.22
29	48	49	86	.322	.370	.549	1,447	.314	2,669	.579	32.36	75.15	31.56	76.94	216.01	55.17
6	43	46	169	.255	.345	.482	1,752	.287	3,216	.527	39.19	68.69	38.03	69.99	215.89	55.13
13	35	25	75	.333	.413	.624	1,004	.358	1,813	.647	22.46	85.80	21.44	86.01	215.70	55.09
52	92	30	122	.315	.385	.463	1,730	.274	3,351	.531	38.69	65.59	39.62	70.52	214.43	54.76
9	38	43	75	.260	.345	.476	1,677	.284	3,131	.530	37.51	67.96	37.02	70.43	212.92	54.38
17	30	18	143	.276	.360	.500	1,483	.301	2,672	.542	33.17	72.05	31.60	72.06	208.87	53.34
26	37	26	46	.303	.416	.563	1,051	.319	2,063	.626	23.51	76.43	24.39	83.27	207.60	53.02
38	34	35	131	.307	.364	.525	1,327	.306	2,409	.555	28.14	73.22	27.13	74.12	202.60	51.74
9	28	-	-	.287	.380	.478	1,294	.285	2,558	.563	28.94	68.25	30.25	74.89	202.33	51.67

Actual Career Statistics Listed by Total Offensive Production Ranking

Actual Career Statistics

Actual Career Statistics A-H

Rank	Player	Years	G	AB	H	1B	2B	3B	HR	RUN	RBI	BB	SO	SB
						Actual Career Statistics Listed Alphabetically								
4	Aaron, Hank	1954-1976	3,298	12,364	3,771	2,294	624	98	755	2,174	2,297	1,402	1,383	240
84	Allen, Dick	1963-1977	1,749	6,332	1,848	1,098	320	79	351	1,099	1,119	894	1,556	133
11	Anson, Cap	1871-1897	2,500	10,260	3,504	2,677	583	147	97	1,989	2,076	983	302	295
71	Averill, Earl	1929-1941	1,668	6,353	2,019	1,252	401	128	238	1,224	1,164	774	518	70
25	Bagwell, Jeff**	1991-2004	2,111	7,697	2,289	1,327	484	32	446	1,506	1,510	1,383	1,537	202
61	Banks, Ernie	1953-1971	2,528	9,421	2,583	1,574	407	90	512	1,305	1,636	763	1,236	50
78	Belle, Albert	1989-2000	1,539	5,853	1,726	935	389	21	381	974	1,239	683	961	88
95	Bench, Johnny	1967-1983	2,158	7,658	2,048	1,254	381	24	389	1,091	1,376	891	1,278	68
125	Berkman, Lance**	1999-2004	775	2,683	814	446	195	17	156	516	535	501	542	40
81	Berra, Yogi	1946-1965	2,120	7,555	2,150	1,422	321	49	358	1,175	1,430	704	415	30
108	Bichette, Dante	1988-2001	1,704	6,381	1,906	1,204	401	27	274	934	1,141	355	1,078	152
2	Bonds, Barry **	1986-2004	2,716	9,098	2,730	1,387	563	77	703	2,070	1,843	2,302	1,428	506
74	Bottomley, Jim	1922-1937	1,991	7,471	2,313	1,478	465	151	219	1,177	1,422	664	591	58
39	Brett, George	1973-1993	2,707	10,349	3,154	2,035	665	137	317	1,583	1,595	1,096	908	201
28	Brouthers, Dan	1879-1904	1,658	6,725	2,349	1,583	449	211	106	1,507	1,296	840	238	263
68	Burkett, Jesse	1890-1905	2,062	8,389	2,872	2,298	314	185	75	1,708	952	1,029	230	392
124	Campanella, Roy	1948-1957	1,215	4,205	1,161	723	178	18	242	627	856	533	501	25
65	Canseco, Jose	1985-2001	1,887	7,057	1,877	1,061	340	14	462	1,186	1,407	906	1,942	200
86	Cepeda, Orlando	1958-1974	2,124	7,927	2,351	1,528	417	27	379	1,131	1,365	588	1,169	142
83	Clemente, Roberto	1955-1972	2,433	9,454	3,000	2,154	440	166	240	1,416	1,305	621	1,230	83
5	Cobb, Ty	1905-1928	3,033	11,429	4,191	3,053	724	297	117	2,245	1,937	1,249	357	892
31	Collins, Eddie	1906-1930	2,826	9,951	3,314	2,642	438	187	47	1,820	1,300	1,503	286	743
34	Conner, Roger	1880-1897	1,987	7,807	2,535	1,741	429	227	138	1,607	1,322	1,002	449	252
127	Cravath, Gavy	1908-1920	1,220	3,951	1,134	700	232	83	119	575	719	561	514	89
63	Crawford, Sam	1899-1917	2,505	9,579	2,964	2,098	457	312	97	1,392	1,525	760	104	363
62	Dawson, Andre	1976-1996	2,627	9,927	2,774	1,735	503	98	438	1,373	1,591	589	1,509	314
21	Delahanty, Ed	1888-1903	1,825	7,493	2,593	1,801	510	181	101	1,596	1,464	741	244	481
94	Delgado, Carlos**	1993-2004	1,423	5,008	1,413	723	343	11	336	889	1,058	827	1,242	9
99	Dickey, Bill*	1928-1946	1,789	6,300	1,969	1,352	343	72	202	930	1,209	678	289	36
22	DiMaggio, Joe*	1936-1951	1,736	6,821	2,214	1,333	389	131	361	1,390	1,537	790	369	30
36	Duffy, Hugh	1888-1906	1,722	6,999	2,307	1,774	310	117	106	1,545	1,302	662	211	597
120	Fielder, Cecil	1985-1998	1,470	5,157	1,313	787	200	7	319	744	1,008	693	1,316	2
104	Foster, George	1969-1986	1,977	7,023	1,925	1,223	307	47	348	986	1,239	666	1,419	51
7	Foxx, Jimmie*	1925-1944	2,317	8,134	2,646	1,529	458	125	534	1,751	1,922	1,452	1,311	88
77	Galarraga, Andres**	1985-2004	2,257	8,096	2,333	1,458	444	32	399	1,195	1,425	583	2,003	128
119	Garciaparra, Nomar**	1996-2004	1,009	4,133	1,330	805	293	50	182	737	710	295	420	86
3	Gehrig, Lou	1923-1938	2,164	8,001	2,721	1,531	534	163	493	1,888	1,995	1,509	790	102
29	Gehringer, Charlie	1924-1941	2,323	8,860	2,839	1,935	574	146	184	1,774	1,427	1,185	372	182
101	Giambi, Jason**	1995-2004	1,344	4,757	1,413	828	296	8	281	851	944	871	916	13
69	Gonzalez, Juan **	1989-2004	1,688	6,555	1,936	1,089	388	25	434	1,061	1,404	457	1,273	26
32	Goslin, Goose	1921-1938	2,287	8,656	2,735	1,814	500	173	248	1,483	1,609	949	585	175
41	Greenberg, Hank*	1930-1947	1,394	5,193	1,628	847	379	71	331	1,051	1,276	852	844	58
43	Griffey, Ken **	1989-2004	1,997	7,379	2,156	1,219	400	36	501	1,320	1,444	984	1,323	178
106	Guerrero, Vladimir**	1996-2004	1,160	4,375	1,421	847	265	36	273	765	828	433	558	138
115	Hafey, Chick	1924-1937	1,283	4,625	1,466	894	341	67	164	777	833	372	477	70
47	Hamilton, Billy	1888-1901	1,578	6,262	2,157	1,798	225	94	40	1,691	736	1,187	218	937
44	Heilmann, Harry	1914-1932	2,146	7,787	2,660	1,784	542	151	183	1,291	1,539	856	550	112
96	Helton, Todd**	1997-2004	1,135	4,051	1,372	771	328	22	251	832	836	667	542	30
13	Henderson, Rickey	1979-2003	3,081	10,961	3,055	2,182	510	66	297	2,295	1,115	2,190	1,694	1,406
100	Herman, Babe	1926-1945	1,552	5,603	1,818	1,128	399	110	181	882	997	520	553	94

Actual Career Statistics Listed Alphabetically

CS	HBP	SF	GDP	AVG	OBP	SLG	Total Offensive Production Statistics				TRP Rating	RPA Rating	TNB Rating	TBA Rating	TOP Composite	
							TRP	RPA	TNB	TBA					TOP	Rating
73	32	121	328	.305	.374	.555	4,471	.314	8,457	.594	100.00	75.15	100.00	78.90	354.05	90.42
52	16	53	164	.292	.378	.534	2,218	.297	4,370	.586	49.61	71.20	51.67	77.88	250.36	63.94
16	32	-	-	.342	.401	.455	4,065	.361	5,966	.529	90.92	86.33	70.55	70.33	318.13	81.24
57	33	-	7	.318	.395	.534	2,388	.333	4,210	.587	53.41	79.79	49.78	78.08	261.06	66.67
78	127	98	220	.297	.408	.542	3,016	.317	5,809	.610	67.46	75.82	68.69	81.07	293.03	74.84
53	70	96	229	.274	.330	.500	2,941	.278	5,536	.523	65.78	66.57	65.46	69.56	267.37	68.28
41	55	78	193	.295	.369	.564	2,213	.323	4,085	.595	49.50	77.23	48.30	79.13	254.16	64.91
43	19	90	201	.267	.342	.476	2,467	.278	4,579	.517	55.18	66.68	54.14	68.71	244.71	62.49
26	37	26	46	.303	.416	.563	1,051	.319	2,063	.626	23.51	76.43	24.39	83.27	207.60	53.02
26	49	44	146	.285	.348	.482	2,605	.307	4,400	.518	58.26	73.40	52.03	68.82	252.52	64.49
73	41	73	176	.299	.336	.499	2,075	.295	3,658	.521	46.41	70.72	43.25	69.21	229.59	58.63
141	93	87	142	.300	.443	.611	3,913	.334	8,316	.709	87.52	79.93	98.33	94.30	360.09	91.96
15	43	-	33	.310	.369	.500	2,599	.317	4,487	.546	58.13	75.79	53.06	72.64	259.62	66.30
97	33	120	235	.305	.369	.487	3,178	.269	6,277	.530	71.08	64.31	74.22	70.51	280.13	71.54
-	105	-	-	.349	.429	.526	2,803	.365	4,746	.619	62.69	87.51	56.12	82.25	288.57	73.70
-	75	-	-	.342	.419	.451	2,660	.280	5,277	.556	59.49	67.10	62.40	73.89	262.88	67.13
17	30	18	143	.276	.360	.500	1,483	.301	2,672	.542	33.17	72.05	31.60	72.06	208.87	53.34
88	84	81	178	.266	.353	.515	2,593	.312	4,733	.570	58.00	74.75	55.97	75.74	264.46	67.54
80	102	74	218	.297	.350	.499	2,496	.280	4,711	.529	55.83	67.09	55.71	70.29	248.91	63.57
46	35	66	275	.317	.359	.475	2,721	.260	5,185	.496	60.86	62.34	61.31	65.95	250.46	63.96
212	94	-	-	.367	.433	.513	4,182	.327	7,883	.617	93.54	78.41	93.21	82.04	347.20	88.67
173	77	-	-	.333	.424	.429	3,120	.271	6,417	.556	69.78	64.79	75.88	73.97	284.42	72.64
-	38	-	-	.325	.404	.491	2,929	.331	5,124	.579	65.51	79.28	60.59	76.99	282.36	72.11
9	28	-	-	.287	.380	.478	1,294	.285	2,558	.563	28.94	68.25	30.25	74.89	202.33	51.67
30	23	-	-	.309	.362	.453	2,917	.282	5,452	.526	65.24	67.41	64.47	69.94	267.06	68.20
109	111	118	217	.279	.323	.482	2,964	.270	5,692	.519	66.29	64.75	67.31	69.02	267.37	68.28
-	94	-	-	.346	.412	.503	3,060	.367	5,084	.610	68.44	87.99	60.12	81.15	297.69	76.02
7	122	61	93	.282	.392	.556	1,947	.319	3,737	.612	43.55	76.29	44.19	81.29	245.31	62.65
29	31	-	49	.313	.382	.486	2,139	.303	3,778	.535	47.84	72.57	44.67	71.15	236.24	60.33
9	46	-	130	.325	.398	.579	2,927	.376	4,805	.617	65.47	90.01	56.82	82.02	294.31	75.16
-	29	-	-	.330	.390	.453	2,847	.370	4,457	.580	63.68	88.65	52.70	77.04	282.07	72.04
6	43	46	169	.255	.345	.482	1,752	.287	3,216	.527	39.19	68.69	38.03	69.99	215.89	55.13
31	52	68	196	.274	.338	.480	2,225	.278	4,108	.513	49.77	66.56	48.58	68.21	233.11	59.53
72	13	-	69	.325	.428	.609	3,673	.380	6,437	.666	82.15	90.97	76.11	88.50	337.74	86.25
81	178	58	179	.288	.347	.499	2,620	.288	4,846	.533	58.60	68.99	57.30	70.83	255.72	65.31
29	48	49	86	.322	.370	.549	1,447	.314	2,669	.579	32.36	75.15	31.56	76.94	216.01	55.17
101	45	-	2	.340	.447	.632	3,883	.406	6,615	.692	86.85	97.29	78.22	92.01	354.36	90.50
89	51	-	27	.320	.404	.480	3,201	.316	5,586	.552	71.59	75.72	66.05	73.35	286.71	73.22
10	92	62	115	.297	.411	.540	1,795	.304	3,534	.599	40.15	72.89	41.79	79.66	234.48	59.88
19	62	78	182	.295	.343	.561	2,465	.336	4,202	.573	55.13	80.48	49.69	76.16	261.46	66.77
89	56	-	-	.316	.387	.500	3,092	.320	5,416	.561	69.16	76.64	64.04	74.52	284.35	72.62
26	16	-	66	.313	.412	.605	2,327	.380	4,042	.660	52.05	90.94	47.79	87.69	278.48	71.12
66	71	75	139	.292	.377	.560	2,764	.320	5,298	.613	59.38	76.67	60.27	81.71	278.03	71.00
74	58	34	141	.325	.390	.589	1,593	.316	3,132	.621	35.63	75.67	37.03	82.59	230.92	58.97
7	33	-	28	.317	.372	.526	1,610	.318	2,901	.574	36.01	76.22	34.30	76.24	222.77	56.89
-	89	-	-	.344	.455	.430	2,427	.322	4,903	.650	54.28	77.10	57.98	86.46	275.82	70.44
64	40	-	-	.342	.410	.520	2,830	.326	4,997	.575	63.30	78.04	59.09	76.50	276.93	70.72
23	31	47	98	.339	.432	.616	1,668	.341	3,202	.654	37.31	81.61	37.86	86.97	243.75	62.25
335	98	67	172	.279	.401	.419	3,410	.253	7,947	.589	76.27	60.54	93.97	78.32	309.10	78.94
-	11	-	43	.324	.383	.532	1,879	.304	3,605	.584	42.03	72.84	42.63	77.58	235.07	60.03

Actual Career Statistics A-H

Actual Career Statistics H-R

Rank	Player	Years	G	AB	H	1B	2B	3B	HR	RUN	RBI	BB	SO	SB
								Actual Career Statistics Listed Alphabetically						
16	Hornsby, Rogers	1915-1937	2,259	8,173	2,930	1,919	541	169	301	1,579	1,584	1,038	679	135
112	Howard, Frank	1958-1973	1,895	6,491	1,774	1,112	245	35	382	864	1,119	782	1,460	8
111	Jackson, Joe	1908-1920	1,330	4,981	1,772	1,243	307	168	54	873	785	519	158	202
27	Jackson, Reggie	1967-1987	2,820	9,864	2,584	1,509	463	49	563	1,551	1,702	1,376	2,597	228
109	Jennings, Hughie	1891-1918	1,262	4,842	1,520	1,189	225	88	18	989	840	347	117	374
122	Jeter, Derek**	1995-2004	1,366	5,513	1,734	1,259	283	42	150	1,037	693	559	972	201
70	Johnson, Robert	1933-1945	1,863	6,920	2,051	1,272	396	95	288	1,239	1,283	1,075	851	96
90	Jones, Chipper**	1993-2004	1,542	5,616	1,705	1,043	325	27	310	1,035	1,039	937	877	118
38	Kaline, Al	1953-1974	2,833	10,116	3,007	2,035	498	75	399	1,622	1,583	1,277	1,020	139
91	Keeler, Willie	1892-1910	2,124	8,564	2,955	2,537	232	153	33	1,720	810	524	810	519
116	Keller, Charlie*	1939-1952	1,170	3,790	1,085	658	166	72	189	725	760	784	499	45
60	Kelley, Joe	1891-1908	1,835	6,991	2,245	1,638	353	189	65	1,417	1,194	910	160	440
82	Kelly, King	1878-1892	1,434	5,922	1,853	1,324	351	109	69	1,359	950	550	420	368
46	Killebrew, Harmon	1954-1975	2,435	8,147	2,086	1,199	290	24	573	1,283	1,584	1,559	1,699	19
89	Kiner, Ralph	1946-1956	1,472	5,205	1,451	827	216	39	369	971	1,015	1,011	749	22
72	Klein, Chuck	1928-1944	1,753	6,486	2,076	1,304	398	74	300	1,168	1,201	601	521	79
117	Kluszewski, Ted	1947-1961	1,718	5,929	1,766	1,168	290	29	279	848	1,028	492	365	20
42	Lajoie, Nap	1896-1916	2,475	9,589	3,252	2,359	648	163	82	1,506	1,599	516	85	395
14	Mantle, Mickey	1951-1968	2,401	8,102	2,415	1,463	344	72	536	1,677	1,509	1,735	1,713	153
123	Maris, Roger	1957-1968	1,463	5,101	1,325	813	195	42	275	826	851	652	733	21
73	Martinez, Edgar**	1987-2004	2,055	7,213	2,247	1,409	514	15	309	1,219	1,261	1,283	1,202	49
37	Matthews, Eddie	1952-1968	2,391	8,537	2,315	1,377	354	72	512	1,509	1,453	1,444	1,487	68
113	Mattingly, Don	1982-1995	1,785	7,003	2,153	1,469	442	20	222	1,007	1,099	588	444	14
8	Mays, Willie*	1951-1973	2,992	10,881	3,283	1,960	523	140	660	2,062	1,903	1,463	1,526	338
50	McCovey, Willie	1959-1980	2,588	8,197	2,211	1,291	353	46	521	1,229	1,555	1,345	1,550	26
48	McGriff, Fred **	1986-2004	2,460	8,757	2,490	1,532	441	24	493	1,349	1,550	1,305	1,882	72
35	McGwire, Mark	1986-2001	1,874	6,187	1,626	785	252	6	583	1,167	1,414	1,317	1,596	12
79	Medwick, Joe	1932-1948	1,984	7,635	2,471	1,613	540	113	205	1,198	1,383	437	551	42
110	Meusel, Bob	1920-1930	1,407	5,475	1,693	1,074	368	95	156	826	1,067	375	619	142
57	Mize, Johnny*	1936-1953	1,884	6,443	2,011	1,202	367	83	359	1,118	1,337	857	524	28
53	Morgan, Joe	1963-1984	2,649	9,277	2,517	1,704	449	96	268	1,650	1,133	1,865	1,015	689
93	Murphy, Dale	1976-1993	2,180	7,960	2,111	1,324	350	39	398	1,197	1,266	986	1,748	161
23	Murray, Eddie	1977-1997	3,026	11,336	3,255	2,156	560	35	504	1,627	1,917	1,333	1,516	110
9	Musial, Stan*	1941-1963	3,026	10,972	3,630	2,253	725	177	475	1,949	1,951	1,599	696	78
114	O'Neill, Tip	1883-1892	1,054	4,305	1,436	1,070	222	92	52	880	757	421	146	161
126	Ordonez, Magglio**	1997-2004	1,001	3,807	1,167	725	240	15	187	624	703	333	431	82
10	Ott, Mel	1926-1947	2,730	9,456	2,876	1,805	488	72	511	1,859	1,860	1,708	896	89
19	Palmiero, Rafael**	1986-2004	2,721	10,103	2,922	1,761	572	38	551	1,616	1,775	1,310	1,305	95
80	Parker, Dave	1973-1991	2,466	9,358	2,712	1,772	526	75	339	1,272	1,493	683	1,537	154
75	Perez, Tony	1964-1986	2,777	9,778	2,732	1,769	505	79	379	1,272	1,652	925	1,867	49
92	Piazza, Mike**	1992-2004	1,590	5,805	1,829	1,160	285	6	378	935	1,161	666	919	17
121	Pujols, Albert**	2001-2004	629	2,363	787	429	189	9	160	500	504	304	279	13
54	Ramirez, Manny**	1993-2004	1,535	5,572	1,760	975	381	14	390	1,067	1,270	874	1,230	33
76	Rice, Jim	1974-1989	2,089	8,225	2,452	1,618	373	79	382	1,249	1,451	670	1,423	58
49	Ripkin, Cal, Jr.	1981-2001	3,001	11,551	3,184	2,106	603	44	431	1,647	1,695	1,129	1,305	36
12	Robinson, Frank	1956-1976	2,808	10,006	2,943	1,757	528	72	586	1,829	1,812	1,420	1,532	204
118	Robinson, Jackie	1947-1956	1,382	4,877	1,518	1,054	273	54	137	947	734	740	291	197
67	Rodriguez, Alex**	1994-2004	1,430	5,590	1,707	993	309	24	381	1,121	1,096	639	1,126	205
40	Rose, Pete	1963-1986	3,562	14,053	4,256	3,215	746	135	160	2,165	1,314	1,566	1,143	198
1	Ruth, Babe	1914-1935	2,503	8,399	2,873	1,517	506	136	714	2,174	2,213	2,062	1,330	123

Actual Career Statistics Listed Alphabetically

CS	HBP	SF	GDP	AVG	OBP	SLG	Total Offensive Production Statistics				TRP Rating	RPA Rating	TNB Rating	TBA Rating	TOP Composite	
							TRP	RPA	TNB	TBA					TOP	Rating
64	48	3	-	.358	.434	.577	3,163	.342	5,869	.634	70.74	81.78	69.40	84.23	306.15	78.18
9	33	43	219	.273	.352	.498	1,983	.262	4,049	.535	44.35	62.74	47.88	71.12	226.09	57.74
61	59	-	-	.356	.423	.517	1,658	.298	3,296	.593	37.08	71.42	38.97	78.81	226.29	57.79
115	96	68	183	.262	.356	.490	3,253	.281	6,419	.554	72.76	67.23	75.90	73.64	289.52	73.94
-	287	-	-	.314	.393	.408	1,829	.334	2,983	.545	40.91	79.98	35.27	72.41	228.57	58.37
52	92	30	122	.315	.385	.463	1,730	.274	3,351	.531	38.69	65.59	39.62	70.52	214.43	54.76
64	24	-	102	.296	.393	.506	2,522	.311	4,632	.570	56.41	74.36	54.77	75.82	261.36	66.75
40	14	64	150	.304	.401	.537	2,074	.306	4,043	.596	46.39	73.24	47.81	79.25	246.69	63.00
80	55	104	271	.297	.376	.480	3,205	.271	6,243	.528	71.68	64.91	73.82	70.19	280.61	71.66
36	129	-	-	.345	.391	.419	2,530	.274	4,728	.513	56.59	65.73	55.91	68.19	246.41	62.93
23	10	-	50	.286	.410	.518	1,485	.320	2,778	.599	33.21	76.74	32.85	79.69	222.48	56.82
-	82	-	-	.321	.405	.454	2,611	.327	4,603	.577	58.40	78.32	54.43	76.64	267.79	68.39
-	12	-	-	.313	.372	.444	2,309	.356	3,559	.549	51.64	85.27	42.08	72.96	251.96	64.35
18	48	77	243	.256	.376	.509	2,867	.285	5,751	.571	64.12	68.15	68.00	75.88	276.16	70.53
2	24	7	126	.279	.398	.548	1,986	.312	3,907	.613	44.42	74.62	46.20	81.49	246.73	63.01
-	12	-	55	.320	.379	.543	2,369	.331	4,214	.589	52.99	79.29	49.83	78.30	260.41	66.50
10	23	23	143	.298	.353	.498	1,876	.284	3,476	.526	41.96	67.96	41.10	69.90	220.92	56.42
21	134	-	-	.339	.381	.466	3,105	.303	5,496	.537	69.45	72.62	64.99	71.35	278.40	71.10
38	13	47	113	.298	.421	.557	3,186	.318	6,374	.637	71.26	76.21	75.37	84.64	307.48	78.53
9	38	43	75	.260	.345	.476	1,677	.284	3,131	.530	37.51	67.96	37.02	70.43	212.92	54.38
30	89	77	190	.312	.418	.515	2,480	.280	5,109	.577	55.47	67.09	60.41	76.72	259.69	66.32
39	26	58	123	.271	.376	.509	2,962	.291	5,848	.574	66.25	69.62	69.15	76.30	281.32	71.84
9	21	96	191	.307	.358	.471	2,106	.267	3,915	.496	47.10	63.84	46.29	65.88	223.12	56.98
103	44	91	251	.302	.384	.557	3,965	.311	7,808	.613	88.68	74.58	92.34	81.53	337.13	86.10
22	69	70	176	.270	.374	.515	2,784	.282	5,637	.572	62.27	67.63	66.65	76.02	272.57	69.61
38	39	71	226	.284	.377	.509	2,899	.279	5,836	.561	64.84	66.76	69.01	74.61	275.21	70.28
8	75	78	147	.263	.394	.588	2,581	.331	5,035	.645	57.73	79.20	59.54	85.76	282.22	72.07
2	26	-	203	.324	.362	.505	2,581	.311	4,355	.525	57.73	74.45	51.50	69.74	253.41	64.72
102	21	-	-	.309	.356	.497	1,893	.322	3,155	.537	42.34	77.21	37.31	71.43	228.29	58.30
2	52	-	99	.312	.397	.562	2,455	.329	4,556	.611	54.91	78.89	53.86	81.25	268.91	68.67
162	40	96	105	.271	.392	.427	2,783	.244	6,394	.562	62.25	58.54	75.61	74.67	271.06	69.22
68	28	60	209	.265	.346	.469	2,463	.266	4,840	.524	55.09	63.81	57.23	69.60	245.73	62.76
43	18	128	316	.287	.359	.476	3,544	.270	6,815	.519	79.27	64.63	80.58	68.99	293.47	74.95
35	53	53	243	.331	.417	.559	3,900	.302	7,829	.606	87.23	72.28	92.57	80.55	332.63	84.95
-	44	-	-	.334	.399	.464	1,637	.343	2,624	.550	36.61	82.18	31.03	73.12	222.94	56.94
38	34	35	131	.307	.364	.525	1,327	.306	2,409	.555	28.14	73.22	27.13	74.12	202.60	51.74
2	64	-	82	.304	.414	.533	3,719	.329	6,900	.610	83.11	78.68	81.59	81.09	324.47	82.86
40	85	111	222	.289	.372	.517	3,391	.287	6,673	.564	75.84	68.62	78.91	74.96	298.33	76.19
113	56	86	209	.290	.339	.471	2,765	.266	5,185	.499	61.84	63.71	61.31	66.32	253.19	64.66
33	43	106	268	.279	.341	.463	2,924	.263	5,516	.496	65.40	62.97	65.22	65.94	259.52	66.28
20	24	40	199	.315	.385	.562	2,096	.311	3,947	.586	46.88	74.53	46.67	77.91	245.99	62.82
13	35	25	75	.333	.413	.624	1,004	.358	1,813	.647	22.46	85.80	21.44	86.01	215.70	55.09
30	67	60	159	.316	.411	.599	2,337	.347	4,283	.636	52.27	83.13	50.64	84.57	270.61	69.11
34	64	94	315	.298	.352	.502	2,700	.288	4,887	.522	60.39	69.02	57.79	69.34	256.53	65.51
39	66	127	350	.276	.340	.447	3,342	.253	6,360	.481	74.75	60.52	75.20	63.93	274.41	70.08
77	198	102	269	.294	.389	.537	3,641	.304	7,118	.593	81.44	72.69	84.17	78.88	317.17	81.00
54	72	9	113	.311	.409	.474	1,681	.289	3,265	.562	37.60	69.27	38.61	74.69	220.16	56.22
50	82	58	128	.305	.381	.574	2,217	.341	4,083	.628	49.59	81.71	48.28	83.54	263.11	67.19
149	107	79	247	.303	.375	.409	3,479	.217	7,474	.466	77.81	51.90	88.38	61.89	279.98	71.50
117	42	-	2	.342	.474	.690	4,387	.418	7,903	.752	98.12	100.00	93.45	100.00	391.57	100.00

Actual Career Statistics H-R

Actual Career Statistics Listed Alphabetically

Rank	Player	Years	G	AB	H	1B	2B	3B	HR	RUN	RBI	BB	SO	SB
24	Schmidt, Mike	1972-1989	2,404	8,352	2,234	1,219	408	59	548	1,506	1,595	1,507	1,883	174
51	Sheffield, Gary**	1988-2004	2,036	7,302	2,175	1,350	386	24	415	1,307	1,353	1,202	879	205
20	Simmons, Al*	1924-1944	2,215	8,763	2,927	1,932	539	149	307	1,507	1,827	615	737	87
88	Sisler, George	1915-1930	2,055	8,267	2,812	2,121	425	164	102	1,284	1,175	472	327	375
58	Snider, Duke	1947-1964	2,143	7,161	2,116	1,266	358	85	407	1,259	1,333	971	1,237	99
33	Sosa, Sammy**	1989-2004	2,138	8,021	2,220	1,263	340	43	574	1,383	1,530	856	2,110	233
15	Speaker, Tris	1907-1928	2,789	10,195	3,515	2,382	793	223	117	1,881	1,529	1,381	220	434
55	Stargell, Willie	1962-1982	2,360	7,927	2,232	1,279	423	55	475	1,195	1,540	937	1,936	17
66	Stovey, Harry	1880-1893	1,487	6,194	1,826	1,183	347	174	122	1,492	908	663	343	509
97	Terry, Bill	1923-1936	1,721	6,428	2,193	1,554	373	112	154	1,120	1,078	537	449	56
30	Thomas, Frank **	1990-2004	1,925	6,851	2,113	1,222	444	11	436	1,308	1,439	1,450	1,134	32
64	Thome, Jim**	1991-2004	1,679	5,726	1,625	861	317	24	423	1,125	1,163	1,212	1,703	18
52	Thompson, Sam	1885-1906	1,405	6,004	2,016	1,418	326	146	126	1,259	1,299	450	226	236
98	Traynor, Pie	1920-1937	1,941	7,559	2,416	1,823	371	164	58	1,183	1,273	472	278	158
105	Trosky, Hal*	1933-1946	1,347	5,161	1,561	944	331	58	228	835	1,012	545	440	28
103	Vaughn, Mo	1991-2003	1,512	5,532	1,620	1,012	270	10	328	861	1,064	725	1,429	30
17	Wagner, Honus	1897-1917	2,787	10,427	3,430	2,426	651	252	101	1,740	1,732	963	327	722
45	Walker, Larry **	1989-2004	1,886	6,592	2,069	1,189	451	61	368	1,289	1,259	872	1,167	228
56	Waner, Paul	1927-1945	2,549	9,459	3,152	2,242	606	191	113	1,627	1,309	1,091	376	104
87	Williams, Bernie**	1991-2004	1,804	6,964	2,097	1,379	401	54	263	1,248	1,132	983	1,085	144
59	Williams, Billy	1959-1976	2,488	9,350	2,711	1,763	434	88	426	1,410	1,475	1,045	1,046	90
102	Williams, Ken*	1915-1929	1,397	4,862	1,552	994	285	77	196	860	913	566	287	154
6	Williams, Ted*	1939-1960	2,292	7,706	2,654	1,537	525	71	521	1,798	1,839	2,021	709	24
85	Wilson, Hack	1923-1934	1,348	4,760	1,461	884	266	67	244	884	1,063	674	713	52
26	Winfield, Dave	1973-1995	2,973	11,003	3,110	2,017	540	88	465	1,669	1,833	1,216	1,686	223
18	Yastrzemski, Carl	1961-1983	3,308	11,988	3,419	2,262	646	59	452	1,816	1,844	1,845	1,394	168
107	York, Rudy	1934-1948	1,603	5,891	1,621	1,001	291	52	277	876	1,152	791	867	38

* Player missed time for military service
** Active player. Statistics through 2004 season
TOP ranking for players with less than 70% rating is based upon comparison to listed players only.

Actual Career Statistics S-Y

Actual Career Statistics Listed Alphabetically

CS	HBP	SF	GDP	AVG	OBP	SLG	Total Offensive Production Statistics				TRP Rating	RPA Rating	TNB Rating	TBA Rating	TOP Composite	
							TRP	RPA	TNB	TBA					TOP	Rating
92	79	108	156	.267	.380	.527	3,101	.304	6,072	.595	69.36	72.79	71.80	79.11	293.06	74.84
93	110	96	179	.298	.400	.528	2,660	.299	5,278	.594	59.49	71.66	62.41	78.93	272.49	69.59
64	30	-	23	.334	.380	.535	3,334	.354	5,353	.568	74.57	84.65	63.30	75.45	297.97	76.09
127	48	-	-	.340	.379	.468	2,459	.280	4,639	.528	55.00	67.01	54.85	70.18	247.04	63.09
55	21	32	166	.295	.380	.540	2,592	.310	4,901	.587	57.97	74.32	57.95	78.01	268.26	68.51
106	54	70	175	.277	.348	.545	2,913	.317	5,405	.589	65.15	76.02	63.91	78.30	283.38	72.37
129	103	-	-	.345	.428	.501	3,410	.292	6,894	.590	76.27	69.92	81.52	78.46	306.17	78.19
16	78	75	143	.282	.360	.529	2,735	.299	5,206	.568	61.17	71.50	61.56	75.55	269.77	68.90
-	31	-	-	.295	.366	.466	2,400	.348	4,090	.594	53.68	83.43	48.36	78.93	264.40	67.52
6	9	-	38	.341	.393	.506	2,198	.313	3,848	.549	49.16	75.06	45.50	72.95	242.67	61.97
23	71	106	187	.308	.429	.567	2,747	.317	5,417	.625	61.44	75.91	64.05	83.10	284.51	72.66
19	48	52	101	.284	.410	.569	2,288	.320	4,518	.633	51.17	76.74	53.42	84.12	265.46	67.79
-	63	-	-	.336	.388	.502	2,558	.393	3,761	.577	57.21	93.99	44.47	76.71	272.39	69.56
46	31	-	47	.320	.362	.435	2,456	.303	3,904	.481	54.93	72.53	46.16	64.00	237.62	60.68
23	16	-	43	.302	.371	.522	1,847	.320	3,258	.565	41.31	76.72	38.52	75.12	231.67	59.17
18	108	45	135	.293	.383	.523	1,925	.294	3,739	.571	43.06	70.43	44.21	75.94	233.63	59.67
23	124	-	-	.329	.392	.469	3,472	.302	6,674	.580	77.66	72.21	78.92	77.05	305.83	78.10
75	129	63	144	.314	.401	.568	2,548	.327	4,900	.628	56.99	78.22	57.94	83.50	276.66	70.65
1	38	-	127	.333	.404	.474	2,936	.274	5,711	.533	65.67	65.61	67.53	70.85	269.66	68.87
85	36	52	193	.301	.388	.488	2,380	.289	4,473	.544	53.23	69.26	52.89	72.26	247.65	63.25
49	43	73	200	.290	.361	.492	2,885	.269	5,728	.535	64.53	64.50	67.73	71.08	267.84	68.40
106	28	-	-	.319	.393	.530	1,773	.325	3,221	.590	39.66	77.81	38.09	78.47	234.03	59.77
17	39	20	197	.344	.482	.634	3,637	.364	6,951	.696	81.35	87.24	82.19	92.55	343.33	87.68
5	20	-	15	.307	.395	.545	1,947	.356	3,334	.610	43.55	85.25	39.42	81.03	249.25	63.65
96	25	95	319	.283	.353	.475	3,502	.277	6,589	.521	78.33	66.25	77.91	69.19	291.68	74.49
116	40	105	323	.285	.379	.462	3,660	.256	7,476	.523	81.86	61.28	88.40	69.49	301.03	76.88
26	12	-	155	.275	.362	.483	2,028	.296	3,662	.535	45.36	70.90	43.30	71.07	230.64	58.90

380 of the Greatest Seasons Ever

D-1
Players Listed by Total Offensive Production

D-2
Players Listed Alphabetically

(Rating and Ranking of Total Offensive Production Statistics in Chapter 7)

★ ★ ★ **THE BEST** ★ ★ ★

The Greatest 300 Single Seasons and Others Listed by Total Offensive Production

Rank	Player	Player Season	Year	G	AB	H	1B	2B	3B	HR	RUN	RBI	BB	SO
1	Ruth, Babe	1st	1921	152	540	204	85	44	16	59	177	171	145	81
2	Ruth, Babe	2nd	1927	151	540	192	95	29	8	60	158	164	137	89
3	Ruth, Babe	3rd	1920	142	458	172	73	36	9	54	158	137	150	80
4	Gehrig, Lou	1st	1927	155	584	218	101	52	18	47	149	175	109	84
5	Wilson, Hack	1st	1930	155	585	208	111	35	6	56	146	191	105	84
6	Gehrig, Lou	2nd	1931	155	619	211	119	31	15	46	163	184	117	56
7	Foxx, Jimmie*	1st	1932	154	585	213	113	33	9	58	151	169	116	96
8	Bonds, Barry **	1st	2001	153	476	156	49	32	2	73	129	137	177	93
9	Duffy, Hugh	1st	1894	124	539	236	155	50	13	18	160	145	66	15
10	Gehrig, Lou	3rd	1930	154	581	220	120	42	17	41	143	174	101	63
11	Gehrig, Lou	4th	1936	155	579	205	112	37	7	49	167	152	130	46
12	Ruth, Babe	4th	1930	145	518	186	100	28	9	49	150	153	136	61
13	Foxx, Jimmie*	2nd	1938	149	565	197	105	33	9	50	139	175	119	76
14	Simmons, Al*	1st	1930	138	554	211	118	41	16	36	152	165	39	34
15	Ruth, Babe	5th	1931	145	534	199	119	31	3	46	149	163	128	51
16	Klein, Chuck	1st	1930	156	648	250	143	59	8	40	158	170	54	50
17	Ruth, Babe	6th	1928	154	536	173	82	29	8	54	163	142	137	87
18	Sosa, Sammy**	1st	2001	160	577	189	86	34	5	64	146	160	116	153
19	Greenberg, Hank*	1st	1937	154	594	200	97	49	14	40	137	183	102	101
20	Ruth, Babe	7th	1923	152	522	205	106	45	13	41	151	131	170	93
21	O'Neill, Tip	1st	1887	124	567	275	190	52	19	14	167	123	50	-
22	Ruth, Babe	8th	1926	152	495	184	102	30	5	47	139	146	144	76
23	DiMaggio, Joe*	1st	1937	151	621	215	119	35	15	46	151	167	64	37
24	McGwire, Mark	1st	1998	155	509	152	61	21	-	70	130	147	162	155
25	Gehrig, Lou	5th	1934	154	579	210	115	40	6	49	128	165	109	31
26	Hornsby, Rogers	1st	1922	154	623	250	148	46	14	42	141	152	65	50
27	Hornsby, Rogers	2nd	1929	156	602	229	135	47	8	39	156	149	87	65
28	Hornsby, Rogers	3rd	1925	138	504	203	113	41	10	39	133	143	83	39
29	Williams, Ted*	1st	1949	155	566	194	109	39	3	43	150	159	162	48
30	Thompson, Sam	1st	1895	118	533	210	128	42	22	18	131	165	31	11
31	Greenberg, Hank*	2nd	1938	155	556	175	90	23	4	58	144	146	119	92
32	Foxx, Jimmie*	3rd	1933	149	573	204	110	37	9	48	125	163	96	93
33	Cobb, Ty	1st	1911	146	591	248	169	47	24	8	147	127	44	-
34	Walker, Larry **	1st	1997	153	568	208	109	46	4	49	143	130	78	90
35	Hamilton, Billy	1st	1894	131	559	223	183	22	14	4	196	87	126	17
36	Gehrig, Lou	6th	1937	157	569	200	117	37	9	37	138	159	127	49
37	Ruth, Babe	9th	1924	153	529	200	108	39	7	46	143	121	142	81
38	Bonds, Barry **	2nd	2004	147	373	135	60	27	3	45	129	101	232	41
39	Helton, Todd**	1st	2000	160	580	216	113	59	2	42	138	147	103	61
40	Ramirez, Manny**	1st	1999	147	522	174	93	34	3	44	131	165	96	131
41	Ruth, Babe	10th	1929	135	499	172	94	26	6	46	121	154	72	60
42	Ott, Mel	1st	1929	150	545	179	98	37	2	42	138	151	113	38
43	Kelley, Joe	1st	1894	129	509	199	128	48	17	6	167	111	107	36
44	Klein, Chuck	2nd	1932	154	650	226	123	50	15	38	152	137	60	49
45	Kelley, Joe	2nd	1895	131	510	189	132	26	21	10	148	134	77	29
46	Bonds, Barry **	3rd	2002	143	403	149	70	31	2	46	117	110	198	47
47	Herman, Babe	1st	1930	153	614	241	147	48	11	35	143	130	66	56
48	Williams, Ted*	2nd	1941	143	456	185	112	33	3	37	135	120	147	27
49	Mantle, Mickey	1st	1956	150	533	188	109	22	5	52	132	130	112	99
50	Helton, Todd**	2nd	2001	159	587	197	92	54	2	49	132	146	98	104

The Greatest 300 Single Seasons and Others Listed by Total Offensive Production

SB	CS	HBP	SF	GDP	AVG	OBP	SLG	Total Offensive Production Statistics				TRP Rating	RPA Rating	TNB Rating	TBA Rating	TOP Composite	
								TRP	RPA	TNB	TBA					TOP	Rating
17	13	4	-	-	.378	.512	.846	348	.505	610	.885	100.00	94.64	100.00	97.58	392.22	100.00
7	6	-	-	-	.356	.486	.772	322	.476	555	.820	92.53	89.12	90.98	90.35	362.99	92.55
14	14	3	-	-	.376	.532	.847	295	.483	541	.885	84.77	90.47	88.69	97.59	361.52	92.17
10	8	3	-	-	.373	.474	.765	324	.466	561	.806	93.10	87.23	91.97	88.84	361.14	92.08
3	-	1	-	-	.356	.454	.723	337	.488	532	.770	96.84	91.39	87.21	84.85	360.29	91.86
17	12	-	-	-	.341	.446	.662	347	.471	532	.723	99.71	88.34	87.21	79.67	354.94	90.49
3	7	-	-	-	.364	.469	.749	320	.456	550	.785	91.95	85.54	90.16	86.47	354.13	90.29
13	3	9	2	5	.328	.515	.863	266	.398	607	.907	76.44	74.50	99.51	100.00	350.45	89.35
49	-	1	-	-	.438	.500	.679	305	.503	482	.795	87.64	94.31	79.02	87.66	348.63	88.89
12	14	3	-	-	.379	.473	.721	317	.463	521	.761	91.09	86.72	85.41	83.83	347.04	88.48
3	4	7	-	-	.354	.478	.696	319	.446	539	.753	91.67	83.48	88.36	82.97	346.48	88.34
10	10	1	-	-	.359	.493	.732	303	.463	516	.788	87.07	86.68	84.59	86.83	345.17	88.00
5	4	-	-	-	.349	.462	.704	314	.459	518	.757	90.23	86.02	84.92	83.47	344.63	87.87
9	2	1	-	-	.381	.423	.708	317	.534	439	.739	91.09	100.00	71.97	81.45	344.51	87.84
5	4	-	-	-	.373	.494	.700	312	.471	503	.760	89.66	88.31	82.46	83.74	344.17	87.75
4	-	4	-	-	.386	.436	.687	328	.465	507	.718	94.25	87.06	83.11	79.15	343.57	87.60
4	5	3	-	-	.323	.463	.709	305	.451	519	.768	87.64	84.54	85.08	84.62	341.89	87.17
-	2	6	12	6	.328	.437	.737	306	.427	545	.760	87.93	79.97	89.34	83.78	341.02	86.95
8	3	3	-	-	.337	.436	.668	320	.458	507	.725	91.95	85.78	83.11	79.94	340.79	86.89
17	21	4	-	-	.393	.545	.764	282	.405	569	.818	81.03	75.92	93.28	90.10	340.34	86.77
30	-	5	-	-	.485	.531	.718	290	.466	492	.791	83.33	87.36	80.66	87.18	338.53	86.31
11	9	3	-	-	.372	.516	.737	285	.444	514	.801	81.90	83.18	84.26	88.24	337.58	86.07
3	-	5	-	-	.346	.412	.673	318	.461	490	.710	91.38	86.36	80.33	78.27	336.33	85.75
1	-	6	4	8	.299	.470	.752	277	.402	552	.801	79.60	75.33	90.49	88.30	333.72	85.09
9	5	2	-	-	.363	.465	.706	293	.425	524	.759	84.20	79.57	85.90	83.70	333.37	84.99
17	12	1	-	-	.401	.459	.722	293	.425	521	.756	84.20	79.68	85.41	83.34	332.63	84.81
2	-	1	-	-	.380	.459	.679	305	.442	499	.723	87.64	82.83	81.80	79.71	331.98	84.64
5	3	2	-	-	.403	.489	.756	276	.469	468	.795	79.31	87.81	76.72	87.57	331.41	84.50
1	1	2	-	22	.343	.490	.650	309	.411	532	.707	88.79	77.00	87.21	77.97	330.97	84.38
24	-	5	-	-	.394	.432	.657	296	.520	410	.721	85.06	97.48	67.21	79.42	329.16	83.92
7	5	3	-	-	.315	.438	.683	290	.428	504	.743	83.33	80.15	82.62	81.93	328.03	83.64
2	2	1	-	-	.356	.449	.703	288	.430	500	.746	82.76	80.55	81.97	82.25	327.52	83.50
83	-	8	-	-	.420	.467	.621	274	.426	502	.781	78.74	79.85	82.30	86.05	326.93	83.35
33	8	14	4	15	.366	.452	.720	273	.402	526	.775	78.45	75.34	86.23	85.38	325.40	82.96
99	-	9	-	-	.399	.516	.510	283	.408	519	.748	81.32	76.41	85.08	82.42	325.24	82.92
4	3	4	-	-	.351	.473	.643	297	.424	498	.711	85.34	79.50	81.64	78.41	324.90	82.84
9	13	4	-	-	.378	.513	.739	264	.391	533	.790	75.86	73.29	87.38	87.03	323.55	82.49
6	1	9	3	5	.362	.609	.812	230	.370	549	.883	66.09	69.29	90.00	97.28	322.66	82.27
5	3	4	10	12	.372	.463	.698	285	.402	514	.725	81.90	75.32	84.26	79.90	321.38	81.94
2	4	13	9	12	.333	.442	.663	296	.454	453	.695	85.06	85.07	74.26	76.58	320.96	81.83
5	3	3	-	-	.345	.430	.697	275	.479	425	.740	79.02	89.77	69.67	81.60	320.07	81.61
6	-	6	-	-	.328	.449	.635	289	.435	471	.709	83.05	81.56	77.21	78.18	319.99	81.59
46	-	5	-	-	.391	.501	.587	278	.448	457	.736	79.89	83.88	74.92	81.11	319.80	81.53
20	-	1	-	-	.348	.404	.646	289	.406	501	.705	83.05	76.17	82.13	77.66	319.00	81.33
54	-	10	-	-	.371	.462	.563	282	.472	428	.717	81.03	88.51	70.16	79.01	318.72	81.26
9	2	9	2	4	.370	.582	.799	227	.369	536	.870	65.23	69.05	87.87	95.90	318.05	81.09
18	-	4	-	-	.393	.455	.678	273	.399	504	.737	78.45	74.79	82.62	81.21	317.07	80.84
2	4	3	-	10	.406	.553	.735	255	.414	483	.784	73.28	77.57	79.18	86.42	316.44	80.68
10	1	2	4	4	.353	.464	.705	262	.400	499	.762	75.29	74.95	81.80	83.96	316.01	80.57
7	5	5	5	14	.336	.432	.685	278	.392	507	.715	79.89	73.47	83.11	78.81	315.29	80.38

Single Season Statistics

The Greatest 300 Single Seasons and Others Listed by Total Offensive Production

Rank	Player	Player Season	Year	G	AB	H	1B	2B	3B	HR	RUN	RBI	BB	SO
51	Delahanty, Ed	1st	1893	132	588	218	148	31	20	19	145	146	47	20
52	Williams, Ted*	3rd	1942	150	522	186	111	34	5	36	141	137	145	51
53	Wilson, Hack	2nd	1929	150	574	198	124	30	5	39	135	159	78	83
54	Williams, Ken*	1st	1922	153	585	194	110	34	11	39	128	155	74	31
55	Thompson, Sam	2nd	1894	102	458	185	117	29	26	13	115	141	40	13
56	Mantle, Mickey	2nd	1961	153	514	163	87	16	6	54	132	128	126	112
57	Sosa, Sammy**	2nd	1998	159	643	198	112	20	-	66	134	158	73	171
58	Greenberg, Hank*	3rd	1935	152	619	203	105	46	16	36	121	170	87	91
59	Greenberg, Hank*	4th	1940	148	573	195	96	50	8	41	129	150	93	75
60	McGwire, Mark	2nd	1999	153	521	145	58	21	1	65	118	147	133	141
61	Gonzalez, Luis**	1st	2001	162	609	198	98	36	7	57	128	142	100	83
62	Foxx, Jimmie*	4th	1930	153	562	188	105	33	13	37	127	156	93	66
63	Browning, Pete	1st	1887	134	547	220	165	35	16	4	137	118	55	-
64	Musial, Stan*	1st	1948	155	611	230	127	46	18	39	135	131	79	34
65	Williams, Ted*	4th	1946	150	514	176	93	37	8	38	142	123	156	44
66	Gehrig, Lou	7th	1932	156	596	208	123	42	9	34	138	151	108	38
67	Gehrig, Lou	8th	1928	154	562	210	123	47	13	27	139	142	94	69
68	Lajoie, Nap	1st	1901	131	543	229	154	48	13	14	145	125	24	-
69	Jennings, Hughie	1st	1895	131	528	204	152	40	8	4	159	125	24	17
70	Foxx, Jimmie*	5th	1936	155	585	198	117	32	8	41	130	143	105	119
71	Trosky, Hal*	1st	1936	151	629	216	120	45	9	42	124	162	36	58
72	Delahanty, Ed	2nd	1894	114	497	199	143	36	16	4	149	131	60	16
73	Ruth, Babe	11th	1932	133	457	156	97	13	5	41	120	137	130	62
74	Delahanty, Ed	3rd	1895	116	481	192	126	47	8	11	148	106	86	31
75	Bonds, Barry **	4th	1993	159	539	181	93	38	4	46	129	123	126	79
76	Bagwell, Jeff**	1st	2000	159	590	183	98	37	1	47	152	132	107	116
77	Cuyler, Kiki	1st	1930	156	642	228	148	50	17	13	155	134	72	49
78	Klein, Chuck	3rd	1929	149	616	219	125	45	6	43	126	145	54	61
79	Thompson, Sam	3rd	1887	127	576	234	172	29	23	10	118	166	32	19
80	Burks, Ellis	1st	1996	156	613	211	118	45	8	40	142	128	61	114
81	Delahanty, Ed	4th	1896	122	505	199	130	42	14	13	131	126	62	22
82	Kelley, Joe	3rd	1896	130	516	191	139	27	17	8	147	100	91	19
83	Griffey, Ken **	1st	1997	157	608	185	92	34	3	56	125	147	76	121
84	Stovey, Harry	1st	1889	137	556	171	101	38	13	19	152	119	77	68
85	Bonds, Barry **	5th	1996	158	517	159	87	27	3	42	122	129	151	76
86	Bagwell, Jeff**	2nd	1999	162	562	171	94	35	-	42	143	126	149	127
87	Delahanty, Ed	5th	1899	145	573	234	160	56	9	9	133	137	55	-
88	Williams, Ted*	5th	1939	149	565	185	99	44	11	31	131	145	107	64
89	O'Doul, Lefty	1st	1929	154	638	254	181	35	6	32	152	122	76	19
90	Belle, Albert	1st	1996	158	602	187	98	38	3	48	124	148	99	87
91	Pujols, Albert**	1st	2003	157	591	212	117	51	1	43	137	124	79	65
92	Foxx, Jimmie*	6th	1934	150	539	180	102	28	6	44	120	130	111	75
93	Griffey, Ken **	2nd	1996	140	545	165	88	26	2	49	125	140	78	104
94	Cash, Norm	1st	1961	159	535	193	122	22	8	41	119	132	124	85
95	Gehrig, Lou	9th	1933	152	593	198	113	41	12	32	138	139	92	42
96	Delgado, Carlos**	1st	2000	162	569	196	97	57	1	41	115	137	123	104
97	Brouthers, Dan	1st	1887	122	570	239	172	35	20	12	153	101	71	9
98	Simmons, Al*	2nd	1929	143	581	212	128	41	9	34	114	157	31	38
99	Mize, Johnny*	1st	1947	154	586	177	98	26	2	51	137	138	74	42
100	Robinson, Frank	1st	1962	162	609	208	116	51	2	39	134	136	76	62

The Greatest 300 Single Seasons and Others Listed by Total Offensive Production

SB	CS	HBP	SF	GDP	AVG	OBP	SLG	Total Offensive Production Statistics				TRP Rating	RPA Rating	TNB Rating	TBA Rating	TOP Composite	
								TRP	RPA	TNB	TBA					TOP	Rating
36	-	10	-	-	.371	.426	.588	291	.451	439	.681	83.62	84.54	71.97	75.01	315.14	80.35
3	2	4	-	12	.356	.499	.648	278	.407	488	.714	79.89	76.27	80.00	78.75	314.90	80.29
3	-	2	-	-	.345	.425	.618	294	.450	438	.670	84.48	84.24	71.80	73.81	314.34	80.14
37	20	7	-	-	.332	.413	.627	283	.425	465	.698	81.32	79.62	76.23	76.95	314.13	80.09
29	-	1	-	-	.404	.453	.666	256	.513	375	.752	73.56	96.13	61.48	82.83	314.00	80.06
12	1	-	5	2	.317	.448	.687	260	.402	490	.757	74.71	75.30	80.33	83.47	313.81	80.01
18	9	1	5	20	.308	.377	.647	292	.394	499	.673	83.91	73.74	81.80	74.12	313.57	79.95
4	3	-	-	-	.328	.411	.628	291	.412	477	.676	83.62	77.24	78.20	74.46	313.52	79.93
6	3	1	-	15	.340	.433	.670	279	.409	481	.705	80.17	76.66	78.85	77.73	313.41	79.91
-	-	2	5	12	.278	.424	.697	265	.394	498	.740	76.15	73.78	81.64	81.56	313.13	79.83
1	1	14	5	14	.325	.429	.688	270	.364	533	.718	77.59	68.18	87.38	79.17	312.32	79.63
7	7	-	-	-	.335	.429	.637	283	.432	451	.689	81.32	80.96	73.93	75.89	312.10	79.57
103	-	8	-	-	.402	.464	.547	255	.418	465	.762	73.28	78.33	76.23	84.02	311.85	79.51
7	-	3	-	18	.376	.450	.702	266	.374	518	.729	76.44	70.10	84.92	80.30	311.75	79.48
-	-	2	-	12	.342	.497	.667	265	.387	501	.732	76.15	72.60	82.13	80.73	311.60	79.45
4	11	3	-	-	.349	.451	.621	289	.409	474	.670	83.05	76.60	77.70	73.89	311.24	79.35
4	11	4	-	-	.374	.467	.648	281	.426	455	.689	80.75	79.78	74.59	75.98	311.10	79.32
27	-	13	-	-	.422	.459	.635	270	.466	409	.705	77.59	87.23	67.05	77.72	309.58	78.93
60	-	32	-	-	.386	.445	.515	284	.486	388	.664	81.61	91.12	63.61	73.22	309.56	78.93
13	4	1	-	-	.338	.440	.631	273	.395	484	.700	78.45	74.03	79.34	77.20	309.02	78.79
6	5	3	-	-	.343	.382	.644	286	.428	445	.666	82.18	80.23	72.95	73.42	308.78	78.73
29	-	7	-	-	.400	.472	.561	280	.496	375	.665	80.46	93.03	61.48	73.28	308.24	78.59
2	2	2	-	-	.341	.489	.661	257	.436	434	.737	73.85	81.76	71.15	81.21	307.97	78.52
46	-	6	-	-	.399	.496	.599	254	.443	426	.743	72.99	83.06	69.84	81.94	307.83	78.48
29	12	2	7	11	.336	.458	.677	252	.368	510	.745	72.41	68.93	83.61	82.06	307.01	78.28
9	6	15	7	19	.310	.424	.615	284	.385	488	.661	81.61	72.11	80.00	72.88	306.60	78.17
37	-	10	-	-	.355	.428	.547	289	.399	470	.649	83.05	74.80	77.05	71.55	306.44	78.13
5	-	-	-	-	.356	.407	.657	271	.404	464	.693	77.87	75.79	76.07	76.33	306.06	78.03
22	-	9	-	-	.406	.446	.589	284	.460	402	.652	81.61	86.25	65.90	71.81	305.57	77.91
32	6	6	2	19	.344	.408	.639	270	.385	485	.692	77.59	72.17	79.51	76.25	305.52	77.90
37	-	9	-	-	.394	.469	.610	257	.446	416	.722	73.85	83.61	68.20	79.60	305.25	77.83
87	-	12	-	-	.370	.475	.535	247	.399	466	.753	70.98	74.77	76.39	82.97	305.11	77.79
15	4	8	12	12	.304	.382	.646	272	.380	488	.682	78.16	71.18	80.00	75.12	304.46	77.63
63	-	1	-	-	.308	.393	.525	271	.427	433	.683	77.87	80.10	70.98	75.27	304.22	77.56
40	7	1	6	10	.308	.461	.615	251	.366	503	.734	72.13	68.66	82.46	80.93	304.18	77.55
30	11	11	7	18	.304	.454	.591	269	.360	511	.684	77.30	67.48	83.77	75.39	303.94	77.49
38	-	4	-	-	.408	.464	.585	270	.427	432	.684	77.59	80.05	70.82	75.34	303.79	77.46
2	1	2	-	10	.327	.436	.609	276	.404	454	.664	79.31	75.61	74.43	73.15	302.50	77.13
2	-	4	-	-	.398	.465	.622	274	.382	479	.667	78.74	71.51	78.52	73.53	302.30	77.07
11	-	7	7	20	.311	.410	.623	272	.370	492	.669	78.16	69.34	80.66	73.78	301.94	76.98
5	1	10	5	13	.359	.439	.667	261	.374	487	.698	75.00	70.07	79.84	76.90	301.80	76.95
11	2	1	-	-	.334	.449	.653	250	.384	473	.727	71.84	71.96	77.54	80.08	301.42	76.85
16	1	7	7	7	.303	.392	.628	265	.411	442	.686	76.15	77.11	72.46	75.64	301.36	76.83
11	5	9	2	16	.361	.487	.662	251	.366	493	.719	72.13	68.56	80.82	79.21	300.71	76.67
9	13	1	-	-	.334	.424	.605	277	.404	448	.653	79.60	75.66	73.44	71.98	300.68	76.66
-	1	15	4	12	.344	.470	.664	252	.349	515	.712	72.41	65.31	84.43	78.51	300.66	76.66
34	-	6	-	-	.419	.488	.614	254	.393	461	.713	72.99	73.56	75.57	78.53	300.65	76.65
4	2	1	-	-	.365	.398	.642	271	.442	407	.664	77.87	82.84	66.72	73.18	300.61	76.64
2	-	4	-	6	.302	.384	.614	275	.410	440	.657	79.02	76.91	72.13	72.38	300.44	76.60
18	9	11	5	13	.342	.421	.624	270	.378	476	.667	77.59	70.86	78.03	73.48	299.95	76.48

Single Season Statistics

Single Season Statistics

Rank	Player	Player Season	Year	G	AB	H	1B	2B	3B	HR	RUN	RBI	BB	SO
101	Sisler, George	1st	1920	154	631	257	171	49	18	19	137	122	46	19
102	Mays, Willie*	1st	1962	162	621	189	99	36	5	49	130	141	78	85
103	Brouthers, Dan	2nd	1894	123	528	182	115	33	25	9	137	128	67	9
104	Rodriguez, Alex**	1st	2001	162	632	201	114	34	1	52	133	135	75	131
105	Maris, Roger	1st	1961	161	590	159	78	16	4	61	132	142	94	67
106	Mays, Willie*	2nd	1955	152	580	185	103	18	13	51	123	127	79	60
107	Rodriguez, Alex**	2nd	2002	162	624	187	101	27	2	57	125	142	87	122
108	Bottomley, Jim	1st	1928	149	576	187	94	42	20	31	123	136	71	54
109	Terry, Bill	1st	1930	154	633	254	177	39	15	23	139	129	57	33
110	Belle, Albert	2nd	1998	163	609	200	101	48	2	49	113	152	81	84
111	Snider, Duke	1st	1955	148	538	166	84	34	6	42	126	136	104	87
112	Rodriguez, Alex**	3rd	2000	148	554	175	98	34	2	41	134	132	100	121
113	Foster, George	1st	1977	158	615	197	112	31	2	52	124	149	61	107
114	Bonds, Barry **	6th	2000	143	480	147	66	28	4	49	129	106	117	77
115	Griffey, Ken **	3rd	1998	161	633	180	88	33	3	56	120	146	76	121
116	Averill, Earl	1st	1931	155	627	209	131	36	10	32	140	143	68	38
117	Hamilton, Billy	2nd	1895	121	517	203	171	19	6	7	166	74	96	30
118	Speaker, Tris	1st	1923	150	574	218	131	59	11	17	133	130	93	15
119	Kiner, Ralph	1st	1949	152	549	170	92	19	5	54	116	127	117	61
120	Snider, Duke	2nd	1953	153	590	198	114	38	4	42	132	126	82	90
121	Medwick, Joe	1st	1937	156	633	237	140	56	10	31	111	154	41	50
122	Giambi, Jason**	1st	2000	152	510	170	97	29	1	43	108	137	137	96
123	Rodriguez, Alex**	4th	1996	146	601	215	124	54	1	36	141	123	59	104
124	Bagwell, Jeff**	3rd	1994	110	400	147	74	32	2	39	104	116	65	65
125	Belle, Albert	3rd	1995	143	546	173	70	52	1	50	121	126	73	80
126	Averill, Earl	2nd	1936	152	614	232	150	39	15	28	136	126	65	35
127	Hornsby, Rogers	4th	1921	154	592	235	152	44	18	21	131	126	60	48
128	Simmons, Al*	3rd	1932	154	670	216	144	28	9	35	144	151	47	76
129	Pujols, Albert**	2nd	2004	154	592	196	97	51	2	46	133	123	84	52
130	Williams, Ted*	6th	1948	137	509	188	116	44	3	25	124	127	126	41
131	Anson, Cap	1st	1886	125	504	187	132	34	11	10	117	147	55	19
132	Thomas, Frank **	1st	2000	159	582	191	104	44	-	43	115	143	112	94
133	Brown, Tom	1st	1891	137	589	189	133	30	21	5	177	72	70	96
134	Delgado, Carlos**	2nd	2003	161	570	172	91	38	1	42	117	145	109	137
135	Williams, Ted*	7th	1947	156	528	181	100	40	9	32	125	114	162	47
136	Galarraga, Andres**	1st	1996	159	626	190	101	39	3	47	119	150	40	157
137	Foxx, Jimmie*	7th	1939	124	467	168	92	31	10	35	130	105	89	72
138	Musial, Stan*	2nd	1949	157	612	207	117	41	13	36	128	123	107	38
139	Mize, Johnny*	2nd	1940	155	579	182	95	31	13	43	111	137	82	49
140	Sheffield, Gary**	1st	2003	155	576	190	112	37	2	39	126	132	86	55
141	DiMaggio, Joe*	2nd	1941	139	541	193	109	43	11	30	122	125	76	13
142	Hornsby, Rogers	5th	1927	155	568	205	138	32	9	26	133	125	86	38
143	Bonds, Barry **	7th	2003	130	390	133	65	22	1	45	111	90	148	58
144	DiMaggio, Joe*	3rd	1938	145	599	194	117	32	13	32	129	140	59	21
145	McGwire, Mark	3rd	1996	130	423	132	59	21	-	52	104	113	116	112
146	Clolavito, Rocky	1st	1961	163	583	169	92	30	2	45	129	140	113	75
147	Snider, Duke	3rd	1954	149	584	199	110	39	10	40	120	130	84	96
148	Bagwell, Jeff**	4th	1997	162	566	162	77	40	2	43	109	135	127	122
149	Ott, Mel	2nd	1936	150	534	175	108	28	6	33	120	135	111	41
150	Gonzalez, Juan **	1st	1998	154	606	193	96	50	2	45	110	157	46	126

The Greatest 300 Single Seasons and Others Listed by Total Offensive Production

The Greatest 300 Single Seasons and Others Listed by Total Offensive Production

SB	CS	HBP	SF	GDP	AVG	OBP	SLG	Total Offensive Production Statistics				TRP Rating	RPA Rating	TNB Rating	TBA Rating	TOP Composite	
								TRP	RPA	TNB	TBA					TOP	Rating
42	17	2	-	-	.407	.449	.632	259	.381	472	.695	74.43	71.48	77.38	76.61	299.89	76.46
18	2	4	3	19	.304	.384	.615	271	.374	480	.662	77.87	70.04	78.69	72.97	299.57	76.38
40	-	5	-	-	.345	.423	.553	265	.442	404	.673	76.15	82.76	66.23	74.21	299.35	76.32
18	3	16	9	17	.318	.399	.622	268	.358	499	.666	77.01	67.05	81.80	73.43	299.29	76.31
-	-	7	7	16	.269	.372	.620	274	.384	467	.654	78.74	71.91	76.56	72.09	299.29	76.31
24	4	4	7	12	.319	.400	.659	250	.367	485	.711	71.84	68.69	79.51	78.38	298.41	76.08
9	4	10	4	14	.300	.392	.623	267	.361	491	.664	76.72	67.70	80.49	73.23	298.14	76.01
10	-	3	-	-	.325	.402	.628	259	.398	446	.686	74.43	74.66	73.11	75.62	297.83	75.93
8	-	1	-	-	.401	.452	.619	268	.388	458	.663	77.01	72.67	75.08	73.05	297.82	75.93
6	4	1	15	17	.328	.399	.655	265	.367	483	.668	76.15	68.68	79.18	73.63	297.64	75.89
9	7	1	6	9	.309	.418	.628	262	.398	445	.676	75.29	74.61	72.95	74.54	297.39	75.82
15	4	7	11	10	.316	.420	.606	266	.390	454	.666	76.44	73.08	74.43	73.37	297.32	75.80
6	4	5	8	17	.320	.382	.631	273	.387	456	.646	78.45	72.46	74.75	71.19	296.85	75.68
11	3	3	7	6	.306	.440	.688	235	.383	458	.747	67.53	71.83	75.08	82.35	296.79	75.67
20	5	7	4	14	.284	.365	.611	266	.362	485	.661	76.44	67.91	79.51	72.83	296.68	75.64
9	9	6	-	-	.333	.404	.576	283	.404	435	.621	81.32	75.65	71.31	68.39	296.67	75.64
95	-	7	-	-	.393	.494	.493	240	.387	453	.731	68.97	72.53	74.26	80.53	296.29	75.54
10	9	4	-	-	.380	.469	.610	263	.392	448	.668	75.57	73.44	73.44	73.59	296.05	75.48
6	-	1	-	10	.310	.432	.658	243	.359	485	.716	69.83	67.26	79.51	78.96	295.55	75.35
16	7	3	-	10	.336	.419	.627	258	.377	464	.677	74.14	70.58	76.07	74.66	295.44	75.32
4	-	2	-	11	.374	.414	.641	265	.386	453	.659	76.15	72.28	74.26	72.67	295.37	75.31
2	-	9	8	9	.333	.476	.647	245	.364	478	.710	70.40	68.21	78.36	78.28	295.26	75.28
15	4	4	7	15	.358	.414	.631	264	.385	453	.660	75.86	72.11	74.26	72.78	295.02	75.22
15	4	4	10	12	.368	.451	.750	220	.448	380	.774	63.22	83.96	62.30	85.30	294.77	75.15
5	2	6	4	24	.317	.401	.690	247	.378	459	.703	70.98	70.88	75.25	77.47	294.57	75.10
3	3	1	-	-	.378	.438	.627	262	.385	451	.663	75.29	72.20	73.93	73.10	294.50	75.09
13	13	7	-	-	.397	.458	.639	257	.390	445	.675	73.85	73.08	72.95	74.42	294.30	75.03
4	2	1	-	-	.322	.368	.548	295	.411	417	.581	84.77	76.99	68.36	64.01	294.13	74.99
5	5	7	9	21	.331	.415	.657	256	.359	480	.673	73.56	67.28	78.69	74.20	293.73	74.89
4	-	3	-	10	.369	.497	.615	251	.387	446	.688	72.13	72.58	73.11	75.86	293.68	74.88
29	-	-	-	-	.371	.433	.542	264	.472	357	.639	75.86	88.50	58.52	70.39	293.27	74.77
1	3	5	8	13	.328	.436	.625	258	.358	479	.665	74.14	67.15	78.52	73.32	293.13	74.74
106	-	4	-	-	.321	.397	.469	249	.376	456	.688	71.55	70.37	74.75	75.80	292.48	74.57
-	-	19	7	9	.302	.426	.593	262	.367	466	.653	75.29	68.76	76.39	71.93	292.37	74.54
-	1	2	-	10	.343	.499	.634	239	.340	498	.709	68.68	63.80	81.64	78.19	292.30	74.52
18	8	17	8	6	.304	.357	.601	269	.386	443	.636	77.30	72.32	72.62	70.05	292.29	74.52
4	3	2	-	17	.360	.464	.694	235	.409	416	.723	67.53	76.58	68.20	79.74	292.05	74.46
3	-	2	-	12	.338	.438	.624	251	.342	494	.674	72.13	64.16	80.98	74.28	291.55	74.33
7	-	5	-	10	.314	.404	.636	248	.367	462	.683	71.26	68.74	75.74	75.32	291.07	74.21
18	4	8	8	16	.330	.419	.604	258	.372	456	.657	74.14	69.66	74.75	72.42	290.97	74.19
4	2	4	-	6	.357	.440	.643	247	.394	430	.686	70.98	73.82	70.49	75.59	290.87	74.16
9	-	4	-	-	.361	.448	.586	258	.392	432	.657	74.14	73.47	70.82	72.36	290.79	74.14
7	-	10	2	7	.341	.529	.749	201	.361	457	.820	57.76	67.62	74.92	90.43	290.72	74.12
6	1	2	-	-	.324	.386	.581	269	.408	414	.627	77.30	76.37	67.87	69.13	290.67	74.11
-	-	8	1	14	.312	.467	.730	217	.386	433	.770	62.36	72.35	70.98	84.92	290.61	74.09
1	2	2	8	14	.290	.402	.580	269	.374	452	.628	77.30	70.01	74.10	69.19	290.60	74.09
6	6	4	6	12	.341	.423	.647	250	.362	466	.675	71.84	67.89	76.39	74.43	290.56	74.08
31	10	16	8	10	.286	.425	.592	244	.336	499	.686	70.11	62.89	81.80	75.65	290.46	74.05
6	-	5	-	8	.328	.448	.588	255	.388	436	.663	73.28	72.62	71.48	73.03	290.40	74.04
2	1	6	11	20	.318	.366	.630	267	.388	435	.631	76.72	72.61	71.31	69.58	290.23	74.00

Single Season Statistics

The Greatest 300 Single Seasons and Others Listed by Total Offensive Production

Rank	Player	Player Season	Year	G	AB	H	1B	2B	3B	HR	RUN	RBI	BB	SO
151	Rosen, Al	1st	1953	155	599	201	126	27	5	43	115	145	85	48
152	Bonds, Barry **	8th	1998	156	552	167	79	44	7	37	120	122	130	92
153	Cuyler, Kiki	2nd	1925	153	617	220	133	43	26	18	144	102	58	56
154	Gehrig, Lou	10th	1929	154	553	166	89	32	10	35	127	126	124	68
155	Kiner, Ralph	2nd	1947	152	565	177	99	23	4	51	118	127	98	81
156	Sosa, Sammy**	3rd	1999	162	625	180	91	24	2	63	114	141	78	171
157	Griffey, Ken **	4th	1999	160	606	173	96	26	3	48	123	134	91	108
158	Foxx, Jimmie*	8th	1929	149	517	183	118	23	9	33	123	118	103	70
159	Sheffield, Gary**	2nd	1996	161	519	163	87	33	1	42	118	120	142	66
160	Kelly, King	1st	1886	118	451	175	129	31	11	4	155	79	83	33
161	Helton, Todd**	3rd	2003	160	583	209	122	49	5	33	135	117	111	72
162	Walker, Larry **	2nd	1999	127	438	166	99	26	4	37	108	115	57	52
163	Duffy, Hugh	2nd	1893	131	537	203	167	23	7	6	149	118	50	13
164	Williams, Billy	1st	1970	161	636	205	125	34	4	42	137	129	72	65
165	Greenberg, Hank*	5th	1934	153	593	201	105	63	7	26	118	139	63	93
166	Aaron, Hank	1st	1962	156	592	191	112	28	6	45	127	128	66	73
167	Jackson, Reggie	1st	1969	152	549	151	65	36	3	47	123	118	115	142
168	DiMaggio, Joe*	4th	1939	120	462	176	108	32	6	30	108	126	52	20
169	DiMaggio, Joe*	5th	1948	153	594	190	114	26	11	39	110	155	67	30
170	Matthews, Eddie	1st	1953	157	579	175	89	31	8	47	110	135	99	83
171	Goslin, Goose	1st	1930	148	584	180	95	36	12	37	115	138	67	54
172	Mantle, Mickey	3rd	1957	144	474	173	105	28	6	34	121	94	146	75
173	Aaron, Hank	2nd	1963	161	631	201	124	29	4	44	121	130	78	94
174	Foxx, Jimmie*	9th	1935	147	535	185	109	33	7	36	118	115	114	99
175	Vaughn, Mo	1st	1996	161	635	207	133	29	1	44	118	143	95	154
176	Morgan, Joe	1st	1976	141	472	151	89	30	5	27	113	111	114	41
177	Walker, Larry **	3rd	2001	142	497	174	98	35	3	38	107	123	82	103
178	Trosky, Hal*	2nd	1934	154	625	206	117	45	9	35	117	142	58	49
179	Stovey, Harry	2nd	1890	118	481	143	95	25	11	12	142	84	81	38
180	Sosa, Sammy**	4th	2000	156	604	193	104	38	1	50	106	138	91	168
181	Giambi, Jason**	2nd	2001	154	520	178	91	47	2	38	109	120	129	83
182	Killebrew, Harmon	1st	1969	162	555	153	82	20	2	49	106	140	145	84
183	Jennings, Hughie	2nd	1896	129	523	208	175	24	9	-	125	121	19	11
184	Lowe, Bobby	1st	1894	133	613	212	150	34	11	17	158	115	50	25
185	Gehrig, Lou	11th	1935	149	535	176	110	26	10	30	125	119	132	38
186	McGraw, John	1st	1894	124	512	174	141	18	14	1	156	92	91	12
187	Kluszewski, Ted	1st	1954	149	573	187	107	28	3	49	104	141	78	35
188	Kiner, Ralph	3rd	1951	151	531	164	85	31	6	42	124	109	137	57
189	Ott, Mel	3rd	1932	154	566	180	104	30	8	38	119	123	100	39
190	Jones, Chipper**	1st	1999	157	567	181	94	41	1	45	116	110	126	94
191	Robinson, Frank	2nd	1966	155	576	182	97	34	2	49	122	122	87	90
192	Alomar, Roberto**	1st	1999	159	563	182	115	40	3	24	138	120	99	96
193	Cobb, Ty	2nd	1915	156	563	208	161	31	13	3	144	99	118	43
194	Ruth, Babe	12th	1919	130	432	139	64	34	12	29	103	114	101	58
195	Rice, Jim	1st	1978	163	677	213	127	25	15	46	121	139	58	126
196	Sisler, George	2nd	1922	142	586	246	178	42	18	8	134	105	49	14
197	Conner, Roger	1st	1890	123	484	180	126	25	15	14	134	103	88	32
198	Galarraga, Andres**	2nd	1997	154	600	191	116	31	3	41	120	140	54	141
199	Wilson, Hack	3rd	1927	146	551	175	103	30	12	30	119	129	71	70
200	Palmiero, Rafael**	1st	1999	158	565	183	105	30	1	47	96	148	97	69

The Greatest 300 Single Seasons and Others Listed by Total Offensive Production

SB	CS	HBP	SF	GDP	AVG	OBP	SLG	Total Offensive Production Statistics				TRP Rating	RPA Rating	TNB Rating	TBA Rating	TOP Composite	
								TRP	RPA	TNB	TBA					TOP	Rating
8	7	4	-	19	.336	.422	.613	260	.368	457	.646	74.71	68.91	74.92	71.24	289.78	73.88
28	12	8	6	15	.303	.438	.609	242	.340	490	.689	69.54	63.78	80.33	75.96	289.60	73.84
41	13	13	-	-	.357	.423	.598	246	.358	468	.680	70.69	67.00	76.72	74.97	289.38	73.78
4	4	5	-	-	.300	.433	.584	253	.371	452	.663	72.70	69.51	74.10	73.05	289.36	73.77
1	-	2	-	12	.313	.417	.639	245	.362	462	.682	70.40	67.81	75.74	75.21	289.16	73.73
7	8	3	6	17	.288	.367	.635	255	.350	477	.654	73.28	65.55	78.20	72.12	289.13	73.72
24	7	7	2	8	.285	.384	.576	257	.360	464	.650	73.85	67.45	76.07	71.62	288.99	73.68
10	7	2	-	-	.354	.463	.625	241	.387	431	.693	69.25	72.60	70.66	76.37	288.88	73.65
16	9	10	6	16	.314	.465	.624	238	.343	483	.697	68.39	64.35	79.18	76.82	288.74	73.62
53	-	-	-	-	.388	.483	.532	234	.438	376	.704	67.24	82.11	61.64	77.60	288.60	73.58
-	4	2	7	19	.358	.458	.630	252	.349	476	.659	72.41	65.40	78.03	72.66	288.51	73.56
11	4	12	6	12	.379	.458	.710	223	.425	387	.737	64.08	79.59	63.44	81.24	288.36	73.52
50	-	1	-	-	.378	.432	.480	267	.454	359	.611	76.72	85.09	58.85	67.29	287.95	73.42
7	1	2	4	13	.322	.391	.586	266	.366	453	.623	76.44	68.56	74.26	68.68	287.94	73.41
9	5	2	-	-	.339	.404	.600	257	.391	425	.646	73.85	73.19	69.67	71.19	287.90	73.40
15	7	3	6	14	.323	.390	.618	255	.374	443	.651	73.28	70.16	72.62	71.70	287.76	73.37
13	5	12	1	8	.275	.411	.608	241	.352	469	.685	69.25	65.93	76.89	75.46	287.52	73.31
3	-	4	-	11	.381	.448	.671	234	.442	369	.698	67.24	82.89	60.49	76.88	287.50	73.30
1	1	8	-	20	.320	.396	.598	265	.385	430	.624	76.15	72.07	70.49	68.78	287.50	73.30
1	3	2	-	6	.302	.406	.627	245	.357	462	.673	70.40	66.92	75.74	74.23	287.29	73.25
17	11	3	-	-	.308	.382	.601	253	.387	427	.653	72.70	72.49	70.00	71.96	287.15	73.21
16	3	-	3	5	.365	.512	.665	215	.342	474	.755	61.78	64.15	77.70	83.19	286.83	73.13
31	5	5	5	11	.319	.391	.586	251	.346	474	.654	72.13	64.87	77.70	72.06	286.76	73.11
6	4	-	-	-	.346	.461	.636	233	.359	456	.703	66.95	67.27	74.75	77.44	286.42	73.03
2	-	14	8	17	.326	.420	.583	261	.339	481	.625	75.00	63.60	78.85	68.94	286.39	73.02
60	9	1	12	2	.320	.444	.576	224	.373	438	.729	64.37	69.84	71.80	80.32	286.33	73.00
14	5	14	8	9	.350	.449	.662	230	.377	434	.711	66.09	70.65	71.15	78.41	286.31	73.00
2	2	2	-	-	.330	.388	.598	259	.378	434	.634	74.43	70.85	71.15	69.83	286.25	72.98
97	-	5	-	-	.297	.404	.470	226	.399	409	.721	64.94	74.69	67.05	79.50	286.18	72.96
7	4	2	8	12	.320	.406	.634	244	.340	479	.668	70.11	63.77	78.52	73.63	286.04	72.93
2	-	13	9	17	.342	.477	.660	229	.333	487	.708	65.80	62.37	79.84	78.02	286.03	72.92
8	2	5	4	16	.276	.427	.584	246	.339	480	.662	70.69	63.58	78.69	72.97	285.93	72.90
73	-	51	-	-	.398	.469	.478	246	.415	393	.663	70.69	77.73	64.43	73.04	285.89	72.89
23	-	6	-	-	.346	.401	.520	273	.408	398	.595	78.45	76.47	65.25	65.57	285.73	72.85
8	7	5	-	-	.329	.466	.583	244	.363	450	.670	70.11	68.04	73.77	73.80	285.73	72.85
78	-	13	-	-	.340	.451	.436	248	.403	405	.657	71.26	75.44	66.39	72.46	285.56	72.81
-	2	3	5	12	.326	.407	.642	245	.365	447	.666	70.40	68.42	73.28	73.42	285.52	72.80
2	1	2	-	10	.309	.452	.627	233	.343	473	.696	66.95	64.21	77.54	76.66	285.36	72.76
6	-	4	-	-	.318	.424	.601	242	.361	450	.672	69.54	67.68	73.77	74.02	285.02	72.67
25	3	2	6	20	.319	.441	.633	226	.313	509	.706	64.94	58.74	83.44	77.81	284.93	72.64
8	5	10	7	24	.316	.410	.637	244	.347	467	.663	70.11	64.94	76.56	73.11	284.73	72.59
37	6	7	13	13	.323	.422	.533	258	.371	437	.629	74.14	69.56	71.64	69.30	284.64	72.57
96	38	10	-	-	.369	.486	.487	243	.352	460	.666	69.83	65.90	75.41	73.37	284.50	72.54
7	-	6	-	-	.322	.456	.657	217	.403	398	.738	62.36	75.44	65.25	81.38	284.42	72.52
7	5	5	5	15	.315	.370	.600	260	.342	471	.620	74.71	64.10	77.21	68.30	284.33	72.49
51	19	3	-	-	.420	.467	.594	239	.375	432	.677	68.68	70.19	70.82	74.63	284.32	72.49
23	-	1	-	-	.372	.469	.572	237	.414	389	.679	68.10	77.50	63.77	74.82	284.20	72.46
15	8	17	3	16	.318	.389	.585	260	.377	429	.622	74.71	70.61	70.33	68.52	284.17	72.45
13	-	6	-	-	.318	.401	.579	248	.395	409	.651	71.26	74.00	67.05	71.78	284.09	72.43
2	4	3	9	12	.324	.420	.630	244	.356	454	.662	70.11	66.55	74.43	72.83	283.93	72.39

Single Season Statistics

			The Greatest 300 Single Seasons and Others Listed by Total Offensive Production											
Rank	Player	Player Season	Year	G	AB	H	1B	2B	3B	HR	RUN	RBI	BB	SO
201	Ott, Mel	4th	1934	153	582	190	116	29	10	35	119	135	85	43
202	Thome, Jim**	1st	2002	147	480	146	73	19	2	52	101	118	122	139
203	Heilmann, Harry	1st	1923	144	524	211	138	44	11	18	121	115	74	40
204	Martinez, Edgar**	1st	1995	145	511	182	101	52	-	29	121	113	116	87
205	Stephens, Vern	1st	1949	155	610	177	105	31	2	39	113	159	101	73
206	Thomas, Frank **	2nd	1996	141	527	184	118	26	-	40	110	134	109	70
207	McCovey, Willie	1st	1969	149	491	157	84	26	2	45	101	126	121	66
208	Thome, Jim**	2nd	1996	151	505	157	86	28	5	38	122	116	123	141
209	Bagwell, Jeff**	5th	2001	161	600	173	87	43	4	39	126	130	106	135
210	Robinson, Frank	3rd	1961	153	545	176	100	32	7	37	117	124	71	64
211	Heilmann, Harry	2nd	1921	149	602	237	161	43	14	19	114	139	53	37
212	Duffy, Hugh	3rd	1891	121	511	174	132	23	10	9	124	110	61	29
213	Lynn, Fred	1st	1979	147	531	177	95	42	1	39	116	122	82	79
214	Rodriguez, Alex**	5th	2003	161	607	181	98	30	6	47	124	118	87	126
215	Speaker, Tris	2nd	1912	153	580	222	147	53	12	10	136	90	82	-
216	Ott, Mel	5th	1930	148	521	182	118	34	5	25	122	119	103	35
217	Gehringer, Charlie	1st	1936	154	641	227	140	60	12	15	144	116	83	13
218	Bonds, Barry **	9th	1997	159	532	155	84	26	5	40	123	101	145	87
219	Mays, Willie*	3rd	1961	154	572	176	101	32	3	40	129	123	81	77
220	Latham, Artie	1st	1887	136	627	198	151	35	10	2	163	83	45	-
221	Anderson, Brady**	1st	1996	149	579	172	80	37	5	50	117	110	76	106
222	Campanella, Roy	1st	1953	144	519	162	92	26	3	41	103	142	67	58
223	Conner, Roger	2nd	1889	131	496	157	95	32	17	13	117	130	93	46
224	Conner, Roger	3rd	1887	127	546	209	144	26	22	17	113	104	75	50
225	Williams, Ted*	8th	1940	144	561	193	113	43	14	23	134	113	96	54
226	Hornsby, Rogers	6th	1924	143	536	227	145	43	14	25	121	94	89	32
227	Bonds, Barry **	10th	1992	140	473	147	72	36	5	34	109	103	127	69
228	Thomas, Frank **	3rd	1994	113	399	141	68	34	1	38	106	101	109	61
229	Ramirez, Manny**	2nd	1998	150	571	168	86	35	2	45	108	145	76	121
230	Duffy, Hugh	4th	1897	134	554	189	145	23	10	11	131	129	52	-
231	Ramirez, Manny**	3rd	2000	118	439	154	80	34	2	38	92	122	86	117
232	Simmons, Al*	4th	1931	128	513	200	128	37	13	22	105	128	47	45
233	Mays, Willie*	4th	1954	151	565	195	108	33	13	41	119	110	66	57
234	Musial, Stan*	3rd	1954	153	591	195	110	41	9	35	120	126	103	39
235	Giambi, Jason**	3rd	2002	155	560	176	100	34	1	41	120	122	109	112
236	Musial, Stan*	4th	1953	157	593	200	108	53	9	30	127	113	105	32
237	Mays, Willie*	5th	1965	157	558	177	101	21	3	52	118	112	76	71
238	Berkman, Lance**	1st	2001	156	577	191	97	55	5	34	110	126	92	121
239	Burkett, Jesse	1st	1895	132	555	235	194	21	15	5	149	83	74	31
240	Guerrero, Vladimir**	1st	2004	156	612	206	126	39	2	39	124	126	52	74
241	Murphy, Dale	1st	1983	162	589	178	114	24	4	36	131	121	90	110
242	Hafey, Chick	1st	1930	120	446	150	73	39	12	26	108	107	46	51
243	Yastrzemski, Carl	1st	1967	161	579	189	110	31	4	44	112	121	91	69
244	Canseco, Jose	1st	1988	158	610	187	111	34	-	42	120	124	78	128
245	Thompson, Sam	4th	1893	130	583	220	162	33	14	11	130	126	50	17
246	Aaron, Hank	3rd	1959	154	629	223	131	46	7	39	116	123	51	54
247	Banks, Ernie	1st	1958	154	617	193	112	23	11	47	119	129	52	87
248	Rodriguez, Alex**	6th	1998	161	686	213	131	35	5	42	123	124	45	121
249	Duffy, Hugh	5th	1890	137	591	194	140	33	14	7	161	82	59	20
250	Aaron, Hank	4th	1957	151	615	198	121	27	6	44	118	132	57	58

The Greatest 300 Single Seasons and Others Listed by Total Offensive Production

SB	CS	HBP	SF	GDP	AVG	OBP	SLG	Total Offensive Production Statistics				TRP Rating	RPA Rating	TNB Rating	TBA Rating	TOP Composite	
								TRP	RPA	TNB	TBA					TOP	Rating
-	-	3	-	10	.326	.415	.591	254	.374	432	.635	72.99	69.99	70.82	70.02	283.82	72.36
1	2	5	6	5	.304	.445	.677	219	.354	451	.730	62.93	66.40	73.93	80.43	283.70	72.33
8	7	5	-	-	.403	.481	.632	236	.391	411	.682	67.82	73.34	67.38	75.12	283.65	72.32
4	3	8	4	11	.356	.479	.628	234	.360	446	.686	67.24	67.46	73.11	75.62	283.44	72.26
2	2	-	-	19	.290	.391	.539	272	.373	430	.589	78.16	69.82	70.49	64.92	283.39	72.25
1	1	5	8	25	.349	.459	.626	244	.362	444	.659	70.11	67.84	72.79	72.60	283.34	72.24
-	-	4	7	11	.320	.453	.656	227	.358	447	.705	65.23	67.09	73.28	77.71	283.31	72.23
2	2	6	2	13	.311	.450	.612	238	.367	438	.675	68.39	68.72	71.80	74.38	283.29	72.23
11	3	6	5	20	.288	.397	.568	256	.347	461	.626	73.56	65.09	75.57	68.94	283.16	72.20
22	3	10	10	15	.323	.404	.611	241	.370	433	.665	69.25	69.37	70.98	73.31	282.91	72.13
2	6	2	-	-	.394	.444	.606	253	.385	416	.633	72.70	72.16	68.20	69.79	282.84	72.11
83	-	4	-	-	.341	.415	.477	234	.406	392	.681	67.24	76.12	64.26	75.01	282.63	72.06
2	2	4	5	9	.333	.423	.637	238	.377	424	.672	68.39	70.68	69.51	74.06	282.63	72.06
17	3	15	6	16	.298	.396	.600	242	.331	480	.657	69.54	62.03	78.69	72.37	282.63	72.06
52	-	6	-	-	.383	.464	.567	226	.338	469	.702	64.94	63.40	76.89	77.38	282.60	72.05
9	-	2	-	-	.349	.458	.578	241	.385	415	.663	69.25	72.14	68.03	73.07	282.49	72.02
4	1	4	-	-	.354	.431	.555	260	.357	446	.613	74.71	66.92	73.11	67.52	282.27	71.97
37	8	8	5	13	.291	.446	.585	224	.319	493	.701	64.37	59.71	80.82	77.29	282.18	71.95
18	9	2	4	14	.308	.393	.584	252	.374	426	.633	72.41	70.16	69.84	69.76	282.18	71.94
129	-	5	-	-	.316	.366	.413	246	.363	438	.647	70.69	68.09	71.80	71.31	281.89	71.87
21	8	22	4	11	.297	.396	.637	227	.328	480	.694	65.23	61.47	78.69	76.45	281.84	71.86
4	2	4	-	13	.312	.395	.611	245	.406	390	.647	70.40	76.13	63.93	71.28	281.75	71.84
21	-	2	-	-	.317	.426	.528	247	.418	378	.640	70.98	78.31	61.97	70.49	281.75	71.83
43	-	8	-	-	.383	.464	.604	217	.345	456	.725	62.36	64.65	74.75	79.90	281.66	71.81
4	4	3	-	13	.344	.442	.594	247	.367	432	.642	70.98	68.77	70.82	70.75	281.31	71.72
5	12	2	-	-	.424	.507	.696	215	.343	457	.729	61.78	64.25	74.92	80.33	281.28	71.72
39	8	5	7	9	.311	.456	.624	212	.341	458	.738	60.92	63.97	75.08	81.29	281.26	71.71
2	3	2	7	15	.353	.487	.729	207	.389	401	.754	59.48	72.91	65.74	83.07	281.21	71.70
5	3	6	10	18	.294	.377	.599	253	.372	426	.626	72.70	69.61	69.84	68.94	281.10	71.67
45	-	6	-	-	.341	.404	.478	260	.425	368	.601	74.71	79.61	60.33	66.27	280.92	71.62
1	1	3	4	9	.351	.457	.697	214	.396	395	.730	61.49	74.12	64.75	80.47	280.84	71.60
3	3	3	-	-	.390	.444	.641	233	.414	379	.673	66.95	77.55	62.13	74.19	280.83	71.60
8	5	2	7	12	.345	.411	.667	229	.351	448	.687	65.80	65.81	73.44	75.73	280.79	71.59
1	4	4	7	20	.330	.428	.607	246	.339	463	.639	70.69	63.58	75.90	70.39	280.56	71.53
2	2	15	5	18	.314	.435	.598	242	.342	459	.649	69.54	64.14	75.25	71.55	280.48	71.51
3	7	-	-	10	.337	.437	.609	240	.339	462	.653	68.97	63.52	75.74	71.92	280.14	71.42
9	4	-	2	11	.317	.398	.645	230	.355	441	.682	66.09	66.61	72.30	75.12	280.12	71.42
7	9	13	6	8	.331	.430	.620	236	.339	461	.662	67.82	63.54	75.57	73.00	279.93	71.37
47	-	8	-	-	.423	.498	.542	232	.364	430	.675	66.67	68.25	70.49	74.40	279.80	71.34
15	3	8	8	19	.337	.391	.598	250	.358	438	.627	71.84	67.02	71.80	69.06	279.72	71.32
30	4	2	6	15	.302	.393	.540	252	.359	436	.621	72.41	67.27	71.48	68.45	279.61	71.29
12	-	7	-	-	.336	.407	.652	215	.431	356	.713	61.78	80.74	58.36	78.63	279.51	71.26
10	8	4	5	5	.326	.418	.622	233	.341	457	.668	66.95	63.83	74.92	73.64	279.34	71.22
40	16	10	6	15	.307	.391	.569	244	.339	459	.638	70.11	63.59	75.25	70.36	279.31	71.21
18	-	6	-	-	.377	.432	.539	256	.401	388	.607	73.56	75.07	63.61	66.92	279.16	71.17
8	-	4	9	19	.355	.401	.636	239	.336	463	.650	68.68	62.90	75.90	71.67	279.15	71.17
4	4	4	8	14	.313	.366	.614	248	.357	435	.626	71.26	66.86	71.31	68.98	278.42	70.99
46	13	10	4	12	.310	.360	.560	247	.326	472	.624	70.98	61.14	77.38	68.72	278.21	70.93
79	-	2	-	-	.328	.391	.467	243	.373	416	.638	69.83	69.84	68.20	70.32	278.18	70.93
1	1	-	3	13	.322	.378	.600	250	.363	426	.619	71.84	68.09	69.84	68.24	278.01	70.88

Single Season Statistics

The Greatest 300 Single Seasons and Others Listed by Total Offensive Production

Rank	Player	Player Season	Year	G	AB	H	1B	2B	3B	HR	RUN	RBI	BB	SO
251	Gehringer, Charlie	2nd	1934	154	601	214	146	50	7	11	134	127	99	25
252	DiMaggio, Joe*	6th	1936	138	637	206	118	44	15	29	132	125	24	39
253	Thomas, Frank **	4th	1997	146	530	184	114	35	-	35	110	125	109	69
254	Mays, Willie*	6th	1964	157	578	171	94	21	9	47	121	111	82	72
255	Gonzalez, Juan **	2nd	1996	134	541	170	88	33	2	47	89	144	45	82
256	Ordonez, Magglio**	1st	2002	153	590	189	103	47	1	38	116	135	53	77
257	Stargell, Willie	1st	1973	148	522	156	66	43	3	44	106	119	80	129
258	Mantle, Mickey	4th	1958	150	519	158	94	21	1	42	127	97	129	123
259	Martinez, Edgar**	2nd	2000	153	556	180	112	31	-	37	100	145	96	95
260	Bagwell, Jeff**	6th	1996	162	568	179	98	48	2	31	111	120	135	114
261	Musial, Stan*	5th	1951	152	578	205	131	30	12	32	124	108	98	40
262	Hafey, Chick	2nd	1929	134	517	175	90	47	9	29	101	125	45	42
263	Thomas, Frank **	5th	1993	153	549	174	97	36	-	41	106	128	112	54
264	Holmes, Tommy	1st	1945	154	636	224	143	47	6	28	125	117	70	9
265	Stargell, Willie	2nd	1971	141	511	151	77	26	-	48	104	125	83	154
266	Cepeda, Orlando	1st	1961	152	585	182	104	28	4	46	105	142	39	91
267	Keeler, Willie	1st	1896	127	546	214	175	22	13	4	154	82	37	82
268	Gehrig, Lou	12th	1926	155	572	179	96	47	20	16	135	112	105	73
269	Yastrzemski, Carl	2nd	1970	161	566	186	117	29	-	40	125	102	128	66
270	Heilmann, Harry	3rd	1927	141	505	201	128	50	9	14	106	120	72	16
271	Averill, Earl	3rd	1934	154	598	187	102	48	6	31	128	113	99	44
272	Klein, Chuck	4th	1931	148	594	200	125	34	10	31	121	121	59	49
273	McCovey, Willie	2nd	1970	152	495	143	63	39	2	39	98	126	137	75
274	Keeler, Willie	2nd	1894	128	593	218	166	25	22	5	164	94	40	94
275	Davis, Tommy	1st	1962	163	665	230	167	27	9	27	120	153	33	65
276	Thome, Jim**	3rd	2001	156	526	153	77	26	1	49	101	124	111	185
277	Greenberg, Hank*	6th	1939	138	500	156	74	42	7	33	112	112	91	95
278	Palmiero, Rafael**	2nd	1996	162	626	181	100	40	2	39	110	142	95	96
279	Delgado, Carlos**	3rd	1999	152	573	156	73	39	-	44	113	134	86	141
280	Burkett, Jesse	2nd	1893	124	480	179	135	23	15	6	144	82	98	23
281	Rice, Jim	2nd	1979	158	619	201	117	39	6	39	117	130	57	97
282	Thome, Jim**	4th	2003	159	578	154	74	30	3	47	111	131	111	182
283	Medwick, Joe	2nd	1935	154	634	224	142	46	13	23	132	126	30	59
284	Speaker, Tris	3rd	1920	150	552	214	145	50	11	8	137	107	97	13
285	Ott, Mel	6th	1938	150	527	164	99	23	6	36	116	116	118	47
286	Bottomley, Jim	2nd	1929	146	560	176	104	31	12	29	108	137	70	54
287	Kelley, Joe	4th	1897	129	503	196	151	31	9	5	113	118	70	-
288	Simmons, Al*	5th	1925	153	658	253	174	43	12	24	122	129	35	41
289	Guerrero, Vladimir**	2nd	2000	154	571	197	114	28	11	44	101	123	58	74
290	Hamilton, Billy	3rd	1889	137	532	160	127	15	15	3	145	77	87	41
291	Ramirez, Manny**	4th	2004	152	568	175	88	44	-	43	108	130	82	124
292	Cobb, Ty	3rd	1909	156	573	216	164	33	10	9	116	107	48	-
293	Pujols, Albert**	3rd	2001	161	590	194	106	47	4	37	112	130	69	93
294	Mantle, Mickey	5th	1955	147	517	158	85	25	11	37	121	99	113	97
295	Jennings, Hughie	3rd	1894	128	505	168	117	27	20	4	136	109	37	17
296	Mitchell, Kevin	1st	1989	154	543	158	71	34	6	47	100	125	87	115
297	Piazza, Mike**	1st	1997	152	556	201	128	32	1	40	104	124	69	77
298	Schmidt, Mike	1st	1980	150	548	157	76	25	8	48	104	121	89	119
299	Keeler, Willie	3rd	1897	128	562	243	199	25	19	-	147	74	35	74
300	York, Rudy	1st	1940	155	588	186	101	46	6	33	105	134	89	88

Single Season Statistics

The Greatest 300 Single Seasons and Others Listed by Total Offensive Production

SB	CS	HBP	SF	GDP	AVG	OBP	SLG	TRP	RPA	TNB	TBA	TRP Rating	RPA Rating	TNB Rating	TBA Rating	TOP	Rating
11	8	3	-	-	.356	.450	.517	261	.371	416	.592	75.00	69.57	68.20	65.22	277.98	70.87
4	-	4	-	-	.323	.352	.576	257	.386	399	.600	73.85	72.42	65.41	66.13	277.81	70.83
1	1	3	7	15	.347	.456	.611	235	.354	436	.657	67.53	66.32	71.48	72.37	277.69	70.80
19	5	1	3	11	.296	.383	.607	232	.344	448	.664	66.67	64.40	73.44	73.15	277.66	70.79
2	-	3	3	10	.314	.368	.643	233	.387	398	.661	66.95	72.52	65.25	72.87	277.59	70.77
7	5	7	3	21	.320	.381	.597	251	.372	414	.614	72.13	69.78	67.87	67.70	277.48	70.74
-	-	3	4	6	.299	.392	.646	225	.366	420	.683	64.66	68.55	68.85	75.27	277.33	70.71
18	3	2	2	11	.304	.443	.592	224	.338	453	.683	64.37	63.31	74.26	75.30	277.24	70.69
3	-	5	8	13	.324	.423	.579	245	.361	426	.628	70.40	67.71	69.84	69.25	277.20	70.67
21	7	10	6	15	.315	.451	.570	231	.315	483	.658	66.38	58.97	79.18	72.53	277.06	70.64
4	7	1	-	6	.355	.449	.614	232	.340	451	.660	66.67	63.65	73.93	72.78	277.03	70.63
7	-	2	-	-	.338	.394	.632	226	.401	381	.676	64.94	75.09	62.46	74.45	276.94	70.61
4	2	2	13	10	.317	.426	.607	234	.341	449	.655	67.24	63.92	73.61	72.14	276.90	70.60
15	-	4	-	11	.352	.420	.577	242	.336	456	.632	69.54	62.89	74.75	69.71	276.89	70.60
-	-	7	5	8	.295	.398	.628	229	.373	411	.669	65.80	69.89	67.38	73.78	276.84	70.58
12	8	9	3	21	.311	.362	.609	247	.376	408	.621	70.98	70.45	66.89	68.44	276.75	70.56
73	9	7	-	-	.392	.437	.502	236	.400	382	.647	67.82	74.95	62.62	71.36	276.75	70.56
6	5	1	-	-	.313	.420	.549	247	.364	421	.621	70.98	68.26	69.02	68.44	276.69	70.55
23	13	1	2	12	.329	.452	.592	227	.320	474	.669	65.23	59.99	77.70	73.68	276.61	70.52
11	5	2	-	-	.398	.475	.616	226	.390	391	.675	64.94	73.14	64.10	74.43	276.61	70.52
5	3	4	-	-	.313	.414	.569	241	.344	445	.635	69.25	64.42	72.95	69.96	276.59	70.52
7	-	1	-	-	.337	.398	.584	242	.370	414	.633	69.54	69.34	67.87	69.77	276.51	70.50
-	-	3	3	13	.289	.444	.612	224	.344	443	.680	64.37	64.48	72.62	75.00	276.47	70.49
30	6	18	-	-	.368	.424	.509	258	.396	384	.590	74.14	74.26	62.95	65.01	276.36	70.46
18	6	2	8	17	.346	.374	.535	273	.377	403	.556	78.45	70.56	66.07	61.26	276.34	70.45
-	1	4	3	9	.291	.416	.624	225	.345	442	.677	64.66	64.56	72.46	74.60	276.28	70.44
8	3	2	-	8	.312	.420	.622	224	.373	409	.681	64.37	69.84	67.05	75.00	276.26	70.44
8	-	3	8	9	.289	.381	.546	252	.340	448	.605	72.41	63.72	73.44	66.63	276.22	70.42
1	1	15	7	11	.272	.377	.571	247	.357	428	.618	70.98	66.88	70.16	68.17	276.19	70.42
39	-	7	-	-	.373	.485	.521	226	.386	394	.674	64.94	72.39	64.59	74.23	276.15	70.41
9	4	4	8	16	.325	.381	.596	247	.351	435	.618	70.98	65.74	71.31	68.10	276.13	70.40
-	3	4	5	5	.266	.385	.573	242	.344	443	.630	69.54	64.50	72.62	69.45	276.12	70.40
4	-	4	-	15	.353	.386	.576	258	.378	403	.590	74.14	70.78	66.07	65.03	276.02	70.37
10	13	5	-	-	.388	.483	.562	244	.373	409	.625	70.11	69.91	67.05	68.93	276.00	70.37
2	-	5	-	8	.311	.442	.583	232	.353	432	.657	66.67	66.07	70.82	72.36	275.91	70.35
3	-	1	-	-	.314	.391	.568	245	.388	392	.621	70.40	72.76	64.26	68.47	275.89	70.34
44	-	7	-	-	.390	.471	.517	231	.398	381	.657	66.38	74.63	62.46	72.40	275.87	70.33
7	14	1	-	-	.384	.416	.596	251	.362	421	.607	72.13	67.77	69.02	66.86	275.77	70.31
9	10	8	4	15	.345	.410	.664	224	.341	444	.677	64.37	63.98	72.79	74.60	275.73	70.30
117	-	14	-	-	.301	.412	.402	222	.351	432	.682	63.79	65.72	70.82	75.22	275.55	70.25
2	4	6	7	17	.308	.397	.613	238	.350	434	.638	68.39	65.58	71.15	70.34	275.46	70.23
76	-	6	-	-	.377	.431	.517	223	.356	426	.679	64.08	66.64	69.84	74.88	275.44	70.23
1	3	9	7	21	.329	.403	.610	242	.348	436	.626	69.54	65.15	71.48	69.04	275.21	70.17
8	1	3	3	4	.306	.431	.611	220	.344	439	.686	63.22	64.41	71.97	75.60	275.20	70.16
36	-	27	-	-	.333	.408	.489	245	.431	347	.610	70.40	80.68	56.89	67.21	275.18	70.16
3	4	3	7	6	.291	.388	.635	225	.348	434	.672	64.66	65.26	71.15	74.04	275.11	70.14
5	1	3	5	18	.362	.431	.638	228	.350	431	.662	65.52	65.63	70.66	72.97	274.77	70.05
12	5	2	13	6	.286	.380	.624	225	.342	440	.669	64.66	64.07	72.13	73.70	274.56	70.00
63	-	7	-	-	.432	.472	.544	221	.366	411	.680	63.51	68.56	67.38	75.00	274.44	69.97
3	2	4	-	12	.316	.410	.583	239	.345	437	.631	68.68	64.62	71.64	69.50	274.44	69.97

Single Season Statistics

Rank	Player	Player Season	Year	G	AB	H	1B	2B	3B	HR	RUN	RBI	BB	SO
301	Henderson, Rickey	1st	1985	143	547	172	115	28	5	24	146	72	99	65
302	Bell, George	1st	1987	156	610	188	105	32	4	47	111	134	39	75
303	Vaughn, Greg	1st	1998	158	573	156	74	28	4	50	112	119	79	121
304	Keeler, Willie	4th	1895	131	560	221	179	23	15	4	161	78	37	78
305	Robinson, Jackie	1st	1949	156	593	203	137	38	12	16	122	124	86	27
306	Perez, Tony	1st	1970	158	587	186	112	28	6	40	107	129	83	134
307	Fielder, Cecil	1st	1990	159	573	159	82	25	1	51	104	132	90	182
308	Allen, Dick	1st	1966	141	524	166	91	25	10	40	112	110	68	136
309	Bench, Johnny	1st	1970	158	605	177	93	35	4	45	97	148	54	102
310	Castilla, Vinny**	1st	1998	162	645	206	128	28	4	46	108	144	40	89
311	Cronin, Joe	1st	1930	154	587	203	140	41	9	13	127	126	72	36
312	McGwire, Mark	4th	1997	156	540	148	63	27	-	58	86	123	101	159
313	Jackson, Joe	1st	1911	147	571	233	162	45	19	7	126	83	56	-
314	Yount, Robin	1st	1982	156	635	210	123	46	12	29	129	114	54	63
315	Waner, Paul	1st	1927	155	623	237	168	42	18	9	114	131	60	14
316	Beltre, Adrian**	1st	2004	156	598	200	120	32	-	48	104	121	53	87
317	Mattingly, Don	1st	1985	159	652	211	125	48	3	35	107	145	56	41
318	Jeter, Derek**	1st	1999	158	627	219	149	37	9	24	134	102	91	116
319	Keller, Charlie*	1st	1941	140	507	151	84	24	10	33	102	122	102	65
320	Belle, Albert	4th	1994	106	412	147	74	35	2	36	90	101	58	71
321	Bichette, Dante	1st	1996	159	633	198	125	39	3	31	114	141	45	105
322	Williams, Ted*	9th	1957	132	420	163	96	28	1	38	96	87	119	43
323	Burkett, Jesse	3rd	1896	133	585	240	192	26	16	6	159	72	49	19
324	Brett, George	1st	1980	117	449	175	109	33	9	24	87	118	58	22
325	Meusel, Bob	1st	1921	149	598	190	110	40	16	24	104	135	34	88
326	Johnson, Robert	1st	1939	150	544	184	122	30	9	23	115	114	99	59
327	Martinez, Tino**	1st	1997	158	594	176	99	31	2	44	96	141	75	75
328	Berger, Wally	1st	1930	151	555	172	93	27	14	38	98	119	54	69
329	Killebrew, Harmon	2nd	1961	150	541	156	83	20	7	46	94	122	107	109
330	Carew, Rod	1st	1977	155	616	239	171	38	16	14	128	100	69	55
331	Olerud, John	1st	1993	158	551	200	120	54	2	24	109	107	114	65
332	Crawford, Sam	1st	1911	146	574	217	160	36	14	7	109	115	61	-
333	Wagner, Honus	1st	1908	151	568	201	133	39	19	10	100	109	54	-
334	Williams, Bernie**	1st	2000	141	537	165	92	37	6	30	108	121	71	84
335	Vaughan, Arky	1st	1935	137	499	192	129	34	10	19	108	99	97	18
336	Appling, Luke	1st	1936	138	526	204	160	31	7	6	111	128	85	25
337	McGraw, John	2nd	1899	117	399	156	139	13	3	1	156	33	124	-
338	Parker, Dave	1st	1978	148	581	194	120	32	12	30	102	117	57	92
339	Sheckard, Jimmy	1st	1901	133	554	196	137	29	19	11	116	104	47	-
340	Dickey, Bill*	1st	1936	112	423	153	97	26	8	22	99	107	46	16
341	Anson, Cap	2nd	1887	122	532	224	171	33	13	7	107	102	60	18
342	Garciaparra, Nomar**	1st	1998	143	604	195	115	37	8	35	111	122	33	62
343	Hartnett, Gabby	1st	1930	141	508	172	101	31	3	37	84	122	55	62
344	Heath, Jeff	1st	1938	126	502	172	102	31	18	21	104	112	33	55
345	Minoso, Minnie	1st	1954	153	568	182	116	29	18	19	119	116	77	46
346	Kelly, King	2nd	1887	114	525	207	154	34	11	8	119	63	55	40
347	Howard, Frank	1st	1969	161	592	175	108	17	2	48	111	111	102	96
348	Torre, Joe	1st	1971	161	634	230	164	34	8	24	97	137	63	70
349	Berra, Yogi	1st	1950	151	597	192	128	30	6	28	116	124	55	12
350	Seymour, Cy	1st	1905	149	581	219	150	40	21	8	95	121	51	-

The Greatest 300 Single Seasons and Others Listed by Total Offensive Production

SB	CS	HBP	SF	GDP	AVG	OBP	SLG	TRP	RPA	TNB	TBA	TRP Rating	RPA Rating	TNB Rating	TBA Rating	TOP	Rating
80	10	3	5	8	.314	.419	.516	218	.329	454	.686	62.64	61.71	74.43	75.58	274.36	69.95
5	1	7	9	17	.308	.352	.605	245	.359	419	.614	70.40	67.31	68.69	67.71	274.12	69.89
11	4	5	4	7	.272	.363	.597	231	.346	433	.648	66.38	64.80	70.98	71.44	273.60	69.76
57	12	14	-	-	.395	.445	.511	239	.391	382	.625	68.68	73.30	62.62	68.91	273.50	69.73
37	14	8	-	22	.342	.432	.528	246	.347	430	.606	70.69	65.02	70.49	66.84	273.04	69.61
8	3	4	7	15	.317	.401	.589	236	.339	438	.629	67.82	63.54	71.80	69.36	272.52	69.48
-	1	5	5	15	.277	.377	.592	236	.343	433	.629	67.82	64.28	70.98	69.36	272.44	69.46
10	6	3	4	9	.317	.396	.632	222	.365	406	.668	63.79	68.42	66.56	73.60	272.37	69.44
5	2	-	11	12	.293	.345	.587	245	.359	412	.604	70.40	67.31	67.54	66.58	271.84	69.31
5	9	6	6	24	.319	.362	.589	252	.350	422	.585	72.41	65.49	69.18	64.51	271.59	69.25
17	10	5	-	-	.346	.422	.513	253	.381	385	.580	72.70	71.40	63.11	63.90	271.12	69.12
3	-	9	7	9	.274	.393	.646	209	.314	462	.694	60.06	58.80	75.74	76.45	271.05	69.11
41	-	8	-	-	.408	.468	.590	209	.329	442	.696	60.06	61.67	72.46	76.72	270.91	69.07
14	3	1	10	19	.331	.379	.578	243	.338	433	.602	69.83	63.33	70.98	66.37	270.51	68.97
5	-	3	-	-	.380	.437	.549	245	.357	410	.598	70.40	66.92	67.21	65.87	270.41	68.94
7	2	2	4	15	.334	.388	.629	225	.335	436	.649	64.66	62.74	71.48	71.51	270.38	68.94
2	2	2	15	15	.324	.371	.567	252	.341	428	.578	72.41	63.81	70.16	63.75	270.13	68.87
19	8	12	6	12	.349	.438	.552	236	.316	460	.615	67.82	59.12	75.41	67.78	270.13	68.87
6	4	1	-	3	.298	.416	.580	224	.365	399	.651	64.37	68.47	65.41	71.74	269.99	68.84
9	6	5	4	5	.357	.438	.714	191	.395	360	.744	54.89	73.95	59.02	81.98	269.83	68.79
31	12	6	10	18	.313	.359	.531	255	.358	406	.570	73.28	67.11	66.56	62.85	269.79	68.79
-	1	5	2	11	.388	.526	.731	183	.329	430	.772	52.59	61.56	70.49	85.08	269.73	68.77
32	-	7	-	-	.410	.462	.540	231	.360	404	.630	66.38	67.53	66.23	69.46	269.60	68.74
15	6	1	7	11	.390	.454	.664	205	.390	366	.696	58.91	73.03	60.00	76.69	268.63	68.49
17	6	2	-	-	.318	.356	.559	239	.377	381	.601	68.68	70.64	62.46	66.23	268.01	68.33
15	5	-	-	12	.338	.440	.553	229	.350	410	.626	65.80	65.51	67.21	68.99	267.52	68.21
3	1	3	13	15	.296	.371	.577	237	.339	423	.604	68.10	63.44	69.34	66.60	267.49	68.20
3	-	4	-	-	.310	.375	.614	217	.354	402	.656	62.36	66.33	65.90	72.28	266.87	68.04
1	2	3	5	11	.288	.405	.606	216	.324	437	.655	62.07	60.68	71.64	72.21	266.60	67.97
23	13	3	5	6	.388	.449	.570	228	.326	433	.619	65.52	61.12	70.98	68.27	265.89	67.79
-	2	7	7	12	.363	.473	.599	216	.313	449	.650	62.07	58.57	73.61	71.62	265.86	67.78
37	-	-	-	-	.378	.438	.526	224	.353	400	.630	64.37	66.10	65.57	69.43	265.47	67.68
53	-	5	-	-	.354	.415	.542	209	.333	420	.670	60.06	62.46	68.85	73.83	265.20	67.61
13	5	5	3	15	.307	.391	.566	229	.363	388	.615	65.80	68.00	63.61	67.77	265.19	67.61
4	-	7	-	5	.385	.491	.607	207	.340	411	.676	59.48	63.80	67.38	74.50	265.16	67.60
10	6	-	-	-	.388	.473	.508	239	.391	356	.583	68.68	73.30	58.36	64.22	264.55	67.45
73	-	14	-	-	.391	.547	.446	189	.352	389	.724	54.31	65.95	63.77	79.84	263.87	67.28
20	7	2	2	8	.334	.394	.585	219	.337	412	.634	62.93	63.13	67.54	69.86	263.46	67.17
35	-	3	-	-	.354	.407	.534	220	.364	381	.631	63.22	68.25	62.46	69.52	263.45	67.17
-	2	3	-	-	.362	.428	.617	206	.436	308	.653	59.20	81.78	50.49	71.92	263.39	67.15
27	-	1	-	-	.421	.481	.571	209	.352	392	.661	60.06	66.04	64.26	72.86	263.22	67.11
12	6	8	7	20	.323	.362	.584	233	.347	400	.595	66.95	64.97	65.57	65.60	263.10	67.08
-	-	1	-	-	.339	.404	.630	206	.365	376	.667	59.20	68.44	61.64	73.48	262.75	66.99
3	1	-	-	-	.343	.383	.602	216	.404	337	.630	62.07	75.65	55.25	69.42	262.39	66.90
18	11	16	8	20	.320	.411	.535	235	.341	404	.586	67.53	63.91	66.23	64.62	262.29	66.87
84	-	1	-	-	.394	.453	.547	182	.313	427	.735	52.30	58.70	70.00	81.00	262.00	66.80
1	-	5	3	29	.296	.402	.574	222	.304	448	.613	63.79	56.91	73.44	67.55	261.69	66.72
4	1	4	5	18	.363	.421	.555	234	.323	422	.583	67.24	60.56	69.18	64.24	261.23	66.60
4	2	1	-	11	.322	.380	.533	240	.361	376	.566	68.97	67.73	61.64	62.41	260.74	66.48
21	-	2	-	-	.377	.429	.559	216	.341	399	.629	62.07	63.84	65.41	69.36	260.68	66.46

Single Season Statistics

The Greatest 300 Single Seasons and Others Listed by Total Offensive Production

Rank	Player	Player Season	Year	G	AB	H	1B	2B	3B	HR	RUN	RBI	BB	SO	
351	Boggs, Wade	1st	1987	147	551	200	130	40	6	24	108	105	105	48	
352	Murray, Eddie	1st	1985	156	583	173	104	37	1	31	111	124	84	68	
353	Cobb, Ty	4th	1912	140	553	227	167	30	23	7	119	83	43	-	
354	Kingman, Dave	1st	1979	145	532	153	81	19	5	48	97	115	45	131	
355	Dawson, Andre	1st	1987	153	621	178	103	24	2	49	90	137	32	103	
356	Erstad, Darin**	1st	2000	157	676	240	170	39	6	25	121	100	64	82	
357	Sievers, Roy	1st	1957	152	572	172	102	23	5	42	99	114	76	55	
358	Winfield, Dave	1st	1979	159	597	184	113	27	10	34	97	118	85	71	
359	Kaline, Al	1st	1955	152	588	200	141	24	8	27	121	102	82	57	
360	Kelly, George	1st	1924	144	571	185	118	37	9	21	91	136	38	52	
361	Manush, Heinie	1st	1928	154	638	241	161	47	20	13	104	106	39	14	
362	Cravath, Gavy	1st	1913	147	525	179	112	34	14	19	78	128	55	63	
363	Ripkin, Cal, Jr.	1st	1991	162	650	210	125	46	5	34	99	114	53	46	
364	Collins, Eddie	1st	1912	153	543	189	153	25	11	-	137	64	101	-	
365	McGriff, Fred **	1st	1993	151	557	162	94	29	2	37	111	101	76	106	
366	Zimmerman, Heinie	1st	1912	145	557	207	138	41	14	14	95	99	38	60	
367	English, Woody	1st	1930	156	638	214	147	36	17	14	152	59	100	72	
368	Clemente, Roberto	1st	1966	154	638	202	131	31	11	29	105	119	46	109	
369	Puckett, Kirby	1st	1988	158	657	234	163	42	5	24	109	121	23	83	
370	Traynor, Pie	1st	1930	130	497	182	140	22	11	9	90	119	48	19	
371	Oliva, Tony	1st	1964	161	672	217	133	43	9	32	109	94	34	68	
372	Tucker, Tuck	1st	1894	80	339	141	110	21	9	1	91	82	23	13	
373	Carty, Rico	1st	1970	136	478	175	124	23	3	25	84	101	77	46	
374	Rose, Pete	1st	1969	156	627	218	158	33	11	16	120	82	88	65	
375	Wheat, Zack	1st	1922	152	600	201	144	29	12	16	92	112	45	22	
376	Gwynn, Tony	1st	1987	157	589	218	162	36	13	7	119	54	82	35	
377	Burkett, Jesse	4th	1899	138	567	228	194	17	10	7	115	71	67	-	
378	Suzuki, Ichiro**	1st	2001	157	692	242	192	34	8	8	127	69	30	53	
379	Dunlap, Fred	1st	1884	101	449	185	125	39	8	13	160	-	29	-	
380	Suzuki, Ichiro**	2nd	2004	161	704	262	225	24	5	8	101	60	49	63	

* Player missed time for military service

** Active player. Statistics through 2004 season

TOP ranking for players with less than 70% rating is based upon comparison to listed players only.

The Greatest 300 Single Seasons and Others Listed by Total Offensive Production

SB	CS	HBP	SF	GDP	AVG	OBP	SLG	Total Offensive Production Statistics				TRP Rating	RPA Rating	TNB Rating	TBA Rating	TOP Composite	
								TRP	RPA	TNB	TBA					TOP	Rating
1	3	2	8	13	.363	.461	.588	213	.314	429	.632	61.21	58.78	70.33	69.63	259.95	66.28
5	2	2	8	8	.297	.383	.523	235	.343	394	.575	67.53	64.28	64.59	63.39	259.80	66.24
61	34	5	-	-	.410	.458	.586	202	.336	399	.664	58.05	62.98	65.41	73.17	259.61	66.19
4	2	4	8	7	.288	.343	.613	212	.356	377	.633	60.92	66.65	61.80	69.72	259.09	66.06
11	3	7	2	15	.287	.328	.568	227	.335	400	.591	65.23	62.83	65.57	65.12	258.75	65.97
28	8	1	4	8	.355	.409	.541	221	.293	451	.599	63.51	55.00	73.93	66.01	258.45	65.89
1	1	7	2	9	.301	.388	.579	213	.320	414	.622	61.21	59.93	67.87	68.51	257.52	65.66
15	9	2	2	9	.308	.395	.558	215	.309	426	.613	61.78	57.97	69.84	67.56	257.14	65.56
6	8	5	6	13	.340	.421	.546	223	.321	406	.585	64.08	60.21	66.56	64.48	255.33	65.10
7	2	5	-	-	.324	.371	.531	227	.370	351	.572	65.23	69.28	57.54	63.01	255.05	65.03
17	5	-	-	-	.378	.414	.575	210	.310	418	.617	60.34	58.12	68.52	68.05	255.04	65.03
10	-	3	-	-	.341	.407	.568	206	.353	366	.628	59.20	66.21	60.00	69.19	254.60	64.91
6	1	5	9	19	.323	.374	.566	213	.289	431	.586	61.21	54.23	70.66	64.54	250.63	63.90
63	-	-	-	-	.348	.450	.435	201	.312	400	.621	57.76	58.48	65.57	68.46	250.27	63.81
5	3	2	5	14	.291	.375	.549	212	.324	386	.590	60.92	60.74	63.28	65.05	249.99	63.74
23	-	6	-	-	.372	.418	.571	194	.323	385	.641	55.75	60.49	63.11	70.60	249.95	63.73
3	-	6	-	-	.335	.430	.511	211	.284	435	.585	60.63	53.14	71.31	64.44	249.53	63.62
7	5	-	5	14	.317	.360	.536	224	.319	390	.555	64.37	59.71	63.93	61.14	249.15	63.52
6	7	2	9	17	.356	.375	.545	230	.325	382	.540	66.09	60.87	62.62	59.47	249.05	63.50
7	-	1	-	-	.366	.423	.509	209	.383	309	.566	60.06	71.73	50.66	62.37	244.81	62.42
12	6	6	3	9	.323	.359	.557	203	.280	420	.580	58.33	52.54	68.85	63.94	243.66	62.12
11	-	2	-	-	.416	.456	.540	173	.475	219	.602	49.71	89.06	35.90	66.31	240.98	61.44
1	2	2	3	19	.366	.454	.584	185	.320	357	.617	53.16	59.87	58.52	67.96	239.51	61.07
7	10	5	6	13	.348	.428	.512	202	.273	411	.556	58.05	51.22	67.38	61.30	237.94	60.66
9	6	7	-	-	.335	.388	.503	204	.313	357	.548	58.62	58.63	58.52	60.35	236.12	60.20
56	12	3	4	13	.370	.447	.511	173	.250	430	.622	49.71	46.91	70.49	68.58	235.70	60.09
22	-	2	-	-	.402	.467	.504	186	.292	377	.593	53.45	54.80	61.80	65.33	235.38	60.01
56	14	8	4	3	.350	.381	.457	196	.266	396	.537	56.32	49.83	64.92	59.22	230.29	58.72
-	-	-	-	-	.412	.448	.621	160	.335	308	.644	45.98	62.72	50.49	71.02	230.21	58.69
36	11	4	3	6	.372	.414	.455	161	.210	398	.520	46.26	39.38	65.25	57.27	208.16	53.07

Single Season Statistics

The Greatest 300 Single Seasons and Others Listed Alphabetically

Rank	Player	Player Season	Year	G	AB	H	1B	2B	3B	HR	RUN	RBI	BB	SO
166	Aaron, Hank	1st	1962	156	592	191	112	28	6	45	127	128	66	73
173	Aaron, Hank	2nd	1963	161	631	201	124	29	4	44	121	130	78	94
246	Aaron, Hank	3rd	1959	154	629	223	131	46	7	39	116	123	51	54
250	Aaron, Hank	4th	1957	151	615	198	121	27	6	44	118	132	57	58
308	Allen, Dick	1st	1966	141	524	166	91	25	10	40	112	110	68	136
192	Alomar, Roberto**	1st	1999	159	563	182	115	40	3	24	138	120	99	96
221	Anderson, Brady**	1st	1996	149	579	172	80	37	5	50	117	110	76	106
131	Anson, Cap	1st	1886	125	504	187	132	34	11	10	117	147	55	19
341	Anson, Cap	2nd	1887	122	532	224	171	33	13	7	107	102	60	18
336	Appling, Luke	1st	1936	138	526	204	160	31	7	6	111	128	85	25
116	Averill, Earl	1st	1931	155	627	209	131	36	10	32	140	143	68	38
126	Averill, Earl	2nd	1936	152	614	232	150	39	15	28	136	126	65	35
271	Averill, Earl	3rd	1934	154	598	187	102	48	6	31	128	113	99	44
76	Bagwell, Jeff**	1st	2000	159	590	183	98	37	1	47	152	132	107	116
86	Bagwell, Jeff**	2nd	1999	162	562	171	94	35	-	42	143	126	149	127
124	Bagwell, Jeff**	3rd	1994	110	400	147	74	32	2	39	104	116	65	65
148	Bagwell, Jeff**	4th	1997	162	566	162	77	40	2	43	109	135	127	122
209	Bagwell, Jeff**	5th	2001	161	600	173	87	43	4	39	126	130	106	135
260	Bagwell, Jeff**	6th	1996	162	568	179	98	48	2	31	111	120	135	114
247	Banks, Ernie	1st	1958	154	617	193	112	23	11	47	119	129	52	87
302	Bell, George	1st	1987	156	610	188	105	32	4	47	111	134	39	75
90	Belle, Albert	1st	1996	158	602	187	98	38	3	48	124	148	99	87
110	Belle, Albert	2nd	1998	163	609	200	101	48	2	49	113	152	81	84
125	Belle, Albert	3rd	1995	143	546	173	70	52	1	50	121	126	73	80
320	Belle, Albert	4th	1994	106	412	147	74	35	2	36	90	101	58	71
316	Beltre, Adrian**	1st	2004	156	598	200	120	32	-	48	104	121	53	87
309	Bench, Johnny	1st	1970	158	605	177	93	35	4	45	97	148	54	102
328	Berger, Wally	1st	1930	151	555	172	93	27	14	38	98	119	54	69
238	Berkman, Lance**	1st	2001	156	577	191	97	55	5	34	110	126	92	121
349	Berra, Yogi	1st	1950	151	597	192	128	30	6	28	116	124	55	12
321	Bichette, Dante	1st	1996	159	633	198	125	39	3	31	114	141	45	105
351	Boggs, Wade	1st	1987	147	551	200	130	40	6	24	108	105	105	48
8	Bonds, Barry **	1st	2001	153	476	156	49	32	2	73	129	137	177	93
38	Bonds, Barry **	2nd	2004	147	373	135	60	27	3	45	129	101	232	41
46	Bonds, Barry **	3rd	2002	143	403	149	70	31	2	46	117	110	198	47
75	Bonds, Barry **	4th	1993	159	539	181	93	38	4	46	129	123	126	79
85	Bonds, Barry **	5th	1996	158	517	159	87	27	3	42	122	129	151	76
114	Bonds, Barry **	6th	2000	143	480	147	66	28	4	49	129	106	117	77
143	Bonds, Barry **	7th	2003	130	390	133	65	22	1	45	111	90	148	58
152	Bonds, Barry **	8th	1998	156	552	167	79	44	7	37	120	122	130	92
218	Bonds, Barry **	9th	1997	159	532	155	84	26	5	40	123	101	145	87
227	Bonds, Barry **	10th	1992	140	473	147	72	36	5	34	109	103	127	69
108	Bottomley, Jim	1st	1928	149	576	187	94	42	20	31	123	136	71	54
286	Bottomley, Jim	2nd	1929	146	560	176	104	31	12	29	108	137	70	54
324	Brett, George	1st	1980	117	449	175	109	33	9	24	87	118	58	22
97	Brouthers, Dan	1st	1887	122	570	239	172	35	20	12	153	101	71	9
103	Brouthers, Dan	2nd	1894	123	528	182	115	33	25	9	137	128	67	9
133	Brown, Tom	1st	1891	137	589	189	133	30	21	5	177	72	70	96
63	Browning, Pete	1st	1887	134	547	220	165	35	16	4	137	118	55	-
239	Burkett, Jesse	1st	1895	132	555	235	194	21	15	5	149	83	74	31

The Greatest 300 Single Seasons and Others Listed Alphabetically

SB	CS	HBP	SF	GDP	AVG	OBP	SLG	TRP	RPA	TNB	TBA	TRP Rating	RPA Rating	TNB Rating	TBA Rating	TOP	Rating
15	7	3	6	14	.323	.390	.618	255	.374	443	.651	73.28	70.16	72.62	71.70	287.76	73.37
31	5	-	5	11	.319	.391	.586	251	.346	474	.654	72.13	64.87	77.70	72.06	286.76	73.11
8	-	4	9	19	.355	.401	.636	239	.336	463	.650	68.68	62.90	75.90	71.67	279.15	71.17
1	1	-	3	13	.322	.378	.600	250	.363	426	.619	71.84	68.09	69.84	68.24	278.01	70.88
10	6	3	4	9	.317	.396	.632	222	.365	406	.668	63.79	68.42	66.56	73.60	272.37	69.44
37	6	7	13	13	.323	.422	.533	258	.371	437	.629	74.14	69.56	71.64	69.30	284.64	72.57
21	8	22	4	11	.297	.396	.637	227	.328	480	.694	65.23	61.47	78.69	76.45	281.84	71.86
29	-	-	-	-	.371	.433	.542	264	.472	357	.639	75.86	88.50	58.52	70.39	293.27	74.77
27	-	1	-	-	.421	.481	.571	209	.352	392	.661	60.06	66.04	64.26	72.86	263.22	67.11
10	6	-	-	-	.388	.473	.508	239	.391	356	.583	68.68	73.30	58.36	64.22	264.55	67.45
9	9	6	-	-	.333	.404	.576	283	.404	435	.621	81.32	75.65	71.31	68.39	296.67	75.64
3	3	1	-	-	.378	.438	.627	262	.385	451	.663	75.29	72.20	73.93	73.10	294.52	75.09
5	3	4	-	-	.313	.414	.569	241	.344	445	.635	69.25	64.42	72.95	69.96	276.59	70.52
9	6	15	7	19	.310	.424	.615	284	.385	488	.661	81.61	72.11	80.00	72.88	306.60	78.17
30	11	11	7	18	.304	.454	.591	269	.360	511	.684	77.30	67.48	83.77	75.39	303.94	77.49
15	4	4	10	12	.368	.451	.750	220	.448	380	.774	63.22	83.96	62.30	85.30	294.77	75.15
31	10	16	8	10	.286	.425	.592	244	.336	499	.686	70.11	62.89	81.80	75.65	290.46	74.05
11	3	6	5	20	.288	.397	.568	256	.347	461	.626	73.56	65.09	75.57	68.94	283.16	72.20
21	7	10	6	15	.315	.451	.570	231	.315	483	.658	66.38	58.97	79.18	72.53	277.06	70.64
4	4	4	8	14	.313	.366	.614	248	.357	435	.626	71.26	66.86	71.31	68.98	278.42	70.99
5	1	7	9	17	.308	.352	.605	245	.359	419	.614	70.40	67.31	68.69	67.71	274.12	69.89
11	-	7	7	20	.311	.410	.623	272	.370	492	.669	78.16	69.34	80.66	73.78	301.94	76.98
6	4	1	15	17	.328	.399	.655	265	.367	483	.668	76.15	68.68	79.18	73.63	297.64	75.89
5	2	6	4	24	.317	.401	.690	247	.378	459	.703	70.98	70.88	75.25	77.47	294.57	75.10
9	6	5	4	5	.357	.438	.714	191	.395	360	.744	54.89	73.95	59.02	81.98	269.83	68.79
7	2	2	4	15	.334	.388	.629	225	.335	436	.649	64.66	62.74	71.48	71.51	270.38	68.94
5	2	-	11	12	.293	.345	.587	245	.359	412	.604	70.40	67.31	67.54	66.58	271.84	69.31
3	-	4	-	-	.310	.375	.614	217	.354	402	.656	62.36	66.33	65.90	72.28	266.87	68.04
7	9	13	6	8	.331	.430	.620	236	.339	461	.662	67.82	63.54	75.57	73.00	279.93	71.37
4	2	1	-	11	.322	.380	.533	240	.361	376	.566	68.97	67.73	61.64	62.41	260.74	66.48
31	12	6	10	18	.313	.359	.531	255	.358	406	.570	73.28	67.11	66.56	62.85	269.79	68.79
1	3	2	8	13	.363	.461	.588	213	.314	429	.632	61.21	58.78	70.33	69.63	259.95	66.28
13	3	9	2	5	.328	.515	.863	266	.398	607	.907	76.44	74.50	99.51	100.00	350.45	89.35
6	1	9	3	5	.362	.609	.812	230	.370	549	.883	66.09	69.29	90.00	97.28	322.66	82.27
9	2	9	2	4	.370	.582	.799	227	.369	536	.870	65.23	69.05	87.87	95.90	318.05	81.09
29	12	2	7	11	.336	.458	.677	252	.368	510	.745	72.41	68.93	83.61	82.06	307.01	78.28
40	7	1	6	10	.308	.461	.615	251	.366	503	.734	72.13	68.66	82.46	80.93	304.18	77.55
11	3	3	7	6	.306	.440	.688	235	.383	458	.747	67.53	71.83	75.08	82.35	296.79	75.67
7	-	10	2	7	.341	.529	.749	201	.361	457	.820	57.76	67.62	74.92	90.43	290.72	74.12
28	12	8	6	15	.303	.438	.609	242	.340	490	.689	69.54	63.78	80.33	75.96	289.60	73.84
37	8	8	5	13	.291	.446	.585	224	.319	493	.701	64.37	59.71	80.82	77.29	282.18	71.95
39	8	5	7	9	.311	.456	.624	212	.341	458	.738	60.92	63.97	75.08	81.29	281.26	71.71
10	-	3	-	-	.325	.402	.628	259	.398	446	.686	74.43	74.66	73.11	75.62	297.83	75.93
3	-	1	-	-	.314	.391	.568	245	.388	392	.621	70.40	72.76	64.26	68.47	275.89	70.34
15	6	1	7	11	.390	.454	.664	205	.390	366	.696	58.91	73.03	60.00	76.69	268.63	68.49
34	-	6	-	-	.419	.488	.614	254	.393	461	.713	72.99	73.56	75.57	78.53	300.65	76.65
40	-	5	-	-	.345	.423	.553	265	.442	404	.673	76.15	82.76	66.23	74.21	299.35	76.32
106	-	4	-	-	.321	.397	.469	249	.376	456	.688	71.55	70.37	74.75	75.80	292.48	74.57
103	-	8	-	-	.402	.464	.547	255	.418	465	.762	73.28	78.33	76.23	84.02	311.85	79.51
47	-	8	-	-	.423	.498	.542	232	.364	430	.675	66.67	68.25	70.49	74.40	279.80	71.34

Single Season Statistics A-B

The Greatest 300 Single Seasons and Others Listed Alphabetically

Single Season Statistics B-E

Rank	Player	Player Season	Year	G	AB	H	1B	2B	3B	HR	RUN	RBI	BB	SO
280	Burkett, Jesse	2nd	1893	124	480	179	135	23	15	6	144	82	98	23
323	Burkett, Jesse	3rd	1896	133	585	240	192	26	16	6	159	72	49	19
377	Burkett, Jesse	4th	1899	138	567	228	194	17	10	7	115	71	67	-
80	Burks, Ellis	1st	1996	156	613	211	118	45	8	40	142	128	61	114
222	Campanella, Roy	1st	1953	144	519	162	92	26	3	41	103	142	67	58
244	Canseco, Jose	1st	1988	158	610	187	111	34	-	42	120	124	78	128
330	Carew, Rod	1st	1977	155	616	239	171	38	16	14	128	100	69	55
373	Carty, Rico	1st	1970	136	478	175	124	23	3	25	84	101	77	46
94	Cash, Norm	1st	1961	159	535	193	122	22	8	41	119	132	124	85
310	Castilla, Vinny**	1st	1998	162	645	206	128	28	4	46	108	144	40	89
266	Cepeda, Orlando	1st	1961	152	585	182	104	28	4	46	105	142	39	91
368	Clemente, Roberto	1st	1966	154	638	202	131	31	11	29	105	119	46	109
146	Clolavito, Rocky	1st	1961	163	583	169	92	30	2	45	129	140	113	75
33	Cobb, Ty	1st	1911	146	591	248	169	47	24	8	147	127	44	-
193	Cobb, Ty	2nd	1915	156	563	208	161	31	13	3	144	99	118	43
292	Cobb, Ty	3rd	1909	156	573	216	164	33	10	9	116	107	48	-
353	Cobb, Ty	4th	1912	140	553	227	167	30	23	7	119	83	43	-
364	Collins, Eddie	1st	1912	153	543	189	153	25	11	-	137	64	101	-
197	Conner, Roger	1st	1890	123	484	180	126	25	15	14	134	103	88	32
223	Conner, Roger	2nd	1889	131	496	157	95	32	17	13	117	130	93	46
224	Conner, Roger	3rd	1887	127	546	209	144	26	22	17	113	104	75	50
362	Cravath, Gavy	1st	1913	147	525	179	112	34	14	19	78	128	55	63
332	Crawford, Sam	1st	1911	146	574	217	160	36	14	7	109	115	61	-
311	Cronin, Joe	1st	1930	154	587	203	140	41	9	13	127	126	72	36
77	Cuyler, Kiki	1st	1930	156	642	228	148	50	17	13	155	134	72	49
153	Cuyler, Kiki	2nd	1925	153	617	220	133	43	26	18	144	102	58	56
275	Davis, Tommy	1st	1962	163	665	230	167	27	9	27	120	153	33	65
355	Dawson, Andre	1st	1987	153	621	178	103	24	2	49	90	137	32	103
51	Delahanty, Ed	1st	1893	132	588	218	148	31	20	19	145	146	47	20
72	Delahanty, Ed	2nd	1894	114	497	199	143	36	16	4	149	131	60	16
74	Delahanty, Ed	3rd	1895	116	481	192	126	47	8	11	148	106	86	31
81	Delahanty, Ed	4th	1896	122	505	199	130	42	14	13	131	126	62	22
87	Delahanty, Ed	5th	1899	145	573	234	160	56	9	9	133	137	55	-
96	Delgado, Carlos**	1st	2000	162	569	196	97	57	1	41	115	137	123	104
134	Delgado, Carlos**	2nd	2003	161	570	172	91	38	1	42	117	145	109	137
279	Delgado, Carlos**	3rd	1999	152	573	156	73	39	-	44	113	134	86	141
340	Dickey, Bill*	1st	1936	112	423	153	97	26	8	22	99	107	46	16
23	DiMaggio, Joe*	1st	1937	151	621	215	119	35	15	46	151	167	64	37
141	DiMaggio, Joe*	2nd	1941	139	541	193	109	43	11	30	122	125	76	13
144	DiMaggio, Joe*	3rd	1938	145	599	194	117	32	13	32	129	140	59	21
168	DiMaggio, Joe*	4th	1939	120	462	176	108	32	6	30	108	126	52	20
169	DiMaggio, Joe*	5th	1948	153	594	190	114	26	11	39	110	155	67	30
252	DiMaggio, Joe*	6th	1936	138	637	206	118	44	15	29	132	125	24	39
9	Duffy, Hugh	1st	1894	124	539	236	155	50	13	18	160	145	66	15
163	Duffy, Hugh	2nd	1893	131	537	203	167	23	7	6	149	118	50	13
212	Duffy, Hugh	3rd	1891	121	511	174	132	23	10	9	124	110	61	29
230	Duffy, Hugh	4th	1897	134	554	189	145	23	10	11	131	129	52	-
249	Duffy, Hugh	5th	1890	137	591	194	140	33	14	7	161	82	59	20
379	Dunlap, Fred	1st	1884	101	449	185	125	39	8	13	160	-	29	-
367	English, Woody	1st	1930	156	638	214	147	36	17	14	152	59	100	72

The Greatest 300 Single Seasons and Others Listed Alphabetically

SB	CS	HBP	SF	GDP	AVG	OBP	SLG	TRP	RPA	TNB	TBA	TRP Rating	RPA Rating	TNB Rating	TBA Rating	TOP	Rating
39	-	7	-	-	.373	.485	.521	226	.386	394	.674	64.94	72.39	64.59	74.23	276.15	70.41
32	-	7	-	-	.410	.462	.540	231	.360	404	.630	66.38	67.53	66.23	69.46	269.60	68.74
22	-	2	-	-	.402	.467	.504	186	.292	377	.593	53.45	54.80	61.80	65.33	235.38	60.01
32	6	6	2	19	.344	.408	.639	270	.385	485	.692	77.59	72.17	79.51	76.25	305.52	77.90
4	2	4	-	13	.312	.395	.611	245	.406	390	.647	70.40	76.13	63.93	71.28	281.75	71.84
40	16	10	6	15	.307	.391	.569	244	.339	459	.638	70.11	63.59	75.25	70.36	279.31	71.21
23	13	3	5	6	.388	.449	.570	228	.326	433	.619	65.52	61.12	70.98	68.27	265.89	67.79
1	2	2	3	19	.366	.454	.584	185	.320	357	.617	53.16	59.87	58.52	67.96	239.51	61.07
11	5	9	2	16	.361	.487	.662	251	.366	493	.719	72.13	68.56	80.82	79.21	300.71	76.67
5	9	6	6	24	.319	.362	.589	252	.350	422	.585	72.41	65.49	69.18	64.51	271.59	69.25
12	8	9	3	21	.311	.362	.609	247	.376	408	.621	70.98	70.45	66.89	68.44	276.75	70.56
7	5	-	5	14	.317	.360	.536	224	.319	390	.555	64.37	59.71	63.93	61.14	249.15	63.52
1	2	2	8	14	.290	.402	.580	269	.374	452	.628	77.30	70.01	74.10	69.19	290.60	74.09
83	-	8	-	-	.420	.467	.621	274	.426	502	.781	78.74	79.85	82.30	86.05	326.93	83.35
96	38	10	-	-	.369	.486	.487	243	.352	460	.666	69.83	65.90	75.41	73.37	284.50	72.54
76	-	6	-	-	.377	.431	.517	223	.356	426	.679	64.08	66.64	69.84	74.88	275.44	70.23
61	34	5	-	-	.410	.458	.586	202	.336	399	.664	58.05	62.98	65.41	73.17	259.61	66.19
63	-	-	-	-	.348	.450	.435	201	.312	400	.621	57.76	58.48	65.57	68.46	250.27	63.81
23	-	1	-	-	.372	.469	.572	237	.414	389	.679	68.10	77.50	63.77	74.82	284.20	72.46
21	-	2	-	-	.317	.426	.528	247	.418	378	.640	70.98	78.31	61.97	70.49	281.75	71.83
43	-	8	-	-	.383	.464	.604	217	.345	456	.725	62.36	64.65	74.75	79.90	281.66	71.81
10	-	3	-	-	.341	.407	.568	206	.353	366	.628	59.20	66.21	60.00	69.19	254.60	64.91
37	-	-	-	-	.378	.438	.526	224	.353	400	.630	64.37	66.10	65.57	69.43	265.47	67.68
17	10	5	-	-	.346	.422	.513	253	.381	385	.580	72.70	71.40	63.11	63.90	271.12	69.12
37	-	10	-	-	.355	.428	.547	289	.399	470	.649	83.05	74.80	77.05	71.55	306.44	78.13
41	13	13	-	-	.357	.423	.598	246	.358	468	.680	70.69	67.00	76.72	74.97	289.38	73.78
18	6	2	8	17	.346	.374	.535	273	.377	403	.556	78.45	70.56	66.07	61.26	276.34	70.45
11	3	7	2	15	.287	.328	.568	227	.335	400	.591	65.52	62.83	65.57	65.12	258.75	65.97
36	-	10	-	-	.371	.426	.588	291	.451	439	.681	83.62	84.54	71.97	75.01	315.14	80.35
29	-	7	-	-	.400	.472	.561	280	.496	375	.665	80.46	93.03	61.48	73.28	308.24	78.59
46	-	6	-	-	.399	.496	.599	254	.443	426	.743	72.99	83.06	69.84	81.94	307.83	78.48
37	-	9	-	-	.394	.469	.610	257	.446	416	.722	73.85	83.61	68.20	79.60	305.25	77.83
38	-	4	-	-	.408	.464	.585	270	.427	432	.684	77.59	80.05	70.82	75.34	303.79	77.46
-	1	15	4	12	.344	.470	.664	252	.349	515	.712	72.41	65.31	84.43	78.51	300.66	76.66
-	-	19	7	9	.302	.426	.593	262	.367	466	.653	75.29	68.76	76.39	71.93	292.37	74.54
1	1	15	7	11	.272	.377	.571	247	.357	428	.618	70.98	66.88	70.16	68.17	276.19	70.42
-	2	3	-	-	.362	.428	.617	206	.436	308	.653	59.20	81.78	50.49	71.92	263.39	67.15
3	-	5	-	-	.346	.412	.673	318	.461	490	.710	91.38	86.36	80.33	78.27	336.33	85.75
4	2	4	-	6	.357	.440	.643	247	.394	430	.686	70.98	73.82	70.49	75.59	290.87	74.16
6	1	2	-	-	.324	.386	.581	269	.408	414	.627	77.30	76.37	67.87	69.13	290.67	74.11
3	-	4	-	11	.381	.448	.671	234	.442	369	.698	67.24	82.89	60.49	76.88	287.50	73.30
1	1	8	-	20	.320	.396	.598	265	.385	430	.624	76.15	72.07	70.49	68.78	287.50	73.30
4	-	4	-	-	.323	.352	.576	257	.386	399	.600	73.85	72.42	65.41	66.13	277.81	70.83
49	-	1	-	-	.438	.500	.679	305	.503	482	.795	87.64	94.31	79.02	87.66	348.63	88.89
50	-	1	-	-	.378	.432	.480	267	.454	359	.611	76.72	85.09	58.85	67.29	287.95	73.42
83	-	4	-	-	.341	.415	.477	234	.406	392	.681	67.24	76.12	64.26	75.01	282.63	72.06
45	-	6	-	-	.341	.404	.478	260	.425	368	.601	74.71	79.61	60.33	66.27	280.92	71.62
79	-	2	-	-	.328	.391	.467	243	.373	416	.638	69.83	69.84	68.20	70.32	278.18	70.93
-	-	-	-	-	.412	.448	.621	160	.335	308	.644	45.98	62.72	50.49	71.02	230.21	58.69
3	-	6	-	-	.335	.430	.511	211	.284	435	.585	60.63	53.14	71.31	64.44	249.53	63.62

The Greatest 300 Single Seasons and Others Listed Alphabetically

Rank	Player	Player Season	Year	G	AB	H	1B	2B	3B	HR	RUN	RBI	BB	SO	
356	Erstad, Darin**	1st	2000	157	676	240	170	39	6	25	121	100	64	82	
307	Fielder, Cecil	1st	1990	159	573	159	82	25	1	51	104	132	90	182	
113	Foster, George	1st	1977	158	615	197	112	31	2	52	124	149	61	107	
7	Foxx, Jimmie*	1st	1932	154	585	213	113	33	9	58	151	169	116	96	
13	Foxx, Jimmie*	2nd	1938	149	565	197	105	33	9	50	139	175	119	76	
32	Foxx, Jimmie*	3rd	1933	149	573	204	110	37	9	48	125	163	96	93	
62	Foxx, Jimmie*	4th	1930	153	562	188	105	33	13	37	127	156	93	66	
70	Foxx, Jimmie*	5th	1936	155	585	198	117	32	8	41	130	143	105	119	
92	Foxx, Jimmie*	6th	1934	150	539	180	102	28	6	44	120	130	111	75	
137	Foxx, Jimmie*	7th	1939	124	467	168	92	31	10	35	130	105	89	72	
158	Foxx, Jimmie*	8th	1929	149	517	183	118	23	9	33	123	118	103	70	
174	Foxx, Jimmie*	9th	1935	147	535	185	109	33	7	36	118	115	114	99	
136	Galarraga, Andres**	1st	1996	159	626	190	101	39	3	47	119	150	40	157	
198	Galarraga, Andres**	2nd	1997	154	600	191	116	31	3	41	120	140	54	141	
342	Garciaparra, Nomar**	1st	1998	143	604	195	115	37	8	35	111	122	33	62	
4	Gehrig, Lou	1st	1927	155	584	218	101	52	18	47	149	175	109	84	
6	Gehrig, Lou	2nd	1931	155	619	211	119	31	15	46	163	184	117	56	
10	Gehrig, Lou	3rd	1930	154	581	220	120	42	17	41	143	174	101	63	
11	Gehrig, Lou	4th	1936	155	579	205	112	37	7	49	167	152	130	46	
25	Gehrig, Lou	5th	1934	154	579	210	115	40	6	49	128	165	109	31	
36	Gehrig, Lou	6th	1937	157	569	200	117	37	9	37	138	159	127	49	
66	Gehrig, Lou	7th	1932	156	596	208	123	42	9	34	138	151	108	38	
67	Gehrig, Lou	8th	1928	154	562	210	123	47	13	27	139	142	94	69	
95	Gehrig, Lou	9th	1933	152	593	198	113	41	12	32	138	139	92	42	
154	Gehrig, Lou	10th	1929	154	553	166	89	32	10	35	127	126	124	68	
185	Gehrig, Lou	11th	1935	149	535	176	110	26	10	30	125	119	132	38	
268	Gehrig, Lou	12th	1926	155	572	179	96	47	20	16	135	112	105	73	
217	Gehringer, Charlie	1st	1936	154	641	227	140	60	12	15	144	116	83	13	
251	Gehringer, Charlie	2nd	1934	154	601	214	146	50	7	11	134	127	99	25	
122	Giambi, Jason**	1st	2000	152	510	170	97	29	1	43	108	137	137	96	
181	Giambi, Jason**	2nd	2001	154	520	178	91	47	2	38	109	120	129	83	
235	Giambi, Jason**	3rd	2002	155	560	176	100	34	1	41	120	122	109	112	
150	Gonzalez, Juan **	1st	1998	154	606	193	96	50	2	45	110	157	46	126	
255	Gonzalez, Juan **	2nd	1996	134	541	170	88	33	2	47	89	144	45	82	
61	Gonzalez, Luis**	1st	2001	162	609	198	98	36	7	57	128	142	100	83	
171	Goslin, Goose	1st	1930	148	584	180	95	36	12	37	115	138	67	54	
19	Greenberg, Hank*	1st	1937	154	594	200	97	49	14	40	137	183	102	101	
31	Greenberg, Hank*	2nd	1938	155	556	175	90	23	4	58	144	146	119	92	
58	Greenberg, Hank*	3rd	1935	152	619	203	105	46	16	36	121	170	87	91	
59	Greenberg, Hank*	4th	1940	148	573	195	96	50	8	41	129	150	93	75	
165	Greenberg, Hank*	5th	1934	153	593	201	105	63	7	26	118	139	63	93	
277	Greenberg, Hank*	6th	1939	138	500	156	74	42	7	33	112	112	91	95	
83	Griffey, Ken **	1st	1997	157	608	185	92	34	3	56	125	147	76	121	
93	Griffey, Ken **	2nd	1996	140	545	165	88	26	2	49	125	140	78	104	
115	Griffey, Ken **	3rd	1998	161	633	180	88	33	3	56	120	146	76	121	
157	Griffey, Ken **	4th	1999	160	606	173	96	26	3	48	123	134	91	108	
240	Guerrero, Vladimir**	1st	2004	156	612	206	126	39	2	39	124	126	52	74	
289	Guerrero, Vladimir**	2nd	2000	154	571	197	114	28	11	44	101	123	58	74	
376	Gwynn, Tony	1st	1987	157	589	218	162	36	13	7	119	54	82	35	
242	Hafey, Chick	1st	1930	120	446	150	73	39	12	26	108	107	46	51	

The Greatest 300 Single Seasons and Others Listed Alphabetically

SB	CS	HBP	SF	GDP	AVG	OBP	SLG	Total Offensive Production Statistics				TRP Rating	RPA Rating	TNB Rating	TBA Rating	TOP Composite	
								TRP	RPA	TNB	TBA					TOP	Rating
28	8	1	4	8	.355	.409	.541	221	.293	451	.599	63.51	55.00	73.93	66.01	258.45	65.89
-	1	5	5	15	.277	.377	.592	236	.343	433	.629	67.82	64.28	70.98	69.36	272.44	69.46
6	4	5	8	17	.320	.382	.631	273	.387	456	.646	78.45	72.46	74.75	71.19	296.85	75.68
3	7	-	-	-	.364	.469	.749	320	.456	550	.785	91.95	85.54	90.16	86.47	354.13	90.29
5	4	-	-	-	.349	.462	.704	314	.459	518	.757	90.23	86.02	84.92	83.47	344.63	87.87
2	2	1	-	-	.356	.449	.703	288	.430	500	.746	82.76	80.55	81.97	82.25	327.52	83.50
7	7	-	-	-	.335	.429	.637	283	.432	451	.689	81.32	80.96	73.93	75.89	312.10	79.57
13	4	1	-	-	.338	.440	.631	273	.395	484	.700	78.45	74.03	79.34	77.20	309.02	78.79
11	2	1	-	-	.334	.449	.653	250	.384	473	.727	71.84	71.96	77.54	80.08	301.42	76.85
4	3	2	-	17	.360	.464	.694	235	.409	416	.723	67.53	76.58	68.20	79.74	292.05	74.46
10	7	2	-	-	.354	.463	.625	241	.387	431	.693	69.25	72.60	70.66	76.37	288.88	73.65
6	4	-	-	-	.346	.461	.636	233	.359	456	.703	66.95	67.27	74.75	77.44	286.42	73.03
18	8	17	8	6	.304	.357	.601	269	.386	443	.636	77.30	72.32	72.62	70.05	292.29	74.52
15	8	17	3	16	.318	.389	.585	260	.377	429	.622	74.71	70.61	70.33	68.52	284.17	72.45
12	6	8	7	20	.323	.362	.584	233	.347	400	.595	66.95	64.97	65.57	65.60	263.10	67.08
10	8	3	-	-	.373	.474	.765	324	.466	561	.806	93.10	87.23	91.97	88.84	361.14	92.08
17	12	-	-	-	.341	.446	.662	347	.471	532	.723	99.71	88.34	87.21	79.67	354.94	90.49
12	14	3	-	-	.379	.473	.721	317	.463	521	.761	91.09	86.72	85.41	83.83	347.04	88.48
3	4	7	-	-	.354	.478	.696	319	.446	539	.753	91.67	83.48	88.36	82.97	346.48	88.34
9	5	2	-	-	.363	.465	.706	293	.425	524	.759	84.20	79.57	85.90	83.70	333.37	84.99
4	3	4	-	-	.351	.473	.643	297	.424	498	.711	85.34	79.50	81.64	78.41	324.90	82.84
4	11	3	-	-	.349	.451	.621	289	.409	474	.670	83.05	76.60	77.70	73.89	311.24	79.35
4	11	4	-	-	.374	.467	.648	281	.426	455	.689	80.75	79.78	74.59	75.98	311.10	79.32
9	13	1	-	-	.334	.424	.605	277	.404	448	.653	79.60	75.66	73.44	71.98	300.68	76.66
4	4	5	-	-	.300	.433	.584	253	.371	452	.663	72.70	69.51	74.10	73.05	289.36	73.77
8	7	5	-	-	.329	.466	.583	244	.363	450	.670	70.11	68.04	73.77	73.80	285.73	72.85
6	5	1	-	-	.313	.420	.549	247	.364	421	.621	70.98	68.26	69.02	68.44	276.69	70.55
4	1	4	-	-	.354	.431	.555	260	.357	446	.613	74.71	69.63	73.11	67.52	282.27	71.97
11	8	3	-	-	.356	.450	.517	261	.371	416	.592	75.00	69.57	68.20	65.22	277.98	70.87
2	-	9	8	9	.333	.476	.647	245	.364	478	.710	70.40	68.21	78.36	78.28	295.26	75.28
2	-	13	9	17	.342	.477	.660	229	.333	487	.708	65.80	62.37	79.84	78.02	286.03	72.92
2	2	15	5	18	.314	.435	.598	242	.342	459	.649	69.54	64.14	75.25	71.55	280.48	71.51
2	1	6	11	20	.318	.366	.630	267	.388	435	.631	76.72	72.61	71.31	69.58	290.23	74.00
2	-	3	3	10	.314	.368	.643	233	.387	398	.661	66.95	72.52	65.25	72.87	277.59	70.77
1	1	14	5	14	.325	.429	.688	270	.364	533	.718	77.59	68.18	87.38	79.17	312.32	79.63
17	11	3	-	-	.308	.382	.601	253	.387	427	.653	72.70	72.49	70.00	71.96	287.15	73.21
8	3	3	-	-	.337	.436	.668	320	.458	507	.725	91.95	85.78	83.11	79.94	340.79	86.89
7	5	3	-	-	.315	.438	.683	290	.428	504	.743	83.33	80.15	82.62	81.93	328.03	83.64
4	3	-	-	-	.328	.411	.628	291	.412	477	.676	83.62	77.24	78.20	74.46	313.52	79.93
6	3	1	-	15	.340	.433	.670	279	.409	481	.705	80.17	76.66	78.85	77.73	313.41	79.91
9	5	2	-	-	.339	.404	.600	257	.391	425	.646	73.85	73.19	69.67	71.19	287.90	73.40
8	3	2	-	8	.312	.420	.622	224	.373	409	.681	64.37	69.84	67.05	75.00	276.26	70.44
15	4	8	12	12	.304	.382	.646	272	.380	488	.682	78.16	71.18	80.00	75.12	304.46	77.63
16	1	7	7	7	.303	.392	.628	265	.411	442	.686	76.15	77.11	72.46	75.64	301.36	76.83
20	5	7	4	14	.284	.365	.611	266	.362	485	.661	76.44	67.91	79.51	72.83	296.68	75.64
24	7	7	2	8	.285	.384	.576	257	.360	464	.650	73.85	67.45	76.07	71.62	288.99	73.68
15	3	8	8	19	.337	.391	.598	250	.358	438	.627	71.84	67.02	71.80	69.06	279.72	71.32
9	10	8	4	15	.345	.410	.664	224	.341	444	.677	64.37	63.98	72.79	74.60	275.73	70.30
56	12	3	4	13	.370	.447	.511	173	.250	430	.622	49.71	46.91	70.49	68.58	235.70	60.09
12	-	7	-	-	.336	.407	.652	215	.431	356	.713	61.78	80.74	58.36	78.63	279.51	71.26

Single Season Statistics E-H

The Greatest 300 Single Seasons and Others Listed Alphabetically

Rank	Player	Player Season	Year	G	AB	H	1B	2B	3B	HR	RUN	RBI	BB	SO
262	Hafey, Chick	2nd	1929	134	517	175	90	47	9	29	101	125	45	42
35	Hamilton, Billy	1st	1894	131	559	223	183	22	14	4	196	87	126	17
117	Hamilton, Billy	2nd	1895	121	517	203	171	19	6	7	166	74	96	30
290	Hamilton, Billy	3rd	1889	137	532	160	127	15	15	3	145	77	87	41
343	Hartnett, Gabby	1st	1930	141	508	172	101	31	3	37	84	122	55	62
344	Heath, Jeff	1st	1938	126	502	172	102	31	18	21	104	112	33	55
203	Heilmann, Harry	1st	1923	144	524	211	138	44	11	18	121	115	74	40
211	Heilmann, Harry	2nd	1921	149	602	237	161	43	14	19	114	139	53	37
270	Heilmann, Harry	3rd	1927	141	505	201	128	50	9	14	106	120	72	16
39	Helton, Todd**	1st	2000	160	580	216	113	59	2	42	138	147	103	61
50	Helton, Todd**	2nd	2001	159	587	197	92	54	2	49	132	146	98	104
161	Helton, Todd**	3rd	2003	160	583	209	122	49	5	33	135	117	111	72
301	Henderson, Rickey	1st	1985	143	547	172	115	28	5	24	146	72	99	65
47	Herman, Babe	1st	1930	153	614	241	147	48	11	35	143	130	66	56
264	Holmes, Tommy	1st	1945	154	636	224	143	47	6	28	125	117	70	9
26	Hornsby, Rogers	1st	1922	154	623	250	148	46	14	42	141	152	65	50
27	Hornsby, Rogers	2nd	1929	156	602	229	135	47	8	39	156	149	87	65
28	Hornsby, Rogers	3rd	1925	138	504	203	113	41	10	39	133	143	83	39
127	Hornsby, Rogers	4th	1921	154	592	235	152	44	18	21	131	126	60	48
142	Hornsby, Rogers	5th	1927	155	568	205	138	32	9	26	133	125	86	38
226	Hornsby, Rogers	6th	1924	143	536	227	145	43	14	25	121	94	89	32
347	Howard, Frank	1st	1969	161	592	175	108	17	2	48	111	111	102	96
313	Jackson, Joe	1st	1911	147	571	233	162	45	19	7	126	83	56	-
167	Jackson, Reggie	1st	1969	152	549	151	65	36	3	47	123	118	115	142
69	Jennings, Hughie	1st	1895	131	528	204	152	40	8	4	159	125	24	17
183	Jennings, Hughie	2nd	1896	129	523	208	175	24	9	-	125	121	19	11
295	Jennings, Hughie	3rd	1894	128	505	168	117	27	20	4	136	109	37	17
318	Jeter, Derek**	1st	1999	158	627	219	149	37	9	24	134	102	91	116
326	Johnson, Robert	1st	1939	150	544	184	122	30	9	23	115	114	99	59
190	Jones, Chipper**	1st	1999	157	567	181	94	41	1	45	116	110	126	94
359	Kaline, Al	1st	1955	152	588	200	141	24	8	27	121	102	82	57
267	Keeler, Willie	1st	1896	127	546	214	175	22	13	4	154	82	37	82
274	Keeler, Willie	2nd	1894	128	593	218	166	25	22	5	164	94	40	94
299	Keeler, Willie	3rd	1897	128	562	243	199	25	19	-	147	74	35	74
304	Keeler, Willie	4th	1895	131	560	221	179	23	15	4	161	78	37	78
319	Keller, Charlie*	1st	1941	140	507	151	84	24	10	33	102	122	102	65
43	Kelley, Joe	1st	1894	129	509	199	128	48	17	6	167	111	107	36
45	Kelley, Joe	2nd	1895	131	510	189	132	26	21	10	148	134	77	29
82	Kelley, Joe	3rd	1896	130	516	191	139	27	17	8	147	100	91	19
287	Kelley, Joe	4th	1897	129	503	196	151	31	9	5	113	118	70	-
360	Kelly, George	1st	1924	144	571	185	118	37	9	21	91	136	38	52
160	Kelly, King	1st	1886	118	451	175	129	31	11	4	155	79	83	33
346	Kelly, King	2nd	1887	114	525	207	154	34	11	8	119	63	55	40
182	Killebrew, Harmon	1st	1969	162	555	153	82	20	2	49	106	140	145	84
329	Killebrew, Harmon	2nd	1961	150	541	156	83	20	7	46	94	122	107	109
119	Kiner, Ralph	1st	1949	152	549	170	92	19	5	54	116	127	117	61
155	Kiner, Ralph	2nd	1947	152	565	177	99	23	4	51	118	127	98	81
188	Kiner, Ralph	3rd	1951	151	531	164	85	31	6	42	124	109	137	57
354	Kingman, Dave	1st	1979	145	532	153	81	19	5	48	97	115	45	131
16	Klein, Chuck	1st	1930	156	648	250	143	59	8	40	158	170	54	50

The Greatest 300 Single Seasons and Others Listed Alphabetically

SB	CS	HBP	SF	GDP	AVG	OBP	SLG	Total Offensive Production Statistics				TRP Rating	RPA Rating	TNB Rating	TBA Rating	TOP Composite	
								TRP	RPA	TNB	TBA					TOP	Rating
7	-	2	-	-	.338	.394	.632	226	.401	381	.676	64.94	75.09	62.46	74.45	276.94	70.61
99	-	9	-	-	.399	.516	.510	283	.408	519	.748	81.32	76.41	85.08	82.42	325.24	82.92
95	-	7	-	-	.393	.494	.493	240	.387	453	.731	68.97	72.53	74.26	80.53	296.29	75.54
117	-	14	-	-	.301	.412	.402	222	.351	432	.682	63.79	65.72	70.82	75.22	275.55	70.25
-	-	1	-	-	.339	.404	.630	206	.365	376	.667	59.20	68.44	61.64	73.48	262.75	66.99
3	1	-	-	-	.343	.383	.602	216	.404	337	.630	62.07	75.65	55.25	69.42	262.39	66.90
8	7	5	-	-	.403	.481	.632	236	.391	411	.682	67.82	73.34	67.38	75.12	283.65	72.32
2	6	2	-	-	.394	.444	.606	253	.385	416	.633	72.70	72.16	68.20	69.79	282.84	72.11
11	5	2	-	-	.398	.475	.616	226	.390	391	.675	64.94	73.14	64.10	74.43	276.61	70.52
5	3	4	10	12	.372	.463	.698	285	.402	514	.725	81.90	75.32	84.26	79.90	321.38	81.94
7	5	5	5	14	.336	.432	.685	278	.392	507	.715	79.89	73.47	83.11	78.81	315.29	80.38
-	4	2	7	19	.358	.458	.630	252	.349	476	.659	72.41	65.40	78.03	72.66	288.51	73.56
80	10	3	5	8	.314	.419	.516	218	.329	454	.686	62.64	61.71	74.43	75.58	274.36	69.95
18	-	4	-	-	.393	.455	.678	273	.399	504	.737	78.45	74.79	82.62	81.21	317.07	80.84
15	-	4	-	11	.352	.420	.577	242	.336	456	.632	69.54	62.89	74.75	69.71	276.89	70.60
17	12	1	-	-	.401	.459	.722	293	.425	521	.756	84.20	79.68	85.41	83.34	332.63	84.81
2	-	1	-	-	.380	.459	.679	305	.442	499	.723	87.64	82.83	81.80	79.71	331.98	84.64
5	3	2	-	-	.403	.489	.756	276	.469	468	.795	79.31	87.81	76.72	87.57	331.41	84.50
13	13	7	-	-	.397	.458	.639	257	.390	445	.675	73.85	73.08	72.95	74.42	294.30	75.03
9	-	4	-	-	.361	.448	.586	258	.392	432	.657	74.14	73.47	70.82	72.36	290.79	74.14
5	12	2	-	-	.424	.507	.696	215	.343	457	.729	61.78	64.25	74.92	80.33	281.28	71.72
1	-	5	3	29	.296	.402	.574	222	.304	448	.613	63.79	56.91	73.44	67.55	261.69	66.72
41	-	8	-	-	.408	.468	.590	209	.329	442	.696	60.06	61.67	72.46	76.72	270.91	69.07
13	5	12	1	8	.275	.411	.608	241	.352	469	.685	69.25	65.93	76.89	75.46	287.52	73.31
60	-	32	-	-	.386	.445	.515	284	.486	388	.664	81.61	91.12	63.61	73.22	309.56	78.93
73	-	51	-	-	.398	.469	.478	246	.415	393	.663	70.69	77.73	64.43	73.04	285.89	72.89
36	-	27	-	-	.333	.408	.489	245	.431	347	.610	70.40	80.68	56.89	67.21	275.18	70.16
19	8	12	6	12	.349	.438	.552	236	.316	460	.615	67.82	59.12	75.41	67.78	270.13	68.87
15	5	-	-	12	.338	.440	.553	229	.350	410	.626	65.80	65.51	67.21	68.99	267.52	68.21
25	3	2	6	20	.319	.441	.633	226	.313	509	.706	64.94	58.74	83.44	77.81	284.93	72.64
6	8	5	6	13	.340	.421	.546	223	.321	406	.585	64.08	60.21	66.56	64.48	255.33	65.10
73	9	7	-	-	.392	.437	.502	236	.400	382	.647	67.82	74.95	62.62	71.36	276.75	70.56
30	6	18	-	-	.368	.424	.509	258	.396	384	.590	74.14	74.26	62.95	65.01	276.36	70.46
63	-	7	-	-	.432	.472	.544	221	.366	411	.680	63.51	68.56	67.38	70.04	274.44	69.97
57	12	14	-	-	.395	.445	.511	239	.391	382	.625	68.68	73.30	62.62	68.91	273.50	69.73
6	4	1	-	3	.298	.416	.580	224	.365	399	.651	64.37	68.47	65.41	71.74	269.99	68.84
46	-	5	-	-	.391	.501	.587	278	.448	457	.736	79.89	83.88	74.92	81.11	319.80	81.53
54	-	10	-	-	.371	.462	.563	282	.472	428	.717	81.03	88.51	70.16	79.01	318.72	81.26
87	-	12	-	-	.370	.475	.535	247	.399	466	.753	70.98	74.77	76.39	82.97	305.11	77.79
44	-	7	-	-	.390	.471	.517	231	.398	381	.657	66.38	74.63	62.46	72.40	275.87	70.33
7	2	5	-	-	.324	.371	.531	227	.370	351	.572	65.23	69.28	57.54	63.01	255.05	65.03
53	-	-	-	-	.388	.483	.532	234	.438	376	.704	67.24	82.11	61.64	77.60	288.60	73.58
84	-	1	-	-	.394	.453	.547	182	.313	427	.735	52.30	58.70	70.00	81.00	262.00	66.80
8	2	5	4	16	.276	.427	.584	246	.339	480	.662	70.69	63.58	78.69	72.97	285.93	72.90
1	2	3	5	11	.288	.405	.606	216	.324	437	.655	62.07	60.68	71.64	72.21	266.60	67.97
6	-	1	-	10	.310	.432	.658	243	.359	485	.716	69.83	67.26	79.51	78.96	295.55	75.35
1	-	2	-	12	.313	.417	.639	245	.362	462	.682	70.40	67.81	75.74	75.21	289.16	73.73
2	1	2	-	10	.309	.452	.627	233	.343	473	.696	66.95	64.21	77.54	76.66	285.36	72.76
4	2	4	8	7	.288	.343	.613	212	.356	377	.633	60.92	66.65	61.80	69.72	259.09	66.06
4	-	4	-	-	.386	.436	.687	328	.465	507	.718	94.25	87.06	83.11	79.15	343.57	87.60

Single Season Statistics H-K

The Greatest 300 Single Seasons and Others Listed Alphabetically

Rank	Player	Player Season	Year	G	AB	H	1B	2B	3B	HR	RUN	RBI	BB	SO
44	Klein, Chuck	2nd	1932	154	650	226	123	50	15	38	152	137	60	49
78	Klein, Chuck	3rd	1929	149	616	219	125	45	6	43	126	145	54	61
272	Klein, Chuck	4th	1931	148	594	200	125	34	10	31	121	121	59	49
187	Kluszewski, Ted	1st	1954	149	573	187	107	28	3	49	104	141	78	35
68	Lajoie, Nap	1st	1901	131	543	229	154	48	13	14	145	125	24	-
220	Latham, Artie	1st	1887	136	627	198	151	35	10	2	163	83	45	-
184	Lowe, Bobby	1st	1894	133	613	212	150	34	11	17	158	115	50	25
213	Lynn, Fred	1st	1979	147	531	177	95	42	1	39	116	122	82	79
49	Mantle, Mickey	1st	1956	150	533	188	109	22	5	52	132	130	112	99
56	Mantle, Mickey	2nd	1961	153	514	163	87	16	6	54	132	128	126	112
172	Mantle, Mickey	3rd	1957	144	474	173	105	28	6	34	121	94	146	75
258	Mantle, Mickey	4th	1958	150	519	158	94	21	1	42	127	97	129	123
294	Mantle, Mickey	5th	1955	147	517	158	85	25	11	37	121	99	113	97
361	Manush, Heinie	1st	1928	154	638	241	161	47	20	13	104	106	39	14
105	Maris, Roger	1st	1961	161	590	159	78	16	4	61	132	142	94	67
204	Martinez, Edgar**	1st	1995	145	511	182	101	52	-	29	121	113	116	87
259	Martinez, Edgar**	2nd	2000	153	556	180	112	31	-	37	100	145	96	95
327	Martinez, Tino**	1st	1997	158	594	176	99	31	2	44	96	141	75	75
170	Matthews, Eddie	1st	1953	157	579	175	89	31	8	47	110	135	99	83
317	Mattingly, Don	1st	1985	159	652	211	125	48	3	35	107	145	56	41
102	Mays, Willie*	1st	1962	162	621	189	99	36	5	49	130	141	78	85
106	Mays, Willie*	2nd	1955	152	580	185	103	18	13	51	123	127	79	60
219	Mays, Willie*	3rd	1961	154	572	176	101	32	3	40	129	123	81	77
233	Mays, Willie*	4th	1954	151	565	195	108	33	13	41	119	110	66	57
237	Mays, Willie*	5th	1965	157	558	177	101	21	3	52	118	112	76	71
254	Mays, Willie*	6th	1964	157	578	171	94	21	9	47	121	111	82	72
207	McCovey, Willie	1st	1969	149	491	157	84	26	2	45	101	126	121	66
273	McCovey, Willie	2nd	1970	152	495	143	63	39	2	39	98	126	137	75
186	McGraw, John	1st	1894	124	512	174	141	18	14	1	156	92	91	12
337	McGraw, John	2nd	1899	117	399	156	139	13	3	1	156	33	124	-
365	McGriff, Fred **	1st	1993	151	557	162	94	29	2	37	111	101	76	106
24	McGwire, Mark	1st	1998	155	509	152	61	21	-	70	130	147	162	155
60	McGwire, Mark	2nd	1999	153	521	145	58	21	1	65	118	147	133	141
145	McGwire, Mark	3rd	1996	130	423	132	59	21	-	52	104	113	116	112
312	McGwire, Mark	4th	1997	156	540	148	63	27	-	58	86	123	101	159
121	Medwick, Joe	1st	1937	156	633	237	140	56	10	31	111	154	41	50
283	Medwick, Joe	2nd	1935	154	634	224	142	46	13	23	132	126	30	59
325	Meusel, Bob	1st	1921	149	598	190	110	40	16	24	104	135	34	88
345	Minoso, Minnie	1st	1954	153	568	182	116	29	18	19	119	116	77	46
296	Mitchell, Kevin	1st	1989	154	543	158	71	34	6	47	100	125	87	115
99	Mize, Johnny*	1st	1947	154	586	177	98	26	2	51	137	138	74	42
139	Mize, Johnny*	2nd	1940	155	579	182	95	31	13	43	111	137	82	49
176	Morgan, Joe	1st	1976	141	472	151	89	30	5	27	113	111	114	41
241	Murphy, Dale	1st	1983	162	589	178	114	24	4	36	131	121	90	110
352	Murray, Eddie	1st	1985	156	583	173	104	37	1	31	111	124	84	68
64	Musial, Stan*	1st	1948	155	611	230	127	46	18	39	135	131	79	34
138	Musial, Stan*	2nd	1949	157	612	207	117	41	13	36	128	123	107	38
234	Musial, Stan*	3rd	1954	153	591	195	110	41	9	35	120	126	103	39
236	Musial, Stan*	4th	1953	157	593	200	108	53	9	30	127	113	105	32
261	Musial, Stan*	5th	1951	152	578	205	131	30	12	32	124	108	98	40

The Greatest 300 Single Seasons and Others Listed Alphabetically

SB	CS	HBP	SF	GDP	AVG	OBP	SLG	TRP	RPA	TNB	TBA	TRP Rating	RPA Rating	TNB Rating	TBA Rating	TOP	Rating
20	-	1	-	-	.348	.404	.646	289	.406	501	.705	83.05	76.17	82.13	77.66	319.00	81.33
5	-	-	-	-	.356	.407	.657	271	.404	464	.693	77.87	75.79	76.07	76.33	306.06	78.03
7	-	1	-	-	.337	.398	.584	242	.370	414	.633	69.54	69.34	67.87	69.77	276.51	70.50
-	2	3	5	12	.326	.407	.642	245	.365	447	.666	70.40	68.42	73.28	73.42	285.52	72.80
27	-	13	-	-	.422	.459	.635	270	.466	409	.705	77.59	87.23	67.05	77.72	309.58	78.93
129	-	5	-	-	.316	.366	.413	246	.363	438	.647	70.69	68.09	71.80	71.31	281.89	71.87
23	-	6	-	-	.346	.401	.520	273	.408	398	.595	78.45	76.47	65.25	65.57	285.73	72.85
2	2	4	5	9	.333	.423	.637	238	.377	424	.672	68.39	70.68	69.51	74.06	282.63	72.06
10	1	2	4	4	.353	.464	.705	262	.400	499	.762	75.29	74.95	81.80	83.96	316.01	80.57
12	1	-	5	2	.317	.448	.687	260	.402	490	.757	74.71	75.30	80.33	83.47	313.81	80.01
16	3	-	3	5	.365	.512	.665	215	.342	474	.755	61.78	64.15	77.70	83.19	286.83	73.13
18	3	2	2	11	.304	.443	.592	224	.338	453	.683	64.37	63.31	74.26	75.30	277.24	70.69
8	1	3	3	4	.306	.431	.611	220	.344	439	.686	63.22	64.41	71.97	75.60	275.20	70.16
17	5	-	-	-	.378	.414	.575	210	.310	418	.617	60.34	58.12	68.52	68.05	255.04	65.03
-	-	7	7	16	.269	.372	.620	274	.384	467	.654	78.74	71.91	76.56	72.09	299.29	76.31
4	3	8	4	11	.356	.479	.628	234	.360	446	.686	67.24	67.46	73.11	75.62	283.44	72.26
3	-	5	8	13	.324	.423	.579	245	.361	426	.628	70.40	67.71	69.84	69.25	277.20	70.67
3	1	3	13	15	.296	.371	.577	237	.339	423	.604	68.10	63.44	69.34	66.60	267.49	68.20
1	3	2	-	6	.302	.406	.627	245	.357	462	.673	70.40	66.92	75.74	74.23	287.29	73.25
2	2	2	15	15	.324	.371	.567	252	.341	428	.578	72.41	63.81	70.16	63.75	270.13	68.87
18	2	4	3	19	.304	.384	.615	271	.374	480	.662	77.87	70.04	78.69	72.97	299.57	76.38
24	4	4	7	12	.319	.400	.659	250	.367	485	.711	71.84	68.69	79.51	78.38	298.41	76.08
18	9	2	4	14	.308	.393	.584	252	.374	426	.633	72.41	70.16	69.84	69.76	282.18	71.94
8	5	2	7	12	.345	.411	.667	229	.351	448	.687	65.80	65.81	73.44	75.73	280.79	71.59
9	4	-	2	11	.317	.398	.645	230	.355	441	.682	66.09	66.61	72.30	75.12	280.12	71.42
19	5	1	3	11	.296	.383	.607	232	.344	448	.664	66.67	64.40	73.44	73.15	277.66	70.79
-	-	4	7	11	.320	.453	.656	227	.358	447	.705	65.23	67.09	73.28	77.71	283.31	72.23
-	-	3	3	13	.289	.444	.612	224	.344	443	.680	64.37	64.48	72.62	75.00	276.47	70.49
78	-	13	-	-	.340	.451	.436	248	.403	405	.657	71.26	75.44	66.39	72.46	285.56	72.81
73	-	14	-	-	.391	.547	.446	189	.352	389	.724	54.31	65.95	63.77	79.84	263.87	67.28
5	3	2	5	14	.291	.375	.549	212	.324	386	.590	60.92	60.74	63.28	65.05	249.99	63.74
1	-	6	4	8	.299	.470	.752	277	.402	552	.801	79.60	75.33	90.49	88.30	333.72	85.09
-	-	2	5	12	.278	.424	.697	265	.394	498	.740	76.15	73.78	81.64	81.56	313.13	79.83
-	-	8	1	14	.312	.467	.730	217	.386	433	.770	62.36	72.35	70.98	84.92	290.61	74.09
3	-	9	7	9	.274	.393	.646	209	.314	462	.694	60.06	58.80	75.74	76.45	271.05	69.11
4	-	2	-	11	.374	.414	.641	265	.386	453	.659	76.15	72.28	74.26	72.67	295.37	75.31
4	-	4	-	15	.353	.386	.576	258	.378	403	.590	74.14	70.78	66.07	65.03	276.02	70.37
17	6	2	-	-	.318	.356	.559	239	.377	381	.601	68.68	70.64	62.46	66.23	268.01	68.33
18	11	16	8	20	.320	.411	.535	235	.341	404	.586	67.53	63.91	66.23	64.62	262.29	66.87
3	4	3	7	6	.291	.388	.635	225	.348	434	.672	64.66	65.26	71.15	74.04	275.11	70.14
2	-	4	-	6	.302	.384	.614	275	.410	440	.657	79.02	76.91	72.13	72.38	300.44	76.60
7	-	5	-	10	.314	.404	.636	248	.367	462	.683	71.26	68.74	75.74	75.32	291.07	74.21
60	9	1	12	2	.320	.444	.576	224	.373	438	.729	64.37	69.84	71.80	80.32	286.33	73.00
30	4	2	6	15	.302	.393	.540	252	.359	436	.621	72.41	67.27	71.48	68.45	279.61	71.29
5	2	2	8	8	.297	.383	.523	235	.343	394	.575	67.53	64.28	64.59	63.39	259.80	66.24
7	-	3	-	18	.376	.450	.702	266	.374	518	.729	76.44	70.10	84.92	80.30	311.75	79.48
3	-	2	-	12	.338	.438	.624	251	.342	494	.674	72.13	64.16	80.98	74.28	291.55	74.33
1	4	4	7	20	.330	.428	.607	246	.339	463	.639	70.69	63.58	75.90	70.39	280.56	71.53
3	7	-	-	10	.337	.437	.609	240	.339	462	.653	68.97	63.52	75.74	71.92	280.14	71.42
4	7	1	-	6	.355	.449	.614	232	.340	451	.660	66.67	63.65	73.93	72.78	277.03	70.63

Single Season Statistics O-R

Rank	Player	Player Season	Year	G	AB	H	1B	2B	3B	HR	RUN	RBI	BB	SO	
								The Greatest 300 Single Seasons and Others Listed Alphabetically							
89	O'Doul, Lefty	1st	1929	154	638	254	181	35	6	32	152	122	76	19	
331	Olerud, John	1st	1993	158	551	200	120	54	2	24	109	107	114	65	
371	Oliva, Tony	1st	1964	161	672	217	133	43	9	32	109	94	34	68	
21	O'Neill, Tip	1st	1887	124	567	275	190	52	19	14	167	123	50	-	
256	Ordonez, Magglio**	1st	2002	153	590	189	103	47	1	38	116	135	53	77	
42	Ott, Mel	1st	1929	150	545	179	98	37	2	42	138	151	113	38	
149	Ott, Mel	2nd	1936	150	534	175	108	28	6	33	120	135	111	41	
189	Ott, Mel	3rd	1932	154	566	180	104	30	8	38	119	123	100	39	
201	Ott, Mel	4th	1934	153	582	190	116	29	10	35	119	135	85	43	
216	Ott, Mel	5th	1930	148	521	182	118	34	5	25	122	119	103	35	
285	Ott, Mel	6th	1938	150	527	164	99	23	6	36	116	116	118	47	
200	Palmiero, Rafael**	1st	1999	158	565	183	105	30	1	47	96	148	97	69	
278	Palmiero, Rafael**	2nd	1996	162	626	181	100	40	2	39	110	142	95	96	
338	Parker, Dave	1st	1978	148	581	194	120	32	12	30	102	117	57	92	
306	Perez, Tony	1st	1970	158	587	186	112	28	6	40	107	129	83	134	
297	Piazza, Mike**	1st	1997	152	556	201	128	32	1	40	104	124	69	77	
369	Puckett, Kirby	1st	1988	158	657	234	163	42	5	24	109	121	23	83	
91	Pujols, Albert**	1st	2003	157	591	212	117	51	1	43	137	124	79	65	
129	Pujols, Albert**	2nd	2004	154	592	196	97	51	2	46	133	123	84	52	
293	Pujols, Albert**	3rd	2001	161	590	194	106	47	4	37	112	130	69	93	
40	Ramirez, Manny**	1st	1999	147	522	174	93	34	3	44	131	165	96	131	
229	Ramirez, Manny**	2nd	1998	150	571	168	86	35	2	45	108	145	76	121	
231	Ramirez, Manny**	3rd	2000	118	439	154	80	34	2	38	92	122	86	117	
291	Ramirez, Manny**	4th	2004	152	568	175	88	44	-	43	108	130	82	124	
195	Rice, Jim	1st	1978	163	677	213	127	25	15	46	121	139	58	126	
281	Rice, Jim	2nd	1979	158	619	201	117	39	6	39	117	130	57	97	
363	Ripkin, Cal, Jr.	1st	1991	162	650	210	125	46	5	34	99	114	53	46	
100	Robinson, Frank	1st	1962	162	609	208	116	51	2	39	134	136	76	62	
191	Robinson, Frank	2nd	1966	155	576	182	97	34	2	49	122	122	87	90	
210	Robinson, Frank	3rd	1961	153	545	176	100	32	7	37	117	124	71	64	
305	Robinson, Jackie	1st	1949	156	593	203	137	38	12	16	122	124	86	27	
104	Rodriguez, Alex**	1st	2001	162	632	201	114	34	1	52	133	135	75	131	
107	Rodriguez, Alex**	2nd	2002	162	624	187	101	27	2	57	125	142	87	122	
112	Rodriguez, Alex**	3rd	2000	148	554	175	98	34	2	41	134	132	100	121	
123	Rodriguez, Alex**	4th	1996	146	601	215	124	54	1	36	141	123	59	104	
214	Rodriguez, Alex**	5th	2003	161	607	181	98	30	6	47	124	118	87	126	
248	Rodriguez, Alex**	6th	1998	161	686	213	131	35	5	42	123	124	45	121	
374	Rose, Pete	1st	1969	156	627	218	158	33	11	16	120	82	88	65	
151	Rosen, Al	1st	1953	155	599	201	126	27	5	43	115	145	85	48	
1	Ruth, Babe	1st	1921	152	540	204	85	44	16	59	177	171	145	81	
2	Ruth, Babe	2nd	1927	151	540	192	95	29	8	60	158	164	137	89	
3	Ruth, Babe	3rd	1920	142	458	172	73	36	9	54	158	137	150	80	
12	Ruth, Babe	4th	1930	145	518	186	100	28	9	49	150	153	136	61	
15	Ruth, Babe	5th	1931	145	534	199	119	31	3	46	149	163	128	51	
17	Ruth, Babe	6th	1928	154	536	173	82	29	8	54	163	142	137	87	
20	Ruth, Babe	7th	1923	152	522	205	106	45	13	41	151	131	170	93	
22	Ruth, Babe	8th	1926	152	495	184	102	30	5	47	139	146	144	76	
37	Ruth, Babe	9th	1924	153	529	200	108	39	7	46	143	121	142	81	
41	Ruth, Babe	10th	1929	135	499	172	94	26	6	46	121	154	72	60	
73	Ruth, Babe	11th	1932	133	457	156	97	13	5	41	120	137	130	62	

The Greatest 300 Single Seasons and Others Listed Alphabetically

SB	CS	HBP	SF	GDP	AVG	OBP	SLG	Total Offensive Production Statistics				TRP Rating	RPA Rating	TNB Rating	TBA Rating	TOP Composite	
								TRP	RPA	TNB	TBA					TOP	Rating
2	-	4	-	-	.398	.465	.622	274	.382	479	.667	78.74	71.51	78.52	73.53	302.30	77.07
-	2	7	7	12	.363	.473	.599	216	.313	449	.650	62.07	58.57	73.61	71.62	265.86	67.78
12	6	6	3	9	.323	.359	.557	203	.280	420	.580	58.33	52.54	68.85	63.94	243.66	62.12
30	-	5	-	-	.485	.531	.718	290	.466	492	.791	83.33	87.36	80.66	87.18	338.53	86.31
7	5	7	3	21	.320	.381	.597	251	.372	414	.614	72.13	69.78	67.87	67.70	277.48	70.74
6	-	6	-	-	.328	.449	.635	289	.435	471	.709	83.05	81.56	77.21	78.18	319.99	81.59
6	-	5	-	8	.328	.448	.588	255	.388	436	.663	73.28	72.62	71.48	73.03	290.40	74.04
6	-	4	-	-	.318	.424	.601	242	.361	450	.672	69.54	67.68	73.77	74.02	285.02	72.67
-	-	3	-	10	.326	.415	.591	254	.374	432	.635	72.99	69.99	70.82	70.02	283.82	72.36
9	-	2	-	-	.349	.458	.578	241	.385	415	.663	69.25	72.14	68.03	73.07	282.49	72.02
2	-	5	-	8	.311	.442	.583	232	.353	432	.657	66.67	66.07	70.82	72.36	275.91	70.35
2	4	3	9	12	.324	.420	.630	244	.356	454	.662	70.11	66.55	74.43	72.83	283.93	72.39
8	-	3	8	9	.289	.381	.546	252	.340	448	.605	72.41	63.72	73.44	66.63	276.22	70.42
20	7	2	2	8	.334	.394	.585	219	.337	412	.634	62.93	63.13	67.54	69.86	263.46	67.17
8	3	4	7	15	.317	.401	.589	236	.339	438	.629	67.82	63.54	71.80	69.36	272.52	69.48
5	1	3	5	18	.362	.431	.638	228	.350	431	.662	65.52	65.63	70.66	72.97	274.77	70.05
6	7	2	9	17	.356	.375	.545	230	.325	382	.540	66.09	60.87	62.62	59.47	249.05	63.50
5	1	10	5	13	.359	.439	.667	261	.374	487	.698	75.00	70.07	79.84	76.90	301.80	76.95
5	5	7	9	21	.331	.415	.657	256	.359	480	.673	73.56	67.28	78.69	74.20	293.73	74.89
1	3	9	7	21	.329	.403	.610	242	.348	436	.626	69.54	65.15	71.48	69.04	275.21	70.17
2	4	13	9	12	.333	.442	.663	296	.454	453	.695	85.06	85.07	74.26	76.58	320.96	81.83
5	3	6	10	18	.294	.377	.599	253	.372	426	.626	72.70	69.61	69.84	68.94	281.10	71.67
1	1	3	4	9	.351	.457	.697	214	.396	395	.730	61.49	74.12	64.75	80.47	280.84	71.60
2	4	6	7	17	.308	.397	.613	238	.350	434	.638	68.39	65.58	71.15	70.34	275.46	70.23
7	5	5	5	15	.315	.370	.600	260	.342	471	.620	74.71	64.10	77.21	68.30	284.33	72.49
9	4	4	8	16	.325	.381	.596	247	.351	435	.618	70.98	65.74	71.31	68.10	276.13	70.40
6	1	5	9	19	.323	.374	.566	213	.289	431	.586	61.21	54.23	70.66	64.54	250.63	63.90
18	9	11	5	13	.342	.421	.624	270	.378	476	.667	77.59	70.86	78.03	73.48	299.95	76.48
8	5	10	7	24	.316	.410	.637	244	.347	467	.663	70.11	64.94	76.56	73.11	284.73	72.59
22	3	10	10	15	.323	.404	.611	241	.370	433	.665	69.25	69.37	70.98	73.31	282.91	72.13
37	14	8	-	22	.342	.432	.528	246	.347	430	.606	70.69	65.02	70.49	66.84	273.04	69.61
18	3	16	9	17	.318	.399	.622	268	.358	499	.666	77.01	67.05	81.80	73.43	299.29	76.31
9	4	10	4	14	.300	.392	.623	267	.361	491	.664	76.72	67.70	80.49	73.23	298.14	76.01
15	4	7	11	10	.316	.420	.606	266	.390	454	.666	76.44	73.08	74.43	73.37	297.32	75.80
15	4	4	7	15	.358	.414	.631	264	.385	453	.660	75.86	72.11	74.26	72.78	295.02	75.22
17	3	15	6	16	.298	.396	.600	242	.331	480	.657	69.54	62.03	78.69	72.37	282.63	72.06
46	13	10	4	12	.310	.360	.560	247	.326	472	.624	70.98	61.14	77.38	68.72	278.21	70.93
7	10	5	6	13	.348	.428	.512	202	.273	411	.556	58.05	51.22	67.38	61.30	237.94	60.66
8	7	4	-	19	.336	.422	.613	260	.368	457	.646	74.71	68.91	74.92	71.24	289.78	73.88
17	13	4	-	-	.378	.512	.846	348	.505	610	.885	100.00	94.64	100.00	97.58	392.22	100.00
7	6	-	-	-	.356	.486	.772	322	.476	555	.820	92.53	89.12	90.98	90.35	362.99	92.55
14	14	3	-	-	.376	.532	.847	295	.483	541	.885	84.77	90.47	88.69	97.59	361.52	92.17
10	10	1	-	-	.359	.493	.732	303	.463	516	.788	87.07	86.68	84.59	86.83	345.17	88.00
5	4	-	-	-	.373	.494	.700	312	.471	503	.760	89.66	88.31	82.46	83.74	344.17	87.75
4	5	3	-	-	.323	.463	.709	305	.451	519	.768	87.64	84.54	85.08	84.62	341.89	87.17
17	21	4	-	-	.393	.545	.764	282	.405	569	.818	81.03	75.92	93.28	90.10	340.34	86.77
11	9	3	-	-	.372	.516	.737	285	.444	514	.801	81.90	83.18	84.26	88.24	337.58	86.07
9	13	4	-	-	.378	.513	.739	264	.391	533	.790	75.86	73.29	87.38	87.03	323.55	82.49
5	3	3	-	-	.345	.430	.697	275	.479	425	.740	79.02	89.77	69.67	81.60	320.07	81.61
2	2	2	-	-	.341	.489	.661	257	.436	434	.737	73.85	81.76	71.15	81.21	307.97	78.52

Single Season Statistics O-R

The Greatest 300 Single Seasons and Others Listed Alphabetically

Rank	Player	Player Season	Year	G	AB	H	1B	2B	3B	HR	RUN	RBI	BB	SO
194	Ruth, Babe	12th	1919	130	432	139	64	34	12	29	103	114	101	58
298	Schmidt, Mike	1st	1980	150	548	157	76	25	8	48	104	121	89	119
350	Seymour, Cy	1st	1905	149	581	219	150	40	21	8	95	121	51	-
339	Sheckard, Jimmy	1st	1901	133	554	196	137	29	19	11	116	104	47	-
140	Sheffield, Gary**	1st	2003	155	576	190	112	37	2	39	126	132	86	55
159	Sheffield, Gary**	2nd	1996	161	519	163	87	33	1	42	118	120	142	66
357	Sievers, Roy	1st	1957	152	572	172	102	23	5	42	99	114	76	55
14	Simmons, Al*	1st	1930	138	554	211	118	41	16	36	152	165	39	34
98	Simmons, Al*	2nd	1929	143	581	212	128	41	9	34	114	157	31	38
128	Simmons, Al*	3rd	1932	154	670	216	144	28	9	35	144	151	47	76
232	Simmons, Al*	4th	1931	128	513	200	128	37	13	22	105	128	47	45
288	Simmons, Al*	5th	1925	153	658	253	174	43	12	24	122	129	35	41
101	Sisler, George	1st	1920	154	631	257	171	49	18	19	137	122	46	19
196	Sisler, George	2nd	1922	142	586	246	178	42	18	8	134	105	49	14
111	Snider, Duke	1st	1955	148	538	166	84	34	6	42	126	136	104	87
120	Snider, Duke	2nd	1953	153	590	198	114	38	4	42	132	126	82	90
147	Snider, Duke	3rd	1954	149	584	199	110	39	10	40	120	130	84	96
18	Sosa, Sammy**	1st	2001	160	577	189	86	34	5	64	146	160	116	153
57	Sosa, Sammy**	2nd	1998	159	643	198	112	20	-	66	134	158	73	171
156	Sosa, Sammy**	3rd	1999	162	625	180	91	24	2	63	114	141	78	171
180	Sosa, Sammy**	4th	2000	156	604	193	104	38	1	50	106	138	91	168
118	Speaker, Tris	1st	1923	150	574	218	131	59	11	17	133	130	93	15
215	Speaker, Tris	2nd	1912	153	580	222	147	53	12	10	136	90	82	-
284	Speaker, Tris	3rd	1920	150	552	214	145	50	11	8	137	107	97	13
257	Stargell, Willie	1st	1973	148	522	156	66	43	3	44	106	119	80	129
265	Stargell, Willie	2nd	1971	141	511	151	77	26	-	48	104	125	83	154
205	Stephens, Vern	1st	1949	155	610	177	105	31	2	39	113	159	101	73
84	Stovey, Harry	1st	1889	137	556	171	101	38	13	19	152	119	77	68
179	Stovey, Harry	2nd	1890	118	481	143	95	25	11	12	142	84	81	38
378	Suzuki, Ichiro**	1st	2001	157	692	242	192	34	8	8	127	69	30	53
380	Suzuki, Ichiro**	2nd	2004	161	704	262	225	24	5	8	101	60	49	63
109	Terry, Bill	1st	1930	154	633	254	177	39	15	23	139	129	57	33
132	Thomas, Frank **	1st	2000	159	582	191	104	44	-	43	115	143	112	94
206	Thomas, Frank **	2nd	1996	141	527	184	118	26	-	40	110	134	109	70
228	Thomas, Frank **	3rd	1994	113	399	141	68	34	1	38	106	101	109	61
253	Thomas, Frank **	4th	1997	146	530	184	114	35	-	35	110	125	109	69
263	Thomas, Frank **	5th	1993	153	549	174	97	36	-	41	106	128	112	54
202	Thome, Jim**	1st	2002	147	480	146	73	19	2	52	101	118	122	139
208	Thome, Jim**	2nd	1996	151	505	157	86	28	5	38	122	116	123	141
276	Thome, Jim**	3rd	2001	156	526	153	77	26	1	49	101	124	111	185
282	Thome, Jim**	4th	2003	159	578	154	74	30	3	47	111	131	111	182
30	Thompson, Sam	1st	1895	118	533	210	128	42	22	18	131	165	31	11
55	Thompson, Sam	2nd	1894	102	458	185	117	29	26	13	115	141	40	13
79	Thompson, Sam	3rd	1887	127	576	234	172	29	23	10	118	166	32	19
245	Thompson, Sam	4th	1893	130	583	220	162	33	14	11	130	126	50	17
348	Torre, Joe	1st	1971	161	634	230	164	34	8	24	97	137	63	70
370	Traynor, Pie	1st	1930	130	497	182	140	22	11	9	90	119	48	19
71	Trosky, Hal*	1st	1936	151	629	216	120	45	9	42	124	162	36	58
178	Trosky, Hal*	2nd	1934	154	625	206	117	45	9	35	117	142	58	49
372	Tucker, Tuck	1st	1894	80	339	141	110	21	9	1	91	82	23	13

The Greatest 300 Single Seasons and Others Listed Alphabetically

SB	CS	HBP	SF	GDP	AVG	OBP	SLG	TRP	RPA	TNB	TBA	TRP Rating	RPA Rating	TNB Rating	TBA Rating	TOP	Rating
7	-	6	-	-	.322	.456	.657	217	.403	398	.738	62.36	75.44	65.25	81.38	284.42	72.52
12	5	2	13	6	.286	.380	.624	225	.342	440	.669	64.66	64.07	72.13	73.70	274.56	70.00
21	-	2	-	-	.377	.429	.559	216	.341	399	.629	62.07	63.84	65.41	69.36	260.68	66.46
35	-	3	-	-	.354	.407	.534	220	.364	381	.631	63.22	68.25	62.46	69.52	263.45	67.17
18	4	8	8	16	.330	.419	.604	258	.372	456	.657	74.14	69.66	74.75	72.42	290.97	74.19
16	9	10	6	16	.314	.465	.624	238	.343	483	.697	68.39	64.35	79.18	76.82	288.74	73.62
1	1	7	2	9	.301	.388	.579	213	.320	414	.622	61.21	59.93	67.87	68.51	257.52	65.66
9	2	1	-	-	.381	.423	.708	317	.534	439	.739	91.09	100.00	71.97	81.45	344.51	87.84
4	2	1	-	-	.365	.398	.642	271	.442	407	.664	77.87	82.84	66.72	73.18	300.61	76.64
4	2	1	-	-	.322	.368	.548	295	.411	417	.581	84.77	76.99	68.36	64.01	294.13	74.99
3	3	3	-	-	.390	.444	.641	233	.414	379	.673	66.95	77.55	62.13	74.19	280.83	71.60
7	14	1	-	-	.384	.416	.596	251	.362	421	.607	72.13	67.77	69.02	66.86	275.77	70.31
42	17	2	-	-	.407	.449	.632	259	.381	472	.695	74.43	71.48	77.38	76.61	299.89	76.46
51	19	3	-	-	.420	.467	.594	239	.375	432	.677	68.68	70.19	70.82	74.63	284.32	72.49
9	7	1	6	9	.309	.418	.628	262	.398	445	.676	75.29	74.61	72.95	74.54	297.39	75.82
16	7	3	-	10	.336	.419	.627	258	.377	464	.677	74.14	70.58	76.07	74.66	295.44	75.32
6	6	4	6	12	.341	.423	.647	250	.362	466	.675	71.84	67.89	76.39	74.43	290.56	74.08
-	2	6	12	6	.328	.437	.737	306	.427	545	.760	87.93	79.97	89.34	83.78	341.02	86.95
18	9	1	5	20	.308	.377	.647	292	.394	499	.673	83.91	73.74	81.80	74.12	313.57	79.95
7	8	3	6	17	.288	.367	.635	255	.350	477	.654	73.28	65.55	78.20	72.12	289.13	73.72
7	4	2	8	12	.320	.406	.634	244	.340	479	.668	70.11	63.77	78.52	73.63	286.04	72.93
10	9	4	-	-	.380	.469	.610	263	.392	448	.668	75.57	73.44	73.44	73.59	296.05	75.48
52	-	6	-	-	.383	.464	.567	226	.338	469	.702	64.94	63.40	76.89	77.38	282.60	72.05
10	13	5	-	-	.388	.483	.562	244	.373	409	.625	70.11	69.91	67.05	68.93	276.00	70.37
-	-	3	4	6	.299	.392	.646	225	.366	420	.683	64.66	68.55	68.85	75.27	277.33	70.71
-	-	7	5	8	.295	.398	.628	229	.373	411	.669	65.80	69.89	67.38	73.78	276.84	70.58
2	2	-	-	19	.290	.391	.539	272	.373	430	.589	78.16	69.82	70.49	64.92	283.39	72.25
63	-	1	-	-	.308	.393	.525	271	.427	433	.683	77.87	80.10	70.98	75.27	304.22	77.56
97	-	5	-	-	.297	.404	.470	226	.399	409	.721	64.94	74.69	67.05	79.50	286.18	72.96
56	14	8	4	3	.350	.381	.457	196	.266	396	.537	56.32	49.83	64.92	59.22	230.29	58.72
36	11	4	3	6	.372	.414	.455	161	.210	398	.520	46.26	39.38	65.25	57.27	208.16	53.07
8	-	1	-	-	.401	.452	.619	268	.388	458	.663	77.01	72.67	75.08	73.05	297.82	75.93
1	3	5	8	13	.328	.436	.625	258	.358	479	.665	74.14	67.15	78.52	73.32	293.13	74.74
1	1	5	8	25	.349	.459	.626	244	.362	444	.659	70.11	67.84	72.79	72.60	283.34	72.24
2	3	2	7	15	.353	.487	.729	207	.389	401	.754	59.48	72.91	65.74	83.07	281.21	71.70
1	1	3	7	15	.347	.456	.611	235	.354	436	.657	67.53	66.32	71.48	72.37	277.69	70.80
4	2	2	13	10	.317	.426	.607	234	.341	449	.655	67.24	63.92	73.61	72.14	276.90	70.60
1	2	5	6	5	.304	.445	.677	219	.354	451	.730	62.93	66.40	73.93	80.43	283.70	72.33
2	2	6	2	13	.311	.450	.612	238	.367	438	.675	68.39	68.72	71.80	74.38	283.29	72.23
-	1	4	3	9	.291	.416	.624	225	.345	442	.677	64.66	64.56	72.46	74.60	276.28	70.44
-	3	4	5	5	.266	.385	.573	242	.344	443	.630	69.54	64.50	72.62	69.45	276.12	70.40
24	-	5	-	-	.394	.432	.657	296	.520	410	.721	85.06	97.48	67.21	79.42	329.16	83.92
29	-	1	-	-	.404	.453	.666	256	.513	375	.752	73.56	96.13	61.48	82.83	314.00	80.06
22	-	9	-	-	.406	.446	.589	284	.460	402	.652	81.61	86.25	65.90	71.81	305.57	77.91
18	-	6	-	-	.377	.432	.539	256	.401	388	.607	73.56	75.07	63.61	66.92	279.16	71.17
4	1	4	5	18	.363	.421	.555	234	.323	422	.583	67.24	60.56	69.18	64.24	261.23	66.60
7	-	1	-	-	.366	.423	.509	209	.383	309	.566	60.06	71.73	50.66	62.37	244.81	62.42
6	5	3	-	-	.343	.382	.644	286	.428	445	.666	82.18	80.23	72.95	73.42	308.78	78.73
2	2	2	-	-	.330	.388	.598	259	.378	434	.634	74.43	70.85	71.15	69.83	286.25	72.98
11	-	2	-	-	.416	.456	.540	173	.475	219	.602	49.71	89.06	35.90	66.31	240.98	61.44

Single Season Statistics R-T

The Greatest 300 Single Seasons and Others Listed Alphabetically

Rank	Player	Player Season	Year	G	AB	H	1B	2B	3B	HR	RUN	RBI	BB	SO
335	Vaughan, Arky	1st	1935	137	499	192	129	34	10	19	108	99	97	18
303	Vaughn, Greg	1st	1998	158	573	156	74	28	4	50	112	119	79	121
175	Vaughn, Mo	1st	1996	161	635	207	133	29	1	44	118	143	95	154
333	Wagner, Honus	1st	1908	151	568	201	133	39	19	10	100	109	54	-
34	Walker, Larry **	1st	1997	153	568	208	109	46	4	49	143	130	78	90
162	Walker, Larry **	2nd	1999	127	438	166	99	26	4	37	108	115	57	52
177	Walker, Larry **	3rd	2001	142	497	174	98	35	3	38	107	123	82	103
315	Waner, Paul	1st	1927	155	623	237	168	42	18	9	114	131	60	14
375	Wheat, Zack	1st	1922	152	600	201	144	29	12	16	92	112	45	22
334	Williams, Bernie**	1st	2000	141	537	165	92	37	6	30	108	121	71	84
164	Williams, Billy	1st	1970	161	636	205	125	34	4	42	137	129	72	65
54	Williams, Ken*	1st	1922	153	585	194	110	34	11	39	128	155	74	31
29	Williams, Ted*	1st	1949	155	566	194	109	39	3	43	150	159	162	48
48	Williams, Ted*	2nd	1941	143	456	185	112	33	3	37	135	120	147	27
52	Williams, Ted*	3rd	1942	150	522	186	111	34	5	36	141	137	145	51
65	Williams, Ted*	4th	1946	150	514	176	93	37	8	38	142	123	156	44
88	Williams, Ted*	5th	1939	149	565	185	99	44	11	31	131	145	107	64
130	Williams, Ted*	6th	1948	137	509	188	116	44	3	25	124	127	126	41
135	Williams, Ted*	7th	1947	156	528	181	100	40	9	32	125	114	162	47
225	Williams, Ted*	8th	1940	144	561	193	113	43	14	23	134	113	96	54
322	Williams, Ted*	9th	1957	132	420	163	96	28	1	38	96	87	119	43
5	Wilson, Hack	1st	1930	155	585	208	111	35	6	56	146	191	105	84
53	Wilson, Hack	2nd	1929	150	574	198	124	30	5	39	135	159	78	83
199	Wilson, Hack	3rd	1927	146	551	175	103	30	12	30	119	129	71	70
358	Winfield, Dave	1st	1979	159	597	184	113	27	10	34	97	118	85	71
243	Yastrzemski, Carl	1st	1967	161	579	189	110	31	4	44	112	121	91	69
269	Yastrzemski, Carl	2nd	1970	161	566	186	117	29	-	40	125	102	128	66
300	York, Rudy	1st	1940	155	588	186	101	46	6	33	105	134	89	88
314	Yount, Robin	1st	1982	156	635	210	123	46	12	29	129	114	54	63
366	Zimmerman, Heinie	1st	1912	145	557	207	138	41	14	14	95	99	38	60

Single Season Statistics V-Z

* Player missed time for military service
** Active player. Statistics through 2004 season
TOP ranking for players with less than 70% rating is based upon comparison to listed players only.

The Greatest 300 Single Seasons and Others Listed Alphabetically

SB	CS	HBP	SF	GDP	AVG	OBP	SLG	Total Offensive Production Statistics				TRP Rating	RPA Rating	TNB Rating	TBA Rating	TOP Composite	
								TRP	RPA	TNB	TBA					TOP	Rating
4	-	7	-	5	.385	.491	.607	207	.340	411	.676	59.48	63.80	67.38	74.50	265.16	67.60
11	4	5	4	7	.272	.363	.597	231	.346	433	.648	66.38	64.80	70.98	71.44	273.60	69.76
2	-	14	8	17	.326	.420	.583	261	.339	481	.625	75.00	63.60	78.85	68.94	286.39	73.02
53	-	5	-	-	.354	.415	.542	209	.333	420	.670	60.06	62.46	68.85	73.83	265.20	67.61
33	8	14	4	15	.366	.452	.720	273	.402	526	.775	78.45	75.34	86.23	85.38	325.40	82.96
11	4	12	6	12	.379	.458	.710	223	.425	387	.737	64.08	79.59	63.44	81.24	288.36	73.52
14	5	14	8	9	.350	.449	.662	230	.377	434	.711	66.09	70.65	71.15	78.41	286.31	73.00
5	-	3	-	-	.380	.437	.549	245	.357	410	.598	70.40	66.92	67.21	65.87	270.41	68.94
9	6	7	-	-	.335	.388	.503	204	.313	357	.548	58.62	58.63	58.52	60.35	236.12	60.20
13	5	5	3	15	.307	.391	.566	229	.363	388	.615	65.80	68.00	63.61	67.77	265.19	67.61
7	1	2	4	13	.322	.391	.586	266	.366	453	.623	76.44	68.56	74.26	68.68	287.94	73.41
37	20	7	-	-	.332	.413	.627	283	.425	465	.698	81.32	79.62	76.23	76.95	314.13	80.09
1	1	2	-	22	.343	.490	.650	309	.411	532	.707	88.79	77.00	87.21	77.97	330.97	84.38
2	4	3	-	10	.406	.553	.735	255	.414	483	.784	73.28	77.57	79.18	86.42	316.44	80.68
3	2	4	-	12	.356	.499	.648	278	.407	488	.714	79.89	76.27	80.00	78.75	314.90	80.29
-	-	2	-	12	.342	.497	.667	265	.387	501	.732	76.15	72.60	82.13	80.73	311.60	79.45
2	1	2	-	10	.327	.436	.609	276	.404	454	.664	79.31	75.61	74.43	73.15	302.50	77.13
4	-	3	-	10	.369	.497	.615	251	.387	446	.688	72.13	72.58	73.11	75.86	293.68	74.88
-	1	2	-	10	.343	.499	.634	239	.340	498	.709	68.68	63.80	81.64	78.19	292.30	74.52
4	4	3	-	13	.344	.442	.594	247	.367	432	.642	70.98	68.77	70.82	70.75	281.31	71.72
-	1	5	2	11	.388	.526	.731	183	.329	430	.772	52.59	61.56	70.49	85.08	269.73	68.77
3	-	1	-	-	.356	.454	.723	337	.488	532	.770	96.84	91.39	87.21	84.85	360.29	91.86
3	-	2	-	-	.345	.425	.618	294	.450	438	.670	84.48	84.24	71.80	73.81	314.34	80.14
13	-	6	-	-	.318	.401	.579	248	.395	409	.651	71.26	74.00	67.05	71.78	284.09	72.43
15	9	2	2	9	.308	.395	.558	215	.309	426	.613	61.78	57.97	69.84	67.56	257.14	65.56
10	8	4	5	5	.326	.418	.622	233	.341	457	.668	66.95	63.83	74.92	73.64	279.34	71.22
23	13	1	2	12	.329	.452	.592	227	.320	474	.669	65.23	59.99	77.70	73.68	276.61	70.52
3	2	4	-	12	.316	.410	.583	239	.345	437	.631	68.68	64.62	71.64	69.50	274.44	69.97
14	3	1	10	19	.331	.379	.578	243	.338	433	.602	69.83	63.33	70.98	66.37	270.51	68.97
23	-	6	-	-	.372	.418	.571	194	.323	385	.641	55.75	60.49	63.11	70.60	249.95	63.73

125 of the Greatest Hitters Best 5 Consecutive Seasons:

E-1
Players Listed by Total Offensive Production

E-2
Players Listed Alphabetically

(Rating and Ranking of Total Offensive Production Statistics in Chapter 8)

5 Consecutive Year Statistics & Analysis Listed by Total Offensive Production Ranking

Rank	Player	Years	G	AB	H	1B	2B	3B	HR	RUN	RBI	BB	SO	SB
1	Ruth, Babe	1927-1931	730	2,627	922	490	143	34	255	741	776	610	348	31
N/R	Ruth, Babe	1920-1924	709	2,455	909	433	188	53	235	723	659	691	415	59
2	Gehrig, Lou	1927-1931	772	2,899	1,025	552	204	73	196	721	801	545	340	47
N/R	Gehrig, Lou	1933-1937	767	2,855	989	567	181	44	197	696	734	590	206	33
3	Foxx, Jimmie*	1932-1936	755	2,817	980	551	163	39	227	644	720	542	482	35
4	Bonds, Barry **	2000-2004	716	2,122	720	310	140	12	258	615	544	872	316	46
5	Williams, Ted*	1942-1949	748	2,639	925	529	194	28	174	682	660	751	231	8
6	Klein, Chuck	1929-1933	759	3,114	1,118	660	232	46	180	658	693	283	245	51
7	Sosa, Sammy**	1998-2002	787	3,005	920	483	135	10	292	622	705	461	807	34
8	Delahanty, Ed	1893-1897	613	2,601	1,008	690	193	73	52	683	605	315	89	176
9	Hornsby, Rogers	1921-1925	696	2,679	1,078	662	206	66	144	615	598	352	198	43
10	DiMaggio, Joe*	1937-1941	687	2,731	957	564	170	54	169	603	691	312	121	17
11	Wilson, Hack	1926-1930	738	2,759	914	534	163	40	177	586	708	400	392	33
12	Greenberg, Hank*	1937-1945	692	2,560	828	416	189	36	187	581	663	463	415	33
13	Kelley, Joe	1893-1897	643	2,528	928	653	157	80	38	695	539	422	128	264
14	Bagwell, Jeff**	1997-2001	791	2,858	853	452	188	8	205	654	634	598	590	100
15	McGwire, Mark	1995-1999	698	2,310	664	276	103	1	284	513	620	600	644	5
16	Helton, Todd**	2000-2004	789	2,850	994	543	250	15	186	627	615	538	400	20
17	Simmons, Al*	1928-1932	682	2,782	1,002	624	180	56	142	593	708	195	223	21
18	Griffey, Ken **	1996-2000	763	2,912	844	440	141	14	249	593	685	415	571	81
19	Rodriguez, Alex**	1999-2003	762	2,919	887	487	150	11	239	626	638	405	609	80
20	Duffy, Hugh	1890-1894	659	2,787	991	735	154	57	45	719	536	296	114	322
21	Mantle, Mickey	1954-1958	737	2,586	840	500	113	35	192	630	522	602	501	57
22	Ramirez, Manny**	1998-2002	677	2,497	810	433	167	9	201	508	664	412	601	8
23	Kiner, Ralph	1947-1951	761	2,747	807	434	113	26	234	574	604	586	339	12
24	Mays, Willie*	1961-1965	787	2,925	900	505	142	27	226	613	590	383	388	72
25	Hamilton, Billy	1894-1898	617	2,522	943	785	100	38	20	779	324	524	76	416
26	Musial, Stan*	1948-1952	764	2,934	1,028	616	200	56	156	597	562	467	177	26
27	Aaron, Hank	1959-1963	779	3,045	984	582	162	38	202	581	627	311	348	91
28	Belle, Albert	1994-1998	731	2,803	881	441	218	9	213	538	643	364	427	35
29	Snider, Duke	1953-1957	740	2,762	860	455	169	29	207	581	585	446	478	37
30	Jennings, Hughie	1894-1898	646	2,525	907	704	137	55	11	687	521	200	45	260
31	Giambi, Jason**	1999-2003	775	2,700	839	467	171	5	196	549	609	609	537	9
32	Thomas, Frank **	1993-1998	698	2,498	835	482	158	1	194	534	599	575	328	11
33	Thompson, Sam	1892-1896	620	2,693	956	654	162	77	63	588	636	208	73	112
34	Ott, Mel	1929-1933	742	2,709	850	509	160	24	157	581	611	471	204	32
35	Delgado, Carlos**	1999-2003	780	2,791	824	421	199	5	199	550	626	531	644	5
36	Cobb, Ty	1908-1912	732	2,807	1,075	767	182	90	36	576	516	233	-	324
37	Stovey, Harry	1887-1891	643	2,664	816	530	150	76	60	664	440	355	175	378
38	Gehringer, Charlie	1934-1938	754	2,984	1,025	699	214	33	79	667	554	463	100	51
39	Walker, Larry **	1997-2001	639	2,271	810	459	174	21	156	535	486	327	346	77
40	Thome, Jim**	1999-2003	766	2,635	740	378	135	9	218	520	587	589	848	2
41	Heilmann, Harry	1921-1925	714	2,724	1,032	690	199	62	81	531	594	330	173	37
42	Trosky, Hal*	1934-1938	762	3,041	957	561	199	43	154	535	655	272	267	17
43	Medwick, Joe	1934-1938	760	3,113	1,072	646	253	62	111	568	646	168	266	14
44	Burkett, Jesse	1893-1897	641	2,657	1,038	819	123	69	27	714	391	381	100	177
45	Bottomley, Jim	1925-1929	754	2,932	944	564	188	73	119	516	645	320	245	28
46	Guerrero, Vladimir**	1998-2002	793	3,017	982	572	184	29	197	524	582	299	389	111
47	Brouthers, Dan	1887-1891	623	2,499	900	643	153	70	34	603	491	391	65	149
48	Williams, Ken*	1921-1925	662	2,496	847	519	154	39	135	510	552	333	136	105

5 Consecutive Year Statistics & Analysis Listed by Total Offensive Production Ranking

CS	HBP	SF	GDP	AVG	OBP	SLG	Total Offensive Production Statistics				TRP Rating	RPA Rating	TNB Rating	TBA Rating	TOP Composite	
							TRP	RPA	TNB	TBA					TOP	Rating
28	7	-	-	.351	.474	.722	1,517	.468	2,518	.776	99.67	100.00	96.55	94.11	390.33	100.00
66	16	-	-	.370	.511	.777	1,382	.437	2,608	.825	90.80	93.46	100.00	100.00	384.27	98.45
49	15	-	-	.354	.458	.677	1,522	.440	2,521	.729	100.00	94.09	96.66	88.36	379.12	97.13
32	19	-	-	.346	.461	.648	1,430	.413	2,459	.710	93.96	88.28	94.29	86.07	362.59	92.89
19	3	-	-	.348	.454	.675	1,364	.406	2,463	.733	89.62	86.76	94.44	88.82	359.64	92.14
9	40	16	27	.339	.535	.781	1,159	.377	2,607	.847	76.15	80.55	99.96	102.72	359.38	92.07
4	13	-	66	.351	.496	.643	1,342	.387	2,465	.711	88.17	82.73	94.52	86.15	351.57	90.07
-	7	-	3	.359	.414	.636	1,351	.397	2,323	.682	88.76	84.80	89.07	82.67	345.30	88.46
23	15	35	69	.306	.397	.649	1,327	.370	2,438	.680	87.19	79.15	93.48	82.45	342.28	87.69
-	35	-	-	.388	.460	.578	1,288	.436	2,029	.688	84.63	93.33	77.80	83.36	339.12	86.88
47	15	-	-	.402	.474	.690	1,213	.398	2,211	.726	79.70	85.16	84.78	88.01	337.64	86.50
5	18	-	33	.350	.420	.638	1,294	.418	2,084	.674	85.02	89.44	79.91	81.66	336.03	86.09
-	17	-	-	.331	.419	.612	1,294	.407	2,138	.673	85.02	87.13	81.98	81.62	335.74	86.02
15	9	-	33	.323	.429	.645	1,244	.406	2,140	.698	81.73	86.79	82.06	84.65	335.23	85.89
-	38	-	-	.367	.465	.538	1,234	.413	2,083	.697	81.08	88.31	79.87	84.52	333.78	85.51
37	55	32	81	.298	.425	.585	1,288	.355	2,388	.659	84.63	76.00	91.56	79.89	332.08	85.08
1	36	23	52	.287	.438	.702	1,133	.375	2,261	.748	74.44	80.20	86.69	90.74	332.08	85.08
13	19	38	67	.349	.450	.643	1,242	.354	2,396	.682	81.60	75.62	91.87	82.72	331.81	85.01
13	9	-	-	.360	.404	.618	1,301	.436	1,932	.647	85.48	93.17	74.08	78.45	331.18	84.85
21	38	33	48	.290	.382	.604	1,278	.371	2,273	.660	83.97	79.31	87.15	79.97	330.40	84.65
21	53	38	69	.304	.394	.608	1,264	.363	2,293	.658	83.05	77.58	87.92	79.80	328.35	84.12
-	9	-	-	.356	.419	.500	1,255	.406	2,021	.654	82.46	86.80	77.49	79.25	325.99	83.52
10	7	16	27	.325	.451	.618	1,152	.356	2,255	.696	75.69	76.08	86.46	84.44	322.67	82.67
9	38	26	61	.324	.424	.640	1,172	.386	2,047	.675	77.00	82.61	78.49	81.80	319.90	81.96
1	11	-	69	.294	.420	.609	1,178	.345	2,282	.669	77.40	73.81	87.50	81.07	319.77	81.92
23	9	19	70	.308	.387	.606	1,203	.353	2,215	.650	79.04	75.53	84.93	78.85	318.35	81.56
-	26	-	-	.374	.486	.467	1,103	.359	2,145	.698	72.47	76.78	82.25	84.66	316.15	81.00
16	11	-	58	.350	.441	.616	1,159	.334	2,296	.662	76.15	71.42	88.04	80.22	315.83	80.91
28	11	41	68	.323	.383	.600	1,208	.348	2,213	.637	79.37	74.32	84.85	77.19	315.73	80.89
16	25	38	92	.314	.393	.626	1,181	.356	2,164	.651	77.60	76.02	82.98	78.98	315.57	80.85
27	10	19	64	.311	.407	.618	1,166	.353	2,174	.659	76.61	75.54	83.36	79.85	315.35	80.79
-	202	-	-	.359	.447	.470	1,208	.413	1,849	.632	79.37	88.26	70.90	76.59	315.11	80.73
4	65	35	64	.311	.444	.596	1,158	.333	2,287	.659	76.08	71.30	87.69	79.84	314.92	80.68
9	18	47	79	.334	.455	.631	1,133	.352	2,172	.675	74.44	75.31	83.28	81.86	314.90	80.67
-	29	-	-	.355	.407	.543	1,224	.418	1,810	.618	80.42	89.33	69.40	74.90	314.05	80.46
-	16	-	10	.314	.418	.564	1,192	.372	2,048	.639	78.32	79.51	78.53	77.45	313.80	80.39
2	78	29	49	.295	.418	.584	1,176	.338	2,242	.645	77.27	72.31	85.97	78.16	313.69	80.37
34	29	-	-	.383	.436	.550	1,092	.356	2,097	.683	71.75	76.09	80.41	82.84	311.09	79.70
-	18	-	-	.306	.392	.487	1,104	.364	2,049	.675	72.54	77.74	78.57	81.80	310.64	79.58
18	15	-	-	.343	.434	.517	1,221	.353	2,053	.593	80.22	75.42	78.72	71.90	306.26	78.46
26	53	23	59	.357	.445	.658	1,021	.374	1,925	.704	67.08	79.89	73.81	85.40	306.18	78.44
6	21	23	33	.281	.413	.587	1,107	.335	2,153	.652	72.73	71.71	82.55	79.08	306.08	78.42
28	15	-	-	.379	.449	.587	1,125	.367	1,952	.636	73.92	78.39	74.85	77.11	304.27	77.95
11	8	-	-	.315	.372	.560	1,190	.358	1,990	.599	78.19	76.63	76.30	72.65	303.77	77.82
-	13	-	76	.344	.380	.572	1,214	.360	1,977	.587	79.76	77.03	75.81	71.13	303.73	77.81
-	30	-	-	.391	.472	.519	1,105	.360	1,968	.641	72.60	77.02	75.46	77.77	302.85	77.59
4	15	-	-	.322	.391	.558	1,161	.355	1,994	.610	76.28	75.99	76.46	74.00	302.73	77.56
62	37	19	92	.325	.391	.602	1,106	.319	2,200	.635	72.67	68.28	84.36	77.00	302.30	77.45
-	74	-	-	.360	.461	.518	1,094	.369	1,909	.644	71.88	78.93	73.20	78.09	302.09	77.39
70	17	-	-	.339	.421	.595	1,062	.373	1,869	.657	69.78	79.80	71.66	79.62	300.86	77.08

Best 5 Consecutive Seasons

	5 Consecutive Year Statistics & Analysis Listed by Total Offensive Production Ranking													
Rank	Player	Years	G	AB	H	1B	2B	3B	HR	RUN	RBI	BB	SO	SB
49	Jones, Chipper**	1998-2002	790	2,867	917	549	176	13	179	560	530	522	422	72
50	Palmiero, Rafael**	1998-2002	793	2,895	842	456	162	5	219	493	617	484	421	18
51	Terry, Bill	1928-1932	760	3,062	1,103	751	199	62	91	587	576	248	163	37
52	Averill, Earl	1930-1934	752	2,989	955	583	193	54	125	569	591	352	199	32
53	Robinson, Frank	1958-1962	748	2,712	839	468	172	25	174	533	551	360	366	81
54	Gonzalez, Juan **	1995-1999	655	2,594	808	435	163	10	200	457	642	192	486	7
55	Keeler, Willie	1894-1898	642	2,825	1,110	920	105	71	14	752	372	180	372	249
56	Galarraga, Andres**	1994-1998	712	2,752	838	487	147	10	194	508	602	208	683	60
57	Conner, Roger	1889-1893	671	2,505	794	534	140	63	57	594	505	471	182	125
58	Mize, Johnny*	1936-1940	728	2,648	898	519	179	58	142	479	553	354	234	10
59	Sheffield, Gary**	2000-2004	728	2,657	830	498	145	8	179	528	546	445	329	49
60	Matthews, Eddie	1953-1957	735	2,678	774	425	124	28	197	526	528	502	407	23
61	Lajoie, Nap	1897-1901	578	2,457	900	613	174	71	42	530	541	82	-	121
62	Morgan, Joe	1973-1977	746	2,579	781	501	144	22	114	556	432	594	281	301
63	O'Neill, Tip	1887-1891	654	2,728	972	717	157	57	41	610	501	293	106	138
64	Martinez, Edgar**	1995-1999	735	2,610	872	511	220	5	136	518	512	561	452	17
65	Schmidt, Mike	1979-1983	714	2,491	686	355	111	21	199	503	522	517	584	54
66	Anson, Cap	1886-1890	654	2,573	922	701	131	47	43	526	557	361	103	140
67	Banks, Ernie	1955-1959	758	2,934	877	494	136	40	207	509	576	283	378	29
68	Sisler, George	1918-1922	680	2,762	1,053	743	181	78	51	561	455	196	97	201
69	Johnson, Robert	1935-1939	740	2,732	845	524	147	43	131	514	565	450	344	41
70	Hafey, Chick	1927-1931	617	2,279	771	422	193	40	116	466	501	206	230	50
71	Waner, Paul	1926-1930	747	2,946	1,057	717	202	92	46	605	473	349	91	55
72	Berkman, Lance**	2000-2004	741	2,590	792	430	193	17	152	506	520	489	521	35
73	Herman, Babe	1929-1933	735	2,878	984	600	207	71	106	505	520	281	268	69
74	Vaughn, Mo	1994-1998	707	2,715	865	537	137	7	184	479	562	367	714	19
75	Goslin, Goose	1924-1928	734	2,785	968	651	163	77	77	497	572	282	164	87
76	Williams, Bernie**	1996-2000	699	2,687	871	554	156	30	131	540	535	400	412	69
77	Murphy, Dale	1983-1987	805	2,992	869	521	144	22	182	547	520	449	662	82
78	Piazza, Mike**	1996-2000	728	2,680	887	562	137	2	186	469	577	317	389	12
79	Wagner, Honus	1900-1904	673	2,624	927	633	191	81	22	506	493	240	-	228
80	Bichette, Dante	1995-1999	761	3,028	964	606	194	11	153	498	642	179	451	70
81	Ordonez, Magglio**	1999-2003	783	3,001	935	563	201	11	160	510	590	287	348	72
82	McCovey, Willie	1966-1970	734	2,467	727	398	124	18	187	438	544	477	422	9
83	Speaker, Tris	1920-1924	698	2,544	943	597	245	53	48	556	448	407	64	35
84	Kelly, King	1884-1888	551	2,302	801	573	139	46	43	603	383	261	160	193
85	Rice, Jim	1975-1979	778	3,085	958	592	147	48	171	509	570	232	588	39
86	Stargell, Willie	1971-1975	691	2,497	741	392	166	11	172	446	542	373	627	1
87	Kluszewski, Ted	1952-1956	724	2,769	874	556	116	15	187	470	550	295	168	7
88	Foster, George	1976-1980	725	2,749	816	497	117	26	176	454	581	317	538	28
89	Keller, Charlie*	1939-1943	682	2,461	725	450	102	51	122	494	492	509	300	41
90	Yastrzemski, Carl	1966-1971	801	2,881	856	524	159	10	163	504	488	523	376	69
91	Killebrew, Harmon	1960-1964	729	2,627	701	383	89	10	219	446	535	449	597	3
92	Williams, Billy	1968-1972	794	3,088	948	599	158	33	158	512	537	318	291	24
93	Henderson, Rickey	1982-1986	732	2,706	772	525	135	25	87	613	303	493	401	471
94	Mattingly, Don	1984-1988	759	3,100	1,028	662	220	9	137	502	571	242	176	5
95	Robinson, Jackie	1949-1953	738	2,653	874	600	161	33	80	540	463	425	148	115
96	York, Rudy	1937-1941	651	2,345	693	394	136	15	148	419	543	355	352	15
97	Cepeda, Orlando	1959-1963	772	2,963	917	577	158	16	166	483	554	180	449	68
98	Collins, Eddie	1911-1915	740	2,617	907	719	115	61	12	594	372	464	95	260

5 Consecutive Year Statistics & Analysis Listed by Total Offensive Production Ranking

CS	HBP	SF	GDP	AVG	OBP	SLG	Total Offensive Production Statistics				TRP Rating	RPA Rating	TNB Rating	TBA Rating	TOP Composite	
							TRP	RPA	TNB	TBA					TOP	Rating
28	9	34	82	.320	.422	.578	1,090	.310	2,231	.635	71.62	66.33	85.54	76.98	300.47	76.98
13	26	33	58	.291	.393	.577	1,110	.318	2,186	.625	72.93	67.88	83.82	75.79	300.42	76.96
-	4	-	-	.360	.409	.555	1,163	.351	1,988	.600	76.41	75.05	76.23	72.73	300.42	76.96
28	23	-	-	.320	.395	.546	1,160	.345	2,010	.598	76.22	73.74	77.07	72.44	299.47	76.72
27	45	31	75	.309	.395	.584	1,084	.336	2,042	.634	71.22	71.92	78.30	76.82	298.26	76.41
4	16	41	66	.311	.357	.613	1,099	.378	1,802	.619	72.21	80.79	69.10	75.10	297.20	76.14
27	49	-	-	.393	.438	.495	1,124	.368	1,850	.606	73.85	78.70	70.94	73.44	296.93	76.07
27	80	26	54	.305	.367	.577	1,110	.356	1,908	.612	72.93	76.08	73.10	74.14	296.31	75.91
-	16	-	-	.317	.428	.491	1,099	.367	1,843	.616	72.21	78.55	70.67	74.68	296.10	75.86
-	19	-	42	.339	.421	.611	1,032	.337	2,002	.654	67.81	72.05	76.76	79.24	295.86	75.80
22	38	31	73	.312	.414	.575	1,074	.331	2,038	.628	70.57	70.80	78.14	76.17	295.68	75.75
11	6	19	30	.289	.400	.577	1,054	.326	2,065	.638	69.25	69.67	79.18	77.39	295.50	75.70
-	50	-	-	.366	.399	.546	1,071	.414	1,595	.616	70.37	88.46	61.16	74.69	294.68	75.50
56	13	32	29	.303	.431	.508	988	.304	2,163	.666	64.91	65.07	82.94	80.77	293.69	75.24
-	28	-	-	.356	.424	.501	1,111	.364	1,825	.599	73.00	77.92	69.98	72.57	293.46	75.18
13	36	24	72	.334	.455	.579	1,030	.312	2,111	.639	67.67	66.68	80.94	77.49	292.79	75.01
29	15	36	49	.275	.398	.576	1,025	.330	1,993	.641	67.35	70.52	76.42	77.75	292.03	74.82
-	13	-	-	.358	.440	.496	1,083	.367	1,790	.607	71.16	78.59	68.63	73.64	292.02	74.81
24	16	28	67	.299	.361	.584	1,085	.326	2,018	.606	71.29	69.72	77.38	73.52	291.90	74.78
47	20	-	-	.381	.426	.559	1,016	.341	1,913	.642	66.75	72.96	73.35	77.88	290.95	74.54
30	7	-	12	.309	.408	.538	1,079	.337	1,939	.606	70.89	72.08	74.35	73.44	290.77	74.49
-	19	-	-	.338	.398	.611	967	.386	1,667	.666	63.53	82.58	63.92	80.72	290.75	74.49
-	19	-	-	.359	.430	.537	1,078	.325	2,004	.605	70.83	69.56	76.84	73.32	290.54	74.44
25	37	25	44	.306	.420	.569	1,026	.322	2,011	.631	67.41	68.89	77.11	76.55	289.96	74.29
-	4	-	15	.342	.401	.574	1,025	.323	2,005	.631	67.35	68.97	76.88	76.49	289.69	74.22
10	58	20	64	.319	.408	.578	1,041	.323	2,002	.621	68.40	69.05	76.76	75.29	289.50	74.17
39	31	-	-	.348	.413	.544	1,069	.345	1,877	.606	70.24	73.79	71.97	73.46	289.45	74.16
36	8	27	70	.324	.410	.551	1,075	.337	1,921	.602	70.63	72.02	73.66	72.97	289.27	74.11
27	14	20	63	.290	.383	.536	1,067	.302	2,121	.599	70.11	64.49	81.33	72.68	288.61	73.94
8	10	21	96	.331	.401	.592	1,046	.335	1,917	.614	68.73	71.60	73.50	74.40	288.23	73.84
-	39	-	-	.353	.415	.513	999	.344	1,853	.638	65.64	73.59	71.05	77.39	287.67	73.70
36	16	38	84	.318	.355	.541	1,140	.341	1,868	.558	74.90	72.88	71.63	67.71	287.11	73.56
27	22	30	107	.312	.372	.546	1,100	.319	1,992	.578	72.27	68.24	76.38	70.07	286.96	73.52
6	24	26	50	.295	.410	.587	982	.323	1,952	.641	64.52	68.99	74.85	77.75	286.10	73.30
36	16	-	-	.371	.460	.565	1,004	.338	1,860	.627	65.97	72.36	71.32	76.01	285.73	73.18
-	5	-	-	.348	.415	.504	986	.384	1,620	.631	64.78	82.11	62.12	76.48	285.49	73.14
23	25	35	89	.311	.360	.556	1,079	.311	1,987	.573	70.89	66.57	76.19	69.51	283.16	72.54
3	21	24	38	.297	.389	.579	988	.335	1,837	.622	64.91	71.55	70.44	75.42	282.32	72.33
6	18	14	59	.316	.383	.571	1,020	.323	1,895	.601	67.02	69.13	72.66	72.82	281.64	72.15
13	20	30	71	.297	.370	.550	1,035	.325	1,865	.585	68.00	69.45	71.51	70.95	279.91	71.71
16	3	-	30	.295	.416	.526	986	.328	1,832	.610	64.78	70.21	70.25	73.96	279.21	71.53
43	9	14	60	.297	.405	.529	992	.284	2,082	.597	65.18	60.84	79.83	72.39	278.23	71.28
4	19	22	66	.267	.375	.558	981	.308	1,934	.608	64.45	65.91	74.16	73.67	278.18	71.27
10	17	25	72	.307	.372	.533	1,049	.298	1,995	.567	68.92	63.73	76.50	68.72	277.86	71.19
107	16	13	43	.285	.397	.450	916	.280	2,091	.639	60.18	59.88	80.18	77.50	277.75	71.16
7	8	50	76	.332	.376	.541	1,073	.309	1,925	.554	70.50	66.01	73.81	67.14	277.47	71.08
33	43	-	71	.329	.430	.505	1,003	.314	1,891	.592	65.90	67.19	72.51	71.83	277.43	71.08
7	9	-	36	.296	.390	.556	962	.350	1,675	.610	63.21	74.94	64.23	73.98	276.36	70.80
30	38	21	76	.309	.354	.542	1,037	.316	1,861	.568	68.13	67.65	71.36	68.83	275.97	70.70
60	33	-	-	.347	.451	.451	966	.310	1,877	.603	63.47	66.34	71.97	73.08	274.86	70.42

Best 5 Consecutive Seasons

	5 Consecutive Year Statistics & Analysis Listed by Total Offensive Production Ranking														
Rank	Player	Years	G	AB	H	1B	2B	3B	HR	RUN	RBI	BB	SO	SB	
99	Dickey, Bill*	1935-1939	632	2,335	741	465	137	23	116	422	541	306	108	12	
100	Murray, Eddie	1981-1985	724	2,681	816	515	144	10	147	467	533	387	370	29	
101	Allen, Dick	1966-1970	655	2,405	699	387	113	37	162	455	467	352	676	51	
102	Jackson, Reggie	1973-1977	736	2,661	742	418	158	10	156	457	515	357	586	109	
103	Jeter, Derek**	1998-2002	762	3,104	1,005	730	154	24	97	614	408	345	547	130	
104	Canseco, Jose	1987-1991	667	2,520	694	392	124	7	171	439	517	301	664	106	
105	McGriff, Fred **	1990-1994	722	2,597	763	458	124	9	172	446	493	421	533	29	
106	Fielder, Cecil	1990-1994	739	2,789	730	428	111	3	188	433	596	381	719	-	
107	Maris, Roger	1958-1962	726	2,695	709	401	108	23	177	478	506	354	348	9	
108	Meusel, Bob	1921-1925	701	2,734	854	531	169	60	94	418	568	191	296	82	
109	Parker, Dave	1975-1979	751	2,935	942	597	184	47	114	475	490	250	469	84	
110	Bench, Johnny	1970-1974	766	2,883	771	457	131	13	170	455	567	366	442	22	
111	Berra, Yogi	1950-1954	722	2,765	827	554	117	22	134	473	543	271	117	11	
112	Winfield, Dave	1982-1986	742	2,902	835	517	149	31	138	484	540	285	414	51	
113	Crawford, Sam	1908-1912	757	2,923	945	672	160	84	29	458	521	224	-	143	
114	Kaline, Al	1955-1959	735	2,836	901	612	138	31	120	470	499	321	239	37	
115	Campanella, Roy	1949-1953	671	2,365	700	423	118	10	149	401	518	299	255	17	
116	Jackson, Joe	1911-1915	697	2,585	951	667	170	89	25	480	378	283	83	140	
117	Howard, Frank	1967-1971	782	2,824	785	472	105	10	198	411	515	425	638	3	
118	Garciaparra, Nomar**	1997-2001	592	2,432	815	495	177	26	117	453	428	187	252	53	
119	Brett, George	1979-1983	627	2,457	806	488	172	47	99	439	443	264	171	52	
120	Traynor, Pie	1927-1931	708	2,794	945	707	156	59	23	449	560	182	75	49	
121	Perez, Tony	1967-1971	792	3,050	885	580	134	25	146	453	536	281	579	19	
122	Ripkin, Cal, Jr.	1983-1987	809	3,197	921	592	179	18	132	535	477	347	391	11	
123	Cravath, Gavy	1913-1916	723	2,497	745	465	142	53	85	383	496	358	358	50	
124	Dawson, Andre	1979-1983	716	2,851	845	526	159	39	121	468	439	178	411	159	
125	Clemente, Roberto	1963-1967	760	3,034	1,008	726	141	50	91	471	457	212	441	41	
126	Rose, Pete	1965-1969	771	3,162	1,018	732	180	41	65	514	358	306	344	33	

* Consecutive excluding or consolidating years of military service

** Active player. Statistics through 2004 season

TOP ranking for players with less than 70% rating is based upon comparison to listed players only.

N/R = Not Rated

Best 5 Consecutive Seasons

5 Consecutive Year Statistics & Analysis Listed by Total Offensive Production Ranking

CS	HBP	SF	GDP	AVG	OBP	SLG	Total Offensive Production Statistics				TRP Rating	RPA Rating	TNB Rating	TBA Rating	TOP Composite	
							TRP	RPA	TNB	TBA					TOP	Rating
5	19	-	9	.317	.401	.545	963	.361	1,604	.601	63.27	77.16	61.50	72.86	274.80	70.40
10	9	34	57	.304	.390	.530	1,000	.316	1,836	.580	65.70	67.50	70.40	70.27	273.87	70.16
25	7	16	44	.291	.381	.570	922	.326	1,757	.622	60.58	69.82	67.37	75.43	273.20	69.99
31	21	27	51	.279	.365	.522	972	.312	1,844	.592	63.86	66.68	70.71	71.73	272.98	69.94
24	46	16	66	.324	.398	.483	1,022	.286	1,995	.558	67.15	61.10	76.50	67.62	272.36	69.78
38	28	32	60	.275	.355	.534	956	.325	1,742	.592	62.81	69.51	66.79	71.81	270.93	69.41
16	8	23	57	.294	.391	.547	939	.302	1,863	.600	61.70	64.65	71.43	72.72	270.50	69.30
2	19	25	85	.262	.352	.506	1,029	.312	1,809	.548	67.61	66.70	69.36	66.48	270.16	69.21
5	21	24	35	.263	.350	.517	984	.314	1,773	.567	64.65	67.25	67.98	68.70	268.58	68.81
57	13	-	-	.312	.360	.521	986	.336	1,654	.563	64.78	71.77	63.42	68.26	268.23	68.72
43	25	20	56	.321	.377	.532	965	.294	1,878	.572	63.40	62.80	72.01	69.29	267.50	68.53
14	5	39	85	.267	.347	.499	1,022	.303	1,817	.538	67.15	64.70	69.67	65.22	266.73	68.33
13	15	7	51	.299	.364	.503	1,016	.327	1,674	.538	66.75	69.88	64.19	65.28	266.11	68.17
25	4	30	101	.288	.349	.503	1,024	.308	1,775	.534	67.28	65.92	68.06	64.78	266.04	68.16
-	7	-	-	.323	.373	.465	979	.310	1,734	.550	64.32	66.38	66.49	66.66	263.84	67.60
26	15	28	62	.318	.387	.515	969	.297	1,808	.554	63.67	63.52	69.33	67.20	263.71	67.56
10	16	-	82	.296	.379	.543	919	.333	1,607	.582	60.38	71.15	61.62	70.54	263.69	67.56
35	36	-	-	.368	.437	.532	858	.295	1,798	.619	56.37	63.18	68.94	75.07	263.56	67.52
3	20	20	108	.278	.374	.533	926	.273	1,949	.574	60.84	58.29	74.73	69.56	263.43	67.49
21	25	25	49	.335	.385	.574	881	.324	1,639	.603	57.88	69.31	62.85	73.11	263.15	67.42
24	4	23	47	.328	.391	.557	882	.316	1,665	.596	57.95	67.48	63.84	72.22	261.50	66.99
-	8	-	-	.338	.380	.461	1,009	.338	1,527	.512	66.29	72.31	58.55	62.04	259.20	66.40
11	17	31	82	.290	.350	.494	989	.286	1,813	.524	64.98	61.11	69.52	63.51	259.12	66.38
15	8	32	110	.288	.356	.479	1,012	.274	1,883	.510	66.49	58.58	72.20	61.80	259.08	66.37
9	18	-	-	.298	.390	.500	879	.306	1,665	.580	57.75	65.43	63.84	70.26	257.28	65.91
44	36	43	47	.296	.341	.507	907	.287	1,774	.562	59.59	61.48	68.02	68.17	257.26	65.91
10	14	19	79	.332	.376	.502	928	.276	1,779	.530	60.97	59.10	68.21	64.23	252.51	64.69
35	21	15	55	.322	.384	.466	872	.245	1,800	.506	57.29	52.39	69.02	61.32	240.03	61.49

Best 5 Consecutive Seasons

5 Consecutive Year Statistics & Analysis Listed Alphabetically

Rank	Player	Years	G	AB	H	1B	2B	3B	HR	RUN	RBI	BB	SO	SB
27	Aaron, Hank	1959-1963	779	3,045	984	582	162	38	202	581	627	311	348	91
101	Allen, Dick	1966-1970	655	2,405	699	387	113	37	162	455	467	352	676	51
66	Anson, Cap	1886-1890	654	2,573	922	701	131	47	43	526	557	361	103	140
52	Averill, Earl	1930-1934	752	2,989	955	583	193	54	125	569	591	352	199	32
14	Bagwell, Jeff**	1997-2001	791	2,858	853	452	188	8	205	654	634	598	590	100
67	Banks, Ernie	1955-1959	758	2,934	877	494	136	40	207	509	576	283	378	29
28	Belle, Albert**	1994-1998	731	2,803	881	441	218	9	213	538	643	364	427	35
110	Bench, Johnny	1970-1974	766	2,883	771	457	131	13	170	455	567	366	442	22
72	Berkman, Lance**	2000-2004	741	2,590	792	430	193	17	152	506	520	489	521	35
111	Berra, Yogi	1950-1954	722	2,765	827	554	117	22	134	473	543	271	117	11
80	Bichette, Dante	1995-1999	761	3,028	964	606	194	11	153	498	642	179	451	70
4	Bonds, Barry **	2000-2004	716	2,122	720	310	140	12	258	615	544	872	316	46
45	Bottomley, Jim	1925-1929	754	2,932	944	564	188	73	119	516	645	320	245	28
119	Brett, George	1979-1983	627	2,457	806	488	172	47	99	439	443	264	171	52
47	Brouthers, Dan	1887-1891	623	2,499	900	643	153	70	34	603	491	391	65	149
44	Burkett, Jesse	1893-1897	641	2,657	1,038	819	123	69	27	714	391	381	100	177
115	Campanella, Roy	1949-1953	671	2,365	700	423	118	10	149	401	518	299	255	17
104	Canseco, Jose	1987-1991	667	2,520	694	392	124	7	171	439	517	301	664	106
97	Cepeda, Orlando	1959-1963	772	2,963	917	577	158	16	166	483	554	180	449	68
125	Clemente, Roberto	1963-1967	760	3,034	1,008	726	141	50	91	471	457	212	441	41
36	Cobb, Ty	1908-1912	732	2,807	1,075	767	182	90	36	576	516	233	-	324
98	Collins, Eddie	1911-1915	740	2,617	907	719	115	61	12	594	372	464	95	260
57	Conner, Roger	1889-1893	671	2,505	794	534	140	63	57	594	505	471	182	125
123	Cravath, Gavy	1913-1916	723	2,497	745	465	142	53	85	383	496	358	358	50
113	Crawford, Sam	1908-1912	757	2,923	945	672	160	84	29	458	521	224	-	143
124	Dawson, Andre	1979-1983	716	2,851	845	526	159	39	121	468	439	178	411	159
8	Delahanty, Ed	1893-1897	613	2,601	1,008	690	193	73	52	683	605	315	89	176
35	Delgado, Carlos**	1999-2003	780	2,791	824	421	199	5	199	550	626	531	644	5
99	Dickey, Bill*	1935-1939	632	2,335	741	465	137	23	116	422	541	306	108	12
10	DiMaggio, Joe*	1937-1941	687	2,731	957	564	170	54	169	603	691	312	121	17
20	Duffy, Hugh	1890-1894	659	2,787	991	735	154	57	45	719	536	296	114	322
106	Fielder, Cecil	1990-1994	739	2,789	730	428	111	3	188	433	596	381	719	-
88	Foster, George	1976-1980	725	2,749	816	497	117	26	176	454	581	317	538	28
3	Foxx, Jimmie*	1932-1936	755	2,817	980	551	163	39	227	644	720	542	482	35
56	Galarraga, Andres**	1994-1998	712	2,752	838	487	147	10	194	508	602	208	683	60
118	Garciaparra, Nomar**	1997-2001	592	2,432	815	495	177	26	117	453	428	187	252	53
2	Gehrig, Lou	1927-1931	772	2,899	1,025	552	204	73	196	721	801	545	340	47
N/R	Gehrig, Lou	1933-1937	767	2,855	989	567	181	44	197	696	734	590	206	33
38	Gehringer, Charlie	1934-1938	754	2,984	1,025	699	214	33	79	667	554	463	100	51
31	Giambi, Jason**	1999-2003	775	2,700	839	467	171	5	196	549	609	609	537	9
54	Gonzalez, Juan **	1995-1999	655	2,594	808	435	163	10	200	457	642	192	486	7
75	Goslin, Goose	1924-1928	734	2,785	968	651	163	77	77	497	572	282	164	87
12	Greenberg, Hank*	1937-1945	692	2,560	828	416	189	36	187	581	663	463	415	33
18	Griffey, Ken **	1996-2000	763	2,912	844	440	141	14	249	593	685	415	571	81
46	Guerrero, Vladimir**	1998-2002	793	3,017	982	572	184	29	197	524	582	299	389	111
70	Hafey, Chick	1927-1931	617	2,279	771	422	193	40	116	466	501	206	230	50
25	Hamilton, Billy	1894-1898	617	2,522	943	785	100	38	20	779	324	524	76	416
41	Heilmann, Harry	1921-1925	714	2,724	1,032	690	199	62	81	531	594	330	173	37
16	Helton, Todd**	2000-2004	789	2,850	994	543	250	15	186	627	615	538	400	20
93	Henderson, Rickey	1982-1986	732	2,706	772	525	135	25	87	613	303	493	401	471

5 Consecutive Year Statistics & Analysis Listed Alphabetically

CS	HBP	SF	GDP	AVG	OBP	SLG	Total Offensive Production Statistics				TRP Rating	RPA Rating	TNB Rating	TBA Rating	TOP Composite	
							TRP	RPA	TNB	TBA					TOP	Rating
28	11	41	68	.323	.383	.600	1,208	.348	2,213	.637	79.37	74.32	84.85	77.19	315.73	80.89
25	7	16	44	.291	.381	.570	922	.326	1,757	.622	60.58	69.82	67.37	75.43	273.20	69.99
-	13	-	-	.358	.440	.496	1,083	.367	1,790	.607	71.16	78.59	68.63	73.64	292.02	74.81
28	23	-	-	.320	.395	.546	1,160	.345	2,010	.598	76.22	73.74	77.07	72.44	299.47	76.72
37	55	32	81	.298	.425	.585	1,288	.355	2,388	.659	84.63	76.00	91.56	79.89	332.08	85.08
24	16	28	67	.299	.361	.584	1,085	.326	2,018	.606	71.29	69.72	77.38	73.52	291.90	74.78
16	25	38	92	.314	.393	.626	1,181	.356	2,164	.651	77.60	76.02	82.98	78.98	315.57	80.85
14	5	39	85	.267	.347	.499	1,022	.303	1,817	.538	67.15	64.70	69.67	65.22	266.73	68.33
25	37	25	44	.306	.420	.569	1,026	.322	2,011	.631	67.41	68.89	77.11	76.55	289.96	74.29
13	15	7	51	.299	.364	.503	1,016	.327	1,674	.538	66.75	69.88	64.19	65.28	266.11	68.17
36	16	38	84	.318	.355	.541	1,140	.341	1,868	.558	74.90	72.88	71.63	67.71	287.11	73.56
9	40	16	27	.339	.535	.781	1,159	.377	2,607	.847	76.15	80.55	99.96	102.72	359.38	92.07
4	15	-	-	.322	.391	.558	1,161	.355	1,994	.610	76.28	75.99	76.46	74.00	302.73	77.56
24	4	23	47	.328	.391	.557	882	.316	1,665	.596	57.95	67.48	63.84	72.22	261.50	66.99
-	74	-	-	.360	.461	.518	1,094	.369	1,909	.644	71.88	78.93	73.20	78.09	302.09	77.39
-	30	-	-	.391	.472	.519	1,105	.360	1,968	.641	72.60	77.02	75.46	77.77	302.85	77.59
10	16	-	82	.296	.379	.543	919	.333	1,607	.582	60.38	71.15	61.62	70.54	263.69	67.56
38	28	32	60	.275	.355	.534	956	.325	1,742	.592	62.81	69.51	66.79	71.81	270.93	69.41
30	38	21	76	.309	.354	.542	1,037	.316	1,861	.568	68.13	67.65	71.36	68.83	275.97	70.70
10	14	19	79	.332	.376	.502	928	.276	1,779	.530	60.97	59.10	68.21	64.23	252.51	64.69
34	29	-	-	.383	.436	.550	1,092	.356	2,097	.683	71.75	76.09	80.41	82.84	311.09	79.70
60	33	-	-	.347	.451	.451	966	.310	1,877	.603	63.47	66.34	71.97	73.08	274.86	70.42
-	16	-	-	.317	.428	.491	1,099	.367	1,843	.616	72.21	78.55	70.67	74.68	296.10	75.86
9	18	-	-	.298	.390	.500	879	.306	1,665	.580	57.75	65.43	63.84	70.26	257.28	65.91
-	7	-	-	.323	.373	.465	979	.310	1,734	.550	64.32	66.38	66.49	66.66	263.84	67.60
44	36	43	47	.296	.341	.507	907	.287	1,774	.562	59.59	61.48	68.02	68.17	257.26	65.91
-	35	-	-	.388	.460	.578	1,288	.436	2,029	.688	84.63	93.33	77.80	83.36	339.12	86.88
2	78	29	49	.295	.418	.584	1,176	.338	2,242	.645	77.27	72.31	85.97	78.16	313.69	80.37
5	19	-	9	.317	.401	.545	963	.361	1,604	.601	63.27	77.16	61.50	72.86	274.80	70.40
5	18	-	33	.350	.420	.638	1,294	.418	2,084	.674	85.02	89.44	79.91	81.66	336.03	86.09
-	9	-	-	.356	.419	.500	1,255	.406	2,021	.654	82.46	86.80	77.49	79.25	325.99	83.52
2	19	25	85	.262	.352	.506	1,029	.312	1,809	.548	67.61	66.70	69.36	66.48	270.16	69.21
13	20	30	71	.297	.370	.550	1,035	.325	1,865	.585	68.00	69.45	71.51	70.95	279.91	71.71
19	3	-	-	.348	.454	.675	1,364	.406	2,463	.733	89.62	86.76	94.44	88.82	359.64	92.14
27	80	26	54	.305	.367	.577	1,110	.356	1,908	.612	72.93	76.08	73.16	74.14	296.31	75.91
21	25	25	49	.335	.385	.574	881	.324	1,639	.603	57.88	69.31	62.85	73.11	263.15	67.42
49	15	-	-	.354	.458	.677	1,522	.440	2,521	.729	100.00	94.09	96.66	88.36	379.12	97.13
32	19	-	-	.346	.461	.648	1,430	.413	2,459	.710	93.96	88.28	94.29	86.07	362.59	92.89
18	15	-	-	.343	.434	.517	1,221	.353	2,053	.593	80.22	75.42	78.72	71.90	306.26	78.46
4	65	35	64	.311	.444	.596	1,158	.333	2,287	.659	76.08	71.30	87.69	79.84	314.92	80.68
4	16	41	66	.311	.357	.613	1,099	.378	1,802	.619	72.21	80.79	69.10	75.10	297.20	76.14
39	31	-	-	.348	.413	.544	1,069	.345	1,877	.606	70.24	73.79	71.97	73.46	289.45	74.16
15	9	-	33	.323	.429	.645	1,244	.406	2,140	.698	81.73	86.79	82.06	84.65	335.23	85.89
21	38	33	48	.290	.382	.604	1,278	.371	2,273	.660	83.97	79.31	87.15	79.97	330.40	84.65
62	37	19	92	.325	.391	.602	1,106	.319	2,200	.635	72.67	68.28	84.36	77.00	302.30	77.45
-	19	-	-	.338	.398	.611	967	.386	1,667	.666	63.53	82.58	63.92	80.72	290.75	74.49
-	26	-	-	.374	.486	.467	1,103	.359	2,145	.698	72.47	76.78	82.25	84.66	316.15	81.00
28	15	-	-	.379	.449	.587	1,125	.367	1,952	.636	73.92	78.39	74.85	77.11	304.27	77.95
13	19	38	67	.349	.450	.643	1,242	.354	2,396	.682	81.60	75.62	91.87	82.72	331.81	85.01
107	16	13	43	.285	.397	.450	916	.280	2,091	.639	60.18	59.88	80.18	77.50	277.75	71.16

Best 5 Consecutive Seasons A-H

	5 Consecutive Year Statistics & Analysis Listed Alphabetically													
Rank	Player	Years	G	AB	H	1B	2B	3B	HR	RUN	RBI	BB	SO	SB
73	Herman, Babe	1929-1933	735	2,878	984	600	207	71	106	505	520	281	268	69
9	Hornsby, Rogers	1921-1925	696	2,679	1,078	662	206	66	144	615	598	352	198	43
117	Howard, Frank	1967-1971	782	2,824	785	472	105	10	198	411	515	425	638	3
116	Jackson, Joe	1911-1915	697	2,585	951	667	170	89	25	480	378	283	83	140
102	Jackson, Reggie	1973-1977	736	2,661	742	418	158	10	156	457	515	357	586	109
30	Jennings, Hughie	1894-1898	646	2,525	907	704	137	55	11	687	521	200	45	260
103	Jeter, Derek**	1998-2002	762	3,104	1,005	730	154	24	97	614	408	345	547	130
69	Johnson, Robert	1935-1939	740	2,732	845	524	147	43	131	514	565	450	344	41
49	Jones, Chipper**	1998-2002	790	2,867	917	549	176	13	179	560	530	522	422	72
114	Kaline, Al	1955-1959	735	2,836	901	612	138	31	120	470	499	321	239	37
55	Keeler, Willie	1894-1898	642	2,825	1,110	920	105	71	14	752	372	180	372	249
89	Keller, Charlie*	1939-1943	682	2,461	725	450	102	51	122	494	492	509	300	41
13	Kelley, Joe	1893-1897	643	2,528	928	653	157	80	38	695	539	422	128	264
84	Kelly, King	1884-1888	551	2,302	801	573	139	46	43	603	383	261	160	193
91	Killebrew, Harmon	1960-1964	729	2,627	701	383	89	10	219	446	535	449	597	3
23	Kiner, Ralph	1947-1951	761	2,747	807	434	113	26	234	574	604	586	339	12
6	Klein, Chuck	1929-1933	759	3,114	1,118	660	232	46	180	658	693	283	245	51
87	Kluszewski, Ted	1952-1956	724	2,769	874	556	116	15	187	470	550	295	168	7
61	Lajoie, Nap	1897-1901	578	2,457	900	613	174	71	42	530	541	82	-	121
21	Mantle, Mickey	1954-1958	737	2,586	840	500	113	35	192	630	522	602	501	57
107	Maris, Roger	1958-1962	726	2,695	709	401	108	23	177	478	506	354	348	9
64	Martinez, Edgar**	1995-1999	735	2,610	872	511	220	5	136	518	512	561	452	17
60	Matthews, Eddie	1953-1957	735	2,678	774	425	124	28	197	526	528	502	407	23
94	Mattingly, Don	1984-1988	759	3,100	1,028	662	220	9	137	502	571	242	176	5
24	Mays, Willie*	1961-1965	787	2,925	900	505	142	27	226	613	590	383	388	72
82	McCovey, Willie	1966-1970	734	2,467	727	398	124	18	187	438	544	477	422	9
105	McGriff, Fred **	1990-1994	722	2,597	763	458	124	9	172	446	493	421	533	29
15	McGwire, Mark	1995-1999	698	2,310	664	276	103	1	284	513	620	600	644	5
43	Medwick, Joe	1934-1938	760	3,113	1,072	646	253	62	111	568	646	168	266	14
108	Meusel, Bob	1921-1925	701	2,734	854	531	169	60	94	418	568	191	296	82
58	Mize, Johnny*	1936-1940	728	2,648	898	519	179	58	142	479	553	354	234	10
62	Morgan, Joe	1973-1977	746	2,579	781	501	144	22	114	556	432	594	281	301
77	Murphy, Dale	1983-1987	805	2,992	869	521	144	22	182	547	520	449	662	82
100	Murray, Eddie	1981-1985	724	2,681	816	515	144	10	147	467	533	387	370	29
26	Musial, Stan*	1948-1952	764	2,934	1,028	616	200	56	156	597	562	467	177	26
63	O'Neill, Tip	1887-1891	654	2,728	972	717	157	57	41	610	501	293	106	138
81	Ordonez, Magglio**	1999-2003	783	3,001	935	563	201	11	160	510	590	287	348	72
34	Ott, Mel	1929-1933	742	2,709	850	509	160	24	157	581	611	471	204	32
50	Palmiero, Rafael**	1998-2002	793	2,895	842	456	162	5	219	493	617	484	421	18
109	Parker, Dave	1975-1979	751	2,935	942	597	184	47	114	475	490	250	469	84
121	Perez, Tony	1967-1971	792	3,050	885	580	134	25	146	453	536	281	579	19
78	Piazza, Mike**	1996-2000	728	2,680	887	562	137	2	186	469	577	317	389	12
22	Ramirez, Manny**	1998-2002	677	2,497	810	433	167	9	201	508	664	412	601	8
85	Rice, Jim	1975-1979	778	3,085	958	592	147	48	171	509	570	232	588	39
122	Ripkin, Cal, Jr.	1983-1987	809	3,197	921	592	179	18	132	535	477	347	391	11
53	Robinson, Frank	1958-1962	748	2,712	839	468	172	25	174	533	551	360	366	81
95	Robinson, Jackie	1949-1953	738	2,653	874	600	161	33	80	540	463	425	148	115
19	Rodriguez, Alex**	1999-2003	762	2,919	887	487	150	11	239	626	638	405	609	80
126	Rose, Pete	1965-1969	771	3,162	1,018	732	180	41	65	514	358	306	344	33
1	Ruth, Babe	1927-1931	730	2,627	922	490	143	34	255	741	776	610	348	31

5 Consecutive Year Statistics & Analysis Listed Alphabetically

CS	HBP	SF	GDP	AVG	OBP	SLG	Total Offensive Production Statistics				TRP Rating	RPA Rating	TNB Rating	TBA Rating	TOP Composite	
							TRP	RPA	TNB	TBA					TOP	Rating
-	4	-	15	.342	.401	.574	1,025	.323	2,005	.631	67.35	68.97	76.88	76.49	289.69	74.22
47	15	-	-	.402	.474	.690	1,213	.398	2,211	.726	79.70	85.16	84.78	88.01	337.64	86.50
3	20	20	108	.278	.374	.533	926	.273	1,949	.574	60.84	58.29	74.73	69.56	263.43	67.49
35	36	-	-	.368	.437	.532	858	.295	1,798	.619	56.37	63.18	68.94	75.07	263.56	67.52
31	21	27	51	.279	.365	.522	972	.312	1,844	.592	63.86	66.68	70.71	71.73	272.98	69.94
-	202	-	-	.359	.447	.470	1,208	.413	1,849	.632	79.37	88.26	70.90	76.59	315.11	80.73
24	46	16	66	.324	.398	.483	1,022	.286	1,995	.558	67.15	61.10	76.50	67.62	272.36	69.78
30	7	-	12	.309	.408	.538	1,079	.337	1,939	.606	70.89	72.08	74.35	73.44	290.77	74.49
28	9	34	82	.320	.422	.578	1,090	.310	2,231	.635	71.62	66.33	85.54	76.98	300.47	76.98
26	15	28	62	.318	.387	.515	969	.297	1,808	.554	63.67	63.52	69.33	67.20	263.71	67.56
27	49	-	-	.393	.438	.495	1,124	.368	1,850	.606	73.85	78.70	70.94	73.44	296.93	76.07
16	3	-	30	.295	.416	.526	986	.328	1,832	.610	64.78	70.21	70.25	73.96	279.21	71.53
-	38	-	-	.367	.465	.538	1,234	.413	2,083	.697	81.08	88.31	79.87	84.52	333.78	85.51
-	5	-	-	.348	.415	.504	986	.384	1,620	.631	64.78	82.11	62.12	76.48	285.49	73.14
4	19	22	66	.267	.375	.558	981	.308	1,934	.608	64.45	65.91	74.16	73.67	278.18	71.27
1	11	-	69	.294	.420	.609	1,178	.345	2,282	.669	77.40	73.81	87.50	81.07	319.77	81.92
-	7	-	3	.359	.414	.636	1,351	.397	2,323	.682	88.76	84.80	89.07	82.67	345.30	88.46
6	18	14	59	.316	.383	.571	1,020	.323	1,895	.601	67.02	69.13	72.66	72.82	281.64	72.15
-	50	-	-	.366	.399	.546	1,071	.414	1,595	.616	70.37	88.46	61.16	74.69	294.68	75.50
10	7	16	27	.325	.451	.618	1,152	.356	2,255	.696	75.69	76.08	86.46	84.44	322.67	82.67
5	21	24	35	.263	.350	.517	984	.314	1,773	.567	64.65	67.25	67.98	68.70	268.58	68.81
13	36	24	72	.334	.455	.579	1,030	.312	2,111	.639	67.67	66.68	80.94	77.49	292.79	75.01
11	6	19	30	.289	.400	.577	1,054	.326	2,065	.638	69.25	69.67	79.18	77.39	295.50	75.70
7	8	50	76	.332	.376	.541	1,073	.309	1,925	.554	70.50	66.01	73.81	67.14	277.47	71.08
23	9	19	70	.308	.387	.606	1,203	.353	2,215	.650	79.04	75.53	84.93	78.85	318.35	81.56
6	24	26	50	.295	.410	.587	982	.323	1,952	.641	64.52	68.99	74.85	77.75	286.10	73.30
16	8	23	57	.294	.391	.547	939	.302	1,863	.600	61.70	64.65	71.43	72.72	270.50	69.30
1	36	23	52	.287	.438	.702	1,133	.375	2,261	.748	74.44	80.20	86.69	90.74	332.08	85.08
-	13	-	76	.344	.380	.572	1,214	.360	1,977	.587	79.76	77.03	75.81	71.13	303.73	77.81
57	13	-	-	.312	.360	.521	986	.336	1,654	.563	64.78	71.77	63.42	68.26	268.23	68.72
-	19	-	42	.339	.421	.611	1,032	.337	2,002	.654	67.81	72.05	76.76	79.24	295.86	75.80
56	13	32	29	.303	.431	.508	988	.304	2,163	.666	64.91	65.07	82.94	80.77	293.69	75.24
27	14	20	63	.290	.383	.536	1,067	.302	2,121	.599	70.11	64.49	81.33	72.68	288.61	73.94
10	9	34	57	.304	.390	.530	1,000	.316	1,836	.580	65.70	67.50	70.40	70.27	273.87	70.16
16	11	-	58	.350	.441	.616	1,159	.334	2,296	.662	76.15	71.42	80.04	80.22	315.83	80.91
-	28	-	-	.356	.424	.501	1,111	.364	1,825	.599	73.00	77.92	69.98	72.57	293.46	75.18
27	22	30	107	.312	.372	.546	1,100	.319	1,992	.578	72.27	68.24	76.38	70.07	286.96	73.52
-	16	-	10	.314	.418	.564	1,192	.372	2,048	.639	78.32	79.51	78.53	77.45	313.80	80.39
13	26	33	58	.291	.393	.577	1,110	.318	2,186	.625	72.93	67.88	83.82	75.79	300.42	76.96
43	25	20	56	.321	.377	.532	965	.294	1,878	.572	63.40	62.80	72.01	69.29	267.50	68.53
11	17	31	82	.290	.350	.494	989	.286	1,813	.524	64.98	61.11	69.52	63.51	259.12	66.38
8	10	21	96	.331	.401	.592	1,046	.335	1,917	.614	68.73	71.60	73.50	74.40	288.23	73.84
9	38	26	61	.324	.424	.640	1,172	.386	2,047	.675	77.00	82.61	78.49	81.80	319.90	81.96
23	25	35	89	.311	.360	.556	1,079	.311	1,987	.573	70.89	66.57	76.19	69.51	283.16	72.54
15	8	32	110	.288	.356	.479	1,012	.274	1,883	.510	66.49	58.58	72.20	61.80	259.08	66.37
27	45	31	75	.309	.395	.584	1,084	.336	2,042	.634	71.22	71.92	78.30	76.82	298.26	76.41
33	43	-	71	.329	.430	.505	1,003	.314	1,891	.592	65.90	67.19	72.51	71.83	277.43	71.08
21	53	38	69	.304	.394	.608	1,264	.363	2,293	.658	83.05	77.58	87.92	79.80	328.35	84.12
35	21	15	55	.322	.384	.466	872	.245	1,800	.506	57.29	52.39	69.02	61.32	240.03	61.49
28	7	-	-	.351	.474	.722	1,517	.468	2,518	.776	99.67	100.00	96.55	94.11	390.33	100.00

Best 5 Consecutive Seasons H-R

Rank	Player	Years	G	AB	H	1B	2B	3B	HR	RUN	RBI	BB	SO	SB	

5 Consecutive Year Statistics & Analysis Listed Alphabetically

Rank	Player	Years	G	AB	H	1B	2B	3B	HR	RUN	RBI	BB	SO	SB
N/R	Ruth, Babe	1920-1924	709	2,455	909	433	188	53	235	723	659	691	415	59
65	Schmidt, Mike	1979-1983	714	2,491	686	355	111	21	199	503	522	517	584	54
59	Sheffield, Gary**	2000-2004	728	2,657	830	498	145	8	179	528	546	445	329	49
17	Simmons, Al*	1928-1932	682	2,782	1,002	624	180	56	142	593	708	195	223	21
68	Sisler, George	1918-1922	680	2,762	1,053	743	181	78	51	561	455	196	97	201
29	Snider, Duke	1953-1957	740	2,762	860	455	169	29	207	581	585	446	478	37
7	Sosa, Sammy**	1998-2002	787	3,005	920	483	135	10	292	622	705	461	807	34
83	Speaker, Tris	1920-1924	698	2,544	943	597	245	53	48	556	448	407	64	35
86	Stargell, Willie	1971-1975	691	2,497	741	392	166	11	172	446	542	373	627	1
37	Stovey, Harry	1887-1891	643	2,664	816	530	150	76	60	664	440	355	175	378
51	Terry, Bill	1928-1932	760	3,062	1,103	751	199	62	91	587	576	248	163	37
32	Thomas, Frank **	1993-1998	698	2,498	835	482	158	1	194	534	599	575	328	11
40	Thome, Jim**	1999-2003	766	2,635	740	378	135	9	218	520	587	589	848	2
33	Thompson, Sam	1892-1896	620	2,693	956	654	162	77	63	588	636	208	73	112
120	Traynor, Pie	1927-1931	708	2,794	945	707	156	59	23	449	560	182	75	49
42	Trosky, Hal*	1934-1938	762	3,041	957	561	199	43	154	535	655	272	267	17
74	Vaughn, Mo	1994-1998	707	2,715	865	537	137	7	184	479	562	367	714	19
79	Wagner, Honus	1900-1904	673	2,624	927	633	191	81	22	506	493	240	-	228
39	Walker, Larry **	1997-2001	639	2,271	810	459	174	21	156	535	486	327	346	77
71	Waner, Paul	1926-1930	747	2,946	1,057	717	202	92	46	605	473	349	91	55
76	Williams, Bernie**	1996-2000	699	2,687	871	554	156	30	131	540	535	400	412	69
92	Williams, Billy	1968-1972	794	3,088	948	599	158	33	158	512	537	318	291	24
48	Williams, Ken*	1921-1925	662	2,496	847	519	154	39	135	510	552	333	136	105
5	Williams, Ted*	1942-1949	748	2,639	925	529	194	28	174	682	660	751	231	8
11	Wilson, Hack	1926-1930	738	2,759	914	534	163	40	177	586	708	400	392	33
112	Winfield, Dave	1982-1986	742	2,902	835	517	149	31	138	484	540	285	414	51
90	Yastrzemski, Carl	1966-1971	801	2,881	856	524	159	10	163	504	488	523	376	69
96	York, Rudy	1937-1941	651	2,345	693	394	136	15	148	419	543	355	352	15

* Consecutive excluding or consolidating years of military service
** Active player. Statistics through 2004 season
TOP ranking for players with less than 70% rating is based upon comparison to listed players only.
N/R = Not Rated

Best 5 Consecutive Seasons R-Y

5 Consecutive Year Statistics & Analysis Listed Alphabetically

CS	HBP	SF	GDP	AVG	OBP	SLG	Total Offensive Production Statistics				TRP Rating	RPA Rating	TNB Rating	TBA Rating	TOP Composite	
							TRP	RPA	TNB	TBA					TOP	Rating
66	16	-	-	.370	.511	.777	1,382	.437	2,608	.825	90.80	93.46	100.00	100.00	384.27	98.45
29	15	36	49	.275	.398	.576	1,025	.330	1,993	.641	67.35	70.52	76.42	77.75	292.03	74.82
22	38	31	73	.312	.414	.575	1,074	.331	2,038	.628	70.57	70.80	78.14	76.17	295.68	75.75
13	9	-	-	.360	.404	.618	1,301	.436	1,932	.647	85.48	93.17	74.08	78.45	331.18	84.85
47	20	-	-	.381	.426	.559	1,016	.341	1,913	.642	66.75	72.96	73.35	77.88	290.95	74.54
27	10	19	64	.311	.407	.618	1,166	.353	2,174	.659	76.61	75.54	83.36	79.85	315.35	80.79
23	15	35	69	.306	.397	.649	1,327	.370	2,438	.680	87.19	79.15	93.48	82.45	342.28	87.69
36	16	-	-	.371	.460	.565	1,004	.338	1,860	.627	65.97	72.36	71.32	76.01	285.65	73.18
3	21	24	38	.297	.389	.579	988	.335	1,837	.622	64.91	71.55	70.44	75.42	282.32	72.33
-	18	-	-	.306	.392	.487	1,104	.364	2,049	.675	72.54	77.74	78.57	81.80	310.64	79.58
-	4	-	-	.360	.409	.555	1,163	.351	1,988	.600	76.41	75.05	76.23	72.73	300.42	76.96
9	18	47	79	.334	.455	.631	1,133	.352	2,172	.675	74.44	75.31	83.28	81.86	314.90	80.67
6	21	23	33	.281	.413	.587	1,107	.335	2,153	.652	72.73	71.71	82.55	79.08	306.08	78.42
-	29	-	-	.355	.407	.543	1,224	.418	1,810	.618	80.42	89.33	69.40	74.90	314.05	80.46
-	8	-	-	.338	.380	.461	1,009	.338	1,527	.512	66.29	72.31	58.55	62.04	259.20	66.40
11	8	-	-	.315	.372	.560	1,190	.358	1,990	.599	78.19	76.63	76.30	72.65	303.77	77.82
10	58	20	64	.319	.408	.578	1,041	.323	2,002	.621	68.40	69.05	76.76	75.29	289.50	74.17
-	39	-	-	.353	.415	.513	999	.344	1,853	.638	65.64	73.59	71.05	77.39	287.67	73.70
26	53	23	59	.357	.445	.658	1,021	.374	1,925	.704	67.08	79.89	73.81	85.40	306.18	78.44
-	19	-	-	.359	.430	.537	1,078	.325	2,004	.605	70.83	69.56	76.84	73.32	290.54	74.44
36	8	27	70	.324	.410	.551	1,075	.337	1,921	.602	70.63	72.02	73.66	72.97	289.27	74.11
10	17	25	72	.307	.372	.533	1,049	.298	1,995	.567	68.92	63.73	76.50	68.72	277.86	71.19
70	17	-	-	.339	.421	.595	1,062	.373	1,869	.657	69.78	79.80	71.66	79.62	300.86	77.08
4	13	-	66	.351	.496	.643	1,342	.387	2,465	.711	88.17	82.73	94.52	86.15	351.57	90.07
-	17	-	-	.331	.419	.612	1,294	.407	2,138	.673	85.02	87.13	81.98	81.62	335.74	86.02
25	4	30	101	.288	.349	.503	1,024	.308	1,775	.534	67.28	65.92	68.06	64.78	266.04	68.16
43	9	14	60	.297	.405	.529	992	.284	2,082	.597	65.18	60.84	79.83	72.39	278.23	71.28
7	9	-	36	.296	.390	.556	962	.350	1,675	.610	63.21	74.94	64.23	73.98	276.36	70.80

Best 5 Consecutive Seasons R-Y

120 of the Greatest Hitters Best 10 Consecutive Seasons

F-1
Players Listed by Total Offensive Production

F-2
Players Listed Alphabetically

(Rating and Ranking of Total Offensive Production Statistics in Chapter 9)

★ ★ ★ THE BEST ★ ★ ★

10 Consecutive Year Statistics & Analysis Listed by Total Offensive Production

Rank	Player	Years	G	AB	H	1B	2B	3B	HR	RUN	RBI	BB	SO	SB
1	Ruth, Babe	1920-1929	1,399	4,884	1,734	871	314	82	467	1,365	1,331	1,240	795	88
2	Gehrig, Lou	1927-1936	1,538	5,781	2,022	1,125	390	117	390	1,417	1,527	1,116	535	80
3	Foxx, Jimmie*	1930-1939	1,470	5,495	1,845	1,027	316	87	415	1,244	1,403	1,015	876	65
4	Williams, Ted*	1939-1951	1,421	5,086	1,763	1,013	366	61	323	1,273	1,261	1,327	442	20
5	Bonds, Barry **	1995-2004	1,435	4,584	1,443	676	287	36	444	1,180	1,083	1,491	716	197
6	Hornsby, Rogers	1920-1929	1,430	5,451	2,085	1,315	405	115	250	1,195	1,153	753	431	74
7	Delahanty, Ed	1893-1902	1,291	5,275	1,968	1,351	399	133	85	1,221	1,144	615	89	335
8	DiMaggio, Joe*	1936-1948	1,405	5,609	1,853	1,119	320	111	303	1,146	1,277	594	282	30
9	Ott, Mel	1929-1938	1,498	5,490	1,730	1,052	301	54	323	1,148	1,206	969	462	54
10	Bagwell, Jeff**	1994-2003	1,495	5,450	1,643	903	358	16	366	1,160	1,155	1,066	1,120	166
11	Mantle, Mickey	1953-1962	1,437	5,006	1,559	928	208	55	368	1,186	1,000	1,135	1,032	121
12	Mays, Willie*	1954-1963	1,536	5,867	1,876	1,088	309	97	382	1,182	1,088	718	673	237
13	Musial, Stan*	1944-1954	1,525	5,897	2,031	1,217	425	121	268	1,193	1,093	918	331	48
14	Simmons, Al*	1925-1934	1,372	5,592	2,005	1,290	377	106	232	1,078	1,277	401	450	56
15	Greenberg, Hank*	1933-1946	1,268	4,790	1,528	787	366	69	306	980	1,202	748	771	58
16	Duffy, Hugh	1889-1898	1,342	5,559	1,892	1,459	252	91	90	1,297	1,075	568	179	538
17	Sosa, Sammy**	1995-2004	1,480	5,704	1,633	888	247	19	479	1,053	1,226	716	1,525	108
18	Ramirez, Manny**	1995-2004	1,422	5,229	1,673	930	358	14	371	1,011	1,205	830	1,150	29
19	Aaron, Hank	1957-1966	1,536	6,004	1,914	1,170	316	52	376	1,137	1,165	625	678	163
20	Hamilton, Billy	1889-1898	1,228	4,967	1,759	1,457	185	82	35	1,439	607	940	218	847
21	Thomas, Frank **	1991-2000	1,470	5,283	1,692	998	350	7	337	1,044	1,152	1,144	781	29
22	Rodriguez, Alex**	1995-2004	1,413	5,536	1,696	982	309	24	381	1,117	1,094	636	1,106	202
23	Griffey, Ken **	1991-2000	1,398	5,300	1,584	867	291	26	400	1,011	1,129	734	937	141
24	Thome, Jim**	1995-2004	1,467	5,036	1,449	757	279	20	393	1,024	1,068	1,122	1,533	10
25	Cobb, Ty	1908-1917	1,404	5,273	2,003	1,456	328	163	56	1,079	909	605	169	630
26	Brouthers, Dan	1885-1894	1,192	4,778	1,699	1,168	308	155	68	1,140	933	694	140	254
27	Thompson, Sam	1887-1896	1,195	5,140	1,750	1,217	293	130	110	1,082	1,145	393	173	221
28	Averill, Earl	1929-1938	1,485	5,854	1,888	1,173	369	121	225	1,146	1,077	719	458	66
29	Heilmann, Harry	1921-1930	1,414	5,201	1,909	1,243	412	102	152	975	1,135	640	342	68
30	Mize, Johnny*	1936-1948	1,403	5,185	1,679	987	313	82	297	960	1,096	714	423	26
31	Palmiero, Rafael**	1993-2002	1,527	5,722	1,666	930	328	13	395	993	1,154	835	839	63
32	Robinson, Frank	1958-1967	1,484	5,399	1,641	938	319	48	336	1,029	1,067	748	776	153
33	Klein, Chuck	1928-1937	1,318	5,243	1,783	1,104	342	65	272	1,024	1,041	473	427	67
34	Kelley, Joe	1893-1902	1,246	4,861	1,675	1,202	269	146	58	1,108	944	690	128	378
35	Belle, Albert	1991-2000	1,468	5,612	1,673	902	381	17	373	951	1,199	670	900	86
36	Gehringer, Charlie	1929-1938	1,471	5,857	1,948	1,300	416	89	143	1,224	1,023	761	212	125
37	Wagner, Honus	1899-1908	1,399	5,320	1,879	1,291	385	150	53	1,023	969	492	-	489
38	Matthews, Eddie	1953-1962	1,489	5,474	1,562	907	225	56	374	1,058	1,024	972	861	53
39	Schmidt, Mike	1974-1983	1,493	5,262	1,417	741	258	48	370	1,023	1,019	1,019	1,276	154
40	Stovey, Harry	1883-1892	1,189	4,937	1,488	963	280	137	108	1,222	790	565	226	486
41	Walker, Larry **	1993-2002	1,228	4,399	1,454	805	331	41	277	945	921	588	699	161
42	Conner, Roger	1885-1894	1,281	4,934	1,629	1,095	268	162	104	1,105	909	770	316	227
43	Snider, Duke	1949-1958	1,438	5,401	1,652	973	291	62	326	1,011	1,035	709	872	88
44	Jones, Chipper**	1995-2004	1,534	5,613	1,703	1,042	324	27	310	1,033	1,039	936	876	118
45	Goslin, Goose	1923-1932	1,478	5,685	1,852	1,211	326	133	182	982	1,109	627	380	142
46	McGwire, Mark	1992-2001	1,097	3,531	979	427	146	1	405	750	910	880	1,004	6
47	Kiner, Ralph	1947-1956	1,472	5,205	1,451	827	216	39	369	971	1,015	1,011	749	22
48	Sheffield, Gary**	1995-2004	1,369	4,819	1,470	889	255	12	314	954	969	959	629	128
49	Gonzalez, Juan **	1992-2001	1,312	5,129	1,548	861	302	20	365	862	1,161	367	972	19
50	Burkett, Jesse	1892-1901	1,356	5,610	2,079	1,683	208	131	57	1,288	713	705	159	313

Best 10 Consecutive Seasons

10 Consecutive Year Statistics & Analysis Listed by Total Offensive Production

CS	HBP	SF	GDP	AVG	OBP	SLG	Total Offensive Production Statistics				TRP Rating	RPA Rating	TNB Rating	TBA Rating	TOP Composite	
							TRP	RPA	TNB	TBA					TOP	Rating
93	27	-	-	.355	.488	.740	2,696	.438	4,875	.793	91.58	99.95	98.35	100.00	389.87	100.00
89	33	-	-	.350	.458	.660	2,944	.425	4,956	.715	100.00	96.88	99.98	90.23	387.09	99.29
44	7	-	17	.336	.440	.652	2,647	.405	4,623	.708	89.91	92.38	93.26	89.27	364.83	93.58
14	21	-	121	.347	.484	.633	2,534	.387	4,574	.698	86.07	88.16	92.27	88.04	354.54	90.94
48	65	40	83	.315	.485	.684	2,263	.361	4,839	.773	76.87	82.40	97.62	97.49	354.37	90.89
62	24	-	-	.382	.460	.637	2,348	.377	4,259	.684	79.76	85.97	85.92	86.28	337.93	86.68
-	65	-	-	.373	.445	.547	2,365	.397	3,903	.655	80.33	90.57	78.74	82.70	332.33	85.24
8	37	-	89	.330	.398	.589	2,423	.383	3,957	.625	82.30	87.30	79.83	78.89	328.32	84.21
-	35	-	44	.315	.421	.566	2,354	.360	4,166	.637	79.96	82.11	84.04	80.40	326.51	83.75
60	91	66	158	.301	.420	.574	2,315	.339	4,394	.643	78.63	77.28	88.64	81.16	325.72	83.55
21	11	30	53	.311	.438	.595	2,186	.351	4,227	.678	74.25	79.95	85.27	85.54	325.02	83.36
72	23	58	139	.320	.393	.601	2,270	.334	4,431	.651	77.11	76.07	89.39	82.16	324.72	83.29
27	27	7	120	.344	.435	.594	2,286	.328	4,468	.641	77.65	74.80	90.14	80.89	323.48	82.97
35	16	-	-	.359	.403	.588	2,355	.392	3,728	.620	79.99	89.37	75.21	78.28	322.85	82.81
26	12	-	50	.319	.412	.616	2,182	.390	3,742	.668	74.12	88.85	75.49	84.31	322.77	82.79
-	24	-	-	.340	.404	.467	2,372	.386	3,726	.606	80.57	87.94	75.17	76.43	320.11	82.11
48	34	54	130	.286	.366	.588	2,279	.343	4,165	.627	77.41	78.29	84.02	79.17	318.89	81.79
28	67	56	150	.320	.416	.607	2,216	.350	4,070	.643	75.27	79.81	82.11	81.10	318.29	81.64
41	14	65	153	.319	.381	.577	2,302	.336	4,223	.616	78.19	76.51	85.19	77.66	317.56	81.45
-	77	-	-	.354	.464	.446	2,046	.342	4,077	.681	69.50	77.97	82.25	85.96	315.68	80.97
20	44	87	159	.320	.439	.581	2,196	.327	4,264	.635	74.59	74.55	86.02	80.10	315.26	80.86
50	82	57	128	.306	.383	.577	2,211	.343	4,066	.631	75.10	78.30	82.03	79.67	315.11	80.82
46	52	56	98	.299	.386	.590	2,140	.343	4,008	.642	72.69	78.21	80.86	81.04	312.79	80.23
14	41	44	80	.288	.418	.585	2,092	.331	4,106	.649	71.06	75.45	82.83	81.93	311.28	79.84
113	55	-	-	.380	.449	.536	1,988	.335	4,002	.675	67.53	76.41	80.73	85.11	309.78	79.46
-	101	-	-	.356	.448	.528	2,073	.372	3,570	.641	70.41	84.82	72.02	80.83	308.08	79.02
-	63	-	-	.340	.394	.512	2,227	.398	3,310	.591	75.65	90.75	66.77	74.63	307.80	78.95
54	31	-	-	.323	.399	.542	2,223	.337	3,936	.596	75.51	76.76	79.40	75.20	306.87	78.71
49	24	-	-	.367	.439	.573	2,110	.360	3,664	.625	71.67	82.04	73.92	78.82	306.45	78.60
-	38	-	76	.324	.409	.588	2,056	.342	3,825	.636	69.84	77.97	77.16	80.26	305.24	78.29
22	44	67	112	.291	.382	.560	2,147	.317	4,125	.608	72.49	72.20	83.22	76.75	305.10	78.26
59	103	57	143	.304	.395	.568	2,096	.325	4,009	.622	71.20	74.10	80.88	78.42	304.60	78.13
-	12	-	33	.340	.396	.586	2,065	.358	3,623	.629	70.14	81.74	73.09	79.35	304.32	78.06
-	58	-	-	.345	.432	.496	2,052	.366	3,536	.630	69.70	83.43	71.33	79.54	304.00	77.98
39	53	76	188	.298	.374	.571	2,150	.326	3,977	.603	73.03	74.30	80.23	76.04	303.60	77.87
58	34	-	-	.333	.412	.507	2,247	.338	3,833	.576	76.32	77.03	77.32	72.70	303.38	77.82
-	77	-	-	.353	.416	.512	1,992	.338	3,781	.642	67.66	77.14	76.28	81.01	302.09	77.48
24	17	43	74	.285	.392	.552	2,082	.316	4,039	.614	70.72	72.16	81.48	77.45	301.81	77.41
76	47	66	81	.269	.388	.548	2,042	.315	4,025	.622	69.36	71.92	81.20	78.43	300.91	77.18
-	31	-	-	.301	.377	.479	2,012	.364	3,448	.623	68.34	82.92	69.56	78.63	299.45	76.81
48	93	47	103	.331	.416	.613	1,866	.357	3,492	.668	63.38	81.36	70.45	84.24	299.44	76.80
-	34	-	-	.330	.424	.513	2,014	.351	3,564	.621	68.41	80.04	71.90	78.37	298.72	76.62
48	15	23	132	.306	.386	.564	2,046	.326	3,809	.607	69.50	74.29	76.84	76.53	297.16	76.22
40	14	64	150	.303	.400	.536	2,072	.306	4,039	.596	70.38	69.72	81.48	75.20	296.78	76.12
70	45	-	-	.326	.397	.526	2,091	.329	3,734	.587	71.03	75.01	75.33	74.11	295.48	75.79
3	52	41	77	.277	.424	.663	1,660	.362	3,277	.715	56.39	82.63	66.11	90.26	295.39	75.76
2	24	7	126	.279	.398	.548	1,986	.312	3,907	.613	67.46	71.06	78.82	77.35	294.69	75.59
54	79	59	116	.305	.424	.558	1,923	.319	3,803	.630	65.32	72.70	76.72	79.55	294.29	75.48
12	49	71	142	.302	.350	.582	2,023	.351	3,408	.592	68.72	80.12	68.75	74.68	292.27	74.96
-	55	-	-	.371	.446	.485	2,001	.314	3,793	.595	67.97	71.63	76.52	75.13	291.25	74.70

Best 10 Consecutive Seasons

10 Consecutive Year Statistics & Analysis Listed by Total Offensive Production

Rank	Player	Years	G	AB	H	1B	2B	3B	HR	RUN	RBI	BB	SO	SB
51	Johnson, Robert	1933-1942	1,459	5,428	1,617	986	307	72	252	997	1,040	853	678	78
52	Wilson, Hack	1924-1933	1,271	4,558	1,412	846	261	67	238	860	1,033	631	675	52
53	Delgado, Carlos**	1995-2004	1,378	4,877	1,385	706	341	11	327	872	1,034	801	1,196	8
54	Medwick, Joe	1933-1942	1,476	5,986	1,967	1,238	441	106	182	1,010	1,131	341	462	31
55	Killebrew, Harmon	1961-1970	1,462	5,079	1,352	748	184	17	403	876	1,046	1,027	1,007	11
56	Piazza, Mike**	1993-2002	1,372	5,047	1,625	1,025	248	6	346	846	1,066	559	789	17
57	Waner, Paul	1927-1936	1,494	5,950	2,074	1,425	417	143	89	1,127	878	675	212	83
58	Bottomley, Jim	1922-1931	1,301	5,003	1,635	1,021	328	116	170	876	1,057	484	397	48
59	Martinez, Edgar**	1994-2003	1,351	4,787	1,526	909	362	7	248	859	981	962	843	31
60	Anson, Cap	1884-1893	1,261	4,987	1,660	1,230	271	79	80	948	1,052	634	200	189
61	Williams, Billy	1963-1972	1,605	6,272	1,882	1,192	316	67	307	1,006	1,013	647	657	63
62	Lajoie, Nap	1897-1906	1,148	4,702	1,709	1,174	360	112	63	910	933	199	-	224
63	Williams, Bernie**	1995-2004	1,410	5,408	1,678	1,096	308	43	231	1,019	947	792	832	102
64	Henderson, Rickey	1982-1991	1,387	5,118	1,478	1,015	258	37	168	1,146	565	976	708	805
65	Rice, Jim	1977-1986	1,469	5,915	1,807	1,168	275	61	303	931	1,089	496	961	37
66	Speaker, Tris	1916-1925	1,369	5,007	1,801	1,201	434	100	66	983	798	763	131	147
67	Giambi, Jason**	1995-2004	1,344	4,757	1,413	828	296	8	281	851	944	871	916	13
68	Allen, Dick	1964-1973	1,353	4,961	1,484	870	254	73	287	884	887	718	1,254	103
69	Keeler, Willie	1894-1903	1,322	5,618	2,094	1,769	176	128	21	1,305	614	321	614	411
70	Terry, Bill	1926-1935	1,429	5,540	1,926	1,366	325	99	136	982	945	457	358	51
71	Banks, Ernie	1955-1964	1,493	5,675	1,599	921	259	64	355	873	1,036	513	750	37
72	Morgan, Joe	1969-1978	1,478	5,238	1,468	971	267	51	179	1,029	731	1,088	546	509
73	Jackson, Reggie	1971-1980	1,434	5,217	1,463	856	271	26	310	870	967	685	1,234	158
74	McGriff, Fred **	1988-1997	1,492	5,393	1,548	935	275	19	319	887	964	820	1,141	57
75	Murray, Eddie	1978-1987	1,499	5,631	1,677	1,083	295	21	278	892	1,018	734	745	56
76	Kelly, King	1882-1891	1,049	4,328	1,384	972	269	81	62	1,049	705	462	327	341
77	Stargell, Willie	1965-1974	1,394	4,947	1,416	798	271	33	314	797	978	621	1,201	11
78	McCovey, Willie	1962-1971	1,372	4,493	1,272	724	193	29	326	775	916	769	824	15
79	Trosky, Hal*	1933-1944	1,259	4,862	1,485	885	319	55	226	813	981	511	403	24
80	Winfield, Dave	1979-1988	1,473	5,579	1,625	1,032	285	51	257	901	1,017	637	793	114
81	Williams, Ken*	1919-1928	1,240	4,476	1,448	923	261	71	193	816	874	533	255	148
82	Murphy, Dale	1980-1989	1,537	5,694	1,553	957	257	31	308	938	929	784	1,268	134
83	Herman, Babe	1926-1935	1,379	5,169	1,697	1,052	370	108	167	815	914	475	504	88
84	York, Rudy	1937-1946	1,419	5,250	1,476	906	266	48	256	816	1,055	725	762	37
85	Vaughn, Mo	1991-2000	1,346	4,966	1,479	920	250	10	299	784	977	652	1,262	30
86	Kaline, Al	1955-1964	1,426	5,447	1,691	1,129	279	56	227	907	912	628	466	90
87	Yastrzemski, Carl	1965-1974	1,507	5,393	1,574	1,014	293	23	244	902	872	975	644	110
88	Berra, Yogi	1948-1957	1,384	5,193	1,508	994	224	41	249	853	1,027	500	240	21
89	Brett, George	1979-1988	1,282	4,841	1,529	942	319	64	204	820	878	639	400	82
90	Bichette, Dante	1991-2000	1,419	5,457	1,664	1,048	347	25	244	835	1,016	313	892	142
91	Canseco, Jose	1986-1995	1,216	4,615	1,246	713	226	12	295	780	938	556	1,236	152
92	Bench, Johnny	1969-1978	1,453	5,297	1,424	843	268	19	294	802	1,023	669	909	58
93	Traynor, Pie	1922-1931	1,447	5,691	1,845	1,376	282	134	53	929	1,022	370	181	141
94	Jackson, Joe	1911-1920	1,300	4,866	1,737	1,216	305	163	53	855	768	510	158	198
95	Collins, Eddie	1909-1918	1,454	5,209	1,715	1,377	201	117	20	1,008	658	823	160	523
96	Cepeda, Orlando	1958-1967	1,388	5,193	1,606	1,029	287	22	268	808	936	355	779	112
97	Sisler, George	1918-1927	1,280	5,274	1,850	1,361	282	123	84	920	802	308	195	270
98	Perez, Tony	1967-1976	1,513	5,763	1,647	1,052	288	46	261	822	1,028	575	1,118	38
99	Meusel, Bob	1920-1929	1,294	5,032	1,565	994	338	87	146	764	1,005	349	556	133
100	Crawford, Sam	1905-1914	1,510	5,835	1,846	1,299	313	176	58	850	936	470	59	245

10 Consecutive Year Statistics & Analysis Listed by Total Offensive Production

CS	HBP	SF	GDP	AVG	OBP	SLG	Total Offensive Production Statistics				TRP Rating	RPA Rating	TNB Rating	TBA Rating	TOP Composite	
							TRP	RPA	TNB	TBA					TOP	Rating
49	16	-	64	.298	.395	.520	2,037	.320	3,722	.585	69.19	73.03	75.09	73.83	291.13	74.67
5	20	-	8	.310	.396	.553	1,893	.363	3,219	.617	64.30	82.75	64.94	77.85	289.84	74.34
6	119	60	88	.284	.394	.560	1,906	.321	3,651	.614	64.74	73.11	73.65	77.49	288.99	74.13
-	21	-	160	.329	.367	.529	2,141	.329	3,559	.547	72.72	75.02	71.80	69.00	288.54	74.01
11	36	48	151	.266	.390	.547	1,922	.303	3,842	.606	65.29	69.12	77.51	76.45	288.36	73.96
20	20	34	173	.322	.389	.579	1,912	.328	3,499	.600	64.95	74.75	70.59	75.69	285.97	73.35
-	31	-	55	.349	.418	.512	2,005	.299	3,833	.571	68.10	68.13	77.32	72.06	285.62	73.26
15	30	-	-	.327	.390	.541	1,933	.350	3,252	.589	65.66	79.90	65.60	74.37	285.54	73.24
18	66	57	121	.319	.435	.553	1,840	.307	3,687	.615	62.50	70.01	74.38	77.62	284.52	72.98
-	19	-	-	.333	.410	.467	2,000	.355	3,171	.562	67.93	80.87	63.97	70.94	283.71	72.77
30	30	48	140	.300	.366	.519	2,019	.283	3,963	.555	68.58	64.51	79.95	70.06	283.10	72.61
-	75	-	-	.363	.399	.528	1,843	.370	2,980	.599	62.60	84.46	60.12	75.56	282.74	72.52
56	27	44	156	.310	.398	.511	1,966	.306	3,630	.565	66.78	69.76	73.23	71.26	281.03	72.08
170	35	28	87	.289	.404	.452	1,711	.274	3,960	.634	58.12	62.49	79.89	80.02	280.51	71.95
22	44	60	232	.305	.360	.526	2,020	.299	3,668	.544	68.61	68.27	74.00	68.59	279.48	71.68
65	42	-	-	.360	.448	.526	1,781	.306	3,520	.606	60.50	69.88	71.01	76.42	277.80	71.25
10	92	62	115	.297	.411	.540	1,795	.304	3,534	.599	60.97	69.41	71.29	75.61	277.29	71.12
42	12	36	110	.299	.387	.553	1,771	.303	3,536	.606	60.16	69.19	71.33	76.44	277.11	71.08
27	92	-	-	.373	.416	.461	1,919	.318	3,386	.561	65.18	72.56	68.31	70.84	276.89	71.02
-	8	-	31	.348	.398	.516	1,927	.319	3,373	.559	65.46	72.80	68.05	70.51	276.81	71.00
35	36	64	134	.282	.342	.538	1,909	.297	3,602	.561	64.84	67.79	72.66	70.77	276.07	70.81
113	24	60	60	.280	.402	.453	1,760	.272	3,882	.600	59.78	62.03	78.31	75.70	275.83	70.75
70	48	45	95	.280	.366	.521	1,837	.302	3,537	.581	62.40	68.79	71.35	73.28	275.82	70.75
30	27	47	147	.287	.381	.523	1,851	.288	3,692	.574	62.87	65.61	74.48	72.40	275.36	70.63
21	14	62	138	.298	.376	.506	1,910	.290	3,631	.552	64.88	66.20	73.25	69.64	273.97	70.27
-	12	-	-	.320	.387	.462	1,754	.365	2,816	.586	59.58	83.30	56.81	73.99	273.67	70.20
8	51	48	92	.286	.368	.545	1,775	.308	3,370	.585	60.29	70.29	67.98	73.83	272.40	69.87
17	50	42	89	.283	.391	.557	1,691	.311	3,318	.610	57.44	70.85	66.94	76.91	272.14	69.80
20	16	-	32	.305	.373	.533	1,794	.331	3,123	.576	60.94	75.47	63.00	72.69	272.09	69.79
52	11	47	175	.291	.362	.499	1,918	.297	3,493	.542	65.15	67.82	70.47	68.34	271.78	69.71
98	26	-	-	.324	.399	.543	1,690	.336	3,039	.604	57.40	76.54	61.31	76.16	271.41	69.61
56	22	37	129	.273	.361	.491	1,867	.280	3,680	.552	63.42	63.87	74.24	69.66	271.18	69.56
-	9	-	31	.328	.386	.539	1,729	.304	3,356	.590	58.73	69.37	67.70	74.50	270.30	69.33
26	12	-	131	.281	.370	.496	1,871	.306	3,354	.548	63.55	69.74	67.66	69.17	270.13	69.29
17	96	42	118	.298	.387	.533	1,761	.300	3,407	.580	59.82	68.37	68.73	73.18	270.10	69.28
36	30	49	137	.310	.382	.507	1,819	.289	3,475	.552	61.79	65.94	70.10	69.70	267.52	68.62
74	18	49	134	.292	.399	.490	1,774	.270	3,674	.559	60.26	61.58	74.12	70.57	266.53	68.36
21	35	21	98	.290	.355	.493	1,880	.322	3,096	.530	63.86	73.32	62.46	66.81	266.45	68.34
35	15	58	101	.316	.393	.535	1,698	.300	3,289	.582	57.68	68.48	66.35	73.40	265.91	68.20
69	35	64	151	.305	.343	.512	1,851	.307	3,214	.534	62.87	70.12	64.84	67.36	265.19	68.02
66	57	55	123	.270	.352	.516	1,718	.318	3,080	.570	58.36	72.47	62.13	71.89	264.85	67.93
28	15	71	132	.269	.348	.493	1,825	.295	3,326	.538	61.99	67.30	67.10	67.86	264.25	67.78
43	21	-	-	.324	.368	.449	1,951	.321	3,043	.500	66.27	73.15	61.39	63.13	263.94	67.70
61	59	-	-	.357	.424	.519	1,623	.299	3,233	.595	55.13	68.10	65.22	75.05	263.50	67.59
81	51	-	-	.329	.426	.424	1,666	.274	3,526	.580	56.59	62.46	71.13	73.14	263.31	67.54
56	75	56	136	.309	.359	.528	1,744	.300	3,227	.555	59.24	68.39	65.10	70.02	262.75	67.39
91	30	-	-	.351	.390	.499	1,722	.307	3,147	.561	58.49	69.97	63.49	70.75	262.70	67.38
24	30	61	143	.286	.350	.488	1,850	.281	3,429	.522	62.84	64.19	69.17	65.83	262.04	67.21
102	20	-	-	.311	.358	.500	1,769	.328	2,915	.540	60.09	74.69	58.81	68.10	261.68	67.12
16	14	-	-	.316	.369	.460	1,786	.283	3,398	.538	60.67	64.45	68.55	67.85	261.52	67.08

Best 10 Consecutive Seasons

	10 Consecutive Year Statistics & Analysis Listed by Total Offensive Production															
Rank	Player	Years	G	AB	H	1B	2B	3B	HR	RUN	RBI	BB	SO	SB	
101	Jennings, Hughie	1891-1900	1,092	4,225	1,350	1,065	186	83	16	917	766	307	117	352	
102	Galarraga, Andres**	1989-1998	1,341	5,073	1,468	903	268	19	278	792	944	354	1,238	94	
103	Foster, George	1975-1984	1,421	5,330	1,507	956	228	37	286	794	995	526	1,042	38	
104	Dickey, Bill*	1930-1939	1,213	4,474	1,431	960	247	56	168	722	937	485	187	26	
105	Robinson, Jackie	1947-1956	1,382	4,877	1,518	1,054	273	54	137	947	734	740	291	197	
106	Dawson, Andre	1979-1988	1,433	5,621	1,610	1,001	296	59	254	839	910	354	838	226	
107	Ripkin, Cal, Jr.	1983-1992	1,617	6,305	1,759	1,148	337	29	245	952	921	705	694	29	
108	Clemente, Roberto	1960-1969	1,464	5,723	1,877	1,342	259	99	177	916	862	428	795	61	
109	O'Neill, Tip	1883-1892	1,054	4,305	1,436	1,070	222	92	52	880	757	421	146	161	
110	Jeter, Derek**	1995-2004	1,366	5,513	1,734	1,259	283	42	150	1,037	693	559	972	201	
111	Mattingly, Don	1984-1993	1,462	5,882	1,827	1,234	375	13	205	852	966	467	353	14	
112	Howard, Frank	1962-1971	1,475	5,179	1,429	880	200	29	320	714	922	656	1,191	7	
113	Keller, Charlie*	1939-1949	1,064	3,676	1,053	637	163	69	184	712	723	760	480	45	
114	Kluszewski, Ted	1948-1957	1,330	4,951	1,498	980	244	23	251	744	884	405	290	20	
115	Hafey, Chick	1925-1934	1,155	4,218	1,356	826	319	59	152	718	761	341	422	66	
116	Rose, Pete	1969-1978	1,597	6,522	2,055	1,507	387	70	91	1,098	603	776	497	92	
117	Parker, Dave	1977-1986	1,366	5,273	1,582	1,021	315	45	201	777	859	415	823	109	
118	Maris, Roger	1957-1966	1,238	4,381	1,139	686	159	33	261	737	751	576	634	21	
119	Fielder, Cecil	1987-1996	1,191	4,223	1,086	637	162	6	281	642	850	577	1,075	2	
120	Campanella, Roy	1948-1957	1,215	4,205	1,161	723	178	18	242	627	856	533	501	25	

* Consecutive excluding or consolidating years of military service
** Active player. Statistics through 2004 season
TOP ranking for players with less than 70% rating is based upon comparison to listed players only.

10 Consecutive Year Statistics & Analysis Listed by Total Offensive Production

CS	HBP	SF	GDP	AVG	OBP	SLG	Total Offensive Production Statistics				TRP Rating	RPA Rating	TNB Rating	TBA Rating	TOP Composite	
							TRP	RPA	TNB	TBA					TOP	Rating
-	263	-	-	.320	.400	.414	1,683	.351	2,672	.557	57.17	80.04	53.90	70.31	261.42	67.05
47	113	43	103	.289	.347	.514	1,736	.305	3,122	.549	58.97	69.62	62.98	69.28	260.85	66.91
18	38	55	143	.283	.348	.500	1,789	.294	3,251	.534	60.77	66.97	65.58	67.33	260.65	66.86
18	23	-	9	.320	.389	.513	1,659	.332	2,810	.563	56.35	75.80	56.69	71.04	259.88	66.66
54	72	9	113	.311	.409	.474	1,681	.289	3,265	.562	57.10	65.97	65.87	70.89	259.83	66.64
72	59	71	112	.286	.331	.496	1,749	.281	3,353	.539	59.41	64.15	67.64	68.05	259.25	66.50
24	30	71	186	.279	.351	.458	1,873	.257	3,629	.497	63.62	58.53	73.21	62.75	258.11	66.20
24	24	40	168	.328	.375	.501	1,778	.279	3,354	.525	60.39	63.52	67.66	66.30	257.88	66.14
-	44	-	-	.334	.399	.464	1,637	.343	2,624	.550	55.60	78.26	52.94	69.41	256.21	65.72
52	92	30	122	.315	.385	.463	1,730	.274	3,351	.531	58.76	62.46	67.60	66.94	255.77	65.60
7	19	81	156	.311	.359	.483	1,818	.275	3,336	.505	61.75	62.77	67.30	63.73	255.55	65.55
6	28	38	170	.276	.358	.511	1,636	.269	3,332	.549	55.57	61.45	67.22	69.25	253.49	65.02
23	10	-	50	.286	.410	.518	1,435	.319	2,698	.600	48.74	72.78	54.43	75.72	251.67	64.55
8	22	14	121	.303	.357	.513	1,628	.295	2,980	.541	55.30	67.34	60.12	68.20	250.96	64.37
7	29	-	21	.321	.376	.533	1,479	.321	2,678	.581	50.24	73.18	54.02	73.31	250.75	64.32
59	53	35	106	.315	.390	.438	1,701	.227	3,717	.496	57.78	51.78	74.98	62.60	247.14	63.39
82	28	48	105	.300	.351	.491	1,636	.279	3,060	.521	55.57	63.57	61.73	65.79	246.65	63.27
9	33	34	62	.260	.348	.490	1,488	.293	2,768	.544	50.54	66.72	55.84	68.67	241.77	62.01
5	31	36	132	.257	.348	.498	1,492	.298	2,708	.542	50.68	68.06	54.63	68.35	241.72	62.00
17	30	18	143	.276	.360	.500	1,483	.301	2,672	.542	50.37	68.61	53.90	68.40	241.29	61.89

Best 10 Consecutive Seasons

10 Consecutive Year Statistics & Analysis Listed Alphabetically

Rank	Player	Years	G	AB	H	1B	2B	3B	HR	RUN	RBI	BB	SO	SB
19	Aaron, Hank	1957-1966	1,536	6,004	1,914	1,170	316	52	376	1,137	1,165	625	678	163
68	Allen, Dick	1964-1973	1,353	4,961	1,484	870	254	73	287	884	887	718	1,254	103
60	Anson, Cap	1884-1893	1,261	4,987	1,660	1,230	271	79	80	948	1,052	634	200	189
28	Averill, Earl	1929-1938	1,485	5,854	1,888	1,173	369	121	225	1,146	1,077	719	458	66
10	Bagwell, Jeff**	1994-2003	1,495	5,450	1,643	903	358	16	366	1,160	1,155	1,066	1,120	166
71	Banks, Ernie	1955-1964	1,493	5,675	1,599	921	259	64	355	873	1,036	513	750	37
35	Belle, Albert	1991-2000	1,468	5,612	1,673	902	381	17	373	951	1,199	670	900	86
92	Bench, Johnny	1969-1978	1,453	5,297	1,424	843	268	19	294	802	1,023	669	909	58
88	Berra, Yogi	1948-1957	1,384	5,193	1,508	994	224	41	249	853	1,027	500	240	21
90	Bichette, Dante	1991-2000	1,419	5,457	1,664	1,048	347	25	244	835	1,016	313	892	142
5	Bonds, Barry **	1995-2004	1,435	4,584	1,443	676	287	36	444	1,180	1,083	1,491	716	197
58	Bottomley, Jim	1922-1931	1,301	5,003	1,635	1,021	328	116	170	876	1,057	484	397	48
89	Brett, George	1979-1988	1,282	4,841	1,529	942	319	64	204	820	878	639	400	82
26	Brouthers, Dan	1885-1894	1,192	4,778	1,699	1,168	308	155	68	1,140	933	694	140	254
50	Burkett, Jesse	1892-1901	1,356	5,610	2,079	1,683	208	131	57	1,288	713	705	159	313
120	Campanella, Roy	1948-1957	1,215	4,205	1,161	723	178	18	242	627	856	533	501	25
91	Canseco, Jose	1986-1995	1,216	4,615	1,246	713	226	12	295	780	938	556	1,236	152
96	Cepeda, Orlando	1958-1967	1,388	5,193	1,606	1,029	287	22	268	808	936	355	779	112
108	Clemente, Roberto	1960-1969	1,464	5,723	1,877	1,342	259	99	177	916	862	428	795	61
25	Cobb, Ty	1908-1917	1,404	5,273	2,003	1,456	328	163	56	1,079	909	605	169	630
95	Collins, Eddie	1909-1918	1,454	5,209	1,715	1,377	201	117	20	1,008	658	823	160	523
42	Conner, Roger	1885-1894	1,281	4,934	1,629	1,095	268	162	104	1,105	909	770	316	227
100	Crawford, Sam	1905-1914	1,510	5,835	1,846	1,299	313	176	58	850	936	470	59	245
106	Dawson, Andre	1979-1988	1,433	5,621	1,610	1,001	296	59	254	839	910	354	838	226
7	Delahanty, Ed	1893-1902	1,291	5,275	1,968	1,351	399	133	85	1,221	1,144	615	89	335
53	Delgado, Carlos**	1995-2004	1,378	4,877	1,385	706	341	11	327	872	1,034	801	1,196	8
104	Dickey, Bill*	1930-1939	1,213	4,474	1,431	960	247	56	168	722	937	485	187	26
8	DiMaggio, Joe*	1936-1948	1,405	5,609	1,853	1,119	320	111	303	1,146	1,277	594	282	30
16	Duffy, Hugh	1889-1898	1,342	5,559	1,892	1,459	252	91	90	1,297	1,075	568	179	538
119	Fielder, Cecil	1987-1996	1,191	4,223	1,086	637	162	6	281	642	850	577	1,075	2
103	Foster, George	1975-1984	1,421	5,330	1,507	956	228	37	286	794	995	526	1,042	38
3	Foxx, Jimmie*	1930-1939	1,470	5,495	1,845	1,027	316	87	415	1,244	1,403	1,015	876	65
102	Galarraga, Andres**	1989-1998	1,341	5,073	1,468	903	268	19	278	792	944	354	1,238	94
2	Gehrig, Lou	1927-1936	1,538	5,781	2,022	1,125	390	117	390	1,417	1,527	1,116	535	80
36	Gehringer, Charlie	1929-1938	1,471	5,857	1,948	1,300	416	89	143	1,224	1,023	761	212	125
67	Giambi, Jason**	1995-2004	1,344	4,757	1,413	828	296	8	281	851	944	871	916	13
49	Gonzalez, Juan **	1992-2001	1,312	5,129	1,548	861	302	20	365	862	1,161	367	972	19
45	Goslin, Goose	1923-1932	1,478	5,685	1,852	1,211	326	133	182	982	1,109	627	380	142
15	Greenberg, Hank*	1933-1946	1,268	4,790	1,528	787	366	69	306	980	1,202	748	771	58
23	Griffey, Ken **	1991-2000	1,398	5,300	1,584	867	291	26	400	1,011	1,129	734	937	141
115	Hafey, Chick	1925-1934	1,155	4,218	1,356	826	319	59	152	718	761	341	422	66
20	Hamilton, Billy	1889-1898	1,228	4,967	1,759	1,457	185	82	35	1,439	607	940	218	847
29	Heilmann, Harry	1921-1930	1,414	5,201	1,909	1,243	412	102	152	975	1,135	640	342	68
64	Henderson, Rickey	1982-1991	1,387	5,118	1,478	1,015	258	37	168	1,146	565	976	708	805
83	Herman, Babe	1926-1935	1,379	5,169	1,697	1,052	370	108	167	815	914	475	504	88
6	Hornsby, Rogers	1920-1929	1,430	5,451	2,085	1,315	405	115	250	1,195	1,153	753	431	74
112	Howard, Frank	1962-1971	1,475	5,179	1,429	880	200	29	320	714	922	656	1,191	7
94	Jackson, Joe	1911-1920	1,300	4,866	1,737	1,216	305	163	53	855	768	510	158	198
73	Jackson, Reggie	1971-1980	1,434	5,217	1,463	856	271	26	310	870	967	685	1,234	158
101	Jennings, Hughie	1891-1900	1,092	4,225	1,350	1,065	186	83	16	917	766	307	117	352

10 Consecutive Year Statistics & Analysis Listed Alphabetically

CS	HBP	SF	GDP	AVG	OBP	SLG	Total Offensive Production Statistics				TRP Rating	RPA Rating	TNB Rating	TBA Rating	TOP Composite	
							TRP	RPA	TNB	TBA					TOP	Rating
41	14	65	153	.319	.381	.577	2,302	.336	4,223	.616	78.19	76.51	85.19	77.66	317.56	81.45
42	12	36	110	.299	.387	.553	1,771	.303	3,536	.606	60.16	69.19	71.33	76.44	277.11	71.08
-	19	-	-	.333	.410	.467	2,000	.355	3,171	.562	67.93	80.87	63.97	70.94	283.71	72.77
54	31	-	-	.323	.399	.542	2,223	.337	3,936	.596	75.51	76.76	79.40	75.20	306.87	78.71
60	91	66	158	.301	.420	.574	2,315	.339	4,394	.643	78.63	77.28	88.64	81.16	325.72	83.55
35	36	64	134	.282	.342	.538	1,909	.297	3,602	.561	64.84	67.79	72.66	70.77	276.07	70.81
39	53	76	188	.298	.374	.571	2,150	.326	3,977	.603	73.03	74.30	80.23	76.04	303.60	77.87
28	15	71	132	.269	.348	.493	1,825	.295	3,326	.538	61.99	67.30	67.10	67.86	264.25	67.78
21	35	21	98	.290	.355	.493	1,880	.322	3,096	.530	63.86	73.32	62.46	66.81	266.45	68.34
69	35	64	151	.305	.343	.512	1,851	.307	3,214	.534	62.87	70.12	64.84	67.36	265.19	68.02
48	65	40	83	.315	.485	.684	2,263	.361	4,839	.773	76.87	82.40	97.62	97.49	354.37	90.89
15	30	-	-	.327	.390	.541	1,933	.350	3,252	.589	65.66	79.90	65.60	74.37	285.54	73.24
35	15	58	101	.316	.393	.535	1,698	.300	3,289	.582	57.68	68.48	66.35	73.40	265.91	68.20
-	101	-	-	.356	.448	.528	2,073	.372	3,570	.641	70.41	84.82	72.02	80.83	308.08	79.02
-	55	-	-	.371	.446	.485	2,001	.314	3,793	.595	67.97	71.63	76.52	75.13	291.25	74.70
17	30	18	143	.276	.360	.500	1,483	.301	2,672	.542	50.37	68.61	53.90	68.40	241.29	61.89
66	57	55	123	.270	.352	.516	1,718	.318	3,080	.570	58.36	72.47	62.13	71.89	264.85	67.93
56	75	56	136	.309	.359	.528	1,744	.300	3,227	.555	59.24	68.39	65.10	70.02	262.75	67.39
24	24	40	168	.328	.375	.501	1,778	.279	3,354	.525	60.39	63.52	67.66	66.30	257.88	66.14
113	55	-	-	.380	.449	.536	1,988	.335	4,002	.675	67.53	76.41	80.73	85.11	309.78	79.46
81	51	-	-	.329	.426	.424	1,666	.274	3,526	.580	56.59	62.46	71.13	73.14	263.31	67.54
-	34	-	-	.330	.424	.513	2,014	.351	3,564	.621	68.41	80.04	71.90	78.37	298.72	76.62
16	14	-	-	.316	.369	.460	1,786	.283	3,398	.538	60.67	64.45	68.55	67.85	261.52	67.08
72	59	71	112	.286	.331	.496	1,749	.281	3,353	.539	59.41	64.15	67.64	68.05	259.25	66.50
-	65	-	-	.373	.445	.547	2,365	.397	3,903	.655	80.33	90.57	78.74	82.70	332.33	85.24
6	119	60	88	.284	.394	.560	1,906	.321	3,651	.614	64.74	73.11	73.65	77.49	288.99	74.13
18	23	-	9	.320	.389	.513	1,659	.332	2,810	.563	56.35	75.80	56.69	71.04	259.88	66.66
8	37	-	89	.330	.398	.589	2,423	.383	3,957	.625	82.30	87.30	79.83	78.89	328.32	84.21
-	24	-	-	.340	.404	.467	2,372	.386	3,726	.606	80.57	87.94	75.17	76.43	320.11	82.11
5	31	36	132	.257	.348	.498	1,492	.298	2,708	.542	50.68	68.06	54.63	68.35	241.72	62.00
18	38	55	143	.283	.348	.500	1,789	.294	3,251	.534	60.77	66.97	65.58	67.33	260.65	66.86
44	7	-	17	.336	.440	.652	2,647	.405	4,623	.708	89.91	92.38	93.26	89.27	364.83	93.58
47	113	43	103	.289	.347	.514	1,736	.305	3,122	.549	58.97	69.62	62.98	69.28	260.85	66.91
89	33	-	-	.350	.458	.660	2,944	.425	4,956	.715	100.00	96.88	99.98	90.23	387.09	99.29
58	34	-	-	.333	.412	.507	2,247	.338	3,833	.576	76.32	77.03	77.32	72.70	303.38	77.82
10	92	62	115	.297	.411	.540	1,795	.304	3,534	.599	60.97	69.41	71.29	75.61	277.29	71.12
12	49	71	142	.302	.350	.582	2,023	.351	3,408	.592	68.72	80.12	68.75	74.68	292.27	74.96
70	45	-	-	.326	.397	.526	2,091	.329	3,734	.587	71.03	75.01	75.33	74.11	295.48	75.79
26	12	-	50	.319	.412	.616	2,182	.390	3,742	.668	74.12	88.85	75.49	84.31	322.77	82.79
46	52	56	98	.299	.386	.590	2,140	.343	4,008	.642	72.69	78.21	80.86	81.04	312.79	80.23
7	29	-	21	.321	.376	.533	1,479	.321	2,678	.581	50.24	73.18	54.02	73.31	250.75	64.32
-	77	-	-	.354	.464	.446	2,046	.342	4,077	.681	69.50	77.97	82.25	85.96	315.68	80.97
49	24	-	-	.367	.439	.573	2,110	.360	3,664	.625	71.67	82.04	73.92	78.82	306.45	78.60
170	35	28	87	.289	.404	.452	1,711	.274	3,960	.634	58.12	62.49	79.89	80.02	280.51	71.95
-	9	-	31	.328	.386	.539	1,729	.304	3,356	.590	58.73	69.37	67.70	74.50	270.30	69.33
62	24	-	-	.382	.460	.637	2,348	.377	4,259	.684	79.76	85.97	85.92	86.28	337.93	86.68
6	28	38	170	.276	.358	.511	1,636	.269	3,332	.549	55.57	61.45	67.22	69.25	253.49	65.02
61	59	-	-	.357	.424	.519	1,623	.299	3,233	.595	55.13	68.10	65.22	75.05	263.50	67.59
70	48	45	95	.280	.366	.521	1,837	.302	3,537	.581	62.40	68.79	71.35	73.28	275.82	70.75
-	263	-	-	.320	.400	.414	1,683	.351	2,672	.557	57.17	80.04	53.90	70.31	261.42	67.05

Best 10 Consecutive Seasons A-J

Rank	Player	Years	G	AB	H	1B	2B	3B	HR	RUN	RBI	BB	SO	SB	
110	Jeter, Derek**	1995-2004	1,366	5,513	1,734	1,259	283	42	150	1,037	693	559	972	201	
51	Johnson, Robert	1933-1942	1,459	5,428	1,617	986	307	72	252	997	1,040	853	678	78	
44	Jones, Chipper**	1995-2004	1,534	5,613	1,703	1,042	324	27	310	1,033	1,039	936	876	118	
86	Kaline, Al	1955-1964	1,426	5,447	1,691	1,129	279	56	227	907	912	628	466	90	
69	Keeler, Willie	1894-1903	1,322	5,618	2,094	1,769	176	128	21	1,305	614	321	614	411	
113	Keller, Charlie*	1939-1949	1,064	3,676	1,053	637	163	69	184	712	723	760	480	45	
34	Kelley, Joe	1893-1902	1,246	4,861	1,675	1,202	269	146	58	1,108	944	690	128	378	
76	Kelly, King	1882-1891	1,049	4,328	1,384	972	269	81	62	1,049	705	462	327	341	
55	Killebrew, Harmon	1961-1970	1,462	5,079	1,352	748	184	17	403	876	1,046	1,027	1,007	11	
47	Kiner, Ralph	1947-1956	1,472	5,205	1,451	827	216	39	369	971	1,015	1,011	749	22	
33	Klein, Chuck	1928-1937	1,318	5,243	1,783	1,104	342	65	272	1,024	1,041	473	427	67	
114	Kluszewski, Ted	1948-1957	1,330	4,951	1,498	980	244	23	251	744	884	405	290	20	
62	Lajoie, Nap	1897-1906	1,148	4,702	1,709	1,174	360	112	63	910	933	199	-	224	
11	Mantle, Mickey	1953-1962	1,437	5,006	1,559	928	208	55	368	1,186	1,000	1,135	1,032	121	
118	Maris, Roger	1957-1966	1,238	4,381	1,139	686	159	33	261	737	751	576	634	21	
59	Martinez, Edgar**	1994-2003	1,351	4,787	1,526	909	362	7	248	859	981	962	843	31	
38	Matthews, Eddie	1953-1962	1,489	5,474	1,562	907	225	56	374	1,058	1,024	972	861	53	
111	Mattingly, Don	1984-1993	1,462	5,882	1,827	1,234	375	13	205	852	966	467	353	14	
12	Mays, Willie*	1954-1963	1,536	5,867	1,876	1,088	309	97	382	1,182	1,088	718	673	237	
78	McCovey, Willie	1962-1971	1,372	4,493	1,272	724	193	29	326	775	916	769	824	15	
74	McGriff, Fred **	1988-1997	1,492	5,393	1,548	935	275	19	319	887	964	820	1,141	57	
46	McGwire, Mark	1992-2001	1,097	3,531	979	427	146	1	405	750	910	880	1,004	6	
54	Medwick, Joe	1933-1942	1,476	5,986	1,967	1,238	441	106	182	1,010	1,131	341	462	31	
99	Meusel, Bob	1920-1929	1,294	5,032	1,565	994	338	87	146	764	1,005	349	556	133	
30	Mize, Johnny*	1936-1948	1,403	5,185	1,679	987	313	82	297	960	1,096	714	423	26	
72	Morgan, Joe	1969-1978	1,478	5,238	1,468	971	267	51	179	1,029	731	1,088	546	509	
82	Murphy, Dale	1980-1989	1,537	5,694	1,553	957	257	31	308	938	929	784	1,268	134	
75	Murray, Eddie	1978-1987	1,499	5,631	1,677	1,083	295	21	278	892	1,018	734	745	56	
13	Musial, Stan*	1944-1954	1,525	5,897	2,031	1,217	425	121	268	1,193	1,093	918	331	48	
109	O'Neill, Tip	1883-1892	1,054	4,305	1,436	1,070	222	92	52	880	757	421	146	161	
9	Ott, Mel	1929-1938	1,498	5,490	1,730	1,052	301	54	323	1,148	1,206	969	462	54	
31	Palmiero, Rafael**	1993-2002	1,527	5,722	1,666	930	328	13	395	993	1,154	835	839	63	
117	Parker, Dave	1977-1986	1,366	5,273	1,582	1,021	315	45	201	777	859	415	823	109	
98	Perez, Tony	1967-1976	1,513	5,763	1,647	1,052	288	46	261	822	1,028	575	1,118	38	
56	Piazza, Mike**	1993-2002	1,372	5,047	1,625	1,025	248	6	346	846	1,066	559	789	17	
18	Ramirez, Manny**	1995-2004	1,422	5,229	1,673	930	358	14	371	1,011	1,205	830	1,150	29	
65	Rice, Jim	1977-1986	1,469	5,915	1,807	1,168	275	61	303	931	1,089	496	961	37	
107	Ripkin, Cal, Jr.	1983-1992	1,617	6,305	1,759	1,148	337	29	245	952	921	705	694	29	
32	Robinson, Frank	1958-1967	1,484	5,399	1,641	938	319	48	336	1,029	1,067	748	776	153	
105	Robinson, Jackie	1947-1956	1,382	4,877	1,518	1,054	273	54	137	947	734	740	291	197	
22	Rodriguez, Alex**	1995-2004	1,413	5,536	1,696	982	309	24	381	1,117	1,094	636	1,106	202	
116	Rose, Pete	1969-1978	1,597	6,522	2,055	1,507	387	70	91	1,098	603	776	497	92	
1	Ruth, Babe	1920-1929	1,399	4,884	1,734	871	314	82	467	1,365	1,331	1,240	795	88	
39	Schmidt, Mike	1974-1983	1,493	5,262	1,417	741	258	48	370	1,023	1,019	1,019	1,276	154	
48	Sheffield, Gary**	1995-2004	1,369	4,819	1,470	889	255	12	314	954	969	959	629	128	
14	Simmons, Al*	1925-1934	1,372	5,592	2,005	1,290	377	106	232	1,078	1,277	401	450	56	
97	Sisler, George	1918-1927	1,280	5,274	1,850	1,361	282	123	84	920	802	308	195	270	
43	Snider, Duke	1949-1958	1,438	5,401	1,652	973	291	62	326	1,011	1,035	709	872	88	
17	Sosa, Sammy**	1995-2004	1,480	5,704	1,633	888	247	19	479	1,053	1,226	716	1,525	108	
66	Speaker, Tris	1916-1925	1,369	5,007	1,801	1,201	434	100	66	983	798	763	131	147	

10 Consecutive Year Statistics & Analysis Listed Alphabetically

10 Consecutive Year Statistics & Analysis Listed Alphabetically

CS	HBP	SF	GDP	AVG	OBP	SLG	Total Offensive Production Statistics				TRP Rating	RPA Rating	TNB Rating	TBA Rating	TOP Composite	
							TRP	RPA	TNB	TBA					TOP	Rating
52	92	30	122	.315	.385	.463	1,730	.274	3,351	.531	58.76	62.46	67.60	66.94	255.77	65.60
49	16	-	64	.298	.395	.520	2,037	.320	3,722	.585	69.19	73.03	75.09	73.83	291.13	74.67
40	14	64	150	.303	.400	.536	2,072	.306	4,039	.596	70.38	69.72	81.48	75.20	296.78	76.12
36	30	49	137	.310	.382	.507	1,819	.289	3,475	.552	61.79	65.94	70.10	69.70	267.52	68.62
27	92	-	-	.373	.416	.461	1,919	.318	3,386	.561	65.18	72.56	68.31	70.84	276.89	71.02
23	10	-	50	.286	.410	.518	1,435	.319	2,698	.600	48.74	72.78	54.43	75.72	251.67	64.55
-	58	-	-	.345	.432	.496	2,052	.366	3,536	.630	69.70	83.43	71.33	79.54	304.00	77.98
-	12	-	-	.320	.387	.462	1,754	.365	2,816	.586	59.58	83.30	56.81	73.99	273.67	70.20
11	36	48	151	.266	.390	.547	1,922	.303	3,842	.606	65.29	69.12	77.51	76.45	288.36	73.96
2	24	7	126	.279	.398	.548	1,986	.312	3,907	.613	67.46	71.06	78.82	77.35	294.69	75.59
-	12	-	33	.340	.396	.586	2,065	.358	3,623	.629	70.14	81.74	73.09	79.35	304.32	78.06
8	22	14	121	.303	.357	.513	1,628	.295	2,980	.541	55.30	67.34	60.12	68.20	250.96	64.37
-	75	-	-	.363	.399	.528	1,843	.370	2,980	.599	62.60	84.46	60.12	75.56	282.74	72.52
21	11	30	53	.311	.438	.595	2,186	.351	4,227	.678	74.25	79.95	85.27	85.54	325.02	83.36
9	33	34	62	.260	.348	.490	1,488	.293	2,768	.544	50.54	66.72	55.84	68.67	241.77	62.01
18	66	57	121	.319	.435	.553	1,840	.307	3,687	.615	62.50	70.01	74.38	77.62	284.52	72.98
24	17	43	74	.285	.392	.552	2,082	.316	4,039	.614	70.72	72.16	81.48	77.45	301.81	77.41
7	19	81	156	.311	.359	.483	1,818	.275	3,336	.505	61.75	62.77	67.30	63.73	255.55	65.55
72	23	58	139	.320	.393	.601	2,270	.334	4,431	.651	77.11	76.07	89.39	82.16	324.72	83.29
17	50	42	89	.283	.391	.557	1,691	.311	3,318	.610	57.44	70.85	66.94	76.91	272.14	69.80
30	27	47	147	.287	.381	.523	1,851	.288	3,692	.574	62.87	65.61	74.48	72.40	275.36	70.63
3	52	41	77	.277	.424	.663	1,660	.362	3,277	.715	56.39	82.63	66.11	90.26	295.39	75.76
-	21	-	160	.329	.367	.529	2,141	.329	3,559	.547	72.72	75.02	71.80	69.00	288.54	74.01
102	20	-	-	.311	.358	.500	1,769	.328	2,915	.540	60.09	74.69	58.81	68.10	261.68	67.12
-	38	-	76	.324	.409	.588	2,056	.342	3,825	.636	69.84	77.97	77.16	80.26	305.24	78.29
113	24	60	60	.280	.402	.453	1,760	.272	3,882	.600	59.78	62.03	78.31	75.70	275.83	70.75
56	22	37	129	.273	.361	.491	1,867	.280	3,680	.552	63.42	63.87	74.24	69.66	271.18	69.56
21	14	62	138	.298	.376	.506	1,910	.290	3,631	.552	64.88	66.20	73.25	69.64	273.97	70.27
27	27	7	120	.344	.435	.594	2,286	.328	4,468	.641	77.65	74.80	90.14	80.89	323.48	82.97
-	44	-	-	.334	.399	.464	1,637	.343	2,624	.550	55.60	78.26	52.94	69.41	256.21	65.72
-	35	-	44	.315	.421	.566	2,354	.360	4,166	.637	79.96	82.11	84.04	80.40	326.51	83.75
22	44	67	112	.291	.382	.560	2,147	.317	4,125	.608	72.93	72.20	83.22	76.75	305.10	78.26
82	28	48	105	.300	.351	.491	1,636	.279	3,060	.521	55.57	63.57	61.73	65.79	246.65	63.27
24	30	61	143	.286	.350	.488	1,850	.281	3,429	.522	62.84	64.19	69.17	65.83	262.04	67.21
20	20	34	173	.322	.389	.579	1,912	.328	3,499	.600	64.95	74.75	70.59	75.69	285.97	73.35
28	67	56	150	.320	.416	.607	2,216	.350	4,070	.643	75.27	79.81	82.11	81.10	318.29	81.64
22	44	60	232	.305	.360	.526	2,020	.299	3,668	.544	68.61	68.27	74.00	68.59	279.48	71.68
24	30	71	186	.279	.351	.458	1,873	.257	3,629	.497	63.62	58.53	73.21	62.75	258.11	66.20
59	103	57	143	.304	.395	.568	2,096	.325	4,009	.622	71.20	74.10	80.88	78.42	304.60	78.13
54	72	9	113	.311	.409	.474	1,681	.289	3,265	.562	57.10	65.97	65.87	70.89	259.83	66.64
50	82	57	128	.306	.383	.577	2,211	.343	4,066	.631	75.10	78.30	82.03	79.67	315.11	80.82
59	53	35	106	.315	.390	.438	1,701	.227	3,717	.496	57.78	51.78	74.98	62.60	247.14	63.39
93	27	-	-	.355	.488	.740	2,696	.438	4,875	.793	91.58	99.95	98.35	100.00	389.87	100.00
76	47	66	81	.269	.388	.548	2,042	.315	4,025	.622	69.36	71.92	81.20	78.43	300.91	77.18
54	79	59	116	.305	.424	.558	1,923	.319	3,803	.630	65.32	72.70	76.72	79.55	294.29	75.48
35	16	-	-	.359	.403	.588	2,355	.392	3,728	.620	79.99	89.37	75.21	78.28	322.85	82.81
91	30	-	-	.351	.390	.499	1,722	.307	3,147	.561	58.49	69.97	63.49	70.75	262.70	67.38
48	15	23	132	.306	.386	.564	2,046	.326	3,809	.607	69.50	74.29	76.84	76.53	297.16	76.22
48	34	54	130	.286	.366	.588	2,279	.343	4,165	.627	77.41	78.29	84.02	79.17	318.89	81.79
65	42	-	-	.360	.448	.526	1,781	.306	3,520	.606	60.50	69.88	71.01	76.42	277.80	71.25

Best 10 Consecutive Seasons J-S

10 Consecutive Year Statistics & Analysis Listed Alphabetically														
Rank	Player	Years	G	AB	H	1B	2B	3B	HR	RUN	RBI	BB	SO	SB
77	Stargell, Willie	1965-1974	1,394	4,947	1,416	798	271	33	314	797	978	621	1,201	11
40	Stovey, Harry	1883-1892	1,189	4,937	1,488	963	280	137	108	1,222	790	565	226	486
70	Terry, Bill	1926-1935	1,429	5,540	1,926	1,366	325	99	136	982	945	457	358	51
21	Thomas, Frank **	1991-2000	1,470	5,283	1,692	998	350	7	337	1,044	1,152	1,144	781	29
24	Thome, Jim**	1995-2004	1,467	5,036	1,449	757	279	20	393	1,024	1,068	1,122	1,533	10
27	Thompson, Sam	1887-1896	1,195	5,140	1,750	1,217	293	130	110	1,082	1,145	393	173	221
93	Traynor, Pie	1922-1931	1,447	5,691	1,845	1,376	282	134	53	929	1,022	370	181	141
79	Trosky, Hal*	1933-1944	1,259	4,862	1,485	885	319	55	226	813	981	511	403	24
85	Vaughn, Mo	1991-2000	1,346	4,966	1,479	920	250	10	299	784	977	652	1,262	30
37	Wagner, Honus	1899-1908	1,399	5,320	1,879	1,291	385	150	53	1,023	969	492	-	489
41	Walker, Larry **	1993-2002	1,228	4,399	1,454	805	331	41	277	945	921	588	699	161
57	Waner, Paul	1927-1936	1,494	5,950	2,074	1,425	417	143	89	1,127	878	675	212	83
63	Williams, Bernie**	1995-2004	1,410	5,408	1,678	1,096	308	43	231	1,019	947	792	832	102
61	Williams, Billy	1963-1972	1,605	6,272	1,882	1,192	316	67	307	1,006	1,013	647	657	63
81	Williams, Ken*	1919-1928	1,240	4,476	1,448	923	261	71	193	816	874	533	255	148
4	Williams, Ted*	1939-1951	1,421	5,086	1,763	1,013	366	61	323	1,273	1,261	1,327	442	20
52	Wilson, Hack	1924-1933	1,271	4,558	1,412	846	261	67	238	860	1,033	631	675	52
80	Winfield, Dave	1979-1988	1,473	5,579	1,625	1,032	285	51	257	901	1,017	637	793	114
87	Yastrzemski, Carl	1965-1974	1,507	5,393	1,574	1,014	293	23	244	902	872	975	644	110
84	York, Rudy	1937-1946	1,419	5,250	1,476	906	266	48	256	816	1,055	725	762	37

* Consecutive excluding or consolidating years of military service
** Active player. Statistics through 2004 season
TOP ranking for players with less than 70% rating is based upon comparison to listed players only.

10 Consecutive Year Statistics & Analysis Listed Alphabetically

CS	HBP	SF	GDP	AVG	OBP	SLG	Total Offensive Production Statistics				TRP Rating	RPA Rating	TNB Rating	TBA Rating	TOP Composite	
							TRP	RPA	TNB	TBA					TOP	Rating
8	51	48	92	.286	.368	.545	1,775	.308	3,370	.585	60.29	70.29	67.98	73.83	272.40	69.87
-	31	-	-	.301	.377	.479	2,012	.364	3,448	.623	68.34	82.92	69.56	78.63	299.45	76.81
-	8	-	31	.348	.398	.516	1,927	.319	3,373	.559	65.46	72.80	68.05	70.51	276.81	71.00
20	44	87	159	.320	.439	.581	2,196	.327	4,264	.635	74.59	74.55	86.02	80.10	315.26	80.86
14	41	44	80	.288	.418	.585	2,092	.331	4,106	.649	71.06	75.45	82.83	81.93	311.28	79.84
-	63	-	-	.340	.394	.512	2,227	.398	3,310	.591	75.65	90.75	66.77	74.63	307.80	78.95
43	21	-	-	.324	.368	.449	1,951	.321	3,043	.500	66.27	73.15	61.39	63.13	263.94	67.70
20	16	-	32	.305	.373	.533	1,794	.331	3,123	.576	60.94	75.47	63.00	72.69	272.09	69.79
17	96	42	118	.298	.387	.533	1,761	.300	3,407	.580	59.82	68.37	68.73	73.18	270.10	69.28
-	77	-	-	.353	.416	.512	1,992	.338	3,781	.642	67.66	77.14	76.28	81.01	302.09	77.48
48	93	47	103	.331	.416	.613	1,866	.357	3,492	.668	63.38	81.36	70.45	84.24	299.44	76.80
-	31	-	55	.349	.418	.512	2,005	.299	3,833	.571	68.10	68.13	77.32	72.06	285.62	73.26
56	27	44	156	.310	.398	.511	1,966	.306	3,630	.565	66.78	69.76	73.23	71.26	281.03	72.08
30	30	48	140	.300	.366	.519	2,019	.283	3,963	.555	68.58	64.51	79.95	70.06	283.10	72.61
98	26	-	-	.324	.399	.543	1,690	.336	3,039	.604	57.40	76.54	61.31	76.16	271.41	69.61
14	21	-	121	.347	.484	.633	2,534	.387	4,574	.698	86.07	88.16	92.27	88.04	354.54	90.94
5	20	-	8	.310	.396	.553	1,893	.363	3,219	.617	64.30	82.75	64.94	77.85	289.84	74.34
52	11	47	175	.291	.362	.499	1,918	.297	3,493	.542	65.15	67.82	70.47	68.34	271.78	69.71
74	18	49	134	.292	.399	.490	1,774	.270	3,674	.559	60.26	61.58	74.12	70.57	266.53	68.36
26	12	-	131	.281	.370	.496	1,871	.306	3,354	.548	63.55	69.74	67.66	69.17	270.13	69.29

Career Statistics of over 125 of the Greatest Players, Listed Alphabetically:

Including all TOP Statistics:

Total Run Production (TRP), Run Production Average (RPA), Total Net Bases (TNB), Total Base Average (TBA) and Total Offensive Production (TOP)

Analyzed for Career, Adjusted Career, 10 Consecutive Year, 5 Consecutive Year and Best Single Season Statistics based on TOP Statistics and Ratings

Total Career Statistics & Adjusted Career, 10 year, 5 year, and Single Year Analysis

Aaron, Hank: *Henry Louis "Hammerin' Hank" Aaron; born Feb 5, 1934, Mobile, AL*

Rating Category	Year	Ranked Seasons & Adjustment	G	AB	H	1B	2B	3B	HR	RUN	RBI	BB	SO	SB
	1954		122	468	131	85	27	6	13	58	69	28	39	2
	1955		153	602	189	116	37	9	27	105	106	49	61	3
	1956		153	609	200	126	34	14	26	106	92	37	54	2
10 Year Total	1957	4th	151	615	198	121	27	6	44	118	132	57	58	1
	1958		153	601	196	128	34	4	30	109	95	59	49	4
5 Year Total	1959	3rd	154	629	223	131	46	7	39	116	123	51	54	8
	1960		153	590	172	101	20	11	40	102	126	60	63	16
	1961		155	603	197	114	39	10	34	115	120	56	64	21
	1962	1st	156	592	191	112	28	6	45	127	128	66	73	15
	1963	2nd	161	631	201	124	29	4	44	121	130	78	94	31
	1964		145	570	187	131	30	2	24	103	95	62	46	22
	1965		150	570	181	108	40	1	32	109	89	60	81	24
	1966		158	603	168	100	23	1	44	117	127	76	96	21
	1967		155	600	184	105	37	3	39	113	109	63	97	17
	1968		160	606	174	108	33	4	29	84	86	64	62	28
	1969		147	547	164	87	30	3	44	100	97	87	47	9
	1970		150	516	154	89	26	1	38	103	118	74	63	9
	1971		139	495	162	90	22	3	47	95	118	71	58	1
	1972		129	449	119	75	10	0	34	75	77	92	55	4
	1973		120	392	118	65	12	1	40	84	96	68	51	1
	1974		112	340	91	55	16	0	20	47	69	39	29	1
	1975		137	465	109	79	16	2	12	45	60	70	51	0
	1976		85	271	62	44	8	0	10	22	35	35	38	0
Career Total	1954-1976		3,298	12,364	3,771	2,294	624	98	755	2,174	2,297	1,402	1,383	240
Career Adj. to 10,000 BO	1954-1976	0.701902155	2,315	8,678	2,647	1,610	438	69	530	1,526	1,612	984	971	168
Career Adj. to 10,000 AB	1954-1976	0.808799741	2,667	10,000	3,050	1,855	505	79	611	1,758	1,858	1,134	1,119	194
10 Year Total	1957-1966		1,536	6,004	1,914	1,170	316	52	376	1,137	1,165	625	678	163
5 Year Total	1959-1963		779	3,045	984	582	162	38	202	581	627	311	348	91
Best Single Year	1962		156	592	191	112	28	6	45	127	128	66	73	15
2nd Best Year	1963		161	631	201	124	29	4	44	121	130	78	94	31
3rd Best Year	1959		154	629	223	131	46	7	39	116	123	51	54	8
4th Best Year	1957		151	615	198	121	27	6	44	118	132	57	58	1

Total Career Statistics & Adjusted Career, 10 year, 5 year, and Single Year Analysis

Aaron, Hank

CS	HBP	SF	GDP	AVG	OBP	SLG	Total Offensive Production Statistics				TRP Rating	RPA Rating	TNB Rating	TBA Rating	TOP Composite		
							TRP	RPA	TNB	TBA					TOP	Rating	Ranking
2	3	4	13	.280	.322	.447	127	.246	240	.465	36.49	46.12	39.34	51.26	173.22	44.16	
1	3	4	20	.314	.366	.540	211	.311	379	.559	60.63	58.31	62.13	61.61	242.69	61.88	
4	2	7	21	.328	.365	.558	198	.293	377	.558	56.90	54.88	61.80	61.47	235.05	59.93	
1	0	3	13	.322	.378	.600	250	.363	426	.619	71.84	68.09	69.84	68.24	278.01	70.88	
1	1	3	21	.326	.386	.546	204	.298	391	.571	58.62	55.80	64.10	62.91	241.43	61.56	
0	4	9	19	.355	.401	.636	239	.336	463	.650	68.68	62.90	75.90	71.67	279.15	71.17	
7	2	12	8	.292	.352	.566	228	.339	405	.603	65.52	63.58	66.39	66.42	261.91	66.78	
9	2	9	16	.327	.381	.594	235	.343	428	.624	67.53	64.19	70.16	68.76	270.65	69.00	
7	3	6	14	.323	.390	.618	255	.374	443	.651	73.28	70.16	72.62	71.70	287.76	73.37	
5	0	5	11	.319	.391	.586	251	.346	474	.654	72.13	64.87	77.70	72.06	286.76	73.11	
4	0	2	22	.328	.393	.514	198	.302	373	.569	56.90	56.56	61.15	62.67	237.27	60.49	
4	1	8	15	.318	.379	.560	198	.303	400	.612	56.90	56.73	65.57	67.41	246.61	62.88	
3	1	8	14	.279	.356	.539	244	.348	420	.598	70.11	65.13	68.85	65.94	270.04	68.85	
6	0	6	11	.307	.369	.573	222	.326	418	.615	63.79	61.17	68.52	67.75	261.24	66.61	
5	1	5	21	.287	.354	.498	170	.244	390	.560	48.85	45.70	63.93	61.67	220.16	56.13	
10	2	3	14	.300	.396	.607	197	.302	420	.643	56.61	56.53	68.85	70.89	252.88	64.47	
0	2	6	13	.298	.385	.574	221	.362	381	.624	63.51	67.78	62.46	68.73	262.47	66.92	
1	2	5	9	.327	.410	.669	213	.366	404	.694	61.21	68.58	66.23	76.51	272.52	69.48	
0	1	2	17	.265	.390	.514	152	.271	328	.585	43.68	50.77	53.77	64.44	212.66	54.22	
1	1	4	7	.301	.402	.643	180	.381	321	.680	51.72	71.46	52.62	74.95	250.76	63.93	
0	0	2	6	.268	.341	.491	116	.300	207	.535	33.33	56.17	33.93	58.95	182.39	46.50	
1	1	6	15	.234	.332	.355	105	.189	235	.422	30.17	35.32	38.52	46.50	150.52	38.38	
1	0	2	8	.229	.315	.369	57	.180	134	.424	16.38	33.80	21.97	46.74	118.88	30.31	
73	32	121	328	.305	.374	.555	4,471	.314	8,457	.594	100.00	75.15	100.00	78.90	354.05	90.42	4
51	22	85	230	.305	.374	.555	3,138	.314	5,936	.594	75.15	75.15	78.90	78.90	308.10	77.03	49
59	26	98	265	.305	.374	.555	3,616	.314	6,840	.594	69.23	75.15	72.69	78.90	295.98	73.99	51
41	14	65	153	.319	.381	.577	2,302	.336	4,223	.616	78.19	76.51	85.19	77.66	317.56	81.45	19
28	11	41	68	.323	.383	.600	1,208	.348	2,213	.637	79.37	74.32	84.85	77.19	315.73	80.89	27
7	3	6	14	.323	.390	.618	255	.374	443	.651	73.28	70.16	72.62	71.70	287.76	73.37	166
5	-	5	11	.319	.391	.586	251	.346	474	.654	72.13	64.87	77.70	72.06	286.76	73.11	173
-	4	9	19	.355	.401	.636	239	.336	463	.650	68.68	62.90	75.90	71.67	279.15	71.17	246
1	-	3	13	.322	.378	.600	250	.363	426	.619	71.84	68.09	69.84	68.24	278.01	70.88	250

Complete Career Statistics A

Complete Career Statistics A

Total Career Statistics & Adjusted Career, 10 year, 5 year, and Single Year Analysis

Allen, Dick: *Richard Anthonry Allen, b. March 8, 1942; Wampum, PA*

Rating Category			Year	Ranked Seasons & Adjustment	G	AB	H	1B	2B	3B	HR	RUN	RBI	BB	SO	SB
10 Year Total	5 Year Total		1963		10	24	7	4	2	1	-	6	2	-	5	-
			1964		162	632	201	121	38	13	29	125	91	67	138	3
			1965		161	619	187	122	31	14	20	93	85	74	150	15
			1966	1st	141	524	166	91	25	10	40	112	110	68	136	10
			1967		122	463	142	78	31	10	23	89	77	75	117	20
			1968		152	521	137	78	17	9	33	87	90	74	161	7
			1969		118	438	126	68	23	3	32	79	89	64	144	9
			1970		122	459	128	72	17	5	34	88	101	71	118	5
			1971		155	549	162	114	24	1	23	82	90	93	113	8
			1972		148	506	156	86	28	5	37	90	113	99	126	19
			1973		72	250	79	40	20	3	16	39	41	33	51	7
			1974		128	462	139	83	23	1	32	84	88	57	89	7
			1975		119	416	97	61	21	3	12	54	62	58	109	11
			1976		85	298	80	48	16	1	15	52	49	37	63	11
			1977		54	171	41	32	4	-	5	19	31	24	36	1
Career Total			1963-1977		1,749	6,332	1,848	1,098	320	79	351	1,099	1,119	894	1,556	133
Career Adj. to 10,000 BO			1963-1977	1.340662287	2,345	8,489	2,478	1,472	429	106	471	1,473	1,500	1,199	2,086	178
Career Adj. to 10,000 AB			1963-1977	1.579279848	2,762	10,000	2,919	1,734	505	125	554	1,736	1,767	1,412	2,457	210
10 Year Total			1964-1973		1,353	4,961	1,484	870	254	73	287	884	887	718	1,254	103
5 Year Total			1966-1970		655	2,405	699	387	113	37	162	455	467	352	676	51
Best Single Year			1966		141	524	166	91	25	10	40	112	110	68	136	10

Total Career Statistics & Adjusted Career, 10 year, 5 year, and Single Year Analysis

Allen, Dick

CS	HBP	SF	GDP	AVG	OBP	SLG	Total Offensive Production Statistics				TRP Rating	RPA Rating	TNB Rating	TBA Rating	TOP Composite		
							TRP	RPA	TNB	TBA					TOP	Rating	Ranking
-	-	1	2	.292	.280	.458	8	.296	11	.407	2.30	55.52	1.80	44.90	104.52	26.65	
4	-	3	8	.318	.382	.557	216	.304	418	.589	62.07	57.01	68.52	64.89	252.49	64.37	
2	2	6	13	.302	.375	.494	178	.249	395	.553	51.15	46.71	64.75	60.97	223.59	57.01	
6	3	4	9	.317	.396	.632	222	.365	406	.668	63.79	68.42	66.56	73.60	272.37	69.44	
5	1	-	9	.307	.404	.566	166	.303	353	.644	47.70	56.76	57.87	71.00	233.33	59.49	
7	1	7	7	.263	.352	.520	177	.290	346	.567	50.86	54.37	56.72	62.51	224.47	57.23	
3	-	4	10	.288	.375	.573	168	.326	321	.622	48.28	61.01	52.62	68.56	230.47	58.76	
4	2	1	9	.279	.377	.560	189	.349	331	.611	54.31	65.34	54.26	67.31	241.22	61.50	
1	1	5	23	.295	.395	.468	172	.256	358	.534	49.43	48.03	58.69	58.80	214.95	54.80	
8	1	3	13	.308	.420	.603	203	.326	416	.669	58.33	61.16	68.20	73.71	261.40	66.65	
2	1	3	9	.316	.394	.612	80	.270	192	.649	22.99	50.64	31.48	71.49	176.60	45.03	
1	1	5	16	.301	.375	.563	172	.318	324	.599	49.43	59.57	53.11	66.01	228.12	58.16	
2	2	4	19	.233	.327	.385	116	.232	229	.459	33.33	43.56	37.54	50.58	165.01	42.07	
4	-	3	13	.268	.346	.480	101	.288	187	.533	29.02	53.92	30.66	58.72	172.32	43.93	
3	1	4	4	.240	.330	.351	50	.245	83	.407	14.37	45.93	13.61	44.84	118.74	30.27	
52	16	53	164	.292	.378	.534	2,218	.297	4,370	.586	49.61	71.20	51.67	77.88	250.36	63.94	84
70	21	71	220	.292	.378	.534	2,974	.297	5,859	.586	71.20	71.20	77.88	77.88	298.16	74.54	68
82	25	84	259	.292	.378	.534	3,503	.297	6,901	.586	67.06	71.20	73.35	77.88	289.49	72.37	61
42	12	36	110	.299	.387	.553	1,771	.303	3,536	.606	60.16	69.19	71.33	76.44	277.11	71.08	68
25	7	16	44	.291	.381	.570	922	.326	1,757	.622	60.58	69.82	67.37	75.43	273.20	69.99	101
6	3	4	9	.317	.396	.632	222	.365	406	.668	63.79	68.42	66.56	73.60	272.37	69.44	308

Complete Career Statistics A

Total Career Statistics & Adjusted Career, 10 year, 5 year, and Single Year Analysis

Anson, Cap: Adrian Constantine "Pop" Anson; b. April 17+B107, 1852, Marshalltown, IA

Complete Career Statistics A

Rating Category	Year	Ranked Seasons & Adjustment	G	AB	H	1B	2B	3B	HR	RUN	RBI	BB	SO	SB
	1871		25	120	39	25	11	3	-	29	16	2	1	6
	1872		46	217	90	73	10	7	-	60	50	16	3	6
	1873		52	254	101	90	9	2	-	53	36	5	1	-
	1874		55	259	87	76	8	3	-	51	37	4	1	6
	1875		69	326	106	88	15	3	-	84	58	4	2	11
	1876		66	321	110	89	13	6	2	63	59	12	8	-
	1877		47	200	67	46	20	1	-	36	32	9	3	-
	1878		59	256	86	72	12	2	-	54	40	13	1	-
	1879		49	221	90	67	22	1	-	41	34	2	2	-
	1880		84	346	117	93	22	1	1	52	74	14	12	-
	1881		84	343	137	104	25	7	1	67	82	26	4	-
	1882		82	348	126	87	30	8	1	69	83	20	7	-
	1883		98	413	127	88	33	6	-	69	68	18	9	-
	1884		111	471	159	101	32	5	21	108	102	29	13	-
	1885		112	464	144	96	35	6	7	100	108	34	13	-
10 Year Total / 5 Year Total	1886	1st	125	504	187	132	34	11	10	117	147	55	19	29
	1887	2nd	122	532	224	171	33	13	7	107	102	60	18	27
	1888		134	515	177	135	17	13	12	101	84	47	24	28
	1889		134	518	177	134	30	6	7	99	117	86	19	27
	1890		139	504	157	129	17	4	7	102	107	113	23	29
	1891		136	537	158	116	25	9	8	82	120	75	29	21
	1892		147	561	154	121	23	9	1	62	74	67	30	15
	1893		101	381	123	95	25	3	-	70	91	68	12	13
	1894		83	347	137	100	26	6	5	87	99	40	15	17
	1895		122	476	161	130	23	6	2	88	91	55	23	16
	1896		106	403	135	113	17	3	2	72	90	49	10	28
	1897		112	423	128	106	16	3	3	66	75	60	-	16
Career Total	1871-1897		2,500	10,260	3,504	2,677	583	147	97	1,989	2,076	983	302	295
Career Adj. to 10,000 BO	1871-1897	0.886918	2,217	9,100	3,108	2,374	517	130	86	1,764	1,841	872	268	262
Career Adj. to 10,000 AB	1871-1897	0.974659	2,437	10,000	3,415	2,609	568	143	95	1,939	2,023	958	294	288
10 Year Total	1884-1893		1,261	4,987	1,660	1,230	271	79	80	948	1,052	634	200	189
5 Year Total	1886-1890		654	2,573	922	701	131	47	43	526	557	361	103	140
Best Single Year	1886		125	504	187	132	34	11	10	117	147	55	19	29
2nd Best Year	1887		122	532	224	171	33	13	7	107	102	60	18	27

Total Career Statistics & Adjusted Career, 10 year, 5 year, and Single Year Analysis

Anson, Cap

CS	HBP	SF	GDP	AVG	OBP	SLG	Total Offensive Production Statistics				TRP Rating	RPA Rating	TNB Rating	TBA Rating	TOP Composite		
							TRP	RPA	TNB	TBA					TOP	Rating	Ranking
2	-	-	-	.325	.336	.467	45	.369	62	.508	12.93	69.12	10.16	56.01	148.22	37.79	
6	-	-	-	.415	.455	.525	110	.472	130	.558	31.61	88.46	21.31	61.49	202.88	51.73	
2	-	-	-	.398	.409	.449	89	.344	117	.452	25.57	64.39	19.18	49.79	158.93	40.52	
-	-	-	-	.336	.346	.390	88	.335	111	.422	25.29	62.70	18.20	46.52	152.70	38.93	
6	-	-	-	.325	.333	.390	142	.430	136	.412	40.80	80.63	22.30	45.42	189.15	48.23	
-	-	-	-	.343	.366	.439	122	.366	153	.459	35.06	68.65	25.08	50.64	179.43	45.75	
-	-	-	-	.335	.364	.445	68	.325	98	.469	19.54	60.97	16.07	51.68	148.25	37.80	
-	-	-	-	.336	.368	.398	94	.349	115	.428	27.01	65.48	18.85	47.12	158.46	40.40	
-	-	-	-	.407	.413	.516	75	.336	116	.520	21.55	63.02	19.02	57.33	160.92	41.03	
-	-	-	-	.338	.364	.416	126	.350	158	.439	36.21	65.58	25.90	48.37	176.06	44.89	
-	-	-	-	.399	.442	.522	149	.404	205	.556	42.82	75.66	33.61	61.23	213.32	54.39	
-	-	-	-	.362	.397	.503	152	.413	195	.530	43.68	77.40	31.97	58.40	211.44	53.91	
-	-	-	-	.308	.336	.416	137	.318	190	.441	39.37	59.56	31.15	48.59	178.66	45.55	
-	-	-	-	.338	.376	.561	210	.420	293	.586	60.34	78.70	48.03	64.59	251.66	64.16	
-	-	-	-	.310	.357	.457	208	.418	246	.494	59.77	78.26	40.33	54.44	232.80	59.36	
-	-	-	-	.371	.433	.542	264	.472	357	.639	75.86	88.50	58.52	70.39	293.27	74.77	
-	1	-	-	.421	.481	.571	209	.352	392	.661	60.06	66.04	64.26	72.86	263.22	67.11	
-	1	-	-	.344	.400	.497	185	.329	332	.590	53.16	61.57	54.43	64.99	234.15	59.70	
-	5	-	-	.342	.440	.463	216	.355	358	.588	62.07	66.46	58.69	64.79	252.01	64.25	
-	6	-	-	.312	.443	.403	209	.335	351	.563	60.06	62.86	57.54	62.10	242.56	61.84	
-	1	-	-	.294	.382	.419	202	.330	322	.525	58.05	61.75	52.62	57.71	230.13	58.67	
-	4	-	-	.275	.356	.353	136	.215	284	.449	39.08	40.32	46.56	49.53	175.49	44.74	
-	1	-	-	.323	.427	.404	161	.358	236	.524	46.26	67.04	38.69	57.80	209.80	53.49	
-	3	-	-	.395	.462	.548	186	.477	250	.641	53.45	89.37	40.98	70.65	254.45	64.87	
-	3	-	-	.338	.410	.424	179	.335	276	.517	51.44	62.81	45.25	56.96	216.46	55.19	
-	3	-	-	.335	.411	.407	162	.356	244	.536	46.55	66.72	40.00	59.10	212.37	54.15	
-	4	-	-	.303	.394	.376	141	.290	239	.491	40.52	54.25	39.18	54.09	188.04	47.94	
16	32	-	-	.342	.401	.455	4,065	.361	5,966	.529	90.92	86.33	70.55	70.33	318.13	81.24	11
14	28	-	-	.342	.401	.455	3,605	.361	5,291	.529	86.33	86.33	70.33	70.33	313.33	78.33	37
16	31	-	-	.342	.401	.455	3,962	.361	5,815	.529	75.85	86.33	61.80	70.33	294.32	73.58	54
-	19	-	-	.333	.410	.467	2,000	.355	3,171	.562	67.93	80.87	63.97	70.94	283.71	72.77	60
-	13	-	-	.358	.440	.496	1,083	.367	1,790	.607	71.16	78.59	68.63	73.64	292.02	74.81	66
-	-	-	-	.371	.433	.542	264	.472	357	.639	75.86	88.50	58.52	70.39	293.27	74.77	131
-	1	-	-	.421	.481	.571	209	.352	392	.661	60.06	66.04	64.26	72.86	263.22	67.11	341

Complete Career Statistics A

Total Career Statistics & Adjusted Career, 10 year, 5 year, and Single Year Analysis

Averill, Earl: *Howard Earl Averill; b. May 21, 1902, Snohomish, WA*

Complete Career Statistics A

		Rating Category	Year	Ranked Seasons & Adjustment	G	AB	H	1B	2B	3B	HR	RUN	RBI	BB	SO	SB
10 Year Total	5 Year Total		1929		151	597	198	124	43	13	18	110	96	63	53	13
			1930		139	534	181	121	33	8	19	102	119	56	48	10
			1931	1st	155	627	209	131	36	10	32	140	143	68	38	9
			1932		153	631	198	115	37	14	32	116	124	75	40	5
			1933		151	599	180	114	39	16	11	83	92	54	29	3
			1934	3rd	154	598	187	102	48	6	31	128	113	99	44	5
			1935		140	563	162	96	34	13	19	109	79	70	58	8
			1936	2nd	152	614	232	150	39	15	28	136	126	65	35	3
			1937		156	609	182	117	33	11	21	121	92	88	65	5
			1938		134	482	159	103	27	15	14	101	93	81	48	5
			1939		111	364	96	51	28	6	11	66	65	49	42	4
			1940		64	118	33	26	4	1	2	10	20	5	14	-
			1941		8	17	2	2	-	-	-	2	2	1	4	-
Career Total			1929-1941		1,668	6,353	2,019	1,252	401	128	238	1,224	1,164	774	518	70
Career Adj. to 10,000 BO			1929-1941	1.39528394	2,327	8,864	2,817	1,747	560	179	332	1,708	1,624	1,080	723	98
Career Adj. to 10,000 AB			1929-1941	1.574059499	2,626	10,000	3,178	1,971	631	201	375	1,927	1,832	1,218	815	110
10 Year Total			1929-1938		1,485	5,854	1,888	1,173	369	121	225	1,146	1,077	719	458	66
5 Year Total			1930-1934		752	2,989	955	583	193	54	125	569	591	352	199	32
Best Single Year			1931		155	627	209	131	36	10	32	140	143	68	38	9
2nd Best Year			1936		152	614	232	150	39	15	28	136	126	65	35	3
3rd Best Year			1934		154	598	187	102	48	6	31	128	113	99	44	5

Total Career Statistics & Adjusted Career, 10 year, 5 year, and Single Year Analysis

Averill, Earl

CS	HBP	SF	GDP	AVG	OBP	SLG	Total Offensive Production Statistics				TRP Rating	RPA Rating	TNB Rating	TBA Rating	TOP Composite		
							TRP	RPA	TNB	TBA					TOP	Rating	Ranking
13	3	-	-	.332	.398	.538	206	.311	387	.584	59.20	58.22	63.44	64.33	245.19	62.51	
7	2	-	-	.339	.404	.537	221	.373	348	.588	63.51	69.95	57.05	64.79	255.29	65.09	
9	6	-	-	.333	.404	.576	283	.404	435	.621	81.32	75.65	71.31	68.39	296.67	75.64	
8	6	-	-	.314	.392	.569	240	.337	437	.614	68.97	63.16	71.64	67.65	271.41	69.20	
1	5	-	-	.301	.363	.474	175	.266	345	.524	50.29	49.84	56.56	57.79	214.47	54.68	
3	4	-	-	.313	.414	.569	241	.344	445	.635	69.25	64.42	72.95	69.96	276.59	70.52	
4	1	-	-	.288	.368	.496	188	.297	354	.558	54.02	55.56	58.03	61.54	229.16	58.43	
3	1	-	-	.378	.438	.627	262	.385	451	.663	75.29	72.20	73.93	73.10	294.52	75.09	
4	-	-	-	.299	.387	.493	213	.306	389	.558	61.21	57.26	63.77	61.51	243.75	62.15	
2	3	-	-	.330	.429	.535	194	.343	345	.610	55.75	64.23	56.56	67.18	243.71	62.14	
3	1	-	4	.264	.353	.464	131	.313	220	.526	37.64	58.72	36.07	58.01	190.44	48.55	
-	-	-	3	.280	.309	.381	30	.238	50	.397	8.62	44.61	8.20	43.74	105.17	26.81	
-	1	-	-	.118	.211	.118	4	.211	4	.211	1.15	39.45	0.66	23.20	64.46	16.43	
57	33	-	7	.318	.395	.534	2,388	.333	4,210	.587	53.41	79.79	49.78	78.08	261.06	66.67	71
80	46	-	10	.318	.395	.534	3,332	.333	5,874	.587	79.79	79.79	78.08	78.08	315.73	78.93	33
90	52	-	11	.318	.395	.534	3,759	.333	6,627	.587	71.96	79.79	70.43	78.08	300.26	75.06	38
54	31	-	-	.323	.399	.542	2,223	.337	3,936	.596	75.51	76.76	79.40	75.20	306.87	78.71	28
28	23	-	-	.320	.395	.546	1,160	.345	2,010	.598	76.22	73.74	77.07	72.44	299.47	76.72	52
9	6	-	-	.333	.404	.576	283	.404	435	.621	81.32	75.65	71.31	68.39	296.67	75.64	116
3	1	-	-	.378	.438	.627	262	.385	451	.663	75.29	72.20	73.93	73.10	294.52	75.09	126
3	4	-	-	.313	.414	.569	241	.344	445	.635	69.25	64.42	72.95	69.96	276.59	70.52	271

Complete Career Statistics A

Complete Career Statistics B

Total Career Statistics & Adjusted Career, 10 year, 5 year, and Single Year Analysis

Bagwell, Jeff: *Jeffrey Robert Bagwell; b, May 27, 1968, Boston, MA*

Rating Category			Year	Ranked Seasons & Adjustment	G	AB	H	1B	2B	3B	HR	RUN	RBI	BB	SO	SB
			1991		156	554	163	118	26	4	15	79	82	75	116	7
			1992		162	586	160	102	34	6	18	87	96	84	97	10
			1993		142	535	171	110	37	4	20	76	88	62	73	13
10 Year Total			1994	3rd	110	400	147	74	32	2	39	104	116	65	65	15
			1995		114	448	130	80	29	-	21	88	87	79	102	12
			1996	6th	162	568	179	98	48	2	31	111	120	135	114	21
	5 Year Total		1997	4th	162	566	162	77	40	2	43	109	135	127	122	31
			1998		147	540	164	96	33	1	34	124	111	109	90	19
			1999	2nd	162	562	171	94	35	-	42	143	126	149	127	30
			2000	1st	159	590	183	98	37	1	47	152	132	107	116	9
			2001	5th	161	600	173	87	43	4	39	126	130	106	135	11
			2002		158	571	166	100	33	2	31	94	98	101	130	7
			2003		160	605	168	99	28	2	39	109	100	88	119	11
			2004		156	572	152	94	29	2	27	104	89	96	131	6
Career Total**			1991-2004		2,111	7,697	2,289	1,327	484	32	446	1,506	1,510	1,383	1,537	202
Career Adj. to 10,000 BO**			1991-2004	1.049869	2,216	8,081	2,403	1,393	508	34	468	1,581	1,585	1,452	1,614	212
Career Adj. to 10,000 AB**			1991-2004	1.299207	2,743	10,000	2,974	1,724	629	42	579	1,957	1,962	1,797	1,997	262
10 Year Total**			1994-2003		1,495	5,450	1,643	903	358	16	366	1,160	1,155	1,066	1,120	166
5 Year Total**			1997-2001		791	2,858	853	452	188	8	205	654	634	598	590	100
Best Single Year**			2000		159	590	183	98	37	1	47	152	132	107	116	9
2nd Best Year**			1999		162	562	171	94	35	-	42	143	126	149	127	30
3rd Best Year**			1994		110	400	147	74	32	2	39	104	116	65	65	15
4th Best Year**			1997		162	566	162	77	40	2	43	109	135	127	122	31
5th Best Year**			2001		161	600	173	87	43	4	39	126	130	106	135	11
6th Best Year**			1996		162	568	179	98	48	2	31	111	120	135	114	21

Total Career Statistics & Adjusted Career, 10 year, 5 year, and Single Year Analysis

Bagwell, Jeff

CS	HBP	SF	GDP	AVG	OBP	SLG	Total Offensive Production Statistics				TRP Rating	RPA Rating	TNB Rating	TBA Rating	TOP Composite		
							TRP	RPA	TNB	TBA					TOP	Rating	Ranking
4	13	7	12	.294	.387	.437	161	.244	333	.504	46.26	45.64	54.59	55.52	202.02	51.51	
6	12	13	17	.273	.368	.444	183	.257	360	.506	52.59	48.16	59.02	55.73	215.49	54.94	
4	3	9	21	.320	.388	.516	164	.260	350	.556	47.13	48.86	57.38	61.33	214.69	54.74	
4	4	10	12	.368	.451	.750	220	.448	380	.774	63.22	83.96	62.30	85.30	294.77	75.15	
5	6	6	9	.290	.399	.496	175	.319	314	.573	50.29	59.84	51.48	63.15	224.75	57.30	
7	10	6	15	.315	.451	.570	231	.315	483	.658	66.38	58.97	79.18	72.53	277.06	70.64	
10	16	8	10	.286	.425	.592	244	.336	499	.686	70.11	62.89	81.80	75.65	290.46	74.05	
7	7	5	14	.304	.424	.557	235	.348	429	.636	67.53	65.24	70.33	70.05	273.14	69.64	
11	11	7	18	.304	.454	.591	269	.360	511	.684	77.30	67.48	83.77	75.39	303.94	77.49	
6	15	7	19	.310	.424	.615	284	.385	488	.661	81.61	72.11	80.00	72.88	306.60	78.17	
3	6	5	20	.288	.397	.568	256	.347	461	.626	73.56	65.09	75.57	68.94	283.16	72.20	
3	10	9	16	.291	.401	.518	192	.272	411	.581	55.17	50.89	67.38	64.07	237.51	60.55	
4	6	3	25	.278	.373	.524	209	.287	418	.575	60.06	53.87	68.52	63.37	245.82	62.67	
4	8	3	12	.266	.377	.465	193	.279	372	.538	55.46	52.34	45.57	44.34	197.71	50.41	
78	127	98	220	.297	.408	.542	3,016	.317	5,809	.610	67.46	75.82	68.69	81.07	293.03	74.84	25
82	133	103	231	.297	.408	.542	3,166	.317	6,099	.610	75.82	75.82	81.07	81.07	313.78	78.44	36
101	165	127	286	.297	.408	.542	3,918	.317	7,547	.610	75.02	75.82	80.21	81.07	312.11	78.03	25
60	91	66	158	.301	.420	.574	2,315	.339	4,394	.643	78.63	77.28	88.64	81.16	325.72	83.55	10
37	55	32	81	.298	.425	.585	1,288	.355	2,388	.659	84.63	76.00	91.56	79.89	332.08	85.08	14
6	15	7	19	.310	.424	.615	284	.385	488	.661	81.61	72.11	80.00	72.88	306.60	78.17	76
11	11	7	18	.304	.454	.591	269	.360	511	.684	77.30	67.48	83.77	75.39	303.94	77.49	86
4	4	10	12	.368	.451	.750	220	.448	380	.774	63.22	83.96	62.30	85.30	294.77	75.15	124
10	16	8	10	.286	.425	.592	244	.336	499	.686	70.11	62.89	81.80	75.65	290.46	74.05	148
3	6	5	20	.288	.397	.568	256	.347	461	.626	73.56	65.09	75.57	68.94	283.16	72.20	209
7	10	6	15	.315	.451	.570	231	.315	483	.658	66.38	58.97	79.18	72.53	277.06	70.64	260

Complete Career Statistics B

Total Career Statistics & Adjusted Career, 10 year, 5 year, and Single Year Analysis

Banks, Ernie: *Ernest Banks; b. January 31, 1931, Dallas, TX*

Rating Category		Year	Ranked Seasons & Adjustment	G	AB	H	1B	2B	3B	HR	RUN	RBI	BB	SO	SB	
		1953		10	35	11	7	1	1	2	3	6	4	5	-	
		1954		154	593	163	118	19	7	19	70	79	40	50	6	
		1955		154	596	176	98	25	9	44	98	117	45	72	9	
		1956		139	538	160	95	29	8	28	82	85	52	62	6	
	5 Year Total	1957		156	594	169	86	34	6	43	113	102	70	85	8	
10 Year Total		1958	1st	154	617	193	112	23	11	47	119	129	52	87	4	
		1959		155	589	179	103	25	6	45	97	143	64	72	2	
		1960		156	597	162	82	32	7	41	94	117	71	69	1	
		1961		138	511	142	87	22	4	29	75	80	54	75	1	
		1962		154	610	164	101	20	6	37	87	104	30	71	5	
		1963		130	432	98	59	20	1	18	41	64	39	73	-	
		1964		157	591	156	98	29	6	23	67	95	36	84	1	
		1965		163	612	162	106	25	3	28	79	106	55	64	3	
		1966		141	511	139	94	23	7	15	52	75	29	59	-	
		1967		151	573	158	105	26	4	23	68	95	27	93	2	
		1968		150	552	136	77	27	-	32	71	83	27	67	2	
		1969		155	565	143	99	19	2	23	60	106	42	101	-	
		1970		72	222	56	36	6	2	12	25	44	20	33	-	
		1971		39	83	16	11	2	-	3	4	6	6	14	-	
Career Total		1953-1971		2,528	9,421	2,583	1,574	407	90	512	1,305	1,636	763	1,236	50	
Career Adj. to 10,000 BO		1953-1971	0.945268929	2,390	8,905	2,442	1,488	385	85	484	1,234	1,546	721	1,168	47	
Career Adj. to 10,000 AB		1953-1971	1.061458444	2,683	10,000	2,742	1,671	432	96	543	1,385	1,737	810	1,312	53	
10 Year Total		1955-1964		1,493	5,675	1,599	921	259	64	355	873	1,036	513	750	37	
5 Year Total		1955-1959		758	2,934	877	494	136	40	207	509	576	283	378	29	
Best Single Year		1958		154	617	193	112	23	11	47	119	129	52	87	4	

Total Career Statistics & Adjusted Career, 10 year, 5 year, and Single Year Analysis

Banks, Ernie

CS	HBP	SF	GDP	AVG	OBP	SLG	Total Offensive Production Statistics				TRP Rating	RPA Rating	TNB Rating	TBA Rating	TOP Composite		
							TRP	RPA	TNB	TBA					TOP	Rating	Ranking
-	-	-	-	.314	.385	.571	9	.231	24	.615	2.59	43.24	3.93	67.82	117.59	29.98	
10	7	4	11	.275	.326	.427	149	.227	296	.452	42.82	42.63	48.52	49.81	183.77	46.85	
3	2	3	16	.295	.345	.589	215	.325	404	.610	61.78	60.86	66.23	67.26	256.13	65.30	
9	-	3	7	.297	.358	.537	167	.278	338	.563	47.99	52.15	55.41	62.09	217.64	55.49	
4	3	5	12	.285	.360	.579	215	.314	421	.615	61.78	58.90	69.02	67.84	257.53	65.66	
4	4	8	14	.313	.366	.614	248	.357	435	.626	71.26	66.86	71.31	68.98	278.42	70.99	
4	7	9	18	.304	.374	.596	240	.349	420	.611	68.97	65.46	68.85	67.38	270.66	69.01	
3	4	6	14	.271	.350	.554	211	.305	404	.584	60.63	57.14	66.23	64.34	248.34	63.32	
2	2	6	11	.278	.346	.507	155	.265	314	.538	44.54	49.73	51.48	59.26	205.01	52.27	
1	7	10	19	.269	.306	.503	191	.283	348	.515	54.89	52.94	57.05	56.74	221.62	56.50	
3	4	8	7	.227	.292	.403	105	.214	214	.437	30.17	40.15	35.08	48.13	153.54	39.15	
2	3	6	16	.264	.307	.450	162	.248	304	.466	46.55	46.56	49.84	51.39	194.33	49.55	
5	6	7	16	.265	.328	.453	185	.266	336	.483	53.16	49.81	55.08	53.21	211.26	53.86	
1	5	5	15	.272	.315	.432	127	.225	254	.450	36.49	42.12	41.64	49.55	169.80	43.29	
2	3	4	20	.276	.310	.455	163	.260	291	.464	46.84	48.71	47.70	51.15	194.41	49.57	
-	5	2	12	.246	.287	.469	154	.258	293	.490	44.25	48.26	48.03	54.00	194.54	49.60	
-	7	7	15	.253	.309	.416	166	.261	284	.447	47.70	48.91	46.56	49.22	192.38	49.05	
-	1	3	5	.252	.313	.459	69	.275	123	.490	19.83	51.51	20.16	54.01	145.51	37.10	
-	-	-	1	.193	.247	.325	10	.111	33	.367	2.87	20.82	5.41	40.41	69.52	17.72	
53	70	96	229	.274	.330	.500	2,941	.278	5,536	.523	65.78	66.57	65.46	69.56	267.37	68.28	61
50	66	91	216	.274	.330	.500	2,780	.278	5,233	.523	66.57	66.57	69.56	69.56	272.26	68.06	107
56	74	102	243	.274	.330	.500	3,122	.278	5,876	.523	59.77	66.57	62.45	69.56	258.35	64.59	111
35	36	64	134	.282	.342	.538	1,909	.297	3,602	.561	64.84	67.79	72.66	70.77	276.07	70.81	71
24	16	28	67	.299	.361	.584	1,085	.326	2,018	.606	71.29	69.72	77.38	73.52	291.90	74.78	67
4	4	8	14	.313	.366	.614	248	.357	435	.626	71.26	66.86	71.31	68.98	278.42	70.99	247

Complete Career Statistics B

Complete Career Statistics B

Total Career Statistics & Adjusted Career, 10 year, 5 year, and Single Year Analysis

Belle, Albert: *Albert Jojuan "Joey" Belle; b. Aug. 25, 1966, Shreveport, LA.*

Rating Category	Year	Ranked Seasons & Adjustment	G	AB	H	1B	2B	3B	HR	RUN	RBI	BB	SO	SB
	1989		62	218	49	30	8	4	7	22	37	12	55	2
	1990		9	23	4	3	-	-	1	1	3	1	6	-
	1991		123	461	130	69	31	2	28	60	95	25	99	3
	1992		153	585	152	94	23	1	34	81	112	52	128	8
	1993		159	594	172	95	36	3	38	93	129	76	96	23
	1994	4th	106	412	147	74	35	2	36	90	101	58	71	9
	1995	3rd	143	546	173	70	52	1	50	121	126	73	80	5
	1996	1st	158	602	187	98	38	3	48	124	148	99	87	11
	1997		161	634	174	98	45	1	30	90	116	53	105	4
	1998	2nd	163	609	200	101	48	2	49	113	152	81	84	6
	1999		161	610	181	107	36	1	37	108	117	101	82	17
	2000		141	559	157	96	37	1	23	71	103	52	68	-
Career Total	1989-2000		1,539	5,853	1,726	935	389	21	381	974	1,239	683	961	88
Career Adj. to 10,000 BO	1989-2000	1.457301078	2,243	8,530	2,515	1,363	567	31	555	1,419	1,806	995	1,400	128
Career Adj. to 10,000 AB	1989-2000	1.708525542	2,629	10,000	2,949	1,597	665	36	651	1,664	2,117	1,167	1,642	150
10 Year Total	1991-2000		1,468	5,612	1,673	902	381	17	373	951	1,199	670	900	86
5 Year Total	1994-1998		731	2,803	881	441	218	9	213	538	643	364	427	35
Best Single Year	1996		158	602	187	98	38	3	48	124	148	99	87	11
2nd Best Year	1998		163	609	200	101	48	2	49	113	152	81	84	6
3rd Best Year	1995		143	546	173	70	52	1	50	121	126	73	80	5
4th Best Year	1994		106	412	147	74	35	2	36	90	101	58	71	9

10 Year Total — *5 Year Total*

Total Career Statistics & Adjusted Career, 10 year, 5 year, and Single Year Analysis

Belle, Albert

CS	HBP	SF	GDP	AVG	OBP	SLG	Total Offensive Production Statistics				TRP Rating	RPA Rating	TNB Rating	TBA Rating	TOP Composite		
							TRP	RPA	TNB	TBA					TOP	Rating	Ranking
2	2	2	4	.225	.269	.394	59	.248	100	.420	16.95	46.45	16.39	46.31	126.11	32.15	
-	-	-	1	.174	.208	.304	4	.160	8	.320	1.15	29.98	1.31	35.27	67.71	17.26	
1	5	5	24	.282	.323	.540	155	.298	281	.540	44.54	55.85	46.07	59.56	206.02	52.53	
2	4	8	18	.260	.320	.477	193	.289	341	.511	55.46	54.22	55.90	56.35	221.93	56.58	
12	8	14	18	.290	.370	.552	222	.313	423	.596	63.79	58.59	69.34	65.66	257.39	65.62	
6	5	4	5	.357	.438	.714	191	.395	360	.744	54.89	73.95	59.02	81.98	269.83	68.79	
2	6	4	24	.317	.401	.690	247	.378	459	.703	70.98	70.88	75.25	77.47	294.57	75.10	
-	7	7	20	.311	.410	.623	272	.370	492	.669	78.16	69.34	80.66	73.78	301.94	76.98	
4	6	8	26	.274	.332	.491	206	.283	370	.509	59.20	53.10	60.66	56.09	229.04	58.40	
4	1	15	17	.328	.399	.655	265	.367	483	.668	76.15	68.68	79.18	73.63	297.64	75.89	
3	7	4	19	.297	.400	.541	225	.304	452	.610	64.66	56.90	74.10	67.23	262.88	67.02	
5	4	7	17	.281	.342	.474	174	.272	316	.495	50.00	51.02	51.80	54.50	207.33	52.86	
41	55	78	193	.295	.369	.564	2,213	.323	4,085	.595	49.50	77.23	48.30	79.13	254.16	64.91	78
60	80	114	281	.295	.369	.564	3,225	.323	5,953	.595	77.23	77.23	79.13	79.13	312.71	78.18	40
70	94	133	330	.295	.369	.564	3,781	.323	6,979	.595	72.39	77.23	74.17	79.13	302.92	75.73	36
39	53	76	188	.298	.374	.571	2,150	.326	3,977	.603	73.03	74.30	80.23	76.04	303.60	77.87	35
16	25	38	92	.314	.393	.626	1,181	.356	2,164	.651	77.60	76.02	82.98	78.98	315.57	80.85	28
-	7	7	20	.311	.410	.623	272	.370	492	.669	78.16	69.34	80.66	73.78	301.94	76.98	90
4	1	15	17	.328	.399	.655	265	.367	483	.668	76.15	68.68	79.18	73.63	297.64	75.89	110
2	6	4	24	.317	.401	.690	247	.378	459	.703	70.98	70.88	75.25	77.47	294.57	75.10	125
6	5	4	5	.357	.438	.714	191	.395	360	.744	54.89	73.95	59.02	81.98	269.83	68.79	320

Complete Career Statistics B

Total Career Statistics & Adjusted Career, 10 year, 5 year, and Single Year Analysis

Bench, Johnny: *Johnny Lee Bench; b. Dec. 7, 1947, Oklahoma City, OK*

Rating Category		Year	Ranked Seasons & Adjustment	G	AB	H	1B	2B	3B	HR	RUN	RBI	BB	SO	SB
		1967		26	86	14	9	3	1	1	7	6	5	19	-
		1968		154	564	155	98	40	2	15	67	82	31	96	1
		1969		148	532	156	106	23	1	26	83	90	49	86	6
10 Year Total	5 Year Total	1970	1st	158	605	177	93	35	4	45	97	148	54	102	5
		1971		149	562	134	86	19	2	27	80	61	49	83	2
		1972		147	538	145	81	22	2	40	87	125	100	84	6
		1973		152	557	141	96	17	3	25	83	104	83	83	4
		1974		160	621	174	101	38	2	33	108	129	80	90	5
		1975		142	530	150	82	39	1	28	83	110	65	108	11
		1976		135	465	109	68	24	1	16	62	74	81	95	13
		1977		142	494	136	69	34	2	31	67	109	58	95	2
		1978		120	393	102	61	17	1	23	52	73	50	83	4
		1979		130	464	128	87	19	-	22	73	80	67	73	4
		1980		114	360	90	54	12	-	24	52	68	41	64	4
		1981		52	178	55	39	8	-	8	14	25	17	21	-
		1982		119	399	103	74	16	-	13	44	38	37	58	1
		1983		110	310	79	50	15	2	12	32	54	24	38	-
Career Total		1967-1983		2,158	7,658	2,048	1,254	381	24	389	1,091	1,376	891	1,278	68
Career Adj. to 10,000 BO		1967-1983	1.128795575	2,436	8,644	2,312	1,416	430	27	439	1,232	1,553	1,006	1,443	77
Career Adj. to 10,000 AB		1967-1983	1.305823975	2,818	10,000	2,674	1,638	498	31	508	1,425	1,797	1,163	1,669	89
10 Year Total		1969-1978		1,453	5,297	1,424	843	268	19	294	802	1,023	669	909	58
5 Year Total		1970-1974		766	2,883	771	457	131	13	170	455	567	366	442	22
Best Single Year		1970		158	605	177	93	35	4	45	97	148	54	102	5

Complete Career Statistics B

Total Career Statistics & Adjusted Career, 10 year, 5 year, and Single Year Analysis

Bench, Johnny

CS	HBP	SF	GDP	AVG	OBP	SLG	TRP	RPA	TNB	TBA	TRP Rating	RPA Rating	TNB Rating	TBA Rating	TOP	Rating	Ranking
1	-	1	4	.163	.207	.256	13	.135	26	.271	3.74	25.37	4.26	29.85	63.22	16.12	
5	2	8	14	.275	.311	.433	149	.241	273	.441	42.82	45.10	44.75	48.61	181.28	46.22	
6	4	7	7	.293	.353	.487	173	.289	312	.521	49.71	54.12	51.15	57.41	212.39	54.15	
2	-	11	12	.293	.345	.587	245	.359	412	.604	70.40	67.31	67.54	66.58	271.84	69.31	
1	-	2	20	.238	.299	.423	141	.223	288	.455	40.52	41.74	47.21	50.14	179.61	45.79	
6	2	12	18	.270	.379	.541	212	.316	393	.587	60.92	59.29	64.43	64.65	249.28	63.56	
1	-	10	22	.253	.345	.429	187	.278	325	.484	53.74	52.14	53.28	53.30	212.46	54.17	
4	3	4	13	.280	.363	.507	237	.329	399	.553	68.10	61.59	65.41	60.99	256.10	65.29	
-	2	8	12	.283	.359	.519	193	.313	353	.572	55.46	58.61	57.87	63.06	235.00	59.91	
2	2	4	9	.234	.348	.394	136	.242	277	.494	39.08	45.43	45.41	54.42	184.34	47.00	
4	1	7	10	.275	.348	.540	176	.309	324	.568	50.57	57.86	53.11	62.65	224.20	57.16	
2	1	6	9	.260	.340	.483	125	.272	243	.529	35.92	51.03	39.84	58.35	185.13	47.20	
2	-	4	11	.276	.364	.459	153	.280	282	.516	43.97	52.51	46.23	56.92	199.63	50.90	
2	2	4	9	.250	.327	.483	120	.288	219	.526	34.48	54.05	35.90	58.02	182.46	46.52	
2	-	-	4	.309	.369	.489	39	.196	102	.513	11.21	36.72	16.72	56.49	121.14	30.89	
2	-	2	14	.258	.320	.396	82	.181	194	.429	23.56	33.99	31.80	47.30	136.66	34.84	
1	-	-	13	.255	.308	.432	86	.248	157	.452	24.71	46.44	25.74	49.87	146.76	37.42	
43	19	90	201	.267	.342	.476	2,467	.278	4,579	.517	55.18	66.68	54.14	68.71	244.71	62.49	95
49	21	102	227	.267	.342	.476	2,785	.278	5,169	.517	66.68	66.68	68.71	68.71	270.78	67.69	111
56	25	118	262	.267	.342	.476	3,221	.278	5,979	.517	61.68	66.68	63.55	68.71	260.61	65.15	106
28	15	71	132	.269	.348	.493	1,825	.295	3,326	.538	61.99	67.30	67.10	67.86	264.25	67.78	92
14	5	39	85	.267	.347	.499	1,022	.303	1,817	.538	67.15	64.70	69.67	65.22	266.73	68.33	110
2	-	11	12	.293	.345	.587	245	.359	412	.604	70.40	67.31	67.54	66.58	271.84	69.31	309

Complete Career Statistics B

Total Career Statistics & Adjusted Career, 10 year, 5 year, and Single Year Analysis

Berkman, Lance: *William Lance Berkman; b. Feb. 10, 1976, Waco, TX*

Rating Category		Year	Ranked Seasons & Adjustment	G	AB	H	1B	2B	3B	HR	RUN	RBI	BB	SO	SB	
		1999		34	93	22	16	2	-	4	10	15	12	21	5	
	5 Year Total	2000		114	353	105	55	28	1	21	76	67	56	73	6	
		2001	1st	156	577	191	97	55	5	34	110	126	92	121	7	
		2002		158	578	169	90	35	2	42	106	128	107	118	8	
		2003		153	538	155	89	35	6	25	110	93	107	108	5	
		2004		160	544	172	99	40	3	30	104	106	127	101	9	
Career Total**		1999-2004		775	2,683	814	446	195	17	156	516	535	501	542	40	
Career Adj. to 10,000 BO**		1999-2004	3.03674461	2,353	8,148	2,472	1,354	592	52	474	1,567	1,625	1,521	1,646	121	
Career Adj. to 10,000 AB**		1999-2004	3.727171077	2,889	10,000	3,034	1,662	727	63	581	1,923	1,994	1,867	2,020	149	
10 Year Total**		n/a														
5 Year Total**		2000-2004		741	2,590	792	430	193	17	152	506	520	489	521	35	
Best Single Year**		2001		156	577	191	97	55	5	34	110	126	92	121	7	

Total Career Statistics & Adjusted Career, 10 year, 5 year, and Single Year Analysis

Berkman, Lance

CS	HBP	SF	GDP	AVG	OBP	SLG	Total Offensive Production Statistics				TRP Rating	RPA Rating	TNB Rating	TBA Rating	TOP Composite		
							TRP	RPA	TNB	TBA					TOP	Rating	Ranking
1	-	1	2	.237	.321	.387	25	.231	52	.481	7.18	43.38	8.52	53.07	112.15	28.59	
2	1	7	6	.297	.388	.561	143	.338	259	.612	41.09	63.35	42.46	67.48	214.38	54.66	
9	13	6	8	.331	.430	.620	236	.339	461	.662	67.82	63.54	75.57	73.00	279.93	71.37	
4	4	3	10	.292	.405	.578	234	.333	449	.640	67.24	62.46	73.61	70.49	273.80	69.81	
3	9	3	10	.288	.412	.515	203	.304	395	.592	58.33	57.03	64.75	65.27	245.39	62.56	
7	10	6	10	.316	.450	.566	210	.301	447	.641	60.34	56.46	73.28	70.68	260.76	66.48	
26	37	26	46	.303	.416	.563	1,051	.319	2,063	.626	23.51	76.43	24.39	83.27	207.60	53.02	125
79	112	79	140	.303	.416	.563	3,192	.319	6,265	.626	76.43	76.43	83.27	83.27	319.40	79.85	28
97	138	97	171	.303	.416	.563	3,917	.319	7,689	.626	75.00	76.43	81.72	83.27	316.41	79.10	22
25	37	25	44	.306	.420	.569	1,026	.322	2,011	.631	67.41	68.89	77.11	76.55	289.96	74.29	72
9	13	6	8	.331	.430	.620	236	.339	461	.662	67.82	63.54	75.57	73.00	279.93	71.37	238

Complete Career Statistics   B

Total Career Statistics & Adjusted Career, 10 year, 5 year, and Single Year Analysis

Berra, Yogi: *Lawrence Peter Berra; b. May 12, 1925, St. Louis, MO*

Rating Category	Year	Ranked Seasons & Adjustment	G	AB	H	1B	2B	3B	HR	RUN	RBI	BB	SO	SB	
	1946		7	22	8	5	1	-	2	3	4	1	1	-	
	1947		83	293	82	53	15	3	11	41	54	13	12	-	
	1948		125	469	143	95	24	10	14	70	98	25	24	3	
	1949		116	415	115	73	20	2	20	59	91	22	25	2	
	1950	1st	151	597	192	128	30	6	28	116	124	55	12	4	
10 Year Total / 5 Year Total	1951		141	547	161	111	19	4	27	92	88	44	20	5	
	1952		142	534	146	98	17	1	30	97	98	66	24	2	
	1953		137	503	149	94	23	5	27	80	108	50	32	-	
	1954		151	584	179	123	28	6	22	88	125	56	29	-	
	1955		147	541	147	97	20	3	27	84	108	60	20	1	
	1956		140	521	155	94	29	2	30	93	105	65	29	3	
	1957		134	482	121	81	14	2	24	74	82	57	25	1	
	1958		122	433	115	73	17	3	22	60	90	35	35	3	
	1959		131	472	134	89	25	1	19	64	69	43	38	1	
	1960		120	359	99	69	14	1	15	46	62	38	23	2	
	1961		119	395	107	74	11	-	22	62	61	35	28	2	
	1962		86	232	52	34	8	-	10	25	35	24	18	-	
	1963		64	147	43	29	6	-	8	20	28	15	17	1	
	1965		4	9	2	2	-	-	-	1	-	-	3	-	
Career Total	1946-1965		2,120	7,555	2,150	1,422	321	49	358	1,175	1,430	704	415	30	
Career Adj. to 10,000 BO	1946-1965	1.17674747	2,495	8,890	2,530	1,673	378	58	421	1,383	1,683	828	488	35	
Career Adj. to 10,000 AB	1946-1965	1.323626737	2,806	10,000	2,846	1,882	425	65	474	1,555	1,893	932	549	40	
10 Year Total	1948-1957		1,384	5,193	1,508	994	224	41	249	853	1,027	500	240	21	
5 Year Total	1950-1954		722	2,765	827	554	117	22	134	473	543	271	117	11	
Best Single Year	1950		151	597	192	128	30	6	28	116	124	55	12	4	

Complete Career Statistics B

Total Career Statistics & Adjusted Career, 10 year, 5 year, and Single Year Analysis

Berra, Yogi

CS	HBP	SF	GDP	AVG	OBP	SLG	Total Offensive Production Statistics				TRP Rating	RPA Rating	TNB Rating	TBA Rating	TOP Composite		
							TRP	RPA	TNB	TBA					TOP	Rating	Ranking
-	-	-	-	.364	.391	.682	7	.304	16	.696	2.01	57.03	2.62	76.67	138.33	35.27	
1	-	-	7	.280	.310	.464	95	.304	148	.473	27.30	56.87	24.26	52.11	160.55	40.93	
3	1	-	9	.305	.341	.488	168	.333	255	.506	48.28	62.46	41.80	55.76	208.30	53.11	
1	6	-	6	.277	.323	.480	150	.334	228	.508	43.10	62.60	37.38	55.97	199.05	50.75	
2	1	-	11	.322	.380	.533	240	.361	376	.566	68.97	67.73	61.64	62.41	260.74	66.48	
4	3	-	16	.294	.350	.492	180	.295	317	.520	51.72	55.29	51.97	57.28	216.26	55.14	
3	4	-	8	.273	.358	.478	195	.319	324	.529	56.03	59.70	53.11	58.35	227.20	57.93	
3	3	-	7	.296	.363	.523	188	.334	313	.556	54.02	62.57	51.31	61.27	229.18	58.43	
1	4	7	9	.307	.367	.488	213	.323	344	.521	61.21	60.47	56.39	57.44	235.52	60.05	
-	7	5	13	.272	.349	.470	192	.307	322	.514	55.17	57.47	52.79	56.69	222.12	56.63	
2	5	5	8	.298	.378	.534	198	.328	349	.578	56.90	61.43	57.21	63.68	239.22	60.99	
2	1	4	11	.251	.329	.438	156	.281	268	.483	44.83	52.67	43.93	53.22	194.65	49.63	
-	2	6	6	.266	.319	.471	150	.311	244	.506	43.10	58.31	40.00	55.79	197.21	50.28	
2	4	2	6	.284	.347	.462	133	.252	264	.501	38.22	47.29	43.28	55.21	184.00	46.91	
1	3	4	11	.276	.347	.446	108	.260	202	.487	31.03	48.76	33.11	53.65	166.56	42.47	
-	2	5	7	.271	.330	.466	123	.277	223	.502	35.34	51.91	36.56	55.36	179.17	45.68	
1	2	5	7	.224	.297	.388	60	.222	115	.426	17.24	41.64	18.85	46.94	124.68	31.79	
-	1	1	4	.293	.360	.497	48	.286	90	.536	13.79	53.54	14.75	59.04	141.13	35.98	
-	-	-	-	.222	.222	.222	1	.111	2	.222	0.29	20.82	0.33	24.49	45.93	11.71	
26	49	44	146	.285	.348	.482	2,605	.307	4,400	.518	58.26	73.40	52.03	68.82	252.52	64.49	81
31	58	52	172	.285	.348	.482	3,065	.307	5,178	.518	73.40	73.40	68.82	68.82	284.46	71.11	88
34	65	58	193	.285	.348	.482	3,448	.307	5,824	.518	66.01	73.40	61.89	68.82	270.14	67.53	91
21	35	21	98	.290	.355	.493	1,880	.322	3,096	.530	63.86	73.32	62.46	66.81	266.45	68.34	88
13	15	7	51	.299	.364	.503	1,016	.327	1,674	.538	66.75	69.88	64.19	65.28	266.11	68.17	111
2	1	-	11	.322	.380	.533	240	.361	376	.566	68.97	67.73	61.64	62.41	260.74	66.48	349

Complete Career Statistics B

Complete Career Statistics B

Total Career Statistics & Adjusted Career, 10 year, 5 year, and Single Year Analysis

Bichette, Dante: *Alphonse Dante Bichette; b. Nov. 18, 1963, West Palm Beach, FL*

Rating Category	Year	Ranked Seasons & Adjustment	G	AB	H	1B	2B	3B	HR	RUN	RBI	BB	SO	SB
	1988		21	46	12	10	2	-	-	1	8	-	7	-
	1989		48	138	29	19	7	-	3	13	15	6	24	3
	1990		109	349	89	58	15	1	15	40	53	16	79	5
	1991		134	445	106	70	18	3	15	53	59	22	107	14
	1992		112	387	111	77	27	2	5	37	41	16	74	18
	1993		141	538	167	98	43	5	21	93	89	28	99	14
	1994		116	484	147	85	33	2	27	74	95	19	70	21
	1995		139	579	197	117	38	2	40	102	128	22	96	13
	1996	1st	159	633	198	125	39	3	31	114	141	45	105	31
	1997		151	561	173	114	31	2	26	81	118	30	90	6
	1998		161	662	219	147	48	2	22	97	122	28	76	14
	1999		151	593	177	103	38	2	34	104	133	54	84	6
	2000		155	575	169	112	32	2	23	80	90	49	91	5
	2001		107	391	112	69	30	1	12	45	49	20	76	2
Career Total	1988-2001		1,704	6,381	1,906	1,204	401	27	274	934	1,141	355	1,078	152
Career Adj. to 10,000 BO	1988-2001	1.423284942	2,425	9,082	2,713	1,714	571	38	390	1,329	1,624	505	1,534	216
Career Adj. to 10,000 AB	1988-2001	1.567152484	2,670	10,000	2,987	1,887	628	42	429	1,464	1,788	556	1,689	238
10 Year Total	1991-2000		1,419	5,457	1,664	1,048	347	25	244	835	1,016	313	892	142
5 Year Total	1995-1999		761	3,028	964	606	194	11	153	498	642	179	451	70
Best Single Year	1996		159	633	198	125	39	3	31	114	141	45	105	31

10 Year Total · *5 Year Total*

Total Career Statistics & Adjusted Career, 10 year, 5 year, and Single Year Analysis

Bichette, Dante

CS	HBP	SF	GDP	AVG	OBP	SLG	Total Offensive Production Statistics				TRP Rating	RPA Rating	TNB Rating	TBA Rating	TOP Composite		
							TRP	RPA	TNB	TBA					TOP	Rating	Ranking
-	-	4	-	.261	.240	.304	9	.180	14	.280	2.59	33.73	2.30	30.86	69.47	17.71	
-	-	2	3	.210	.240	.326	28	.188	54	.362	8.05	35.21	8.85	39.94	92.05	23.47	
2	3	2	9	.255	.292	.433	93	.245	173	.456	26.72	45.98	28.36	50.31	151.37	38.59	
8	1	6	9	.238	.272	.393	112	.232	204	.422	32.18	43.45	33.44	46.55	155.63	39.68	
7	3	3	13	.287	.318	.406	78	.185	187	.443	22.41	34.63	30.66	48.84	136.54	34.81	
8	7	8	7	.310	.348	.526	182	.310	324	.551	52.30	58.00	53.11	60.73	224.14	57.15	
8	4	2	17	.304	.334	.548	169	.321	301	.572	48.56	60.20	49.34	63.07	221.18	56.39	
9	4	7	16	.340	.364	.620	230	.366	389	.619	66.09	68.63	63.77	68.27	266.76	68.01	
12	6	10	18	.313	.359	.531	255	.358	406	.570	73.28	67.11	66.56	62.85	269.79	68.79	
5	3	7	13	.308	.343	.510	199	.324	320	.521	57.18	60.73	52.46	57.44	227.81	58.08	
4	1	4	22	.331	.357	.509	219	.305	376	.524	62.93	57.23	61.64	57.80	239.60	61.09	
6	2	10	15	.298	.354	.541	237	.352	377	.559	68.10	65.89	61.80	61.65	257.44	65.64	
2	4	7	21	.294	.350	.477	170	.259	330	.503	48.85	48.56	54.10	55.44	206.95	52.76	
2	3	1	13	.286	.325	.460	94	.220	203	.474	27.01	41.15	33.28	52.27	153.72	39.19	
73	41	73	176	.299	.336	.499	2,075	.295	3,658	.521	46.41	70.72	43.25	69.21	229.59	58.63	108
104	58	104	250	.299	.336	.499	2,953	.295	5,206	.521	70.72	70.72	69.21	69.21	279.85	69.96	94
114	64	114	276	.299	.336	.499	3,252	.295	5,733	.521	62.26	70.72	60.92	69.21	263.11	65.78	101
69	35	64	151	.305	.343	.512	1,851	.307	3,214	.534	62.87	70.12	64.84	67.36	265.19	68.02	90
36	16	38	84	.318	.355	.541	1,140	.341	1,868	.558	74.90	72.88	71.63	67.71	287.11	73.56	80
12	6	10	18	.313	.359	.531	255	.358	406	.570	73.28	67.11	66.56	62.85	269.79	68.79	321

Complete Career Statistics B

Complete Career Statistics B

Total Career Statistics & Adjusted Career, 10 year, 5 year, and Single Year Analysis

Bonds, Barry: *Barry Lamar Bonds; b. July 24, 1964, Riverside, CA*

Rating Category	Year	Ranked Seasons & Adjustment	G	AB	H	1B	2B	3B	HR	RUN	RBI	BB	SO	SB
	1986		113	413	92	47	26	3	16	72	48	65	102	36
	1987		150	551	144	76	34	9	25	99	59	54	88	32
	1988		144	538	152	93	30	5	24	97	58	72	82	17
	1989		159	580	144	85	34	6	19	96	58	93	93	32
	1990		151	519	156	88	32	3	33	104	114	93	83	52
	1991		153	510	149	91	28	5	25	95	116	107	73	43
	1992	10th	140	473	147	72	36	5	34	109	103	127	69	39
	1993	4th	159	539	181	93	38	4	46	129	123	126	79	29
	1994		112	391	122	66	18	1	37	89	81	74	43	29
10 Year Total	1995		144	506	149	79	30	7	33	109	104	120	83	31
	1996	5th	158	517	159	87	27	3	42	122	129	151	76	40
	1997	9th	159	532	155	84	26	5	40	123	101	145	87	37
	1998	8th	156	552	167	79	44	7	37	120	122	130	92	28
	1999		102	355	93	37	20	2	34	91	83	73	62	15
5 Year Total	2000	6th	143	480	147	66	28	4	49	129	106	117	77	11
	2001	1st	153	476	156	49	32	2	73	129	137	177	93	13
	2002	3rd	143	403	149	70	31	2	46	117	110	198	47	9
	2003	7th	130	390	133	65	22	1	45	111	90	148	58	7
	2004	2nd	147	373	135	60	27	3	45	129	101	232	41	6
Career Total**	1986-2004		2,716	9,098	2,730	1,387	563	77	703	2,070	1,843	2,302	1,428	506
Career Adj. to 10,000 BO**	1986-2004	0.853096741	2,317	7,761	2,329	1,183	480	66	600	1,766	1,572	1,964	1,218	432
Career Adj. to 10,000 AB**	1986-2004	1.099142669	2,985	10,000	3,001	1,525	619	85	773	2,275	2,026	2,530	1,570	556
10 Year Total**	1995-2004		1,435	4,584	1,443	676	287	36	444	1,180	1,083	1,491	716	197
5 Year Total**	2000-2004		716	2,122	720	310	140	12	258	615	544	872	316	46
Best Single Year**	2001		153	476	156	49	32	2	73	129	137	177	93	13
2nd Best Year**	2004		147	373	135	60	27	3	45	129	101	232	41	6
3rd Best Year**	2002		143	403	149	70	31	2	46	117	110	198	47	9
4th Best Year**	1993		159	539	181	93	38	4	46	129	123	126	79	29
5th Best Year**	1996		158	517	159	87	27	3	42	122	129	151	76	40
6th Best Year**	2000		143	480	147	66	28	4	49	129	106	117	77	11
7th Best Year**	2003		130	390	133	65	22	1	45	111	90	148	58	7
8th Best Year**	1998		156	552	167	79	44	7	37	120	122	130	92	28
9th Best Year**	1997		159	532	155	84	26	5	40	123	101	145	87	37
10th Best Year**	1992		140	473	147	72	36	5	34	109	103	127	69	39

Total Career Statistics & Adjusted Career, 10 year, 5 year, and Single Year Analysis

Bonds, Barry

| CS | HBP | SF | GDP | AVG | OBP | SLG | Total Offensive Production Statistics | | | | TRP Rating | RPA Rating | TNB Rating | TBA Rating | TOP Composite | | |
							TRP	RPA	TNB	TBA					TOP	Rating	Ranking
7	2	2	4	.223	.330	.416	120	.247	268	.551	34.48	46.27	43.93	60.78	185.46	47.28	
10	3	3	4	.261	.329	.492	158	.257	350	.569	45.40	48.14	57.38	62.72	213.64	54.47	
11	2	2	3	.283	.368	.491	155	.251	344	.558	44.54	47.07	56.39	61.45	209.46	53.40	
10	1	4	9	.248	.351	.426	154	.224	363	.528	44.25	42.00	59.51	58.24	204.00	52.01	
13	3	6	8	.301	.406	.565	218	.347	428	.680	62.64	64.94	70.16	74.99	272.75	69.54	
13	4	13	8	.292	.410	.514	211	.329	403	.628	60.63	61.58	66.07	69.18	257.47	65.64	
8	5	7	9	.311	.456	.624	212	.341	458	.738	60.92	63.97	75.08	81.29	281.26	71.71	
12	2	7	11	.336	.458	.677	252	.368	510	.745	72.41	68.93	83.61	82.06	307.01	78.28	
9	6	3	3	.312	.426	.647	170	.356	353	.740	48.85	66.78	57.87	81.56	255.06	65.03	
10	5	4	12	.294	.431	.577	213	.329	438	.677	61.21	61.69	71.80	74.61	269.31	68.66	
7	1	6	10	.308	.461	.615	251	.366	503	.734	72.13	68.66	82.46	80.93	304.18	77.55	
8	8	5	13	.291	.446	.585	224	.319	493	.701	64.37	59.71	80.82	77.29	282.18	71.95	
12	8	6	15	.303	.438	.609	242	.340	490	.689	69.54	63.78	80.33	75.96	289.60	73.84	
2	3	3	6	.262	.389	.617	174	.395	308	.700	50.00	74.10	50.49	77.15	251.74	64.18	
3	3	7	6	.306	.440	.688	235	.383	458	.747	67.53	71.83	75.08	82.35	296.79	75.67	
3	9	2	5	.328	.515	.863	266	.398	607	.907	76.44	74.50	99.51	100.00	350.45	89.35	
2	9	2	4	.370	.582	.799	227	.369	536	.870	65.23	69.05	87.87	95.90	318.05	81.09	
-	10	2	7	.341	.529	.749	201	.361	457	.820	57.76	67.62	74.92	90.43	290.72	74.12	
1	9	3	5	.362	.609	.812	230	.370	549	.883	66.09	69.29	90.00	97.28	322.66	82.27	
141	93	87	142	.300	.443	.611	3,913	.334	8,316	.709	87.52	79.93	98.33	94.30	360.09	91.96	2
120	79	74	121	.300	.443	.611	3,338	.334	7,094	.709	79.93	79.93	94.30	94.30	348.47	87.12	6
155	102	96	156	.300	.443	.611	4,301	.334	9,140	.709	82.34	79.93	97.14	94.30	353.72	88.43	4
48	65	40	83	.315	.485	.684	2,263	.361	4,839	.773	76.87	82.40	97.62	97.49	354.37	90.89	5
9	40	16	27	.339	.535	.781	1,159	.377	2,607	.847	76.15	80.55	99.96	102.72	359.38	92.07	4
3	9	2	5	.328	.515	.863	266	.398	607	.907	76.44	74.50	99.51	100.00	350.45	89.35	8
1	9	3	5	.362	.609	.812	230	.370	549	.883	66.09	69.29	90.00	97.28	322.66	82.27	38
2	9	2	4	.370	.582	.799	227	.369	536	.870	65.23	69.05	87.87	95.90	318.05	81.09	46
12	2	7	11	.336	.458	.677	252	.368	510	.745	72.41	68.93	83.61	82.06	307.01	78.28	75
7	1	6	10	.308	.461	.615	251	.366	503	.734	72.13	68.66	82.46	80.93	304.18	77.55	85
3	3	7	6	.306	.440	.688	235	.383	458	.747	67.53	71.83	75.08	82.35	296.79	75.67	114
-	10	2	7	.341	.529	.749	201	.361	457	.820	57.76	67.62	74.92	90.43	290.72	74.12	143
12	8	6	15	.303	.438	.609	242	.340	490	.689	69.54	63.78	80.33	75.96	289.60	73.84	152
8	8	5	13	.291	.446	.585	224	.319	493	.701	64.37	59.71	80.82	77.29	282.18	71.95	218
8	5	7	9	.311	.456	.624	212	.341	458	.738	60.92	63.97	75.08	81.29	281.26	71.71	227

Complete Career Statistics B

Total Career Statistics & Adjusted Career, 10 year, 5 year, and Single Year Analysis

Bottomley, Jim: *James Leroy "Sunny Jim" Bottomley, b. April 23, 1900, Oglesby, IL*

Rating Category	Year	Ranked Seasons & Adjustment	G	AB	H	1B	2B	3B	HR	RUN	RBI	BB	SO	SB
	1922		37	151	49	31	8	5	5	29	35	6	13	3
	1923		134	523	194	138	34	14	8	79	94	45	44	4
	1924		137	528	167	110	31	12	14	87	111	35	35	5
	1925		153	619	227	150	44	12	21	92	128	47	36	3
	1926		154	603	180	107	40	14	19	98	120	58	52	4
	1927		152	574	174	109	31	15	19	95	124	74	49	8
	1928	1st	149	576	187	94	42	20	31	123	136	71	54	10
	1929	2nd	146	560	176	104	31	12	29	108	137	70	54	3
	1930		131	487	148	93	33	7	15	92	97	44	36	5
	1931		108	382	133	85	34	5	9	73	75	34	24	3
	1932		91	311	92	62	16	3	11	45	48	25	32	2
	1933		145	549	137	92	23	9	13	57	83	42	28	3
	1934		142	556	158	105	31	11	11	72	78	33	40	1
	1935		107	399	103	80	21	1	1	44	49	18	24	3
	1936		140	544	162	100	39	11	12	72	95	44	55	-
	1937		65	109	26	18	7	-	1	11	12	18	15	1
Career Total	1922-1937		1,991	7,471	2,313	1,478	465	151	219	1,177	1,422	664	591	58
Career Adj. to 10,000 BO	1922-1937	1.217878456	2,425	9,099	2,817	1,800	566	184	267	1,433	1,732	809	720	71
Career Adj. to 10,000 AB	1922-1937	1.338508901	2,665	10,000	3,096	1,978	622	202	293	1,575	1,903	889	791	78
10 Year Total	1922-1931		1,301	5,003	1,635	1,021	328	116	170	876	1,057	484	397	48
5 Year Total	1925-1929		754	2,932	944	564	188	73	119	516	645	320	245	28
Best Single Year	1928		149	576	187	94	42	20	31	123	136	71	54	10
2nd Best Year	1929		146	560	176	104	31	12	29	108	137	70	54	3

Complete Career Statistics B

10 Year Total · *5 Year Total*

Total Career Statistics & Adjusted Career, 10 year, 5 year, and Single Year Analysis

Bottomley, Jim

CS	HBP	SF	GDP	AVG	OBP	SLG	Total Offensive Production Statistics				TRP Rating	RPA Rating	TNB Rating	TBA Rating	TOP Composite		
							TRP	RPA	TNB	TBA					TOP	Rating	Ranking
1	2	-	-	.325	.358	.543	64	.403	92	.579	18.39	75.42	15.08	63.77	172.67	44.02	
6	4	-	-	.371	.425	.535	173	.302	327	.572	49.71	56.67	53.61	63.01	223.00	56.86	
4	3	-	-	.316	.362	.500	198	.350	303	.535	56.90	65.55	49.67	59.00	231.12	58.93	
4	2	-	-	.367	.413	.578	220	.329	406	.608	63.22	61.71	66.56	66.99	258.47	65.90	
-	4	-	-	.299	.364	.506	218	.328	371	.558	62.64	61.43	60.82	61.49	246.38	62.82	
-	5	-	-	.303	.387	.509	219	.335	379	.580	62.93	62.84	62.13	63.97	251.87	64.22	
-	3	-	-	.325	.402	.628	259	.398	446	.686	74.43	74.66	73.11	75.62	297.83	75.93	
-	1	-	-	.314	.391	.568	245	.388	392	.621	70.40	72.76	64.26	68.47	275.89	70.34	
-	5	-	-	.304	.368	.493	189	.353	294	.549	54.31	66.07	48.20	60.45	229.03	58.39	
-	1	-	-	.348	.403	.534	148	.355	242	.580	42.53	66.50	39.67	63.96	212.67	54.22	
-	1	-	-	.296	.350	.473	93	.276	175	.519	26.72	51.71	28.69	57.23	164.36	41.90	
-	7	-	13	.250	.311	.395	140	.229	269	.440	40.23	42.94	44.10	48.52	175.79	44.82	
-	-	-	9	.284	.324	.439	150	.251	278	.465	43.10	47.00	45.57	51.24	186.92	47.66	
-	2	-	11	.258	.294	.323	93	.216	152	.353	26.72	40.53	24.92	38.96	131.13	33.43	
-	3	-	-	.298	.354	.476	167	.283	306	.518	47.99	52.95	50.16	57.07	208.17	53.07	
-	-	-	-	.239	.346	.330	23	.181	55	.433	6.61	33.94	9.02	47.73	97.29	24.81	
15	43	-	33	.310	.369	.500	2,599	.317	4,487	.546	58.13	75.79	53.06	72.64	259.62	66.30	74
18	52	-	40	.310	.369	.500	3,165	.317	5,465	.546	75.79	75.79	72.64	72.64	296.87	74.22	71
20	58	-	44	.310	.369	.500	3,479	.317	6,006	.546	66.60	75.79	63.83	72.64	278.86	69.72	80
15	30	-	-	.327	.390	.541	1,933	.350	3,252	.589	65.66	79.90	65.60	74.37	285.54	73.24	58
4	15	-	-	.322	.391	.558	1,161	.355	1,994	.610	76.28	75.99	76.46	74.00	302.73	77.56	45
-	3	-	-	.325	.402	.628	259	.398	446	.686	74.43	74.66	73.11	75.62	297.83	75.93	108
-	1	-	-	.314	.391	.568	245	.388	392	.621	70.40	72.76	64.26	68.47	275.89	70.34	286

Complete Career Statistics   B

Total Career Statistics & Adjusted Career, 10 year, 5 year, and Single Year Analysis

Brett, George: *George Howard Brett, b. May 15, 1953, Glen Dale, WV*

Complete Career Statistics B

Rating Category	Year	Ranked Seasons & Adjustment	G	AB	H	1B	2B	3B	HR	RUN	RBI	BB	SO	SB
	1973		13	40	5	3	2	-	-	2	-	-	5	-
	1974		133	457	129	101	21	5	2	49	47	21	38	8
	1975		159	634	195	136	35	13	11	84	89	46	49	13
	1976		159	645	215	160	34	14	7	94	67	49	36	21
	1977		139	564	176	109	32	13	22	105	88	55	24	14
	1978		128	510	150	88	45	8	9	79	62	39	35	23
5 Year Total	1979		154	645	212	127	42	20	23	119	107	51	36	17
	1980	1st	117	449	175	109	33	9	24	87	118	58	22	15
10 Year Total	1981		89	347	109	69	27	7	6	42	43	27	23	14
	1982		144	552	166	104	32	9	21	101	82	71	51	6
	1983		123	464	144	79	38	2	25	90	93	57	39	-
	1984		104	377	107	70	21	3	13	42	69	38	37	-
	1985		155	550	184	111	38	5	30	108	112	103	49	9
	1986		124	441	128	80	28	4	16	70	73	80	45	1
	1987		115	427	124	82	18	2	22	71	78	72	47	6
	1988		157	589	180	111	42	3	24	90	103	82	51	14
	1989		124	457	129	88	26	3	12	67	80	59	47	14
	1990		142	544	179	113	45	7	14	82	87	56	63	9
	1991		131	505	129	77	40	2	10	77	61	58	75	2
	1992		152	592	169	122	35	5	7	55	61	35	69	8
	1993		145	560	149	96	31	3	19	69	75	39	67	7
Career Total	1973-1993		2,707	10,349	3,154	2,035	665	137	317	1,583	1,595	1,096	908	201
Career Adj. to 10,000 BO	1973-1993	0.845094228	2,288	8,746	2,665	1,720	562	116	268	1,338	1,348	926	767	170
Career Adj. to 10,000 AB	1973-1993	0.966276935	2,616	10,000	3,048	1,966	643	132	306	1,530	1,541	1,059	877	194
10 Year Total	1979-1988		1,282	4,841	1,529	942	319	64	204	820	878	639	400	82
5 Year Total	1979-1983		627	2,457	806	488	172	47	99	439	443	264	171	52
Best Single Year	1980		117	449	175	109	33	9	24	87	118	58	22	15

Total Career Statistics & Adjusted Career, 10 year, 5 year, and Single Year Analysis

Brett, George

CS	HBP	SF	GDP	AVG	OBP	SLG	Total Offensive Production Statistics				TRP Rating	RPA Rating	TNB Rating	TBA Rating	TOP Composite		
							TRP	RPA	TNB	TBA					TOP	Rating	Ranking
-	-	-	-	.125	.125	.175	2	.050	7	.175	0.57	9.37	1.15	19.29	30.38	7.75	
5	-	2	9	.282	.313	.363	96	.196	190	.389	27.59	36.79	31.15	42.82	138.34	35.27	
10	2	6	8	.308	.353	.456	173	.249	340	.489	49.71	46.58	55.74	53.84	205.87	52.49	
11	1	8	8	.333	.377	.462	161	.226	358	.504	46.26	42.43	58.69	55.49	202.88	51.73	
12	2	3	12	.312	.373	.532	193	.303	359	.564	55.46	56.86	58.85	62.21	233.39	59.50	
7	1	5	6	.294	.342	.467	141	.251	294	.524	40.52	47.10	48.20	57.76	193.57	49.35	
10	-	4	8	.329	.376	.563	226	.319	421	.595	64.94	59.81	69.02	65.54	259.31	66.11	
6	1	7	11	.390	.454	.664	205	.390	366	.696	58.91	73.03	60.00	76.69	268.63	68.49	
6	1	4	7	.314	.361	.484	85	.220	204	.528	24.43	41.26	33.44	58.25	157.38	40.13	
1	1	5	12	.301	.378	.505	183	.285	356	.555	52.59	53.50	58.36	61.21	225.65	57.53	
1	1	3	9	.310	.385	.563	183	.343	318	.596	52.59	64.22	52.13	65.63	234.57	59.80	
2	-	7	11	.284	.344	.459	111	.256	209	.483	31.90	48.04	34.26	53.20	167.39	42.68	
1	3	9	12	.335	.436	.585	220	.325	436	.644	63.22	60.89	71.48	70.98	266.57	67.96	
2	4	4	6	.290	.401	.481	143	.267	295	.551	41.09	50.09	48.36	60.77	200.31	51.07	
3	1	8	10	.290	.388	.496	149	.288	288	.556	42.82	53.90	47.21	61.28	205.21	52.32	
3	3	7	15	.306	.389	.509	193	.277	396	.569	55.46	51.96	64.92	62.71	235.05	59.93	
4	3	9	18	.282	.362	.431	147	.269	269	.493	42.24	50.45	44.10	54.30	191.09	48.72	
2	-	7	18	.329	.387	.515	169	.270	343	.549	48.56	50.67	56.23	60.49	215.95	55.06	
-	-	8	20	.255	.327	.402	138	.234	263	.445	39.66	43.75	43.11	49.05	175.57	44.76	
6	6	4	15	.285	.330	.397	116	.178	278	.426	33.33	33.34	45.57	46.99	159.24	40.60	
5	3	10	20	.266	.312	.434	144	.228	287	.454	41.38	42.69	47.05	50.05	181.17	46.19	
97	33	120	235	.305	.369	.487	3,178	.269	6,277	.530	71.08	64.31	74.22	70.51	280.13	71.54	39
82	28	101	199	.305	.369	.487	2,686	.269	5,305	.530	64.31	64.31	70.51	70.51	269.65	67.41	113
94	32	116	227	.305	.369	.487	3,071	.269	6,065	.530	58.79	64.31	64.46	70.51	258.07	64.52	112
35	15	58	101	.316	.393	.535	1,698	.300	3,289	.582	57.68	68.48	66.35	73.40	265.91	68.20	89
24	4	23	47	.328	.391	.557	882	.316	1,665	.596	57.95	67.48	63.84	72.22	261.50	66.99	119
6	1	7	11	.390	.454	.664	205	.390	366	.696	58.91	73.03	60.00	76.69	268.63	68.49	324

Complete Career Statistics B

Complete Career Statistics   B

Total Career Statistics & Adjusted Career, 10 year, 5 year, and Single Year Analysis

Brouthers, Dan: *Dennis Joseph "Big Dan" Brouthers, b. May 8, 1858, Sylvan Lake, NY*

Rating Category	Year	Ranked Seasons & Adjustment	G	AB	H	1B	2B	3B	HR	RUN	RBI	BB	SO	SB
	1879		39	168	46	28	13	1	4	17	17	1	18	-
	1880		3	13	2	2	-	-	-	-	1	1	-	-
	1881		65	270	86	56	15	7	8	60	45	18	22	-
	1882		84	351	129	87	25	11	6	71	63	21	7	-
	1883		97	420	156	97	39	17	3	83	97	16	17	-
	1884		90	381	124	72	22	16	14	80	79	33	20	-
	1885		98	407	146	99	27	13	7	87	59	34	10	-
	1886		121	489	181	113	41	16	11	139	72	66	16	21
	1887	1st	122	570	239	172	35	20	12	153	101	71	9	34
	1888		129	522	160	103	35	13	9	118	66	68	13	34
	1889		126	485	181	141	25	8	7	105	118	66	6	22
	1890		123	464	160	118	32	9	1	116	97	99	17	26
	1891		123	458	160	109	26	20	5	111	109	87	20	33
	1892		152	588	197	139	33	20	5	121	124	84	30	36
	1893		75	267	93	59	21	11	2	53	59	52	10	8
	1894	2nd	123	528	182	115	33	25	9	137	128	67	9	40
	1895		29	121	35	20	12	1	2	15	20	12	3	1
	1896		57	218	72	53	15	3	1	41	41	44	11	8
	1904		2	5	-	-	-	-	-	-	-	-	-	-
Career Total	1879-1904		1,658	6,725	2,349	1,583	449	211	106	1,507	1,296	840	238	263
Career Adj. to 10,000 BO	1879-1904	1.303780965	2,162	8,768	3,063	2,064	585	275	138	1,965	1,690	1,095	310	343
Career Adj. to 10,000 AB	1879-1904	1.486988848	2,465	10,000	3,493	2,354	668	314	158	2,241	1,927	1,249	354	391
10 Year Total	1885-1894		1,192	4,778	1,699	1,168	308	155	68	1,140	933	694	140	254
5 Year Total	1887-1891		623	2,499	900	643	153	70	34	603	491	391	65	149
Best Single Year	1887		122	570	239	172	35	20	12	153	101	71	9	34
2nd Best Year	1894		123	528	182	115	33	25	9	137	128	67	9	40

(side labels: 10 Year Total, 5 Year Total)

Total Career Statistics & Adjusted Career, 10 year, 5 year, and Single Year Analysis

Brouthers, Dan

CS	HBP	SF	GDP	AVG	OBP	SLG	Total Offensive Production Statistics				TRP Rating	RPA Rating	TNB Rating	TBA Rating	TOP Composite		
							TRP	RPA	TNB	TBA					TOP	Rating	Ranking
-	-	-	-	.274	.278	.435	34	.201	74	.438	4.89	18.85	12.13	48.26	84.12	21.45	
-	-	-	-	.154	.214	.154	1	.071	3	.214	-	-	0.49	23.62	24.11	6.15	
-	-	-	-	.319	.361	.515	105	.365	157	.545	17.24	39.04	25.74	60.08	142.10	36.23	
-	-	-	-	.368	.403	.553	134	.360	215	.578	20.40	35.76	35.25	63.70	155.11	39.55	
-	-	-	-	.371	.394	.567	180	.413	254	.583	23.85	35.67	41.64	64.21	165.37	42.16	
-	-	-	-	.325	.379	.577	159	.384	253	.611	22.99	36.21	41.48	67.35	168.03	42.84	
-	-	-	-	.359	.408	.541	146	.331	254	.576	41.95	62.04	41.64	63.48	209.11	53.31	
-	-	-	-	.370	.445	.587	211	.380	374	.674	60.63	71.24	61.31	74.27	267.45	68.19	
-	6	-	-	.419	.488	.614	254	.393	461	.713	72.99	73.56	75.57	78.53	300.65	76.65	
-	12	-	-	.307	.399	.475	184	.306	362	.601	52.87	57.27	59.34	66.27	235.77	60.11	
-	14	-	-	.373	.462	.501	223	.395	345	.611	64.08	73.96	56.56	67.30	261.89	66.77	
-	18	-	-	.345	.477	.459	213	.367	356	.613	61.21	68.70	58.36	67.53	255.80	65.22	
-	24	-	-	.349	.476	.526	220	.387	385	.677	63.22	72.45	63.11	74.57	273.36	69.69	
-	16	-	-	.335	.432	.485	245	.356	421	.612	70.40	66.73	69.02	67.44	273.59	69.75	
-	6	-	-	.348	.465	.532	112	.345	208	.640	32.18	64.57	34.10	70.54	201.39	51.35	
-	5	-	-	.345	.423	.553	265	.442	404	.673	76.15	82.76	66.23	74.21	299.35	76.32	
-	-	-	-	.289	.353	.455	35	.263	68	.511	4.31	21.13	11.15	56.35	92.94	23.70	
-	4	-	-	.330	.451	.440	82	.308	152	.571	11.78	28.88	24.92	62.98	128.56	32.78	
-	-	-	-	.000	.000	.000	-	.000	-	.000	-	-	-	-	-	-	
-	105	-	-	.349	.429	.526	2,803	.365	4,746	.619	62.69	87.51	56.12	82.25	288.57	73.70	28
-	137	-	-	.349	.429	.526	3,654	.365	6,188	.619	87.51	87.51	82.25	82.25	339.52	84.88	10
-	156	-	-	.349	.429	.526	4,168	.365	7,057	.619	79.80	87.51	75.00	82.25	324.56	81.14	12
-	101	-	-	.356	.448	.528	2,073	.372	3,570	.641	70.41	84.82	72.02	80.83	308.08	79.02	26
-	74	-	-	.360	.461	.518	1,094	.369	1,909	.644	71.88	78.93	73.20	78.09	302.09	77.39	47
-	6	-	-	.419	.488	.614	254	.393	461	.713	72.99	73.56	75.57	78.53	300.65	76.65	97
-	5	-	-	.345	.423	.553	265	.442	404	.673	76.15	82.76	66.23	74.21	299.35	76.32	103

Complete Career Statistics B

Total Career Statistics & Adjusted Career, 10 year, 5 year, and Single Year Analysis

Burkett, Jesse: *Jesse Cail "Crab" Burkett, b. Dec. 4, 1868, Wheeling, WV*

Complete Career Statistics B

Rating Category			Year	Ranked Seasons & Adjustment	G	AB	H	1B	2B	3B	HR	RUN	RBI	BB	SO	SB
			1890		101	401	124	86	22	12	4	67	60	33	52	14
			1891		40	166	45	34	7	4	-	30	13	23	19	2
			1892		145	605	168	133	15	14	6	117	66	67	59	36
		5 Year Total	1893	2nd	124	480	179	135	23	15	6	144	82	98	23	39
	10 Year Total		1894		124	518	185	137	25	15	8	134	94	84	27	32
			1895	1st	132	555	235	194	21	15	5	149	83	74	31	47
			1896	3rd	133	585	240	192	26	16	6	159	72	49	19	32
			1897		128	519	199	161	28	8	2	128	60	76	-	27
			1898		148	624	215	188	18	9	-	115	42	69	-	20
			1899	4th	138	567	228	194	17	10	7	115	71	67	-	22
			1900		142	560	202	169	14	12	7	88	68	62	-	31
			1901		142	597	228	180	21	17	10	139	75	59	-	27
			1902		137	549	168	125	29	9	5	99	52	71	-	22
			1903		133	514	152	122	20	7	3	74	40	52	-	16
			1904		147	576	157	131	15	9	2	72	27	78	-	12
			1905		148	573	147	117	13	13	4	78	47	67	-	13
Career Total			1890-1905		2,062	8,389	2,872	2,298	314	185	75	1,708	952	1,029	230	392
Career Adj. to 10,000 BO			1890-1905	1.053407774	2,172	8,837	3,025	2,421	331	195	79	1,799	1,003	1,084	242	413
Career Adj. to 10,000 AB			1890-1905	1.192037192	2,458	10,000	3,424	2,739	374	221	89	2,036	1,135	1,227	274	467
10 Year Total			1892-1901		1,356	5,610	2,079	1,683	208	131	57	1,288	713	705	159	313
5 Year Total			1893-1897		641	2,657	1,038	819	123	69	27	714	391	381	100	177
Best Single Year			1895		132	555	235	194	21	15	5	149	83	74	31	47
2nd Best Year			1893		124	480	179	135	23	15	6	144	82	98	23	39
3rd Best Year			1896		133	585	240	192	26	16	6	159	72	49	19	32
4th Best Year			1899		138	567	228	194	17	10	7	115	71	67	-	22

Total Career Statistics & Adjusted Career, 10 year, 5 year, and Single Year Analysis

Burkett, Jesse

CS	HBP	SF	GDP	AVG	OBP	SLG	TRP	RPA	TNB	TBA	TRP Rating	RPA Rating	TNB Rating	TBA Rating	TOP	Rating	Ranking
-	3	-	-	.309	.366	.454	127	.291	232	.531	36.49	54.46	38.03	58.51	187.50	47.80	
-	-	-	-	.271	.360	.361	43	.228	85	.450	12.36	42.63	13.93	49.57	118.49	30.21	
-	1	-	-	.278	.351	.379	183	.272	333	.495	52.59	50.95	54.59	54.53	212.66	54.22	
-	7	-	-	.373	.485	.521	226	.386	394	.674	64.94	72.39	64.59	74.23	276.15	70.41	
-	1	-	-	.357	.448	.510	228	.378	381	.632	65.52	70.85	62.46	69.64	268.46	68.45	
-	8	-	-	.423	.498	.542	232	.364	430	.675	66.67	68.25	70.49	74.40	279.80	71.34	
-	7	-	-	.410	.462	.540	231	.360	404	.630	66.38	67.53	66.23	69.46	269.60	68.74	
-	7	-	-	.383	.468	.480	188	.312	359	.596	54.02	58.52	58.85	65.73	237.12	60.46	
-	9	-	-	.345	.417	.402	157	.224	349	.497	45.11	41.91	57.21	54.79	199.03	50.74	
-	2	-	-	.402	.467	.504	186	.292	377	.593	53.45	54.80	61.80	65.33	235.38	60.01	
-	3	-	-	.361	.427	.466	156	.250	357	.571	44.83	46.77	58.52	62.95	213.08	54.33	
-	10	-	-	.382	.446	.524	214	.321	409	.614	61.49	60.21	67.05	67.68	256.44	65.38	
-	5	-	-	.306	.390	.419	151	.242	328	.525	43.39	45.27	53.77	57.84	200.27	51.06	
-	3	-	-	.296	.364	.379	114	.200	266	.467	32.76	37.54	43.61	51.52	165.43	42.18	
-	5	-	-	.273	.364	.340	99	.150	291	.442	28.45	28.15	47.70	48.67	152.97	39.00	
-	4	-	-	.257	.339	.346	125	.194	282	.438	35.92	36.37	46.23	48.26	166.78	42.52	
-	75	-	-	.342	.419	.451	2,660	.280	5,277	.556	59.49	67.10	62.40	73.89	262.88	67.13	68
-	79	-	-	.342	.419	.451	2,802	.280	5,559	.556	67.10	67.10	73.89	73.89	281.98	70.49	92
-	89	-	-	.342	.419	.451	3,171	.280	6,290	.556	60.71	67.10	66.85	73.89	268.55	67.14	94
-	55	-	-	.371	.446	.485	2,001	.314	3,793	.595	67.97	71.63	76.52	75.13	291.25	74.70	50
-	30	-	-	.391	.472	.519	1,105	.360	1,968	.641	72.60	77.02	75.46	77.77	302.85	77.59	44
-	8	-	-	.423	.498	.542	232	.364	430	.675	66.67	68.25	70.49	74.40	279.80	71.34	239
-	7	-	-	.373	.485	.521	226	.386	394	.674	64.94	72.39	64.59	74.23	276.15	70.41	280
-	7	-	-	.410	.462	.540	231	.360	404	.630	66.38	67.53	66.23	69.46	269.60	68.74	323
-	2	-	-	.402	.467	.504	186	.292	377	.593	53.45	54.80	61.80	65.33	235.38	60.01	377

Complete Career Statistics   B

Complete Career Statistics C

Total Career Statistics & Adjusted Career, 10 year, 5 year, and Single Year Analysis

Campanella, Roy: *Roy Campanella, b. Nov. 19, 1921, Philadelphia, PA*

Rating Category	Year	Ranked Seasons & Adjustment	G	AB	H	1B	2B	3B	HR	RUN	RBI	BB	SO	SB
	1948		83	279	72	49	11	3	9	32	45	36	45	3
	1949		130	436	125	79	22	2	22	65	82	67	36	3
	1950		126	437	123	70	19	3	31	70	89	55	51	1
	1951		143	505	164	97	33	1	33	90	108	53	51	1
	1952		128	468	126	85	18	1	22	73	97	57	59	8
	1953	1st	144	519	162	92	26	3	41	103	142	67	58	4
	1954		111	397	82	46	14	3	19	43	51	42	49	1
	1955		123	446	142	89	20	1	32	81	107	56	41	2
	1956		124	388	85	58	6	1	20	39	73	66	61	1
	1957		103	330	80	58	9	-	13	31	62	34	50	1
Career Total	1948-1957		1,215	4,205	1,161	723	178	18	242	627	856	533	501	25
Career Adj. to 10,000 BO	1948-1957	2.028809089	2,465	8,531	2,355	1,467	361	37	491	1,272	1,737	1,081	1,016	51
Career Adj. to 10,000 AB	1948-1957	2.378121284	2,889	10,000	2,761	1,719	423	43	576	1,491	2,036	1,268	1,191	59
10 Year Total	1948-1957		1,215	4,205	1,161	723	178	18	242	627	856	533	501	25
5 Year Total	1949-1953		671	2,365	700	423	118	10	149	401	518	299	255	17
Best Single Year	1953		144	519	162	92	26	3	41	103	142	67	58	4

(5 Year Total spans 1949–1953; 10 Year Total spans 1948–1957)

Total Career Statistics & Adjusted Career, 10 year, 5 year, and Single Year Analysis

Campanella, Roy

CS	HBP	SF	GDP	AVG	OBP	SLG	Total Offensive Production Statistics				TRP Rating	RPA Rating	TNB Rating	TBA Rating	TOP Composite		
							TRP	RPA	TNB	TBA					TOP	Rating	Ranking
-	1	-	3	.258	.345	.416	77	.241	156	.489	22.13	45.23	25.57	53.90	146.83	37.44	
2	3	-	11	.287	.385	.498	147	.284	288	.557	42.24	53.28	47.21	61.40	204.13	52.04	
-	2	-	17	.281	.364	.551	159	.311	299	.585	45.69	58.30	49.02	64.49	217.50	55.45	
2	4	-	19	.325	.393	.590	198	.341	354	.609	56.90	63.86	58.03	67.15	245.94	62.70	
4	3	-	22	.269	.352	.453	170	.309	276	.502	48.85	57.92	45.25	55.31	207.32	52.86	
2	4	-	13	.312	.395	.611	245	.406	390	.647	70.40	76.13	63.93	71.28	281.75	71.84	
4	2	1	13	.207	.285	.401	94	.207	200	.440	27.01	38.71	32.79	48.45	146.96	37.47	
3	6	9	14	.318	.395	.583	188	.354	321	.605	54.02	66.34	52.62	66.63	239.61	61.09	
-	1	2	20	.219	.333	.394	112	.235	221	.463	32.18	44.00	36.23	51.06	163.47	41.68	
-	4	6	11	.242	.316	.388	93	.242	167	.434	26.72	45.26	27.38	47.81	147.17	37.52	
17	30	18	143	.276	.360	.500	1,483	.301	2,672	.542	33.17	72.05	31.60	72.06	208.87	53.34	124
34	61	37	290	.276	.360	.500	3,009	.301	5,421	.542	72.05	72.05	72.06	72.06	288.21	72.05	79
40	71	43	340	.276	.360	.500	3,527	.301	6,354	.542	67.52	72.05	67.53	72.06	279.16	69.79	79
17	30	18	143	.276	.360	.500	1,483	.301	2,672	.542	50.37	68.61	53.90	68.40	241.29	61.89	120
10	16	-	82	.296	.379	.543	919	.333	1,607	.582	60.38	71.15	61.62	70.54	263.69	67.56	115
2	4	-	13	.312	.395	.611	245	.406	390	.647	70.40	76.13	63.93	71.28	281.75	71.84	222

Total Career Statistics & Adjusted Career, 10 year, 5 year, and Single Year Analysis

Canseco, Jose; *Jose Canceco (Capas), b. July 2, 1964, Havana, Cuba*

Rating Category	Year	Ranked Seasons & Adjustment	G	AB	H	1B	2B	3B	HR	RUN	RBI	BB	SO	SB
	1985		29	96	29	21	3	-	5	16	13	4	31	1
	1986		157	600	144	81	29	1	33	85	117	65	175	15
	1987		159	630	162	93	35	3	31	81	113	50	157	15
	1988	1st	158	610	187	111	34	-	42	120	124	78	128	40
	1989		65	227	61	34	9	1	17	40	57	23	69	6
	1990		131	481	132	79	14	2	37	83	101	72	158	19
	1991		154	572	152	75	32	1	44	115	122	78	152	26
	1992		119	439	107	66	15	-	26	74	87	63	128	6
	1993		60	231	59	34	14	1	10	30	46	16	62	6
	1994		111	429	121	69	19	2	31	88	90	69	114	15
	1995		102	396	121	71	25	1	24	64	81	42	93	4
	1996		96	360	104	53	22	1	28	68	82	63	82	3
	1997		108	388	91	49	19	-	23	56	74	51	122	8
	1998		151	583	138	66	26	-	46	98	107	65	159	29
	1999		113	430	120	67	18	1	34	75	95	58	135	3
	2000		98	329	83	50	18	-	15	47	49	64	102	2
	2001		76	256	66	42	8	-	16	46	49	45	75	2
Career Total	1985-2001		1,887	7,057	1,877	1,061	340	14	462	1,186	1,407	906	1,942	200
Career Adj. to 10,000 BO	1985-2001	1.203948953	2,272	8,496	2,260	1,277	409	17	556	1,428	1,694	1,091	2,338	241
Career Adj. to 10,000 AB	1985-2001	1.417032733	2,674	10,000	2,660	1,503	482	20	655	1,681	1,994	1,284	2,752	283
10 Year Total	1986-1995		1,216	4,615	1,246	713	226	12	295	780	938	556	1,236	152
5 Year Total	1987-1991		667	2,520	694	392	124	7	171	439	517	301	664	106
Best Single Year	1988		158	610	187	111	34	-	42	120	124	78	128	40

Side labels: 10 Year Total / 5 Year Total

Vertical tab: Complete Career Statistics C

Total Career Statistics & Adjusted Career, 10 year, 5 year, and Single Year Analysis

Canseco, Jose

CS	HBP	SF	GDP	AVG	OBP	SLG	Total Offensive Production Statistics				TRP Rating	RPA Rating	TNB Rating	TBA Rating	TOP Composite		
							TRP	RPA	TNB	TBA					TOP	Rating	Ranking
1	-	-	1	.302	.330	.490	29	.287	51	.505	8.33	53.80	8.36	55.65	126.15	32.16	
7	8	9	12	.240	.318	.457	202	.291	355	.512	58.05	54.54	58.20	56.38	227.16	57.92	
3	2	9	16	.257	.310	.470	194	.274	360	.509	55.75	51.42	59.02	56.12	222.30	56.68	
16	10	6	15	.307	.391	.569	244	.339	459	.638	70.11	63.59	75.25	70.36	279.31	71.21	
3	2	6	4	.269	.333	.542	97	.370	151	.576	27.87	69.37	24.75	63.52	185.52	47.30	
10	5	5	9	.274	.371	.543	184	.322	347	.607	52.87	60.28	56.89	66.86	236.90	60.40	
6	9	6	16	.266	.359	.556	237	.348	425	.624	68.10	65.21	69.67	68.78	271.77	69.29	
7	6	4	16	.244	.344	.456	161	.305	268	.508	46.26	57.14	43.93	55.94	203.28	51.83	
6	3	3	6	.255	.308	.455	76	.293	124	.479	21.84	54.98	20.33	52.77	149.92	38.22	
8	5	2	20	.282	.386	.552	178	.339	318	.606	51.15	63.53	52.13	66.76	233.57	59.55	
-	7	5	9	.306	.378	.556	145	.316	273	.595	41.67	59.19	44.75	65.55	211.17	53.84	
1	6	3	7	.289	.400	.589	150	.342	283	.645	43.10	64.03	46.39	71.05	224.57	57.26	
2	3	4	15	.235	.325	.461	130	.282	239	.518	37.36	52.84	39.18	57.14	186.52	47.55	
17	6	4	7	.237	.318	.518	205	.308	385	.579	58.91	57.76	63.11	63.81	243.60	62.11	
-	7	7	14	.279	.369	.563	170	.329	310	.601	48.85	61.73	50.82	66.21	227.62	58.03	
-	4	4	7	.252	.377	.444	96	.235	216	.529	27.59	44.09	35.41	58.35	165.43	42.18	
1	1	4	4	.258	.366	.477	95	.306	169	.545	27.30	57.42	27.70	60.08	172.51	43.98	
88	84	81	178	.266	.353	.515	2,593	.312	4,733	.570	58.00	74.75	55.97	75.74	264.46	67.54	65
106	101	98	214	.266	.353	.515	3,122	.312	5,698	.570	74.75	74.75	75.74	75.74	301.00	75.25	63
125	119	115	252	.266	.353	.515	3,674	.312	6,707	.570	70.35	74.75	71.28	75.74	292.12	73.03	58
66	57	55	123	.270	.352	.516	1,718	.318	3,080	.570	58.36	72.47	62.13	71.89	264.85	67.93	91
38	28	32	60	.275	.355	.534	956	.325	1,742	.592	62.81	69.51	66.79	71.81	270.93	69.41	104
16	10	6	15	.307	.391	.569	244	.339	459	.638	70.11	63.59	75.25	70.36	279.31	71.21	244

Complete Career Statistics   C

Total Career Statistics & Adjusted Career, 10 year, 5 year, and Single Year Analysis

Cepeda, Orlando; *Orlando Manuel "Baby Bull" Cepeda (Penne), b. Sept. 17, 1937, Ponce, Puerto Rico*

Rating Category	Year	Ranked Seasons & Adjustment	G	AB	H	1B	2B	3B	HR	RUN	RBI	BB	SO	SB
	1958		148	603	188	121	38	4	25	88	96	29	84	15
	1959		151	605	192	126	35	4	27	92	105	33	100	23
	1960		151	569	169	106	36	3	24	81	96	34	91	15
	1961	1st	152	585	182	104	28	4	46	105	142	39	91	12
	1962		162	625	191	129	26	1	35	105	114	37	97	10
	1963		156	579	183	112	33	4	34	100	97	37	70	8
	1964		142	529	161	101	27	2	31	75	97	43	83	9
	1965		33	34	6	4	1	-	1	1	5	3	9	-
	1966		142	501	151	105	26	-	20	70	73	38	79	9
	1967		151	563	183	121	37	-	25	91	111	62	75	11
	1968		157	600	149	105	26	2	16	71	73	43	96	8
	1969		154	573	147	95	28	2	22	74	88	55	76	12
	1970		148	567	173	106	33	-	34	87	111	47	75	6
	1971		71	250	69	44	10	1	14	31	44	22	29	3
	1972		31	87	25	18	3	-	4	6	9	7	17	-
	1973		142	550	159	114	25	-	20	51	86	50	81	-
	1974		33	107	23	17	5	-	1	3	18	9	16	1
Career Total	1958-1974		2,124	7,927	2,351	1,528	417	27	379	1,131	1,365	588	1,169	142
Career Adj. to 10,000 BO	1958-1974	1.122460433	2,384	8,898	2,639	1,715	468	30	425	1,270	1,532	660	1,312	159
Career Adj. to 10,000 AB	1958-1974	1.261511291	2,679	10,000	2,966	1,928	526	34	478	1,427	1,722	742	1,475	179
10 Year Total	1958-1967		1,388	5,193	1,606	1,029	287	22	268	808	936	355	779	112
5 Year Total	1959-1963		772	2,963	917	577	158	16	166	483	554	180	449	68
Best Single Year	1961		152	585	182	104	28	4	46	105	142	39	91	12

10 Year Total

5 Year Total

Complete Career Statistics C

Total Career Statistics & Adjusted Career, 10 year, 5 year, and Single Year Analysis

Cepeda, Orlando

CS	HBP	SF	GDP	AVG	OBP	SLG	Total Offensive Production Statistics				TRP Rating	RPA Rating	TNB Rating	TBA Rating	TOP Composite		
							TRP	RPA	TNB	TBA					TOP	Rating	Ranking
11	3	9	18	.312	.342	.512	184	.278	345	.521	52.87	52.08	56.56	57.44	218.95	55.82	
9	5	4	10	.317	.355	.522	197	.300	368	.560	56.61	56.19	60.33	61.73	234.86	59.88	
6	8	4	11	.297	.343	.497	177	.283	334	.534	50.86	52.98	54.75	58.80	217.40	55.43	
8	9	3	21	.311	.362	.609	247	.376	408	.621	70.98	70.45	66.89	68.44	276.75	70.56	
4	6	7	16	.306	.347	.518	219	.317	373	.540	62.93	59.39	61.15	59.49	242.96	61.94	
3	10	3	18	.316	.366	.563	197	.304	378	.584	56.61	57.05	61.97	64.39	240.02	61.20	
4	8	7	13	.304	.361	.539	172	.287	341	.568	49.43	53.72	55.90	62.64	221.68	56.52	
-	-	3	1	.176	.225	.294	6	.146	13	.317	1.72	27.42	2.13	34.95	66.22	16.88	
9	14	9	12	.301	.361	.473	143	.249	289	.503	41.09	46.68	47.38	55.49	190.64	48.61	
2	12	7	16	.325	.399	.524	202	.306	378	.573	58.05	57.35	61.97	63.12	240.49	61.31	
6	9	4	13	.248	.306	.378	144	.215	281	.420	41.38	40.33	46.07	46.29	174.07	44.38	
5	5	3	12	.257	.325	.428	162	.250	312	.481	46.55	46.85	51.15	53.07	197.61	50.38	
5	9	4	15	.305	.365	.543	198	.308	365	.569	56.90	57.79	59.84	62.66	237.18	60.47	
6	-	4	12	.276	.330	.492	75	.260	142	.493	21.55	48.80	23.28	54.34	147.97	37.73	
-	-	-	1	.287	.340	.460	15	.158	47	.495	4.31	29.59	7.70	54.53	96.13	24.51	
2	3	3	24	.289	.350	.444	137	.217	295	.468	39.37	40.75	48.36	51.61	180.08	45.91	
-	1	-	5	.215	.282	.290	21	.172	42	.344	6.03	32.25	6.89	37.94	83.12	21.19	
80	102	74	218	.297	.350	.499	2,496	.280	4,711	.529	55.83	67.09	55.71	70.29	248.91	63.57	86
90	114	83	245	.297	.350	.499	2,802	.280	5,288	.529	67.09	67.09	70.29	70.29	274.75	68.69	102
101	129	93	275	.297	.350	.499	3,149	.280	5,943	.529	60.28	67.09	63.16	70.29	260.82	65.20	103
56	75	56	136	.309	.359	.528	1,744	.300	3,227	.555	59.24	68.39	65.10	70.02	262.75	67.39	96
30	38	21	76	.309	.354	.542	1,037	.316	1,861	.568	68.13	67.65	71.36	68.83	275.97	70.70	97
8	9	3	21	.311	.362	.609	247	.376	408	.621	70.98	70.45	66.89	68.44	276.75	70.56	266

Complete Career Statistics C

Total Career Statistics & Adjusted Career, 10 year, 5 year, and Single Year Analysis

Clemente, Roberto: *Roberto "Bob" Clemente (Walker), b. August 18, 1934, Carolina, Puerto Rice*

Complete Career Statistics C

Rating Category	Year	Ranked Seasons & Adjustment	G	AB	H	1B	2B	3B	HR	RUN	RBI	BB	SO	SB
	1955		124	474	121	82	23	11	5	48	47	18	60	2
	1956		147	543	169	125	30	7	7	66	60	13	58	6
	1957		111	451	114	86	17	7	4	42	30	23	45	-
	1958		140	519	150	110	24	10	6	69	50	31	41	8
	1959		105	432	128	100	17	7	4	60	50	15	51	2
	1960		144	570	179	135	22	6	16	89	94	39	72	4
	1961		146	572	201	138	30	10	23	100	89	35	59	4
10 Year Total	1962		144	538	168	121	28	9	10	95	74	35	73	6
	1963		152	600	192	144	23	8	17	77	76	31	64	12
	1964	5 Year Total	155	622	211	152	40	7	12	95	87	51	87	5
	1965		152	589	194	149	21	14	10	91	65	43	78	8
	1966	1st	154	638	202	131	31	11	29	105	119	46	109	7
	1967		147	585	209	150	26	10	23	103	110	41	103	9
	1968		132	502	146	98	18	12	18	74	57	51	77	2
	1969		138	507	175	124	20	12	19	87	91	56	73	4
	1970		108	412	145	99	22	10	14	65	60	38	66	3
	1971		132	522	178	128	29	8	13	82	86	26	65	1
	1972		102	378	118	82	19	7	10	68	60	29	49	-
Career Total	1955-1972		2,433	9,454	3,000	2,154	440	166	240	1,416	1,305	621	1,230	83
Career Adj. to 10,000 BO	1955-1972	0.956846235	2,328	9,046	2,871	2,061	421	159	230	1,355	1,249	594	1,177	79
Career Adj. to 10,000 AB	1955-1972	1.057753332	2,574	10,000	3,173	2,278	465	176	254	1,498	1,380	657	1,301	88
10 Year Total	1960-1969		1,464	5,723	1,877	1,342	259	99	177	916	862	428	795	61
5 Year Total	1963-1967		760	3,034	1,008	726	141	50	91	471	457	212	441	41
Best Single Year	1966		154	638	202	131	31	11	29	105	119	46	109	7

Total Career Statistics & Adjusted Career, 10 year, 5 year, and Single Year Analysis

Clemente, Roberto

CS	HBP	SF	GDP	AVG	OBP	SLG	Total Offensive Production Statistics				TRP Rating	RPA Rating	TNB Rating	TBA Rating	TOP Composite		
							TRP	RPA	TNB	TBA					TOP	Rating	Ranking
5	2	3	14	.255	.284	.382	95	.186	198	.387	27.30	34.84	32.46	42.71	137.30	35.01	
6	4	4	14	.311	.330	.431	126	.218	251	.434	36.21	40.85	41.15	47.86	166.06	42.34	
4	-	1	13	.253	.288	.348	72	.148	176	.361	20.69	27.65	28.85	39.75	116.94	29.81	
2	-	3	15	.289	.327	.408	119	.210	249	.438	34.20	39.26	40.82	48.32	162.59	41.45	
3	3	3	10	.296	.322	.396	110	.238	188	.406	31.61	44.52	30.82	44.75	151.70	38.68	
5	2	5	21	.314	.357	.458	183	.287	301	.473	52.59	53.83	49.34	52.08	207.84	52.99	
1	3	3	18	.351	.390	.559	189	.300	361	.572	54.31	56.13	59.18	63.05	232.67	59.32	
4	1	6	18	.312	.352	.454	169	.283	282	.472	48.56	52.96	46.23	51.97	199.72	50.92	
2	4	3	24	.320	.356	.470	153	.231	327	.494	43.97	43.31	53.61	54.44	195.32	49.80	
2	2	5	9	.339	.388	.484	182	.264	357	.518	52.30	49.50	58.52	57.11	217.43	55.44	
-	5	3	17	.329	.378	.463	156	.237	329	.501	44.83	44.49	53.93	55.19	198.45	50.60	
5	-	5	14	.317	.360	.536	224	.319	390	.555	64.37	59.71	63.93	61.14	249.15	63.52	
1	3	3	15	.357	.400	.554	213	.329	376	.581	61.21	61.69	61.64	64.05	248.58	63.38	
3	1	3	13	.291	.355	.482	131	.230	293	.514	37.64	43.06	48.03	56.65	185.40	47.27	
1	3	4	19	.345	.411	.544	178	.302	338	.574	51.15	56.63	55.41	63.25	226.43	57.73	
-	2	2	7	.352	.407	.556	125	.271	272	.590	35.92	50.81	44.59	65.03	196.35	50.06	
2	-	4	19	.341	.370	.502	168	.294	287	.503	48.28	55.13	47.05	55.40	205.85	52.48	
-	-	6	15	.312	.356	.479	128	.299	210	.491	36.78	56.04	34.43	54.08	181.32	46.23	
46	35	66	275	.317	.359	.475	2,721	.260	5,185	.496	60.86	62.34	61.31	65.95	250.46	63.96	83
44	33	63	263	.317	.359	.475	2,604	.260	4,961	.496	62.34	62.34	65.95	65.95	256.58	64.15	125
49	37	70	291	.317	.359	.475	2,878	.260	5,484	.496	55.10	62.34	58.29	65.95	241.68	60.42	125
24	24	40	168	.328	.375	.501	1,778	.279	3,354	.525	60.39	63.52	67.66	66.30	257.88	66.14	108
10	14	19	79	.332	.376	.502	928	.276	1,779	.530	60.97	59.10	68.21	64.23	252.51	64.69	125
5	-	5	14	.317	.360	.536	224	.319	390	.555	64.37	59.71	63.93	61.14	249.15	63.52	368

Complete Career Statistics C

Total Career Statistics & Adjusted Career, 10 year, 5 year, and Single Year Analysis

Cobb, Ty: *Tyrus Ramond "The Georgia Peach" Cobb; b. Dec. 18, 1886, Narrows, GA.*

Rating Category	Year	Ranked Seasons & Adjustment	G	AB	H	1B	2B	3B	HR	RUN	RBI	BB	SO	SB
	1905		41	150	36	29	6	-	1	19	15	10	-	2
	1906		98	350	112	91	13	7	1	45	34	19	-	23
	1907		150	605	212	163	29	15	5	97	119	24	-	49
	1908		150	581	188	128	36	20	4	88	108	34	-	39
	1909	3rd	156	573	216	164	33	10	9	116	107	48	-	76
	1910		140	509	196	139	36	13	8	106	91	64	-	65
	1911	1st	146	591	248	169	47	24	8	147	127	44	-	83
	1912	4th	140	553	227	167	30	23	7	119	83	43	-	61
	1913		122	428	167	129	18	16	4	70	67	58	31	52
	1914		97	345	127	92	22	11	2	69	57	57	22	35
	1915	2nd	156	563	208	161	31	13	3	144	99	118	43	96
	1916		145	542	201	155	31	10	5	113	68	78	39	68
	1917		152	588	225	152	44	23	6	107	102	61	34	55
	1918		111	421	161	125	19	14	3	83	64	41	21	34
	1919		124	497	191	141	36	13	1	92	70	38	22	28
	1920		112	428	143	105	28	8	2	86	63	58	28	14
	1921		128	507	197	132	37	16	12	124	101	56	19	22
	1922		137	526	211	149	42	16	4	99	99	55	24	9
	1923		145	556	189	136	40	7	6	103	88	66	14	9
	1924		155	625	211	159	38	10	4	115	78	85	18	23
	1925		121	415	157	102	31	12	12	97	102	65	12	13
	1926		79	233	79	52	18	5	4	48	62	26	2	9
	1927		133	490	175	131	32	7	5	104	93	67	12	22
	1928		95	353	114	82	27	4	1	54	40	34	16	5
Career Total	1905-1928		3,033	11,429	4,191	3,053	724	297	117	2,245	1,937	1,249	357	892
Career Adj. to 10,000 BO	1905-1928	0.782962731	2,375	8,948	3,281	2,390	567	233	92	1,758	1,517	978	280	698
Career Adj. to 10,000 AB	1905-1928	0.874967189	2,654	10,000	3,667	2,671	633	260	102	1,964	1,695	1,093	312	780
10 Year Total	1908-1917		1,404	5,273	2,003	1,456	328	163	56	1,079	909	605	169	630
5 Year Total	1908-1912		732	2,807	1,075	767	182	90	36	576	516	233	-	324
Best Single Year	1911		146	591	248	169	47	24	8	147	127	44	-	83
2nd Best Year	1915		156	563	208	161	31	13	3	144	99	118	43	96
3rd Best Year	1909		156	573	216	164	33	10	9	116	107	48	-	76
4th Best Year	1912		140	553	227	167	30	23	7	119	83	43	-	61

(Left margin: Complete Career Statistics C; 10 Year Total; 5 Year Total)

Total Career Statistics & Adjusted Career, 10 year, 5 year, and Single Year Analysis

Cobb, Ty

CS	HBP	SF	GDP	AVG	OBP	SLG	TRP	RPA	TNB	TBA	TRP Rating	RPA Rating	TNB Rating	TBA Rating	TOP	Rating	Ranking
-	-	-	-	.240	.288	.300	34	.213	57	.356	9.77	39.82	9.34	39.26	98.20	25.04	
-	3	-	-	.320	.360	.406	79	.212	187	.503	22.70	39.79	30.66	55.40	148.55	37.88	
-	5	-	-	.350	.380	.473	216	.341	364	.574	62.07	63.84	59.67	63.28	248.86	63.45	
-	6	-	-	.324	.367	.475	196	.316	355	.572	56.32	59.14	58.20	63.00	236.66	60.34	
-	6	-	-	.377	.431	.517	223	.356	426	.679	64.08	66.64	69.84	74.88	275.44	70.23	
-	4	-	-	.385	.458	.554	197	.341	415	.719	56.61	63.98	68.03	79.27	267.89	68.30	
-	8	-	-	.420	.467	.621	274	.426	502	.781	78.74	79.85	82.30	86.05	326.93	83.35	
34	5	-	-	.410	.458	.586	202	.336	399	.664	58.05	62.98	65.41	73.17	259.61	66.19	
-	4	-	-	.390	.467	.535	137	.280	343	.700	39.37	52.39	56.23	77.15	225.14	57.40	
17	6	-	-	.368	.466	.513	126	.309	258	.632	36.21	57.87	42.30	69.69	206.06	52.54	
38	10	-	-	.369	.486	.487	243	.352	460	.666	69.83	65.90	75.41	73.37	284.50	72.54	
24	2	-	-	.371	.452	.493	181	.291	391	.629	52.01	54.53	64.10	69.28	239.92	61.17	
-	4	-	-	.383	.444	.566	209	.320	453	.694	60.06	59.97	74.26	76.46	270.75	69.03	
-	2	-	-	.382	.440	.515	147	.317	294	.634	42.24	59.36	48.20	69.83	219.64	56.00	
-	1	-	-	.384	.429	.515	162	.302	323	.603	46.55	56.63	52.95	66.42	222.55	56.74	
10	2	-	-	.334	.416	.451	149	.305	257	.527	42.82	57.21	42.13	58.04	200.20	51.04	
15	3	-	-	.389	.452	.596	225	.398	368	.650	64.66	74.49	60.33	71.66	271.13	69.13	
13	4	-	-	.401	.462	.565	198	.338	352	.602	56.90	63.42	57.70	66.32	244.34	62.30	
10	3	-	-	.340	.413	.469	191	.306	329	.526	54.89	57.26	53.93	58.02	224.10	57.14	
14	1	-	-	.338	.418	.450	193	.271	376	.529	55.46	50.86	61.64	58.28	226.25	57.68	
9	5	-	-	.378	.468	.598	199	.410	322	.664	57.18	76.88	52.79	73.17	260.03	66.30	
4	1	-	-	.339	.408	.511	110	.423	151	.581	31.61	79.28	24.75	64.01	199.65	50.90	
16	5	-	-	.357	.440	.482	197	.351	314	.559	56.61	65.68	51.48	61.58	235.35	60.00	
8	4	-	-	.323	.389	.431	94	.240	187	.478	27.01	45.05	30.66	52.71	155.43	39.63	
212	94	-	-	.367	.433	.513	4,182	.327	7,883	.617	93.54	78.41	93.21	82.04	347.20	88.67	5
166	74	-	-	.367	.433	.513	3,274	.327	6,172	.617	78.41	78.41	82.04	82.04	320.90	80.22	24
185	82	-	-	.367	.433	.513	3,659	.327	6,897	.617	70.05	78.41	73.30	82.04	303.81	75.95	34
113	55	-	-	.380	.449	.536	1,988	.335	4,002	.675	67.53	76.41	80.73	85.11	309.78	79.46	25
34	29	-	-	.383	.436	.550	1,092	.356	2,097	.683	71.75	76.09	80.41	82.84	311.09	79.70	36
-	8	-	-	.420	.467	.621	274	.426	502	.781	78.74	79.85	82.30	86.05	326.93	83.35	33
38	10	-	-	.369	.486	.487	243	.352	460	.666	69.83	65.90	75.41	73.37	284.50	72.54	193
-	6	-	-	.377	.431	.517	223	.356	426	.679	64.08	66.64	69.84	74.88	275.44	70.23	292
34	5	-	-	.410	.458	.586	202	.336	399	.664	58.05	62.98	65.41	73.17	259.61	66.19	353

Complete Career Statistics C

Complete Career Statistics C

Total Career Statistics & Adjusted Career, 10 year, 5 year, and Single Year Analysis

Collins, Eddie: *Edward Trowbridge Collins, Sr.; b. May 2, 1887, Millerton, NY*

Rating Category	Year	Ranked Seasons & Adjustment	G	AB	H	1B	2B	3B	HR	RUN	RBI	BB	SO	SB
	1906		6	17	4	4	-	-	-	1	-	-	-	1
	1907		14	23	6	5	-	1	-	-	2	-	-	-
	1908		102	330	90	64	18	7	1	39	40	16	-	8
10 Year Total	1909		153	572	198	155	30	10	3	104	56	62	-	67
	1910		153	581	188	154	16	15	3	81	81	49	-	81
5 Year Total	1911		132	493	180	142	22	13	3	92	73	62	-	38
	1912	1st	153	543	189	153	25	11	-	137	64	101	-	63
	1913		148	534	184	145	23	13	3	125	73	85	37	55
	1914		152	526	181	142	23	14	2	122	85	97	31	58
	1915		155	521	173	137	22	10	4	118	77	119	27	46
	1916		155	545	168	137	14	17	-	87	52	86	36	40
	1917		156	564	163	133	18	12	-	91	67	89	16	53
	1918		97	330	91	79	8	2	2	51	30	73	13	22
	1919		140	518	165	135	19	7	4	87	80	68	27	33
	1920		153	602	224	170	38	13	3	117	76	69	19	19
	1921		139	526	177	145	20	10	2	79	58	66	11	12
	1922		154	598	194	161	20	12	1	92	69	73	16	20
	1923		145	505	182	150	22	5	5	89	67	84	8	47
	1924		152	556	194	154	27	7	6	108	86	89	16	42
	1925		118	425	147	115	26	3	3	80	80	87	8	19
	1926		106	375	129	92	32	4	1	66	62	62	8	13
	1927		95	225	76	62	12	1	1	50	15	60	9	6
	1928		36	33	10	7	3	-	-	3	7	4	4	-
	1929		9	7	-	-	-	-	-	-	-	2	-	-
	1930		3	2	1	1	-	-	-	1	-	-	-	-
Career Total	1906-1930		2,826	9,951	3,314	2,642	438	187	47	1,820	1,300	1,503	286	743
Career Adj. to 10,000 BO	1906-1930	0.867227474	2,451	8,630	2,874	2,291	380	162	41	1,578	1,127	1,303	248	644
Career Adj. to 10,000 AB	1906-1930	1.004924128	2,840	10,000	3,330	2,655	440	188	47	1,829	1,306	1,510	287	747
10 Year Total	1909-1918		1,454	5,209	1,715	1,377	201	117	20	1,008	658	823	160	523
5 Year Total	1911-1915		740	2,617	907	719	115	61	12	594	372	464	95	260
Best Single Year	1912		153	543	189	153	25	11	-	137	64	101	-	63

Total Career Statistics & Adjusted Career, 10 year, 5 year, and Single Year Analysis

Collins, Eddie

CS	HBP	SF	GDP	AVG	OBP	SLG	Total Offensive Production Statistics				TRP Rating	RPA Rating	TNB Rating	TBA Rating	TOP Composite		
							TRP	RPA	TNB	TBA					TOP	Rating	Ranking
-	-	-	-	.235	.235	.235	1	.059	5	.294	0.29	11.02	0.82	32.42	44.55	11.36	
-	-	-	-	.261	.261	.348	2	.087	8	.348	0.57	16.29	1.31	38.34	56.52	14.41	
-	3	-	-	.273	.312	.379	79	.226	152	.436	22.70	42.42	24.92	48.00	138.04	35.19	
-	6	-	-	.346	.416	.449	160	.250	392	.613	45.98	46.85	64.26	67.51	224.59	57.26	
-	6	-	-	.324	.382	.418	162	.255	379	.596	46.55	47.73	62.13	65.68	222.09	56.62	
-	15	-	-	.365	.451	.481	165	.289	352	.618	47.41	54.24	57.70	68.06	227.42	57.98	
-	-	-	-	.348	.450	.435	201	.312	400	.621	57.76	58.48	65.57	68.46	250.27	63.81	
-	7	-	-	.345	.441	.453	198	.316	389	.621	56.90	59.27	63.77	68.49	248.42	63.34	
30	6	-	-	.344	.452	.452	207	.329	369	.587	59.48	61.67	60.49	64.66	246.30	62.80	
30	5	-	-	.332	.460	.436	195	.302	367	.569	56.03	56.65	60.16	62.71	235.56	60.06	
21	3	-	-	.308	.405	.396	139	.219	324	.511	39.94	41.08	53.11	56.32	190.46	48.56	
-	3	-	-	.289	.389	.363	158	.241	350	.534	45.40	45.13	57.38	58.80	206.71	52.70	
-	-	-	-	.276	.407	.330	81	.201	204	.506	23.28	37.66	33.44	55.79	150.17	38.29	
-	2	-	-	.319	.400	.405	167	.284	313	.532	47.99	53.22	51.31	58.67	211.19	53.84	
8	2	-	-	.372	.438	.493	193	.287	379	.563	55.46	53.74	62.13	62.07	233.39	59.51	
10	2	-	-	.337	.412	.424	137	.231	293	.493	39.37	43.22	48.03	54.36	184.98	47.16	
12	3	-	-	.324	.401	.403	161	.239	325	.482	46.26	44.76	53.28	53.14	197.45	50.34	
29	4	-	-	.360	.455	.453	156	.263	335	.565	44.83	49.29	54.92	62.26	211.30	53.87	
17	3	-	-	.349	.441	.455	194	.299	370	.571	55.75	56.10	60.66	62.93	235.43	60.03	
6	4	-	-	.346	.461	.442	160	.310	292	.566	45.98	58.10	47.87	62.37	214.32	54.64	
8	3	-	-	.344	.441	.459	128	.291	242	.550	36.78	54.51	39.67	60.62	191.58	48.85	
2	-	-	-	.338	.477	.413	65	.228	157	.551	18.68	42.74	25.74	60.71	147.87	37.70	
-	-	-	-	.303	.378	.394	10	.270	17	.459	2.87	50.64	2.79	50.64	106.94	27.27	
-	-	-	-	.000	.222	.000	-	.000	2	.222	-	-	0.33	24.49	24.82	6.33	
-	-	-	-	.500	.500	.500	1	.500	1	.500	0.29	93.69	0.16	55.11	149.25	38.05	
173	77	-	-	.333	.424	.429	3,120	.271	6,417	.556	69.78	64.79	75.88	73.97	284.42	72.64	31
150	67	-	-	.333	.424	.429	2,706	.271	5,565	.556	64.79	64.79	73.97	73.97	277.53	69.38	97
174	77	-	-	.333	.424	.429	3,135	.271	6,449	.556	60.03	64.79	68.53	73.97	267.32	66.83	95
81	51	-	-	.329	.426	.424	1,666	.274	3,526	.580	56.59	62.46	71.13	73.14	263.31	67.54	95
60	33	-	-	.347	.451	.451	966	.310	1,877	.603	63.47	66.34	71.97	73.08	274.86	70.42	98
-	-	-	-	.348	.450	.435	201	.312	400	.621	57.76	58.48	65.57	68.46	250.27	63.81	364

Complete Career Statistics C

Total Career Statistics & Adjusted Career, 10 year, 5 year, and Single Year Analysis

Conner, Roger: *Roger Conner, b. July 1, 1857, Waterbury, CT*

Rating Category	Year	Ranked Seasons & Adjustment	G	AB	H	1B	2B	3B	HR	RUN	RBI	BB	SO	SB
	1880		83	340	113	83	17	10	3	53	47	13	21	-
	1881		84	361	104	79	17	6	2	54	31	15	20	-
	1882		79	339	111	68	22	17	4	63	42	13	20	-
	1883		96	401	145	102	28	14	1	80	50	25	16	-
	1884		112	462	146	111	27	4	4	93	82	38	32	-
	1885		110	455	169	130	23	15	1	102	65	51	8	-
	1886		118	485	172	116	30	19	7	105	71	41	15	17
	1887	3rd	127	546	209	144	26	22	17	113	104	75	50	43
	1888		134	481	140	94	15	17	14	98	71	73	44	27
	1889	2nd	131	496	157	95	32	17	13	117	130	93	46	21
	1890	1st	123	484	180	126	25	15	14	134	103	88	32	23
	1891		129	477	140	94	27	12	7	110	94	83	39	32
	1892		153	558	159	105	31	11	12	122	73	116	39	20
	1893		135	490	158	114	25	8	11	111	105	91	26	29
	1894		121	462	145	77	34	26	8	93	93	59	17	15
	1895		104	402	131	88	28	7	8	78	77	63	10	8
	1896		126	485	137	101	19	6	11	68	72	52	14	14
	1897		22	83	19	14	3	1	1	13	12	13	-	3
Career Total	1880-1897		1,987	7,807	2,535	1,741	429	227	138	1,607	1,322	1,002	449	252
Career Adj. to 10,000 BO	1880-1897	1.130326664	2,246	8,824	2,865	1,968	485	257	156	1,816	1,494	1,133	508	285
Career Adj. to 10,000 AB	1880-1897	1.280901755	2,545	10,000	3,247	2,230	550	291	177	2,058	1,693	1,283	575	323
10 Year Total	1885-1894		1,281	4,934	1,629	1,095	268	162	104	1,105	909	770	316	227
5 Year Total	1889-1893		671	2,505	794	534	140	63	57	594	505	471	182	125
Best Single Year	1890		123	484	180	126	25	15	14	134	103	88	32	23
2nd Best Year	1889		131	496	157	95	32	17	13	117	130	93	46	21
3rd Best Year	1887		127	546	209	144	26	22	17	113	104	75	50	43

10 Year Total

5 Year Total

Total Career Statistics & Adjusted Career, 10 year, 5 year, and Single Year Analysis

Conner, Roger

CS	HBP	SF	GDP	AVG	OBP	SLG	Total Offensive Production Statistics				TRP Rating	RPA Rating	TNB Rating	TBA Rating	TOP Composite		
							TRP	RPA	TNB	TBA					TOP	Rating	Ranking
-	-	-	-	.332	.357	.468	100	.283	172	.487	28.74	53.08	28.20	53.70	163.72	41.74	
-	-	-	-	.288	.316	.385	85	.226	154	.410	24.43	42.36	25.25	45.14	137.17	34.97	
-	-	-	-	.327	.352	.528	105	.298	192	.545	30.17	55.90	31.48	60.12	177.66	45.30	
-	-	-	-	.362	.399	.509	130	.305	229	.538	37.36	57.18	37.54	59.25	191.33	48.78	
-	-	-	-	.316	.368	.418	175	.350	231	.462	50.29	65.58	37.87	50.92	204.66	52.18	
-	-	-	-	.371	.435	.495	167	.330	276	.545	47.99	61.84	45.25	60.12	215.19	54.87	
-	-	-	-	.355	.405	.538	176	.335	319	.606	50.57	62.70	52.30	66.84	232.41	59.25	
-	8	-	-	.383	.464	.604	217	.345	456	.725	62.36	64.65	74.75	79.90	281.66	71.81	
-	4	-	-	.291	.389	.480	169	.303	335	.600	48.56	56.75	54.92	66.17	226.40	57.72	
-	2	-	-	.317	.426	.528	247	.418	378	.640	70.98	78.31	61.97	70.49	281.75	71.83	
-	1	-	-	.372	.469	.572	237	.414	389	.679	68.10	77.50	63.77	74.82	284.20	72.46	
-	4	-	-	.294	.402	.444	204	.362	331	.587	58.62	67.78	54.26	64.68	245.34	62.55	
-	6	-	-	.285	.413	.444	195	.287	390	.574	56.03	53.73	63.93	63.21	236.91	60.40	
-	3	-	-	.322	.432	.473	216	.370	355	.608	62.07	69.31	58.20	67.00	256.57	65.41	
-	6	-	-	.314	.398	.552	186	.353	335	.636	53.45	66.13	54.92	70.06	244.56	62.35	
-	2	-	-	.326	.420	.490	155	.332	270	.578	44.54	62.19	44.26	63.72	214.72	54.74	
-	2	-	-	.282	.354	.414	140	.260	269	.499	40.23	48.67	44.10	55.00	188.00	47.93	
-	-	-	-	.229	.333	.325	25	.260	43	.448	7.18	48.80	7.05	49.37	112.40	28.66	
-	38	-	-	.325	.404	.491	2,929	.331	5,124	.579	65.51	79.28	60.59	76.99	282.36	72.11	34
-	43	-	-	.325	.404	.491	3,311	.331	5,792	.579	79.28	79.28	76.99	76.99	312.53	78.13	42
-	49	-	-	.325	.404	.491	3,752	.331	6,563	.579	71.83	79.28	69.75	76.99	297.85	74.46	42
-	34	-	-	.330	.424	.513	2,014	.351	3,564	.621	68.41	80.04	71.90	78.37	298.72	76.62	42
-	16	-	-	.317	.428	.491	1,099	.367	1,843	.616	72.21	78.55	70.67	74.68	296.10	75.86	57
-	1	-	-	.372	.469	.572	237	.414	389	.679	68.10	77.50	63.77	74.82	284.20	72.46	197
-	2	-	-	.317	.426	.528	247	.418	378	.640	70.98	78.31	61.97	70.49	281.75	71.83	223
-	8	-	-	.383	.464	.604	217	.345	456	.725	62.36	64.65	74.75	79.90	281.66	71.81	224

Complete Career Statistics C

Total Career Statistics & Adjusted Career, 10 year, 5 year, and Single Year Analysis

Cravath, Gavvy: *Clifford Carlton Cactus Cravath; b. March 23, 1881, Escondido, CA*

Rating Category	Year	Ranked Seasons & Adjustment	G	AB	H	1B	2B	3B	HR	RUN	RBI	BB	SO	SB
	1908		94	277	71	49	10	11	1	43	34	38	-	6
	1909		23	56	9	8	-	-	1	7	9	20	-	3
	1912		130	436	124	74	30	9	11	63	70	47	77	15
5 Year Total	1913	1st	147	525	179	112	34	14	19	78	128	55	63	10
	1914		149	499	149	95	27	8	19	76	100	83	72	14
	1915		150	522	149	87	31	7	24	89	115	86	77	11
	1916		137	448	127	87	21	8	11	70	70	64	89	9
	1917		140	503	141	84	29	16	12	70	83	70	57	6
	1918		121	426	99	59	27	5	8	43	54	54	46	7
	1919		83	214	73	38	18	5	12	34	45	35	21	8
	1920		46	45	13	7	5	-	1	2	11	9	12	-
Career Total	1908-1920		1,220	3,951	1,134	700	232	83	119	575	719	561	514	89
Career Adj. to 10,000 BO	1908-1920	2.202643172	2,687	8,703	2,498	1,542	511	183	262	1,267	1,584	1,236	1,132	196
Career Adj. to 10,000 AB	1908-1920	2.531004809	3,088	10,000	2,870	1,772	587	210	301	1,455	1,820	1,420	1,301	225
10 Year Total	n/a	n/a												
5 Year Total	1913-1916		723	2,497	745	465	142	53	85	383	496	358	358	50
Best Single Year	1913		147	525	179	112	34	14	19	78	128	55	63	10

Total Career Statistics & Adjusted Career, 10 year, 5 year, and Single Year Analysis

Cravath, Gavvy

CS	HBP	SF	GDP	AVG	OBP	SLG	Total Offensive Production Statistics				TRP Rating	RPA Rating	TNB Rating	TBA Rating	TOP Composite		
							TRP	RPA	TNB	TBA					TOP	Rating	Ranking
-	4	-	-	.256	.354	.383	77	.241	154	.483	22.13	45.23	25.25	53.21	145.81	37.18	
-	-	-	-	.161	.382	.214	16	.211	35	.461	4.60	39.45	5.74	50.76	100.54	25.63	
-	3	-	-	.284	.358	.470	133	.274	270	.556	38.22	51.28	44.26	61.23	194.99	49.71	
-	3	-	-	.341	.407	.568	206	.353	366	.628	59.20	66.21	60.00	69.19	254.60	64.91	
-	3	-	-	.299	.402	.499	176	.301	349	.597	50.57	56.37	57.21	65.75	229.91	58.62	
9	6	-	-	.285	.393	.510	204	.332	360	.586	58.62	62.26	59.02	64.62	244.51	62.34	
-	5	-	-	.283	.379	.440	140	.271	275	.532	40.23	50.74	45.08	58.62	194.68	49.63	
-	1	-	-	.280	.369	.473	153	.267	315	.549	43.97	49.95	51.64	60.48	206.03	52.53	
-	1	-	-	.232	.320	.376	97	.202	222	.462	27.87	37.79	36.39	50.87	152.92	38.99	
-	2	-	-	.341	.438	.640	79	.315	182	.725	22.70	58.98	29.84	79.92	191.43	48.81	
-	-	-	-	.289	.407	.467	13	.241	30	.556	3.74	45.11	4.92	61.23	114.99	29.32	
9	28	-	-	.287	.380	.478	1,294	.285	2,558	.563	28.94	68.25	30.25	74.89	202.33	51.67	127
20	62	-	-	.287	.380	.478	2,850	.285	5,634	.563	68.25	68.25	74.89	74.89	286.29	71.57	87
23	71	-	-	.287	.380	.478	3,275	.285	6,474	.563	62.70	68.25	68.81	74.89	274.65	68.66	87
9	18	-	-	.298	.390	.500	879	.306	1,665	.580	57.75	65.43	63.84	70.26	257.28	65.91	123
-	3	-	-	.341	.407	.568	206	.353	366	.628	59.20	66.21	60.00	69.19	254.60	64.91	362

Complete Career Statistics C

Complete Career Statistics C

	Total Career Statistics & Adjusted Career, 10 year, 5 year, and Single Year Analysis

Crawford, Sam: *Samuel Earl "Wahoo Sam" Crawford; b. April 18, 1880, Wahoo, NE*

Rating Category		Year	Ranked Seasons & Adjustment	G	AB	H	1B	2B	3B	HR	RUN	RBI	BB	SO	SB
		1899		31	127	39	28	2	8	1	25	20	2	-	3
		1900		96	385	104	68	14	15	7	67	59	28	-	14
		1901		124	523	175	121	22	16	16	89	104	37	-	13
		1902		140	555	185	143	16	23	3	94	78	47	-	16
		1903		137	545	181	129	23	25	4	93	89	25	-	18
		1904		150	571	141	101	21	17	2	46	73	44	-	20
10 Year Total		1905		154	575	171	115	40	10	6	73	75	50	-	22
		1906		145	563	166	123	25	16	2	65	72	38	-	24
		1907		144	582	188	133	34	17	4	102	81	37	-	18
	5 Year Total	1908		152	591	184	128	33	16	7	102	80	37	-	15
		1909		156	589	185	130	35	14	6	83	97	47	-	30
		1910		154	588	170	120	26	19	5	83	120	37	-	20
		1911	1st	146	574	217	160	36	14	7	109	115	61	-	37
		1912		149	581	189	134	30	21	4	81	109	42	-	41
		1913		153	610	193	129	32	23	9	78	83	52	28	13
		1914		157	582	183	127	22	26	8	74	104	69	31	25
		1915		156	612	183	129	31	19	4	81	112	66	29	24
		1916		100	322	92	68	11	13	-	41	42	37	10	10
		1917		61	104	18	12	4	-	2	6	12	4	6	-
Career Total		1899-1917		2,505	9,579	2,964	2,098	457	312	97	1,392	1,525	760	104	363
Career Adj. to 10,000 BO		1899-1917	0.965064659	2,417	9,244	2,860	2,025	441	301	94	1,343	1,472	733	100	350
Career Adj. to 10,000 AB		1899-1917	1.043950308	2,615	10,000	3,094	2,190	477	326	101	1,453	1,592	793	109	379
10 Year Total		1905-1914		1,510	5,835	1,846	1,299	313	176	58	850	936	470	59	245
5 Year Total		1908-1912		757	2,923	945	672	160	84	29	458	521	224	-	143
Best Single Year		1911		146	574	217	160	36	14	7	109	115	61	-	37

Total Career Statistics & Adjusted Career, 10 year, 5 year, and Single Year Analysis

Crawford, Sam

CS	HBP	SF	GDP	AVG	OBP	SLG	TRP	RPA	TNB	TBA	TRP Rating	RPA Rating	TNB Rating	TBA Rating	TOP	Rating	Ranking
-	-	-	-	.307	.318	.472	45	.349	65	.504	12.93	65.37	10.66	55.53	144.49	36.84	
-	3	-	-	.270	.325	.439	126	.303	214	.514	36.21	56.76	35.08	56.70	184.74	47.10	
-	3	-	-	.335	.382	.530	193	.343	330	.586	55.46	64.24	54.10	64.60	238.40	60.78	
-	1	-	-	.333	.386	.461	172	.285	320	.531	49.43	53.45	52.46	58.49	213.82	54.52	
-	2	-	-	.332	.364	.488	182	.318	311	.544	52.30	59.62	50.98	59.92	222.83	56.81	
-	-	-	-	.247	.301	.354	119	.193	266	.433	34.20	36.26	43.61	47.67	161.73	41.23	
-	3	-	-	.297	.357	.433	148	.236	324	.516	42.53	44.16	53.11	56.86	196.67	50.14	
-	1	-	-	.295	.341	.407	137	.228	292	.485	39.37	42.64	47.87	53.46	183.34	46.74	
-	2	-	-	.323	.366	.460	183	.295	325	.523	52.59	55.22	53.28	57.68	218.76	55.78	
-	3	-	-	.311	.355	.457	182	.288	325	.515	52.30	54.05	53.28	56.77	216.39	55.17	
-	1	-	-	.314	.366	.452	180	.283	344	.540	51.72	52.95	56.39	59.52	220.59	56.24	
-	1	-	-	.289	.332	.423	203	.324	307	.490	58.33	60.76	50.33	54.05	223.48	56.98	
-	-	-	-	.378	.438	.526	224	.353	400	.630	64.37	66.10	65.57	69.43	265.47	67.68	
-	2	-	-	.325	.373	.470	190	.304	358	.573	54.60	56.96	58.69	63.13	233.38	59.50	
-	-	-	-	.316	.370	.489	161	.243	363	.548	46.26	45.57	59.51	60.43	211.78	53.99	
16	1	-	-	.314	.388	.483	178	.273	360	.552	51.15	51.16	59.02	60.85	222.18	56.65	
14	-	-	-	.299	.367	.431	193	.285	340	.501	55.46	53.34	55.74	55.27	219.81	56.04	
-	-	-	-	.286	.359	.401	83	.231	176	.490	23.85	43.32	28.85	54.03	150.06	38.26	
-	-	-	-	.173	.204	.269	18	.167	32	.296	5.17	31.23	5.25	32.66	74.30	18.94	
30	23	-	-	.309	.362	.453	2,917	.282	5,452	.526	65.24	67.41	64.47	69.94	267.06	68.20	63
29	22	-	-	.309	.362	.453	2,815	.282	5,262	.526	67.41	67.41	69.94	69.94	274.70	68.67	103
31	24	-	-	.309	.362	.453	3,045	.282	5,692	.526	58.30	67.41	60.49	69.94	256.14	64.03	116
16	14	-	-	.316	.369	.460	1,786	.283	3,398	.538	60.67	64.45	68.55	67.85	261.52	67.08	100
-	7	-	-	.323	.373	.465	979	.310	1,734	.550	64.32	66.38	66.49	66.66	263.84	67.60	113
-	-	-	-	.378	.438	.526	224	.353	400	.630	64.37	66.10	65.57	69.43	265.47	67.68	332

Complete Career Statistics   C

Complete Career Statistics   D

Total Career Statistics & Adjusted Career, 10 year, 5 year, and Single Year Analysis

Dawson, Andre: *Andre Nolan Dawson, b. July 10, 1954, Miami, FL*

Rating Category	Year	Ranked Seasons & Adjustment	G	AB	H	1B	2B	3B	HR	RUN	RBI	BB	SO	SB
	1976		24	85	20	15	4	1	-	9	7	5	13	1
	1977		139	525	148	94	26	9	19	64	65	34	93	21
	1978		157	609	154	97	24	8	25	84	72	30	128	28
	1979		155	639	176	115	24	12	25	90	92	27	115	35
	1980		151	577	178	113	41	7	17	96	87	44	69	34
5 Year Total	1981		103	394	119	71	21	3	24	71	64	35	50	26
	1982		148	608	183	116	37	7	23	107	83	34	96	39
10 Year Total	1983		159	633	189	111	36	10	32	104	113	38	81	25
	1984		138	533	132	86	23	6	17	73	86	41	80	13
	1985		139	529	135	83	27	2	23	65	91	29	92	13
	1986		130	496	141	87	32	2	20	65	78	37	79	18
	1987	1st	153	621	178	103	24	2	49	90	137	32	103	11
	1988		157	591	179	116	31	8	24	78	79	37	73	12
	1989		118	416	105	60	18	6	21	62	77	35	62	8
	1990		147	529	164	104	28	5	27	72	100	42	65	16
	1991		149	563	153	97	21	4	31	69	104	22	80	4
	1992		143	542	150	99	27	2	22	60	90	30	70	6
	1993		121	461	126	83	29	1	13	44	67	17	49	2
	1994		75	292	70	36	18	-	16	34	48	9	53	2
	1995		79	226	58	37	10	3	8	30	37	9	45	-
	1996		42	58	16	12	2	-	2	6	14	2	13	-
Career Total	1976-1996		2,627	9,927	2,774	1,735	503	98	438	1,373	1,591	589	1,509	314
Career Adj. to 10,000 BO	1976-1996	0.912242	2,396	9,056	2,531	1,583	459	89	400	1,253	1,451	537	1,377	286
Career Adj. to 10,000 AB	1976-1996	1.007354	2,646	10,000	2,794	1,748	507	99	441	1,383	1,603	593	1,520	316
10 Year Total	1979-1988		1,433	5,621	1,610	1,001	296	59	254	839	910	354	838	226
5 Year Total	1979-1983		716	2,851	845	526	159	39	121	468	439	178	411	159
Best Single Year	1987		153	621	178	103	24	2	49	90	137	32	103	11

Total Career Statistics & Adjusted Career, 10 year, 5 year, and Single Year Analysis

Dawson, Andre

CS	HBP	SF	GDP	AVG	OBP	SLG	Total Offensive Production Statistics				TRP Rating	RPA Rating	TNB Rating	TBA Rating	TOP Composite		
							TRP	RPA	TNB	TBA					TOP	Rating	Ranking
2	-	-	-	.235	.278	.306	16	.178	30	.333	4.60	33.31	4.92	36.74	79.57	20.29	
7	2	4	6	.282	.326	.474	129	.226	299	.524	37.07	42.33	49.02	57.71	186.13	47.46	
11	12	5	7	.253	.299	.442	156	.235	328	.495	44.83	44.09	53.77	54.53	197.21	50.28	
10	6	4	10	.275	.309	.468	182	.265	357	.520	52.30	49.71	58.52	57.36	217.89	55.55	
9	6	10	9	.308	.358	.492	183	.283	359	.556	52.59	53.08	58.85	61.25	225.77	57.56	
4	7	5	6	.302	.365	.553	135	.302	282	.631	38.79	56.59	46.23	69.53	211.15	53.83	
10	8	6	8	.301	.343	.498	190	.286	374	.563	54.60	53.62	61.31	62.08	231.61	59.05	
11	9	18	14	.299	.338	.539	217	.305	402	.565	62.36	57.11	65.90	62.23	247.59	63.13	
5	2	6	12	.248	.301	.409	159	.268	269	.453	45.69	50.16	44.10	49.91	189.86	48.41	
4	4	7	12	.255	.295	.444	156	.269	277	.477	44.83	50.31	45.41	52.55	193.10	49.23	
12	6	6	13	.284	.338	.478	143	.256	286	.513	41.09	48.02	46.89	56.49	192.49	49.08	
3	7	2	15	.287	.328	.568	227	.335	400	.591	65.23	62.83	65.57	65.12	258.75	65.97	
4	4	7	13	.303	.344	.504	157	.241	347	.532	45.11	45.12	56.89	58.66	205.78	52.47	
5	1	7	16	.252	.307	.476	139	.293	237	.499	39.94	54.83	38.85	54.99	188.62	48.09	
2	2	8	12	.310	.358	.535	172	.290	341	.575	49.43	54.35	55.90	63.38	223.05	56.87	
5	5	6	10	.272	.302	.488	173	.285	301	.497	49.71	53.49	49.34	54.74	207.29	52.85	
2	4	6	13	.277	.316	.456	150	.252	285	.479	43.10	47.24	46.72	52.79	189.86	48.41	
1	13	7	18	.273	.313	.425	111	.215	227	.440	31.90	40.31	37.21	48.49	157.90	40.26	
2	4	1	15	.240	.271	.466	82	.255	149	.464	23.56	47.87	24.43	51.16	147.02	37.48	
-	8	3	7	.257	.305	.434	67	.265	115	.455	19.25	49.62	18.85	50.10	137.83	35.14	
-	1	-	1	.276	.311	.414	20	.323	27	.435	5.75	60.45	4.43	48.00	118.62	30.24	
109	111	118	217	.279	.323	.482	2,964	.270	5,692	.519	66.29	64.75	67.31	69.02	267.37	68.28	62
99	101	108	198	.279	.323	.482	2,704	.270	5,192	.519	64.75	64.75	69.02	69.02	267.53	66.88	117
110	112	119	219	.279	.323	.482	2,986	.270	5,734	.519	57.16	64.75	60.94	69.02	251.87	62.97	120
72	59	71	112	.286	.331	.496	1,749	.281	3,353	.539	59.41	64.15	67.64	68.05	259.25	66.50	106
44	36	43	47	.296	.341	.507	907	.287	1,774	.562	59.59	61.48	68.02	68.17	257.26	65.91	124
3	7	2	15	.287	.328	.568	227	.335	400	.591	65.23	62.83	65.57	65.12	258.75	65.97	355

Complete Career Statistics D

Total Career Statistics & Adjusted Career, 10 year, 5 year, and Single Year Analysis

Delahanty, Ed: *Edward James "Big Ed" Delahanty, b. Oct. 30, 1867, Cleveland, OH*

Rating Category	Year	Ranked Seasons & Adjustment	G	AB	H	1B	2B	3B	HR	RUN	RBI	BB	SO	SB
	1888		74	290	66	53	11	1	1	40	31	12	26	38
	1889		54	246	72	56	13	3	-	37	27	14	17	19
	1890		115	513	152	110	24	15	3	106	64	24	30	24
	1891		128	545	136	103	19	9	5	92	86	33	50	27
	1892		120	470	147	89	33	19	6	78	91	31	32	35
	1893	1st	132	588	218	148	31	20	19	145	146	47	20	36
	1894	2nd	114	497	199	143	36	16	4	149	131	60	16	29
	1895	3rd	116	481	192	126	47	8	11	148	106	86	31	46
	1896	4th	122	505	199	130	42	14	13	131	126	62	22	37
	1897		129	530	200	143	37	15	5	110	96	60	-	28
	1898		142	547	183	131	37	11	4	114	92	77	-	62
	1899	5th	145	573	234	160	56	9	9	133	137	55	-	38
	1900		130	542	173	129	32	10	2	82	109	41	-	14
	1901		138	538	192	130	38	16	8	106	108	65	-	29
	1902		123	474	178	111	43	14	10	103	93	62	-	16
	1903		43	154	52	39	11	1	1	22	21	12	-	3
Career Total	1888-1903		1,825	7,493	2,593	1,801	510	181	101	1,596	1,464	741	244	481
Career Adj. to 10,000 BO	1888-1903	1.200768	2,191	8,997	3,114	2,163	612	217	121	1,916	1,758	890	293	578
Career Adj. to 10,000 AB	1888-1903	1.334579	2,436	10,000	3,461	2,404	681	242	135	2,130	1,954	989	326	642
10 Year Total	1893-1902		1,291	5,275	1,968	1,351	399	133	85	1,221	1,144	615	89	335
5 Year Total	1893-1897		613	2,601	1,008	690	193	73	52	683	605	315	89	176
Best Single Year	1893		132	588	218	148	31	20	19	145	146	47	20	36
2nd Best Year	1894		114	497	199	143	36	16	4	149	131	60	16	29
3rd Best Year	1895		116	481	192	126	47	8	11	148	106	86	31	46
4th Best Year	1896		122	505	199	130	42	14	13	131	126	62	22	37
5th Best Year	1899		145	573	234	160	56	9	9	133	137	55	-	38

Total Career Statistics & Adjusted Career, 10 year, 5 year, and Single Year Analysis

Delahanty, Ed

CS	HBP	SF	GDP	AVG	OBP	SLG	Total Offensive Production Statistics				TRP Rating	RPA Rating	TNB Rating	TBA Rating	TOP Composite		
							TRP	RPA	TNB	TBA					TOP	Rating	Ranking
-	1	-	-	.228	.261	.283	71	.234	133	.439	20.40	43.91	21.80	48.38	134.49	34.29	
-	1	-	-	.293	.333	.370	64	.245	125	.479	18.39	45.95	20.49	52.78	137.62	35.09	
-	8	-	-	.296	.338	.419	170	.312	271	.497	48.85	58.45	44.43	54.80	206.53	52.66	
-	8	-	-	.250	.302	.345	178	.304	256	.437	51.15	56.92	41.97	48.15	198.18	50.53	
-	9	-	-	.313	.367	.502	169	.331	311	.610	48.56	62.09	50.98	67.21	228.85	58.35	
-	10	-	-	.371	.426	.588	291	.451	439	.681	83.62	84.54	71.97	75.01	315.14	80.35	
-	7	-	-	.400	.472	.561	280	.496	375	.665	80.46	93.03	61.48	73.28	308.24	78.59	
-	6	-	-	.399	.496	.599	254	.443	426	.743	72.99	83.06	69.84	81.94	307.83	78.48	
-	9	-	-	.394	.469	.610	257	.446	416	.722	73.85	83.61	68.20	79.60	305.25	77.83	
-	3	-	-	.377	.444	.532	206	.347	373	.629	59.20	65.09	61.15	69.33	254.76	64.95	
-	11	-	-	.335	.427	.464	206	.324	404	.636	59.20	60.79	66.23	70.12	256.33	65.35	
-	4	-	-	.408	.464	.585	270	.427	432	.684	77.59	80.05	70.82	75.34	303.79	77.46	
-	7	-	-	.319	.375	.426	191	.324	293	.497	54.89	60.66	48.03	54.73	218.31	55.66	
-	4	-	-	.357	.430	.532	214	.353	384	.633	61.49	66.06	62.95	69.72	260.23	66.35	
-	4	-	-	.376	.452	.589	196	.363	361	.669	56.32	68.01	59.18	73.68	257.20	65.57	
-	2	-	-	.338	.393	.442	43	.256	85	.506	12.36	47.96	13.93	55.76	130.01	33.15	
-	94	-	-	.346	.412	.503	3,060	.367	5,084	.610	68.44	87.99	60.12	81.15	297.69	76.02	21
-	113	-	-	.346	.412	.503	3,674	.367	6,105	.610	87.99	87.99	81.15	81.15	338.26	84.57	11
-	125	-	-	.346	.412	.503	4,084	.367	6,785	.610	78.19	87.99	72.11	81.15	319.43	79.86	17
-	65	-	-	.373	.445	.547	2,365	.397	3,903	.655	80.33	90.57	78.74	82.70	332.33	85.24	7
-	35	-	-	.388	.460	.578	1,288	.436	2,029	.688	84.63	93.33	77.80	83.36	339.12	86.88	8
-	10	-	-	.371	.426	.588	291	.451	439	.681	83.62	84.54	71.97	75.01	315.14	80.35	51
-	7	-	-	.400	.472	.561	280	.496	375	.665	80.46	93.03	61.48	73.28	308.24	78.59	72
-	6	-	-	.399	.496	.599	254	.443	426	.743	72.99	83.06	69.84	81.94	307.83	78.48	74
-	9	-	-	.394	.469	.610	257	.446	416	.722	73.85	83.61	68.20	79.60	305.25	77.83	81
-	4	-	-	.408	.464	.585	270	.427	432	.684	77.59	80.05	70.82	75.34	303.79	77.46	87

Complete Career Statistics   D

Complete Career Statistics   D

Total Career Statistics & Adjusted Career, 10 year, 5 year, and Single Year Analysis

Delgado, Carlos: *Carlos Juan Hernandez Delgado; b. June 25, 1972, Mayaguez, Puerto Rico*

Rating Category	Year	Ranked Seasons & Adjustment	G	AB	H	1B	2B	3B	HR	RUN	RBI	BB	SO	SB
	1993		2	1	-	-	-	-	-	-	-	1	-	-
	1994		43	130	28	17	2	-	9	17	24	25	46	1
	1995		37	91	15	9	3	-	3	7	11	6	26	-
	1996		138	488	132	77	28	2	25	68	92	58	139	-
	1997		153	519	136	61	42	3	30	79	91	64	133	-
	1998		142	530	155	73	43	1	38	94	115	73	139	3
	1999	3rd	152	573	156	73	39	-	44	113	134	86	141	1
	2000	1st	162	569	196	97	57	1	41	115	137	123	104	-
	2001		162	574	160	89	31	1	39	102	102	111	136	3
	2002		143	505	140	71	34	2	33	103	108	102	126	1
	2003	2nd	161	570	172	91	38	1	42	117	145	109	137	-
	2004		128	458	123	65	26	-	32	74	99	69	115	-
Career Total**	1993-2004		1,423	5,008	1,413	723	343	11	336	889	1,058	827	1,242	9
Career Adj. to 10,000 BO**	1993-2004	1.636393	2,329	8,195	2,312	1,183	561	18	550	1,455	1,731	1,353	2,032	15
Career Adj. to 10,000 AB**	1993-2004	1.996805	2,841	10,000	2,821	1,444	685	22	671	1,775	2,113	1,651	2,480	18
10 Year Total**	1995-2004		1,378	4,877	1,385	706	341	11	327	872	1,034	801	1,196	8
5 Year Total**	1999-2003		780	2,791	824	421	199	5	199	550	626	531	644	5
Best Single Year**	2000		162	569	196	97	57	1	41	115	137	123	104	-
2nd Best Year**	2003		161	570	172	91	38	1	42	117	145	109	137	-
3rd Best Year**	1999		152	573	156	73	39	-	44	113	134	86	141	1

10 Year Total — *5 Year Total*

Total Career Statistics & Adjusted Career, 10 year, 5 year, and Single Year Analysis

Delgado, Carlos

CS	HBP	SF	GDP	AVG	OBP	SLG	Total Offensive Production Statistics				TRP Rating	RPA Rating	TNB Rating	TBA Rating	TOP Composite		
							TRP	RPA	TNB	TBA					TOP	Rating	Ranking
-	-	-	-	.000	.500	.000	-	.000	1	.500	-	-	0.16	55.11	55.27	14.09	
1	3	1	5	.215	.352	.438	41	.250	85	.518	11.78	46.85	13.93	57.12	129.68	33.06	
-	-	2	1	.165	.212	.297	18	.180	33	.330	5.17	33.73	5.41	36.37	80.68	20.57	
-	9	8	13	.270	.353	.490	160	.278	306	.531	45.98	52.05	50.16	58.55	206.74	52.71	
3	8	4	6	.262	.350	.528	170	.283	343	.571	48.85	53.00	56.23	62.90	220.98	56.34	
-	11	6	8	.292	.385	.592	209	.333	401	.639	60.06	62.36	65.74	70.38	258.53	65.92	
1	15	7	11	.272	.377	.571	247	.357	428	.618	70.98	66.88	70.16	68.17	276.19	70.42	
1	15	4	12	.344	.470	.664	252	.349	515	.712	72.41	65.31	84.43	78.51	300.66	76.66	
-	16	3	9	.279	.408	.540	204	.286	440	.617	58.62	53.61	72.13	68.01	252.38	64.35	
-	13	8	8	.277	.406	.549	211	.332	393	.618	60.63	62.17	64.43	68.10	255.33	65.10	
-	19	7	9	.302	.426	.593	262	.367	466	.653	75.29	68.76	76.39	71.93	292.37	74.54	
1	13	11	11	.269	.372	.535	173	.308	326	.580	49.71	57.68	53.44	63.93	224.77	57.31	
7	122	61	93	.282	.392	.556	1,947	.319	3,737	.612	43.55	76.29	44.19	81.29	245.31	62.65	94
11	200	100	152	.282	.392	.556	3,186	.319	6,115	.612	76.29	76.29	81.29	81.29	315.16	78.79	35
14	244	122	186	.282	.392	.556	3,888	.319	7,462	.612	74.43	76.29	79.30	81.29	311.31	77.83	26
6	119	60	88	.284	.394	.560	1,906	.321	3,651	.614	64.74	73.11	73.65	77.49	288.99	74.13	53
2	78	29	49	.295	.418	.584	1,176	.338	2,242	.645	77.27	72.31	85.97	78.16	313.69	80.37	35
1	15	4	12	.344	.470	.664	252	.349	515	.712	72.41	65.31	84.43	78.51	300.66	76.66	96
-	19	7	9	.302	.426	.593	262	.367	466	.653	75.29	68.76	76.39	71.93	292.37	74.54	134
1	15	7	11	.272	.377	.571	247	.357	428	.618	70.98	66.88	70.16	68.17	276.19	70.42	279

Complete Career Statistics   D

Total Career Statistics & Adjusted Career, 10 year, 5 year, and Single Year Analysis

Dickey, Bill: *William Malcolm Dickey, b. June 6, 1907, Bastrop, LA*

Rating Category	Year	Ranked Seasons & Adjustment	G	AB	H	1B	2B	3B	HR	RUN	RBI	BB	SO	SB
	1928		10	15	3	1	1	1	-	1	2	-	2	-
	1929		130	447	145	99	30	6	10	60	65	14	16	4
	1930		109	366	124	87	25	7	5	55	65	21	14	7
	1931		130	477	156	123	17	10	6	65	78	39	20	2
	1932		108	423	131	92	20	4	15	66	84	34	13	2
	1933		130	478	152	106	24	8	14	58	97	47	14	3
	1934		104	395	127	87	24	4	12	56	72	38	18	-
	1935		120	448	125	79	26	6	14	54	81	35	11	1
	1936	1st	112	423	153	97	26	8	22	99	107	46	16	-
	1937		140	530	176	110	35	2	29	87	133	73	22	3
	1938		132	454	142	84	27	4	27	84	115	75	22	3
	1939		128	480	145	95	23	3	24	98	105	77	37	5
	1940		106	372	92	71	11	1	9	45	54	48	32	-
	1941		109	348	99	72	15	5	7	35	71	45	17	2
	1942		82	268	79	63	13	1	2	28	37	26	11	2
	1943		85	242	85	61	18	2	4	29	33	41	12	2
	1946		54	134	35	25	8	-	2	10	10	19	12	-
Career Total*	1928-1946		1,789	6,300	1,969	1,352	343	72	202	930	1,209	678	289	36
Career Adj. to 10,000 BO*	1928-1946	1.416832	2,535	8,926	2,790	1,916	486	102	286	1,318	1,713	961	409	51
Career Adj. to 10,000 AB*	1928-1946	1.587302	2,840	10,000	3,125	2,146	544	114	321	1,476	1,919	1,076	459	57
10 Year Total*	1930-1939		1,213	4,474	1,431	960	247	56	168	722	937	485	187	26
5 Year Total*	1935-1939		632	2,335	741	465	137	23	116	422	541	306	108	12
Best Single Year*	1936		112	423	153	97	26	8	22	99	107	46	16	-

Complete Career Statistics   D

10 Year Total

5 Year Total

Total Career Statistics & Adjusted Career, 10 year, 5 year, and Single Year Analysis

Dickey, Bill

CS	HBP	SF	GDP	AVG	OBP	SLG	Total Offensive Production Statistics				TRP Rating	RPA Rating	TNB Rating	TBA Rating	TOP Composite		
							TRP	RPA	TNB	TBA					TOP	Rating	Ranking
-	-	-	-	.200	.200	.400	3	.200	6	.400	0.86	37.48	0.98	44.09	83.41	21.27	
3	1	-	-	.324	.346	.485	125	.271	233	.504	35.92	50.70	38.20	55.58	180.40	45.99	
1	-	-	-	.339	.375	.486	120	.310	205	.530	34.48	58.10	33.61	58.38	184.57	47.06	
1	-	-	-	.327	.378	.442	143	.277	251	.486	41.09	51.93	41.15	53.61	187.78	47.88	
4	-	-	-	.310	.361	.482	150	.328	236	.516	43.10	61.50	38.69	56.92	200.21	51.05	
4	2	-	-	.318	.381	.490	155	.294	282	.535	44.54	55.11	46.23	58.98	204.86	52.23	
3	2	-	-	.322	.384	.494	128	.294	232	.533	36.78	55.14	38.03	58.78	188.73	48.12	
1	6	-	-	.279	.339	.458	135	.276	246	.503	38.79	51.73	40.33	55.45	186.30	47.50	
2	3	-	-	.362	.428	.617	206	.436	308	.653	59.20	81.78	50.49	71.92	263.39	67.15	
2	4	-	-	.332	.417	.570	220	.362	380	.626	63.22	67.91	62.30	69.00	262.43	66.91	
-	2	-	-	.313	.412	.568	199	.375	338	.637	57.18	70.22	55.41	70.16	252.97	64.50	
-	4	-	9	.302	.403	.513	203	.356	332	.582	58.33	66.73	54.43	64.19	243.69	62.13	
3	2	-	7	.247	.336	.355	99	.231	179	.417	28.45	43.24	29.34	45.99	147.02	37.48	
1	3	-	10	.284	.371	.417	106	.261	194	.478	30.46	48.92	31.80	52.66	163.85	41.77	
2	1	-	12	.295	.359	.373	65	.212	127	.414	18.68	39.67	20.82	45.59	124.76	31.81	
1	-	-	5	.351	.445	.492	62	.215	161	.559	17.82	40.34	26.39	61.61	146.16	37.27	
1	1	-	6	.261	.357	.366	20	.125	68	.425	5.75	23.42	11.15	46.84	87.16	22.22	
29	31	-	49	.313	.382	.486	2,139	.303	3,778	.535	47.84	72.57	44.67	71.15	236.24	60.33	99
41	44	-	69	.313	.382	.486	3,031	.303	5,353	.535	72.57	72.57	71.15	71.15	287.44	71.86	84
46	49	-	78	.313	.382	.486	3,395	.303	5,997	.535	65.00	72.57	63.73	71.15	272.46	68.11	90
18	23	-	9	.320	.389	.513	1,659	.332	2,810	.563	56.35	75.80	56.69	71.04	259.88	66.66	104
5	19	-	9	.317	.401	.545	963	.361	1,604	.601	63.27	77.16	61.50	72.86	274.80	70.40	99
2	3	-	-	.362	.428	.617	206	.436	308	.653	59.20	81.78	50.49	71.92	263.39	67.15	340

Complete Career Statistics D

Total Career Statistics & Adjusted Career, 10 year, 5 year, and Single Year Analysis

DiMaggio, Joe: *Joseph Paul "The Yankee Clipper" DiMaggio; b. Nov. 25, 1914, Martinez, CA*

Rating Category	Year	Ranked Seasons & Adjustment	G	AB	H	1B	2B	3B	HR	RUN	RBI	BB	SO	SB
	1936	6th	138	637	206	118	44	15	29	132	125	24	39	4
	1937	1st	151	621	215	119	35	15	46	151	167	64	37	3
	1938	3rd	145	599	194	117	32	13	32	129	140	59	21	6
	1939	4th	120	462	176	108	32	6	30	108	126	52	20	3
	1940		132	508	179	111	28	9	31	93	133	61	30	1
	1941	2nd	139	541	193	109	43	11	30	122	125	76	13	4
	1942		154	610	186	123	29	13	21	123	114	68	36	4
	1946		132	503	146	93	20	8	25	81	95	59	24	1
	1947		141	534	168	107	31	10	20	97	97	64	32	3
	1948	5th	153	594	190	114	26	11	39	110	155	67	30	1
	1949		76	272	94	60	14	6	14	58	67	55	18	-
	1950		139	525	158	83	33	10	32	114	122	80	33	-
	1951		116	415	109	71	22	4	12	72	71	61	36	-
Career Total*	1936-1951		1,736	6,821	2,214	1,333	389	131	361	1,390	1,537	790	369	30
Career Adj. to 10,000 BO*	1936-1951	1.284192	2,229	8,759	2,843	1,712	500	168	464	1,785	1,974	1,015	474	39
Career Adj. to 10,000 AB*	1936-1951	1.466061	2,545	10,000	3,246	1,954	570	192	529	2,038	2,253	1,158	541	44
10 Year Total*	1936-1948		1,405	5,609	1,853	1,119	320	111	303	1,146	1,277	594	282	30
5 Year Total*	1937-1941		687	2,731	957	564	170	54	169	603	691	312	121	17
Best Single Year*	1937		151	621	215	119	35	15	46	151	167	64	37	3
2nd Best Year*	1941		139	541	193	109	43	11	30	122	125	76	13	4
3rd Best Year*	1938		145	599	194	117	32	13	32	129	140	59	21	6
4th Best Year*	1939		120	462	176	108	32	6	30	108	126	52	20	3
5th Best Year*	1948		153	594	190	114	26	11	39	110	155	67	30	1
6th Best Year*	1936		138	637	206	118	44	15	29	132	125	24	39	4

The rows 1936–1941 are labeled **5 Year Total**; the rows 1936–1948 are labeled **10 Year Total**.

Complete Career Statistics D

Total Career Statistics & Adjusted Career, 10 year, 5 year, and Single Year Analysis

DiMaggio, Joe

CS	HBP	SF	GDP	AVG	OBP	SLG	Total Offensive Production Statistics				TRP Rating	RPA Rating	TNB Rating	TBA Rating	TOP Composite		
							TRP	RPA	TNB	TBA					TOP	Rating	Ranking
-	4	-	-	.323	.352	.576	257	.386	399	.600	73.85	72.42	65.41	66.13	277.81	70.83	
-	5	-	-	.346	.412	.673	318	.461	490	.710	91.38	86.36	80.33	78.27	336.33	85.75	
1	2	-	-	.324	.386	.581	269	.408	414	.627	77.30	76.37	67.87	69.13	290.67	74.11	
-	4	-	11	.381	.448	.671	234	.442	369	.698	67.24	82.89	60.49	76.88	287.50	73.30	
2	3	-	16	.352	.425	.626	226	.384	381	.648	64.94	72.02	62.46	71.41	270.84	69.05	
2	4	-	6	.357	.440	.643	247	.394	430	.686	70.98	73.82	70.49	75.59	290.87	74.16	
2	2	-	9	.305	.376	.498	237	.344	376	.546	68.10	64.45	61.64	60.15	254.34	64.85	
-	2	-	13	.290	.367	.511	176	.305	319	.553	50.57	57.16	52.30	60.93	220.96	56.34	
-	3	-	14	.315	.391	.522	194	.315	349	.567	55.75	59.11	57.21	62.54	234.61	59.82	
1	8	-	20	.320	.396	.598	265	.385	430	.624	76.15	72.07	70.49	68.78	287.50	73.30	
1	2	-	11	.346	.459	.596	125	.368	218	.641	35.92	68.89	35.74	70.67	211.21	53.85	
-	1	-	14	.301	.394	.585	236	.381	388	.626	67.82	71.33	63.61	68.97	271.72	69.28	
-	6	-	16	.263	.365	.422	143	.287	242	.486	41.09	53.81	39.67	53.56	188.13	47.97	
9	46	-	130	.325	.398	.579	2,927	.376	4,805	.617	65.47	90.01	56.82	82.02	294.31	75.16	22
12	59	-	167	.325	.398	.579	3,759	.376	6,171	.617	90.01	90.01	82.02	82.02	344.06	86.01	7
13	67	-	191	.325	.398	.579	4,291	.376	7,044	.617	82.16	90.01	74.87	82.02	329.05	82.26	11
8	37	-	89	.330	.398	.589	2,423	.383	3,957	.625	82.30	87.30	79.83	78.89	328.32	84.21	8
5	18	-	33	.350	.420	.638	1,294	.418	2,084	.674	85.02	89.44	79.91	81.66	336.03	86.09	10
-	5	-	-	.346	.412	.673	318	.461	490	.710	91.38	86.36	80.33	78.27	336.33	85.75	23
2	4	-	6	.357	.440	.643	247	.394	430	.686	70.98	73.82	70.49	75.59	290.87	74.16	141
1	2	-	-	.324	.386	.581	269	.408	414	.627	77.30	76.37	67.87	69.13	290.67	74.11	144
-	4	-	11	.381	.448	.671	234	.442	369	.698	67.24	82.89	60.49	76.88	287.50	73.30	168
1	8	-	20	.320	.396	.598	265	.385	430	.624	76.15	72.07	70.49	68.78	287.50	73.30	169
-	4	-	-	.323	.352	.576	257	.386	399	.600	73.85	72.42	65.41	66.13	277.81	70.83	252

Complete Career Statistics D

Total Career Statistics & Adjusted Career, 10 year, 5 year, and Single Year Analysis

Duffy, Hugh: *Hugh Duffy, b. Nov. 26, 1866, Cranston, RI*

Rating Category	Year	Ranked Seasons & Adjustment	G	AB	H	1B	2B	3B	HR	RUN	RBI	BB	SO	SB
	1888		71	298	84	62	11	4	7	60	41	9	32	13
	1889		136	584	182	142	21	7	12	144	89	46	30	52
	1890	5th	137	591	194	140	33	14	7	161	82	59	20	79
	1891	3rd	121	511	174	132	23	10	9	124	110	61	29	83
	1892		146	609	184	141	25	13	5	125	81	60	37	61
	1893	2nd	131	537	203	167	23	7	6	149	118	50	13	50
	1894	1st	124	539	236	155	50	13	18	160	145	66	15	49
	1895		131	540	190	150	25	6	9	113	100	63	16	42
	1896		131	533	161	131	17	8	5	93	113	52	19	45
	1897	4th	134	554	189	145	23	10	11	131	129	52	-	45
	1898		151	561	179	156	12	3	8	97	108	59	-	32
	1899		147	588	164	126	25	8	5	102	102	39	-	18
	1900		50	181	54	43	5	4	2	28	31	16	-	12
	1901		78	286	88	64	14	8	2	41	45	16	-	13
	1904		18	46	13	11	1	1	-	10	5	13	-	3
	1905		15	40	12	9	2	1	-	7	3	1	-	-
	1906		1	1	-	-	-	-	-	-	-	-	-	-
Career Total	1888-1906		1,722	6,999	2,307	1,774	310	117	106	1,545	1,302	662	211	597
Career Adj. to 10,000 BO	1888-1906	1.300390	2,239	9,101	3,000	2,307	403	152	138	2,009	1,693	861	274	776
Career Adj. to 10,000 AB	1888-1906	1.428776	2,460	10,000	3,296	2,535	443	167	151	2,207	1,860	946	301	853
10 Year Total	1889-1898		1,342	5,559	1,892	1,459	252	91	90	1,297	1,075	568	179	538
5 Year Total	1890-1894		659	2,787	991	735	154	57	45	719	536	296	114	322
Best Single Year	1894		124	539	236	155	50	13	18	160	145	66	15	49
2nd Best Year	1893		131	537	203	167	23	7	6	149	118	50	13	50
3rd Best Year	1891		121	511	174	132	23	10	9	124	110	61	29	83
4th Best Year	1897		134	554	189	145	23	10	11	131	129	52	-	45
5th Best Year	1890		137	591	194	140	33	14	7	161	82	59	20	79

5 Year Total

10 Year Total

Complete Career Statistics D

Total Career Statistics & Adjusted Career, 10 year, 5 year, and Single Year Analysis

Duffy, Hugh

CS	HBP	SF	GDP	AVG	OBP	SLG	Total Offensive Production Statistics				TRP Rating	RPA Rating	TNB Rating	TBA Rating	TOP Composite		
							TRP	RPA	TNB	TBA					TOP	Rating	Ranking
-	1	-	-	.282	.305	.416	101	.328	147	.477	29.02	61.45	24.10	52.60	167.17	42.62	
-	2	-	-	.312	.364	.433	233	.369	353	.559	66.95	69.08	57.87	61.56	255.46	65.13	
-	2	-	-	.328	.391	.467	243	.373	416	.638	69.83	69.84	68.20	70.32	278.18	70.93	
-	4	-	-	.341	.415	.477	234	.406	392	.681	67.24	76.12	64.26	75.01	282.63	72.06	
-	1	-	-	.302	.366	.411	206	.307	372	.555	59.20	57.61	60.98	61.19	238.99	60.93	
-	1	-	-	.378	.432	.480	267	.454	359	.611	76.72	85.09	58.85	67.29	287.95	73.42	
-	1	-	-	.438	.500	.679	305	.503	482	.795	87.64	94.31	79.02	87.66	348.63	88.89	
-	4	-	-	.352	.423	.470	213	.351	363	.598	61.21	65.75	59.51	65.91	252.38	64.35	
-	2	-	-	.302	.366	.392	206	.351	308	.525	59.20	65.76	50.49	57.83	233.28	59.48	
-	6	-	-	.341	.404	.478	260	.425	368	.601	74.71	79.61	60.33	66.27	280.92	71.62	
-	1	-	-	.319	.385	.394	205	.330	313	.504	58.91	61.86	51.31	55.55	227.63	58.04	
-	3	-	-	.279	.327	.374	204	.324	280	.444	58.62	60.68	45.90	48.98	214.18	54.61	
-	-	-	-	.298	.355	.403	59	.299	101	.513	16.95	56.12	16.56	56.51	146.14	37.26	
-	1	-	-	.308	.347	.434	86	.284	154	.508	24.71	53.18	25.25	56.02	159.16	40.58	
-	-	-	-	.283	.441	.348	15	.254	32	.542	4.31	47.64	5.25	59.78	116.97	29.82	
-	-	-	-	.300	.317	.400	10	.244	17	.415	2.87	45.70	2.79	45.70	97.06	24.75	
-	-	-	-	.000	.000	.000	-	.000	-	.000	-	-	-	-	-	-	
-	29	-	-	.330	.390	.453	2,847	.370	4,457	.580	63.68	88.65	52.70	77.04	282.07	72.04	36
-	38	-	-	.330	.390	.453	3,702	.370	5,796	.580	88.65	88.65	77.04	77.04	331.39	82.85	16
-	41	-	-	.330	.390	.453	4,068	.370	6,368	.580	77.88	88.65	67.68	77.04	311.25	77.81	27
-	24	-	-	.340	.404	.467	2,372	.386	3,726	.606	80.57	87.94	75.17	76.43	320.11	82.11	16
-	9	-	-	.356	.419	.500	1,255	.406	2,021	.654	82.46	86.80	77.49	79.25	325.99	83.52	20
-	1	-	-	.438	.500	.679	305	.503	482	.795	87.64	94.31	79.02	87.66	348.63	88.89	9
-	1	-	-	.378	.432	.480	267	.454	359	.611	76.72	85.09	58.85	67.29	287.95	73.42	163
-	4	-	-	.341	.415	.477	234	.406	392	.681	67.24	76.12	64.26	75.01	282.63	72.06	212
-	6	-	-	.341	.404	.478	260	.425	368	.601	74.71	79.61	60.33	66.27	280.92	71.62	230
-	2	-	-	.328	.391	.467	243	.373	416	.638	69.83	69.84	68.20	70.32	278.18	70.93	249

Complete Career Statistics   D

Total Career Statistics & Adjusted Career, 10 year, 5 year, and Single Year Analysis

Fielder, Cecil: *Cecil Grant Fielder, b. Sept. 21, 1963, Los Angeles, CA*

Rating Category	Year	Ranked Seasons & Adjustment	G	AB	H	1B	2B	3B	HR	RUN	RBI	BB	SO	SB
	1985		30	74	23	15	4	-	4	6	16	6	16	-
	1986		34	83	13	7	2	-	4	7	13	6	27	-
	1987		82	175	47	25	7	1	14	30	32	20	48	-
	1988		74	174	40	24	6	1	9	24	23	14	53	-
	1990	1st	159	573	159	82	25	1	51	104	132	90	182	-
	1991		162	624	163	94	25	-	44	102	133	78	151	-
	1992		155	594	145	88	22	-	35	80	124	73	151	-
	1993		154	573	153	100	23	-	30	80	117	90	125	-
	1994		109	425	110	64	16	2	28	67	90	50	110	-
	1995		136	494	120	70	18	1	31	70	82	75	116	-
	1996		160	591	149	90	20	-	39	85	117	87	139	2
	1997		98	361	94	66	15	-	13	40	61	51	87	-
	1998		117	416	97	62	17	1	17	49	68	53	111	-
Career Total	1985-1998		1,470	5,157	1,313	787	200	7	319	744	1,008	693	1,316	2
Career Adj. to 10,000 BO	1985-1998	1.637197	2,407	8,443	2,150	1,288	327	11	522	1,218	1,650	1,135	2,155	3
Career Adj. to 10,000 AB	1985-1998	1.939112	2,850	10,000	2,546	1,526	388	14	619	1,443	1,955	1,344	2,552	4
10 Year Total	1987-1996		1,191	4,223	1,086	637	162	6	281	642	850	577	1,075	2
5 Year Total	1990-1994		739	2,789	730	428	111	3	188	433	596	381	719	-
Best Single Year	1990		159	573	159	82	25	1	51	104	132	90	182	-

10 Year Total

5 Year Total

Total Career Statistics & Adjusted Career, 10 year, 5 year, and Single Year Analysis

Fielder, Cecil

CS	HBP	SF	GDP	AVG	OBP	SLG	Total Offensive Production Statistics				TRP Rating	RPA Rating	TNB Rating	TBA Rating	TOP Composite		
							TRP	RPA	TNB	TBA					TOP	Rating	Ranking
-	-	1	2	.311	.358	.527	22	.265	45	.542	6.32	49.67	7.38	59.75	123.12	31.39	
-	1	-	3	.157	.222	.325	20	.215	34	.366	5.75	40.30	5.57	40.29	91.91	23.43	
1	1	1	6	.269	.345	.560	62	.305	118	.581	17.82	57.23	19.34	64.07	158.46	40.40	
1	1	1	6	.230	.289	.431	47	.240	89	.454	13.51	44.93	14.59	50.05	123.08	31.38	
1	5	5	15	.277	.377	.592	236	.343	433	.629	67.82	64.28	70.98	69.36	272.44	69.46	
-	6	4	17	.261	.347	.513	235	.322	404	.554	67.53	60.40	66.23	61.08	255.24	65.08	
-	2	7	14	.244	.325	.458	204	.296	347	.503	58.62	55.40	56.89	55.43	226.33	57.71	
1	4	5	22	.267	.368	.464	197	.284	359	.517	56.61	53.19	58.85	57.01	225.66	57.54	
-	2	4	17	.259	.337	.504	157	.315	266	.534	45.11	59.07	43.61	58.87	206.67	52.69	
1	5	4	17	.243	.346	.472	152	.255	312	.524	43.68	47.87	51.15	57.79	200.49	51.12	
-	5	5	18	.252	.350	.484	202	.286	380	.538	58.05	53.61	62.30	59.32	233.28	59.48	
-	7	6	14	.260	.358	.410	101	.230	206	.469	29.02	43.11	33.77	51.72	157.62	40.19	
1	4	3	18	.233	.324	.401	117	.237	223	.451	33.62	44.38	36.56	49.75	164.31	41.89	
6	43	46	169	.255	.345	.482	1,752	.287	3,216	.527	39.19	68.69	38.03	69.99	215.89	55.13	120
10	70	75	277	.255	.345	.482	2,868	.287	5,265	.527	68.69	68.69	69.99	69.99	277.35	69.34	98
12	83	89	328	.255	.345	.482	3,397	.287	6,236	.527	65.04	68.69	66.28	69.99	269.99	67.50	92
5	31	36	132	.257	.348	.498	1,492	.298	2,708	.542	50.68	68.06	54.63	68.35	241.72	62.00	119
2	19	25	85	.262	.352	.506	1,029	.312	1,809	.548	67.61	66.70	69.36	66.48	270.16	69.21	106
1	5	5	15	.277	.377	.592	236	.343	433	.629	67.82	64.28	70.98	69.36	272.44	69.46	307

Complete Career Statistics F

Total Career Statistics & Adjusted Career, 10 year, 5 year, and Single Year Analysis

Foster, George: *George Arthur Foster, b. Dec, 1, 1949, Tuscaloosa, AL*

Rating Category	Year	Ranked Seasons & Adjustment	G	AB	H	1B	2B	3B	HR	RUN	RBI	BB	SO	SB
	1969		9	5	2	2	-	-	-	1	1	-	1	-
	1970		9	19	6	3	1	1	1	2	4	2	5	-
	1971		140	473	114	74	23	4	13	50	58	29	120	7
	1972		59	145	29	22	4	1	2	15	12	5	44	2
	1973		17	39	11	4	3	-	4	6	9	4	7	-
	1974		106	276	73	48	18	-	7	31	41	30	52	3
	1975		134	463	139	88	24	4	23	71	78	40	73	2
	1976		144	562	172	113	21	9	29	86	121	52	89	17
	1977	1st	158	615	197	112	31	2	52	124	149	61	107	6
	1978		158	604	170	97	26	7	40	97	120	70	138	4
	1979		121	440	133	82	18	3	30	68	98	59	105	-
	1980		144	528	144	93	21	5	25	79	93	75	99	1
	1981		108	414	122	75	23	2	22	64	90	51	75	4
	1982		151	550	136	98	23	2	13	64	70	50	123	1
	1983		157	601	145	96	19	2	28	74	90	38	111	1
	1984		146	553	149	102	22	1	24	67	86	30	122	2
	1985		129	452	119	73	24	1	21	57	77	46	87	-
	1986		87	284	64	41	6	3	14	30	42	24	61	1
Career Total	1969-1986		1,977	7,023	1,925	1,223	307	47	348	986	1,239	666	1,419	51
Career Adj. to 10,000 BO	1969-1986	1.249219	2,470	8,773	2,405	1,528	384	59	435	1,232	1,548	832	1,773	64
Career Adj. to 10,000 AB	1969-1986	1.423893	2,815	10,000	2,741	1,741	437	67	496	1,404	1,764	948	2,021	73
10 Year Total	1975-1984		1,421	5,330	1,507	956	228	37	286	794	995	526	1,042	38
5 Year Total	1976-1980		725	2,749	816	497	117	26	176	454	581	317	538	28
Best Single Year	1977		158	615	197	112	31	2	52	124	149	61	107	6

10 Year Total

5 Year Total

Complete Career Statistics F

★ ★ ★ *Appendix G* ★ ★ ★

Total Career Statistics & Adjusted Career, 10 year, 5 year, and Single Year Analysis

Foster, George

CS	HBP	SF	GDP	AVG	OBP	SLG	TRP	RPA	TNB	TBA	TRP Rating	RPA Rating	TNB Rating	TBA Rating	TOP	Rating	Ranking
-	-	-	-	.400	.400	.400	2	.400	2	.400	0.57	74.95	0.33	44.09	119.94	30.58	
-	-	-	1	.316	.381	.632	6	.273	14	.636	1.72	51.10	2.30	70.14	125.26	31.94	
7	7	4	20	.241	.292	.389	108	.203	220	.413	31.03	37.97	36.07	45.49	150.56	38.39	
1	1	1	6	.200	.230	.283	27	.171	48	.304	7.76	32.02	7.87	33.48	81.13	20.69	
1	-	-	1	.282	.349	.667	15	.341	29	.659	4.31	63.88	4.75	72.64	145.59	37.12	
2	4	2	8	.264	.343	.406	72	.225	147	.459	20.69	42.16	24.10	50.63	137.58	35.08	
1	3	5	14	.300	.356	.518	149	.284	284	.541	42.82	53.18	46.56	59.62	202.17	51.55	
3	4	9	11	.306	.364	.530	207	.324	368	.577	59.48	60.80	60.33	63.57	244.18	62.26	
4	5	8	17	.320	.382	.631	273	.387	456	.646	78.45	72.46	74.75	71.19	296.85	75.68	
4	7	6	18	.281	.360	.546	217	.308	407	.577	62.36	57.68	66.72	63.63	250.38	63.84	
2	3	3	11	.302	.386	.561	166	.322	307	.595	47.70	60.28	50.33	65.57	223.88	57.08	
-	1	4	14	.273	.362	.473	172	.277	327	.526	49.43	51.82	53.61	57.94	212.79	54.25	
-	3	4	12	.295	.373	.519	154	.318	273	.564	44.25	59.62	44.75	62.17	210.79	53.74	
1	2	6	13	.247	.309	.367	134	.216	254	.409	38.51	40.43	41.64	45.08	165.66	42.24	
1	4	4	19	.241	.289	.419	164	.246	294	.441	47.13	46.14	48.20	48.65	190.12	48.47	
2	6	6	14	.269	.311	.443	153	.251	281	.461	43.97	47.08	46.07	50.85	187.96	47.92	
1	2	4	8	.263	.331	.460	134	.262	255	.498	38.51	49.04	41.80	54.89	184.24	46.97	
1	-	2	9	.225	.284	.415	72	.226	142	.445	20.69	42.29	23.28	49.06	135.32	34.50	
31	52	68	196	.274	.338	.480	2,225	.278	4,108	.513	49.77	66.56	48.58	68.21	233.11	59.53	104
39	65	85	245	.274	.338	.480	2,780	.278	5,132	.513	66.56	66.56	68.21	68.21	269.54	67.39	114
44	74	97	279	.274	.338	.480	3,168	.278	5,849	.513	60.66	66.56	62.16	68.21	257.59	64.40	113
18	38	55	143	.283	.348	.500	1,789	.294	3,251	.534	60.77	66.97	65.58	67.33	260.65	66.86	103
13	20	30	71	.297	.370	.550	1,035	.325	1,865	.585	68.00	69.45	71.51	70.95	279.91	71.71	88
4	5	8	17	.320	.382	.631	273	.387	456	.646	78.45	72.46	74.75	71.19	296.85	75.68	113

Complete Career Statistics F

Total Career Statistics & Adjusted Career, 10 year, 5 year, and Single Year Analysis

Foxx, Jimmie: *James Emory "Beast" "Double X" Foxx; b. Oct. 22, 1907, Sudlersville, MD*

Rating Category	Year	Ranked Seasons & Adjustment	G	AB	H	1B	2B	3B	HR	RUN	RBI	BB	SO	SB
	1925		10	9	6	5	1	-	-	2	-	-	1	-
	1926		26	32	10	7	2	1	-	8	5	1	6	1
	1927		61	130	42	28	6	5	3	23	20	14	11	2
	1928		118	400	131	79	29	10	13	85	79	60	43	3
	1929	8th	149	517	183	118	23	9	33	123	118	103	70	10
	1930	4th	153	562	188	105	33	13	37	127	156	93	66	7
	1931		139	515	150	78	32	10	30	93	120	73	84	4
	1932	1st	154	585	213	113	33	9	58	151	169	116	96	3
	1933	3rd	149	573	204	110	37	9	48	125	163	96	93	2
	1934	6th	150	539	180	102	28	6	44	120	130	111	75	11
	1935	9th	147	535	185	109	33	7	36	118	115	114	99	6
	1936	5th	155	585	198	117	32	8	41	130	143	105	119	13
	1937		150	569	162	96	24	6	36	111	127	99	96	10
	1938	2nd	149	565	197	105	33	9	50	139	175	119	76	5
	1939	7th	124	467	168	92	31	10	35	130	105	89	72	4
	1940		144	515	153	83	30	4	36	106	119	101	87	4
	1941		135	487	146	92	27	8	19	87	105	93	103	2
	1942		100	305	69	49	12	-	8	43	33	40	70	1
	1944		15	20	1	-	1	-	-	-	2	2	5	-
	1945		89	224	60	41	11	1	7	30	38	23	39	-
Career Total*	1925-1944		2,317	8,134	2,646	1,529	458	125	534	1,751	1,922	1,452	1,311	88
Career Adj. to 10,000 BO*	1925-1944	1.034340	2,397	8,413	2,737	1,582	474	129	552	1,811	1,988	1,502	1,356	91
Career Adj. to 10,000 AB*	1925-1944	1.229407	2,849	10,000	3,253	1,880	563	154	657	2,153	2,363	1,785	1,612	108
10 Year Total*	1930-1939		1,470	5,495	1,845	1,027	316	87	415	1,244	1,403	1,015	876	65
5 Year Total*	1932-1936		755	2,817	980	551	163	39	227	644	720	542	482	35
Best Single Year*	1932		154	585	213	113	33	9	58	151	169	116	96	3
2nd Best Year*	1938		149	565	197	105	33	9	50	139	175	119	76	5
3rd Best Year*	1933		149	573	204	110	37	9	48	125	163	96	93	2
4th Best Year*	1930		153	562	188	105	33	13	37	127	156	93	66	7
5th Best Year*	1936		155	585	198	117	32	8	41	130	143	105	119	13
6th Best Year*	1934		150	539	180	102	28	6	44	120	130	111	75	11
7th Best Year*	1939		124	467	168	92	31	10	35	130	105	89	72	4
8th Best Year*	1929		149	517	183	118	23	9	33	123	118	103	70	10
9th Best Year*	1935		147	535	185	109	33	7	36	118	115	114	99	6

10 Year Total (side label)
5 Year Total (side label)

Total Career Statistics & Adjusted Career, 10 year, 5 year, and Single Year Analysis

Foxx, Jimmie

CS	HBP	SF	GDP	AVG	OBP	SLG	Total Offensive Production Statistics				TRP Rating	RPA Rating	TNB Rating	TBA Rating	TOP Composite		
							TRP	RPA	TNB	TBA					TOP	Rating	Ranking
-	-	-	-	.667	.667	.778	2	.222	7	.778	0.57	41.64	1.15	85.72	129.08	32.91	
-	-	-	-	.313	.333	.438	13	.394	16	.485	3.74	73.82	2.62	53.44	133.61	34.07	
1	1	-	-	.323	.393	.515	43	.297	83	.572	12.36	55.57	13.61	63.09	144.62	36.87	
8	1	-	-	.328	.416	.548	164	.356	275	.597	47.13	66.66	45.08	65.75	224.62	57.27	
7	2	-	-	.354	.463	.625	241	.387	431	.693	69.25	72.60	70.66	76.37	288.88	73.65	
7	-	-	-	.335	.429	.637	283	.432	451	.689	81.32	80.96	73.93	75.89	312.10	79.57	
3	1	-	-	.291	.380	.567	213	.362	367	.623	61.21	67.76	60.16	68.67	257.81	65.73	
7	-	-	-	.364	.469	.749	320	.456	550	.785	91.95	85.54	90.16	86.47	354.13	90.29	
2	1	-	-	.356	.449	.703	288	.430	500	.746	82.76	80.55	81.97	82.25	327.52	83.50	
2	1	-	-	.334	.449	.653	250	.384	473	.727	71.84	71.96	77.54	80.08	301.42	76.85	
4	-	-	-	.346	.461	.636	233	.359	456	.703	66.95	67.27	74.75	77.44	286.42	73.03	
4	1	-	-	.338	.440	.631	273	.395	484	.700	78.45	74.03	79.34	77.20	309.02	78.79	
8	1	-	-	.285	.392	.538	238	.356	408	.610	68.39	66.66	66.89	67.22	269.15	68.62	
4	-	-	-	.349	.462	.704	314	.459	518	.757	90.23	86.02	84.92	83.47	344.63	87.87	
3	2	-	17	.360	.464	.694	235	.409	416	.723	67.53	76.58	68.20	79.74	292.05	74.46	
7	-	-	18	.297	.412	.581	225	.355	397	.626	64.66	66.50	65.08	69.01	265.25	67.63	
5	-	-	21	.300	.412	.505	192	.319	336	.559	55.17	59.86	55.08	61.62	231.73	59.08	
-	2	-	10	.226	.320	.344	76	.213	148	.415	21.84	39.89	24.26	45.69	131.68	33.57	
-	-	-	-	.050	.136	.100	2	.091	4	.182	0.57	17.03	0.66	20.04	38.30	9.77	
-	-	-	3	.268	.336	.420	68	.272	117	.468	19.54	50.97	19.18	51.58	141.27	36.02	
72	13	-	69	.325	.428	.609	3,673	.380	6,437	.666	82.15	90.97	76.11	88.50	337.74	86.25	7
74	13	-	71	.325	.428	.609	3,799	.380	6,658	.666	90.97	90.97	88.50	88.50	358.95	89.74	4
89	16	-	85	.325	.428	.609	4,516	.380	7,914	.666	86.45	90.97	84.10	88.50	350.03	87.51	5
44	7	-	17	.336	.440	.652	2,647	.405	4,623	.708	89.91	92.38	93.26	89.27	364.83	93.58	3
19	3	-	-	.348	.454	.675	1,364	.406	2,463	.733	89.62	86.76	94.44	88.82	359.64	92.14	3
7	-	-	-	.364	.469	.749	320	.456	550	.785	91.95	85.54	90.16	86.47	354.13	90.29	7
4	-	-	-	.349	.462	.704	314	.459	518	.757	90.23	86.02	84.92	83.47	344.63	87.87	13
2	1	-	-	.356	.449	.703	288	.430	500	.746	82.76	80.55	81.97	82.25	327.52	83.50	32
7	-	-	-	.335	.429	.637	283	.432	451	.689	81.32	80.96	73.93	75.89	312.10	79.57	62
4	1	-	-	.338	.440	.631	273	.395	484	.700	78.45	74.03	79.34	77.20	309.02	78.79	70
2	1	-	-	.334	.449	.653	250	.384	473	.727	71.84	71.96	77.54	80.08	301.42	76.85	92
3	2	-	17	.360	.464	.694	235	.409	416	.723	67.53	76.58	68.20	79.74	292.05	74.46	137
7	2	-	-	.354	.463	.625	241	.387	431	.693	69.25	72.60	70.66	76.37	288.88	73.65	158
4	-	-	-	.346	.461	.636	233	.359	456	.703	66.95	67.27	74.75	77.44	286.42	73.03	174

Complete Career Statistics F

Total Career Statistics & Adjusted Career, 10 year, 5 year, and Single Year Analysis

Galarraga, Andres: *Andres Jose Galarraga (Podovani), b. June 18, 1961, Caracas, Venezuela*

Rating Category	Year	Ranked Seasons & Adjustment	G	AB	H	1B	2B	3B	HR	RUN	RBI	BB	SO	SB
	1985		24	75	14	11	1	-	2	9	4	3	18	1
	1986		105	321	87	64	13	-	10	39	42	30	79	6
	1987		147	551	168	112	40	3	13	72	90	41	127	7
	1988		157	609	184	105	42	8	29	99	92	39	153	13
	1989		152	572	147	93	30	1	23	76	85	48	158	12
	1990		155	579	148	99	29	-	20	65	87	40	169	10
	1991		107	375	82	58	13	2	9	34	33	23	86	5
	1992		95	325	79	53	14	2	10	38	39	11	69	5
	1993		120	470	174	113	35	4	22	71	98	24	73	2
	1994		103	417	133	81	21	-	31	77	85	19	93	8
	1995		143	554	155	92	29	3	31	89	106	32	146	12
	1996	1st	159	626	190	101	39	3	47	119	150	40	157	18
	1997	2nd	154	600	191	116	31	3	41	120	140	54	141	15
	1998		153	555	169	97	27	1	44	103	121	63	146	7
	2000		141	494	149	95	25	1	28	67	100	36	126	3
	2001		121	399	102	56	28	1	17	50	69	31	117	1
	2002		104	292	76	55	12	-	9	30	40	30	81	2
	2003		110	272	82	55	15	-	12	36	42	19	61	1
	2004		7	10	3	2	-	-	1	1	2	-	3	-
Career Total**	1985-2004		2,257	8,096	2,333	1,458	444	32	399	1,195	1,425	583	2,003	128
Career Adj. to 10,000 BO**	1985-2004	1.099626	2,482	8,903	2,565	1,603	488	35	439	1,314	1,567	641	2,203	141
Career Adj. to 10,000 AB**	1985-2004	1.235178	2,788	10,000	2,882	1,801	548	40	493	1,476	1,760	720	2,474	158
10 Year Total**	1989-1998		1,341	5,073	1,468	903	268	19	278	792	944	354	1,238	94
5 Year Total**	1994-1998		712	2,752	838	487	147	10	194	508	602	208	683	60
Best Single Year**	1996		159	626	190	101	39	3	47	119	150	40	157	18
2nd Best Year**	1997		154	600	191	116	31	3	41	120	140	54	141	15

10 Year Total / 5 Year Total (row labels in left margin)

Complete Career Statistics G (side margin)

Total Career Statistics & Adjusted Career, 10 year, 5 year, and Single Year Analysis

Galarraga, Andres

CS	HBP	SF	GDP	AVG	OBP	SLG	Total Offensive Production Statistics				TRP Rating	RPA Rating	TNB Rating	TBA Rating	TOP Composite		
							TRP	RPA	TNB	TBA					TOP	Rating	Ranking
2	1	-	-	.187	.228	.280	13	.165	24	.304	3.74	30.83	3.93	33.48	71.99	18.35	
5	3	1	8	.271	.338	.405	81	.223	164	.452	23.28	41.81	26.89	49.79	141.77	36.14	
10	10	4	11	.305	.361	.459	162	.263	301	.488	46.55	49.20	49.34	53.77	198.86	50.70	
4	10	3	12	.302	.352	.540	191	.284	387	.575	54.89	53.18	63.44	63.38	234.88	59.89	
5	13	3	12	.257	.327	.434	161	.248	316	.488	46.26	46.56	51.80	53.75	198.37	50.58	
1	4	5	14	.256	.306	.409	152	.237	290	.452	43.68	44.36	47.54	49.79	185.37	47.26	
6	2	-	6	.219	.268	.336	67	.165	150	.369	19.25	30.92	24.59	40.72	115.49	29.44	
4	8	3	8	.243	.282	.391	77	.217	147	.414	22.13	40.64	24.10	45.64	132.51	33.78	
4	6	6	9	.370	.403	.602	169	.328	311	.604	48.56	61.49	50.98	66.56	227.59	58.03	
3	8	5	10	.319	.356	.592	162	.353	279	.608	46.55	66.13	45.74	66.99	225.42	57.47	
2	13	5	14	.280	.331	.511	195	.316	338	.547	56.03	59.13	55.41	60.28	230.85	58.86	
8	17	8	6	.304	.357	.601	269	.386	443	.636	77.30	72.32	72.62	70.05	292.29	74.52	
8	17	3	16	.318	.389	.585	260	.377	429	.622	74.71	70.61	70.33	68.52	284.17	72.45	
6	25	5	8	.305	.397	.595	224	.341	419	.639	64.37	63.98	68.69	70.40	267.44	68.19	
5	17	1	15	.302	.369	.526	167	.297	311	.552	47.99	55.58	50.98	60.88	215.44	54.93	
3	12	3	12	.256	.326	.459	119	.260	224	.490	34.20	48.79	36.72	54.02	173.73	44.29	
2	9	3	8	.260	.344	.394	70	.205	154	.450	20.11	38.35	25.25	49.63	133.34	34.00	
3	2	-	9	.301	.352	.489	78	.258	152	.503	22.41	48.40	24.92	55.47	151.20	38.55	
-	1	-	1	.300	.364	.600	3	.250	7	.583	0.86	46.85	1.15	64.29	113.15	28.85	
81	178	58	179	.288	.347	.499	2,620	.288	4,846	.533	58.60	68.99	57.30	70.83	255.72	65.31	77
89	196	64	197	.288	.347	.499	2,881	.288	5,329	.533	68.99	68.99	70.83	70.83	279.64	69.91	95
100	220	72	221	.288	.347	.499	3,236	.288	5,986	.533	61.96	68.99	63.61	70.83	265.39	66.35	98
47	113	43	103	.289	.347	.514	1,736	.305	3,122	.549	58.97	69.62	62.98	69.28	260.85	66.91	102
27	80	26	54	.305	.367	.577	1,110	.356	1,908	.612	72.93	76.08	73.16	74.14	296.31	75.91	56
8	17	8	6	.304	.357	.601	269	.386	443	.636	77.30	72.32	72.62	70.05	292.29	74.52	136
8	17	3	16	.318	.389	.585	260	.377	429	.622	74.71	70.61	70.33	68.52	284.17	72.45	198

Complete Career Statistics   G

Total Career Statistics & Adjusted Career, 10 year, 5 year, and Single Year Analysis

Garciaparra, Nomar: *Anthony Nomar Garciaparra, b. July 23, 1973, Whittier, CA*

Rating Category	Year	Ranked Seasons & Adjustment	G	AB	H	1B	2B	3B	HR	RUN	RBI	BB	SO	SB
	1996		24	87	21	12	2	3	4	11	16	4	14	5
5 Year Total	1997		153	684	209	124	44	11	30	122	98	35	92	22
	1998	1st	143	604	195	115	37	8	35	111	122	33	62	12
	1999		135	532	190	117	42	4	27	103	104	51	39	14
	2000		140	529	197	122	51	3	21	104	96	61	50	5
	2001		21	83	24	17	3	-	4	13	8	7	9	-
	2002		156	635	197	112	56	5	24	101	120	41	63	5
	2003		156	658	198	120	37	13	28	120	105	39	61	19
	2004		81	321	99	66	21	3	9	52	41	24	30	4
Career Total**	1996-2004		1,009	4,133	1,330	805	293	50	182	737	710	295	420	86
Career Adj. to 10,000 BO**	1996-2004	2.168727	2,188	8,963	2,884	1,746	635	108	395	1,598	1,540	640	911	187
Career Adj. to 10,000 AB**	1996-2004	2.419550	2,441	10,000	3,218	1,948	709	121	440	1,783	1,718	714	1,016	208
10 Year Total**	n/a													
5 Year Total**	1997-2001		592	2,432	815	495	177	26	117	453	428	187	252	53
Best Single Year**	1998		143	604	195	115	37	8	35	111	122	33	62	12

Total Career Statistics & Adjusted Career, 10 year, 5 year, and Single Year Analysis

Garciaparra, Nomar

CS	HBP	SF	GDP	AVG	OBP	SLG	Total Offensive Production Statistics				TRP Rating	RPA Rating	TNB Rating	TBA Rating	TOP Composite		
							TRP	RPA	TNB	TBA					TOP	Rating	Ranking
-	-	1	-	.241	.272	.471	27	.293	50	.543	7.76	54.99	8.20	59.90	130.85	33.36	
9	6	7	9	.306	.342	.534	220	.297	419	.565	63.22	55.63	68.69	62.32	249.86	63.70	
6	8	7	20	.323	.362	.584	233	.347	400	.595	66.95	64.97	65.57	65.60	263.10	67.08	
3	8	4	11	.357	.418	.603	207	.342	391	.645	59.48	64.01	64.10	71.11	258.70	65.96	
2	2	7	8	.372	.434	.599	200	.329	383	.631	57.47	61.74	62.79	69.54	251.54	64.13	
1	1	-	1	.289	.352	.470	21	.228	46	.500	6.03	42.77	7.54	55.11	111.45	28.42	
2	6	11	17	.310	.352	.528	221	.311	385	.542	63.51	58.33	63.11	59.76	244.71	62.39	
5	11	10	10	.301	.345	.524	225	.309	409	.562	64.66	57.91	67.05	61.92	251.54	64.13	
1	6	2	10	.308	.365	.477	93	.256	186	.512	26.72	48.01	30.49	56.47	161.70	41.23	
29	48	49	86	.322	.370	.549	1,447	.314	2,669	.579	32.36	75.15	31.56	76.94	216.01	55.17	119
63	104	106	187	.322	.370	.549	3,138	.314	5,788	.579	75.15	75.15	76.94	76.94	304.17	76.04	57
70	116	119	208	.322	.370	.549	3,501	.314	6,458	.579	67.03	75.15	68.63	76.94	287.75	71.94	62
21	25	25	49	.335	.385	.574	881	.324	1,639	.603	57.88	69.31	62.85	73.11	263.15	67.42	118
6	8	7	20	.323	.362	.584	233	.347	400	.595	66.95	64.97	65.57	65.60	263.10	67.08	342

Complete Career Statistics G

Total Career Statistics & Adjusted Career, 10 year, 5 year, and Single Year Analysis

Gehrig, Lou: *Henry Louis "The Iron Horse" Gehrig, b. June 19, 1903, New York, NY*

Rating Category	Year	Ranked Seasons & Adjustment	G	AB	H	1B	2B	3B	HR	RUN	RBI	BB	SO	SB
	1923		13	26	11	5	4	1	1	6	9	2	5	-
	1924		10	12	6	5	1	-	-	2	5	1	3	-
	1925		126	437	129	76	23	10	20	73	68	46	49	6
	1926	12th	155	572	179	96	47	20	16	135	112	105	73	6
10 Year Total / 5 Year Total	1927	1st	155	584	218	101	52	18	47	149	175	109	84	10
	1928	8th	154	562	210	123	47	13	27	139	142	94	69	4
	1929	10th	154	553	166	89	32	10	35	127	126	124	68	4
	1930	3rd	154	581	220	120	42	17	41	143	174	101	63	12
	1931	2nd	155	619	211	119	31	15	46	163	184	117	56	17
	1932	7th	156	596	208	123	42	9	34	138	151	108	38	4
5 Year Total	1933	9th	152	593	198	113	41	12	32	138	139	92	42	9
	1934	5th	154	579	210	115	40	6	49	128	165	109	31	9
	1935	11th	149	535	176	110	26	10	30	125	119	132	38	8
	1936	4th	155	579	205	112	37	7	49	167	152	130	46	3
	1937	6th	157	569	200	117	37	9	37	138	159	127	49	4
	1938		157	576	170	103	32	6	29	115	114	107	75	6
	1939		8	28	4	4	-	-	-	2	1	5	1	-
Career Total	1923-1938		2,164	8,001	2,721	1,531	534	163	493	1,888	1,995	1,509	790	102
Career Adj. to 10,000 BO	1923-1938	1.046353	2,264	8,372	2,847	1,602	559	171	516	1,976	2,087	1,579	827	107
Career Adj. to 10,000 AB	1923-1938	1.249844	2,705	10,000	3,401	1,914	667	204	616	2,360	2,493	1,886	987	127
10 Year Total	1927-1936		1,538	5,781	2,022	1,125	390	117	390	1,417	1,527	1,116	535	80
5 Year Total	1927-1931		772	2,899	1,025	552	204	73	196	721	801	545	340	47
5 Year Total	1933-1937		767	2,855	989	567	181	44	197	696	734	590	206	33
Best Single Year	1927		155	584	218	101	52	18	47	149	175	109	84	10
2nd Best Year	1931		155	619	211	119	31	15	46	163	184	117	56	17
3rd Best Year	1930		154	581	220	120	42	17	41	143	174	101	63	12
4th Best Year	1936		155	579	205	112	37	7	49	167	152	130	46	3
5th Best Year	1934		154	579	210	115	40	6	49	128	165	109	31	9
6th Best Year	1937		157	569	200	117	37	9	37	138	159	127	49	4
7th Best Year	1932		156	596	208	123	42	9	34	138	151	108	38	4
8th Best Year	1928		154	562	210	123	47	13	27	139	142	94	69	4
9th Best Year	1933		152	593	198	113	41	12	32	138	139	92	42	9
10th Best Year	1929		154	553	166	89	32	10	35	127	126	124	68	4
11th Best Year	1935		149	535	176	110	26	10	30	125	119	132	38	8
12th Best Year	1926		155	572	179	96	47	20	16	135	112	105	73	6

Complete Career Statistics G

Total Career Statistics & Adjusted Career, 10 year, 5 year, and Single Year Analysis

Gehrig, Lou

| CS | HBP | SF | GDP | AVG | OBP | SLG | Total Offensive Production Statistics | | | | TRP Rating | RPA Rating | TNB Rating | TBA Rating | TOP Composite | | |
							TRP	RPA	TNB	TBA					TOP	Rating	Ranking
-	-	-	-	.423	.464	.769	15	.536	22	.786	4.31	100.38	3.61	86.60	194.90	49.69	
-	-	-	-	.500	.538	.583	7	.538	8	.615	2.01	100.90	1.31	67.82	172.04	43.86	
3	2	-	-	.295	.365	.531	141	.291	283	.584	40.52	54.48	46.39	64.31	205.70	52.44	
5	1	-	-	.313	.420	.549	247	.364	421	.621	70.98	68.26	69.02	68.44	276.69	70.55	
8	3	-	-	.373	.474	.765	324	.466	561	.806	93.10	87.23	91.97	88.84	361.14	92.08	
11	4	-	-	.374	.467	.648	281	.426	455	.689	80.75	79.78	74.59	75.98	311.10	79.32	
4	5	-	-	.300	.433	.584	253	.371	452	.663	72.70	69.51	74.10	73.05	289.36	73.77	
14	3	-	-	.379	.473	.721	317	.463	521	.761	91.09	86.72	85.41	83.83	347.04	88.48	
12	-	-	-	.341	.446	.662	347	.471	532	.723	99.71	88.34	87.21	79.67	354.94	90.49	
11	3	-	-	.349	.451	.621	289	.409	474	.670	83.05	76.60	77.70	73.89	311.24	79.35	
13	1	-	-	.334	.424	.605	277	.404	448	.653	79.60	75.66	73.44	71.98	300.68	76.66	
5	2	-	-	.363	.465	.706	293	.425	524	.759	84.20	79.57	85.90	83.70	333.37	84.99	
7	5	-	-	.329	.466	.583	244	.363	450	.670	70.11	68.04	73.77	73.80	285.73	72.85	
4	7	-	-	.354	.478	.696	319	.446	539	.753	91.67	83.48	88.36	82.97	346.48	88.34	
3	4	-	-	.351	.473	.643	297	.424	498	.711	85.34	79.50	81.64	78.41	324.90	82.84	
1	5	-	-	.295	.410	.523	229	.333	418	.608	65.80	62.37	68.52	66.96	263.66	67.22	
-	-	-	2	.143	.273	.143	3	.086	9	.257	0.86	16.06	1.48	28.34	46.74	11.92	
101	45	-	2	.340	.447	.632	3,883	.406	6,615	.692	86.85	97.29	78.22	92.01	354.36	90.50	3
106	47	-	2	.340	.447	.632	4,063	.406	6,922	.692	97.29	97.29	92.01	92.01	378.59	94.65	2
126	56	-	2	.340	.447	.632	4,853	.406	8,268	.692	92.91	97.29	87.87	92.01	370.08	92.52	2
89	33	-	-	.350	.458	.660	2,944	.425	4,956	.715	100.00	96.88	99.98	90.23	387.09	99.29	2
49	15	-	-	.354	.458	.677	1,522	.440	2,521	.729	100.00	94.09	96.66	88.36	379.12	97.13	2
32	19	-	-	.346	.461	.648	1,430	.413	2,459	.710	93.96	88.28	94.29	86.07	362.59	92.89	n/r
8	3	-	-	.373	.474	.765	324	.466	561	.806	93.10	87.23	91.97	88.84	361.14	92.08	4
12	-	-	-	.341	.446	.662	347	.471	532	.723	99.71	88.34	87.21	79.67	354.94	90.49	6
14	3	-	-	.379	.473	.721	317	.463	521	.761	91.09	86.72	85.41	83.83	347.04	88.48	10
4	7	-	-	.354	.478	.696	319	.446	539	.753	91.67	83.48	88.36	82.97	346.48	88.34	11
5	2	-	-	.363	.465	.706	293	.425	524	.759	84.20	79.57	85.90	83.70	333.37	84.99	25
3	4	-	-	.351	.473	.643	297	.424	498	.711	85.34	79.50	81.64	78.41	324.90	82.84	36
11	3	-	-	.349	.451	.621	289	.409	474	.670	83.05	76.60	77.70	73.89	311.24	79.35	66
11	4	-	-	.374	.467	.648	281	.426	455	.689	80.75	79.78	74.59	75.98	311.10	79.32	67
13	1	-	-	.334	.424	.605	277	.404	448	.653	79.60	75.66	73.44	71.98	300.68	76.66	95
4	5	-	-	.300	.433	.584	253	.371	452	.663	72.70	69.51	74.10	73.05	289.36	73.77	154
7	5	-	-	.329	.466	.583	244	.363	450	.670	70.11	68.04	73.77	73.80	285.73	72.85	185
5	1	-	-	.313	.420	.549	247	.364	421	.621	70.98	68.26	69.02	68.44	276.69	70.55	268

Complete Career Statistics G

Total Career Statistics & Adjusted Career, 10 year, 5 year, and Single Year Analysis

Gehringer, Charlie: *Charles Leonard "The Mechanical Man" Gehringer, b. June 11, 1903, Fowlerville, MI*

Rating Category	Year	Ranked Seasons & Adjustment	G	AB	H	1B	2B	3B	HR	RUN	RBI	BB	SO	SB
	1924		5	13	6	6	-	-	-	2	1	-	2	1
	1925		8	18	3	3	-	-	-	3	-	2	-	-
	1926		123	459	127	90	19	17	1	62	48	30	42	9
	1927		133	508	161	117	29	11	4	110	61	52	31	17
	1928		154	603	193	142	29	16	6	108	74	69	22	15
	1929		155	634	215	138	45	19	13	131	106	64	19	28
	1930		154	610	201	123	47	15	16	144	98	69	17	19
	1931		101	383	119	86	24	5	4	67	53	29	15	13
	1932		152	618	184	110	44	11	19	112	107	68	34	9
10 Year Total	1933		155	628	204	144	42	6	12	103	105	68	27	5
	1934	2nd	154	601	214	146	50	7	11	134	127	99	25	11
5 Year Total	1935		150	610	201	142	32	8	19	123	108	79	16	11
	1936	1st	154	641	227	140	60	12	15	144	116	83	13	4
	1937		144	564	209	154	40	1	14	133	96	90	25	11
	1938		152	568	174	117	32	5	20	133	107	112	21	14
	1939		118	406	132	81	29	6	16	86	86	68	16	4
	1940		139	515	161	115	33	3	10	108	81	101	17	10
	1941		127	436	96	70	19	4	3	65	46	95	26	1
	1942		45	45	12	11	-	-	1	6	7	7	4	-
Career Total	1924-1941		2,323	8,860	2,839	1,935	574	146	184	1,774	1,427	1,185	372	182
Career Adj. to 10,000 BO	1924-1941	0.987849	2,295	8,752	2,805	1,911	567	144	182	1,752	1,410	1,171	367	180
Career Adj. to 10,000 AB	1924-1941	1.128668	2,622	10,000	3,204	2,184	648	165	208	2,002	1,611	1,337	420	205
10 Year Total	1929-1938		1,471	5,857	1,948	1,300	416	89	143	1,224	1,023	761	212	125
5 Year Total	1934-1938		754	2,984	1,025	699	214	33	79	667	554	463	100	51
Best Single Year	1936		154	641	227	140	60	12	15	144	116	83	13	4
2nd Best Year	1934		154	601	214	146	50	7	11	134	127	99	25	11

Complete Career Statistics G

Total Career Statistics & Adjusted Career, 10 year, 5 year, and Single Year Analysis

Gehringer, Charlie

CS	HBP	SF	GDP	AVG	OBP	SLG	Total Offensive Production Statistics				TRP Rating	RPA Rating	TNB Rating	TBA Rating	TOP Composite		
							TRP	RPA	TNB	TBA					TOP	Rating	Ranking
1	1	-	-	.462	.500	.462	3	.214	7	.500	0.86	40.15	1.15	55.11	97.27	24.80	
1	-	-	-	.167	.250	.167	3	.150	4	.200	0.86	28.11	0.66	22.04	51.67	13.17	
7	1	-	-	.277	.322	.399	110	.224	216	.441	31.61	42.07	35.41	48.58	157.67	40.20	
8	2	-	-	.317	.383	.441	171	.304	287	.511	49.14	57.01	47.05	56.28	209.49	53.41	
9	6	-	-	.320	.395	.451	182	.268	353	.521	52.30	50.30	57.87	57.38	217.85	55.54	
9	6	-	-	.339	.405	.532	237	.337	426	.605	68.10	63.08	69.84	66.69	267.71	68.26	
15	7	-	-	.330	.404	.534	242	.353	406	.592	69.54	66.10	66.56	65.23	267.43	68.18	
4	-	-	-	.311	.359	.431	120	.291	203	.493	34.48	54.58	33.28	54.30	176.64	45.04	
8	3	-	-	.298	.370	.497	219	.318	379	.550	62.93	59.56	62.13	60.63	245.25	62.53	
4	3	-	-	.325	.393	.468	208	.298	366	.524	59.77	55.76	60.00	57.71	233.24	59.47	
8	3	-	-	.356	.450	.517	261	.371	416	.592	75.00	69.57	68.20	65.22	277.98	70.87	
4	3	-	-	.330	.409	.502	231	.334	395	.571	66.38	62.55	64.75	62.91	256.60	65.42	
1	4	-	-	.354	.431	.555	260	.357	446	.613	74.71	66.92	73.11	67.52	282.27	71.97	
4	1	-	-	.371	.458	.520	229	.350	391	.597	65.80	65.51	64.10	65.79	261.21	66.60	
1	4	-	-	.306	.424	.486	240	.351	405	.592	68.97	65.75	66.39	65.26	266.37	67.91	
3	1	-	7	.325	.423	.544	172	.357	291	.604	49.43	66.87	47.70	66.54	230.54	58.78	
-	3	-	9	.313	.428	.447	189	.301	344	.548	54.31	56.39	56.39	60.37	227.47	58.00	
2	3	-	11	.220	.363	.303	111	.204	229	.420	31.90	38.16	37.54	46.31	153.91	39.24	
-	-	-	-	.267	.365	.333	13	.250	22	.423	3.74	46.85	3.61	46.63	100.82	25.70	
89	51	-	27	.320	.404	.480	3,201	.316	5,586	.552	71.59	75.72	66.05	73.35	286.71	73.22	29
88	50	-	27	.320	.404	.480	3,162	.316	5,518	.552	75.72	75.72	73.35	73.35	298.14	74.53	69
100	58	-	30	.320	.404	.480	3,613	.316	6,305	.552	69.17	75.72	67.00	73.35	285.24	71.31	67
58	34	-	-	.333	.412	.507	2,247	.338	3,833	.576	76.32	77.03	77.32	72.70	303.38	77.82	36
18	15	-	-	.343	.434	.517	1,221	.353	2,053	.593	80.22	75.42	78.72	71.90	306.26	78.46	38
1	4	-	-	.354	.431	.555	260	.357	446	.613	74.71	66.92	73.11	67.52	282.27	71.97	217
8	3	-	-	.356	.450	.517	261	.371	416	.592	75.00	69.57	68.20	65.22	277.98	70.87	251

Complete Career Statistics G

Total Career Statistics & Adjusted Career, 10 year, 5 year, and Single Year Analysis

Giambi, Jason: *Jason Gilbert Giambi, b. Jan. 8, 1971, West Covina, CA*

	Rating Category	Year	Ranked Seasons & Adjustment	G	AB	H	1B	2B	3B	HR	RUN	RBI	BB	SO	SB	
		1995		54	176	45	32	7	-	6	27	25	28	31	2	
		1996		140	536	156	95	40	1	20	84	79	51	95	-	
		1997		142	519	152	89	41	2	20	66	81	55	89	-	
		1998		153	562	166	111	28	-	27	92	110	81	102	2	
10 Year Total	5 Year Total	1999		158	575	181	111	36	1	33	115	123	105	106	1	
		2000	1st	152	510	170	97	29	1	43	108	137	137	96	2	
		2001	2nd	154	520	178	91	47	2	38	109	120	129	83	2	
		2002	3rd	155	560	176	100	34	1	41	120	122	109	112	2	
		2003		156	535	134	68	25	-	41	97	107	129	140	2	
		2004		80	264	55	34	9	-	12	33	40	47	62	-	
Career Total**		1995-2004		1,344	4,757	1,413	828	296	8	281	851	944	871	916	13	
Career Adj. to 10,000 BO**		1995-2004	1.695778	2,279	8,067	2,396	1,404	502	14	477	1,443	1,601	1,477	1,553	22	
Career Adj. to 10,000 AB**		1995-2004	2.102165	2,825	10,000	2,970	1,741	622	17	591	1,789	1,984	1,831	1,926	27	
10 Year Total**		1995-2004		1,344	4,757	1,413	828	296	8	281	851	944	871	916	13	
5 Year Total**		1999-2003		775	2,700	839	467	171	5	196	549	609	609	537	9	
Best Single Year**		2000		152	510	170	97	29	1	43	108	137	137	96	2	
2nd Best Year**		2001		154	520	178	91	47	2	38	109	120	129	83	2	
3rd Best Year**		2002		155	560	176	100	34	1	41	120	122	109	112	2	

Complete Career Statistics G

Total Career Statistics & Adjusted Career, 10 year, 5 year, and Single Year Analysis

Giambi, Jason

CS	HBP	SF	GDP	AVG	OBP	SLG	Total Offensive Production Statistics				TRP Rating	RPA Rating	TNB Rating	TBA Rating	TOP Composite		
							TRP	RPA	TNB	TBA					TOP	Rating	Ranking
1	3	2	4	.256	.364	.398	52	.244	102	.479	14.94	45.75	16.72	52.78	130.19	33.19	
1	5	5	15	.291	.355	.481	163	.266	313	.511	46.84	49.91	51.31	56.37	204.43	52.12	
1	6	8	11	.293	.362	.495	147	.245	317	.529	42.24	45.99	51.97	58.33	198.52	50.61	
2	5	9	16	.295	.384	.489	202	.300	361	.536	58.05	56.24	59.18	59.12	232.59	59.30	
1	7	8	11	.315	.422	.553	238	.337	430	.609	68.39	63.17	70.49	67.13	269.18	68.63	
-	9	8	9	.333	.476	.647	245	.364	478	.710	70.40	68.21	78.36	78.28	295.26	75.28	
-	13	9	17	.342	.477	.660	229	.333	487	.708	65.80	62.37	79.84	78.02	286.03	72.92	
2	15	5	18	.314	.435	.598	242	.342	459	.649	69.54	64.14	75.25	71.55	280.48	71.51	
1	21	5	9	.250	.412	.527	204	.292	433	.619	58.62	54.69	70.98	68.27	252.56	64.39	
1	8	3	5	.208	.342	.379	73	.223	154	.471	20.98	41.83	25.25	51.91	139.96	35.68	
10	92	62	115	.297	.411	.540	1,795	.304	3,534	.599	40.15	72.89	41.79	79.66	234.48	59.88	101
17	156	105	195	.297	.411	.540	3,044	.304	5,993	.599	72.89	72.89	79.66	79.66	305.10	76.27	51
21	193	130	242	.297	.411	.540	3,773	.304	7,429	.599	72.24	72.89	78.95	79.66	303.74	75.94	35
10	92	62	115	.297	.411	.540	1,795	.304	3,534	.599	60.97	69.41	71.29	75.61	277.29	71.12	67
4	65	35	64	.311	.444	.596	1,158	.333	2,287	.659	76.08	71.30	87.69	79.84	314.92	80.68	31
-	9	8	9	.333	.476	.647	245	.364	478	.710	70.40	68.21	78.36	78.28	295.26	75.28	122
-	13	9	17	.342	.477	.660	229	.333	487	.708	65.80	62.37	79.84	78.02	286.03	72.92	181
2	15	5	18	.314	.435	.598	242	.342	459	.649	69.54	64.14	75.25	71.55	280.48	71.51	235

Complete Career Statistics G

Total Career Statistics & Adjusted Career, 10 year, 5 year, and Single Year Analysis

Gonzalez, Juan: *Juan Alberto Gonzalez; b. Oct. 20, 1969, Arecibo, Puerto Rico*

Rating Category		Year	Ranked Seasons & Adjustment	G	AB	H	1B	2B	3B	HR	RUN	RBI	BB	SO	SB
		1989		24	60	9	5	3	-	1	6	7	6	17	-
		1990		25	90	26	14	7	1	4	11	12	2	18	-
		1991		142	545	144	82	34	1	27	78	102	42	118	4
10 Year Total		1992		155	584	152	83	24	2	43	77	109	35	143	-
		1993		140	536	166	86	33	1	46	105	118	37	99	4
		1994		107	422	116	75	18	4	19	57	85	30	66	6
	5 Year Total	1995		90	352	104	55	20	2	27	57	82	17	66	-
		1996	2nd	134	541	170	88	33	2	47	89	144	45	82	2
		1997		133	533	158	89	24	3	42	87	131	33	107	-
		1998	1st	154	606	193	96	50	2	45	110	157	46	126	2
		1999		144	562	183	107	36	1	39	114	128	51	105	3
		2000		115	461	133	79	30	2	22	69	67	32	84	1
		2001		140	532	173	103	34	1	35	97	140	41	94	1
		2002		70	277	78	48	21	1	8	38	35	17	56	2
		2003		82	327	96	54	17	1	24	49	70	14	73	1
		2004		33	127	35	25	4	1	5	17	17	9	19	-
Career Total**		1989-2004		1,688	6,555	1,936	1,089	388	25	434	1,061	1,404	457	1,273	26
Career Adj. to 10,000 BO**		1989-2004	1.363512	2,302	8,938	2,640	1,485	529	34	592	1,447	1,914	623	1,736	35
Career Adj. to 10,000 AB**		1989-2004	1.525553	2,575	10,000	2,953	1,661	592	38	662	1,619	2,142	697	1,942	40
10 Year Total**		1992-2001		1,312	5,129	1,548	861	302	20	365	862	1,161	367	972	19
5 Year Total**		1995-1999		655	2,594	808	435	163	10	200	457	642	192	486	7
Best Single Year**		1998		154	606	193	96	50	2	45	110	157	46	126	2
2nd Best Year**		1996		134	541	170	88	33	2	47	89	144	45	82	2

Total Career Statistics & Adjusted Career, 10 year, 5 year, and Single Year Analysis

Gonzalez, Juan

CS	HBP	SF	GDP	AVG	OBP	SLG	Total Offensive Production Statistics				TRP Rating	RPA Rating	TNB Rating	TBA Rating	TOP Composite		
							TRP	RPA	TNB	TBA					TOP	Rating	Ranking
-	-	-	4	.150	.227	.250	13	.186	21	.300	3.74	34.80	3.44	33.06	75.04	19.13	
1	2	1	2	.289	.316	.522	23	.237	50	.515	6.61	44.43	8.20	56.81	116.05	29.59	
4	5	3	10	.264	.321	.479	180	.298	308	.509	51.72	55.75	50.49	56.11	214.07	54.58	
1	5	8	16	.260	.304	.529	186	.287	348	.537	53.45	53.79	57.05	59.19	223.47	56.98	
1	13	1	11	.310	.368	.632	223	.373	392	.656	64.08	69.88	64.26	72.25	270.47	68.96	
4	7	4	18	.275	.330	.472	142	.295	238	.495	40.80	55.32	39.02	54.53	189.67	48.36	
-	-	5	14	.295	.324	.594	139	.358	226	.582	39.94	67.13	37.05	64.20	208.32	53.11	
-	3	3	10	.314	.368	.643	233	.387	398	.661	66.95	72.52	65.25	72.87	277.59	70.77	
-	3	10	12	.296	.335	.589	218	.369	350	.592	62.64	69.12	57.38	65.27	254.41	64.86	
1	6	11	20	.318	.366	.630	267	.388	435	.631	76.72	72.61	71.31	69.58	290.23	74.00	
3	4	12	10	.326	.378	.601	242	.379	393	.615	69.54	70.96	64.43	67.78	272.72	69.53	
2	2	1	13	.289	.337	.505	136	.267	266	.523	39.08	50.07	43.61	57.60	190.35	48.53	
-	6	16	18	.325	.370	.590	237	.387	362	.591	68.10	72.45	59.34	65.09	264.98	67.56	
-	1	1	11	.282	.324	.451	73	.238	145	.472	20.98	44.56	23.77	52.06	141.36	36.04	
1	4	1	10	.294	.329	.572	119	.334	205	.576	34.20	62.64	33.61	63.47	193.90	49.44	
1	1	1	3	.276	.326	.441	34	.241	65	.461	9.77	45.18	10.66	50.81	116.42	29.68	
19	62	78	182	.295	.343	.561	2,465	.336	4,202	.573	55.13	80.48	49.69	76.16	261.46	66.77	69
26	85	106	248	.295	.343	.561	3,361	.336	5,729	.573	80.48	80.48	76.16	76.16	313.28	78.32	38
29	95	119	278	.295	.343	.561	3,760	.336	6,410	.573	72.00	80.48	68.13	76.16	296.76	74.19	45
12	49	71	142	.302	.350	.582	2,023	.351	3,408	.592	68.72	80.12	68.75	74.68	292.27	74.96	49
4	16	41	66	.311	.357	.613	1,099	.378	1,802	.619	72.21	80.79	69.10	75.10	297.20	76.14	54
1	6	11	20	.318	.366	.630	267	.388	435	.631	76.72	72.61	71.31	69.58	290.23	74.00	150
-	3	3	10	.314	.368	.643	233	.387	398	.661	66.95	72.52	65.25	72.87	277.59	70.77	255

Complete Career Statistics G

Total Career Statistics & Adjusted Career, 10 year, 5 year, and Single Year Analysis

Goslin, Goose: *Leon Allen Goslin, b. Oct. 16, 1900, Salem, NJ*

Rating Category	Year	Ranked Seasons & Adjustment	G	AB	H	1B	2B	3B	HR	RUN	RBI	BB	SO	SB
	1921		14	50	13	10	1	1	1	8	6	6	5	-
	1922		101	358	116	87	19	7	3	44	53	25	26	4
10 Year Total	1923		150	600	180	124	29	18	9	86	99	40	53	7
5 Year Total	1924		154	579	199	140	30	17	12	100	129	68	29	16
	1925		150	601	201	129	34	20	18	116	113	53	50	26
	1926		147	568	201	143	26	15	17	105	108	63	38	8
	1927		148	581	194	129	37	15	13	96	120	50	28	21
	1928		135	456	173	110	36	10	17	80	102	48	19	16
	1929		145	553	159	106	28	7	18	82	91	66	33	10
	1930	1st	148	584	180	95	36	12	37	115	138	67	54	17
	1931		151	591	194	118	42	10	24	114	105	80	41	9
	1932		150	572	171	117	28	9	17	88	104	92	35	12
	1933		132	549	163	108	35	10	10	97	64	42	32	5
	1934		151	614	187	129	38	7	13	106	100	65	38	5
	1935		147	590	172	123	34	6	9	88	109	56	31	5
	1936		147	572	180	115	33	8	24	122	125	85	50	14
	1937		79	181	43	27	11	1	4	30	35	35	18	-
	1938		38	57	9	4	3	-	2	6	8	8	5	-
Career Total	1921-1938		2,287	8,656	2,735	1,814	500	173	248	1,483	1,609	949	585	175
Career Adj. to 10,000 BO	1921-1938	1.0350895	2,367	8,960	2,831	1,878	518	179	257	1,535	1,665	982	606	181
Career Adj. to 10,000 AB	1921-1938	1.1552680	2,642	10,000	3,160	2,096	578	200	287	1,713	1,859	1,096	676	202
10 Year Total	1923-1932		1,478	5,685	1,852	1,211	326	133	182	982	1,109	627	380	142
5 Year Total	1924-1928		734	2,785	968	651	163	77	77	497	572	282	164	87
Best Single Year	1930		148	584	180	95	36	12	37	115	138	67	54	17

Total Career Statistics & Adjusted Career, 10 year, 5 year, and Single Year Analysis

Goslin, Goose

CS	HBP	SF	GDP	AVG	OBP	SLG	Total Offensive Production Statistics				TRP Rating	RPA Rating	TNB Rating	TBA Rating	TOP Composite		
							TRP	RPA	TNB	TBA					TOP	Rating	Ranking
-	1	-	-	.260	.351	.380	14	.246	26	.456	4.02	46.02	4.26	50.27	104.58	26.66	
4	3	-	-	.324	.373	.441	97	.251	186	.482	27.87	47.09	30.49	53.11	158.56	40.43	
2	3	-	-	.300	.347	.453	185	.288	320	.498	53.16	53.91	52.46	54.85	214.38	54.66	
14	9	-	-	.344	.421	.516	229	.349	378	.576	65.80	65.41	61.97	63.51	256.69	65.45	
8	6	-	-	.334	.394	.547	229	.347	406	.615	65.80	65.02	66.56	67.80	265.18	67.61	
8	7	-	-	.354	.425	.542	213	.334	378	.592	61.21	62.56	61.97	65.30	251.03	64.00	
6	5	-	-	.334	.392	.516	216	.340	370	.582	62.07	63.64	60.66	64.12	250.48	63.86	
3	4	-	-	.379	.443	.614	182	.358	345	.679	52.30	67.13	56.56	74.85	250.84	63.95	
3	2	-	-	.288	.366	.461	173	.279	330	.531	49.71	52.20	54.10	58.57	214.58	54.71	
11	3	-	-	.308	.382	.601	253	.387	427	.653	72.70	72.49	70.00	71.96	287.15	73.21	
6	4	-	-	.328	.412	.555	219	.324	415	.615	62.93	60.79	68.03	67.76	259.52	66.17	
9	2	-	-	.299	.398	.469	192	.288	365	.548	55.17	54.02	59.84	60.40	229.43	58.50	
2	1	-	-	.297	.348	.452	161	.272	294	.497	46.26	50.96	48.20	54.73	200.16	51.03	
4	2	-	-	.305	.373	.453	206	.302	346	.508	59.20	56.68	56.72	56.00	228.60	58.28	
4	2	-	-	.292	.355	.415	197	.304	304	.469	56.61	56.97	49.84	51.71	215.12	54.85	
4	-	-	-	.315	.403	.526	247	.376	396	.603	70.98	70.45	64.92	66.43	272.77	69.55	
1	2	-	-	.238	.367	.376	65	.298	104	.477	18.68	55.87	17.05	52.58	144.18	36.76	
-	-	-	-	.158	.262	.316	14	.215	26	.400	4.02	40.36	4.26	44.09	92.73	23.64	
89	56	-	-	.316	.387	.500	3,092	.320	5,416	.561	69.16	76.64	64.04	74.52	284.35	72.62	32
92	58	-	-	.316	.387	.500	3,200	.320	5,606	.561	76.64	76.64	74.52	74.52	302.31	75.58	61
103	65	-	-	.316	.387	.500	3,572	.320	6,257	.561	68.39	76.64	66.50	74.52	286.04	71.51	65
70	45	-	-	.326	.397	.526	2,091	.329	3,734	.587	71.03	75.01	75.33	74.11	295.48	75.79	45
39	31	-	-	.348	.413	.544	1,069	.345	1,877	.606	70.24	73.79	71.97	73.46	289.45	74.16	75
11	3	-	-	.308	.382	.601	253	.387	427	.653	72.70	72.49	70.00	71.96	287.15	73.21	171

Complete Career Statistics G

Total Career Statistics & Adjusted Career, 10 year, 5 year, and Single Year Analysis

Greenberg, Hank: *Henry Benjamin "Hammerin' Hank" Greenberg, b. Jan 1, 1911, New York, NY*

Rating Category	Year	Ranked Seasons & Adjustment	G	AB	H	1B	2B	3B	HR	RUN	RBI	BB	SO	SB
	1930		1	1	-	-	-	-	-	-	-	-	-	-
	1933		117	449	135	87	33	3	12	59	87	46	78	6
	1934	5th	153	593	201	105	63	7	26	118	139	63	93	9
	1935	3rd	152	619	203	105	46	16	36	121	170	87	91	4
	1936		12	46	16	7	6	2	1	10	16	9	6	1
10 Year Total	1937	1st	154	594	200	97	49	14	40	137	183	102	101	8
	1938	2nd	155	556	175	90	23	4	58	144	146	119	92	7
5 Year Total	1939	6th	138	500	156	74	42	7	33	112	112	91	95	8
	1940	4th	148	573	195	96	50	8	41	129	150	93	75	6
	1941-1945		97	337	102	59	25	3	15	59	72	58	52	4
	1946		142	523	145	67	29	5	44	91	127	80	88	5
	1947		125	402	100	60	13	2	25	71	74	104	73	-
Career Total*	1930-1947		1,394	5,193	1,628	847	379	71	331	1,051	1,276	852	844	58
Career Adj. to 10,000 BO*	1930-1947	1.632120	2,275	8,476	2,657	1,382	619	116	540	1,715	2,083	1,391	1,378	95
Career Adj. to 10,000 AB*	1930-1947	1.925669	2,684	10,000	3,135	1,631	730	137	637	2,024	2,457	1,641	1,625	112
10 Year Total*	1933-1946		1,268	4,790	1,528	787	366	69	306	980	1,202	748	771	58
5 Year Total*	1937-1945		692	2,560	828	416	189	36	187	581	663	463	415	33
Best Single Year*	1937		154	594	200	97	49	14	40	137	183	102	101	8
2nd Best Year*	1938		155	556	175	90	23	4	58	144	146	119	92	7
3rd Best Year*	1935		152	619	203	105	46	16	36	121	170	87	91	4
4th Best Year*	1940		148	573	195	96	50	8	41	129	150	93	75	6
5th Best Year*	1934		153	593	201	105	63	7	26	118	139	63	93	9
6th Best Year*	1939		138	500	156	74	42	7	33	112	112	91	95	8

Total Career Statistics & Adjusted Career, 10 year, 5 year, and Single Year Analysis

Greenberg, Hank

CS	HBP	SF	GDP	AVG	OBP	SLG	TRP	RPA	TNB	TBA	TRP Rating	RPA Rating	TNB Rating	TBA Rating	TOP	Rating	Ranking
-	-	-	-	.000	.000	.000	-	.000	-	.000	-	-	-	-	-	-	-
2	1	-	-	.301	.367	.468	146	.294	261	.526	41.95	55.16	42.79	58.00	197.89	50.45	
5	2	-	-	.339	.404	.600	257	.391	425	.646	73.85	73.19	69.67	71.19	287.90	73.40	
3	-	-	-	.328	.411	.628	291	.412	477	.676	83.62	77.24	78.20	74.46	313.52	79.93	
-	-	-	-	.348	.455	.630	26	.473	39	.709	7.47	88.58	6.39	78.15	180.60	46.04	
3	3	-	-	.337	.436	.668	320	.458	507	.725	91.95	85.78	83.11	79.94	340.79	86.89	
5	3	-	-	.315	.438	.683	290	.428	504	.743	83.33	80.15	82.62	81.93	328.03	83.64	
3	2	-	8	.312	.420	.622	224	.373	409	.681	64.37	69.84	67.05	75.00	276.26	70.44	
3	1	-	15	.340	.433	.670	279	.409	481	.705	80.17	76.66	78.85	77.73	313.41	79.91	
1	-	-	10	.303	.405	.528	131	.323	239	.590	37.64	60.61	39.18	65.04	202.47	51.62	
1	-	-	17	.277	.373	.604	218	.352	400	.645	62.64	65.89	65.57	71.11	265.21	67.62	
-	4	-	16	.249	.408	.478	145	.276	300	.570	41.67	51.65	49.18	62.86	205.36	52.36	
26	16	-	66	.313	.412	.605	2,327	.380	4,042	.660	52.05	90.94	47.79	87.69	278.48	71.12	41
42	26	-	108	.313	.412	.605	3,798	.380	6,597	.660	90.94	90.94	87.69	87.69	357.27	89.32	5
50	31	-	127	.313	.412	.605	4,481	.380	7,784	.660	85.79	90.94	82.72	87.69	347.15	86.79	6
26	12	-	50	.319	.412	.616	2,182	.390	3,742	.668	74.12	88.85	75.49	84.31	322.77	82.79	15
15	9	-	33	.323	.429	.645	1,244	.406	2,140	.698	81.73	86.79	82.06	84.65	335.23	85.89	12
3	3	-	-	.337	.436	.668	320	.458	507	.725	91.95	85.78	83.11	79.94	340.79	86.89	19
5	3	-	-	.315	.438	.683	290	.428	504	.743	83.33	80.15	82.62	81.93	328.03	83.64	31
3	-	-	-	.328	.411	.628	291	.412	477	.676	83.62	77.24	78.20	74.46	313.52	79.93	58
3	1	-	15	.340	.433	.670	279	.409	481	.705	80.17	76.66	78.85	77.73	313.41	79.91	59
5	2	-	-	.339	.404	.600	257	.391	425	.646	73.85	73.19	69.67	71.19	287.90	73.40	165
3	2	-	8	.312	.420	.622	224	.373	409	.681	64.37	69.84	67.05	75.00	276.26	70.44	277

Complete Career Statistics G

Total Career Statistics & Adjusted Career, 10 year, 5 year, and Single Year Analysis

Griffey, Jr., Ken: *George Kenneth "Junior" Griffey, Jr.; b. Nov. 21, 1969, Donora, PA*

Rating Category	Year	Ranked Seasons & Adjustment	G	AB	H	1B	2B	3B	HR	RUN	RBI	BB	SO	SB
	1989		127	455	120	81	23	-	16	61	61	44	83	16
	1990		155	597	179	122	28	7	22	91	80	63	81	16
	1991		154	548	179	114	42	1	22	76	100	71	82	18
	1992		142	565	174	104	39	4	27	83	103	44	67	10
	1993		156	582	180	94	38	3	45	113	109	96	91	17
10 Year Total	1994		111	433	140	72	24	4	40	94	90	56	73	11
	1995		72	260	67	43	7	-	17	52	42	52	53	4
5 Year Total	1996	2nd	140	545	165	88	26	2	49	125	140	78	104	16
	1997	1st	157	608	185	92	34	3	56	125	147	76	121	15
	1998	3rd	161	633	180	88	33	3	56	120	146	76	121	20
	1999	4th	160	606	173	96	26	3	48	123	134	91	108	24
	2000		145	520	141	76	22	3	40	100	118	94	117	6
	2001		111	364	104	60	20	2	22	57	65	44	72	2
	2002		70	197	52	36	8	-	8	17	23	28	39	1
	2003		53	166	41	15	12	1	13	34	26	27	44	1
	2004		83	300	76	38	18	-	20	49	60	44	67	1
Career Total**	1989-2004		1,997	7,379	2,156	1,219	400	36	501	1,320	1,444	984	1,323	178
Career Adj. to 10,000 BO**	1989-2004	1.156337	2,309	8,533	2,493	1,410	463	42	579	1,526	1,670	1,138	1,530	206
Career Adj. to 10,000 AB**	1989-2004	1.355197	2,706	10,000	2,922	1,652	542	49	679	1,789	1,957	1,334	1,793	241
10 Year Total**	1991-2000		1,398	5,300	1,584	867	291	26	400	1,011	1,129	734	937	141
5 Year Total**	1996-2000		763	2,912	844	440	141	14	249	593	685	415	571	81
Best Single Year**	1997		157	608	185	92	34	3	56	125	147	76	121	15
2nd Best Year**	1996		140	545	165	88	26	2	49	125	140	78	104	16
3rd Best Year**	1998		161	633	180	88	33	3	56	120	146	76	121	20
4th Best Year**	1999		160	606	173	96	26	3	48	123	134	91	108	24

Total Career Statistics & Adjusted Career, 10 year, 5 year, and Single Year Analysis

Griffey, Jr., Ken

CS	HBP	SF	GDP	AVG	OBP	SLG	Total Offensive Production Statistics				TRP Rating	RPA Rating	TNB Rating	TBA Rating	TOP Composite		
							TRP	RPA	TNB	TBA					TOP	Rating	Ranking
7	2	4	4	.264	.329	.420	122	.240	246	.483	35.06	44.91	40.33	53.27	173.56	44.25	
11	2	4	12	.300	.366	.481	171	.252	357	.527	49.14	47.26	58.52	58.03	212.96	54.29	
6	1	9	10	.327	.399	.527	176	.275	373	.584	50.57	51.61	61.15	64.33	227.67	58.05	
5	5	3	14	.308	.361	.535	186	.295	356	.564	53.45	55.23	58.36	62.18	229.22	58.44	
9	6	7	14	.309	.408	.617	222	.315	469	.665	63.79	59.01	76.89	73.32	273.00	69.60	
3	2	2	8	.323	.402	.674	184	.367	358	.715	52.87	68.82	58.69	78.76	259.14	66.07	
2	-	2	4	.258	.379	.481	94	.296	179	.563	27.01	55.39	29.34	62.04	173.78	44.31	
1	7	7	7	.303	.392	.628	265	.411	442	.686	76.15	77.11	72.46	75.64	301.36	76.83	
4	8	12	12	.304	.382	.646	272	.380	488	.682	78.16	71.18	80.00	75.12	304.46	77.63	
5	7	4	14	.284	.365	.611	266	.362	485	.661	76.44	67.91	79.51	72.83	296.68	75.64	
7	7	2	8	.285	.384	.576	257	.360	464	.650	73.85	67.45	76.07	71.62	288.99	73.68	
4	9	8	7	.271	.387	.556	218	.342	394	.618	62.64	64.03	64.59	68.06	259.32	66.12	
-	4	4	8	.286	.365	.533	122	.288	244	.575	35.06	53.92	40.00	63.43	192.40	49.05	
2	3	4	6	.264	.358	.426	40	.168	114	.479	11.49	31.49	18.69	52.79	114.47	29.18	
-	6	1	3	.247	.370	.566	60	.296	128	.631	17.24	55.38	20.98	69.49	163.10	41.58	
-	2	2	8	.253	.351	.513	109	.306	201	.565	31.32	57.37	32.95	62.23	183.87	46.88	
66	71	75	139	.292	.377	.560	2,764	.320	5,298	.613	59.38	76.67	60.27	81.71	278.03	71.00	43
76	82	87	161	.292	.377	.560	3,196	.320	6,126	.613	76.67	76.67	81.71	81.71	316.76	79.19	30
89	96	102	188	.292	.377	.560	3,746	.320	7,180	.613	71.80	76.67	76.52	81.71	306.70	76.68	32
46	52	56	98	.299	.386	.590	2,140	.343	4,008	.642	72.69	78.21	80.86	81.04	312.79	80.23	23
21	38	33	48	.290	.382	.604	1,278	.371	2,273	.660	83.97	79.31	87.15	79.97	330.40	84.65	18
4	8	12	12	.304	.382	.646	272	.380	488	.682	78.16	71.18	80.00	75.12	304.46	77.63	83
1	7	7	7	.303	.392	.628	265	.411	442	.686	76.15	77.11	72.46	75.64	301.36	76.83	93
5	7	4	14	.284	.365	.611	266	.362	485	.661	76.44	67.91	79.51	72.83	296.68	75.64	115
7	7	2	8	.285	.384	.576	257	.360	464	.650	73.85	67.45	76.07	71.62	288.99	73.68	157

Complete Career Statistics G

Total Career Statistics & Adjusted Career, 10 year, 5 year, and Single Year Analysis

Guerrero, Vladimir: *Vladimir Alvino Guerrero, b. Feb 9., 1976, Nizao Bani, Dominican Republic*

Rating Category	Year	Ranked Seasons & Adjustment	G	AB	H	1B	2B	3B	HR	RUN	RBI	BB	SO	SB
	1996		9	27	5	4	-	-	1	2	1	-	3	-
	1997		90	325	98	63	22	2	11	44	40	19	39	3
5 Year Total	1998		159	623	202	120	37	7	38	108	109	42	95	11
	1999		160	610	193	109	37	5	42	102	131	55	62	14
	2000	2nd	154	571	197	114	28	11	44	101	123	58	74	9
	2001		159	599	184	101	45	4	34	107	108	60	88	37
	2002		161	614	206	128	37	2	39	106	111	84	70	40
	2003		112	394	130	82	20	3	25	71	79	63	53	9
	2004	1st	156	612	206	126	39	2	39	124	126	52	74	15
Career Total**	1996-2004		1,160	4,375	1,421	847	265	36	273	765	828	433	558	138
Career Adj. to 10,000 BO**	1996-2004	1.983733	2,301	8,679	2,819	1,680	526	71	542	1,518	1,643	859	1,107	274
Career Adj. to 10,000 AB**	1996-2004	2.285714	2,651	10,000	3,248	1,936	606	82	624	1,749	1,893	990	1,275	315
10 Year Total**	n/a													
5 Year Total**	1998-2002		793	3,017	982	572	184	29	197	524	582	299	389	111
Best Single Year**	2004		156	612	206	126	39	2	39	124	126	52	74	15
2nd Best Year**	2000		154	571	197	114	28	11	44	101	123	58	74	9

Total Career Statistics & Adjusted Career, 10 year, 5 year, and Single Year Analysis

Guerrero, Vladimir

CS	HBP	SF	GDP	AVG	OBP	SLG	Total Offensive Production Statistics				TRP Rating	RPA Rating	TNB Rating	TBA Rating	TOP Composite		
							TRP	RPA	TNB	TBA					TOP	Rating	Ranking
-	-	-	1	.185	.185	.296	3	.107	8	.286	0.86	20.08	1.31	31.49	53.74	13.70	
4	7	3	11	.302	.350	.483	84	.230	182	.499	24.14	43.12	29.84	54.96	152.05	38.77	
9	7	5	15	.324	.371	.589	217	.314	418	.604	62.36	58.76	68.52	66.57	256.22	65.32	
7	7	2	18	.316	.378	.600	233	.337	435	.629	66.95	63.09	71.31	69.28	270.64	69.00	
10	8	4	15	.345	.410	.664	224	.341	444	.677	64.37	63.98	72.79	74.60	275.73	70.30	
16	9	3	24	.307	.377	.566	215	.309	429	.617	61.78	57.97	70.33	68.03	258.11	65.81	
20	6	5	20	.336	.417	.593	217	.298	474	.650	62.36	55.78	77.70	71.66	267.50	68.20	
5	6	4	18	.330	.426	.586	150	.309	304	.627	43.10	57.95	49.84	69.08	219.98	56.08	
3	8	8	19	.337	.391	.598	250	.358	438	.627	71.84	67.02	71.80	69.06	279.72	71.32	
74	58	34	141	.325	.390	.589	1,593	.316	3,132	.621	35.63	75.67	37.03	82.59	230.92	58.97	106
147	115	67	280	.325	.390	.589	3,160	.316	6,213	.621	75.67	75.67	82.59	82.59	316.51	79.13	31
169	133	78	322	.325	.390	.589	3,641	.316	7,159	.621	69.71	75.67	76.08	82.59	304.05	76.01	33
62	37	19	92	.325	.391	.602	1,106	.319	2,200	.635	72.67	68.28	84.36	77.00	302.30	77.45	46
3	8	8	19	.337	.391	.598	250	.358	438	.627	71.84	67.02	71.80	69.06	279.72	71.32	240
10	8	4	15	.345	.410	.664	224	.341	444	.677	64.37	63.98	72.79	74.60	275.73	70.30	287

Complete Career Statistics G

Total Career Statistics & Adjusted Career, 10 year, 5 year, and Single Year Analysis

Hafey, Chick: *Charles James Hafey, b. Feb 12, 1903, Berkeley, CA*

Rating Category			Year	Ranked Seasons & Adjustment	G	AB	H	1B	2B	3B	HR	RUN	RBI	BB	SO	SB
			1924		24	91	23	14	5	2	2	10	22	4	8	1
			1925		93	358	108	76	25	2	5	36	57	10	29	3
			1926		78	225	61	36	19	2	4	30	38	11	36	2
10 Year Total	5 Year Total		1927		103	346	114	65	26	5	18	62	63	36	41	12
			1928		138	520	175	96	46	6	27	101	111	40	53	8
			1929	2nd	134	517	175	90	47	9	29	101	125	45	42	7
			1930	1st	120	446	150	73	39	12	26	108	107	46	51	12
			1931		122	450	157	98	35	8	16	94	95	39	43	11
			1932		83	253	87	63	19	3	2	34	36	22	20	4
			1933		144	568	172	125	34	6	7	77	62	40	44	3
			1934		140	535	157	104	29	6	18	75	67	52	63	4
			1935		15	59	20	12	6	1	1	10	9	4	5	1
			1937		89	257	67	42	11	5	9	39	41	23	42	2
Career Total			1924-1937		1,283	4,625	1,466	894	341	67	164	777	833	372	477	70
Career Adj. to 10,000 BO			1924-1937	1.977066	2,537	9,144	2,898	1,767	674	132	324	1,536	1,647	735	943	138
Career Adj. to 10,000 AB			1924-1937	2.162162	2,774	10,000	3,170	1,933	737	145	355	1,680	1,801	804	1,031	151
10 Year Total			1925-1934		1,155	4,218	1,356	826	319	59	152	718	761	341	422	66
5 Year Total			1927-1931		617	2,279	771	422	193	40	116	466	501	206	230	50
Best Single Year			1930		120	446	150	73	39	12	26	108	107	46	51	12
2nd Best Year			1929		134	517	175	90	47	9	29	101	125	45	42	7

Complete Career Statistics H

Total Career Statistics & Adjusted Career, 10 year, 5 year, and Single Year Analysis

Hafey, Chick

CS	HBP	SF	GDP	AVG	OBP	SLG	Total Offensive Production Statistics				TRP Rating	RPA Rating	TNB Rating	TBA Rating	TOP Composite		
							TRP	RPA	TNB	TBA					TOP	Rating	Ranking
-	1	-	.000	.253	.292	.418	32	.333	44	.458	9.20	62.46	7.21	50.51	129.38	32.99	
7	-	-	.000	.302	.321	.425	93	.253	158	.429	26.72	47.35	25.90	47.32	147.30	37.56	
-	2	-	.000	.271	.311	.427	68	.286	111	.466	19.54	53.54	18.20	51.40	142.68	36.38	
-	5	-	-	.329	.401	.590	125	.323	257	.664	35.92	60.52	42.13	73.19	211.77	53.99	
-	2	-	-	.337	.386	.604	212	.377	364	.648	60.92	70.68	59.67	71.38	262.66	66.97	
-	2	-	-	.338	.394	.632	226	.401	381	.676	64.94	75.09	62.46	74.45	276.94	70.61	
-	7	-	-	.336	.407	.652	215	.431	356	.713	61.78	80.74	58.36	78.63	279.51	71.26	
-	3	-	-	.349	.404	.569	189	.384	309	.628	54.31	71.98	50.66	69.22	246.17	62.76	
-	3	-	-	.344	.403	.466	70	.252	147	.529	20.11	47.18	24.10	58.28	149.67	38.16	
-	2	-	11	.303	.351	.421	139	.224	284	.457	39.94	41.94	46.56	50.40	178.85	45.60	
-	3	-	10	.293	.359	.471	142	.237	311	.518	40.80	44.35	50.98	57.13	193.26	49.27	
-	2	-	1	.339	.400	.525	19	.288	38	.576	5.46	53.94	6.23	63.46	129.09	32.91	
-	1	-	6	.261	.324	.447	80	.279	141	.491	22.99	52.23	23.11	54.15	152.48	38.88	
7	33	-	28	.317	.372	.526	1,610	.318	2,901	.574	36.01	76.22	34.30	76.24	222.77	56.89	115
14	65	-	55	.317	.372	.526	3,183	.318	5,735	.574	76.22	76.22	76.24	76.24	304.92	76.23	53
15	71	-	61	.317	.372	.526	3,481	.318	6,272	.574	66.65	76.22	66.66	76.24	285.77	71.44	66
7	29	-	21	.321	.376	.533	1,479	.321	2,678	.581	50.24	73.18	54.02	73.31	250.75	64.32	115
-	19	-	-	.338	.398	.611	967	.386	1,667	.666	63.53	82.58	63.92	80.72	290.75	74.49	70
-	7	-	-	.336	.407	.652	215	.431	356	.713	61.78	80.74	58.36	78.63	279.51	71.26	242
-	2	-	-	.338	.394	.632	226	.401	381	.676	64.94	75.09	62.46	74.45	276.94	70.61	262

Complete Career Statistics H

Total Career Statistics & Adjusted Career, 10 year, 5 year, and Single Year Analysis

Hamilton, Billy: *William Robert "Sliding Billy" Hamilton, b. Feb 16, 1866, Newark, NJ*

Rating Category	Year	Ranked Seasons & Adjustment	G	AB	H	1B	2B	3B	HR	RUN	RBI	BB	SO	SB
	1888		35	128	32	24	4	4	-	17	11	4	-	23
	1889	3rd	137	532	160	127	15	15	3	145	77	87	41	117
	1890		123	496	161	140	10	9	2	131	49	83	37	102
	1891		133	529	179	150	21	6	2	142	60	102	28	115
	1892		136	539	178	150	18	7	3	131	53	81	29	56
10 Year Total	1893		82	349	138	105	21	7	5	111	44	63	7	41
	1894	1st	131	559	223	183	22	14	4	196	87	126	17	99
5 Year Total	1895	2nd	121	517	203	171	19	6	7	166	74	96	30	95
	1896		131	523	190	153	26	8	3	153	52	110	29	93
	1897		125	506	174	148	17	6	3	153	61	105	-	70
	1898		109	417	153	130	16	4	3	111	50	87	-	59
	1899		81	294	90	82	6	1	1	62	33	72	-	19
	1900		135	524	174	149	19	5	1	103	47	107	-	29
	1901		99	349	102	86	11	2	3	70	38	64	-	19
Career Total	1888-1901		1,578	6,262	2,157	1,798	225	94	40	1,691	736	1,187	218	937
Career Adj. to 10,000 BO	1888-1901	1.326612	2,093	8,307	2,862	2,385	298	125	53	2,243	976	1,575	289	1,243
Career Adj. to 10,000 AB	1888-1901	1.596934	2,520	10,000	3,445	2,871	359	150	64	2,700	1,175	1,896	348	1,496
10 Year Total	1889-1898		1,228	4,967	1,759	1,457	185	82	35	1,439	607	940	218	847
5 Year Total	1894-1898		617	2,522	943	785	100	38	20	779	324	524	76	416
Best Single Year	1894		131	559	223	183	22	14	4	196	87	126	17	99
2nd Best Year	1895		121	517	203	171	19	6	7	166	74	96	30	95
3rd Best Year	1889		137	532	160	127	15	15	3	145	77	87	41	117

Complete Career Statistics H

Total Career Statistics & Adjusted Career, 10 year, 5 year, and Single Year Analysis

Hamilton, Billy

CS	HBP	SF	GDP	AVG	OBP	SLG	Total Offensive Production Statistics				TRP Rating	RPA Rating	TNB Rating	TBA Rating	TOP Composite		
							TRP	RPA	TNB	TBA					TOP	Rating	Ranking
-	4	-	-	.250	.294	.344	28	.206	75	.551	8.05	38.58	12.30	60.78	119.70	30.52	
-	14	-	-	.301	.412	.402	222	.351	432	.682	63.79	65.72	70.82	75.22	275.55	70.25	
-	9	-	-	.325	.430	.393	180	.306	389	.662	51.72	57.36	63.77	72.91	245.77	62.66	
-	7	-	-	.338	.451	.412	202	.317	442	.693	58.05	59.33	72.46	76.36	266.19	67.87	
-	8	-	-	.330	.425	.406	184	.293	364	.580	52.87	54.90	59.67	63.88	231.33	58.98	
-	13	-	-	.395	.504	.539	155	.365	305	.718	44.54	68.34	50.00	79.09	241.97	61.69	
-	9	-	-	.399	.516	.510	283	.408	519	.748	81.32	76.41	85.08	82.42	325.24	82.92	
-	7	-	-	.393	.494	.493	240	.387	453	.731	68.97	72.53	74.26	80.53	296.29	75.54	
-	2	-	-	.363	.476	.461	205	.323	446	.702	58.91	60.49	73.11	77.41	269.93	68.82	
-	6	-	-	.344	.462	.419	214	.347	393	.637	61.49	64.99	64.43	70.20	261.11	66.57	
-	2	-	-	.367	.478	.446	161	.318	334	.660	46.26	59.62	54.75	72.75	233.39	59.50	
-	1	-	-	.306	.444	.344	95	.259	193	.526	27.30	48.50	31.64	57.96	165.40	42.17	
-	3	-	-	.332	.448	.393	150	.237	345	.544	43.10	44.33	56.56	59.97	203.97	52.00	
-	4	-	-	.292	.408	.361	108	.259	213	.511	31.03	48.53	34.92	56.30	170.78	43.54	
-	89	-	-	.344	.455	.430	2,427	.322	4,903	.650	54.28	77.10	57.98	86.46	275.82	70.44	47
-	118	-	-	.344	.455	.430	3,220	.322	6,504	.650	77.10	77.10	86.46	86.46	327.11	81.78	19
-	142	-	-	.344	.455	.430	3,876	.322	7,830	.650	74.20	77.10	83.21	86.46	320.97	80.24	14
-	77	-	-	.354	.464	.446	2,046	.342	4,077	.681	69.50	77.97	82.25	85.96	315.68	80.97	20
-	26	-	-	.374	.486	.467	1,103	.359	2,145	.698	72.47	76.78	82.25	84.66	316.15	81.00	25
-	9	-	-	.399	.516	.510	283	.408	519	.748	81.32	76.41	85.08	82.42	325.24	82.92	35
-	7	-	-	.393	.494	.493	240	.387	453	.731	68.97	72.53	74.26	80.53	296.29	75.54	117
-	14	-	-	.301	.412	.402	222	.351	432	.682	63.79	65.72	70.82	75.22	275.55	70.25	290

Complete Career Statistics H

Total Career Statistics & Adjusted Career, 10 year, 5 year, and Single Year Analysis

Heilmann, Harry: *Harry Edwin "Slug" Heilmann, b. Aug. 3, 1894, San Francisco, CA*

Rating Category	Year	Ranked Seasons & Adjustment	G	AB	H	1B	2B	3B	HR	RUN	RBI	BB	SO	SB
	1914		67	182	41	30	8	1	2	25	18	22	29	1
	1916		136	451	127	84	30	11	2	57	73	42	40	9
	1917		150	556	156	118	22	11	5	57	86	41	54	11
	1918		79	286	79	58	10	6	5	34	39	35	10	13
	1919		140	537	172	119	30	15	8	74	93	37	41	7
	1920		145	543	168	126	28	5	9	66	89	39	32	3
5 Year Total / 10 Year Total	1921	2nd	149	602	237	161	43	14	19	114	139	53	37	2
	1922		118	455	162	104	27	10	21	92	92	58	28	8
	1923	1st	144	524	211	138	44	11	18	121	115	74	40	8
	1924		153	570	197	126	45	16	10	107	114	78	41	13
	1925		150	573	225	161	40	11	13	97	134	67	27	6
	1926		141	502	184	126	41	8	9	90	103	67	19	6
	1927	3rd	141	505	201	128	50	9	14	106	120	72	16	11
	1928		151	558	183	121	38	10	14	83	107	57	45	7
	1929		125	453	156	93	41	7	15	86	120	50	39	5
	1930		142	459	153	85	43	6	19	79	91	64	50	2
	1932		15	31	8	6	2	-	-	3	6	-	2	-
Career Total	1914-1932		2,146	7,787	2,660	1,784	542	151	183	1,291	1,539	856	550	112
Career Adj. to 10,000 BO	1914-1932	1.151676	2,471	8,968	3,063	2,055	624	174	211	1,487	1,772	986	633	129
Career Adj. to 10,000 AB	1914-1932	1.284192	2,756	10,000	3,416	2,291	696	194	235	1,658	1,976	1,099	706	144
10 Year Total	1921-1930		1,414	5,201	1,909	1,243	412	102	152	975	1,135	640	342	68
5 Year Total	1921-1925		714	2,724	1,032	690	199	62	81	531	594	330	173	37
Best Single Year	1923		144	524	211	138	44	11	18	121	115	74	40	8
2nd Best Year	1921		149	602	237	161	43	14	19	114	139	53	37	2
3rd Best Year	1927		141	505	201	128	50	9	14	106	120	72	16	11

Total Career Statistics & Adjusted Career, 10 year, 5 year, and Single Year Analysis

Heilmann, Harry

CS	HBP	SF	GDP	AVG	OBP	SLG	Total Offensive Production Statistics				TRP Rating	RPA Rating	TNB Rating	TBA Rating	TOP Composite		
							TRP	RPA	TNB	TBA					TOP	Rating	Ranking
8	2	-	-	.225	.316	.313	43	.209	74	.359	12.36	39.11	12.13	39.59	103.19	26.31	
-	5	-	-	.282	.349	.410	130	.261	241	.484	37.36	48.91	39.51	53.34	179.12	45.67	
-	3	-	-	.281	.333	.387	143	.238	270	.450	41.09	44.66	44.26	49.60	179.61	45.79	
-	2	-	-	.276	.359	.406	73	.226	166	.514	20.98	42.35	27.21	56.64	147.18	37.53	
-	2	-	-	.320	.366	.477	167	.290	302	.524	47.99	54.33	49.51	57.79	209.61	53.44	
7	2	-	-	.309	.358	.429	155	.265	270	.462	44.54	49.73	44.26	50.96	189.49	48.31	
6	2	-	-	.394	.444	.606	253	.385	416	.633	72.70	72.16	68.20	69.79	282.84	72.11	
4	3	-	-	.356	.432	.598	184	.357	337	.653	52.87	66.82	55.25	71.98	246.92	62.95	
7	5	-	-	.403	.481	.632	236	.391	411	.682	67.82	73.34	67.38	75.12	283.65	72.32	
5	4	-	-	.346	.428	.533	221	.339	394	.604	63.51	63.51	64.59	66.60	258.21	65.83	
6	1	-	-	.393	.457	.569	231	.360	394	.615	66.38	67.53	64.59	67.74	266.24	67.88	
7	4	-	-	.367	.445	.534	193	.337	338	.590	55.46	63.11	55.41	65.01	239.00	60.93	
5	2	-	-	.398	.475	.616	226	.390	391	.675	64.94	73.14	64.10	74.43	276.61	70.52	
3	-	-	-	.328	.390	.507	190	.309	344	.559	54.60	57.89	56.39	61.65	230.53	58.78	
6	2	-	-	.344	.412	.565	206	.408	307	.608	59.20	76.44	50.33	67.00	252.96	64.49	
-	1	-	-	.333	.416	.577	170	.324	332	.634	48.85	60.79	54.43	69.83	233.90	59.63	
-	-	-	-	.258	.258	.323	9	.290	10	.323	2.59	54.40	1.64	35.55	94.18	24.01	
64	40	-	-	.342	.410	.520	2,830	.326	4,997	.575	63.30	78.04	59.09	76.50	276.93	70.72	44
74	46	-	-	.342	.410	.520	3,259	.326	5,755	.575	78.04	78.04	76.50	76.50	309.08	77.27	47
82	51	-	-	.342	.410	.520	3,634	.326	6,417	.575	69.58	78.04	68.20	76.50	292.32	73.08	57
49	24	-	-	.367	.439	.573	2,110	.360	3,664	.625	71.67	82.04	73.92	78.82	306.45	78.60	29
28	15	-	-	.379	.449	.587	1,125	.367	1,952	.636	73.92	78.39	74.85	77.11	304.27	77.95	41
7	5	-	-	.403	.481	.632	236	.391	411	.682	67.82	73.34	67.38	75.12	283.65	72.32	203
6	2	-	-	.394	.444	.606	253	.385	416	.633	72.70	72.16	68.20	69.79	282.84	72.11	211
5	2	-	-	.398	.475	.616	226	.390	391	.675	64.94	73.14	64.10	74.43	276.61	70.52	270

Total Career Statistics & Adjusted Career, 10 year, 5 year, and Single Year Analysis

Helton, Todd: *Todd Lynn Helton, b. Aug. 20, 1973, Knoxville, TN*

Rating Category	Year	Ranked Seasons & Adjustment	G	AB	H	1B	2B	3B	HR	RUN	RBI	BB	SO	SB
	1997		35	93	26	18	2	1	5	13	11	8	11	-
	1998		152	530	167	104	37	1	25	78	97	53	54	3
	1999		159	578	185	106	39	5	35	114	113	68	77	7
5 Year Total	2000	1st	160	580	216	113	59	2	42	138	147	103	61	5
	2001	2nd	159	587	197	92	54	2	49	132	146	98	104	7
	2002		156	553	182	109	39	4	30	107	109	99	91	5
	2003	3rd	160	583	209	122	49	5	33	135	117	111	72	-
	2004		154	547	190	107	49	2	32	115	96	127	72	3
Career Total**	1997-2004		1,135	4,051	1,372	771	328	22	251	832	836	667	542	30
Career Adj. to 10,000 BO**	1997-2004	2.043318	2,319	8,277	2,803	1,575	670	45	513	1,700	1,708	1,363	1,107	61
Career Adj. to 10,000 AB**	1997-2004	2.468526	2,802	10,000	3,387	1,903	810	54	620	2,054	2,064	1,647	1,338	74
10 Year Total**	n/a													
5 Year Total**	2000-2004		789	2,850	994	543	250	15	186	627	615	538	400	20
Best Single Year**	2000		160	580	216	113	59	2	42	138	147	103	61	5
2nd Best Year**	2001		159	587	197	92	54	2	49	132	146	98	104	7
3rd Best Year**	2003		160	583	209	122	49	5	33	135	117	111	72	-

Complete Career Statistics H

Total Career Statistics & Adjusted Career, 10 year, 5 year, and Single Year Analysis

Helton, Todd

CS	HBP	SF	GDP	AVG	OBP	SLG	Total Offensive Production Statistics				TRP Rating	RPA Rating	TNB Rating	TBA Rating	TOP Composite		
							TRP	RPA	TNB	TBA					TOP	Rating	Ranking
1	-	-	1	.280	.337	.484	24	.235	52	.510	6.90	44.09	8.52	56.19	115.70	29.50	
3	6	5	16	.315	.380	.530	175	.287	340	.557	50.29	53.76	55.74	61.43	221.21	56.40	
6	6	4	14	.320	.395	.587	227	.339	414	.618	65.23	63.49	67.87	68.10	264.69	67.48	
3	4	10	12	.372	.463	.698	285	.402	514	.725	81.90	75.32	84.26	79.90	321.38	81.94	
5	5	5	14	.336	.432	.685	278	.392	507	.715	79.89	73.47	83.11	78.81	315.29	80.38	
1	5	10	10	.329	.429	.577	216	.319	427	.631	62.07	59.79	70.00	69.51	261.37	66.64	
4	2	7	19	.358	.458	.630	252	.349	476	.659	72.41	65.40	78.03	72.66	288.51	73.56	
-	3	6	12	.347	.469	.620	211	.304	472	.679	60.63	56.89	77.38	74.85	269.75	68.77	
23	31	47	98	.339	.432	.616	1,668	.341	3,202	.654	37.31	81.61	37.86	86.97	243.75	62.25	96
47	63	96	200	.339	.432	.616	3,408	.341	6,543	.654	81.61	81.61	86.97	86.97	337.16	84.29	12
57	77	116	242	.339	.432	.616	4,118	.341	7,904	.654	78.83	81.61	84.00	86.97	331.42	82.85	8
13	19	38	67	.349	.450	.643	1,242	.354	2,396	.682	81.60	75.62	91.87	82.72	331.81	85.01	16
3	4	10	12	.372	.463	.698	285	.402	514	.725	81.90	75.32	84.26	79.90	321.38	81.94	39
5	5	5	14	.336	.432	.685	278	.392	507	.715	79.89	73.47	83.11	78.81	315.29	80.38	50
4	2	7	19	.358	.458	.630	252	.349	476	.659	72.41	65.40	78.03	72.66	288.51	73.56	161

Complete Career Statistics H

Total Career Statistics & Adjusted Career, 10 year, 5 year, and Single Year Analysis

Henderson, Rickey: *Rickey Henley Henderson, b. Dec. 25, 1958, Chicago, IL*

Rating Category		Year	Ranked Seasons & Adjustment	G	AB	H	1B	2B	3B	HR	RUN	RBI	BB	SO	SB	
		1979		89	351	96	79	13	3	1	49	26	34	39	33	
		1980		158	591	179	144	22	4	9	111	53	117	54	100	
		1981		108	423	135	104	18	7	6	89	35	64	68	56	
		1982		149	536	143	105	24	4	10	119	51	116	94	130	
	5 Year Total	1983		145	513	150	109	25	7	9	105	48	103	80	108	
10 Year Total		1984		142	502	147	100	27	4	16	113	58	86	81	66	
		1985	1st	143	547	172	115	28	5	24	146	72	99	65	80	
		1986		153	608	160	96	31	5	28	130	74	89	81	87	
		1987		95	358	104	67	17	3	17	78	37	80	52	41	
		1988		140	554	169	131	30	2	6	118	50	82	54	93	
		1989		150	541	148	107	26	3	12	113	57	126	68	77	
		1990		136	489	159	95	33	3	28	119	61	97	60	65	
		1991		134	470	126	90	17	1	18	105	57	98	73	58	
		1992		117	396	112	76	18	3	15	77	46	95	56	48	
		1993		134	481	139	94	22	2	21	114	59	120	65	53	
		1994		87	296	77	58	13	-	6	66	20	72	45	22	
		1995		112	407	122	81	31	1	9	67	54	72	66	32	
		1996		148	465	112	84	17	2	9	110	29	125	90	37	
		1997		120	403	100	78	14	-	8	84	34	97	85	45	
		1998		152	542	128	97	16	1	14	101	57	118	114	66	
		1999		121	438	138	96	30	-	12	89	42	82	82	37	
		2000		123	420	98	78	14	2	4	75	32	88	75	36	
		2001		123	379	86	58	17	3	8	70	42	81	84	25	
		2002		72	179	40	28	6	1	5	40	16	38	47	8	
		2003		30	72	15	12	1	-	2	7	5	11	16	3	
Career Total		1979-2003		3,081	10,961	3,055	2,182	510	66	297	2,295	1,115	2,190	1,694	1,406	
Career Adj. to 10,000 BO		1979-2003	0.741400	2,284	8,126	2,265	1,618	378	49	220	1,702	827	1,624	1,256	1,042	
Career Adj. to 10,000 AB		1979-2003	0.912326	2,811	10,000	2,787	1,991	465	60	271	2,094	1,017	1,998	1,545	1,283	
10 Year Total		1982-1991		1,387	5,118	1,478	1,015	258	37	168	1,146	565	976	708	805	
5 Year Total		1982-1986		732	2,706	772	525	135	25	87	613	303	493	401	471	
Best Single Year		1985		143	547	172	115	28	5	24	146	72	99	65	80	

Total Career Statistics & Adjusted Career, 10 year, 5 year, and Single Year Analysis

Henderson, Rickey

CS	HBP	SF	GDP	AVG	OBP	SLG	TRP	RPA	TNB	TBA	TRP Rating	RPA Rating	TNB Rating	TBA Rating	TOP	Rating	Ranking
11	2	3	4	.274	.338	.336	75	.190	176	.447	21.55	35.67	28.85	49.23	135.31	34.50	
26	5	3	6	.303	.420	.399	164	.227	432	.598	47.13	42.56	70.82	65.95	226.45	57.74	
22	2	4	7	.319	.408	.437	124	.248	285	.570	35.63	46.47	46.72	62.82	191.65	48.86	
42	2	2	5	.267	.398	.382	170	.257	411	.622	48.85	48.19	67.38	68.53	232.95	59.39	
19	4	1	11	.292	.414	.421	153	.242	412	.652	43.97	45.36	67.54	71.85	228.72	58.31	
18	5	3	7	.293	.399	.458	171	.284	369	.612	49.14	53.14	60.49	67.44	230.21	58.69	
10	3	5	8	.314	.419	.516	218	.329	454	.686	62.64	61.71	74.43	75.58	274.36	69.95	
18	2	2	12	.263	.358	.469	204	.286	445	.624	58.62	53.61	72.95	68.79	253.97	64.75	
8	2	-	10	.291	.423	.497	115	.256	293	.651	33.05	47.89	48.03	71.76	200.73	51.18	
13	3	6	6	.305	.394	.399	168	.258	386	.593	48.28	48.36	63.28	65.35	225.26	57.43	
14	3	4	8	.274	.411	.399	170	.249	408	.598	48.85	46.71	66.89	65.93	228.38	58.23	
10	4	2	13	.325	.439	.577	180	.298	438	.724	51.72	55.75	71.80	79.79	259.07	66.05	
18	7	3	7	.268	.400	.423	162	.277	344	.588	46.55	51.89	56.39	64.81	219.65	56.00	
11	6	3	5	.283	.426	.457	123	.244	319	.632	35.34	45.64	52.30	69.62	202.90	51.73	
8	4	4	9	.289	.432	.474	173	.280	397	.642	49.71	52.45	65.08	70.80	238.05	60.69	
7	5	2	-	.260	.411	.365	86	.229	200	.533	24.71	42.97	32.79	58.78	159.25	40.60	
10	4	3	8	.300	.407	.447	121	.245	280	.567	34.77	45.90	45.90	62.47	189.04	48.20	
15	10	2	5	.241	.410	.344	139	.229	317	.522	39.94	42.91	51.97	57.56	192.38	49.05	
8	6	2	10	.248	.400	.342	118	.228	278	.537	33.91	42.69	45.57	59.15	181.32	46.23	
13	5	3	5	.236	.376	.347	158	.235	364	.541	45.40	43.99	59.67	59.61	208.68	53.20	
14	2	3	4	.315	.423	.466	131	.248	311	.588	37.64	46.40	50.98	64.80	199.83	50.95	
11	4	4	11	.233	.368	.305	107	.203	245	.465	30.75	38.05	40.16	51.24	160.19	40.84	
7	3	2	8	.227	.366	.351	112	.237	235	.497	32.18	44.37	38.52	54.76	169.84	43.30	
2	4	1	3	.223	.369	.352	56	.249	111	.493	16.09	46.64	18.20	54.37	135.30	34.50	
-	1	-	-	.208	.321	.306	12	.143	37	.440	3.45	26.77	6.07	48.55	84.83	21.63	
335	98	67	172	.279	.401	.419	3,410	.253	7,947	.589	76.27	60.54	93.97	78.32	309.10	78.94	13
248	73	50	128	.279	.401	.419	2,528	.253	5,892	.589	60.54	60.54	78.32	78.32	277.71	69.43	96
306	89	61	157	.279	.401	.419	3,111	.253	7,250	.589	59.56	60.54	77.05	78.32	275.47	68.87	85
170	35	28	87	.289	.404	.452	1,711	.274	3,960	.634	58.12	62.49	79.89	80.02	280.51	71.95	64
107	16	13	43	.285	.397	.450	916	.280	2,091	.639	60.18	59.88	80.18	77.50	277.75	71.16	93
10	3	5	8	.314	.419	.516	218	.329	454	.686	62.64	61.71	74.43	75.58	274.36	69.95	301

Complete Career Statistics H

Total Career Statistics & Adjusted Career, 10 year, 5 year, and Single Year Analysis

Herman, Babe: *Floyd Caves Herman, b. June 26, 1903, Buffalo, NY*

Rating Category		Year	Ranked Seasons & Adjustment	G	AB	H	1B	2B	3B	HR	RUN	RBI	BB	SO	SB
10 Year Total	5 Year Total	1926		137	496	158	101	35	11	11	64	81	44	53	8
		1927		130	412	112	63	26	9	14	65	73	39	41	4
		1928		134	486	165	110	37	6	12	64	91	38	36	1
		1929		146	569	217	141	42	13	21	105	113	55	45	21
		1930	1st	153	614	241	147	48	11	35	143	130	66	56	18
		1931		151	610	191	114	43	16	18	93	97	50	65	17
		1932		148	577	188	115	38	19	16	87	87	60	45	7
		1933		137	508	147	83	36	12	16	77	93	50	57	6
		1934		125	467	142	89	34	5	14	65	84	35	71	1
		1935		118	430	136	89	31	6	10	52	65	38	35	5
		1936		119	380	106	66	25	2	13	59	71	39	36	4
		1937		17	20	6	3	3	-	-	2	3	1	6	2
		1945		37	34	9	7	1	-	1	6	9	5	7	-
Career Total		1926-1945		1,552	5,603	1,818	1,128	399	110	181	882	997	520	553	94
Career Adj. to 10,000 BO		1926-1945	1.618909	2,513	9,071	2,943	1,826	646	178	293	1,428	1,614	842	895	152
Career Adj. to 10,000 AB		1926-1945	1.784758	2,770	10,000	3,245	2,013	712	196	323	1,574	1,779	928	987	168
10 Year Total		1926-1935		1,379	5,169	1,697	1,052	370	108	167	815	914	475	504	88
5 Year Total		1929-1933		735	2,878	984	600	207	71	106	505	520	281	268	69
Best Single Year		1930		153	614	241	147	48	11	35	143	130	66	56	18

Total Career Statistics & Adjusted Career, 10 year, 5 year, and Single Year Analysis

Herman, Babe

CS	HBP	SF	GDP	AVG	OBP	SLG	Total Offensive Production Statistics				TRP Rating	RPA Rating	TNB Rating	TBA Rating	TOP Composite		
							TRP	RPA	TNB	TBA					TOP	Rating	Ranking
-	1	-	-	.319	.375	.500	145	.268	301	.556	41.67	50.22	49.34	61.32	202.55	51.64	
-	1	-	-	.272	.336	.481	138	.305	242	.535	39.66	57.21	39.67	59.01	195.55	49.86	
-	2	-	-	.340	.390	.514	155	.295	291	.553	44.54	55.22	47.70	60.97	208.44	53.14	
-	-	-	-	.381	.436	.612	218	.349	424	.679	62.64	65.46	69.51	74.89	272.50	69.48	
-	4	-	-	.393	.455	.678	273	.399	504	.737	78.45	74.79	82.62	81.21	317.07	80.84	
-	-	-	-	.313	.365	.525	190	.288	387	.586	54.60	53.94	63.44	64.63	236.61	60.33	
-	-	-	-	.326	.389	.541	174	.273	379	.595	50.00	51.18	62.13	65.57	228.89	58.36	
-	-	-	15	.289	.353	.502	170	.297	311	.543	48.85	55.59	50.98	59.82	215.25	54.88	
-	-	-	9	.304	.353	.488	149	.292	264	.517	42.82	54.64	43.28	56.94	197.67	50.40	
-	1	-	7	.316	.373	.486	117	.246	253	.532	33.62	46.06	41.48	58.58	179.73	45.82	
-	1	-	11	.279	.348	.458	130	.302	218	.506	37.36	56.52	35.74	55.75	185.36	47.26	
-	1	-	-	.300	.364	.450	5	.227	13	.591	1.44	42.59	2.13	65.13	111.28	28.37	
-	-	-	1	.265	.359	.382	15	.375	18	.450	4.31	70.27	2.95	49.60	127.13	32.41	
-	11	-	43	.324	.383	.532	1,879	.304	3,605	.584	42.03	72.84	42.63	77.58	235.07	60.03	100
-	18	-	70	.324	.383	.532	3,042	.304	5,836	.584	72.84	72.84	77.58	77.58	300.84	75.21	64
-	20	-	77	.324	.383	.532	3,354	.304	6,434	.584	64.20	72.84	68.38	77.58	283.00	70.75	73
-	9	-	31	.328	.386	.539	1,729	.304	3,356	.590	58.73	69.37	67.70	74.50	270.30	69.33	83
-	4	-	15	.342	.401	.574	1,025	.323	2,005	.631	67.35	68.97	76.88	76.49	289.69	74.22	73
-	4	-	-	.393	.455	.678	273	.399	504	.737	78.45	74.79	82.62	81.21	317.07	80.84	47

H Complete Career Statistics

Total Career Statistics & Adjusted Career, 10 year, 5 year, and Single Year Analysis

Hornsby, Rogers: *Rogers Rajah Hornsby, b. April 27, 1896, Winters, TX*

Rating Category	Year	Ranked Seasons & Adjustment	G	AB	H	1B	2B	3B	HR	RUN	RBI	BB	SO	SB
	1915		18	57	14	12	2	-	-	5	4	2	6	-
	1916		139	495	155	117	17	15	6	63	65	40	63	17
	1917		145	523	171	122	24	17	8	86	66	45	34	17
	1918		115	416	117	82	19	11	5	51	60	40	43	8
	1919		138	512	163	131	15	9	8	68	71	48	41	17
	1920		149	589	218	145	44	20	9	96	94	60	50	12
	1921	4th	154	592	235	152	44	18	21	131	126	60	48	13
5 Year Total	1922	1st	154	623	250	148	46	14	42	141	152	65	50	17
	1923		107	424	163	104	32	10	17	89	83	55	29	3
	1924	6th	143	536	227	145	43	14	25	121	94	89	32	5
	1925	3rd	138	504	203	113	41	10	39	133	143	83	39	5
10 Year Total	1926		134	527	167	117	34	5	11	96	93	61	39	3
	1927	5th	155	568	205	138	32	9	26	133	125	86	38	9
	1928		140	486	188	118	42	7	21	99	94	107	41	5
	1929	2nd	156	602	229	135	47	8	39	156	149	87	65	2
	1930		42	104	32	24	5	1	2	15	18	12	12	-
	1931		100	357	118	64	37	1	16	64	90	56	23	1
	1932		19	58	13	10	2	-	1	10	7	10	4	-
	1933		57	92	30	20	7	-	3	11	23	14	7	1
	1934		24	23	7	4	2	-	1	2	11	7	4	-
	1935		10	24	5	2	3	-	-	1	3	3	6	-
	1936		2	5	2	2	-	-	-	1	2	1	-	-
	1937		20	56	18	14	3	-	1	7	11	7	5	-
Career Total	1915-1937		2,259	8,173	2,930	1,919	541	169	301	1,579	1,584	1,038	679	135
Career Adj. to 10,000 BO	1915-1937	1.079680	2,439	8,824	3,163	2,072	584	182	325	1,705	1,710	1,121	733	146
Career Adj. to 10,000 AB	1915-1937	1.223541	2,764	10,000	3,585	2,348	662	207	368	1,932	1,938	1,270	831	165
10 Year Total	1920-1929		1,430	5,451	2,085	1,315	405	115	250	1,195	1,153	753	431	74
5 Year Total	1921-1625		696	2,679	1,078	662	206	66	144	615	598	352	198	43
Best Single Year	1922		154	623	250	148	46	14	42	141	152	65	50	17
2nd Best Year	1929		156	602	229	135	47	8	39	156	149	87	65	2
3rd Best Year	1925		138	504	203	113	41	10	39	133	143	83	39	5
4th Best Year	1921		154	592	235	152	44	18	21	131	126	60	48	13
5th Best Year	1927		155	568	205	138	32	9	26	133	125	86	38	9
6th Best Year	1924		143	536	227	145	43	14	25	121	94	89	32	5

Complete Career Statistics **H**

Total Career Statistics & Adjusted Career, 10 year, 5 year, and Single Year Analysis

Hornsby, Rogers

CS	HBP	SF	GDP	AVG	OBP	SLG	Total Offensive Production Statistics				TRP Rating	RPA Rating	TNB Rating	TBA Rating	TOP Composite		
							TRP	RPA	TNB	TBA					TOP	Rating	Ranking
2	-	-	-	.246	.271	.281	9	.153	16	.271	2.59	28.58	2.62	29.89	63.68	16.24	
-	4	-	-	.313	.369	.444	128	.237	281	.521	36.78	44.50	46.07	57.46	184.80	47.12	
-	4	-	-	.327	.385	.484	152	.266	319	.558	43.68	49.79	52.30	61.47	207.23	52.84	
-	3	-	-	.281	.349	.416	111	.242	224	.488	31.90	45.31	36.72	53.79	167.72	42.76	
-	7	-	-	.318	.384	.430	139	.245	292	.515	39.94	45.94	47.87	56.76	190.51	48.57	
15	3	-	-	.370	.431	.559	190	.291	389	.597	54.60	54.61	63.77	65.76	238.73	60.87	
13	7	-	-	.397	.458	.639	257	.390	445	.675	73.85	73.08	72.95	74.42	294.30	75.03	
12	1	-	-	.401	.459	.722	293	.425	521	.756	84.20	79.68	85.41	83.34	332.63	84.81	
7	3	-	-	.384	.459	.627	172	.357	320	.664	49.43	66.87	52.46	73.17	241.92	61.68	
12	2	-	-	.424	.507	.696	215	.343	457	.729	61.78	64.25	74.92	80.33	281.28	71.72	
3	2	-	-	.403	.489	.756	276	.469	468	.795	79.31	87.81	76.72	87.57	331.41	84.50	
-	-	-	-	.317	.388	.463	189	.321	308	.524	54.31	60.23	50.49	57.73	222.76	56.80	
-	4	-	-	.361	.448	.586	258	.392	432	.657	74.14	73.47	70.82	72.36	290.79	74.14	
-	1	-	-	.387	.498	.632	193	.325	420	.707	55.46	60.88	68.85	77.93	263.12	67.09	
-	1	-	-	.380	.459	.679	305	.442	499	.723	87.64	82.83	81.80	79.71	331.98	84.64	
-	1	-	-	.308	.385	.433	33	.282	58	.496	9.48	52.85	9.51	54.64	126.48	32.25	
-	-	-	-	.331	.421	.574	154	.373	262	.634	44.25	69.87	42.95	69.92	226.99	57.87	
-	2	-	-	.224	.357	.310	17	.243	30	.429	4.89	45.51	4.92	47.23	102.54	26.14	
-	2	3	-	.326	.414	.500	34	.306	63	.568	9.77	57.40	10.33	62.55	140.05	35.71	
-	1	-	-	.304	.484	.522	13	.419	20	.645	3.74	78.58	3.28	71.11	156.70	39.95	
-	-	-	-	.208	.296	.333	4	.148	11	.407	1.15	27.76	1.80	44.90	75.62	19.28	
-	-	-	-	.400	.500	.400	3	.500	3	.500	0.86	93.69	0.49	55.11	150.15	38.28	
-	-	-	-	.321	.397	.429	18	.286	31	.492	5.17	53.54	5.08	54.23	118.02	30.09	
64	48	3	-	.358	.434	.577	3,163	.342	5,869	.634	70.74	81.78	69.40	84.23	306.15	78.18	16
69	52	3	-	.358	.434	.577	3,415	.342	6,337	.634	81.78	81.78	84.23	84.23	332.01	83.00	15
78	59	4	-	.358	.434	.577	3,870	.342	7,181	.634	74.09	81.78	76.32	84.23	316.41	79.10	21
62	24	-	-	.382	.460	.637	2,348	.377	4,259	.684	79.76	85.97	85.92	86.28	337.93	86.68	6
47	15	-	-	.402	.474	.690	1,213	.398	2,211	.726	79.70	85.16	84.78	88.01	337.64	86.50	9
12	1	-	-	.401	.459	.722	293	.425	521	.756	84.20	79.68	85.41	83.34	332.63	84.81	26
-	1	-	-	.380	.459	.679	305	.442	499	.723	87.64	82.83	81.80	79.71	331.98	84.64	27
3	2	-	-	.403	.489	.756	276	.469	468	.795	79.31	87.81	76.72	87.57	331.41	84.50	28
13	7	-	-	.397	.458	.639	257	.390	445	.675	73.85	73.08	72.95	74.42	294.30	75.03	127
-	4	-	-	.361	.448	.586	258	.392	432	.657	74.14	73.47	70.82	72.36	290.79	74.14	142
12	2	-	-	.424	.507	.696	215	.343	457	.729	61.78	64.25	74.92	80.33	281.28	71.72	226

H

Complete Career Statistics

Total Career Statistics & Adjusted Career, 10 year, 5 year, and Single Year Analysis

Howard, Frank: *Frank Olvier "Hondo" Howard, b. Aug. 8, 1936, Columbus, OH*

Rating Category	Year	Ranked Seasons & Adjustment	G	AB	H	1B	2B	3B	HR	RUN	RBI	BB	SO	SB
	1958		8	29	7	5	1	-	1	3	2	1	11	-
	1959		9	21	3	1	-	1	1	2	6	2	9	-
	1960		117	448	120	80	15	2	23	54	77	32	108	-
	1961		92	267	79	52	10	2	15	36	45	21	50	-
10 Year Total	1962		141	493	146	84	25	6	31	80	119	39	108	1
	1963		123	417	114	69	16	1	28	58	64	33	116	1
	1964		134	433	98	59	13	2	24	60	69	51	113	1
	1965		149	516	149	100	22	6	21	53	84	55	112	-
	1966		146	496	137	96	19	4	18	52	71	53	104	1
	1967 (5 Year Total)		149	519	133	75	20	2	36	71	89	60	155	-
	1968		158	598	164	89	28	3	44	79	106	54	141	-
	1969	1st	161	592	175	108	17	2	48	111	111	102	96	1
	1970		161	566	160	100	15	1	44	90	126	132	125	1
	1971		153	549	153	100	25	2	26	60	83	77	121	1
	1972		109	320	78	58	10	-	10	29	38	46	63	1
	1973		85	227	58	36	9	1	12	26	29	24	28	-
Career Total	1958-1973		1,895	6,491	1,774	1,112	245	35	382	864	1,119	782	1,460	8
Career Adj. to 10,000 BO	1958-1973	1.321353	2,504	8,577	2,344	1,469	324	46	505	1,142	1,479	1,033	1,929	11
Career Adj. to 10,000 AB	1958-1973	1.540595	2,919	10,000	2,733	1,713	377	54	589	1,331	1,724	1,205	2,249	12
10 Year Total	1962-1971		1,475	5,179	1,429	880	200	29	320	714	922	656	1,191	7
5 Year Total	1967-1971		782	2,824	785	472	105	10	198	411	515	425	638	3
Best Single Year	1969		161	592	175	108	17	2	48	111	111	102	96	1

Total Career Statistics & Adjusted Career, 10 year, 5 year, and Single Year Analysis

Howard, Frank

CS	HBP	SF	GDP	AVG	OBP	SLG	Total Offensive Production Statistics				TRP Rating	RPA Rating	TNB Rating	TBA Rating	TOP Composite		
							TRP	RPA	TNB	TBA					TOP	Rating	Ranking
-	-	-	1	.241	.267	.379	5	.161	12	.387	1.44	30.22	1.97	42.66	76.29	19.45	
-	-	-	-	.143	.217	.381	8	.348	10	.435	2.30	65.18	1.64	47.92	117.03	29.84	
1	3	2	8	.268	.320	.464	131	.266	242	.491	37.64	49.79	39.67	54.10	181.21	46.20	
1	1	2	12	.296	.347	.517	81	.267	159	.525	23.28	50.09	26.07	57.84	157.27	40.10	
-	1	4	18	.296	.346	.560	199	.359	317	.571	57.18	67.19	51.97	62.95	239.29	61.01	
2	4	3	7	.273	.330	.518	122	.263	252	.543	35.06	49.27	41.31	59.86	185.50	47.29	
-	-	7	14	.226	.303	.432	129	.255	239	.473	37.07	47.87	39.18	52.16	176.28	44.94	
-	2	2	9	.289	.358	.477	137	.235	303	.519	39.37	43.96	49.67	57.18	190.18	48.49	
1	1	2	14	.276	.346	.440	123	.217	272	.481	35.34	40.72	44.59	52.97	173.62	44.27	
1	5	1	14	.256	.338	.511	160	.267	329	.549	45.98	50.05	53.93	60.54	210.50	53.67	
-	6	5	13	.274	.338	.552	185	.274	390	.577	53.16	51.28	63.93	63.59	231.96	59.14	
-	5	3	29	.296	.402	.574	222	.304	448	.613	63.79	56.91	73.44	67.55	261.69	66.72	
2	2	6	23	.283	.416	.546	216	.296	442	.606	62.07	55.52	72.46	66.82	256.87	65.49	
-	2	5	29	.279	.367	.474	143	.216	340	.514	41.09	40.48	55.74	56.61	193.91	49.44	
-	1	1	16	.244	.340	.369	67	.174	166	.432	19.25	32.69	27.21	47.64	126.80	32.33	
1	-	-	12	.256	.327	.463	55	.209	128	.487	15.80	39.19	20.98	53.64	129.61	33.05	
9	33	43	219	.273	.352	.498	1,983	.262	4,049	.535	44.35	62.74	47.88	71.12	226.09	57.74	112
12	44	57	289	.273	.352	.498	2,620	.262	5,350	.535	62.74	62.74	71.12	71.12	267.72	66.93	116
14	51	66	337	.273	.352	.498	3,055	.262	6,238	.535	58.49	62.74	66.29	71.12	258.64	64.66	110
6	28	38	170	.276	.358	.511	1,636	.269	3,332	.549	55.57	61.45	67.22	69.25	253.49	65.02	112
3	20	20	108	.278	.374	.533	926	.273	1,949	.574	60.84	58.29	74.73	69.56	263.43	67.49	117
-	5	3	29	.296	.402	.574	222	.304	448	.613	63.79	56.91	73.44	67.55	261.69	66.72	347

Complete Career Statistics   H

Total Career Statistics & Adjusted Career, 10 year, 5 year, and Single Year Analysis

Jackson, Joe: *Joseph Jefferson "Shoeless Joe" Jackson, b. July 16, 1887, Brandon Mills, SC*

Rating Category	Year	Ranked Seasons & Adjustment	G	AB	H	1B	2B	3B	HR	RUN	RBI	BB	SO	SB
	1908		5	23	3	3	-	-	-	-	3	-	-	-
	1909		5	17	3	3	-	-	-	3	3	1	-	-
	1910		20	75	29	21	2	5	1	15	11	8	-	4
	1911	1st	147	571	233	162	45	19	7	126	83	56	-	41
	1912		152	572	226	153	44	26	3	121	90	54	-	35
	1913		148	528	197	134	39	17	7	109	71	80	26	26
	1914		122	453	153	115	22	13	3	61	53	41	34	22
	1915		128	461	142	103	20	14	5	63	81	52	23	16
	1916		155	592	202	138	40	21	3	91	78	46	25	24
	1917		146	538	162	120	20	17	5	91	75	57	25	13
	1918		17	65	23	18	2	2	1	9	20	8	1	3
	1919		139	516	181	129	31	14	7	79	96	60	10	9
	1920		146	570	218	144	42	20	12	105	121	56	14	9
Career Total	1908-1920		1,330	4,981	1,772	1,243	307	168	54	873	785	519	158	202
Career Adj. to 10,000 BO	1908-1920	1.798885	2,393	8,960	3,188	2,236	552	302	97	1,570	1,412	934	284	363
Career Adj. to 10,000 AB	1908-1920	2.007629	2,670	10,000	3,558	2,495	616	337	108	1,753	1,576	1,042	317	406
10 Year Total	1911-1920		1,300	4,866	1,737	1,216	305	163	53	855	768	510	158	198
5 Year Total	1911-1915		697	2,585	951	667	170	89	25	480	378	283	83	140
Best Single Year	1911		147	571	233	162	45	19	7	126	83	56	-	41

5 Year Total (vertical label)
10 Year Total (vertical label)

Total Career Statistics & Adjusted Career, 10 year, 5 year, and Single Year Analysis

Jackson, Joe

CS	HBP	SF	GDP	AVG	OBP	SLG	Total Offensive Production Statistics				TRP Rating	RPA Rating	TNB Rating	TBA Rating	TOP Composite		
							TRP	RPA	TNB	TBA					TOP	Rating	Ranking
-	-	-	-	.130	.130	.130	3	.130	3	.130	0.86	24.44	0.49	14.38	40.17	10.24	
-	-	-	-	.176	.222	.176	6	.333	4	.222	1.72	62.46	0.66	24.49	89.33	22.78	
-	-	-	-	.387	.446	.587	26	.313	56	.675	7.47	58.70	9.18	74.36	149.71	38.17	
-	8	-	-	.408	.468	.590	209	.329	442	.696	60.06	61.67	72.46	76.72	270.91	69.07	
-	12	-	-	.395	.458	.579	211	.331	432	.677	60.63	61.97	70.82	74.63	268.05	68.34	
-	5	-	-	.373	.460	.551	180	.294	402	.656	51.72	55.02	65.90	72.28	244.93	62.45	
15	5	-	-	.338	.399	.464	114	.228	263	.527	32.76	42.81	43.11	58.09	176.77	45.07	
20	6	-	-	.308	.385	.445	144	.277	259	.499	41.38	51.99	42.46	55.00	190.83	48.65	
14	5	-	-	.341	.393	.495	169	.263	354	.551	48.56	49.25	58.03	60.68	216.52	55.20	
-	7	-	-	.301	.375	.429	166	.276	308	.512	47.70	51.67	50.49	56.39	206.25	52.59	
-	-	-	-	.354	.425	.492	29	.397	43	.589	8.33	74.44	7.05	64.92	154.74	39.45	
-	4	-	-	.351	.422	.506	175	.302	334	.576	50.29	56.54	54.75	63.47	225.05	57.38	
12	7	-	-	.382	.444	.589	226	.357	396	.626	64.94	66.90	64.92	68.95	265.71	67.75	
61	59	-	-	.356	.423	.517	1,658	.298	3,296	.593	37.08	71.42	38.97	78.81	226.29	57.79	111
110	106	-	-	.356	.423	.517	2,983	.298	5,929	.593	71.42	71.42	78.81	78.81	300.46	75.12	65
122	118	-	-	.356	.423	.517	3,329	.298	6,617	.593	63.73	71.42	70.32	78.81	284.28	71.07	71
61	59	-	-	.357	.424	.519	1,623	.299	3,233	.595	55.13	68.10	65.22	75.05	263.50	67.59	94
35	36	-	-	.368	.437	.532	858	.295	1,798	.619	56.37	63.18	68.94	75.07	263.56	67.52	116
-	8	-	-	.408	.468	.590	209	.329	442	.696	60.06	61.67	72.46	76.72	270.91	69.07	313

Complete Career Statistics J

Total Career Statistics & Adjusted Career, 10 year, 5 year, and Single Year Analysis

Jackson, Reggie: *Reginald Martinez Jackson, b. May 18, 1946, Wyncote, PA*

Rating Category	Year	Ranked Seasons & Adjustment	G	AB	H	1B	2B	3B	HR	RUN	RBI	BB	SO	SB
	1967		35	118	21	12	4	4	1	13	6	10	46	1
	1968		154	553	138	90	13	6	29	82	74	50	171	14
	1969	1st	152	549	151	65	36	3	47	123	118	115	142	13
	1970		149	426	101	55	21	2	23	57	66	75	135	26
	1971		150	567	157	93	29	3	32	87	80	63	161	16
	1972		135	499	132	80	25	2	25	72	75	59	125	9
	1973		151	539	158	96	28	2	32	99	117	76	111	22
	1974		148	506	146	91	25	1	29	90	93	86	105	25
	1975		157	593	150	72	39	3	36	91	104	67	133	17
	1976		134	498	138	82	27	2	27	84	91	54	108	28
	1977		146	525	150	77	39	2	32	93	110	74	129	17
	1978		139	511	140	95	13	5	27	82	97	58	133	14
	1979		131	465	138	83	24	2	29	78	89	65	107	9
	1980		143	514	154	87	22	4	41	94	111	83	122	1
	1981		94	334	79	46	17	1	15	33	54	46	82	-
	1982		153	530	146	89	17	1	39	92	101	85	156	4
	1983		116	397	77	48	14	1	14	43	49	52	140	-
	1984		143	525	117	73	17	2	25	67	81	55	141	8
	1985		143	460	116	62	27	-	27	64	85	78	138	1
	1986		132	419	101	69	12	2	18	65	58	92	115	1
	1987		115	336	74	44	14	1	15	42	43	33	97	2
Career Total	1967-1987		2,820	9,864	2,584	1,509	463	49	563	1,551	1,702	1,376	2,597	228
Career Adj. to 10,000 BO	1967-1987	0.863036	2,434	8,513	2,230	1,302	400	42	486	1,339	1,469	1,188	2,241	197
Career Adj. to 10,000 AB	1967-1987	1.013788	2,859	10,000	2,620	1,530	469	50	571	1,572	1,725	1,395	2,633	231
10 Year Total	1971-1980		1,434	5,217	1,463	856	271	26	310	870	967	685	1,234	158
5 Year Total	1973-1977		736	2,661	742	418	158	10	156	457	515	357	586	109
Best Single Year	1969		152	549	151	65	36	3	47	123	118	115	142	13

10 Year Total spans 1971–1980. *5 Year Total* spans 1973–1977.

Complete Career Statistics J

Total Career Statistics & Adjusted Career, 10 year, 5 year, and Single Year Analysis

Jackson, Reggie

CS	HBP	SF	GDP	AVG	OBP	SLG	Total Offensive Production Statistics				TRP Rating	RPA Rating	TNB Rating	TBA Rating	TOP Composite		
							TRP	RPA	TNB	TBA					TOP	Rating	Ranking
1	5	1	1	.178	.269	.305	19	.141	51	.378	5.46	26.37	8.36	41.64	81.83	20.86	
4	5	2	3	.250	.316	.452	156	.254	315	.514	44.83	47.69	51.64	56.64	200.79	51.19	
5	12	1	8	.275	.411	.608	241	.352	469	.685	69.25	65.93	76.89	75.46	287.52	73.31	
17	8	3	10	.237	.359	.458	123	.236	287	.550	35.34	44.15	47.05	60.60	187.14	47.71	
10	6	6	7	.277	.352	.508	167	.257	363	.559	47.99	48.22	59.51	61.65	217.36	55.42	
8	8	2	5	.265	.350	.473	147	.257	304	.531	42.24	48.07	49.84	58.47	198.62	50.64	
8	7	7	13	.293	.383	.531	216	.336	383	.597	62.07	63.04	62.79	65.75	253.65	64.67	
5	4	8	8	.289	.391	.514	183	.299	370	.605	52.59	56.03	60.66	66.63	235.91	60.15	
8	3	6	10	.253	.329	.511	195	.287	382	.563	56.03	53.81	62.62	62.01	234.48	59.78	
7	4	2	17	.277	.351	.502	175	.304	329	.572	50.29	57.03	53.93	63.06	224.31	57.19	
3	3	4	3	.286	.375	.550	203	.333	380	.624	58.33	62.46	62.30	68.77	251.86	64.21	
11	9	3	8	.274	.356	.477	179	.304	314	.533	51.44	56.95	51.48	58.76	218.61	55.74	
8	2	5	17	.297	.382	.544	167	.301	321	.579	47.99	56.49	52.62	63.86	220.96	56.34	
2	2	2	7	.300	.398	.597	205	.337	391	.643	58.91	63.18	64.10	70.88	257.06	65.54	
3	1	1	8	.237	.330	.428	87	.223	187	.479	25.00	41.80	30.66	52.85	150.30	38.32	
5	2	4	10	.275	.375	.532	193	.306	368	.583	55.46	57.31	60.33	64.28	237.38	60.52	
2	4	5	5	.194	.290	.340	92	.199	189	.408	26.44	37.23	30.98	44.99	139.64	35.60	
4	3	-	10	.223	.300	.406	148	.250	275	.464	42.53	46.77	45.08	51.11	185.49	47.29	
2	1	2	16	.252	.360	.487	149	.268	302	.542	42.82	50.13	49.51	59.76	202.21	51.55	
1	3	3	14	.241	.379	.408	123	.232	266	.501	35.34	43.40	43.61	55.21	177.57	45.27	
1	4	1	3	.220	.297	.402	85	.225	173	.459	24.43	42.25	28.36	50.58	145.61	37.12	
115	96	68	183	.262	.356	.490	3,253	.281	6,419	.554	72.76	67.23	75.90	73.64	289.52	73.94	27
99	83	59	158	.262	.356	.490	2,807	.281	5,540	.554	67.23	67.23	73.64	73.64	281.73	70.43	93
117	97	69	186	.262	.356	.490	3,298	.281	6,508	.554	63.14	67.23	69.16	73.64	273.16	68.29	89
70	48	45	95	.280	.366	.521	1,837	.302	3,537	.581	62.40	68.79	71.35	73.28	275.82	70.75	73
31	21	27	51	.279	.365	.522	972	.312	1,844	.592	63.86	66.68	70.71	71.73	272.98	69.94	102
5	12	1	8	.275	.411	.608	241	.352	469	.685	69.25	65.93	76.89	75.46	287.52	73.31	167

Complete Career Statistics J

Total Career Statistics & Adjusted Career, 10 year, 5 year, and Single Year Analysis

Jennings, Hughie: *Hugh Ambrose "Ee-Yah" Jennings, b. April 2, 1869, Pittston, PA*

Rating Category	Year	Ranked Seasons & Adjustment	G	AB	H	1B	2B	3B	HR	RUN	RBI	BB	SO	SB
	1891		81	316	95	76	10	8	1	46	58	17	36	14
	1892		152	584	137	116	16	3	2	66	61	30	30	24
	1893		38	135	25	21	3	-	1	12	15	7	6	1
	1894	3rd	128	505	168	117	27	20	4	136	109	37	17	36
	1895	1st	131	528	204	152	40	8	4	159	125	24	17	60
	1896	2nd	129	523	208	175	24	9	-	125	121	19	11	73
	1897		115	436	154	121	22	9	2	131	79	42	-	60
	1898		143	533	173	139	24	9	1	136	87	78	-	31
	1899		63	225	67	54	3	10	-	44	42	22	-	18
	1900		112	440	119	94	17	7	1	62	69	31	-	35
	1901		81	302	83	58	22	2	1	38	39	25	-	13
	1902		78	289	80	60	16	3	1	31	32	14	-	8
	1903		6	17	4	4	-	-	-	2	1	1	-	1
	1907		1	4	1	-	1	-	-	-	-	-	-	-
	1909		2	4	2	2	-	-	-	1	2	-	-	-
	1912		1	1	-	-	-	-	-	-	-	-	-	-
	1918		1		-	-	-	-	-	-	-	-	-	-
Career Total	1891-1918		1,262	4,842	1,520	1,189	225	88	18	989	840	347	117	374
Career Adj. to 10,000 BO	1891-1918	1.826150	2,305	8,842	2,776	2,171	411	161	33	1,806	1,534	634	214	683
Career Adj. to 10,000 AB	1891-1918	2.065262	2,606	10,000	3,139	2,456	465	182	37	2,043	1,735	717	242	772
10 Year Total	1891-1900		1,092	4,225	1,350	1,065	186	83	16	917	766	307	117	352
5 Year Total	1894-1898		646	2,525	907	704	137	55	11	687	521	200	45	260
Best Single Year	1895		131	528	204	152	40	8	4	159	125	24	17	60
2nd Best Year	1896		129	523	208	175	24	9	-	125	121	19	11	73
3rd Best Year	1894		128	505	168	117	27	20	4	136	109	37	17	36

10 Year Total

5 Year Total

Complete Career Statistics J

Total Career Statistics & Adjusted Career, 10 year, 5 year, and Single Year Analysis

Jennings, Hughie

CS	HBP	SF	GDP	AVG	OBP	SLG	Total Offensive Production Statistics				TRP Rating	RPA Rating	TNB Rating	TBA Rating	TOP Composite		
							TRP	RPA	TNB	TBA					TOP	Rating	Ranking
-	9	-	-	.301	.354	.392	104	.304	164	.480	29.89	56.98	26.89	52.85	166.60	42.48	
-	9	-	-	.235	.283	.283	127	.204	228	.366	36.49	38.20	37.38	40.34	152.40	38.86	
-	4	-	-	.185	.247	.230	27	.185	43	.295	7.76	34.65	7.05	32.46	81.92	20.89	
-	27	-	-	.333	.408	.489	245	.431	347	.610	70.40	80.68	56.89	67.21	275.18	70.16	
-	32	-	-	.386	.445	.515	284	.486	388	.664	81.61	91.12	63.61	73.22	309.56	78.93	
-	51	-	-	.398	.469	.478	246	.415	393	.663	70.69	77.73	64.43	73.04	285.89	72.89	
-	46	-	-	.353	.462	.459	210	.401	348	.664	60.34	75.10	57.05	73.20	265.69	67.74	
-	46	-	-	.325	.452	.409	223	.339	373	.568	64.08	63.60	61.15	62.57	251.40	64.10	
-	19	-	-	.298	.406	.400	86	.323	149	.560	24.71	60.58	24.43	61.74	171.46	43.71	
-	20	-	-	.270	.346	.348	131	.267	239	.487	37.64	49.99	39.18	53.65	180.47	46.01	
-	12	-	-	.275	.354	.371	77	.227	162	.478	22.13	42.56	26.56	52.67	143.91	36.69	
-	11	-	-	.277	.334	.363	63	.201	138	.439	18.10	37.60	22.62	48.44	126.76	32.32	
-	1	-	-	.235	.316	.235	3	.158	7	.368	0.86	29.59	1.15	40.61	72.20	18.41	
-	-	-	-	.250	.250	.500	-	.000	2	.500	-	-	0.33	55.11	55.43	14.13	
-	-	-	-	.500	.500	.500	3	.750	2	.500	0.86	140.54	0.33	55.11	196.83	50.18	
-	-	-	-	.000	.000	.000	-	.000	-	.000	-	-	-	-	-	-	
-	-	-	-	.000	.000	.000	-	.000	-	.000	-	-	-	-	-	-	
-	287	-	-	.314	.393	.408	1,829	.334	2,983	.545	40.91	79.98	35.27	72.41	228.57	58.37	109
-	524	-	-	.314	.393	.408	3,340	.334	5,447	.545	79.98	79.98	72.41	72.41	304.78	76.19	55
-	593	-	-	.314	.393	.408	3,777	.334	6,161	.545	72.32	79.98	65.47	72.41	290.18	72.55	60
-	263	-	-	.320	.400	.414	1,683	.351	2,672	.557	57.17	80.04	53.90	70.31	261.42	67.05	101
-	202	-	-	.359	.447	.470	1,208	.413	1,849	.632	79.37	88.26	70.90	76.59	315.11	80.73	30
-	32	-	-	.386	.445	.515	284	.486	388	.664	81.61	91.12	63.61	73.22	309.56	78.93	69
-	51	-	-	.398	.469	.478	246	.415	393	.663	70.69	77.73	64.43	73.04	285.89	72.89	183
-	27	-	-	.333	.408	.489	245	.431	347	.610	70.40	80.68	56.89	67.21	275.18	70.16	295

Complete Career Statistics J

Total Career Statistics & Adjusted Career, 10 year, 5 year, and Single Year Analysis

Jeter, Derek: *Derek Sanderson Jeter, b. June 26, 1974, Pequannock, NJ*

Rating Category			Year	Ranked Seasons & Adjustment	G	AB	H	1B	2B	3B	HR	RUN	RBI	BB	SO	SB
			1995		15	48	12	7	4	1	-	5	7	3	11	-
			1996		157	582	183	142	25	6	10	104	78	48	102	14
			1997		159	654	190	142	31	7	10	116	70	74	125	23
10 Year Total	5 Year Total		1998		149	626	203	151	25	8	19	127	84	57	119	30
			1999	1st	158	627	219	149	37	9	24	134	102	91	116	19
			2000		148	593	201	151	31	4	15	119	73	68	99	22
			2001		150	614	191	132	35	3	21	110	74	56	99	27
			2002		157	644	191	147	26	-	18	124	75	73	114	32
			2003		119	482	156	118	25	3	10	87	52	43	88	11
			2004		154	643	188	120	44	1	23	111	78	46	99	23
Career Total**			1995-2004		1,366	5,513	1,734	1,259	283	42	150	1,037	693	559	972	201
Career Adj. to 10,000 BO**			1995-2004	1.583281	2,163	8,729	2,745	1,993	448	66	237	1,642	1,097	885	1,539	318
Career Adj. to 10,000 AB**			1995-2004	1.813894	2,478	10,000	3,145	2,284	513	76	272	1,881	1,257	1,014	1,763	365
10 Year Total**			1995-2004		1,366	5,513	1,734	1,259	283	42	150	1,037	693	559	972	201
5 Year Total**			1998-2002		762	3,104	1,005	730	154	24	97	614	408	345	547	130
Best Single Year**			1999		158	627	219	149	37	9	24	134	102	91	116	19

Total Career Statistics & Adjusted Career, 10 year, 5 year, and Single Year Analysis

Jeter, Derek

CS	HBP	SF	GDP	AVG	OBP	SLG	TRP	RPA	TNB	TBA	TRP Rating	RPA Rating	TNB Rating	TBA Rating	TOP	Rating	Ranking
-	-	-	-	.250	.294	.375	12	.235	21	.412	3.45	44.09	3.44	45.38	96.36	24.57	
7	9	9	13	.314	.370	.430	182	.275	314	.475	52.30	51.59	51.48	52.36	207.72	52.96	
12	10	2	14	.291	.370	.405	186	.247	360	.477	53.45	46.22	59.02	52.62	211.31	53.88	
6	5	3	13	.324	.384	.481	211	.300	387	.550	60.63	56.16	63.44	60.59	240.82	61.40	
8	12	6	12	.349	.438	.552	236	.316	460	.615	67.82	59.12	75.41	67.78	270.13	68.87	
4	12	3	14	.339	.416	.481	192	.278	383	.555	55.17	52.14	62.79	61.18	231.28	58.97	
3	10	1	13	.311	.377	.480	184	.265	385	.555	52.87	49.68	63.11	61.14	226.81	57.83	
3	7	3	14	.297	.373	.421	199	.269	380	.513	57.18	50.32	62.30	56.52	226.32	57.70	
5	13	1	10	.324	.393	.450	139	.253	279	.508	39.94	47.44	45.74	56.01	189.13	48.22	
4	14	2	19	.292	.352	.471	189	.261	382	.528	54.31	48.92	62.62	58.15	224.00	57.11	
52	92	30	122	.315	.385	.463	1,730	.274	3,351	.531	38.69	65.59	39.62	70.52	214.43	54.76	122
82	146	47	193	.315	.385	.463	2,739	.274	5,306	.531	65.59	65.59	70.52	70.52	272.23	68.06	108
94	167	54	221	.315	.385	.463	3,138	.274	6,078	.531	60.08	65.59	64.60	70.52	260.79	65.20	104
52	92	30	122	.315	.385	.463	1,730	.274	3,351	.531	58.76	62.46	67.60	66.94	255.77	65.60	110
24	46	16	66	.324	.398	.483	1,022	.286	1,995	.558	67.15	61.10	76.50	67.62	272.36	69.78	103
8	12	6	12	.349	.438	.552	236	.316	460	.615	67.82	59.12	75.41	67.78	270.13	68.87	318

Total Career Statistics & Adjusted Career, 10 year, 5 year, and Single Year Analysis

Johnson, Robert: *Robert Lee Indian Bob Johnson, b. Nov. 26, 1906, Pryor, OK*

Rating Category	Year	Ranked Seasons & Adjustment	G	AB	H	1B	2B	3B	HR	RUN	RBI	BB	SO	SB
	1933		142	535	155	86	44	4	21	103	93	85	74	8
	1934		141	547	168	102	26	6	34	111	92	58	60	12
	1935		147	582	174	112	29	5	28	103	109	78	76	2
	1936		153	566	165	97	29	14	25	91	121	88	71	6
	1937		138	477	146	83	32	6	25	91	108	98	65	9
	1938		152	563	176	110	27	9	30	114	113	87	73	9
	1939	1st	150	544	184	122	30	9	23	115	114	99	59	15
	1940		138	512	137	77	25	4	31	93	103	83	64	8
	1941		149	552	152	92	30	8	22	98	107	95	75	6
	1942		149	550	160	105	35	7	13	78	80	82	61	3
	1943		117	438	116	79	22	8	7	65	63	64	50	11
	1944		144	525	170	105	40	8	17	106	106	95	67	2
	1945		143	529	148	102	27	7	12	71	74	63	56	5
Career Total	1933-1945		1,863	6,920	2,051	1,272	396	95	288	1,239	1,283	1,075	851	96
Career Adj. to 10,000 BO	1933-1945	1.231375	2,294	8,521	2,526	1,566	488	117	355	1,526	1,580	1,324	1,048	118
Career Adj. to 10,000 AB	1933-1945	1.445087	2,692	10,000	2,964	1,838	572	137	416	1,790	1,854	1,553	1,230	139
10 Year Total	1933-1942		1,459	5,428	1,617	986	307	72	252	997	1,040	853	678	78
5 Year Total	1935-1939		740	2,732	845	524	147	43	131	514	565	450	344	41
Best Single Year	1939		150	544	184	122	30	9	23	115	114	99	59	15

10 Year Total / 5 Year Total (row span labels on left)

Total Career Statistics & Adjusted Career, 10 year, 5 year, and Single Year Analysis

Johnson, Robert

CS	HBP	SF	GDP	AVG	OBP	SLG	Total Offensive Production Statistics				TRP Rating	RPA Rating	TNB Rating	TBA Rating	TOP Composite		
							TRP	RPA	TNB	TBA					TOP	Rating	Ranking
3	-	-	-	.290	.387	.505	196	.316	360	.581	56.32	59.24	59.02	64.00	238.57	60.83	
8	1	-	-	.307	.375	.563	203	.335	371	.612	58.33	62.77	60.82	67.47	249.40	63.59	
4	2	-	-	.299	.384	.510	212	.320	375	.566	60.92	60.01	61.48	62.43	244.83	62.42	
6	2	-	-	.292	.389	.525	212	.323	387	.590	60.92	60.56	63.44	65.02	249.94	63.72	
7	1	-	-	.306	.425	.556	199	.345	366	.635	57.18	64.74	60.00	70.03	251.95	64.24	
8	2	-	-	.313	.406	.552	227	.348	401	.615	65.23	65.24	65.74	67.79	263.99	67.31	
5	-	-	12	.338	.440	.553	229	.350	410	.626	65.80	65.51	67.21	68.99	267.52	68.21	
2	4	-	20	.268	.374	.514	196	.317	356	.575	56.32	59.33	58.36	63.39	237.40	60.53	
4	3	-	16	.275	.385	.478	205	.308	364	.547	58.91	57.68	59.67	60.24	236.49	60.30	
2	1	-	16	.291	.384	.451	158	.243	332	.512	45.40	45.62	54.43	56.38	201.83	51.46	
5	3	-	11	.265	.362	.400	128	.248	248	.481	36.78	46.48	40.66	52.97	176.89	45.10	
7	4	-	14	.324	.431	.528	212	.332	371	.582	60.92	62.26	60.82	64.09	248.09	63.25	
3	1	-	13	.280	.358	.425	145	.239	291	.480	41.67	44.84	47.70	52.92	187.13	47.71	
64	24	-	102	.296	.393	.506	2,522	.311	4,632	.570	56.41	74.36	54.77	75.82	261.36	66.75	70
79	30	-	126	.296	.393	.506	3,106	.311	5,704	.570	74.36	74.36	75.82	75.82	300.36	75.09	66
92	35	-	147	.296	.393	.506	3,645	.311	6,694	.570	69.77	74.36	71.14	75.82	291.09	72.77	59
49	16	-	64	.298	.395	.520	2,037	.320	3,722	.585	69.19	73.03	75.09	73.83	291.13	74.67	51
30	7	-	12	.309	.408	.538	1,079	.337	1,939	.606	70.89	72.08	74.35	73.44	290.77	74.49	69
5	-	-	12	.338	.440	.553	229	.350	410	.626	65.80	65.51	67.21	68.99	267.52	68.21	326

Complete Career Statistics J

Total Career Statistics & Adjusted Career, 10 year, 5 year, and Single Year Analysis

Jones, Chipper: *Larry Wayne Jones, b. April 24, 1972, DeLand, FL*

Rating Category			Year	Ranked Seasons & Adjustment	G	AB	H	1B	2B	3B	HR	RUN	RBI	BB	SO	SB
			1993		8	3	2	1	1	-	-	2	-	1	1	-
10 Year Total	5 Year Total		1995		140	524	139	91	22	3	23	87	86	73	99	8
			1996		157	598	185	118	32	5	30	114	110	87	88	14
			1997		157	597	176	111	41	3	21	100	111	76	88	20
			1998		160	601	188	120	29	5	34	123	107	96	93	16
			1999	1st	157	567	181	94	41	1	45	116	110	126	94	25
			2000		156	579	180	105	38	1	36	118	111	95	64	14
			2001		159	572	189	113	33	5	38	113	102	98	82	9
			2002		158	548	179	117	35	1	26	90	100	107	89	8
			2003		153	555	169	107	33	2	27	103	106	94	83	2
			2004		137	472	117	66	20	1	30	69	96	84	96	2
Career Total**			1993-2004		1,542	5,616	1,705	1,043	325	27	310	1,035	1,039	937	877	118
Career Adj. to 10,000 BO**			1993-2004	1.474709	2,274	8,282	2,514	1,538	479	40	457	1,526	1,532	1,382	1,293	174
Career Adj. to 10,000 AB**			1993-2004	1.780627	2,746	10,000	3,036	1,857	579	48	552	1,843	1,850	1,668	1,562	210
10 Year Total**			1995-2004		1,534	5,613	1,703	1,042	324	27	310	1,033	1,039	936	876	118
5 Year Total**			1998-2002		790	2,867	917	549	176	13	179	560	530	522	422	72
Best Single Year**			1999		157	567	181	94	41	1	45	116	110	126	94	25

Total Career Statistics & Adjusted Career, 10 year, 5 year, and Single Year Analysis

Jones, Chipper

CS	HBP	SF	GDP	AVG	OBP	SLG	Total Offensive Production Statistics				TRP Rating	RPA Rating	TNB Rating	TBA Rating	TOP Composite		
							TRP	RPA	TNB	TBA					TOP	Rating	Ranking
-	-	-	-	.667	.750	1.000	2	.500	4	1.000	0.57	93.69	0.66	110.21	205.14	52.30	
4	-	4	10	.265	.353	.450	173	.283	313	.512	49.71	53.06	51.31	56.46	210.54	53.68	
1	-	7	14	.309	.393	.530	224	.317	417	.591	64.37	59.45	68.36	65.10	257.28	65.60	
5	-	6	20	.295	.371	.479	211	.302	377	.539	60.63	56.56	61.80	59.44	238.44	60.79	
6	1	8	17	.313	.404	.547	230	.318	436	.603	66.09	59.61	71.48	66.46	263.64	67.22	
3	2	6	20	.319	.441	.633	226	.313	509	.706	64.94	58.74	83.44	77.81	284.93	72.64	
7	2	10	14	.311	.404	.566	229	.327	432	.617	65.80	61.30	70.82	68.02	265.94	67.80	
10	2	5	13	.330	.427	.605	215	.312	445	.645	61.78	58.39	72.95	71.08	264.20	67.36	
2	2	5	18	.327	.435	.536	190	.279	409	.601	54.60	52.36	67.05	66.29	240.29	61.27	
2	1	6	10	.305	.402	.517	209	.314	382	.574	60.06	58.80	62.62	63.22	244.70	62.39	
-	4	7	14	.248	.362	.485	165	.284	319	.549	47.41	53.22	52.30	60.51	213.44	54.42	
40	14	64	150	.304	.401	.537	2,074	.306	4,043	.596	46.39	73.24	47.81	79.25	246.69	63.00	90
59	21	94	221	.304	.401	.537	3,059	.306	5,962	.596	73.24	73.24	79.25	79.25	304.98	76.25	52
71	25	114	267	.304	.401	.537	3,693	.306	7,199	.596	70.70	73.24	76.51	79.25	299.70	74.93	40
40	14	64	150	.303	.400	.536	2,072	.306	4,039	.596	70.38	69.72	81.48	75.20	296.78	76.12	44
28	9	34	82	.320	.422	.578	1,090	.310	2,231	.635	71.62	66.33	85.54	76.98	300.47	76.98	49
3	2	6	20	.319	.441	.633	226	.313	509	.706	64.94	58.74	83.44	77.81	284.93	72.64	190

Complete Career Statistics J

Total Career Statistics & Adjusted Career, 10 year, 5 year, and Single Year Analysis

Kaline, Al: *Albert William Kaline, b. Dec, 19, 1934, Baltimore, MD*

Rating Category	Year	Ranked Seasons & Adjustment	G	AB	H	1B	2B	3B	HR	RUN	RBI	BB	SO	SB
	1953		30	28	7	6	-	-	1	9	2	1	5	1
	1954		138	504	139	114	18	3	4	42	43	22	45	9
	1955	1st	152	588	200	141	24	8	27	121	102	82	57	6
	1956		153	617	194	125	32	10	27	96	128	70	55	6
	1957		149	577	170	114	29	4	23	83	90	43	38	7
	1958		146	543	170	113	34	7	16	84	85	54	47	11
	1959		135	511	167	119	19	2	27	86	94	72	42	7
	1960		147	551	153	105	29	4	15	77	68	65	47	10
	1961		153	586	190	123	41	7	19	116	82	66	42	19
	1962		100	398	121	70	16	6	29	78	94	47	39	14
	1963		145	551	172	118	24	3	27	89	101	54	48	4
	1964		146	525	154	101	31	5	17	77	68	75	51	6
	1965		125	399	112	74	18	2	18	72	72	72	49	6
	1966		142	479	138	79	29	1	29	85	88	81	66	5
	1967		131	458	141	86	28	2	25	94	78	83	47	8
	1968		102	327	94	69	14	1	10	49	53	55	39	6
	1969		131	456	124	86	17	-	21	74	69	54	61	1
	1970		131	467	130	86	24	4	16	64	71	77	49	2
	1971		133	405	119	83	19	2	15	69	54	82	57	4
	1972		106	278	87	64	11	2	10	46	32	28	33	1
	1973		91	310	79	56	13	-	10	40	45	29	28	4
	1974		147	558	146	103	28	2	13	71	64	65	75	2
Career Total	1953-1974		2,833	10,116	3,007	2,035	498	75	399	1,622	1,583	1,277	1,020	139
Career Adj. to 10,000 BO	1953-1974	0.845809	2,396	8,556	2,543	1,721	421	63	337	1,372	1,339	1,080	863	118
Career Adj. to 10,000 AB	1953-1974	0.988533	2,801	10,000	2,973	2,012	492	74	394	1,603	1,565	1,262	1,008	137
10 Year Total	1955-1964		1,426	5,447	1,691	1,129	279	56	227	907	912	628	466	90
5 Year Total	1955-1959		735	2,836	901	612	138	31	120	470	499	321	239	37
Best Single Year	1955		152	588	200	141	24	8	27	121	102	82	57	6

5 Year Total

10 Year Total

Total Career Statistics & Adjusted Career, 10 year, 5 year, and Single Year Analysis

Kaline, Al

CS	HBP	SF	GDP	AVG	OBP	SLG	Total Offensive Production Statistics				TRP Rating	RPA Rating	TNB Rating	TBA Rating	TOP Composite		
							TRP	RPA	TNB	TBA					TOP	Rating	Ranking
-	1	-	1	.250	.300	.357	11	.355	13	.419	3.16	66.49	2.13	46.22	118.00	30.09	
5	-	2	21	.276	.305	.347	85	.155	201	.366	24.43	29.01	32.95	40.35	126.74	32.31	
8	5	6	13	.340	.421	.546	223	.321	406	.585	64.08	60.21	66.56	64.48	255.33	65.10	
1	1	4	10	.314	.383	.530	224	.319	403	.574	64.37	59.79	66.07	63.27	253.50	64.63	
9	3	7	10	.295	.343	.478	173	.270	320	.500	49.71	50.65	52.46	55.11	207.93	53.01	
4	2	5	18	.313	.374	.490	169	.272	329	.529	48.56	50.91	53.93	58.30	211.71	53.98	
4	4	6	11	.327	.410	.530	180	.298	350	.579	51.72	55.84	57.38	63.87	228.81	58.34	
4	3	5	18	.278	.354	.426	145	.226	309	.481	41.67	42.32	50.66	53.05	187.69	47.85	
1	4	5	16	.324	.393	.515	198	.292	390	.576	56.90	54.80	63.93	63.49	239.13	60.97	
-	1	4	17	.304	.376	.593	172	.368	298	.638	49.43	69.01	48.85	70.33	237.62	60.58	
4	4	4	12	.312	.375	.514	190	.304	341	.546	54.60	56.96	55.90	60.13	227.60	58.03	
1	3	3	12	.293	.383	.469	145	.235	329	.532	41.67	43.96	53.93	58.67	198.24	50.54	
6	-	3	9	.281	.388	.471	144	.298	260	.538	41.38	55.87	42.62	59.33	199.20	50.79	
5	5	6	7	.288	.392	.534	173	.299	342	.592	49.71	56.08	56.07	65.21	227.08	57.90	
8	1	6	16	.308	.411	.541	172	.305	332	.589	49.43	57.14	54.43	64.88	225.87	57.59	
6	3	3	4	.287	.392	.428	102	.260	198	.505	29.31	48.76	32.46	55.67	166.20	42.37	
1	1	7	11	.272	.346	.447	143	.270	259	.490	41.09	50.65	42.46	53.96	188.17	47.97	
2	1	7	20	.278	.377	.450	135	.236	288	.503	38.79	44.22	47.21	55.49	185.72	47.35	
4	7	6	12	.294	.416	.462	123	.240	276	.539	35.34	45.02	45.25	59.41	185.02	47.17	
1	2	5	11	.313	.374	.475	78	.241	162	.500	22.41	45.11	26.56	55.11	149.19	38.04	
4	3	5	10	.255	.320	.394	85	.238	154	.431	24.43	44.61	25.25	47.54	141.83	36.16	
2	1	5	12	.262	.337	.389	135	.211	283	.441	38.79	39.46	46.39	48.66	173.31	44.19	
80	55	104	271	.297	.376	.480	3,205	.271	6,243	.528	71.68	64.91	73.82	70.19	280.61	71.66	38
68	47	88	229	.297	.376	.480	2,711	.271	5,280	.528	64.91	64.91	70.19	70.19	270.20	67.55	112
79	54	103	268	.297	.376	.480	3,168	.271	6,171	.528	60.66	64.91	65.59	70.19	261.35	65.34	102
36	30	49	137	.310	.382	.507	1,819	.289	3,475	.552	61.79	65.94	70.10	69.70	267.52	68.62	86
26	15	28	62	.318	.387	.515	969	.297	1,808	.554	63.67	63.52	69.33	67.20	263.71	67.56	114
8	5	6	13	.340	.421	.546	223	.321	406	.585	64.08	60.21	66.56	64.48	255.33	65.10	359

Complete Career Statistics K

Total Career Statistics & Adjusted Career, 10 year, 5 year, and Single Year Analysis

Keeler, Willie: *William Henry "Wee Willie" Keeler (O'Kelleher), b. Mar. 3, 1872, Brooklyn, NY*

Rating Category		Year	Ranked Seasons & Adjustment	G	AB	H	1B	2B	3B	HR	RUN	RBI	BB	SO	SB
		1892		13	49	15	12	3	-	-	6	6	3	6	5
		1893		29	90	30	23	3	2	2	19	16	9	16	7
10 Year Total	5 Year Total	1894	2nd	128	593	218	166	25	22	5	164	94	40	94	30
		1895	4th	131	560	221	179	23	15	4	161	78	37	78	57
		1896	1st	127	546	214	175	22	13	4	154	82	37	82	73
		1897	3rd	128	562	243	199	25	19	-	147	74	35	74	63
		1898		128	564	214	201	10	2	1	126	44	31	44	26
		1899		143	571	215	187	13	14	1	141	61	37	61	44
		1900		137	568	208	179	11	14	4	106	68	30	68	39
		1901		136	589	209	176	16	15	2	124	43	21	43	31
		1902		132	550	188	163	18	7	-	84	38	21	38	23
		1903		132	515	164	144	13	7	-	98	32	32	32	25
		1904		143	539	185	162	13	8	2	76	40	35	40	22
		1905		149	560	169	147	14	4	4	81	38	43	38	19
		1906		152	592	180	167	8	3	2	96	33	40	33	23
		1907		107	423	99	92	5	2	-	50	17	15	17	7
		1908		91	323	85	80	3	1	1	38	14	31	14	14
		1909		99	360	95	82	7	5	1	44	32	24	32	10
		1910		19	10	3	3	-	-	-	5	-	3	-	1
Career Total		1892-1910		2,124	8,564	2,955	2,537	232	153	33	1,720	810	524	810	519
Career Adj. to 10,000 BO		1892-1910	1.084952	2,304	9,292	3,206	2,753	252	166	36	1,866	879	569	879	563
Career Adj. to 10,000 AB		1892-1910	1.167679	2,480	10,000	3,450	2,962	271	179	39	2,008	946	612	946	606
10 Year Total		1894-1903		1,322	5,618	2,094	1,769	176	128	21	1,305	614	321	614	411
5 Year Total		1894-1898		642	2,825	1,110	920	105	71	14	752	372	180	372	249
Best Single Year		1896		127	546	214	175	22	13	4	154	82	37	82	73
2nd Best Year		1894		128	593	218	166	25	22	5	164	94	40	94	30
3rd Best Year		1897		128	562	243	199	25	19	-	147	74	35	74	63
4th Best Year		1895		131	560	221	179	23	15	4	161	78	37	78	57

Total Career Statistics & Adjusted Career, 10 year, 5 year, and Single Year Analysis

Keeler, Willie

CS	HBP	SF	GDP	AVG	OBP	SLG	Total Offensive Production Statistics				TRP Rating	RPA Rating	TNB Rating	TBA Rating	TOP Composite		
							TRP	RPA	TNB	TBA					TOP	Rating	Ranking
3	1	-	-	.306	.358	.367	12	.226	24	.453	3.45	42.43	3.93	49.91	99.72	25.42	
5	1	-	-	.333	.400	.478	35	.350	55	.550	10.06	65.58	9.02	60.62	145.28	37.04	
6	18	-	-	.368	.424	.509	258	.396	384	.590	74.14	74.26	62.95	65.01	276.36	70.46	
12	14	-	-	.395	.445	.511	239	.391	382	.625	68.68	73.30	62.62	68.91	273.50	69.73	
9	7	-	-	.392	.437	.502	236	.400	382	.647	67.82	74.95	62.62	71.36	276.75	70.56	
-	7	-	-	.432	.472	.544	221	.366	411	.680	63.51	68.56	67.38	75.00	274.44	69.97	
-	3	-	-	.379	.415	.410	170	.284	291	.487	48.85	53.27	47.70	53.63	203.46	51.87	
-	9	-	-	.377	.423	.454	202	.327	349	.566	58.05	61.35	57.21	62.34	238.95	60.92	
-	7	-	-	.366	.405	.456	174	.288	335	.554	50.00	53.89	54.92	61.03	219.84	56.05	
-	7	-	-	.355	.384	.443	167	.271	320	.519	47.99	50.72	52.46	57.16	208.33	53.11	
-	7	-	-	.342	.374	.400	122	.211	271	.469	35.06	39.55	44.43	51.67	170.71	43.52	
-	13	-	-	.318	.373	.371	130	.232	261	.466	37.36	43.50	42.79	51.37	175.01	44.62	
-	7	-	-	.343	.391	.408	116	.200	284	.489	33.33	37.41	46.56	53.87	171.18	43.64	
-	5	-	-	.302	.357	.363	119	.196	270	.444	34.20	36.68	44.26	48.94	164.08	41.83	
-	5	-	-	.304	.353	.338	129	.203	268	.421	37.07	37.95	43.93	46.37	165.32	42.15	
-	3	-	-	.234	.265	.255	67	.152	133	.302	19.25	28.47	21.80	33.24	102.76	26.20	
-	5	-	-	.263	.337	.288	52	.145	143	.398	14.94	27.14	23.44	43.90	109.43	27.90	
-	10	-	-	.264	.327	.319	76	.193	159	.404	21.84	36.14	26.07	44.48	128.53	32.77	
1	-	-	-	.300	.462	.300	5	.385	6	.462	1.44	72.07	0.98	50.87	125.36	31.96	
36	129	-	-	.345	.391	.419	2,530	.274	4,728	.513	56.59	65.73	55.91	68.19	246.41	62.93	91
39	140	-	-	.345	.391	.419	2,745	.274	5,130	.513	65.73	65.73	68.19	68.19	267.83	66.96	115
42	151	-	-	.345	.391	.419	2,954	.274	5,521	.513	56.56	65.73	58.67	68.19	249.15	62.29	121
27	92	-	-	.373	.416	.461	1,919	.318	3,386	.561	65.18	72.56	68.31	70.84	276.89	71.02	69
27	49	-	-	.393	.438	.495	1,124	.368	1,850	.606	73.85	78.70	70.94	73.44	296.93	76.07	55
9	7	-	-	.392	.437	.502	236	.400	382	.647	67.82	74.95	62.62	71.36	276.75	70.56	267
6	18	-	-	.368	.424	.509	258	.396	384	.590	74.14	74.26	62.95	65.01	276.36	70.46	274
-	7	-	-	.432	.472	.544	221	.366	411	.680	63.51	68.56	67.38	75.00	274.44	69.97	304
12	14	-	-	.395	.445	.511	239	.391	382	.625	68.68	73.30	62.62	68.91	273.50	69.73	319

Complete Career Statistics K

Total Career Statistics & Adjusted Career, 10 year, 5 year, and Single Year Analysis

Keller, Charlie: *Charles Ernest "King Kong" Keller; b. Sept. 12, 1916, Middletown, MD*

Rating Category	Year	Ranked Seasons & Adjustment	G	AB	H	1B	2B	3B	HR	RUN	RBI	BB	SO	SB
	1939		111	398	133	95	21	6	11	87	83	81	49	6
	1940		138	500	143	89	18	15	21	102	93	106	65	8
5 Year Total	1941	1st	140	507	151	84	24	10	33	102	122	102	65	6
	1942		152	544	159	100	24	9	26	106	108	114	61	14
10 Year Total	1943		141	512	139	82	15	11	31	97	86	106	60	7
	1945		44	163	49	28	7	4	10	26	34	31	21	-
	1946		150	538	148	79	29	10	30	98	101	113	101	1
	1947		45	151	36	16	6	1	13	36	36	41	18	-
	1948		83	247	66	43	15	2	6	41	44	41	25	1
	1949		60	116	29	21	4	1	3	17	16	25	15	2
	1950		50	51	16	10	1	3	2	7	16	13	6	-
	1951		54	62	16	11	2	-	3	6	21	11	12	-
	1952		2	1	-	-	-	-	-	-	-	-	1	-
Career Total	1939-1952		1,170	3,790	1,085	658	166	72	189	725	760	784	499	45
Career Adj. to 10,000 BO*	1939-1952	2.157963	2,525	8,179	2,341	1,420	358	155	408	1,565	1,640	1,692	1,077	97
Career Adj. to 10,000 AB*	1939-1952	2.638522	3,087	10,000	2,863	1,736	438	190	499	1,913	2,005	2,069	1,317	119
10 Year Total*	1939-1949		1,064	3,676	1,053	637	163	69	184	712	723	760	480	45
5 Year Total*	1939-1943		682	2,461	725	450	102	51	122	494	492	509	300	41
Best Single Year	1941		140	507	151	84	24	10	33	102	122	102	65	6

Total Career Statistics & Adjusted Career, 10 year, 5 year, and Single Year Analysis

Keller, Charlie

CS	HBP	SF	GDP	AVG	OBP	SLG	Total Offensive Production Statistics				TRP Rating	RPA Rating	TNB Rating	TBA Rating	TOP Composite		
							TRP	RPA	TNB	TBA					TOP	Rating	Ranking
3	-	-	4	.334	.447	.500	170	.352	283	.586	48.85	65.95	46.39	64.58	225.77	57.56	
2	-	-	11	.286	.411	.508	195	.316	366	.593	56.03	59.22	60.00	65.38	240.63	61.35	
4	1	-	3	.298	.416	.580	224	.365	399	.651	64.37	68.47	65.41	71.74	269.99	68.84	
2	2	-	5	.292	.417	.513	214	.322	407	.612	61.49	60.30	66.72	67.45	255.97	65.26	
5	-	-	7	.271	.396	.525	183	.293	377	.603	52.59	54.87	61.80	66.48	235.74	60.10	
2	-	-	2	.301	.412	.577	60	.306	123	.628	17.24	57.36	20.16	69.17	163.93	41.80	
4	4	-	5	.275	.405	.533	199	.302	401	.608	57.18	56.50	65.74	66.96	246.38	62.82	
-	1	-	3	.238	.404	.550	72	.367	125	.638	20.69	68.83	20.49	70.29	180.31	45.97	
1	-	-	7	.267	.372	.417	85	.288	144	.488	24.43	53.99	23.61	53.80	155.82	39.73	
-	2	-	3	.250	.392	.379	33	.226	73	.500	9.48	42.35	11.97	55.11	118.91	30.32	
-	-	-	-	.314	.453	.569	23	.359	42	.656	6.61	67.34	6.89	72.33	153.16	39.05	
-	-	-	-	.258	.370	.435	27	.370	38	.521	7.76	69.31	6.23	57.37	140.67	35.86	
-	-	-	-	.000	.000	.000	-	.000	-	.000	-	-	-	-	-	-	
23	10	-	50	.286	.410	.518	1,485	.320	2,778	.599	33.21	76.74	32.85	79.69	222.48	56.82	116
50	22	-	108	.286	.410	.518	3,205	.320	5,995	.599	76.74	76.74	79.69	79.69	312.84	78.21	39
61	26	-	132	.286	.410	.518	3,918	.320	7,330	.599	75.01	76.74	77.90	79.69	309.33	77.33	28
23	10	-	50	.286	.410	.518	1,435	.319	2,698	.600	48.74	72.78	54.43	75.72	251.67	64.55	113
16	3	-	30	.295	.416	.526	986	.328	1,832	.610	64.78	70.21	70.25	73.96	279.21	71.53	89
4	1	-	3	.298	.416	.580	224	.365	399	.651	64.37	68.47	65.41	71.74	269.99	68.84	319

Complete Career Statistics K

Total Career Statistics & Adjusted Career, 10 year, 5 year, and Single Year Analysis

Kelley, Joe: *Joseph James Kelley, b. Dec. 9, 1871, Cambridge, MA*

Rating Category			Year	Ranked Seasons & Adjustment	G	AB	H	1B	2B	3B	HR	RUN	RBI	BB	SO	SB
			1891		14	52	12	10	1	1	-	8	3	1	4	-
			1892		66	232	57	45	6	6	-	30	32	21	28	7
10 Year Total	5 Year Total		1893		124	490	153	103	25	16	9	120	76	77	44	33
			1894	1st	129	509	199	128	48	17	6	167	111	107	36	46
			1895	2nd	131	510	189	132	26	21	10	148	134	77	29	54
			1896	3rd	130	516	191	139	27	17	8	147	100	91	19	87
			1897	4th	129	503	196	151	31	9	5	113	118	70	-	44
			1898		124	469	153	119	17	15	2	71	110	56	-	24
			1899		144	540	178	133	27	12	6	107	93	70	-	31
			1900		118	453	144	97	23	18	6	92	91	53	-	26
			1901		120	493	152	115	21	12	4	77	65	40	-	18
			1902		97	378	120	85	24	9	2	66	46	49	-	15
			1903		105	383	121	92	22	4	3	85	45	51	-	18
			1904		123	449	126	92	21	13	-	75	63	49	-	15
			1905		90	321	89	75	7	6	1	43	37	27	-	8
			1906		129	465	106	75	19	11	1	43	53	44	-	9
			1908		62	228	59	47	8	2	2	25	17	27	-	5
Career Total			1891–1908		1,835	6,991	2,245	1,638	353	189	65	1,417	1,194	910	160	440
Career Adj. to 10,000 BO			1891–1908	1.252662	2,299	8,757	2,812	2,052	442	237	81	1,775	1,496	1,140	200	551
Career Adj. to 10,000 AB			1891–1908	1.430411	2,625	10,000	3,211	2,343	505	270	93	2,027	1,708	1,302	229	629
10 Year Total			1893–1902		1,246	4,861	1,675	1,202	269	146	58	1,108	944	690	128	378
5 Year Total			1893–1897		643	2,528	928	653	157	80	38	695	539	422	128	264
Best Single Year			1894		129	509	199	128	48	17	6	167	111	107	36	46
2nd Best Year			1895		131	510	189	132	26	21	10	148	134	77	29	54
3rd Best Year			1896		130	516	191	139	27	17	8	147	100	91	19	87
4th Best Year			1897		129	503	196	151	31	9	5	113	118	70	-	44

Total Career Statistics & Adjusted Career, 10 year, 5 year, and Single Year Analysis

Kelley, Joe

CS	HBP	SF	GDP	AVG	OBP	SLG	Total Offensive Production Statistics				TRP Rating	RPA Rating	TNB Rating	TBA Rating	TOP Composite		
							TRP	RPA	TNB	TBA					TOP	Rating	Ranking
-	-	-	-	.231	.245	.288	11	.208	16	.302	3.16	38.89	2.62	33.27	77.95	19.87	
-	1	-	-	.246	.311	.323	62	.244	104	.409	17.82	45.74	17.05	45.13	125.73	32.06	
-	4	-	-	.312	.410	.484	196	.343	351	.615	56.32	64.32	57.54	67.75	245.93	62.70	
-	5	-	-	.391	.501	.587	278	.448	457	.736	79.89	83.88	74.92	81.11	319.80	81.53	
-	10	-	-	.371	.462	.563	282	.472	428	.717	81.03	88.51	70.16	79.01	318.72	81.26	
-	12	-	-	.370	.475	.535	247	.399	466	.753	70.98	74.77	76.39	82.97	305.11	77.79	
-	7	-	-	.390	.471	.517	231	.398	381	.657	66.38	74.63	62.46	72.40	275.87	70.33	
-	3	-	-	.326	.402	.439	181	.343	289	.547	52.01	64.24	47.38	60.33	223.95	57.10	
-	7	-	-	.330	.413	.457	200	.324	355	.575	57.47	60.74	58.20	63.41	239.82	61.14	
-	6	-	-	.318	.396	.488	183	.357	306	.598	52.59	66.97	50.16	65.87	235.59	60.07	
-	3	-	-	.308	.364	.424	142	.265	270	.504	40.80	49.64	44.26	55.52	190.23	48.50	
-	1	-	-	.317	.397	.444	112	.262	233	.544	32.18	49.03	38.20	60.00	179.41	45.74	
-	4	-	-	.316	.402	.418	130	.297	233	.532	37.36	55.62	38.20	58.63	189.80	48.39	
-	6	-	-	.281	.359	.385	138	.274	243	.482	39.66	51.31	39.84	53.14	183.94	46.90	
-	7	-	-	.277	.346	.346	80	.225	153	.431	22.99	42.23	25.08	47.50	137.80	35.13	
-	4	-	-	.228	.300	.323	96	.187	207	.404	27.59	35.07	33.93	44.47	141.06	35.96	
-	2	-	-	.259	.342	.338	42	.163	111	.432	12.07	30.62	18.20	47.60	108.49	27.66	
-	82	-	-	.321	.405	.454	2,611	.327	4,603	.577	58.40	78.32	54.43	76.64	267.79	68.39	60
-	103	-	-	.321	.405	.454	3,271	.327	5,766	.577	78.32	78.32	76.64	76.64	309.93	77.48	46
-	117	-	-	.321	.405	.454	3,735	.327	6,584	.577	71.50	78.32	69.97	76.64	296.44	74.11	50
-	58	-	-	.345	.432	.496	2,052	.366	3,536	.630	69.70	83.43	71.33	79.54	304.00	77.98	34
-	38	-	-	.367	.465	.538	1,234	.413	2,083	.697	81.08	88.31	79.87	84.52	333.78	85.51	13
-	5	-	-	.391	.501	.587	278	.448	457	.736	79.89	83.88	74.92	81.11	319.80	81.53	43
-	10	-	-	.371	.462	.563	282	.472	428	.717	81.03	88.51	70.16	79.01	318.72	81.26	45
-	12	-	-	.370	.475	.535	247	.399	466	.753	70.98	74.77	76.39	82.97	305.11	77.79	82
-	7	-	-	.390	.471	.517	231	.398	381	.657	66.38	74.63	62.46	72.40	275.87	70.33	287

Complete Career Statistics K

Total Career Statistics & Adjusted Career, 10 year, 5 year, and Single Year Analysis

Kelly, King: *Michael Joseph "King" Kelly; b. Dec. 31, 1857, Troy, NY*

Rating Category	Year	Ranked Seasons & Adjustment	G	AB	H	1B	2B	3B	HR	RUN	RBI	BB	SO	SB
	1878		59	231	65	56	9	-	-	29	27	7	7	-
	1879		76	342	119	81	22	14	2	78	47	8	14	-
	1880		82	335	98	73	13	11	1	71	60	12	22	-
	1881		80	353	114	81	28	3	2	84	55	16	14	-
	1882		84	377	115	73	36	5	1	81	55	10	27	-
	1883		98	430	109	70	27	9	3	92	61	16	35	-
	1884		107	448	153	104	30	6	13	120	95	46	24	-
10 Year Total / 5 Year Total	1885		107	438	126	86	24	7	9	124	75	46	24	-
	1886	1st	118	451	175	129	31	11	4	155	79	83	33	53
	1887	2nd	114	525	207	154	34	11	8	119	63	55	40	84
	1888		105	440	140	100	20	11	9	85	71	31	39	56
	1889		125	507	149	101	32	7	9	120	78	65	40	68
	1890		90	352	114	84	19	7	4	89	66	52	22	40
	1891		101	360	96	71	16	7	2	64	62	58	43	40
	1892		72	279	56	45	9	-	2	40	41	39	31	24
	1892		16	54	17	16	1	-	-	8	15	6	5	3
Career Total	1878-1892		1,434	5,922	1,853	1,324	351	109	69	1,359	950	550	420	368
Career Adj. to 10,000 BO	1878-1892	1.542258	2,212	9,133	2,858	2,042	541	168	106	2,096	1,465	848	648	568
Career Adj. to 10,000 AB	1878-1892	1.688619	2,421	10,000	3,129	2,236	593	184	117	2,295	1,604	929	709	621
10 Year Total	1882-1891		1,049	4,328	1,384	972	269	81	62	1,049	705	462	327	341
5 Year Total	1884-1888		551	2,302	801	573	139	46	43	603	383	261	160	193
Best Single Year	1886		118	451	175	129	31	11	4	155	79	83	33	53
2nd Best Year	1887		114	525	207	154	34	11	8	119	63	55	40	84

Total Career Statistics & Adjusted Career, 10 year, 5 year, and Single Year Analysis

Kelly, King

CS	HBP	SF	GDP	AVG	OBP	SLG	Total Offensive Production Statistics				TRP Rating	RPA Rating	TNB Rating	TBA Rating	TOP Composite		
							TRP	RPA	TNB	TBA					TOP	Rating	Ranking
-	-	-	-	.281	.303	.320	56	.235	81	.340	16.09	44.09	13.28	37.51	110.97	28.29	
-	-	-	-	.348	.363	.512	125	.357	183	.523	35.92	66.92	30.00	57.63	190.47	48.56	
-	-	-	-	.293	.317	.406	131	.378	148	.427	37.64	70.74	24.26	47.01	179.65	45.80	
-	-	-	-	.323	.352	.436	139	.377	170	.461	39.94	70.59	27.87	50.78	189.17	48.23	
-	-	-	-	.305	.323	.435	136	.351	174	.450	39.08	65.85	28.52	49.55	183.01	46.66	
-	-	-	-	.253	.280	.379	153	.343	179	.401	43.97	64.28	29.34	44.23	181.82	46.36	
-	-	-	-	.342	.403	.522	215	.435	280	.567	61.78	81.55	45.90	62.47	251.71	64.17	
-	-	-	-	.288	.355	.436	199	.411	237	.490	57.18	77.04	38.85	53.97	227.05	57.89	
-	-	-	-	.388	.483	.532	234	.438	376	.704	67.24	82.11	61.64	77.60	288.60	73.58	
-	1	-	-	.394	.453	.547	182	.313	427	.735	52.30	58.70	70.00	81.00	262.00	66.80	
-	4	-	-	.318	.368	.475	156	.328	300	.632	44.83	61.54	49.18	69.61	225.16	57.41	
-	2	-	-	.294	.376	.438	198	.345	357	.622	56.90	64.64	58.52	68.55	248.61	63.38	
-	2	-	-	.324	.414	.452	155	.382	253	.623	44.54	71.54	41.48	68.68	226.23	57.68	
-	3	-	-	.267	.373	.367	126	.299	233	.553	36.21	56.08	38.20	61.00	191.48	48.82	
-	-	-	-	.201	.299	.254	81	.255	134	.421	23.28	47.73	21.97	46.44	139.41	35.55	
-	-	-	-	.315	.383	.333	23	.383	27	.450	6.61	71.83	4.43	49.60	132.46	33.77	
-	12	-	-	.313	.372	.444	2,309	.356	3,559	.549	51.64	85.27	42.08	72.96	251.96	64.35	82
-	19	-	-	.313	.372	.444	3,561	.356	5,489	.549	85.27	85.27	72.96	72.96	316.47	79.12	32
-	20	-	-	.313	.372	.444	3,899	.356	6,010	.549	74.65	85.27	63.87	72.96	296.75	74.19	46
-	12	-	-	.320	.387	.462	1,754	.365	2,816	.586	59.58	83.30	56.81	73.99	273.67	70.20	76
-	5	-	-	.348	.415	.504	986	.384	1,620	.631	64.78	82.11	62.12	76.48	285.49	73.14	84
-	-	-	-	.388	.483	.532	234	.438	376	.704	67.24	82.11	61.64	77.60	288.60	73.58	160
-	1	-	-	.394	.453	.547	182	.313	427	.735	52.30	58.70	70.00	81.00	262.00	66.80	346

Complete Career Statistics K

Total Career Statistics & Adjusted Career, 10 year, 5 year, and Single Year Analysis

Killibrew, Harmon: *Harmon Clayton "Killer" Killebrew, b. June 29, 1936, Payette, ID*

Rating Category	Year	Ranked Seasons & Adjustment	G	AB	H	1B	2B	3B	HR	RUN	RBI	BB	SO	SB
	1954		9	13	4	3	1	-	-	1	3	2	3	-
	1955		38	80	16	11	1	-	4	12	7	9	31	-
	1956		44	99	22	15	2	-	5	10	13	10	39	-
	1957		9	31	9	5	2	-	2	4	5	2	8	-
	1958		13	31	6	6	-	-	-	2	2	-	12	-
	1959		153	546	132	68	20	2	42	98	105	90	116	3
	1960		124	442	122	71	19	1	31	84	80	71	106	1
	1961	2nd	150	541	156	83	20	7	46	94	122	107	109	1
	1962		155	552	134	64	21	1	48	85	126	106	142	1
	1963		142	515	133	70	18	-	45	88	96	72	105	1
	1964		158	577	156	95	11	1	49	95	111	93	135	-
	1965		113	401	108	66	16	1	25	78	75	72	69	-
	1966		162	569	160	93	27	1	39	89	110	103	98	-
	1967		163	547	147	78	24	1	44	105	113	131	111	1
	1968		100	295	62	36	7	2	17	40	40	70	70	-
	1969	1st	162	555	153	82	20	2	49	106	140	145	84	8
	1970		157	527	143	81	20	1	41	96	113	128	84	-
	1971		147	500	127	79	19	1	28	61	119	114	96	3
	1972		139	433	100	59	13	2	26	53	74	94	91	-
	1973		69	248	60	45	9	1	5	29	32	41	59	-
	1974		122	333	74	54	7	-	13	28	54	45	61	-
	1975		106	312	62	35	13	-	14	25	44	54	70	1
Career Total	1954-1975		2,435	8,147	2,086	1,199	290	24	573	1,283	1,584	1,559	1,699	19
Career Adj. to 10,000 BO	1954-1975	0.992654	2,417	8,087	2,071	1,190	288	24	569	1,274	1,572	1,548	1,687	19
Career Adj. to 10,000 AB	1954-1975	1.227446	2,989	10,000	2,560	1,472	356	29	703	1,575	1,944	1,914	2,085	23
10 Year Total	1961-1970		1,462	5,079	1,352	748	184	17	403	876	1,046	1,027	1,007	11
5 Year Total	1960-1964		729	2,627	701	383	89	10	219	446	535	449	597	3
Best Single Year	1969		162	555	153	82	20	2	49	106	140	145	84	8
2nd Best Year	1961		150	541	156	83	20	7	46	94	122	107	109	1

10 Year Total · *5 Year Total*

Total Career Statistics & Adjusted Career, 10 year, 5 year, and Single Year Analysis

Killibrew, Harmon

CS	HBP	SF	GDP	AVG	OBP	SLG	Total Offensive Production Statistics				TRP Rating	RPA Rating	TNB Rating	TBA Rating	TOP Composite		
							TRP	RPA	TNB	TBA					TOP	Rating	Ranking
-	-	-	1	.308	.400	.385	4	.250	7	.438	1.15	46.85	1.15	48.22	97.36	24.82	
-	-	-	3	.200	.281	.363	19	.207	38	.413	5.46	38.70	6.23	45.52	95.91	24.45	
-	-	1	2	.222	.291	.394	23	.205	49	.438	6.61	38.48	8.03	48.22	101.34	25.84	
-	-	-	-	.290	.333	.548	9	.273	19	.576	2.59	51.10	3.11	63.46	120.26	30.66	
-	1	1	-	.194	.212	.194	4	.121	7	.212	1.15	22.71	1.15	23.38	48.39	12.34	
2	7	4	12	.242	.354	.516	203	.308	380	.577	58.33	57.72	62.30	63.55	241.90	61.68	
-	1	3	10	.276	.375	.534	164	.311	309	.586	47.13	58.31	50.66	64.62	220.72	56.27	
2	3	5	11	.288	.405	.606	216	.324	437	.655	62.07	60.68	71.64	72.21	266.60	67.97	
2	4	4	14	.243	.366	.545	211	.310	410	.603	60.63	58.14	67.21	66.45	252.44	64.36	
-	3	6	16	.258	.349	.555	184	.301	361	.590	52.87	56.34	59.18	65.01	233.40	59.51	
-	8	4	15	.270	.377	.548	206	.296	417	.598	59.20	55.38	68.36	65.94	248.88	63.45	
-	4	2	10	.269	.384	.501	153	.313	277	.566	43.97	58.63	45.41	62.43	210.44	53.65	
2	2	3	12	.281	.391	.538	199	.289	409	.594	57.18	54.12	67.05	65.42	243.78	62.15	
-	3	8	16	.269	.408	.558	218	.309	440	.624	62.64	57.94	72.13	68.79	261.50	66.67	
-	2	4	13	.210	.361	.420	80	.208	196	.510	22.99	39.04	32.13	56.26	150.41	38.35	
2	5	4	16	.276	.427	.584	246	.339	480	.662	70.69	63.58	78.69	72.97	285.93	72.90	
3	2	8	28	.271	.411	.546	209	.302	415	.599	60.06	56.51	68.03	66.00	250.60	63.89	
2	-	10	21	.254	.386	.464	180	.279	347	.538	51.72	52.29	56.89	59.29	220.20	56.14	
1	1	4	16	.231	.367	.450	127	.232	289	.527	36.49	43.43	47.38	58.12	185.42	47.27	
-	1	-	10	.242	.352	.347	61	.203	128	.427	17.53	38.10	20.98	47.02	123.64	31.52	
-	-	4	12	.222	.312	.360	82	.208	165	.419	23.56	39.00	27.05	46.16	135.77	34.61	
2	1	2	5	.199	.317	.375	69	.184	171	.457	19.83	34.57	28.03	50.39	132.82	33.86	
18	48	77	243	.256	.376	.509	2,867	.285	5,751	.571	64.12	68.15	68.00	75.88	276.16	70.53	46
18	48	76	241	.256	.376	.509	2,846	.285	5,709	.571	68.15	68.15	75.88	75.88	288.06	72.02	80
22	59	95	298	.256	.376	.509	3,519	.285	7,059	.571	67.37	68.15	75.02	75.88	286.43	71.61	64
11	36	48	151	.266	.390	.547	1,922	.303	3,842	.606	65.29	69.12	77.51	76.45	288.36	73.96	55
4	19	22	66	.267	.375	.558	981	.308	1,934	.608	64.45	65.91	74.16	73.67	278.18	71.27	91
2	5	4	16	.276	.427	.584	246	.339	480	.662	70.69	63.58	78.69	72.97	285.93	72.90	182
2	3	5	11	.288	.405	.606	216	.324	437	.655	62.07	60.68	71.64	72.21	266.60	67.97	329

Complete Career Statistics K

Total Career Statistics & Adjusted Career, 10 year, 5 year, and Single Year Analysis

Kiner, Ralph: *Ralph McPherran Kiner, b. Oct. 27, 1922, Santa Rita, NM*

Rating Category			Year	Ranked Seasons & Adjustment	G	AB	H	1B	2B	3B	HR	RUN	RBI	BB	SO	SB	
			1946		144	502	124	81	17	3	23	63	81	74	109	3	
		5 Year Total	1947	2nd	152	565	177	99	23	4	51	118	127	98	81	1	
	10 Year Total		1948		156	555	147	83	19	5	40	104	123	112	61	1	
			1949	1st	152	549	170	92	19	5	54	116	127	117	61	6	
			1950		150	547	149	75	21	6	47	112	118	122	79	2	
			1951	3rd	151	531	164	85	31	6	42	124	109	137	57	2	
			1952		149	516	126	70	17	2	37	90	87	110	77	3	
			1953		158	562	157	99	20	3	35	100	116	100	88	2	
			1954		147	557	159	96	36	5	22	88	73	76	90	2	
			1955		113	321	78	47	13	-	18	56	54	65	46	-	
Career Total			1946-1956		1,472	5,205	1,451	827	216	39	369	971	1,015	1,011	749	22	
Career Adj. to 10,000 BO			1946-1956	1.569120	2,310	8,167	2,277	1,298	339	61	579	1,524	1,593	1,586	1,175	35	
Career Adj. to 10,000 AB			1946-1956	1.921230	2,828	10,000	2,788	1,589	415	75	709	1,866	1,950	1,942	1,439	42	
10 Year Total			1947-1956		1,472	5,205	1,451	827	216	39	369	971	1,015	1,011	749	22	
5 Year Total			1947-1951		761	2,747	807	434	113	26	234	574	604	586	339	12	
Best Single Year			1949		152	549	170	92	19	5	54	116	127	117	61	6	
2nd Best Year			1947		152	565	177	99	23	4	51	118	127	98	81	1	
3rd Best Year			1951		151	531	164	85	31	6	42	124	109	137	57	2	

Total Career Statistics & Adjusted Career, 10 year, 5 year, and Single Year Analysis

Kiner, Ralph

CS	HBP	SF	GDP	AVG	OBP	SLG	Total Offensive Production Statistics				TRP Rating	RPA Rating	TNB Rating	TBA Rating	TOP Composite		
							TRP	RPA	TNB	TBA					TOP	Rating	Ranking
-	1	-	15	.247	.345	.430	144	.243	294	.497	41.38	45.58	48.20	54.73	189.89	48.41	
-	2	-	12	.313	.417	.639	245	.362	462	.682	70.40	67.81	75.74	75.21	289.16	73.73	
-	3	-	15	.265	.391	.533	227	.331	412	.601	65.23	62.10	67.54	66.29	261.16	66.58	
-	1	-	10	.310	.432	.658	243	.359	485	.716	69.83	67.26	79.51	78.96	295.55	75.35	
-	3	-	22	.272	.408	.590	230	.331	450	.648	66.09	62.10	73.77	71.46	273.43	69.71	
1	2	-	10	.309	.452	.627	233	.343	473	.696	66.95	64.21	77.54	76.66	285.36	72.76	
-	7	-	6	.244	.384	.500	177	.277	378	.592	50.86	51.90	61.97	65.20	229.93	58.62	
1	3	-	11	.279	.391	.512	216	.320	392	.580	62.07	59.87	64.26	63.91	250.12	63.77	
-	2	3	17	.285	.371	.487	161	.246	351	.536	46.26	46.06	57.54	59.06	208.93	53.27	
-	-	4	8	.243	.367	.452	110	.276	210	.528	31.61	51.79	34.43	58.15	175.98	44.87	
2	24	7	126	.279	.398	.548	1,986	.312	3,907	.613	44.42	74.62	46.20	81.49	246.73	63.01	89
3	38	11	198	.279	.398	.548	3,116	.312	6,131	.613	74.62	74.62	81.49	81.49	312.22	78.06	44
4	46	13	242	.279	.398	.548	3,816	.312	7,506	.613	73.05	74.62	79.77	81.49	308.93	77.23	29
2	24	7	126	.279	.398	.548	1,986	.312	3,907	.613	67.46	71.06	78.82	77.35	294.69	75.59	47
1	11	-	69	.294	.420	.609	1,178	.345	2,282	.669	77.40	73.81	87.50	81.07	319.77	81.92	23
-	1	-	10	.310	.432	.658	243	.359	485	.716	69.83	67.26	79.51	78.96	295.55	75.35	119
-	2	-	12	.313	.417	.639	245	.362	462	.682	70.40	67.81	75.74	75.21	289.16	73.73	155
1	2	-	10	.309	.452	.627	233	.343	473	.696	66.95	64.21	77.54	76.66	285.36	72.76	188

Complete Career Statistics K

Total Career Statistics & Adjusted Career, 10 year, 5 year, and Single Year Analysis

Klein, Chuck: *Charles Hubert Klein, b. Oct. 7, 1904, Indianapolis, IN*

Rating Category	Year	Ranked Seasons & Adjustment	G	AB	H	1B	2B	3B	HR	RUN	RBI	BB	SO	SB
	1928		64	253	91	62	14	4	11	41	34	14	22	-
	1929	3rd	149	616	219	125	45	6	43	126	145	54	61	5
	1930	1st	156	648	250	143	59	8	40	158	170	54	50	4
	1931	4th	148	594	200	125	34	10	31	121	121	59	49	7
	1932	2nd	154	650	226	123	50	15	38	152	137	60	49	20
	1933		152	606	223	144	44	7	28	101	120	56	36	15
	1934		115	435	131	82	27	2	20	78	80	47	38	3
	1935		119	434	127	88	14	4	21	71	73	41	42	4
	1936		146	601	184	117	35	7	25	102	104	49	59	6
	1937		115	406	132	95	20	2	15	74	57	39	21	3
	1938		129	458	113	81	22	2	8	53	61	38	30	7
	1939		110	317	90	55	18	5	12	45	56	36	21	2
	1940		116	354	77	52	16	2	7	39	37	44	30	2
	1941		50	73	9	8	-	-	1	6	3	10	6	-
	1942		14	14	1	1	-	-	-	-	-	-	2	-
	1943		12	20	2	2	-	-	-	-	3	-	3	1
	1944		4	7	1	1	-	-	-	1	-	-	2	-
Career Total	1928-1944		1,753	6,486	2,076	1,304	398	74	300	1,168	1,201	601	521	79
Career Adj. to 10,000 BO	1928-1944	1.397819	2,450	9,066	2,902	1,823	556	103	419	1,633	1,679	840	728	110
Career Adj. to 10,000 AB	1928-1944	1.541782	2,703	10,000	3,201	2,010	614	114	463	1,801	1,852	927	803	122
10 Year Total	1928-1937		1,318	5,243	1,783	1,104	342	65	272	1,024	1,041	473	427	67
5 Year Total	1929-1933		759	3,114	1,118	660	232	46	180	658	693	283	245	51
Best Single Year	1930		156	648	250	143	59	8	40	158	170	54	50	4
2nd Best Year	1932		154	650	226	123	50	15	38	152	137	60	49	20
3rd Best Year	1929		149	616	219	125	45	6	43	126	145	54	61	5
4th Best Year	1931		148	594	200	125	34	10	31	121	121	59	49	7

(Left margin: 10 Year Total; 5 Year Total)

(Side tab: Complete Career Statistics K)

Total Career Statistics & Adjusted Career, 10 year, 5 year, and Single Year Analysis

Klein, Chuck

CS	HBP	SF	GDP	AVG	OBP	SLG	Total Offensive Production Statistics				TRP Rating	RPA Rating	TNB Rating	TBA Rating	TOP Composite		
							TRP	RPA	TNB	TBA					TOP	Rating	Ranking
-	1	-	-	.360	.396	.577	75	.280	161	.601	21.55	52.44	26.39	66.21	166.59	42.47	
-	-	-	-	.356	.407	.657	271	.404	464	.693	77.87	75.79	76.07	76.33	306.06	78.03	
-	4	-	-	.386	.436	.687	328	.465	507	.718	94.25	87.06	83.11	79.15	343.57	87.60	
-	1	-	-	.337	.398	.584	242	.370	414	.633	69.54	69.34	67.87	69.77	276.51	70.50	
-	1	-	-	.348	.404	.646	289	.406	501	.705	83.05	76.17	82.13	77.66	319.00	81.33	
-	1	-	3	.368	.422	.602	221	.332	437	.656	63.51	62.18	71.64	72.32	269.64	68.75	
-	2	-	6	.301	.372	.510	158	.322	274	.559	45.40	60.42	44.92	61.63	212.37	54.15	
-	1	-	10	.293	.355	.488	144	.296	258	.531	41.38	55.52	42.30	58.51	197.70	50.41	
-	-	-	8	.306	.358	.512	206	.313	363	.552	59.20	58.66	59.51	60.80	238.17	60.72	
-	1	-	6	.325	.386	.495	131	.290	244	.540	37.64	54.31	40.00	59.50	191.45	48.81	
-	-	-	7	.247	.304	.356	114	.227	208	.414	32.76	42.47	34.10	45.58	154.90	39.49	
-	-	-	4	.284	.357	.486	101	.283	192	.538	29.02	53.01	31.48	59.27	172.79	44.05	
-	-	-	8	.218	.304	.333	76	.187	164	.404	21.84	35.08	26.89	44.52	128.32	32.72	
-	-	-	2	.123	.229	.164	9	.106	22	.259	2.59	19.84	3.61	28.53	54.56	13.91	
-	-	-	1	.071	.071	.071	-	.000	1	.067	-	-	0.16	7.35	7.51	1.92	
-	-	-	-	.100	.100	.100	3	.150	3	.150	0.86	28.11	0.49	16.53	45.99	11.73	
-	-	-	-	.143	.143	.143	1	.143	1	.143	0.29	26.77	0.16	15.74	42.96	10.95	
-	12	-	55	.320	.379	.543	2,369	.331	4,214	.589	52.99	79.29	49.83	78.30	260.41	66.50	72
-	17	-	77	.320	.379	.543	3,311	.331	5,890	.589	79.29	79.29	78.30	78.30	315.19	78.80	34
-	19	-	85	.320	.379	.543	3,652	.331	6,497	.589	69.93	79.29	69.05	78.30	296.57	74.14	48
-	12	-	33	.340	.396	.586	2,065	.358	3,623	.629	70.14	81.74	73.09	79.35	304.32	78.06	33
-	7	-	3	.359	.414	.636	1,351	.397	2,323	.682	88.76	84.80	89.07	82.67	345.30	88.46	6
-	4	-	-	.386	.436	.687	328	.465	507	.718	94.25	87.06	83.11	79.15	343.57	87.60	16
-	1	-	-	.348	.404	.646	289	.406	501	.705	83.05	76.17	82.13	77.66	319.00	81.33	44
-	-	-	-	.356	.407	.657	271	.404	464	.693	77.87	75.79	76.07	76.33	306.06	78.03	78
-	1	-	-	.337	.398	.584	242	.370	414	.633	69.54	69.34	67.87	69.77	276.51	70.50	272

Complete Career Statistics K

Total Career Statistics & Adjusted Career, 10 year, 5 year, and Single Year Analysis

Kluszewski, Ted: *Theodore Bernard "Big Klu" Kluszewski, b. Sept. 10, 1924, Argo, IL*

Rating Category	Year	Ranked Seasons & Adjustment	G	AB	H	1B	2B	3B	HR	RUN	RBI	BB	SO	SB
	1947		9	10	1	1	-	-	-	1	2	1	2	-
	1948		113	379	104	65	23	4	12	49	57	18	32	1
	1949		136	531	164	128	26	2	8	63	68	19	24	3
	1950		134	538	165	103	37	-	25	76	111	33	28	3
	1951		154	607	157	107	35	2	13	74	77	35	33	6
10 Year Total	1952		135	497	159	108	24	11	16	62	86	47	28	3
	1953		149	570	180	115	25	-	40	97	108	55	34	2
5 Year Total	1954	1st	149	573	187	107	28	3	49	104	141	78	35	-
	1955		153	612	192	120	25	-	47	116	113	66	40	1
	1956		138	517	156	106	14	1	35	91	102	49	31	1
	1957		69	127	34	21	7	-	6	12	21	5	5	-
	1958		100	301	88	67	13	4	4	29	37	26	16	-
	1959		91	223	62	44	12	2	4	22	27	14	24	-
	1960		81	181	53	39	9	-	5	20	39	22	10	-
	1961		107	263	64	37	12	-	15	32	39	24	23	-
Career Total	1947-1961		1,718	5,929	1,766	1,168	290	29	279	848	1,028	492	365	20
Career Adj. to 10,000 BO	1947-1961	1.512859	2,599	8,970	2,672	1,767	439	44	422	1,283	1,555	744	552	30
Career Adj. to 10,000 AB	1947-1961	1.686625	2,898	10,000	2,979	1,970	489	49	471	1,430	1,734	830	616	34
10 Year Total	1948-1957		1,330	4,951	1,498	980	244	23	251	744	884	405	290	20
5 Year Total	1952-1956		724	2,769	874	556	116	15	187	470	550	295	168	7
Best Single Year	1954		149	573	187	107	28	3	49	104	141	78	35	-

Total Career Statistics & Adjusted Career, 10 year, 5 year, and Single Year Analysis

Kluszewski, Ted

CS	HBP	SF	GDP	AVG	OBP	SLG	Total Offensive Production Statistics				TRP Rating	RPA Rating	TNB Rating	TBA Rating	TOP Composite		
							TRP	RPA	TNB	TBA					TOP	Rating	Ranking
-	-	-	-	.100	.182	.100	3	.273	2	.182	0.86	51.10	0.33	20.04	72.33	18.44	
-	-	-	14	.274	.307	.451	106	.258	190	.462	30.46	48.33	31.15	50.95	160.89	41.02	
-	-	-	10	.309	.333	.411	131	.234	240	.429	37.64	43.83	39.34	47.23	168.06	42.85	
-	1	-	20	.307	.348	.515	187	.316	314	.530	53.74	59.19	51.48	58.46	222.86	56.82	
2	2	-	16	.259	.301	.387	151	.229	276	.418	43.39	42.87	45.25	46.09	177.60	45.28	
3	4	-	13	.320	.383	.509	148	.264	304	.542	42.53	49.43	49.84	59.72	201.52	51.38	
-	4	-	13	.316	.380	.570	205	.319	386	.601	58.91	59.83	63.28	66.27	248.29	63.30	
2	3	5	12	.326	.407	.642	245	.365	447	.666	70.40	68.42	73.28	73.42	285.52	72.80	
1	4	4	10	.314	.382	.585	229	.329	428	.615	65.80	61.65	70.16	67.78	265.40	67.67	
-	3	5	11	.302	.362	.536	193	.330	330	.564	55.46	61.82	54.10	62.17	233.55	59.55	
-	1	-	2	.268	.301	.465	33	.244	65	.481	9.48	45.80	10.66	53.07	119.01	30.34	
-	1	2	8	.292	.348	.402	66	.195	148	.438	18.97	36.59	24.26	48.26	128.08	32.65	
1	-	1	7	.278	.319	.404	49	.200	103	.420	14.08	37.48	16.89	46.33	114.78	29.26	
1	-	3	3	.293	.364	.425	59	.282	98	.469	16.95	52.90	16.07	51.68	137.60	35.08	
-	-	3	4	.243	.303	.460	71	.241	145	.493	20.40	45.25	23.77	54.36	143.78	36.66	
10	23	23	143	.298	.353	.498	1,876	.284	3,476	.526	41.96	67.96	41.10	69.90	220.92	56.42	117
15	35	35	216	.298	.353	.498	2,838	.284	5,259	.526	67.96	67.96	69.90	69.90	275.72	68.93	101
17	39	39	241	.298	.353	.498	3,164	.284	5,863	.526	60.58	67.96	62.31	69.90	260.75	65.19	105
8	22	14	121	.303	.357	.513	1,628	.295	2,980	.541	55.30	67.34	60.12	68.20	250.96	64.37	114
6	18	14	59	.316	.383	.571	1,020	.323	1,895	.601	67.02	69.13	72.66	72.82	281.64	72.15	87
2	3	5	12	.326	.407	.642	245	.365	447	.666	70.40	68.42	73.28	73.42	285.52	72.80	187

Complete Career Statistics K

Total Career Statistics & Adjusted Career, 10 year, 5 year, and Single Year Analysis

Lajoie, Nap: *Napoleon "Larry" Lajoie, b. Sept. 5, 1874, Woonsocket, RI*

Rating Category	Year	Ranked Seasons & Adjustment	G	AB	H	1B	2B	3B	HR	RUN	RBI	BB	SO	SB
	1896		39	174	57	36	11	6	4	37	42	1	11	6
	1897		126	545	198	127	37	25	9	107	127	15	-	22
	1898		147	610	200	144	40	10	6	113	127	21	-	33
	1899		72	308	117	83	17	11	6	70	70	12	-	14
	1900		102	451	156	105	32	12	7	95	92	10	-	25
	1901	1st	131	543	229	154	48	13	14	145	125	24	-	27
	1902		87	352	129	83	34	5	7	81	65	19	-	19
	1903		126	488	173	113	40	13	7	90	93	24	-	22
	1904		140	554	211	142	50	14	5	92	102	27	-	31
	1905		65	249	82	65	13	2	2	29	41	17	-	11
	1906		152	602	214	158	49	7	-	88	91	30	-	20
	1907		137	509	153	115	30	6	2	53	63	30	-	24
	1908		157	581	168	128	32	6	2	77	74	47	-	15
	1909		128	469	152	111	33	7	1	56	47	35	-	13
	1910		159	591	227	165	51	7	4	94	76	60	-	26
	1911		90	315	115	92	20	1	2	36	60	26	-	13
	1912		117	448	165	127	34	4	-	66	90	28	-	18
	1913		137	465	156	128	25	2	1	67	68	33	17	17
	1914		121	419	108	91	14	3	-	37	50	32	15	14
	1915		129	490	137	107	24	5	1	40	61	11	16	10
	1916		113	426	105	85	14	4	2	33	35	14	26	15
Career Total	1896-1916		2,475	9,589	3,252	2,359	648	163	82	1,506	1,599	516	85	395
Career Adj. to 10,000 BO	1896-1916	0.976658	2,417	9,365	3,176	2,304	633	159	80	1,471	1,562	504	83	386
Career Adj. to 10,000 AB	1896-1916	1.042862	2,581	10,000	3,391	2,460	676	170	86	1,571	1,668	538	89	412
10 Year Total	1897-1906		1,148	4,702	1,709	1,174	360	112	63	910	933	199	-	224
5 Year Total	1897-1901		578	2,457	900	613	174	71	42	530	541	82	-	121
Best Single Year	1901		131	543	229	154	48	13	14	145	125	24	-	27

(left margin: 10 Year Total / 5 Year Total)

Complete Career Statistics L

Total Career Statistics & Adjusted Career, 10 year, 5 year, and Single Year Analysis

Lajoie, Nap

CS	HBP	SF	GDP	AVG	OBP	SLG	Total Offensive Production Statistics				TRP Rating	RPA Rating	TNB Rating	TBA Rating	TOP Composite		
							TRP	RPA	TNB	TBA					TOP	Rating	Ranking
-	-	-	-	.328	.331	.529	79	.451	99	.566	22.70	84.59	16.23	62.35	185.87	47.39	
-	12	-	-	.363	.393	.572	234	.409	361	.631	67.24	76.66	59.18	69.56	272.64	69.51	
-	7	-	-	.328	.357	.456	240	.376	339	.531	68.97	70.49	55.57	58.56	253.59	64.66	
-	10	-	-	.380	.421	.565	140	.424	210	.636	40.23	79.50	34.43	70.14	224.29	57.18	
-	8	-	-	.346	.371	.517	187	.399	276	.588	53.74	74.71	45.25	64.86	238.55	60.82	
-	13	-	-	.422	.459	.635	270	.466	409	.705	77.59	87.23	67.05	77.72	309.58	78.93	
-	6	-	-	.366	.408	.551	146	.387	238	.631	41.95	72.57	39.02	69.58	223.12	56.89	
-	3	-	-	.355	.388	.533	183	.355	309	.600	52.59	66.58	50.66	66.13	235.95	60.16	
-	8	-	-	.381	.418	.549	194	.329	370	.628	55.75	61.72	60.66	69.23	247.36	63.07	
-	2	-	-	.329	.377	.422	70	.261	135	.504	20.11	48.94	22.13	55.52	146.71	37.40	
-	6	-	-	.355	.392	.460	179	.281	333	.522	51.44	52.57	54.59	57.53	216.13	55.10	
-	6	-	-	.301	.347	.395	116	.213	261	.479	33.33	39.88	42.79	52.78	168.78	43.03	
-	9	-	-	.289	.352	.375	151	.237	289	.454	43.39	44.42	47.38	50.00	185.19	47.22	
-	6	-	-	.324	.378	.431	103	.202	256	.502	29.60	37.84	41.97	55.32	164.73	42.00	
-	5	-	-	.384	.445	.514	170	.259	395	.602	48.85	48.56	64.75	66.36	228.53	58.27	
-	4	-	-	.365	.420	.454	96	.278	186	.539	27.59	52.14	30.49	59.42	169.64	43.25	
-	7	-	-	.368	.414	.462	156	.323	260	.538	44.83	60.52	42.62	59.33	207.30	52.85	
-	15	-	-	.335	.398	.404	135	.263	253	.493	38.79	49.31	41.48	54.36	183.93	46.90	
15	2	-	-	.258	.313	.305	87	.192	161	.355	25.00	35.99	26.39	39.17	126.55	32.27	
6	4	-	-	.280	.301	.355	101	.200	193	.382	29.02	37.48	31.64	42.12	140.26	35.76	
-	1	-	-	.246	.272	.312	68	.154	163	.370	19.54	28.89	26.72	40.74	115.89	29.55	
21	134	-	-	.339	.381	.466	3,105	.303	5,496	.537	69.45	72.62	64.99	71.35	278.40	71.10	42
21	131	-	-	.339	.381	.466	3,033	.303	5,368	.537	72.62	72.62	71.35	71.35	287.93	71.98	81
22	140	-	-	.339	.381	.466	3,238	.303	5,732	.537	61.99	72.62	60.91	71.35	266.87	66.72	96
-	75	-	-	.363	.399	.528	1,843	.370	2,980	.599	62.60	84.46	60.12	75.56	282.74	72.52	62
-	50	-	-	.366	.399	.546	1,071	.414	1,595	.616	70.37	88.46	61.16	74.69	294.68	75.50	61
-	13	-	-	.422	.459	.635	270	.466	409	.705	77.59	87.23	67.05	77.72	309.58	78.93	68

Complete Career Statistics L

Total Career Statistics & Adjusted Career, 10 year, 5 year, and Single Year Analysis

Mantle, Mickey: *Mickey Charles "The Commerce Comet" Mantle; b. Oct. 20, 1931, Spavinaw, OK*

Rating Category			Year	Ranked Seasons & Adjustment	G	AB	H	1B	2B	3B	HR	RUN	RBI	BB	SO	SB
			1951		96	341	91	62	11	5	13	61	65	43	74	8
			1952		142	549	171	104	37	7	23	94	87	75	111	4
			1953		127	461	136	88	24	3	21	105	92	79	90	8
10 Year Total	5 Year Total		1954		146	543	163	107	17	12	27	129	102	102	107	5
			1955	5th	147	517	158	85	25	11	37	121	99	113	97	8
			1956	1st	150	533	188	109	22	5	52	132	130	112	99	10
			1957	3rd	144	474	173	105	28	6	34	121	94	146	75	16
			1958	4th	150	519	158	94	21	1	42	127	97	129	123	18
			1959		144	541	154	96	23	4	31	104	75	95	126	21
			1960		153	527	145	82	17	6	40	119	94	111	125	14
			1961	2nd	153	514	163	87	16	6	54	132	128	126	112	12
			1962		123	377	121	75	15	1	30	96	89	122	78	9
			1963		65	172	54	31	8	-	15	40	35	40	32	2
			1964		143	465	141	79	25	2	35	92	111	99	102	6
			1965		122	361	92	60	12	1	19	44	46	73	76	4
			1966		108	333	96	60	12	1	23	40	56	57	76	1
			1967		144	440	108	69	17	-	22	63	55	107	113	1
			1968		144	435	103	70	14	1	18	57	54	106	97	6
Career Total			1951-1968		2,401	8,102	2,415	1,463	344	72	536	1,677	1,509	1,735	1,713	153
Career Adj. to 10,000 BO			1951-1968	0.999001	2,399	8,094	2,413	1,462	344	72	535	1,675	1,507	1,733	1,711	153
Career Adj. to 10,000 AB			1951-1968	1.234263	2,963	10,000	2,981	1,806	425	89	662	2,070	1,863	2,141	2,114	189
10 Year Total			1953-1962		1,437	5,006	1,559	928	208	55	368	1,186	1,000	1,135	1,032	121
5 Year Total			1954-1958		737	2,586	840	500	113	35	192	630	522	602	501	57
Best Single Year			1956		150	533	188	109	22	5	52	132	130	112	99	10
2nd Best Year			1961		153	514	163	87	16	6	54	132	128	126	112	12
3rd Best Year			1957		144	474	173	105	28	6	34	121	94	146	75	16
4th Best Year			1958		150	519	158	94	21	1	42	127	97	129	123	18
5th Best Year			1955		147	517	158	85	25	11	37	121	99	113	97	8

Complete Career Statistics   M

Total Career Statistics & Adjusted Career, 10 year, 5 year, and Single Year Analysis

Mantle, Mickey

CS	HBP	SF	GDP	AVG	OBP	SLG	TRP	RPA	TNB	TBA	TRP Rating	RPA Rating	TNB Rating	TBA Rating	TOP	Rating	Ranking
7	-	-	3	.267	.349	.443	126	.326	195	.504	36.21	61.01	31.97	55.53	184.72	47.10	
1	-	-	5	.311	.394	.530	181	.288	369	.587	52.01	53.92	60.49	64.66	231.08	58.92	
4	-	-	2	.295	.398	.497	197	.363	312	.576	56.61	68.11	51.15	63.44	239.31	61.01	
2	-	4	3	.300	.408	.525	231	.354	390	.598	66.38	66.39	63.93	65.93	262.63	66.96	
1	3	3	4	.306	.431	.611	220	.344	439	.686	63.22	64.41	71.97	75.60	275.20	70.16	
1	2	4	4	.353	.464	.705	262	.400	499	.762	75.29	74.95	81.80	83.96	316.01	80.57	
3	-	3	5	.365	.512	.665	215	.342	474	.755	61.78	64.15	77.70	83.19	286.83	73.13	
3	2	2	11	.304	.443	.592	224	.338	453	.683	64.37	63.31	74.26	75.30	277.24	70.69	
3	2	2	7	.285	.392	.514	179	.277	393	.607	51.44	51.84	64.43	66.95	234.65	59.83	
3	1	5	11	.275	.399	.558	213	.325	417	.637	61.21	60.93	68.36	70.17	260.67	66.46	
1	-	5	2	.317	.448	.687	260	.402	490	.757	74.71	75.30	80.33	83.47	313.81	80.01	
-	1	2	4	.321	.486	.605	185	.366	360	.711	53.16	68.51	59.02	78.41	259.10	66.06	
1	-	1	5	.314	.441	.622	75	.344	148	.679	21.55	64.47	24.26	74.82	185.10	47.19	
3	-	3	9	.303	.423	.591	203	.352	377	.655	58.33	66.04	61.80	72.14	258.31	65.86	
1	-	1	11	.255	.379	.452	90	.202	239	.536	25.86	37.81	39.18	59.06	161.92	41.28	
1	-	3	9	.288	.389	.538	96	.239	236	.587	27.59	44.75	38.69	64.70	175.73	44.80	
1	1	5	9	.245	.391	.434	118	.210	299	.532	33.91	39.34	49.02	58.64	180.91	46.12	
2	1	4	9	.237	.385	.398	111	.200	284	.512	31.90	37.48	46.56	56.40	172.33	43.94	
38	13	47	113	.298	.421	.557	3,186	.318	6,374	.637	71.26	76.21	75.37	84.64	307.48	78.53	14
38	13	47	113	.298	.421	.557	3,183	.318	6,368	.637	76.21	76.21	84.64	84.64	321.71	80.43	23
47	16	58	139	.298	.421	.557	3,932	.318	7,867	.637	75.29	76.21	83.61	84.64	319.75	79.94	16
21	11	30	53	.311	.438	.595	2,186	.351	4,227	.678	74.25	79.95	85.27	85.54	325.02	83.36	11
10	7	16	27	.325	.451	.618	1,152	.356	2,255	.696	75.69	76.08	86.46	84.44	322.67	82.67	21
1	2	4	4	.353	.464	.705	262	.400	499	.762	75.29	74.95	81.80	83.96	316.01	80.57	49
1	-	5	2	.317	.448	.687	260	.402	490	.757	74.71	75.30	80.33	83.47	313.81	80.01	56
3	-	3	5	.365	.512	.665	215	.342	474	.755	61.78	64.15	77.70	83.19	286.83	73.13	172
3	2	2	11	.304	.443	.592	224	.338	453	.683	64.37	63.31	74.26	75.30	277.24	70.69	258
1	3	3	4	.306	.431	.611	220	.344	439	.686	63.22	64.41	71.97	75.60	275.20	70.16	294

Complete Career Statistics M

Total Career Statistics & Adjusted Career, 10 year, 5 year, and Single Year Analysis

Maris, Roger: *Roger Eugene Maris (Maras), b. Sept. 10, 1934, Fargo, ND*

Rating Category	Year	Ranked Seasons & Adjustment	G	AB	H	1B	2B	3B	HR	RUN	RBI	BB	SO	SB
	1957		116	358	84	56	9	5	14	61	51	60	79	8
	1958		150	583	140	89	19	4	28	87	80	45	85	4
	1959		122	433	118	74	21	7	16	69	72	58	53	2
	1960		136	499	141	77	18	7	39	98	112	70	65	2
	1961	1st	161	590	159	78	16	4	61	132	142	94	67	-
	1962		157	590	151	83	34	1	33	92	100	87	78	1
	1963		90	312	84	46	14	1	23	53	53	35	40	1
	1964		141	513	144	104	12	2	26	86	71	62	78	3
	1965		46	155	37	22	7	-	8	22	27	29	29	-
	1966		119	348	81	57	9	2	13	37	43	36	60	-
	1967		125	410	107	73	18	7	9	64	55	52	61	-
	1968		100	310	79	54	18	2	5	25	45	24	38	-
Career Total	1957-1968		1,463	5,101	1,325	813	195	42	275	826	851	652	733	21
Career Adj. to 10,000 BO	1957-1968	1.692334	2,476	8,633	2,242	1,376	330	71	465	1,398	1,440	1,103	1,240	36
Career Adj. to 10,000 AB	1957-1968	1.960400	2,868	10,000	2,598	1,594	382	82	539	1,619	1,668	1,278	1,437	41
10 Year Total	1957-1966		1,238	4,381	1,139	686	159	33	261	737	751	576	634	21
5 Year Total	1958-1962		726	2,695	709	401	108	23	177	478	506	354	348	9
Best Single Year	1961		161	590	159	78	16	4	61	132	142	94	67	-

5 Year Total — *10 Year Total*

Complete Career Statistics M

Total Career Statistics & Adjusted Career, 10 year, 5 year, and Single Year Analysis

Maris, Roger

CS	HBP	SF	GDP	AVG	OBP	SLG	Total Offensive Production Statistics				TRP Rating	RPA Rating	TNB Rating	TBA Rating	TOP Composite		
							TRP	RPA	TNB	TBA					TOP	Rating	Ranking
4	1	2	6	.235	.344	.405	112	.262	210	.492	32.18	49.15	34.43	54.20	169.96	43.33	
2	2	5	2	.240	.294	.431	167	.262	300	.471	47.99	49.13	49.18	51.91	198.20	50.53	
1	3	4	4	.273	.359	.464	141	.281	263	.524	40.52	52.63	43.11	57.74	194.00	49.46	
2	3	5	6	.283	.371	.581	210	.360	363	.623	60.34	67.50	59.51	68.62	255.97	65.26	
-	7	7	16	.269	.372	.620	274	.384	467	.654	78.74	71.91	76.56	72.09	299.29	76.31	
-	6	3	7	.256	.356	.485	192	.277	380	.548	55.17	51.92	62.30	60.43	229.82	58.59	
-	2	1	2	.269	.346	.542	106	.301	207	.588	30.46	56.43	33.93	64.81	185.64	47.33	
-	6	2	7	.281	.364	.464	157	.266	309	.524	45.11	49.86	50.66	57.72	203.36	51.85	
-	-	1	4	.239	.357	.439	49	.259	97	.513	14.08	48.58	15.90	56.56	135.13	34.45	
-	3	4	8	.233	.307	.382	80	.201	172	.431	22.99	37.57	28.20	47.51	136.27	34.74	
-	4	5	10	.261	.346	.405	119	.247	222	.462	34.20	46.36	36.39	50.87	167.82	42.79	
-	1	4	3	.255	.307	.374	70	.205	141	.412	20.11	38.35	23.11	45.44	127.02	32.39	
9	38	43	75	.260	.345	.476	1,677	.284	3,131	.530	37.51	67.96	37.02	70.43	212.92	54.38	123
15	64	73	127	.260	.345	.476	2,838	.284	5,299	.530	67.96	67.96	70.43	70.43	276.78	69.20	99
18	74	84	147	.260	.345	.476	3,288	.284	6,138	.530	62.94	67.96	65.23	70.43	266.57	66.64	97
9	33	34	62	.260	.348	.490	1,488	.293	2,768	.544	50.54	66.72	55.84	68.67	241.77	62.01	118
5	21	24	35	.263	.350	.517	984	.314	1,773	.567	64.65	67.25	67.98	68.70	268.58	68.81	107
-	7	7	16	.269	.372	.620	274	.384	467	.654	78.74	71.91	76.56	72.09	299.29	76.31	105

Complete Career Statistics M

Total Career Statistics & Adjusted Career, 10 year, 5 year, and Single Year Analysis

Martinez, Edgar: *Edgar Martinez, b. Jan.2, 1963, New York, NY*

Rating Category	Year	Ranked Seasons & Adjustment	G	AB	H	1B	2B	3B	HR	RUN	RBI	BB	SO	SB
	1987		13	43	16	9	5	2	-	6	5	2	5	-
	1988		14	32	9	5	4	-	-	-	5	4	7	-
	1989		65	171	41	34	5	-	2	20	20	17	26	2
	1990		144	487	147	107	27	2	11	71	49	74	62	1
	1991		150	544	167	117	35	1	14	98	52	84	72	-
	1992		135	528	181	114	46	3	18	100	73	54	61	14
	1993		42	135	32	21	7	-	4	20	13	28	19	-
	1994		89	326	93	56	23	1	13	47	51	53	42	6
	1995	1st	145	511	182	101	52	-	29	121	113	116	87	4
	1996		139	499	163	83	52	2	26	121	103	123	84	3
	1997		155	542	179	115	35	1	28	104	108	119	86	2
	1998		154	556	179	103	46	1	29	86	102	106	96	1
	1999		142	502	169	109	35	1	24	86	86	97	99	7
	2000	2nd	153	556	180	112	31	-	37	100	145	96	95	3
	2001		132	470	144	80	40	1	23	80	116	93	90	4
	2002		97	328	91	53	23	-	15	42	59	67	69	1
	2003		145	497	146	97	25	-	24	72	98	92	95	-
	2004		141	486	128	93	23	-	12	45	63	58	107	1
Career Total**	1987-2004		2,055	7,213	2,247	1,409	514	15	309	1,219	1,261	1,283	1,202	49
Career Adj. to 10,000 BO**	1987-2004	1.129688	2,322	8,148	2,538	1,592	581	17	349	1,377	1,425	1,449	1,358	55
Career Adj. to 10,000 AB**	1987-2004	1.386386	2,849	10,000	3,115	1,953	713	21	428	1,690	1,748	1,779	1,666	68
10 Year Total**	1994-2003		1,351	4,787	1,526	909	362	7	248	859	981	962	843	31
5 Year Total**	1995-1999		735	2,610	872	511	220	5	136	518	512	561	452	17
Best Single Year**	1995		145	511	182	101	52	-	29	121	113	116	87	4
2nd Best Year**	2000		153	556	180	112	31	-	37	100	145	96	95	3

10 Year Total • *5 Year Total*

Complete Career Statistics   M

Total Career Statistics & Adjusted Career, 10 year, 5 year, and Single Year Analysis

Martinez, Edgar

CS	HBP	SF	GDP	AVG	OBP	SLG	Total Offensive Production Statistics				TRP Rating	RPA Rating	TNB Rating	TBA Rating	TOP Composite		
							TRP	RPA	TNB	TBA					TOP	Rating	Ranking
-	1	-	-	.372	.413	.581	11	.239	28	.609	3.16	44.81	4.59	67.09	119.65	30.50	
-	-	1	-	.281	.351	.406	5	.135	17	.459	1.44	25.32	2.79	50.64	80.18	20.44	
1	3	3	3	.240	.314	.304	40	.203	73	.371	11.49	38.05	11.97	40.84	102.35	26.09	
4	5	3	13	.302	.397	.433	120	.206	287	.493	34.48	38.64	47.05	54.35	174.52	44.49	
3	8	4	19	.307	.405	.452	150	.228	335	.508	43.10	42.65	54.92	56.03	196.70	50.15	
4	4	5	15	.343	.404	.544	173	.285	355	.586	49.71	53.49	58.20	64.56	225.97	57.61	
-	-	1	4	.237	.366	.378	33	.196	79	.470	9.48	36.81	12.95	51.83	111.07	28.32	
2	3	3	2	.285	.387	.482	98	.253	217	.561	28.16	47.45	35.57	61.80	172.99	44.10	
3	8	4	11	.356	.479	.628	234	.360	446	.686	67.24	67.46	73.11	75.62	283.44	72.26	
3	8	4	15	.327	.464	.595	224	.345	428	.659	64.37	64.67	70.16	72.68	271.89	69.32	
4	11	6	21	.330	.456	.554	212	.303	428	.612	60.92	56.83	70.16	67.48	255.40	65.12	
1	3	7	13	.322	.429	.565	188	.274	423	.618	54.02	51.43	69.34	68.06	242.85	61.92	
2	6	3	12	.337	.447	.554	172	.277	386	.623	49.43	51.98	63.28	68.62	233.30	59.48	
-	5	8	13	.324	.423	.579	245	.361	426	.628	70.40	67.71	69.84	69.25	277.20	70.67	
1	9	9	11	.306	.423	.543	196	.331	360	.608	56.32	62.04	59.02	67.02	244.40	62.31	
1	6	6	6	.277	.403	.485	101	.245	232	.562	29.02	45.82	38.03	61.91	174.79	44.56	
1	7	7	17	.294	.406	.489	170	.274	341	.550	48.85	51.38	55.90	60.62	216.75	55.26	
-	2	3	15	.263	.342	.385	108	.191	248	.440	31.03	35.88	40.66	48.46	156.03	39.78	
30	89	77	190	.312	.418	.515	2,480	.280	5,109	.577	55.47	67.09	60.41	76.72	259.69	66.32	73
34	101	87	215	.312	.418	.515	2,802	.280	5,772	.577	67.09	67.09	76.72	76.72	287.61	71.90	83
42	123	107	263	.312	.418	.515	3,438	.280	7,083	.577	65.83	67.09	75.28	76.72	284.91	71.23	69
18	66	57	121	.319	.435	.553	1,840	.307	3,687	.615	62.50	70.01	74.38	77.62	284.52	72.98	59
13	36	24	72	.334	.455	.579	1,030	.312	2,111	.639	67.67	66.68	80.94	77.49	292.79	75.01	64
3	8	4	11	.356	.479	.628	234	.360	446	.686	67.24	67.46	73.11	75.62	283.44	72.26	204
-	5	8	13	.324	.423	.579	245	.361	426	.628	70.40	67.71	69.84	69.25	277.20	70.67	259

Complete Career Statistics M

Total Career Statistics & Adjusted Career, 10 year, 5 year, and Single Year Analysis

Matthews, Eddie: *Edwin Lee Matthews, b. Oct. 13, 1931, Texarkana, TX*

Rating Category	Year	Ranked Seasons & Adjustment	G	AB	H	1B	2B	3B	HR	RUN	RBI	BB	SO	SB
	1952		145	528	128	75	23	5	25	80	58	59	115	6
	1953	1st	157	579	175	89	31	8	47	110	135	99	83	1
	1954		138	476	138	73	21	4	40	96	103	113	61	10
	1955		141	499	144	75	23	5	41	108	101	109	98	3
	1956		151	552	150	90	21	2	37	103	95	91	86	6
	1957		148	572	167	98	28	9	32	109	94	90	79	3
	1958		149	546	137	87	18	1	31	97	77	85	85	5
	1959		148	594	182	112	16	8	46	118	114	80	71	2
	1960		153	548	152	87	19	7	39	108	124	111	113	7
	1961		152	572	175	114	23	6	32	103	91	93	95	12
	1962		152	536	142	82	25	6	29	106	90	101	90	4
	1963		158	547	144	90	27	4	23	82	84	124	119	3
	1964		141	502	117	74	19	1	23	83	74	85	100	2
	1965		156	546	137	82	23	-	32	77	95	73	110	1
	1966		134	452	113	72	21	4	16	72	53	63	82	1
	1967		137	436	103	69	16	2	16	53	57	63	88	2
	1968		31	52	11	8	-	-	3	4	8	5	12	-
Career Total	1952-1968		2,391	8,537	2,315	1,377	354	72	512	1,509	1,453	1,444	1,487	68
Career Adj. to 10,000 BO	1952-1968	0.981547	2,347	8,379	2,272	1,352	347	71	503	1,481	1,426	1,417	1,460	67
Career Adj. to 10,000 AB	1952-1968	1.171372	2,801	10,000	2,712	1,613	415	84	600	1,768	1,702	1,691	1,742	80
10 Year Total	1953-1962		1,489	5,474	1,562	907	225	56	374	1,058	1,024	972	861	53
5 Year Total	1953-1957		735	2,678	774	425	124	28	197	526	528	502	407	23
Best Single Year	1953		157	579	175	89	31	8	47	110	135	99	83	1

(Row grouping labels on left side: 5 Year Total covers 1953-1957; 10 Year Total covers 1953-1962)

Total Career Statistics & Adjusted Career, 10 year, 5 year, and Single Year Analysis

Matthews, Eddie

CS	HBP	SF	GDP	AVG	OBP	SLG	Total Offensive Production Statistics				TRP Rating	RPA Rating	TNB Rating	TBA Rating	TOP Composite		
							TRP	RPA	TNB	TBA					TOP	Rating	Ranking
4	1	-	9	.242	.320	.447	138	.231	298	.499	39.66	43.31	48.85	55.01	186.84	47.64	
3	2	-	6	.302	.406	.627	245	.357	462	.673	70.40	66.92	75.74	74.23	287.29	73.25	
3	2	7	9	.290	.423	.603	199	.328	409	.674	57.18	61.43	67.05	74.26	259.93	66.27	
4	1	6	5	.289	.413	.601	209	.337	409	.660	60.06	63.17	67.05	72.71	262.98	67.05	
-	1	4	4	.272	.373	.518	198	.304	384	.589	56.90	56.90	62.95	64.91	241.66	61.61	
1	-	2	6	.292	.387	.540	203	.303	401	.599	58.33	56.77	65.74	65.96	246.81	62.93	
-	2	8	9	.251	.349	.458	174	.268	342	.526	50.00	50.16	56.07	57.99	214.22	54.62	
1	3	2	6	.306	.390	.593	232	.339	436	.636	66.67	63.46	71.48	70.15	271.76	69.29	
3	2	6	8	.277	.397	.551	232	.344	419	.621	66.67	64.40	68.69	68.41	268.17	68.37	
7	2	4	10	.306	.402	.535	194	.285	406	.596	55.75	53.38	66.56	65.71	241.39	61.55	
2	2	4	11	.265	.381	.496	196	.300	371	.567	56.32	56.16	60.82	62.52	235.82	60.12	
4	1	3	9	.263	.399	.453	166	.243	372	.544	47.70	45.48	60.98	59.94	214.10	54.59	
2	1	2	8	.233	.344	.412	157	.263	293	.490	45.11	49.20	48.03	54.00	196.34	50.06	
-	3	3	11	.251	.341	.469	172	.270	333	.524	49.43	50.68	54.59	57.71	212.40	54.15	
1	-	1	6	.250	.341	.420	125	.239	253	.485	35.92	44.87	41.48	53.42	175.68	44.79	
4	3	6	6	.236	.333	.392	110	.214	235	.457	31.61	40.10	38.52	50.39	160.62	40.95	
-	-	-	-	.212	.281	.385	12	.211	25	.439	3.45	39.45	4.10	48.34	95.33	24.31	
39	26	58	123	.271	.376	.509	2,962	.291	5,848	.574	66.25	69.62	69.15	76.30	281.32	71.84	37
38	26	57	121	.271	.376	.509	2,907	.291	5,740	.574	69.62	69.62	76.30	76.30	291.84	72.96	77
46	30	68	144	.271	.376	.509	3,470	.291	6,850	.574	66.43	69.62	72.80	76.30	285.15	71.29	68
24	17	43	74	.285	.392	.552	2,082	.316	4,039	.614	70.72	72.16	81.48	77.45	301.81	77.41	38
11	6	19	30	.289	.400	.577	1,054	.326	2,065	.638	69.25	69.67	79.18	77.39	295.50	75.70	60
3	2	-	6	.302	.406	.627	245	.357	462	.673	70.40	66.92	75.74	74.23	287.29	73.25	170

Total Career Statistics & Adjusted Career, 10 year, 5 year, and Single Year Analysis

Mattingly, Don: *Donald Arthur Mattingly, b. April 20, 1961, Evansville, IN*

Rating Category	Year	Ranked Seasons & Adjustment	G	AB	H	1B	2B	3B	HR	RUN	RBI	BB	SO	SB
	1982		7	12	2	2	-	-	-	-	1	-	1	-
	1983		91	279	79	56	15	4	4	34	32	21	31	-
	1984		153	603	207	138	44	2	23	91	110	41	33	1
	1985	1st	159	652	211	125	48	3	35	107	145	56	41	2
	1986		162	677	238	152	53	2	31	117	113	53	35	-
	1987		141	569	186	116	38	2	30	93	115	51	38	1
	1988		144	599	186	131	37	-	18	94	88	41	29	1
	1989		158	631	191	129	37	2	23	79	113	51	30	3
	1990		102	394	101	80	16	-	5	40	42	28	20	1
	1991		152	587	169	125	35	-	9	64	68	46	42	2
	1992		157	640	184	130	40	-	14	89	86	39	43	3
	1993		134	530	154	108	27	2	17	78	86	61	42	-
	1994		97	372	113	86	20	1	6	62	51	60	24	-
	1995		128	458	132	91	32	2	7	59	49	40	35	-
Career Total	1982-1995		1,785	7,003	2,153	1,469	442	20	222	1,007	1,099	588	444	14
Career Adj. to 10,000 BO	1982-1995	1.265983	2,260	8,866	2,726	1,860	560	25	281	1,275	1,391	744	562	18
Career Adj. to 10,000 AB	1982-1995	1.427959	2,549	10,000	3,074	2,098	631	29	317	1,438	1,569	840	634	20
10 Year Total	1984-1993		1,462	5,882	1,827	1,234	375	13	205	852	966	467	353	14
5 Year Total	1984-1988		759	3,100	1,028	662	220	9	137	502	571	242	176	5
Best Single Year	1985		159	652	211	125	48	3	35	107	145	56	41	2

5 Year Total

10 Year Total

Total Career Statistics & Adjusted Career, 10 year, 5 year, and Single Year Analysis

Mattingly, Don

CS	HBP	SF	GDP	AVG	OBP	SLG	Total Offensive Production Statistics				TRP Rating	RPA Rating	TNB Rating	TBA Rating	TOP Composite		
							TRP	RPA	TNB	TBA					TOP	Rating	Ranking
-	-	1	2	.167	.154	.167	1	.067	2	.133	0.29	12.49	0.33	14.70	27.80	7.09	
-	1	2	8	.283	.333	.409	66	.212	136	.437	18.97	39.77	22.30	48.20	129.22	32.95	
1	1	9	15	.343	.381	.537	201	.300	366	.547	57.76	56.30	60.00	60.30	234.35	59.75	
2	2	15	15	.324	.371	.567	252	.341	428	.578	72.41	63.81	70.16	63.75	270.13	68.87	
-	1	10	17	.352	.394	.573	230	.303	442	.583	66.09	56.86	72.46	64.27	259.68	66.21	
4	1	8	16	.327	.378	.559	208	.322	367	.569	59.77	60.43	60.16	62.71	243.07	61.97	
-	3	8	13	.311	.353	.462	182	.274	322	.485	52.30	51.36	52.79	53.45	209.89	53.51	
-	1	10	15	.303	.351	.477	192	.271	356	.503	55.17	50.82	58.36	55.42	219.77	56.03	
-	3	3	13	.256	.308	.335	82	.186	164	.372	23.56	34.84	26.89	40.99	126.28	32.20	
-	4	9	21	.288	.339	.394	132	.198	283	.424	37.93	37.08	46.39	46.76	168.17	42.88	
-	1	6	11	.288	.327	.416	175	.251	309	.443	50.29	47.05	50.66	48.86	196.85	50.19	
-	2	3	20	.291	.364	.445	164	.266	299	.485	47.13	49.89	49.02	53.50	199.53	50.87	
-	-	4	8	.304	.397	.411	113	.255	213	.480	32.47	47.69	34.92	52.87	167.95	42.82	
2	1	8	17	.288	.341	.413	108	.206	228	.435	31.03	38.62	37.38	47.96	154.99	39.52	
9	21	96	191	.307	.358	.471	2,106	.267	3,915	.496	47.10	63.84	46.29	65.88	223.12	56.98	113
11	27	122	242	.307	.358	.471	2,666	.267	4,956	.496	63.84	63.84	65.88	65.88	259.45	64.86	123
13	30	137	273	.307	.358	.471	3,007	.267	5,590	.496	57.58	63.84	59.41	65.88	246.71	61.68	122
7	19	81	156	.311	.359	.483	1,818	.275	3,336	.505	61.75	62.77	67.30	63.73	255.55	65.55	111
7	8	50	76	.332	.376	.541	1,073	.309	1,925	.554	70.50	66.01	73.81	67.14	277.47	71.08	94
2	2	15	15	.324	.371	.567	252	.341	428	.578	72.41	63.81	70.16	63.75	270.13	68.87	317

Complete Career Statistics M

Total Career Statistics & Adjusted Career, 10 year, 5 year, and Single Year Analysis

Mays, Willie: *Willie Howard "Say Hey" Mays, b. May 6, 1931, Westfield, AL*

Rating Category	Year	Ranked Seasons & Adjustment	G	AB	H	1B	2B	3B	HR	RUN	RBI	BB	SO	SB
	1951		121	464	127	80	22	5	20	59	68	56	60	7
	1952		34	127	30	20	2	4	4	17	23	16	17	4
	1954	4th	151	565	195	108	33	13	41	119	110	66	57	8
	1955	2nd	152	580	185	103	18	13	51	123	127	79	60	24
	1956		152	578	171	100	27	8	36	101	84	68	65	40
	1957		152	585	195	114	26	20	35	112	97	76	62	38
10 Year Total	1958		152	600	208	135	33	11	29	121	96	78	56	31
	1959		151	575	180	98	43	5	34	125	104	65	58	27
	1960		153	595	190	120	29	12	29	107	103	61	70	25
	1961	3rd	154	572	176	101	32	3	40	129	123	81	77	18
	1962	1st	162	621	189	99	36	5	49	130	141	78	85	18
5 Year Total	1963		157	596	187	110	32	7	38	115	103	66	83	8
	1964	6th	157	578	171	94	21	9	47	121	111	82	72	19
	1965	5th	157	558	177	101	21	3	52	118	112	76	71	9
	1966		152	552	159	89	29	4	37	99	103	70	81	5
	1967		141	486	128	82	22	2	22	83	70	51	92	6
	1968		148	498	144	96	20	5	23	84	79	67	81	12
	1969		117	403	114	81	17	3	13	64	58	49	71	6
	1970		139	478	139	94	15	2	28	94	83	79	90	5
	1971		136	417	113	66	24	5	18	82	61	112	123	23
	1972		88	244	61	41	11	1	8	35	22	60	48	4
	1973		66	209	44	28	10	-	6	24	25	27	47	1
Career Total*	1951-1973		2,992	10,881	3,283	1,960	523	140	660	2,062	1,903	1,463	1,526	338
Career Adj. to 10,000 BO*	1951-1973	0.785546	2,350	8,548	2,579	1,540	411	110	518	1,620	1,495	1,149	1,199	266
Career Adj. to 10,000 AB*	1951-1973	0.919033	2,750	10,000	3,017	1,801	481	129	607	1,895	1,749	1,345	1,402	311
10 Year Total*	1954-1963		1,536	5,867	1,876	1,088	309	97	382	1,182	1,088	718	673	237
5 Year Total*	1961-1965		787	2,925	900	505	142	27	226	613	590	383	388	72
Best Single Year	1962		162	621	189	99	36	5	49	130	141	78	85	18
2nd Best Year	1955		152	580	185	103	18	13	51	123	127	79	60	24
3rd Best Year	1961		154	572	176	101	32	3	40	129	123	81	77	18
4th Best Year	1954		151	565	195	108	33	13	41	119	110	66	57	8
5th Best Year	1965		157	558	177	101	21	3	52	118	112	76	71	9
6th Best Year	1964		157	578	171	94	21	9	47	121	111	82	72	19

Complete Career Statistics M

Total Career Statistics & Adjusted Career, 10 year, 5 year, and Single Year Analysis

Mays, Willie

CS	HBP	SF	GDP	AVG	OBP	SLG	Total Offensive Production Statistics				TRP Rating	RPA Rating	TNB Rating	TBA Rating	TOP Composite		
							TRP	RPA	TNB	TBA					TOP	Rating	Ranking
4	2	-	11	.274	.354	.472	127	.238	280	.525	36.49	44.56	46.07	58.00	185.12	47.20	
1	1	-	2	.236	.326	.409	40	.274	72	.493	11.49	51.34	11.80	54.35	128.99	32.89	
5	2	7	12	.345	.411	.667	229	.351	448	.687	65.80	65.81	73.44	75.73	280.79	71.59	
4	4	7	12	.319	.400	.659	250	.367	485	.711	71.84	68.69	79.51	78.38	298.41	76.08	
10	1	3	16	.296	.369	.557	185	.278	421	.632	53.16	52.05	69.02	69.67	243.90	62.18	
19	1	6	14	.333	.407	.626	209	.306	462	.677	60.06	57.42	75.74	74.66	267.88	68.30	
6	1	6	11	.347	.419	.583	217	.312	454	.652	62.36	58.42	74.43	71.89	267.10	68.10	
4	2	6	11	.313	.381	.583	229	.347	425	.645	65.80	65.11	69.67	71.08	271.67	69.26	
10	4	9	15	.319	.381	.555	210	.307	410	.599	60.34	57.53	67.21	66.06	251.15	64.03	
9	2	4	14	.308	.393	.584	252	.374	426	.633	72.41	70.16	69.84	69.76	282.18	71.94	
2	4	3	19	.304	.384	.615	271	.374	480	.662	77.87	70.04	78.69	72.97	299.57	76.38	
3	2	7	15	.314	.380	.582	218	.318	420	.612	62.64	59.55	68.85	67.48	258.52	65.91	
5	1	3	11	.296	.383	.607	232	.344	448	.664	66.67	64.40	73.44	73.15	277.66	70.79	
4	-	2	11	.317	.398	.645	230	.355	441	.682	66.09	66.61	72.30	75.12	280.12	71.42	
1	2	4	13	.288	.368	.556	202	.315	383	.598	58.05	59.05	62.79	65.85	245.74	62.65	
-	2	3	12	.263	.334	.453	153	.276	279	.504	43.97	51.75	45.74	55.50	196.96	50.22	
6	2	6	13	.289	.372	.488	163	.278	318	.543	46.84	52.12	52.13	59.81	210.90	53.77	
2	3	4	8	.283	.362	.437	122	.261	232	.497	35.06	48.95	38.03	54.75	176.80	45.08	
-	3	6	7	.291	.390	.506	177	.309	329	.574	50.86	57.88	53.93	63.28	225.96	57.61	
3	3	4	8	.271	.425	.482	143	.263	336	.618	41.09	49.26	55.08	68.07	213.50	54.43	
5	1	-	9	.250	.400	.402	57	.182	158	.503	16.38	34.02	25.90	55.46	131.75	33.59	
-	1	1	7	.211	.303	.344	49	.200	101	.412	14.08	37.48	16.56	45.44	113.55	28.95	
103	44	91	251	.302	.384	.557	3,965	.311	7,808	.613	88.68	74.58	92.34	81.53	337.13	86.10	8
81	35	71	197	.302	.384	.557	3,115	.311	6,134	.613	74.58	74.58	81.53	81.53	312.23	78.06	43
95	40	84	231	.302	.384	.557	3,644	.311	7,176	.613	69.76	74.58	76.26	81.53	302.14	75.53	37
72	23	58	139	.320	.393	.601	2,270	.334	4,431	.651	77.11	76.07	89.39	82.16	324.72	83.29	12
23	9	19	70	.308	.387	.606	1,203	.353	2,215	.650	79.04	75.53	84.93	78.85	318.35	81.56	24
2	4	3	19	.304	.384	.615	271	.374	480	.662	77.87	70.04	78.69	72.97	299.57	76.38	102
4	4	7	12	.319	.400	.659	250	.367	485	.711	71.84	68.69	79.51	78.38	298.41	76.08	106
9	2	4	14	.308	.393	.584	252	.374	426	.633	72.41	70.16	69.84	69.76	282.18	71.94	219
5	2	7	12	.345	.411	.667	229	.351	448	.687	65.80	65.81	73.44	75.73	280.79	71.59	233
4	-	2	11	.317	.398	.645	230	.355	441	.682	66.09	66.61	72.30	75.12	280.12	71.42	237
5	1	3	11	.296	.383	.607	232	.344	448	.664	66.67	64.40	73.44	73.15	277.66	70.79	254

Complete Career Statistics M

Total Career Statistics & Adjusted Career, 10 year, 5 year, and Single Year Analysis

McCovey, Willie: *Willie Lee "Stretch" McCovey; b. Jan 10, 1938, Mobile, AL*

Rating Category	Year	Ranked Seasons & Adjustment	G	AB	H	1B	2B	3B	HR	RUN	RBI	BB	SO	SB
	1959		52	192	68	41	9	5	13	32	38	22	35	2
	1960		101	260	62	31	15	3	13	37	51	45	53	1
	1961		106	328	89	56	12	3	18	59	50	37	60	1
	1962		91	229	67	40	6	1	20	41	54	29	35	3
	1963		152	564	158	90	19	5	44	103	102	50	119	1
	1964		130	364	80	47	14	1	18	55	54	61	73	2
10 Year Total	1965		160	540	149	89	17	4	39	93	92	88	118	-
	1966		150	502	148	80	26	6	36	85	96	76	100	2
5 Year Total	1967		135	456	126	74	17	4	31	73	91	71	110	3
	1968		148	523	153	97	16	4	36	81	105	72	71	4
	1969	1st	149	491	157	84	26	2	45	101	126	121	66	-
	1970	2nd	152	495	143	63	39	2	39	98	126	137	75	-
	1971		105	329	91	60	13	-	18	45	70	64	57	-
	1972		81	263	56	34	8	-	14	30	35	38	45	-
	1973		130	383	102	56	14	3	29	52	75	105	78	1
	1974		128	344	87	45	19	1	22	53	63	96	76	1
	1975		122	413	104	64	17	-	23	43	68	57	80	1
	1976		82	226	46	30	9	-	7	20	36	24	43	-
	1977		141	478	134	85	21	-	28	54	86	67	106	3
	1978		108	351	80	47	19	2	12	32	64	36	57	1
	1979		117	353	88	64	9	-	15	34	57	36	70	-
	1980		48	113	23	14	8	-	1	8	16	13	23	-
Career Total	1959-1980		2,588	8,197	2,211	1,291	353	46	521	1,229	1,555	1,345	1,550	26
Career Adj. to 10,000 BO	1959-1980	1.014507	2,626	8,316	2,243	1,310	358	47	529	1,247	1,578	1,365	1,572	26
Career Adj. to 10,000 AB	1959-1980	1.219959	3,157	10,000	2,697	1,575	431	56	636	1,499	1,897	1,641	1,891	32
10 Year Total	1962-1971		1,372	4,493	1,272	724	193	29	326	775	916	769	824	15
5 Year Total	1966-1970		734	2,467	727	398	124	18	187	438	544	477	422	9
Best Single Year	1969		149	491	157	84	26	2	45	101	126	121	66	-
2nd Best Year	1970		152	495	143	63	39	2	39	98	126	137	75	-

Complete Career Statistics **M**

Total Career Statistics & Adjusted Career, 10 year, 5 year, and Single Year Analysis

McCovey, Willie

CS	HBP	SF	GDP	AVG	OBP	SLG	Total Offensive Production Statistics				TRP Rating	RPA Rating	TNB Rating	TBA Rating	TOP Composite		
							TRP	RPA	TNB	TBA					TOP	Rating	Ranking
-	4	1	7	.354	.429	.656	70	.310	154	.681	20.11	58.04	25.25	75.10	178.50	45.51	
1	-	2	3	.238	.349	.469	88	.284	167	.539	25.29	53.19	27.38	59.37	165.23	42.13	
2	5	4	8	.271	.350	.491	109	.285	202	.529	31.32	53.47	33.11	58.28	176.18	44.92	
3	-	3	6	.293	.368	.590	95	.356	164	.614	27.30	66.67	26.89	67.70	188.55	48.07	
1	11	1	10	.280	.350	.566	205	.322	380	.597	58.91	60.40	62.30	65.85	247.45	63.09	
1	5	4	9	.220	.336	.412	109	.246	217	.490	31.32	46.11	35.57	53.99	166.99	42.58	
4	6	3	8	.276	.381	.539	185	.287	381	.591	53.16	53.75	62.46	65.10	234.47	59.78	
1	6	4	8	.295	.391	.586	181	.304	377	.633	52.01	56.91	61.80	69.72	240.44	61.30	
3	6	4	8	.276	.378	.535	164	.301	321	.589	47.13	56.39	52.62	64.92	221.05	56.36	
2	5	8	10	.293	.378	.545	186	.301	364	.589	53.45	56.40	59.67	64.92	234.43	59.77	
-	4	7	11	.320	.453	.656	227	.358	447	.705	65.23	67.09	73.28	77.71	283.31	72.23	
-	3	3	13	.289	.444	.612	224	.344	443	.680	64.37	64.48	72.62	75.00	276.47	70.49	
2	4	5	6	.277	.396	.480	115	.282	224	.549	33.05	52.82	36.72	60.51	183.09	46.68	
-	2	1	3	.213	.316	.403	65	.212	146	.476	18.68	39.67	23.93	52.41	134.70	34.34	
-	1	6	6	.266	.420	.546	127	.253	316	.631	36.49	47.50	51.80	69.52	205.31	52.35	
-	1	1	8	.253	.416	.506	116	.258	272	.604	33.33	48.30	44.59	66.62	192.84	49.17	
-	3	2	10	.252	.345	.460	111	.229	251	.518	31.90	42.89	41.15	57.04	172.97	44.10	
-	1	-	4	.204	.283	.336	56	.220	101	.396	16.09	41.15	16.56	43.65	117.45	29.95	
-	-	3	16	.280	.367	.500	140	.248	309	.548	40.23	46.51	50.66	60.38	197.78	50.43	
-	-	2	12	.228	.298	.396	96	.239	176	.439	27.59	44.86	28.85	48.37	149.67	38.16	
2	1	3	7	.249	.318	.402	91	.228	177	.443	26.15	42.63	29.02	48.77	146.56	37.37	
-	1	3	3	.204	.285	.301	24	.180	48	.361	6.90	33.81	7.87	39.78	88.36	22.53	
22	69	70	176	.270	.374	.515	2,784	.282	5,637	.572	62.27	67.63	66.65	76.02	272.57	69.61	50
22	70	71	179	.270	.374	.515	2,824	.282	5,719	.572	67.63	67.63	76.02	76.02	287.30	71.82	85
27	84	85	215	.270	.374	.515	3,396	.282	6,877	.572	65.02	67.63	73.09	76.02	281.76	70.44	76
17	50	42	89	.283	.391	.557	1,691	.311	3,318	.610	57.44	70.85	66.94	76.91	272.14	69.80	78
6	24	26	50	.295	.410	.587	982	.323	1,952	.641	64.52	68.99	74.85	77.75	286.10	73.30	82
-	4	7	11	.320	.453	.656	227	.358	447	.705	65.23	67.09	73.28	77.71	283.31	72.23	207
-	3	3	13	.289	.444	.612	224	.344	443	.680	64.37	64.48	72.62	75.00	276.47	70.49	273

Complete Career Statistics M

Total Career Statistics & Adjusted Career, 10 year, 5 year, and Single Year Analysis

McGriff, Fred: *Frederick Stanley McGriff; b. Oct. 31, 1963, Tampa, FL*

Rating Category	Year	Ranked Seasons & Adjustment	G	AB	H	1B	2B	3B	HR	RUN	RBI	BB	SO	SB
	1986		3	5	1	1	-	-	-	1	-	-	2	-
	1987		107	295	73	37	16	-	20	58	43	60	104	3
	1988		154	536	151	78	35	4	34	100	82	79	149	6
	1989		161	551	148	82	27	3	36	98	92	119	132	7
10 Year Total / 5 Year Total	1990		153	557	167	110	21	1	35	91	88	94	108	5
	1991		153	528	147	96	19	1	31	84	106	105	135	4
	1992		152	531	152	83	30	4	35	79	104	96	108	8
	1993	1st	151	557	162	94	29	2	37	111	101	76	106	5
	1994		113	424	135	75	25	1	34	81	94	50	76	7
	1995		144	528	148	93	27	1	27	85	93	65	99	3
	1996		159	617	182	116	37	1	28	81	107	68	116	7
	1997		152	564	156	108	25	1	22	77	97	68	112	5
	1998		151	564	160	108	33	-	19	73	81	79	118	7
	1999		144	529	164	101	30	1	32	75	104	86	107	1
	2000		158	566	157	112	18	-	27	82	106	91	120	2
	2001		146	513	157	99	25	2	31	67	102	66	106	1
	2002		146	523	143	84	27	2	30	67	103	63	99	1
	2003		86	297	74	47	14	-	13	32	40	31	66	-
	2004		27	72	13	8	3	-	2	7	7	9	19	-
Career Total**	1986-2004		2,460	8,757	2,490	1,532	441	24	493	1,349	1,550	1,305	1,882	72
Career Adj. to 10,000 BO**	1986-2004	0.961723	2,366	8,422	2,395	1,473	424	23	474	1,297	1,491	1,255	1,810	69
Career Adj. to 10,000 AB**	1986-2004	1.141944	2,809	10,000	2,843	1,749	504	27	563	1,540	1,770	1,490	2,149	82
10 Year Total**	1988-1997		1,492	5,393	1,548	935	275	19	319	887	964	820	1,141	57
5 Year Total**	1990-1994		722	2,597	763	458	124	9	172	446	493	421	533	29
Best Single Year**	1993		151	557	162	94	29	2	37	111	101	76	106	5

Total Career Statistics & Adjusted Career, 10 year, 5 year, and Single Year Analysis

McGriff, Fred

CS	HBP	SF	GDP	AVG	OBP	SLG	Total Offensive Production Statistics				TRP Rating	RPA Rating	TNB Rating	TBA Rating	TOP Composite		
							TRP	RPA	TNB	TBA					TOP	Rating	Ranking
-	-	-	-	.200	.200	.200	1	.200	1	.200	0.29	37.48	0.16	22.04	59.97	15.29	
2	1	-	3	.247	.376	.505	101	.281	211	.588	29.02	52.72	34.59	64.78	181.11	46.18	
1	4	4	15	.282	.376	.552	182	.285	384	.602	52.30	53.45	62.95	66.34	235.04	59.93	
4	4	5	14	.269	.399	.525	190	.274	415	.599	54.60	51.37	68.03	66.00	240.01	61.19	
3	2	4	7	.300	.400	.530	179	.270	393	.592	51.44	50.51	64.43	65.23	231.61	59.05	
1	2	7	14	.278	.396	.494	190	.290	371	.566	54.60	54.27	60.82	62.33	232.02	59.16	
6	1	4	14	.286	.394	.556	183	.283	394	.610	52.59	53.08	64.59	67.22	237.48	60.55	
3	2	5	14	.291	.375	.549	212	.324	386	.590	60.92	60.74	63.28	65.05	249.99	63.74	
3	1	3	8	.318	.389	.623	175	.360	319	.656	50.29	67.47	52.30	72.34	242.40	61.80	
6	5	6	19	.280	.361	.489	178	.286	325	.522	51.15	53.54	53.28	57.50	215.46	54.93	
3	2	4	20	.295	.365	.494	188	.264	379	.533	54.02	49.55	62.13	58.75	224.45	57.23	
-	4	5	22	.277	.356	.441	174	.262	326	.492	50.00	49.18	53.44	54.19	206.81	52.73	
2	2	4	14	.284	.371	.443	154	.232	336	.507	44.25	43.52	55.08	55.86	198.71	50.66	
-	1	4	12	.310	.405	.552	179	.283	380	.601	51.44	53.07	62.30	66.27	233.07	59.42	
-	-	7	16	.277	.373	.452	188	.276	349	.513	54.02	51.81	57.21	56.57	219.61	55.99	
2	3	4	13	.306	.386	.544	169	.282	347	.579	48.56	52.87	56.89	63.85	222.16	56.64	
2	4	5	13	.273	.353	.505	170	.280	330	.543	48.85	52.39	54.10	59.82	215.16	54.86	
-	1	-	7	.249	.322	.428	72	.214	159	.473	20.69	40.15	26.07	52.15	139.06	35.46	
-	-	-	1	.181	.272	.306	14	.171	31	.378	4.02	31.99	5.08	41.67	82.76	21.10	
38	39	71	226	.284	.377	.509	2,899	.279	5,836	.561	64.84	66.76	69.01	74.61	275.21	70.28	48
37	38	68	217	.284	.377	.509	2,788	.279	5,613	.561	66.76	66.76	74.61	74.61	282.73	70.68	91
43	45	81	258	.284	.377	.509	3,310	.279	6,664	.561	63.38	66.76	70.83	74.61	275.57	68.89	84
30	27	47	147	.287	.381	.523	1,851	.288	3,692	.574	62.87	65.61	74.48	72.40	275.36	70.63	74
16	8	23	57	.294	.391	.547	939	.302	1,863	.600	61.70	64.65	71.43	72.72	270.50	69.30	105
3	2	5	14	.291	.375	.549	212	.324	386	.590	60.92	60.74	63.28	65.05	249.99	63.74	365

Complete Career Statistics M

Total Career Statistics & Adjusted Career, 10 year, 5 year, and Single Year Analysis

McGwire, Mark: *Mark David McGwire, b. Oct. 1, 1963, Pomona, CA*

Rating Category	Year	Ranked Seasons & Adjustment	G	AB	H	1B	2B	3B	HR	RUN	RBI	BB	SO	SB
	1986		18	53	10	6	1	-	3	10	9	4	18	-
	1987		151	557	161	80	28	4	49	97	118	71	131	1
	1988		155	550	143	88	22	1	32	87	99	76	117	-
	1989		143	490	113	63	17	-	33	74	95	83	94	1
	1990		156	523	123	68	16	-	39	87	108	110	116	2
	1991		154	483	97	53	22	-	22	62	75	93	116	2
	1992		139	467	125	61	22	-	42	87	104	90	105	-
	1993		27	84	28	13	6	-	9	16	24	21	19	-
	1994		47	135	34	22	3	-	9	26	25	37	40	-
	1995		104	317	87	35	13	-	39	75	90	88	77	1
10 Year Total	1996	3rd	130	423	132	59	21	-	52	104	113	116	112	-
5 Year Total	1997	4th	156	540	148	63	27	-	58	86	123	101	159	3
	1998	1st	155	509	152	61	21	-	70	130	147	162	155	1
	1999	2nd	153	521	145	58	21	1	65	118	147	133	141	-
	2000		89	236	72	32	8	-	32	60	73	76	78	1
	2001		97	299	56	23	4	-	29	48	64	56	118	-
Career Total	1986-2001		1,874	6,187	1,626	785	252	6	583	1,167	1,414	1,317	1,596	12
Career Adj. to 10,000 BO	1986-2001	1.281394	2,401	7,928	2,084	1,006	323	8	747	1,495	1,812	1,688	2,045	15
Career Adj. to 10,000 AB	1986-2001	1.616292	3,029	10,000	2,628	1,269	407	10	942	1,886	2,285	2,129	2,580	19
10 Year Total	1992-2001		1,097	3,531	979	427	146	1	405	750	910	880	1,004	6
5 Year Total	1995-1999		698	2,310	664	276	103	1	284	513	620	600	644	5
Best Single Year	1998		155	509	152	61	21	-	70	130	147	162	155	1
2nd Best Year	1999		153	521	145	58	21	1	65	118	147	133	141	-
3rd Best Year	1996		130	423	132	59	21	-	52	104	113	116	112	-
4th Best Year	1997		156	540	148	63	27	-	58	86	123	101	159	3

Total Career Statistics & Adjusted Career, 10 year, 5 year, and Single Year Analysis

McGwire, Mark

CS	HBP	SF	GDP	AVG	OBP	SLG	Total Offensive Production Statistics				TRP Rating	RPA Rating	TNB Rating	TBA Rating	TOP Composite		
							TRP	RPA	TNB	TBA					TOP	Rating	Ranking
1	1	-	-	.189	.259	.377	19	.328	24	.414	5.46	61.38	3.93	45.61	116.38	29.67	
1	5	8	6	.289	.370	.618	215	.332	420	.649	61.78	62.27	68.85	71.55	264.45	67.42	
-	4	4	15	.260	.352	.478	186	.287	343	.529	53.45	53.70	56.23	58.25	221.63	56.51	
1	3	11	23	.231	.339	.467	169	.277	315	.516	48.56	51.91	51.64	56.91	209.03	53.29	
1	7	9	13	.235	.370	.489	195	.295	374	.565	56.03	55.20	61.31	62.27	234.81	59.87	
1	3	5	13	.201	.330	.383	137	.229	282	.472	39.37	43.00	46.23	52.06	180.66	46.06	
1	5	9	10	.268	.385	.585	191	.329	367	.632	54.89	61.60	60.16	69.62	246.27	62.79	
1	1	1	-	.333	.467	.726	40	.374	82	.766	11.49	70.05	13.44	84.46	179.45	45.75	
-	-	-	3	.252	.413	.474	51	.291	101	.577	14.66	54.61	16.56	63.61	149.43	38.10	
1	11	6	9	.274	.441	.685	165	.383	316	.733	47.41	71.74	51.80	80.81	251.76	64.19	
-	8	1	14	.312	.467	.730	217	.386	433	.770	62.36	72.35	70.98	84.92	290.61	74.09	
-	9	7	9	.274	.393	.646	209	.314	462	.694	60.06	58.80	75.74	76.45	271.05	69.11	
-	6	4	8	.299	.470	.752	277	.402	552	.801	79.60	75.33	90.49	88.30	333.72	85.09	
-	2	5	12	.278	.424	.697	265	.394	498	.740	76.15	73.78	81.64	81.56	313.13	79.83	
-	7	2	5	.305	.483	.746	133	.408	260	.798	38.22	76.45	42.62	87.90	245.19	62.51	
-	3	6	7	.187	.316	.492	112	.302	206	.555	32.18	56.57	33.77	61.20	183.72	46.84	
8	75	78	147	.263	.394	.588	2,581	.331	5,035	.645	57.73	79.20	59.54	85.76	282.22	72.07	35
10	96	100	188	.263	.394	.588	3,307	.331	6,452	.645	79.20	79.20	85.76	85.76	329.91	82.48	18
13	121	126	238	.263	.394	.588	4,172	.331	8,138	.645	79.87	79.20	86.49	85.76	331.31	82.83	9
3	52	41	77	.277	.424	.663	1,660	.362	3,277	.715	56.39	82.63	66.11	90.26	295.39	75.76	46
1	36	23	52	.287	.438	.702	1,133	.375	2,261	.748	74.44	80.20	86.69	90.74	332.08	85.08	15
-	6	4	8	.299	.470	.752	277	.402	552	.801	79.60	75.33	90.49	88.30	333.72	85.09	24
-	2	5	12	.278	.424	.697	265	.394	498	.740	76.15	73.78	81.64	81.56	313.13	79.83	60
-	8	1	14	.312	.467	.730	217	.386	433	.770	62.36	72.35	70.98	84.92	290.61	74.09	145
-	9	7	9	.274	.393	.646	209	.314	462	.694	60.06	58.80	75.74	76.45	271.05	69.11	312

Complete Career Statistics   M

Total Career Statistics & Adjusted Career, 10 year, 5 year, and Single Year Analysis

Medwick, Joe: *Joseph Michael "Ducky" Medwick, b. Nov. 24, 1911, Carteret, NJ*

Rating Category	Year	Ranked Seasons & Adjustment	G	AB	H	1B	2B	3B	HR	RUN	RBI	BB	SO	SB
	1932		26	106	37	22	12	1	2	13	12	2	10	3
	1933		148	595	182	114	40	10	18	92	98	26	56	5
	1934		149	620	198	122	40	18	18	110	106	21	83	3
5 Year Total	1935	2nd	154	634	224	142	46	13	23	132	126	30	59	4
	1936		155	636	223	128	64	13	18	115	138	34	33	3
10 Year Total	1937	1st	156	633	237	140	56	10	31	111	154	41	50	4
	1938		146	590	190	114	47	8	21	100	122	42	41	-
	1939		150	606	201	131	48	8	14	98	117	45	44	6
	1940		143	581	175	116	30	12	17	83	86	32	36	2
	1941		133	538	171	110	33	10	18	100	88	38	35	2
	1942		142	553	166	121	37	4	4	69	96	32	25	2
	1943		126	497	138	100	30	3	5	54	70	19	22	1
	1944		128	490	165	131	24	3	7	64	85	38	24	2
	1945		92	310	90	70	17	-	3	31	37	14	14	5
	1946		41	77	24	18	4	-	2	7	18	6	5	-
	1947		75	150	46	30	12	-	4	19	28	16	12	-
	1948		20	19	4	4	-	-	-	-	2	1	2	-
Career Total	1932-1948		1,984	7,635	2,471	1,613	540	113	205	1,198	1,383	437	551	42
Career Adj. to 10,000 BO	1932-1948	1.204674	2,390	9,198	2,977	1,943	651	136	247	1,443	1,666	526	664	51
Career Adj. to 10,000 AB	1932-1948	1.309758	2,599	10,000	3,236	2,113	707	148	269	1,569	1,811	572	722	55
10 Year Total	1933-1942		1,476	5,986	1,967	1,238	441	106	182	1,010	1,131	341	462	31
5 Year Total	1934-1938		760	3,113	1,072	646	253	62	111	568	646	168	266	14
Best Single Year	1937		156	633	237	140	56	10	31	111	154	41	50	4
2nd Best Year	1935		154	634	224	142	46	13	23	132	126	30	59	4

Total Career Statistics & Adjusted Career, 10 year, 5 year, and Single Year Analysis

Medwick, Joe

CS	HBP	SF	GDP	AVG	OBP	SLG	Total Offensive Production Statistics				TRP Rating	RPA Rating	TNB Rating	TBA Rating	TOP Composite		
							TRP	RPA	TNB	TBA					TOP	Rating	Ranking
-	1	-	-	.349	.367	.538	25	.229	63	.578	7.18	42.98	10.33	63.70	124.19	31.66	
-	2	-	15	.306	.337	.497	190	.298	329	.516	54.60	55.80	53.93	56.83	221.17	56.39	
-	1	-	15	.319	.343	.529	216	.329	353	.537	62.07	61.60	57.87	59.22	240.76	61.38	
-	4	-	15	.353	.386	.576	258	.378	403	.590	74.14	70.78	66.07	65.03	276.02	70.37	
-	4	-	14	.351	.387	.577	253	.368	408	.593	72.70	68.91	66.89	65.36	273.85	69.82	
-	2	-	11	.374	.414	.641	265	.386	453	.659	76.15	72.28	74.26	72.67	295.37	75.31	
-	2	-	21	.322	.369	.536	222	.339	360	.550	63.79	63.51	59.02	60.58	246.89	62.95	
-	2	-	15	.332	.380	.507	215	.322	360	.539	61.78	60.31	59.02	59.40	240.50	61.32	
-	3	-	19	.301	.341	.482	169	.266	317	.499	48.56	49.87	51.97	55.02	205.42	52.37	
-	1	-	20	.318	.364	.517	188	.315	319	.534	54.02	59.01	52.30	58.89	224.22	57.17	
-	-	-	15	.300	.338	.403	165	.275	257	.428	47.41	51.53	42.13	47.21	188.28	48.00	
-	1	-	17	.278	.306	.380	124	.232	210	.393	35.63	43.51	34.43	43.34	156.91	40.01	
2	1	-	12	.337	.386	.441	149	.275	255	.471	42.82	51.61	41.80	51.95	188.18	47.98	
-	1	-	9	.290	.323	.374	68	.204	136	.407	19.54	38.15	22.30	44.88	124.86	31.83	
-	1	-	1	.312	.369	.442	25	.294	41	.482	7.18	55.11	6.72	53.16	122.18	31.15	
-	-	-	3	.307	.373	.467	47	.278	86	.509	13.51	52.11	14.10	56.09	135.80	34.62	
-	-	-	1	.211	.250	.211	2	.095	5	.238	0.57	17.85	0.82	26.24	45.48	11.60	
2	26	-	203	.324	.362	.505	2,581	.311	4,355	.525	57.73	74.45	51.50	69.74	253.41	64.72	79
2	31	-	245	.324	.362	.505	3,109	.311	5,246	.525	74.45	74.45	69.74	69.74	288.38	72.10	78
3	34	-	266	.324	.362	.505	3,380	.311	5,704	.525	64.72	74.45	60.62	69.74	269.53	67.38	93
-	21	-	160	.329	.367	.529	2,141	.329	3,559	.547	72.72	75.02	71.80	69.00	288.54	74.01	54
-	13	-	76	.344	.380	.572	1,214	.360	1,977	.587	79.76	77.03	75.81	71.13	303.73	77.81	43
-	2	-	11	.374	.414	.641	265	.386	453	.659	76.15	72.28	74.26	72.67	295.37	75.31	121
-	4	-	15	.353	.386	.576	258	.378	403	.590	74.14	70.78	66.07	65.03	276.02	70.37	283

Complete Career Statistics   M

Total Career Statistics & Adjusted Career, 10 year, 5 year, and Single Year Analysis

Meusel, Bob: *Robert William "Long Bob" Meusel, b. July 19, 1896, San Jose, CA*

Rating Category	Year	Ranked Seasons & Adjustment	G	AB	H	1B	2B	3B	HR	RUN	RBI	BB	SO	SB
	1920		119	460	151	93	40	7	11	75	83	20	72	4
	1921	1st	149	598	190	110	40	16	24	104	135	34	88	17
	1922		121	473	151	98	26	11	16	61	84	40	58	13
5 Year Total	1923		132	460	144	96	29	10	9	59	91	31	52	13
10 Year Total	1924		143	579	188	125	40	11	12	93	120	32	43	26
	1925		156	624	181	102	34	12	33	101	138	54	55	13
	1926		108	413	130	93	22	3	12	73	81	37	32	16
	1927		135	516	174	110	47	9	8	75	103	45	58	24
	1928		131	518	154	93	45	5	11	77	113	39	56	6
	1929		100	391	102	74	15	3	10	46	57	17	42	1
	1930		113	443	128	80	30	8	10	62	62	26	63	9
Career Total	1920-1930		1,407	5,475	1,693	1,074	368	95	156	826	1,067	375	619	142
Career Adj. to 10,000 BO	1920-1930	1.703287	2,397	9,325	2,884	1,829	627	162	266	1,407	1,817	639	1,054	242
Career Adj. to 10,000 AB	1920-1930	1.826484	2,570	10,000	3,092	1,962	672	174	285	1,509	1,949	685	1,131	259
10 Year Total	1920-1929		1,294	5,032	1,565	994	338	87	146	764	1,005	349	556	133
5 Year Total	1921-1925		701	2,734	854	531	169	60	94	418	568	191	296	82
Best Single Year	1921		149	598	190	110	40	16	24	104	135	34	88	17

Total Career Statistics & Adjusted Career, 10 year, 5 year, and Single Year Analysis

Meusel, Bob

CS	HBP	SF	GDP	AVG	OBP	SLG	Total Offensive Production Statistics				TRP Rating	RPA Rating	TNB Rating	TBA Rating	TOP Composite		
							TRP	RPA	TNB	TBA					TOP	Rating	Ranking
4	2	-	-	.328	.359	.517	158	.328	260	.539	45.40	61.42	42.62	59.45	208.90	53.26	
6	2	-	-	.318	.356	.559	239	.377	381	.601	68.68	70.64	62.46	66.23	268.01	68.33	
8	3	-	-	.319	.376	.522	145	.281	295	.572	41.67	52.66	48.36	63.01	205.69	52.44	
15	2	-	-	.313	.359	.478	150	.304	251	.509	43.10	57.01	41.15	56.11	197.38	50.32	
14	5	-	-	.325	.365	.494	213	.346	335	.544	61.21	64.79	54.92	59.94	240.86	61.41	
14	1	-	-	.290	.348	.542	239	.352	392	.577	68.68	65.96	64.26	63.63	262.53	66.93	
17	1	-	-	.315	.373	.470	154	.341	231	.512	44.25	63.98	37.87	56.45	202.56	51.64	
10	2	-	-	.337	.393	.510	178	.316	324	.575	51.15	59.24	53.11	63.43	226.93	57.86	
9	2	-	-	.297	.349	.467	190	.340	280	.501	54.60	63.69	45.90	55.21	219.39	55.94	
5	-	-	-	.261	.292	.391	103	.252	166	.407	29.60	47.30	27.21	44.84	148.96	37.98	
-	1	-	-	.289	.330	.460	124	.264	240	.511	35.63	49.44	39.34	56.28	180.69	46.07	
102	21	-	-	.309	.356	.497	1,893	.322	3,155	.537	42.34	77.21	37.31	71.43	228.29	58.30	110
174	36	-	-	.309	.356	.497	3,224	.322	5,374	.537	77.21	77.21	71.43	71.43	297.28	74.32	70
186	38	-	-	.309	.356	.497	3,458	.322	5,763	.537	66.20	77.21	61.24	71.43	276.08	69.02	83
102	20	-	-	.311	.358	.500	1,769	.328	2,915	.540	60.09	74.69	58.81	68.10	261.68	67.12	99
57	13	-	-	.312	.360	.521	986	.336	1,654	.563	64.78	71.77	63.42	68.26	268.23	68.72	108
6	2	-	-	.318	.356	.559	239	.377	381	.601	68.68	70.64	62.46	66.23	268.01	68.33	325

Complete Career Statistics M

Total Career Statistics & Adjusted Career, 10 year, 5 year, and Single Year Analysis

Mize, Johnny: *John Robert "The Big Cat" Mize, b. Jan. 7, 1913, Demorest, GA*

Rating Category		Year	Ranked Seasons & Adjustment	G	AB	H	1B	2B	3B	HR	RUN	RBI	BB	SO	SB
10 Year Total	5 Year Total	1936		126	414	136	79	30	8	19	76	93	50	32	1
		1937		145	560	204	132	40	7	25	103	113	56	57	2
		1938		149	531	179	102	34	16	27	85	102	74	47	-
		1939		153	564	197	111	44	14	28	104	108	92	49	-
		1940	2nd	155	579	182	95	31	13	43	111	137	82	49	7
		1941		126	473	150	87	39	8	16	67	100	70	45	4
		1942		142	541	165	107	25	7	26	97	110	60	39	3
		1946		101	377	127	84	18	3	22	70	70	62	26	3
		1947	1st	154	586	177	98	26	2	51	137	138	74	42	2
		1948		152	560	162	92	26	4	40	110	125	94	37	4
		1949		119	411	108	73	16	-	19	63	64	54	21	1
		1950		90	274	76	39	12	-	25	43	72	29	24	-
		1951		113	332	86	61	14	1	10	37	49	37	24	1
		1952		78	137	36	23	9	-	4	9	29	11	15	-
		1953		81	104	26	19	3	-	4	6	27	12	17	-
Career Total*		1936-1953		1,884	6,443	2,011	1,202	367	83	359	1,118	1,337	857	524	28
Career Adj. to 10,000 BO*		1936-1953	1.342102	2,529	8,647	2,699	1,613	493	111	482	1,500	1,794	1,150	703	38
Career Adj. to 10,000 AB*		1936-1953	1.552072	2,924	10,000	3,121	1,866	570	129	557	1,735	2,075	1,330	813	43
10 Year Total*		1936-1948		1,403	5,185	1,679	987	313	82	297	960	1,096	714	423	26
5 Year Total*		1936-1940		728	2,648	898	519	179	58	142	479	553	354	234	10
Best Single Year		1947		154	586	177	98	26	2	51	137	138	74	42	2
2nd Best Year		1940		155	579	182	95	31	13	43	111	137	82	49	7

Total Career Statistics & Adjusted Career, 10 year, 5 year, and Single Year Analysis

Mize, Johnny

CS	HBP	SF	GDP	AVG	OBP	SLG	Total Offensive Production Statistics				TRP Rating	RPA Rating	TNB Rating	TBA Rating	TOP Composite		
							TRP	RPA	TNB	TBA					TOP	Rating	Ranking
-	1	-	4	.329	.402	.577	169	.360	291	.620	48.56	67.52	47.70	68.38	232.17	59.19	
-	5	-	5	.364	.427	.595	216	.345	396	.633	62.07	64.66	64.92	69.72	261.36	66.64	
-	4	-	14	.337	.422	.614	187	.300	404	.648	53.74	56.24	66.23	71.47	247.68	63.15	
-	4	-	9	.349	.444	.626	212	.317	449	.671	60.92	59.38	73.61	73.97	267.88	68.30	
-	5	-	10	.314	.404	.636	248	.367	462	.683	71.26	68.74	75.74	75.32	291.07	74.21	
-	1	-	8	.317	.406	.535	167	.303	328	.594	47.99	56.69	53.77	65.49	223.94	57.10	
-	5	-	8	.305	.380	.521	207	.337	350	.570	59.48	63.17	57.38	62.83	242.86	61.92	
-	5	-	5	.337	.437	.576	140	.312	287	.639	40.23	58.43	47.05	70.45	216.15	55.11	
-	4	-	6	.302	.384	.614	275	.410	440	.657	79.02	76.91	72.13	72.38	300.44	76.60	
-	4	-	7	.289	.395	.564	235	.353	418	.629	67.53	66.22	68.52	69.28	271.55	69.23	
1	4	-	5	.263	.354	.440	127	.268	239	.504	36.49	50.21	39.18	55.57	181.45	46.26	
1	2	-	4	.277	.351	.595	115	.372	193	.625	33.05	69.74	31.64	68.84	203.26	51.82	
-	4	-	7	.259	.340	.398	86	.226	174	.458	24.71	42.52	28.36	50.31	145.90	37.20	
-	2	-	6	.263	.327	.416	38	.244	70	.449	10.92	45.07	11.48	48.83	116.29	29.65	
-	2	-	1	.250	.339	.394	33	.277	55	.462	9.48	51.96	9.02	50.94	121.40	30.95	
2	52	-	99	.312	.397	.562	2,455	.329	4,556	.611	54.91	78.89	53.86	81.25	268.91	68.67	57
3	70	-	133	.312	.397	.562	3,295	.329	6,115	.611	78.90	78.90	81.28	81.28	320.35	80.09	25
3	81	-	154	.312	.397	.562	3,810	.329	7,071	.611	72.95	78.90	75.15	81.28	308.28	77.07	30
-	38	-	76	.324	.409	.588	2,056	.342	3,825	.636	69.84	77.97	77.16	80.26	305.24	78.29	30
-	19	-	42	.339	.421	.611	1,032	.337	2,002	.654	67.81	72.05	76.76	79.24	295.86	75.80	58
-	4	-	6	.302	.384	.614	275	.410	440	.657	79.02	76.91	72.13	72.38	300.44	76.60	99
-	5	-	10	.314	.404	.636	248	.367	462	.683	71.26	68.74	75.74	75.32	291.07	74.21	139

Complete Career Statistics M

Total Career Statistics & Adjusted Career, 10 year, 5 year, and Single Year Analysis

Morgan, Joe: *Joe Leonard Morgan, b. Sept. 19, 1943, Bonham, TX*

Rating Category	Year	Ranked Seasons & Adjustment	G	AB	H	1B	2B	3B	HR	RUN	RBI	BB	SO	SB
	1963		8	25	6	5	-	1	-	5	3	5	5	1
	1964		10	37	7	7	-	-	-	4	-	6	7	-
	1965		157	601	163	115	22	12	14	100	40	97	77	20
	1966		122	425	121	94	14	8	5	60	42	89	43	11
	1967		133	494	136	92	27	11	6	73	42	81	51	29
	1968		10	20	5	4	-	1	-	6	-	7	4	3
10 Year Total	1969		147	535	126	88	18	5	15	94	43	110	74	49
	1970		144	548	147	102	28	9	8	102	52	102	55	42
	1971		160	583	149	98	27	11	13	87	56	88	52	40
	1972		149	552	161	118	23	4	16	122	73	115	44	58
	1973		157	576	167	104	35	2	26	116	82	111	61	67
5 Year Total	1974		149	512	150	94	31	3	22	107	67	120	69	58
	1975		146	498	163	113	27	6	17	107	94	132	52	67
	1976	1st	141	472	151	89	30	5	27	113	111	114	41	60
	1977		153	521	150	101	21	6	22	113	78	117	58	49
	1978		132	441	104	64	27	-	13	68	75	79	40	19
	1979		127	436	109	73	26	1	9	70	32	93	45	28
	1980		141	461	112	79	17	5	11	66	49	93	47	24
	1981		90	308	74	49	16	1	8	47	31	66	37	14
	1982		134	463	134	97	19	4	14	68	61	85	60	24
	1983		123	404	93	56	20	1	16	72	59	89	54	18
	1984		116	365	89	62	21	-	6	50	43	66	39	8
Career Total	1963-1984		2,649	9,277	2,517	1,704	449	96	268	1,650	1,133	1,865	1,015	689
Career Adj. to 10,000 BO	1963-1984	0.878503	2,327	8,150	2,211	1,497	394	84	235	1,450	995	1,638	892	605
Career Adj. to 10,000 AB	1963-1984	1.077935	2,855	10,000	2,713	1,837	484	103	289	1,779	1,221	2,010	1,094	743
10 Year Total	1969-1978		1,478	5,238	1,468	971	267	51	179	1,029	731	1,088	546	509
5 Year Total	1973-1977		746	2,579	781	501	144	22	114	556	432	594	281	301
Best Single Year	1976		141	472	151	89	30	5	27	113	111	114	41	60

Total Career Statistics & Adjusted Career, 10 year, 5 year, and Single Year Analysis

Morgan, Joe

CS	HBP	SF	GDP	AVG	OBP	SLG	TRP	RPA	TNB	TBA	TRP Rating	RPA Rating	TNB Rating	TBA Rating	TOP	Rating	Ranking
-	-	-	-	.240	.367	.320	8	.267	14	.467	2.30	49.97	2.30	51.43	106.00	27.02	
1	-	-	-	.189	.302	.189	4	.093	12	.279	1.15	17.43	1.97	30.76	51.30	13.08	
9	3	4	4	.271	.373	.418	140	.197	362	.511	40.23	37.00	59.34	56.27	192.85	49.17	
8	3	2	2	.285	.410	.391	102	.196	261	.501	29.31	36.69	42.79	55.21	164.00	41.81	
5	2	2	2	.275	.378	.411	115	.198	310	.534	33.05	37.09	50.82	58.81	179.76	45.83	
-	-	-	-	.250	.444	.350	6	.222	17	.630	1.72	41.64	2.79	69.39	115.55	29.46	
14	1	4	5	.236	.365	.372	137	.209	345	.527	39.37	39.19	56.56	58.05	193.17	49.25	
13	1	2	11	.268	.383	.396	154	.232	349	.526	44.25	43.46	57.21	57.93	202.85	51.72	
8	1	7	4	.256	.351	.407	143	.209	358	.524	41.09	39.23	58.69	57.77	196.78	50.17	
17	6	4	5	.292	.417	.435	195	.286	402	.589	56.03	53.58	65.90	64.96	240.48	61.31	
15	4	4	12	.290	.406	.493	198	.280	451	.638	56.90	52.48	73.93	70.31	253.61	64.66	
12	3	5	7	.293	.427	.494	174	.269	422	.652	50.00	50.39	69.18	71.89	241.46	61.56	
10	3	6	3	.327	.466	.508	201	.313	445	.693	57.76	58.67	72.95	76.39	265.77	67.76	
9	1	12	2	.320	.444	.576	224	.373	438	.729	64.37	69.84	71.80	80.32	286.33	73.00	
10	2	5	5	.288	.417	.478	191	.294	407	.626	54.89	55.06	66.72	69.01	245.68	62.64	
5	2	11	6	.236	.347	.385	143	.265	265	.492	41.09	49.71	43.44	54.19	188.44	48.04	
6	1	5	8	.250	.379	.376	102	.188	280	.516	29.31	35.20	45.90	56.83	167.24	42.64	
6	-	5	4	.243	.367	.373	115	.204	283	.503	33.05	38.28	46.39	55.40	173.12	44.14	
5	-	3	3	.240	.371	.377	78	.205	191	.503	22.41	38.46	31.31	55.40	147.58	37.63	
4	2	3	3	.289	.400	.438	129	.232	310	.558	37.07	43.48	50.82	61.45	192.81	49.16	
2	4	6	13	.230	.370	.403	131	.254	272	.527	37.64	47.57	44.59	58.10	187.90	47.91	
3	1	6	6	.244	.356	.351	93	.209	200	.450	26.72	39.25	32.79	49.65	148.41	37.84	
162	40	96	105	.271	.392	.427	2,783	.244	6,394	.562	62.25	58.54	75.61	74.67	271.06	69.22	53
142	35	84	92	.271	.392	.427	2,445	.244	5,617	.562	58.54	58.54	74.67	74.67	266.42	66.60	120
175	43	103	113	.271	.392	.427	3,000	.244	6,892	.562	57.43	58.54	73.25	74.67	263.89	65.97	100
113	24	60	60	.280	.402	.453	1,760	.272	3,882	.600	59.78	62.03	78.31	75.70	275.83	70.75	72
56	13	32	29	.303	.431	.508	988	.304	2,163	.666	64.91	65.07	82.94	80.77	293.69	75.24	62
9	1	12	2	.320	.444	.576	224	.373	438	.729	64.37	69.84	71.80	80.32	286.33	73.00	176

Complete Career Statistics M

Total Career Statistics & Adjusted Career, 10 year, 5 year, and Single Year Analysis

Murphy, Dale: *Dale Bryan Murphy, b. Mar. 12, 1956, Portland, OR*

Rating Category	Year	Ranked Seasons & Adjustment	G	AB	H	1B	2B	3B	HR	RUN	RBI	BB	SO	SB
	1976		19	65	17	11	6	-	-	3	9	7	9	-
	1977		18	76	24	13	8	1	2	5	14	-	8	-
	1978		151	530	120	80	14	3	23	66	79	42	145	11
	1979		104	384	106	76	7	2	21	53	57	38	67	6
	1980		156	569	160	98	27	2	33	98	89	59	133	9
	1981		104	369	91	65	12	1	13	43	50	44	72	14
	1982		162	598	168	107	23	2	36	113	109	93	134	23
10 Year Total / 5 Year Total	1983	1st	162	589	178	114	24	4	36	131	121	90	110	30
	1984		162	607	176	100	32	8	36	94	100	79	134	19
	1985		162	616	185	114	32	2	37	118	111	90	141	10
	1986		160	614	163	98	29	7	29	89	83	75	141	7
	1987		159	566	167	95	27	1	44	115	105	115	136	16
	1988		156	592	134	71	35	4	24	77	77	74	125	3
	1989		154	574	131	95	16	-	20	60	84	65	142	3
	1990		154	563	138	90	23	1	24	60	83	61	130	9
	1991		153	544	137	85	33	1	18	66	81	48	93	1
	1992		18	62	10	7	1	-	2	5	7	1	13	-
	1993		26	42	6	5	1	-	-	1	7	5	15	-
Career Total	1976-1993		2,180	7,960	2,111	1,324	350	39	398	1,197	1,266	986	1,748	161
Career Adj. to 10,000 BO	1976-1993	1.081900	2,359	8,612	2,284	1,432	379	42	431	1,295	1,370	1,067	1,891	174
Career Adj. to 10,000 AB	1976-1993	1.256281	2,739	10,000	2,652	1,663	440	49	500	1,504	1,590	1,239	2,196	202
10 Year Total	1980-1989		1,537	5,694	1,553	957	257	31	308	938	929	784	1,268	134
5 Year Total	1983-1987		805	2,992	869	521	144	22	182	547	520	449	662	82
Best Single Year	1983		162	589	178	114	24	4	36	131	121	90	110	30

Total Career Statistics & Adjusted Career, 10 year, 5 year, and Single Year Analysis

Murphy, Dale

CS	HBP	SF	GDP	AVG	OBP	SLG	Total Offensive Production Statistics				TRP Rating	RPA Rating	TNB Rating	TBA Rating	TOP Composite		
							TRP	RPA	TNB	TBA					TOP	Rating	Ranking
-	-	-	-	.262	.333	.354	12	.167	30	.417	3.45	31.23	4.92	45.92	85.52	21.80	
1	-	-	3	.316	.316	.526	19	.241	39	.494	5.46	45.07	6.39	54.41	111.33	28.38	
7	3	5	15	.226	.284	.394	145	.244	258	.434	41.67	45.66	42.30	47.79	177.42	45.23	
1	2	5	12	.276	.340	.469	110	.249	225	.510	31.61	46.74	36.89	56.23	171.47	43.72	
6	1	2	8	.281	.349	.510	187	.293	353	.552	53.74	54.84	57.87	60.89	227.33	57.96	
5	-	2	10	.247	.325	.390	93	.219	197	.464	26.72	41.00	32.30	51.09	151.11	38.53	
11	3	4	10	.281	.378	.507	222	.314	411	.581	63.79	58.76	67.38	63.98	253.91	64.74	
4	2	6	15	.302	.393	.540	252	.359	436	.621	72.41	67.27	71.48	68.45	279.61	71.29	
7	2	3	13	.290	.372	.547	194	.276	425	.604	55.75	51.64	69.67	66.54	243.59	62.11	
3	1	5	14	.300	.388	.539	229	.315	430	.592	65.80	59.11	70.49	65.28	260.68	66.46	
7	2	1	10	.265	.347	.477	172	.245	370	.527	49.43	45.91	60.66	58.09	214.08	54.58	
6	7	5	11	.295	.417	.580	220	.313	460	.653	63.22	58.56	75.41	72.01	269.20	68.63	
5	2	3	24	.226	.313	.421	154	.222	323	.465	44.25	41.52	52.95	51.22	189.95	48.43	
2	2	6	14	.228	.306	.361	144	.218	275	.416	41.38	40.82	45.08	45.85	173.14	44.14	
3	1	4	22	.245	.318	.417	143	.220	303	.465	41.09	41.16	48.20	49.77	180.22	45.95	
-	-	7	20	.252	.309	.415	147	.237	275	.444	42.24	44.50	45.08	48.96	180.79	46.09	
-	-	-	3	.161	.175	.274	12	.182	18	.273	3.45	34.07	2.95	30.06	70.53	17.98	
-	-	2	5	.143	.224	.167	8	.148	12	.222	2.30	27.76	1.97	24.49	56.52	14.41	
68	28	60	209	.265	.346	.469	2,463	.266	4,840	.524	55.09	63.81	57.23	69.60	245.73	62.76	93
74	30	65	226	.265	.346	.469	2,665	.266	5,236	.524	63.81	63.81	69.60	69.60	266.83	66.71	119
85	35	75	263	.265	.346	.469	3,094	.266	6,080	.524	59.24	63.81	64.62	69.60	257.27	64.32	115
56	22	37	129	.273	.361	.491	1,867	.280	3,680	.552	63.42	63.87	74.24	69.66	271.18	69.56	82
27	14	20	63	.290	.383	.536	1,067	.302	2,121	.599	70.11	64.49	81.33	72.68	288.61	73.94	77
4	2	6	15	.302	.393	.540	252	.359	436	.621	72.41	67.27	71.48	68.45	279.61	71.29	241

Complete Career Statistics M

Total Career Statistics & Adjusted Career, 10 year, 5 year, and Single Year Analysis

Murray, Eddie: *Eddie Clarence Murray, b. Feb. 24, 1956, Los Angeles, CA*

Rating Category	Year	Ranked Seasons & Adjustment	G	AB	H	1B	2B	3B	HR	RUN	RBI	BB	SO	SB
	1977		160	611	173	115	29	2	27	81	88	48	104	-
	1978		161	610	174	112	32	3	27	85	95	70	97	6
	1979		159	606	179	122	30	2	25	90	99	72	78	10
	1980		158	621	186	116	36	2	32	100	116	54	71	7
	1981		99	378	111	66	21	2	22	57	78	40	43	2
	1982		151	550	174	111	30	1	32	87	110	70	82	7
	1983		156	582	178	112	30	3	33	115	111	86	90	5
	1984		162	588	180	122	26	3	29	97	110	107	87	10
	1985	1st	156	583	173	104	37	1	31	111	124	84	68	5
	1986		137	495	151	108	25	1	17	61	84	78	49	3
	1987		160	618	171	110	28	3	30	89	91	73	80	1
	1988		161	603	171	114	27	2	28	75	84	75	78	5
	1989		160	594	147	97	29	1	20	66	88	87	85	7
	1990		155	558	184	133	22	3	26	96	95	82	64	8
	1991		153	576	150	107	23	1	19	69	96	55	74	10
	1992		156	551	144	89	37	2	16	64	93	66	74	4
	1993		154	610	174	118	28	1	27	77	100	40	61	2
	1994		108	433	110	71	21	1	17	57	76	31	53	8
	1995		113	436	141	99	21	-	21	68	82	39	65	5
	1996		152	566	147	103	21	1	22	69	79	61	87	4
	1997		55	167	37	27	7	-	3	13	18	15	26	1
Career Total	1977-1997		3,026	11,336	3,255	2,156	560	35	504	1,627	1,917	1,333	1,516	110
Career Adj. to 10,000 BO	1977-1997	0.761557	2,304	8,633	2,479	1,642	426	27	384	1,239	1,460	1,015	1,155	84
Career Adj. to 10,000 AB	1977-1997	0.882145	2,669	10,000	2,871	1,902	494	31	445	1,435	1,691	1,176	1,337	97
10 Year Total	1978-1987		1,499	5,631	1,677	1,083	295	21	278	892	1,018	734	745	56
5 Year Total	1981-1985		724	2,681	816	515	144	10	147	467	533	387	370	29
Best Single Year	1985		156	583	173	104	37	1	31	111	124	84	68	5

10 Year Total / *5 Year Total*

Total Career Statistics & Adjusted Career, 10 year, 5 year, and Single Year Analysis

Murray, Eddie

CS	HBP	SF	GDP	AVG	OBP	SLG	Total Offensive Production Statistics				TRP Rating	RPA Rating	TNB Rating	TBA Rating	TOP Composite		
							TRP	RPA	TNB	TBA					TOP	Rating	Ranking
1	1	6	22	.283	.333	.470	169	.246	335	.487	48.56	46.03	54.92	53.67	203.17	51.80	
5	1	8	15	.285	.356	.480	180	.256	365	.518	51.72	47.91	59.84	57.14	216.61	55.23	
2	2	6	16	.295	.369	.475	189	.269	370	.527	54.31	50.45	60.66	58.09	223.51	56.98	
2	2	6	18	.300	.354	.519	216	.308	383	.546	62.07	57.74	62.79	60.22	242.81	61.91	
3	1	3	10	.294	.360	.534	135	.313	242	.560	38.79	58.56	39.67	61.74	198.76	50.68	
2	1	6	17	.316	.391	.549	197	.306	378	.587	56.61	57.32	61.97	64.69	240.59	61.34	
1	3	9	13	.306	.393	.538	226	.326	406	.586	64.94	61.11	66.56	64.57	257.18	65.57	
2	2	8	9	.306	.410	.509	207	.290	416	.583	59.48	54.32	68.20	64.21	246.22	62.78	
2	2	8	8	.297	.383	.523	235	.343	394	.575	67.53	64.28	64.59	63.39	259.80	66.24	
-	-	5	17	.305	.396	.463	145	.244	310	.521	41.67	45.66	50.82	57.42	195.57	49.86	
2	-	3	15	.277	.352	.477	180	.254	367	.518	51.72	47.57	60.16	57.05	216.51	55.20	
2	-	3	20	.284	.361	.474	159	.227	364	.519	45.69	42.50	59.67	57.23	205.09	52.29	
2	2	7	12	.247	.342	.401	154	.219	332	.473	44.25	41.11	54.43	52.12	191.91	48.93	
5	1	4	19	.330	.414	.520	191	.288	376	.566	54.89	53.90	61.64	62.41	232.84	59.36	
3	-	8	17	.260	.321	.403	165	.252	294	.448	47.41	47.13	48.20	49.39	192.14	48.99	
2	-	8	15	.261	.336	.423	157	.245	301	.470	45.11	45.97	49.34	51.84	192.26	49.02	
2	-	9	24	.285	.325	.467	177	.259	325	.476	50.86	48.56	53.28	52.44	205.15	52.30	
4	-	3	8	.254	.302	.425	133	.280	219	.461	38.22	52.47	35.90	50.81	177.40	45.23	
1	-	5	12	.323	.375	.516	150	.305	268	.545	43.10	57.13	43.93	60.04	204.20	52.06	
-	-	10	19	.260	.327	.417	148	.226	301	.459	42.53	42.28	49.34	50.57	184.72	47.10	
-	-	3	10	.222	.281	.317	31	.159	69	.354	8.91	29.79	11.31	39.00	89.01	22.69	
43	18	128	316	.287	.359	.476	3,544	.270	6,815	.519	79.27	64.63	80.58	68.99	293.47	74.95	23
33	14	97	241	.287	.359	.476	2,699	.270	5,190	.519	64.63	64.63	68.99	68.99	267.23	66.81	118
38	16	113	279	.287	.359	.476	3,126	.270	6,012	.519	59.85	64.63	63.89	68.99	257.36	64.34	114
21	14	62	138	.298	.376	.506	1,910	.290	3,631	.552	64.88	66.20	73.25	69.64	273.97	70.27	75
10	9	34	57	.304	.390	.530	1,000	.316	1,836	.580	65.70	67.50	70.40	70.27	273.87	70.16	100
2	2	8	8	.297	.383	.523	235	.343	394	.575	67.53	64.28	64.59	63.39	259.80	66.24	352

Complete Career Statistics M

Total Career Statistics & Adjusted Career, 10 year, 5 year, and Single Year Analysis

Musial, Stan: *Stanley Frank "Stan the Man" Musial, b. Nov. 21, 1920, Donora, PA*

Rating Category		Year	Ranked Seasons & Adjustment	G	AB	H	1B	2B	3B	HR	RUN	RBI	BB	SO	SB
		1941		12	47	20	15	4	-	1	8	7	2	1	1
		1942		140	467	147	95	32	10	10	87	72	62	25	6
		1943		157	617	220	139	48	20	13	108	81	72	18	9
		1944		146	568	197	120	51	14	12	112	94	90	28	7
		1946		156	624	228	142	50	20	16	124	103	73	31	7
		1947		149	587	183	121	30	13	19	113	95	80	24	4
10 Year Total	5 Year Total	1948	1st	155	611	230	127	46	18	39	135	131	79	34	7
		1949	2nd	157	612	207	117	41	13	36	128	123	107	38	3
		1950		146	555	192	116	41	7	28	105	109	87	36	5
		1951	5th	152	578	205	131	30	12	32	124	108	98	40	4
		1952		154	578	194	125	42	6	21	105	91	96	29	7
		1953	4th	157	593	200	108	53	9	30	127	113	105	32	3
		1954	3rd	153	591	195	110	41	9	35	120	126	103	39	1
		1955		154	562	179	111	30	5	33	97	108	80	39	5
		1956		156	594	184	118	33	6	27	87	109	75	39	2
		1957		134	502	176	106	38	3	29	82	102	66	34	1
		1958		135	472	159	105	35	2	17	64	62	72	26	-
		1959		115	341	87	58	13	2	14	37	44	60	25	-
		1960		116	331	91	56	17	1	17	49	63	41	34	1
		1961		123	372	107	66	22	4	15	46	70	52	35	-
		1962		135	433	143	105	18	1	19	57	82	64	46	3
		1963		124	337	86	62	10	2	12	34	58	35	43	2
Career Total*		1941-1963		3,026	10,972	3,630	2,253	725	177	475	1,949	1,951	1,599	696	78
Career Adj. to 10,000 BO*		1941-1963	0.773994	2,342	8,492	2,810	1,744	561	137	368	1,509	1,510	1,238	539	60
Career Adj. to 10,000 AB*		1941-1963	0.911411	2,758	10,000	3,308	2,053	661	161	433	1,776	1,778	1,457	634	71
10 Year Total*		1944-1954		1,525	5,897	2,031	1,217	425	121	268	1,193	1,093	918	331	48
5 Year Total*		1948-1952		764	2,934	1,028	616	200	56	156	597	562	467	177	26
Best Single Year		1948		155	611	230	127	46	18	39	135	131	79	34	7
2nd Best Year		1949		157	612	207	117	41	13	36	128	123	107	38	3
3rd Best Year		1954		153	591	195	110	41	9	35	120	126	103	39	1
4th Best Year		1953		157	593	200	108	53	9	30	127	113	105	32	3
5th Best Year		1951		152	578	205	131	30	12	32	124	108	98	40	4

Complete Career Statistics **M**

Total Career Statistics & Adjusted Career, 10 year, 5 year, and Single Year Analysis

Musial, Stan

CS	HBP	SF	GDP	AVG	OBP	SLG	TRP	RPA	TNB	TBA	TRP Rating	RPA Rating	TNB Rating	TBA Rating	TOP	Rating	Ranking
-	-	-	-	.426	.449	.574	15	.306	30	.612	4.31	57.36	4.92	67.48	134.07	34.18	
-	2	-	3	.315	.397	.490	159	.298	299	.560	45.69	55.79	49.02	61.71	212.21	54.11	
-	2	-	17	.357	.425	.562	189	.267	430	.607	54.31	50.02	70.49	66.94	241.76	61.64	
-	5	-	7	.347	.440	.549	206	.307	414	.618	59.20	57.61	67.87	68.10	252.78	64.45	
-	3	-	7	.365	.434	.587	227	.321	449	.635	65.23	60.16	73.61	69.99	268.99	68.58	
-	4	-	18	.312	.398	.504	208	.302	384	.557	59.77	56.57	62.95	61.43	240.71	61.37	
-	3	-	18	.376	.450	.702	266	.374	518	.729	76.44	70.10	84.92	80.30	311.75	79.48	
-	2	-	12	.338	.438	.624	251	.342	494	.674	72.13	64.16	80.98	74.28	291.55	74.33	
5	3	-	11	.346	.437	.596	214	.326	421	.642	61.49	61.13	69.02	70.73	262.37	66.89	
7	1	-	6	.355	.449	.614	232	.340	451	.660	66.67	63.65	73.93	72.78	277.03	70.63	
4	2	-	11	.336	.432	.538	196	.285	412	.600	56.32	53.46	67.54	66.10	243.42	62.06	
7	-	-	10	.337	.437	.609	240	.339	462	.653	68.97	63.52	75.74	71.92	280.14	71.42	
4	4	7	20	.330	.428	.607	246	.339	463	.639	70.69	63.58	75.90	70.39	280.56	71.53	
4	8	4	12	.319	.408	.566	205	.308	407	.611	58.91	57.68	66.72	67.35	250.66	63.91	
-	3	7	19	.310	.386	.522	196	.281	390	.559	56.32	52.62	63.93	61.58	234.45	59.78	
1	2	8	13	.351	.422	.612	184	.311	375	.635	52.87	58.34	61.48	69.93	242.62	61.86	
-	1	4	19	.337	.423	.528	126	.222	322	.567	36.21	41.57	52.79	62.48	193.04	49.22	
2	-	3	12	.255	.364	.428	81	.195	204	.490	23.28	36.49	33.44	54.05	147.25	37.54	
1	2	4	5	.275	.354	.486	112	.292	204	.533	32.18	54.80	33.44	58.70	179.13	45.67	
-	1	6	7	.288	.371	.489	116	.265	235	.537	33.33	49.63	38.52	59.13	180.62	46.05	
-	3	5	13	.330	.416	.508	139	.268	290	.560	39.94	50.28	47.54	61.70	199.47	50.86	
-	2	5	3	.255	.325	.404	92	.241	175	.458	26.44	45.13	28.69	50.49	150.74	38.43	
35	53	53	243	.331	.417	.559	3,900	.302	7,829	.606	87.23	72.28	92.57	80.55	332.63	84.95	9
27	41	41	188	.331	.417	.559	3,019	.302	6,060	.606	72.28	72.28	80.55	80.55	305.66	76.41	50
32	48	48	221	.331	.417	.559	3,555	.302	7,135	.606	68.05	72.28	75.83	80.55	296.71	74.18	47
27	27	7	120	.344	.435	.594	2,286	.328	4,468	.641	77.65	74.80	90.14	80.89	323.48	82.97	13
16	11	-	58	.350	.441	.616	1,159	.334	2,296	.662	76.15	71.42	88.04	80.22	315.83	80.91	26
-	3	-	18	.376	.450	.702	266	.374	518	.729	76.44	70.10	84.92	80.30	311.75	79.48	64
-	2	-	12	.338	.438	.624	251	.342	494	.674	72.13	64.16	80.98	74.28	291.55	74.33	138
4	4	7	20	.330	.428	.607	246	.339	463	.639	70.69	63.58	75.90	70.39	280.56	71.53	234
7	-	-	10	.337	.437	.609	240	.339	462	.653	68.97	63.52	75.74	71.92	280.14	71.42	236
7	1	-	6	.355	.449	.614	232	.340	451	.660	66.67	63.65	73.93	72.78	277.03	70.63	261

Complete Career Statistics M

Total Career Statistics & Adjusted Career, 10 year, 5 year, and Single Year Analysis

O'Neill, Tip: *James Edward O'Neill, b. May 25, 1858, Woodstock, Ontario, Canada*

Rating Category	Year	Ranked Seasons & Adjustment	G	AB	H	1B	2B	3B	HR	RUN	RBI	BB	SO	SB	
	1883		23	76	15	12	3	-	-	8	5	3	15	-	
	1884		78	297	82	55	13	11	3	49	54	12	-	-	
	1885		52	206	72	58	7	4	3	44	38	13	-	-	
	1886		138	579	190	145	28	14	3	106	107	47	-	9	
10 Year Total / 5 Year Total	1887	1st	124	567	275	190	52	19	14	167	123	50	-	30	
	1888		130	529	177	138	24	10	5	96	98	44	-	26	
	1889		134	534	179	129	33	8	9	123	110	72	37	28	
	1890		137	577	174	135	20	16	3	112	75	65	36	29	
	1891		129	521	167	125	28	4	10	112	95	62	33	25	
	1892		109	419	105	83	14	6	2	63	52	53	25	14	
Career Total	1883-1892		1,054	4,305	1,436	1,070	222	92	52	880	757	421	146	161	
Career Adj. to 10,000 BO	1883-1892	2.096436	2,210	9,025	3,010	2,243	465	193	109	1,845	1,587	883	306	338	
Career Adj. to 10,000 AB	1883-1892	2.322880	2,448	10,000	3,336	2,485	516	214	121	2,044	1,758	978	339	374	
10 Year Total	1883-1892		1,054	4,305	1,436	1,070	222	92	52	880	757	421	146	161	
5 Year Total	1887-1891		654	2,728	972	717	157	57	41	610	501	293	106	138	
Best Single Year	1887		124	567	275	190	52	19	14	167	123	50	-	30	

Total Career Statistics & Adjusted Career, 10 year, 5 year, and Single Year Analysis

O'Neill, Tip

CS	HBP	SF	GDP	AVG	OBP	SLG	Total Offensive Production Statistics				TRP Rating	RPA Rating	TNB Rating	TBA Rating	TOP Composite		
							TRP	RPA	TNB	TBA					TOP	Rating	Ranking
-	-	-	-	.197	.228	.237	13	.165	21	.266	3.74	30.83	3.44	29.30	67.31	17.16	
-	2	-	-	.276	.309	.424	103	.331	140	.450	29.60	62.06	22.95	49.61	164.22	41.87	
-	4	-	-	.350	.399	.466	82	.368	113	.507	23.56	68.90	18.52	55.85	166.84	42.54	
-	7	-	-	.328	.385	.440	213	.336	318	.502	61.21	63.05	52.13	55.37	231.76	59.09	
-	5	-	-	.485	.531	.718	290	.466	492	.791	83.33	87.36	80.66	87.18	338.53	86.31	
-	4	-	-	.335	.390	.446	194	.336	310	.537	55.75	63.00	50.82	59.21	228.78	58.33	
-	5	-	-	.335	.419	.478	233	.381	360	.589	66.95	71.46	59.02	64.94	262.36	66.89	
-	5	-	-	.302	.377	.407	187	.289	334	.516	53.74	54.16	54.75	56.90	219.54	55.97	
-	9	-	-	.321	.402	.447	207	.350	329	.556	59.48	65.52	53.93	61.25	240.19	61.24	
-	3	-	-	.251	.339	.327	115	.242	207	.436	33.05	45.37	33.93	48.03	160.38	40.89	
-	44	-	-	.334	.399	.464	1,637	.343	2,624	.550	36.61	82.18	31.03	73.12	222.94	56.94	114
-	92	-	-	.334	.399	.464	3,432	.343	5,501	.550	82.18	82.18	73.12	73.12	310.60	77.65	45
-	102	-	-	.334	.399	.464	3,803	.343	6,095	.550	72.80	82.18	64.78	73.12	292.88	73.22	56
-	44	-	-	.334	.399	.464	1,637	.343	2,624	.550	55.60	78.26	52.94	69.41	256.21	65.72	109
-	28	-	-	.356	.424	.501	1,111	.364	1,825	.599	73.00	77.92	69.98	72.57	293.46	75.18	63
-	5	-	-	.485	.531	.718	290	.466	492	.791	83.33	87.36	80.66	87.18	338.53	86.31	21

Complete Career Statistics O

Total Career Statistics & Adjusted Career, 10 year, 5 year, and Single Year Analysis

Ordonez, Magglio: *Magglio Ordonez (Delgado), b. Jan. 28, 1974, Caracas, Venezuela*

Rating Category	Year	Ranked Seasons & Adjustment	G	AB	H	1B	2B	3B	HR	RUN	RBI	BB	SO	SB
	1997		21	69	22	12	6	-	4	12	11	2	8	1
	1998		145	535	151	110	25	2	14	70	65	28	53	9
5 Year Total	1999		157	624	188	121	34	3	30	100	117	47	64	13
	2000		153	588	185	116	34	3	32	102	126	60	64	18
	2001		160	593	181	109	40	1	31	97	113	70	70	25
	2002	1st	153	590	189	103	47	1	38	116	135	53	77	7
	2003		160	606	192	114	46	3	29	95	99	57	73	9
	2004		52	202	59	40	8	2	9	32	37	16	22	-
Career Total**	1997-2004		1,001	3,807	1,167	725	240	15	187	624	703	333	431	82
Career Adj. to 10,000 BO**	1997-2004	2.304147	2,306	8,772	2,689	1,671	553	35	431	1,438	1,620	767	993	189
Career Adj. to 10,000 AB**	1997-2004	2.626740	2,629	10,000	3,065	1,904	630	39	491	1,639	1,847	875	1,132	215
10 Year Total**	n/a		n/a											
5 Year Total**	1999-2003		783	3,001	935	563	201	11	160	510	590	287	348	72
Best Single Year**	2002		153	590	189	103	47	1	38	116	135	53	77	7

Total Career Statistics & Adjusted Career, 10 year, 5 year, and Single Year Analysis

Ordonez, Magglio

CS	HBP	SF	GDP	AVG	OBP	SLG	Total Offensive Production Statistics				TRP Rating	RPA Rating	TNB Rating	TBA Rating	TOP Composite		
							TRP	RPA	TNB	TBA					TOP	Rating	Ranking
2	-	-	1	.319	.338	.580	23	.319	41	.569	6.61	59.86	6.72	62.76	135.95	34.66	
7	9	4	19	.282	.326	.415	135	.227	261	.439	38.79	42.52	42.79	48.35	172.44	43.97	
6	1	5	24	.301	.349	.510	217	.310	373	.532	62.36	58.01	61.15	58.64	240.15	61.23	
4	2	15	28	.315	.371	.546	228	.329	397	.573	65.52	61.65	65.08	63.14	255.39	65.11	
7	5	3	14	.305	.382	.533	210	.307	409	.597	60.34	57.45	67.05	65.81	250.65	63.90	
5	7	3	21	.320	.381	.597	251	.372	414	.614	72.13	69.78	67.87	67.70	277.48	70.74	
5	7	4	20	.317	.380	.546	194	.280	399	.575	55.75	52.38	65.41	63.37	236.90	60.40	
2	3	1	4	.292	.351	.485	69	.305	115	.509	19.83	57.21	18.85	56.08	151.97	38.75	
38	34	35	131	.307	.364	.525	1,327	.306	2,409	.555	28.14	73.22	27.13	74.12	202.60	51.74	126
88	78	81	302	.307	.364	.525	3,058	.306	5,551	.555	73.22	73.22	74.12	74.12	294.68	73.67	74
100	89	92	344	.307	.364	.525	3,486	.306	6,328	.555	66.81	73.22	67.63	74.12	281.78	70.44	75
27	22	30	107	.312	.372	.546	1,100	.319	1,992	.578	72.27	68.24	76.38	70.07	286.96	73.52	81
5	7	3	21	.320	.381	.597	251	.372	414	.614	72.13	69.78	67.87	67.70	277.48	70.74	256

Total Career Statistics & Adjusted Career, 10 year, 5 year, and Single Year Analysis

Ott, Mel: *Melvin Thomas "Master Melvin" Ott, b. Mar. 2, 1909, Gretna, LA*

Rating Category	Year	Ranked Seasons & Adjustment	G	AB	H	1B	2B	3B	HR	RUN	RBI	BB	SO	SB
	1926		35	60	23	21	2	-	-	7	4	1	9	1
	1927		82	163	46	35	7	3	1	23	19	13	9	2
	1928		124	435	140	92	26	4	18	69	77	52	36	3
	1929	1st	150	545	179	98	37	2	42	138	151	113	38	6
	1930	5th	148	521	182	118	34	5	25	122	119	103	35	9
	1931		138	497	145	85	23	8	29	104	115	80	44	10
	1932	3rd	154	566	180	104	30	8	38	119	123	100	39	6
	1933		152	580	164	104	36	1	23	98	103	75	48	1
	1934	4th	153	582	190	116	29	10	35	119	135	85	43	-
	1935		152	593	191	121	33	6	31	113	114	82	58	7
	1936	2nd	150	534	175	108	28	6	33	120	135	111	41	6
	1937		151	545	160	99	28	2	31	99	95	102	69	7
	1938	6th	150	527	164	99	23	6	36	116	116	118	47	2
	1939		125	396	122	70	23	2	27	85	80	100	50	2
	1940		151	536	155	106	27	3	19	89	79	100	50	6
	1941		148	525	150	94	29	-	27	89	90	100	68	5
	1942		152	549	162	111	21	-	30	118	93	109	61	6
	1943		125	380	89	57	12	2	18	65	47	95	48	7
	1944		120	399	115	69	16	4	26	91	82	90	47	2
	1945		135	451	139	95	23	-	21	73	79	71	41	1
	1946		31	68	5	3	1	-	1	2	4	8	15	-
	1947		4	4	-	-	-	-	-	-	-	-	-	-
Career Total	1926-1947		2,730	9,456	2,876	1,805	488	72	511	1,859	1,860	1,708	896	89
Career Adj. to 10,000 BO	1926-1947	0.884173	2,414	8,361	2,543	1,596	431	64	452	1,644	1,645	1,510	792	79
Career Adj. to 10,000 AB	1926-1947	1.057530	2,887	10,000	3,041	1,909	516	76	540	1,966	1,967	1,806	948	94
10 Year Total	1929-1938		1,498	5,490	1,730	1,052	301	54	323	1,148	1,206	969	462	54
5 Year Total	1929-1933		742	2,709	850	509	160	24	157	581	611	471	204	32
Best Single Year	1929		150	545	179	98	37	2	42	138	151	113	38	6
2nd Best Year	1936		150	534	175	108	28	6	33	120	135	111	41	6
3rd Best Year	1932		154	566	180	104	30	8	38	119	123	100	39	6
4th Best Year	1934		153	582	190	116	29	10	35	119	135	85	43	-
5th Best Year	1930		148	521	182	118	34	5	25	122	119	103	35	9
6th Best Year	1938		150	527	164	99	23	6	36	116	116	118	47	2

5 Year Total — *10 Year Total*

Complete Career Statistics O

Total Career Statistics & Adjusted Career, 10 year, 5 year, and Single Year Analysis

Ott, Mel

CS	HBP	SF	GDP	AVG	OBP	SLG	Total Offensive Production Statistics				TRP Rating	RPA Rating	TNB Rating	TBA Rating	TOP Composite		
							TRP	RPA	TNB	TBA					TOP	Rating	Ranking
-	-	-	-	.383	.393	.417	11	.180	27	.443	3.16	33.79	4.43	48.78	90.16	22.99	
-	-	-	-	.282	.335	.380	42	.239	77	.438	12.07	44.72	12.62	48.22	117.63	29.99	
-	2	-	-	.322	.397	.524	146	.299	285	.583	41.95	55.95	46.72	64.24	208.86	53.25	
-	6	-	-	.328	.449	.635	289	.435	471	.709	83.05	81.56	77.21	78.18	319.99	81.59	
-	2	-	-	.349	.458	.578	241	.385	415	.663	69.25	72.14	68.03	73.07	282.49	72.02	
-	2	-	-	.292	.392	.545	219	.378	363	.627	62.93	70.87	59.51	69.10	262.41	66.90	
-	4	-	-	.318	.424	.601	242	.361	450	.672	69.54	67.68	73.77	74.02	285.02	72.67	
-	2	-	10	.283	.367	.467	201	.301	349	.523	57.76	56.47	57.21	57.67	229.11	58.41	
-	3	-	10	.326	.415	.591	254	.374	432	.635	72.99	69.99	70.82	70.02	283.82	72.36	
-	3	-	4	.322	.407	.555	227	.333	421	.617	65.23	62.37	69.02	68.04	264.65	67.48	
-	5	-	8	.328	.448	.588	255	.388	436	.663	73.28	72.62	71.48	73.03	290.40	74.04	
-	3	-	4	.294	.408	.523	194	.297	397	.607	55.75	55.58	65.08	66.90	243.32	62.04	
-	5	-	8	.311	.442	.583	232	.353	432	.657	66.67	66.07	70.82	72.36	275.91	70.35	
-	1	-	5	.308	.449	.581	165	.329	333	.663	47.41	61.59	54.59	73.11	236.70	60.35	
-	6	-	9	.289	.407	.457	168	.258	357	.548	48.28	48.36	58.52	60.44	215.60	54.97	
-	3	-	2	.286	.403	.495	179	.284	368	.584	51.44	53.24	60.33	64.38	229.38	58.48	
-	3	-	8	.295	.415	.497	211	.315	391	.584	60.63	59.10	64.10	64.42	248.25	63.29	
1	3	-	4	.234	.391	.418	112	.232	263	.546	31.32	42.37	43.11	60.14	176.95	45.11	
1	3	-	3	.288	.423	.544	173	.349	311	.628	49.71	65.49	50.98	69.25	235.43	60.03	
-	8	-	6	.308	.411	.499	152	.284	305	.569	43.68	53.14	50.00	62.72	209.53	53.42	
-	-	-	1	.074	.171	.132	6	.078	17	.221	1.72	14.60	2.79	24.33	43.45	11.08	
-	-	-	-	.000	.000	.000	-	.000	-	.000	-	-	-	-	-	-	
2	64	-	82	.304	.414	.533	3,719	.329	6,900	.610	83.11	78.68	81.59	81.09	324.47	82.86	10
2	57	-	73	.304	.414	.533	3,288	.329	6,101	.610	78.74	78.74	81.09	81.09	319.67	79.92	27
2	68	-	87	.304	.414	.533	3,933	.329	7,297	.610	75.30	78.74	77.55	81.09	312.68	78.17	24
-	35	-	44	.315	.421	.566	2,354	.360	4,166	.637	79.96	82.11	84.04	80.40	326.51	83.75	9
-	16	-	10	.314	.418	.564	1,192	.372	2,048	.639	78.32	79.51	78.53	77.45	313.80	80.39	34
-	6	-	-	.328	.449	.635	289	.435	471	.709	83.05	81.56	77.21	78.18	319.99	81.59	42
-	5	-	8	.328	.448	.588	255	.388	436	.663	73.28	72.62	71.48	73.03	290.40	74.04	149
-	4	-	-	.318	.424	.601	242	.361	450	.672	69.54	67.68	73.77	74.02	285.02	72.67	189
-	3	-	10	.326	.415	.591	254	.374	432	.635	72.99	69.99	70.82	70.02	283.82	72.36	201
-	2	-	-	.349	.458	.578	241	.385	415	.663	69.25	72.14	68.03	73.07	282.49	72.02	216
-	5	-	8	.311	.442	.583	232	.353	432	.657	66.67	66.07	70.82	72.36	275.91	70.35	285

Complete Career Statistics O

Total Career Statistics & Adjusted Career, 10 year, 5 year, and Single Year Analysis

Palmiero, Rafael: *Rafael Palmiero (Carrales), b. Sept. 24, 1964, Havana, Cuba*

Complete Career Statistics P

Rating Category	Year	Ranked Seasons & Adjustment	G	AB	H	1B	2B	3B	HR	RUN	RBI	BB	SO	SB
	1986		22	73	18	11	4	-	3	9	12	4	6	1
	1987		84	221	61	31	15	1	14	32	30	20	26	2
	1988		152	580	178	124	41	5	8	75	53	38	34	12
	1989		156	559	154	119	23	4	8	76	64	63	48	4
	1990		154	598	191	136	35	6	14	72	89	40	59	3
	1991		159	631	203	125	49	3	26	115	88	68	72	4
	1992		159	608	163	110	27	4	22	84	85	72	83	2
10 Year Total	1993		160	597	176	97	40	2	37	124	105	73	85	22
	1994		111	436	139	84	32	-	23	82	76	54	63	7
	1995		143	554	172	101	30	2	39	89	104	62	65	3
	1996	2nd	162	626	181	100	40	2	39	110	142	95	96	8
	1997		158	614	156	92	24	2	38	95	110	67	109	5
5 Year Total	1998		162	619	183	103	36	1	43	98	121	79	91	11
	1999	1st	158	565	183	105	30	1	47	96	148	97	69	2
	2000		158	565	163	92	29	3	39	102	120	103	77	2
	2001		160	600	164	84	33	-	47	98	123	101	90	1
	2002		155	546	149	72	34	-	43	99	105	104	94	2
	2003		154	561	146	85	21	2	38	92	112	84	77	2
	2004		154	550	142	90	29	-	23	68	88	86	61	2
Career Total**	1986-2004		2,721	10,103	2,922	1,761	572	38	551	1,616	1,775	1,310	1,305	95
Career Adj. to 10,000 BO**	1986-2004	0.845237	2,300	8,539	2,470	1,488	483	32	466	1,366	1,500	1,107	1,103	80
Career Adj. to 10,000 AB**	1986-2004	0.989805	2,693	10,000	2,892	1,743	566	38	545	1,600	1,757	1,297	1,292	94
10 Year Total**	1993-2002		1,527	5,722	1,666	930	328	13	395	993	1,154	835	839	63
5 Year Total**	1998-2002		793	2,895	842	456	162	5	219	493	617	484	421	18
Best Single Year**	1999		158	565	183	105	30	1	47	96	148	97	69	2
2nd Best Year**	1996		162	626	181	100	40	2	39	110	142	95	96	8

Total Career Statistics & Adjusted Career, 10 year, 5 year, and Single Year Analysis

Palmiero, Rafael

CS	HBP	SF	GDP	AVG	OBP	SLG	Total Offensive Production Statistics				TRP Rating	RPA Rating	TNB Rating	TBA Rating	TOP Composite		
							TRP	RPA	TNB	TBA					TOP	Rating	Ranking
1	1	-	4	.247	.295	.425	21	.256	36	.439	6.03	47.99	5.90	48.39	108.31	27.61	
2	1	2	4	.276	.336	.543	62	.250	141	.569	17.82	46.85	23.11	62.66	150.44	38.36	
2	3	6	11	.307	.349	.436	128	.201	304	.476	36.78	37.59	49.84	52.52	176.73	45.06	
3	6	2	18	.275	.354	.374	140	.216	279	.431	40.23	40.48	45.74	47.45	173.90	44.34	
3	3	8	24	.319	.361	.468	161	.239	323	.480	46.26	44.83	52.95	52.90	196.94	50.21	
3	6	7	17	.322	.389	.532	203	.278	411	.564	58.33	52.11	67.38	62.05	239.87	61.16	
3	10	6	10	.268	.352	.434	169	.239	345	.489	48.56	44.85	56.56	53.86	203.83	51.97	
3	5	9	8	.295	.371	.554	229	.331	428	.618	65.80	62.01	70.16	68.17	266.14	67.86	
3	2	6	11	.319	.392	.550	158	.310	300	.589	45.40	58.17	49.18	64.96	217.71	55.51	
1	3	5	12	.310	.380	.583	193	.303	390	.613	55.46	56.86	63.93	67.58	243.84	62.17	
-	3	8	9	.289	.381	.546	252	.340	448	.605	72.41	63.72	73.44	66.63	276.22	70.42	
2	5	6	14	.254	.329	.485	205	.290	373	.528	58.91	54.41	61.15	58.23	232.69	59.33	
7	7	4	14	.296	.379	.565	219	.303	440	.609	62.93	56.76	72.13	67.07	258.89	66.01	
4	3	9	12	.324	.420	.630	244	.356	454	.662	70.11	66.55	74.43	72.83	283.93	72.39	
1	3	7	14	.288	.397	.558	222	.321	422	.610	63.79	60.11	69.18	67.21	260.30	66.37	
1	7	6	8	.273	.381	.563	221	.306	446	.618	63.51	57.36	73.11	68.08	262.06	66.81	
-	6	7	10	.273	.391	.571	204	.303	424	.630	58.62	56.80	69.51	69.44	254.36	64.85	
-	5	4	7	.260	.359	.508	204	.309	376	.569	58.62	57.83	61.64	62.69	240.78	61.39	
1	6	9	15	.258	.359	.436	156	.234	333	.500	44.83	43.89	54.59	55.11	198.42	50.59	
40	85	111	222	.289	.372	.517	3,391	.287	6,673	.564	75.84	68.62	78.91	74.96	298.33	76.19	19
34	72	94	188	.289	.372	.517	2,866	.287	5,640	.564	68.62	68.62	74.96	74.96	287.16	71.79	86
40	84	110	220	.289	.372	.517	3,356	.287	6,605	.564	64.26	68.62	70.20	74.96	278.04	69.51	81
22	44	67	112	.291	.382	.560	2,147	.317	4,125	.608	72.93	72.20	83.22	76.75	305.10	78.26	31
13	26	33	58	.291	.393	.577	1,110	.318	2,186	.625	72.93	67.88	83.82	75.79	300.42	76.96	50
4	3	9	12	.324	.420	.630	244	.356	454	.662	70.11	66.55	74.43	72.83	283.93	72.39	200
-	3	8	9	.289	.381	.546	252	.340	448	.605	72.41	63.72	73.44	66.63	276.22	70.42	278

Complete Career Statistics   P

Total Career Statistics & Adjusted Career, 10 year, 5 year, and Single Year Analysis

Parker, Dave: *David Gene Parker; b. June 9 1951, Calhoun, MS*

Rating Category	Year	Ranked Seasons & Adjustment	G	AB	H	1B	2B	3B	HR	RUN	RBI	BB	SO	SB
	1973		54	139	40	26	9	1	4	17	14	2	27	1
	1974		73	220	62	45	10	3	4	27	29	10	53	3
	1975		148	558	172	102	35	10	25	75	101	38	89	8
	1976		138	537	168	117	28	10	13	82	90	30	80	19
	1977		159	637	215	142	44	8	21	107	88	58	107	17
	1978	1st	148	581	194	120	32	12	30	102	117	57	92	20
	1979		158	622	193	116	45	7	25	109	94	67	101	20
	1980		139	518	153	104	31	1	17	71	79	25	69	10
10 Year Total	1981		67	240	62	36	14	3	9	29	48	9	25	6
5 Year Total	1982		73	244	66	38	19	3	6	41	29	22	45	7
	1983		144	552	154	109	29	4	12	68	69	28	89	12
	1984		156	607	173	129	28	-	16	73	94	41	89	11
	1985		160	635	198	118	42	4	34	88	125	52	80	5
	1986		162	637	174	109	31	3	31	89	116	56	126	1
	1987		153	589	149	95	28	-	26	77	97	44	104	7
	1988		101	377	97	66	18	1	12	43	55	32	70	-
	1989		144	553	146	97	27	-	22	56	97	38	91	-
	1990		157	610	176	122	30	3	21	71	92	41	102	4
	1991		132	502	120	81	26	2	11	47	59	33	98	3
Career Total	1973-1991		2,466	9,358	2,712	1,772	526	75	339	1,272	1,493	683	1,537	154
Career Adj. to 10,000 BO	1973-1991	0.962279	2,373	9,005	2,610	1,705	506	72	326	1,224	1,437	657	1,479	148
Career Adj. to 10,000 AB	1973-1991	1.068604	2,635	10,000	2,898	1,894	562	80	362	1,359	1,595	730	1,642	165
10 Year Total	1977-1986		1,366	5,273	1,582	1,021	315	45	201	777	859	415	823	109
5 Year Total	1975-1979		751	2,935	942	597	184	47	114	475	490	250	469	84
Best Single Year	1978		148	581	194	120	32	12	30	102	117	57	92	20

Total Career Statistics & Adjusted Career, 10 year, 5 year, and Single Year Analysis

Parker, Dave

CS	HBP	SF	GDP	AVG	OBP	SLG	Total Offensive Production Statistics				TRP Rating	RPA Rating	TNB Rating	TBA Rating	TOP Composite		
							TRP	RPA	TNB	TBA					TOP	Rating	Ranking
1	2	-	2	.288	.308	.453	31	.214	67	.462	8.91	40.06	10.98	50.93	110.88	28.27	
3	3	-	3	.282	.322	.409	56	.237	103	.436	16.09	44.46	16.89	48.10	125.54	32.01	
6	5	1	18	.308	.357	.541	176	.284	347	.560	50.57	53.19	56.89	61.68	222.34	56.69	
7	2	4	16	.313	.349	.475	172	.292	299	.508	49.43	54.72	49.02	55.95	209.11	53.31	
19	7	4	7	.338	.397	.531	195	.273	401	.562	56.03	51.25	65.74	61.99	235.01	59.92	
7	2	2	8	.334	.394	.585	219	.337	412	.634	62.93	63.13	67.54	69.86	263.46	67.17	
4	9	9	7	.310	.380	.526	203	.284	419	.587	58.33	53.28	68.69	64.68	244.97	62.46	
7	2	5	8	.295	.327	.458	150	.269	267	.478	43.10	50.37	41.31	52.74	187.52	47.81	
2	2	3	5	.258	.287	.454	77	.297	124	.479	22.13	55.71	19.51	52.77	150.11	38.27	
5	1	3	7	.270	.330	.447	70	.253	134	.484	20.11	47.35	19.84	53.32	140.62	35.85	
9	-	6	11	.279	.311	.411	137	.229	258	.432	39.37	43.00	40.00	47.63	170.00	43.34	
10	1	6	8	.285	.328	.410	167	.252	292	.440	47.99	47.20	43.11	48.54	186.84	47.64	
13	3	4	26	.312	.365	.551	213	.296	397	.551	61.21	55.43	62.30	60.77	239.71	61.12	
6	1	6	18	.273	.330	.477	205	.286	356	.496	58.91	53.50	52.13	54.65	219.19	55.88	
3	8	6	14	.253	.311	.433	174	.263	311	.470	50.00	49.33	45.57	51.86	196.76	50.16	
1	-	2	3	.257	.314	.406	98	.237	184	.444	28.16	44.36	25.25	48.98	146.75	37.41	
-	1	8	21	.264	.308	.432	153	.246	278	.448	43.97	46.17	41.48	49.34	180.95	46.13	
7	4	14	18	.289	.330	.451	163	.237	317	.461	46.84	44.46	47.05	50.86	189.20	48.24	
3	3	3	9	.239	.288	.365	106	.193	219	.398	30.46	36.11	31.97	43.89	142.43	36.31	
113	56	86	209	.290	.339	.471	2,765	.266	5,185	.499	61.84	63.71	61.31	66.32	253.19	64.66	80
109	54	83	201	.290	.339	.471	2,661	.266	4,989	.499	63.71	63.71	66.32	66.32	260.07	65.02	122
121	60	92	223	.290	.339	.471	2,955	.266	5,541	.499	56.57	63.71	58.88	66.32	245.49	61.37	124
82	28	48	105	.300	.351	.491	1,636	.279	3,060	.521	55.57	63.57	61.73	65.79	246.65	63.27	117
43	25	20	56	.321	.377	.532	965	.294	1,878	.572	63.40	62.80	72.01	69.29	267.50	68.53	109
7	2	2	8	.334	.394	.585	219	.337	412	.634	62.93	63.13	67.54	69.86	263.46	67.17	338

Complete Career Statistics   P

★ ★ ★ THE BEST ★ ★ ★

Complete Career Statistics P

10 Year Total

Total Career Statistics & Adjusted Career, 10 year, 5 year, and Single Year Analysis

Perez, Tony: *Atanasio Perez (Rigal), b. May 14, 1942, Ciego De Avila, Cuba*

Rating Category	Year	Ranked Seasons & Adjustment	G	AB	H	1B	2B	3B	HR	RUN	RBI	BB	SO	SB
	1964		12	25	2	1	1	-	-	1	1	3	9	-
	1965		104	281	73	43	14	4	12	40	47	21	67	-
	1966		99	257	68	50	10	4	4	25	39	14	44	1
5 Year Total	1967		156	600	174	113	28	7	26	78	102	33	102	-
	1968		160	625	176	126	25	7	18	93	92	51	92	3
	1969		160	629	185	115	31	2	37	103	122	63	131	4
	1970	1st	158	587	186	112	28	6	40	107	129	83	134	8
	1971		158	609	164	114	22	3	25	72	91	51	120	4
	1972		136	515	146	85	33	7	21	64	90	55	121	4
	1973		151	564	177	114	33	3	27	73	101	74	117	3
	1974		158	596	158	100	28	2	28	81	101	61	112	1
	1975		137	511	144	93	28	3	20	74	109	54	101	1
	1976		139	527	137	80	32	6	19	77	91	50	88	10
	1977		154	559	158	101	32	6	19	71	91	63	111	4
	1978		148	544	158	103	38	3	14	63	78	38	104	2
	1979		132	489	132	86	29	4	13	58	73	38	82	2
	1980		151	585	161	102	31	3	25	73	105	41	93	1
	1981		84	306	77	54	11	3	9	35	39	27	66	-
	1982		69	196	51	29	14	2	6	18	31	19	48	-
	1983		91	253	61	42	11	2	6	18	43	28	57	1
	1984		71	137	33	24	6	1	2	9	15	11	21	-
	1985		72	183	60	46	8	-	6	25	33	22	22	-
	1986		77	200	51	36	12	1	2	14	29	25	25	-
Career Total	1964-1986		2,777	9,778	2,732	1,769	505	79	379	1,272	1,652	925	1,867	49
Career Adj. to 10,000 BO	1964-1986	0.899281	2,497	8,793	2,457	1,591	454	71	341	1,144	1,486	832	1,679	44
Career Adj. to 10,000 AB	1964-1986	1.022704	2,840	10,000	2,794	1,809	516	81	388	1,301	1,690	946	1,909	50
10 Year Total	1967-1976		1,513	5,763	1,647	1,052	288	46	261	822	1,028	575	1,118	38
5 Year Total	1967-1971		792	3,050	885	580	134	25	146	453	536	281	579	19
Best Single Year	1970		158	587	186	112	28	6	40	107	129	83	134	8

Total Career Statistics & Adjusted Career, 10 year, 5 year, and Single Year Analysis

Perez, Tony

CS	HBP	SF	GDP	AVG	OBP	SLG	Total Offensive Production Statistics				TRP Rating	RPA Rating	TNB Rating	TBA Rating	TOP Composite		
							TRP	RPA	TNB	TBA					TOP	Rating	Ranking
-	-	-	-	.080	.179	.120	2	.071	6	.214	0.57	13.38	0.98	23.62	38.56	9.83	
2	2	1	10	.260	.315	.466	87	.276	152	.483	25.00	51.75	24.92	53.18	154.85	39.48	
-	2	3	12	.265	.304	.381	64	.222	115	.399	18.39	41.64	18.85	44.01	122.89	31.33	
3	4	7	15	.290	.328	.490	180	.273	328	.498	51.72	51.18	53.77	54.86	211.53	53.93	
2	6	7	19	.282	.338	.430	185	.261	327	.462	53.16	48.96	53.61	50.90	206.63	52.68	
2	2	7	20	.294	.357	.526	225	.312	398	.552	64.66	58.48	65.25	60.84	249.22	63.54	
3	4	7	15	.317	.401	.589	236	.339	438	.629	67.82	63.54	71.80	69.36	272.52	69.48	
1	1	3	13	.269	.325	.438	163	.241	322	.476	46.84	45.12	52.79	52.42	197.16	50.27	
2	-	6	9	.283	.349	.497	154	.263	313	.535	44.25	49.33	51.31	58.97	203.86	51.98	
1	3	6	13	.314	.393	.527	174	.264	376	.570	50.00	49.40	61.64	62.79	223.83	57.07	
3	2	8	17	.265	.331	.460	182	.266	335	.490	52.30	49.86	54.92	53.98	211.05	53.81	
2	3	6	12	.282	.350	.466	183	.312	294	.502	52.59	58.52	48.20	55.30	214.59	54.71	
5	5	4	10	.260	.328	.452	168	.282	298	.500	48.28	52.82	48.85	55.11	205.05	52.28	
3	2	9	14	.283	.352	.463	162	.250	325	.502	46.55	46.92	53.28	55.36	202.11	51.53	
-	2	5	10	.290	.336	.449	141	.235	286	.477	40.52	44.11	46.89	52.62	184.13	46.95	
1	3	7	14	.270	.322	.425	131	.238	250	.454	37.64	44.55	40.98	50.01	173.18	44.15	
-	1	8	25	.275	.320	.467	178	.270	316	.479	51.15	50.54	51.80	52.77	206.26	52.59	
-	-	3	9	.252	.310	.395	74	.214	148	.429	21.26	40.19	24.26	47.28	133.00	33.91	
1	-	-	6	.260	.326	.444	49	.222	105	.475	14.08	41.55	17.21	52.36	125.20	31.92	
-	1	3	9	.241	.316	.372	61	.207	124	.422	17.53	38.88	20.33	46.48	123.22	31.42	
-	-	1	8	.241	.295	.343	24	.153	58	.369	6.90	28.64	9.51	40.72	85.77	21.87	
2	-	2	2	.328	.396	.470	58	.278	106	.507	16.67	52.00	17.38	55.90	141.94	36.19	
-	-	3	6	.255	.333	.355	43	.184	96	.410	12.36	34.43	15.74	45.22	107.74	27.47	
33	43	106	268	.279	.341	.463	2,924	.263	5,516	.496	65.40	62.97	65.22	65.94	259.52	66.28	75
30	39	95	241	.279	.341	.463	2,629	.263	4,960	.496	62.97	62.97	65.94	65.94	257.80	64.45	124
34	44	108	274	.279	.341	.463	2,990	.263	5,641	.496	57.25	62.97	59.95	65.94	246.11	61.53	123
24	30	61	143	.286	.350	.488	1,850	.281	3,429	.522	62.84	64.19	69.17	65.83	262.04	67.21	98
11	17	31	82	.290	.350	.494	989	.286	1,813	.524	64.98	61.11	69.52	63.51	259.12	66.38	121
3	4	7	15	.317	.401	.589	236	.339	438	.629	67.82	63.54	71.80	69.36	272.52	69.48	306

Complete Career Statistics P

Complete Career Statistics P

Total Career Statistics & Adjusted Career, 10 year, 5 year, and Single Year Analysis

Piazza, Mike: *Michael Joseph Piazza, b. Sept. 4, 1968, Norristown, PA*

Rating Category			Year	Ranked Seasons & Adjustment	G	AB	H	1B	2B	3B	HR	RUN	RBI	BB	SO	SB
10 Year Total			1992		21	69	16	12	3	-	1	5	7	4	12	-
			1993		149	547	174	113	24	2	35	81	112	46	86	3
			1994		107	405	129	87	18	-	24	64	92	33	65	1
			1995		112	434	150	101	17	-	32	82	93	39	80	1
	5 Year Total		1996		148	547	184	132	16	-	36	87	105	81	93	-
			1997	1st	152	556	201	128	32	1	40	104	124	69	77	5
			1998		151	561	184	113	38	1	32	88	111	58	80	1
			1999		141	534	162	97	25	-	40	100	124	51	70	2
			2000		136	482	156	92	26	-	38	90	113	58	69	4
			2001		141	503	151	86	29	-	36	81	94	67	87	-
			2002		135	478	134	76	23	2	33	69	98	57	82	-
			2003		68	234	67	43	13	-	11	37	34	35	40	-
			2004		129	455	121	80	21	-	20	47	54	68	78	-
Career Total**			1992-2004		1,590	5,805	1,829	1,160	285	6	378	935	1,161	666	919	17
Career Adj. to 10,000 BO**			1992-2004	1.485001	2,361	8,620	2,716	1,723	423	9	561	1,388	1,724	989	1,365	25
Career Adj. to 10,000 AB**			1992-2004	1.722653	2,739	10,000	3,151	1,998	491	10	651	1,611	2,000	1,147	1,583	29
10 Year Total**			1993-2002		1,372	5,047	1,625	1,025	248	6	346	846	1,066	559	789	17
5 Year Total**			1996-2000		728	2,680	887	562	137	2	186	469	577	317	389	12
Best Single Year**			1997		152	556	201	128	32	1	40	104	124	69	77	5

Total Career Statistics & Adjusted Career, 10 year, 5 year, and Single Year Analysis

Piazza, Mike

CS	HBP	SF	GDP	AVG	OBP	SLG	Total Offensive Production Statistics				TRP Rating	RPA Rating	TNB Rating	TBA Rating	TOP Composite		
							TRP	RPA	TNB	TBA					TOP	Rating	Ranking
-	1	-	1	.232	.284	.319	12	.160	27	.360	3.45	29.98	4.43	39.68	77.53	19.77	
4	3	6	10	.318	.370	.561	193	.315	355	.580	55.46	59.09	58.20	63.93	236.68	60.34	
3	1	2	11	.319	.370	.541	156	.345	251	.555	44.83	64.67	41.15	61.20	211.85	54.01	
-	1	1	10	.346	.400	.606	175	.361	304	.627	50.29	67.61	49.84	69.08	236.82	60.38	
3	1	2	21	.336	.422	.563	192	.294	387	.594	55.17	55.18	63.44	65.42	239.21	60.99	
1	3	5	18	.362	.431	.638	228	.350	431	.662	65.52	65.63	70.66	72.97	274.77	70.05	
-	2	5	15	.328	.390	.570	199	.310	381	.594	57.18	58.17	62.46	65.51	243.33	62.04	
2	1	7	27	.303	.361	.575	224	.361	359	.579	64.37	67.70	58.85	63.82	254.74	64.95	
2	3	2	15	.324	.398	.614	203	.363	359	.641	58.33	67.93	58.85	70.66	255.77	65.21	
2	2	1	20	.300	.384	.573	175	.295	355	.599	50.29	55.30	58.20	65.98	229.76	58.58	
3	3	3	26	.280	.359	.544	167	.295	317	.559	47.99	55.19	51.97	61.62	216.76	55.27	
-	1	3	11	.286	.377	.483	71	.250	149	.525	20.40	46.85	24.43	57.82	149.50	38.12	
-	2	3	14	.266	.362	.444	101	.186	272	.502	29.02	34.92	44.59	55.31	163.84	41.77	
20	24	40	199	.315	.385	.562	2,096	.311	3,947	.586	46.88	74.53	46.67	77.91	245.99	62.82	92
30	36	59	296	.315	.385	.562	3,113	.311	5,861	.586	74.53	74.53	77.91	77.91	304.89	76.22	54
34	41	69	343	.315	.385	.562	3,611	.311	6,799	.586	69.13	74.53	72.26	77.91	293.83	73.46	55
20	20	34	173	.322	.389	.579	1,912	.328	3,499	.600	64.95	74.75	70.59	75.69	285.97	73.35	56
8	10	21	96	.331	.401	.592	1,046	.335	1,917	.614	68.73	71.60	73.50	74.40	288.23	73.84	78
1	3	5	18	.362	.431	.638	228	.350	431	.662	65.52	65.63	70.66	72.97	274.77	70.05	297

Complete Career Statistics P

Complete Career Statistics P

Total Career Statistics & Adjusted Career, 10 year, 5 year, and Single Year Analysis

Pujols, Albert: *Jose Albert Pujols, b. Jan 16, 1980, Santo Domingo, Dominican Republic*

Rating Category	Year	Ranked Seasons & Adjustment	G	AB	H	1B	2B	3B	HR	RUN	RBI	BB	SO	SB
	2001	3rd	161	590	194	106	47	4	37	112	130	69	93	1
	2002		157	590	185	109	40	2	34	118	127	72	69	2
	2003	1st	157	591	212	117	51	1	43	137	124	79	65	5
	2004	2nd	154	592	196	97	51	2	46	133	123	84	52	5
Career Total**	2001-2004		629	2,363	787	429	189	9	160	500	504	304	279	13
Career Adj. to 10,000 BO**	2001-2004	3.568879	2,245	8,433	2,809	1,531	675	32	571	1,784	1,799	1,085	996	46
Career Adj. to 10,000 AB**	2001-2004	4.231909	2,662	10,000	3,331	1,815	800	38	677	2,116	2,133	1,287	1,181	55
10 Year Total**	n/a													
5 Year Total**	n/a													
Best Single Year**	2003		157	591	212	117	51	1	43	137	124	79	65	5
2nd Best Year**	2004		154	592	196	97	51	2	46	133	123	84	52	5
3rd Best Year**	2001		161	590	194	106	47	4	37	112	130	69	93	1

Total Career Statistics & Adjusted Career, 10 year, 5 year, and Single Year Analysis

Pujols, Albert

CS	HBP	SF	GDP	AVG	OBP	SLG	Total Offensive Production Statistics				TRP Rating	RPA Rating	TNB Rating	TBA Rating	TOP Composite		
							TRP	RPA	TNB	TBA					TOP	Rating	Ranking
3	9	7	21	.329	.403	.610	242	.348	436	.626	69.54	65.15	71.48	69.04	275.21	70.17	
4	9	4	20	.314	.394	.561	245	.353	410	.590	70.40	66.06	67.21	65.02	268.69	68.50	
1	10	5	13	.359	.439	.667	261	.374	487	.698	75.00	70.07	79.84	76.90	301.80	76.95	
5	7	9	21	.331	.415	.657	256	.359	480	.673	73.56	67.28	78.69	74.20	293.73	74.89	
13	35	25	75	.333	.413	.624	1,004	.358	1,813	.647	22.46	85.80	21.44	86.01	215.70	55.09	121
46	125	89	268	.333	.413	.624	3,583	.358	6,470	.647	85.80	85.80	86.01	86.01	343.62	85.90	8
55	148	106	317	.333	.413	.624	4,249	.358	7,672	.647	81.34	85.80	81.54	86.01	334.69	83.67	7
1	10	5	13	.359	.439	.667	261	.374	487	.698	75.00	70.07	79.84	76.90	301.80	76.95	91
5	7	9	21	.331	.415	.657	256	.359	480	.673	73.56	67.28	78.69	74.20	293.73	74.89	129
3	9	7	21	.329	.403	.610	242	.348	436	.626	69.54	65.15	71.48	69.04	275.21	70.17	293

Complete Career Statistics P

Complete Career Statistics R

Total Career Statistics & Adjusted Career, 10 year, 5 year, and Single Year Analysis																

Ramirez, Manny: *Manuel Aristides Ramirez (Onelcida); b. May 30, 1972, Santo Domingo, Dominican Republic*

Rating Category	Year	Ranked Seasons & Adjustment	G	AB	H	1B	2B	3B	HR	RUN	RBI	BB	SO	SB
	1993		22	53	9	6	1	-	2	5	5	2	8	-
	1994		91	290	78	39	22	-	17	51	60	42	72	4
	1995		137	484	149	91	26	1	31	85	107	75	112	6
	1996		152	550	170	89	45	3	33	94	112	85	104	8
	1997		150	561	184	118	40	-	26	99	88	79	115	2
	1998	2nd	150	571	168	86	35	2	45	108	145	76	121	5
	1999	1st	147	522	174	93	34	3	44	131	165	96	131	2
	2000	3rd	118	439	154	80	34	2	38	92	122	86	117	1
	2001		142	529	162	86	33	2	41	93	125	81	147	-
	2002		120	436	152	88	31	-	33	84	107	73	85	-
	2003		154	569	185	111	36	1	37	117	104	97	94	3
	2004	4th	152	568	175	88	44	-	43	108	130	82	124	2
Career Total**	1993-2004		1,535	5,572	1,760	975	381	14	390	1,067	1,270	874	1,230	33
Career Adj. to 10,000 BO**	1993-2004	1.485443	2,280	8,277	2,614	1,448	566	21	579	1,585	1,887	1,298	1,827	49
Career Adj. to 10,000 AB**	1993-2004	1.794688	2,755	10,000	3,159	1,750	684	25	700	1,915	2,279	1,569	2,207	59
10 Year Total**	1995-2004		1,422	5,229	1,673	930	358	14	371	1,011	1,205	830	1,150	29
5 Year Total**	1998-2002		677	2,497	810	433	167	9	201	508	664	412	601	8
Best Single Year**	1999		147	522	174	93	34	3	44	131	165	96	131	2
2nd Best Year**	1998		150	571	168	86	35	2	45	108	145	76	121	5
3rd Best Year**	2000		118	439	154	80	34	2	38	92	122	86	117	1
4th Best Year**	2004		152	568	175	88	44	-	43	108	130	82	124	2

10 Year Total / 5 Year Total

Total Career Statistics & Adjusted Career, 10 year, 5 year, and Single Year Analysis

Ramirez, Manny

CS	HBP	SF	GDP	AVG	OBP	SLG	Total Offensive Production Statistics				TRP Rating	RPA Rating	TNB Rating	TBA Rating	TOP Composite		
							TRP	RPA	TNB	TBA					TOP	Rating	Ranking
-	-	-	3	.170	.200	.302	10	.172	18	.310	2.87	32.31	2.95	34.20	72.34	18.44	
2	-	4	6	.269	.357	.521	111	.325	195	.570	31.90	60.82	31.97	62.84	187.52	47.81	
6	5	5	13	.308	.402	.558	192	.330	350	.601	55.17	61.82	57.38	66.28	240.65	61.35	
5	3	9	18	.309	.399	.582	206	.310	411	.618	59.20	58.05	67.38	68.12	252.74	64.44	
3	7	4	19	.328	.415	.538	187	.279	387	.578	53.74	52.30	63.44	63.66	233.14	59.44	
3	6	10	18	.294	.377	.599	253	.372	426	.626	72.70	69.61	69.84	68.94	281.10	71.67	
4	13	9	12	.333	.442	.663	296	.454	453	.695	85.06	85.07	74.26	76.58	320.96	81.83	
1	3	4	9	.351	.457	.697	214	.396	395	.730	61.49	74.12	64.75	80.47	280.84	71.60	
1	8	2	9	.306	.405	.609	218	.347	410	.652	62.64	64.94	67.21	71.84	266.64	67.98	
-	8	1	13	.349	.450	.647	191	.360	363	.684	54.89	67.40	59.51	75.34	257.14	65.56	
1	8	5	22	.325	.427	.587	221	.315	441	.629	63.51	59.07	72.30	69.34	264.21	67.36	
4	6	7	17	.308	.397	.613	238	.350	434	.638	68.39	65.58	71.15	70.34	275.46	70.23	
30	67	60	159	.316	.411	.599	2,337	.347	4,283	.636	52.27	83.13	50.64	84.57	270.61	69.11	54
45	100	89	236	.316	.411	.599	3,471	.347	6,362	.636	83.13	83.13	84.57	84.57	335.39	83.85	13
54	120	108	285	.316	.411	.599	4,194	.347	7,687	.636	80.30	83.13	81.69	84.57	329.68	82.42	10
28	67	56	150	.320	.416	.607	2,216	.350	4,070	.643	75.27	79.81	82.11	81.10	318.29	81.64	18
9	38	26	61	.324	.424	.640	1,172	.386	2,047	.675	77.00	82.61	78.49	81.80	319.90	81.96	22
4	13	9	12	.333	.442	.663	296	.454	453	.695	85.06	85.07	74.26	76.58	320.96	81.83	40
3	6	10	18	.294	.377	.599	253	.372	426	.626	72.70	69.61	69.84	68.94	281.10	71.67	228
1	3	4	9	.351	.457	.697	214	.396	395	.730	61.49	74.12	64.75	80.47	280.84	71.60	231
4	6	7	17	.308	.397	.613	238	.350	434	.638	68.39	65.58	71.15	70.34	275.46	70.23	291

Complete Career Statistics R

Total Career Statistics & Adjusted Career, 10 year, 5 year, and Single Year Analysis

Rice, Jim: *James Edward Rice, b. March 8, 1953, Anderson, SC*

Complete Career Statistics   R

Rating Category	Year	Ranked Seasons & Adjustment	G	AB	H	1B	2B	3B	HR	RUN	RBI	BB	SO	SB
	1974		24	67	18	14	2	1	1	6	13	4	12	-
5 Year Total	1975		144	564	174	119	29	4	22	92	102	36	122	10
	1976		153	581	164	106	25	8	25	75	85	28	123	8
	1977		160	644	206	123	29	15	39	104	114	53	120	5
	1978	1st	163	677	213	127	25	15	46	121	139	58	126	7
10 Year Total	1979	2nd	158	619	201	117	39	6	39	117	130	57	97	9
	1980		124	504	148	96	22	6	24	81	86	30	87	8
	1981		108	451	128	92	18	1	17	51	62	34	76	2
	1982		145	573	177	124	24	5	24	86	97	55	98	-
	1983		155	626	191	117	34	1	39	90	126	52	102	-
	1984		159	657	184	124	25	7	28	98	122	44	102	4
	1985		140	546	159	109	20	3	27	85	103	51	75	2
	1986		157	618	200	139	39	2	20	98	110	62	78	-
	1987		108	404	112	85	14	-	13	66	62	45	77	1
	1988		135	485	128	92	18	3	15	57	72	48	89	1
	1989		56	209	49	34	10	2	3	22	28	13	39	1
Career Total	1974-1989		2,089	8,225	2,452	1,618	373	79	382	1,249	1,451	670	1,423	58
Career Adj. to 10,000 BO	1974-1989	1.067464	2,230	8,780	2,617	1,727	398	84	408	1,333	1,549	715	1,519	62
Career Adj. to 10,000 AB	1974-1989	1.215805	2,540	10,000	2,981	1,967	453	96	464	1,519	1,764	815	1,730	71
10 Year Total	1977-1986		1,469	5,915	1,807	1,168	275	61	303	931	1,089	496	961	37
5 Year Total	1975-1979		778	3,085	958	592	147	48	171	509	570	232	588	39
Best Single Year	1978		163	677	213	127	25	15	46	121	139	58	126	7
2nd Best Year	1979		158	619	201	117	39	6	39	117	130	57	97	9

Total Career Statistics & Adjusted Career, 10 year, 5 year, and Single Year Analysis

Rice, Jim

CS	HBP	SF	GDP	AVG	OBP	SLG	Total Offensive Production Statistics				TRP Rating	RPA Rating	TNB Rating	TBA Rating	TOP Composite		
							TRP	RPA	TNB	TBA					TOP	Rating	Ranking
-	1	3	2	.269	.307	.373	19	.247	30	.390	5.46	46.24	4.92	42.94	99.56	25.38	
5	4	8	19	.309	.350	.491	194	.307	322	.510	55.75	57.61	52.79	56.24	222.39	56.70	
5	4	9	18	.282	.315	.482	160	.250	315	.492	45.98	46.85	51.64	54.25	198.71	50.66	
4	8	5	21	.320	.376	.593	218	.298	444	.607	62.64	55.88	72.79	66.94	258.25	65.84	
5	5	5	15	.315	.370	.600	260	.342	471	.620	74.71	64.10	77.21	68.30	284.33	72.49	
4	4	8	16	.325	.381	.596	247	.351	435	.618	70.98	65.74	71.31	68.10	276.13	70.40	
3	4	3	16	.294	.336	.504	167	.300	293	.526	47.99	56.18	48.03	57.98	210.18	53.59	
2	3	7	14	.284	.333	.441	113	.222	236	.464	32.47	41.60	38.69	51.10	163.86	41.78	
1	7	3	29	.309	.375	.494	183	.274	344	.516	52.59	53.00	56.39	58.60	220.58	56.24	
2	6	5	31	.305	.361	.550	216	.300	400	.556	62.07	56.21	65.57	61.23	245.09	62.49	
-	1	6	36	.280	.323	.467	220	.296	356	.478	63.22	55.41	58.36	52.74	229.72	58.57	
-	2	9	35	.291	.349	.487	188	.292	321	.499	54.02	54.79	52.62	55.02	216.45	55.19	
1	4	9	19	.324	.384	.490	208	.292	368	.517	59.77	54.74	60.33	56.96	231.80	59.10	
1	7	3	22	.277	.357	.408	128	.266	217	.451	36.78	49.86	35.57	49.72	171.94	43.84	
1	3	6	18	.264	.330	.406	129	.230	248	.443	37.07	43.16	40.66	48.81	169.70	43.27	
-	1	5	4	.234	.276	.344	50	.216	87	.375	14.37	40.38	14.26	41.33	110.34	28.13	
34	64	94	315	.298	.352	.502	2,700	.288	4,887	.522	60.39	69.02	57.79	69.34	256.53	65.51	76
36	68	100	336	.298	.352	.502	2,882	.288	5,217	.522	69.02	69.02	69.34	69.34	276.72	69.18	100
41	78	114	383	.298	.352	.502	3,283	.288	5,942	.522	62.85	69.02	63.15	69.34	264.35	66.09	99
22	44	60	232	.305	.360	.526	2,020	.299	3,668	.544	68.61	68.27	74.00	68.59	279.48	71.68	65
23	25	35	89	.311	.360	.556	1,079	.311	1,987	.573	70.89	66.57	76.19	69.51	283.16	72.54	85
5	5	5	15	.315	.370	.600	260	.342	471	.620	74.71	64.10	77.21	68.30	284.33	72.49	195
4	4	8	16	.325	.381	.596	247	.351	435	.618	70.98	65.74	71.31	68.10	276.13	70.40	281

Complete Career Statistics R

Complete Career Statistics   R

| | | Total Career Statistics & Adjusted Career, 10 year, 5 year, and Single Year Analysis | | | | | | | | | | | | | |

Ripkin, Cal: *Calvin Edwin Ripkin, Jr., b. Aug. 24, 1960, Havre De Grace, MD*

Rating Category		Year	Ranked Seasons & Adjustment	G	AB	H	1B	2B	3B	HR	RUN	RBI	BB	SO	SB
		1981		23	39	5	5	-	-	-	1	-	1	8	-
		1982		160	598	158	93	32	5	28	90	93	46	95	3
	5 Year Total	1983		162	663	211	135	47	2	27	121	102	58	97	-
		1984		162	641	195	124	37	7	27	103	86	71	89	2
		1985		161	642	181	118	32	5	26	116	110	67	68	2
10 Year Total		1986		162	627	177	116	35	1	25	98	81	70	60	4
		1987		162	624	157	99	28	3	27	97	98	81	77	3
		1988		161	575	152	103	25	1	23	87	81	102	69	2
		1989		162	646	166	115	30	-	21	80	93	57	72	3
		1990		161	600	150	97	28	4	21	78	84	82	66	3
		1991	1st	162	650	210	125	46	5	34	99	114	53	46	6
		1992		162	637	160	116	29	1	14	73	72	64	50	4
		1993		162	641	165	112	26	3	24	87	90	65	58	1
		1994		112	444	140	105	19	3	13	71	75	32	41	1
		1995		144	550	144	92	33	2	17	71	88	52	59	-
		1996		163	640	178	111	40	1	26	94	102	59	78	1
		1997		162	615	166	119	30	-	17	79	84	56	73	1
		1998		161	601	163	121	27	1	14	65	61	51	68	-
		1999		86	332	113	68	27	-	18	51	57	13	31	-
		2000		83	309	79	48	16	-	15	43	56	23	37	-
		2001		128	477	114	84	16	-	14	43	68	26	63	-
Career Total		1981-2001		3,001	11,551	3,184	2,106	603	44	431	1,647	1,695	1,129	1,305	36
Career Adj. to 10,000 BO		1981-2001	0.756258	2,270	8,736	2,408	1,593	456	33	326	1,246	1,282	854	987	27
Career Adj. to 10,000 AB		1981-2001	0.865726	2,598	10,000	2,756	1,823	522	38	373	1,426	1,467	977	1,130	31
10 Year Total		1983-1992		1,617	6,305	1,759	1,148	337	29	245	952	921	705	694	29
5 Year Total		1983-1987		809	3,197	921	592	179	18	132	535	477	347	391	11
Best Single Year		1991		162	650	210	125	46	5	34	99	114	53	46	6

Total Career Statistics & Adjusted Career, 10 year, 5 year, and Single Year Analysis

Ripkin, Cal

CS	HBP	SF	GDP	AVG	OBP	SLG	Total Offensive Production Statistics				TRP Rating	RPA Rating	TNB Rating	TBA Rating	TOP Composite		
							TRP	RPA	TNB	TBA					TOP	Rating	Ranking
-	-	-	4	.128	.150	.128	1	.023	6	.136	0.29	4.26	0.98	15.03	20.56	5.24	
3	3	6	16	.264	.317	.475	183	.274	333	.498	52.59	51.26	54.59	54.86	213.29	54.38	
4	-	5	24	.318	.371	.517	223	.297	397	.529	64.08	55.71	65.08	58.34	243.22	62.01	
1	2	2	16	.304	.374	.510	189	.258	401	.548	54.31	48.38	65.74	60.38	228.81	58.34	
3	1	8	32	.282	.347	.469	226	.301	368	.491	64.94	56.46	60.33	54.08	235.81	60.12	
2	4	6	19	.282	.355	.461	179	.247	365	.503	51.44	46.20	59.84	55.41	212.88	54.28	
5	1	11	19	.252	.333	.436	195	.265	352	.478	56.03	49.65	57.70	52.71	216.10	55.10	
2	2	10	10	.264	.372	.431	168	.240	352	.504	48.28	45.04	57.70	55.50	206.52	52.65	
2	3	6	22	.257	.317	.401	173	.236	320	.436	49.71	44.16	52.46	48.05	194.39	49.56	
1	5	7	12	.250	.341	.415	162	.229	338	.479	46.55	43.00	55.41	52.77	197.72	50.41	
1	5	9	19	.323	.374	.566	213	.289	431	.586	61.21	54.23	70.66	64.54	250.63	63.90	
3	7	7	13	.251	.323	.366	145	.199	305	.419	41.67	37.32	50.00	46.17	175.16	44.66	
4	6	6	17	.257	.329	.420	177	.241	337	.459	50.86	45.12	55.25	50.53	201.77	51.44	
-	4	4	17	.315	.364	.459	146	.291	241	.481	41.95	54.61	39.51	53.02	189.09	48.21	
1	2	8	15	.262	.324	.422	159	.254	285	.455	45.69	47.52	46.72	50.10	190.03	48.45	
2	4	4	28	.278	.341	.466	196	.267	360	.490	56.32	49.97	59.02	53.98	219.29	55.91	
-	5	10	19	.270	.331	.402	163	.231	309	.438	46.84	43.32	50.66	48.31	189.13	48.22	
2	4	2	9	.271	.331	.389	126	.189	287	.430	36.21	35.40	47.05	47.42	166.08	42.34	
1	3	3	14	.340	.368	.584	108	.296	209	.573	31.03	55.44	34.26	63.11	183.85	46.87	
-	3	4	10	.256	.310	.453	99	.284	166	.476	28.45	53.15	27.21	52.42	161.24	41.11	
2	2	9	15	.239	.276	.361	111	.210	198	.374	31.90	39.32	32.46	41.25	144.93	36.95	
39	66	127	350	.276	.340	.447	3,342	.253	6,360	.481	74.75	60.52	75.20	63.93	274.41	70.08	49
29	50	96	265	.276	.340	.447	2,527	.253	4,810	.481	60.52	60.52	63.93	63.93	248.91	62.23	126
34	57	110	303	.276	.340	.447	2,893	.253	5,506	.481	55.39	60.52	58.52	63.93	238.36	59.59	126
24	30	71	186	.279	.351	.458	1,873	.257	3,629	.497	63.62	58.53	73.21	62.75	258.11	66.20	107
15	8	32	110	.288	.356	.479	1,012	.274	1,883	.510	66.49	58.58	72.20	61.80	259.08	66.37	122
1	5	9	19	.323	.374	.566	213	.289	431	.586	61.21	54.23	70.66	64.54	250.63	63.90	363

Complete Career Statistics R

Total Career Statistics & Adjusted Career, 10 year, 5 year, and Single Year Analysis

Complete Career Statistics R

Robinson, Frank: *Frank Robinson, b. Aug. 31, 1935, Beaumont, TX*

Rating Category	Year	Ranked Seasons & Adjustment	G	AB	H	1B	2B	3B	HR	RUN	RBI	BB	SO	SB
	1956		152	572	166	95	27	6	38	122	83	64	95	8
	1957		150	611	197	134	29	5	29	97	75	44	92	10
	1958		148	554	149	87	25	6	31	90	83	62	80	10
	1959		146	540	168	97	31	4	36	106	125	69	93	18
	1960		139	464	138	68	33	6	31	86	83	82	67	13
	1961	3rd	153	545	176	100	32	7	37	117	124	71	64	22
	1962	1st	162	609	208	116	51	2	39	134	136	76	62	18
	1963		140	482	125	82	19	3	21	79	91	81	69	26
	1964		156	568	174	101	38	6	29	103	96	79	67	23
	1965		156	582	172	101	33	5	33	109	113	70	100	13
	1966	2nd	155	576	182	97	34	2	49	122	122	87	90	8
	1967		129	479	149	89	23	7	30	83	94	71	84	2
	1968		130	421	113	70	27	1	15	69	52	73	84	11
	1969		148	539	166	110	19	5	32	111	100	88	62	9
	1970		132	471	144	94	24	1	25	88	78	69	70	2
	1971		133	455	128	82	16	2	28	82	99	72	62	3
	1972		103	342	86	60	6	1	19	41	59	55	76	2
	1973		147	534	142	83	29	-	30	85	97	82	93	1
	1974		144	477	117	65	27	3	22	81	68	85	95	5
	1975		49	118	28	14	5	-	9	19	24	29	15	-
	1976		36	67	15	12	-	-	3	5	10	11	12	-
Career Total	1956-1976		2,808	10,006	2,943	1,757	528	72	586	1,829	1,812	1,420	1,532	204
Career Adj. to 10,000 BO	1956-1976	0.833681	2,341	8,342	2,454	1,465	440	60	489	1,525	1,511	1,184	1,277	170
Career Adj. to 10,000 AB	1956-1976	0.999400	2,806	10,000	2,941	1,756	528	72	586	1,828	1,811	1,419	1,531	204
10 Year Total	1958-1967		1,484	5,399	1,641	938	319	48	336	1,029	1,067	748	776	153
5 Year Total	1958-1962		748	2,712	839	468	172	25	174	533	551	360	366	81
Best Single Year	1962		162	609	208	116	51	2	39	134	136	76	62	18
2nd Best Year	1966		155	576	182	97	34	2	49	122	122	87	90	8
3rd Best Year	1961		153	545	176	100	32	7	37	117	124	71	64	22

(Left margin: 5 Year Total / 10 Year Total)

Total Career Statistics & Adjusted Career, 10 year, 5 year, and Single Year Analysis

Robinson, Frank

CS	HBP	SF	GDP	AVG	OBP	SLG	TRP	RPA	TNB	TBA	TRP Rating	RPA Rating	TNB Rating	TBA Rating	TOP	Rating	Ranking
4	20	4	14	.290	.379	.558	205	.304	407	.604	58.91	56.99	66.72	66.55	249.18	63.53	
2	12	5	13	.322	.376	.529	172	.251	387	.565	49.43	47.05	63.44	62.27	222.19	56.65	
1	7	-	13	.269	.350	.504	173	.272	357	.561	49.71	50.97	58.52	61.87	221.07	56.36	
8	8	9	16	.311	.391	.583	231	.360	402	.626	66.38	67.42	65.90	69.01	268.72	68.51	
6	9	7	18	.297	.407	.595	169	.291	374	.645	48.56	54.60	61.31	71.07	235.54	60.05	
3	10	10	15	.323	.404	.611	241	.370	433	.665	69.25	69.37	70.98	73.31	282.91	72.13	
9	11	5	13	.342	.421	.624	270	.378	476	.667	77.59	70.86	78.03	73.48	299.95	76.48	
10	14	3	7	.259	.379	.442	170	.290	324	.552	48.85	54.27	53.11	60.83	217.07	55.34	
5	9	6	13	.306	.396	.548	199	.295	417	.618	57.18	55.24	68.36	68.09	248.88	63.45	
9	18	4	14	.296	.386	.540	222	.323	406	.590	63.79	60.46	66.56	65.04	255.85	65.23	
5	10	7	24	.316	.410	.637	244	.347	467	.663	70.11	64.94	76.56	73.11	284.73	72.59	
3	7	6	10	.311	.403	.576	177	.309	353	.616	50.86	57.88	57.87	67.90	234.51	59.79	
2	12	2	15	.268	.390	.444	121	.231	281	.537	34.77	43.35	46.07	59.22	183.40	46.76	
3	13	3	12	.308	.415	.540	211	.322	398	.608	60.63	60.36	65.25	66.97	253.21	64.56	
1	7	6	13	.306	.398	.520	166	.293	322	.569	47.70	54.96	52.79	62.70	218.15	55.62	
-	9	8	21	.281	.384	.510	181	.320	316	.559	52.01	60.03	51.80	61.64	225.49	57.49	
3	2	6	9	.251	.353	.442	100	.242	207	.500	28.74	45.26	33.93	55.11	163.04	41.57	
1	10	3	13	.266	.372	.489	182	.283	353	.550	52.30	53.12	57.87	60.60	223.89	57.08	
2	10	6	11	.245	.367	.453	149	.253	314	.533	42.82	47.40	51.48	58.76	200.45	51.11	
-	-	1	2	.237	.385	.508	43	.287	89	.593	12.36	53.72	14.59	65.39	146.06	37.24	
-	-	1	3	.224	.329	.358	15	.183	35	.427	4.31	34.28	5.74	47.04	91.37	23.30	
77	198	102	269	.294	.389	.537	3,641	.304	7,118	.593	81.44	72.69	84.17	78.88	317.17	81.00	12
64	165	85	224	.294	.389	.537	3,035	.304	5,934	.593	72.69	72.69	78.88	78.88	303.13	75.78	60
77	198	102	269	.294	.389	.537	3,639	.304	7,114	.593	69.67	72.69	75.60	78.88	296.83	74.21	44
59	103	57	143	.304	.395	.568	2,096	.325	4,009	.622	71.20	74.10	80.88	78.42	304.60	78.13	32
27	45	31	75	.309	.395	.584	1,084	.336	2,042	.634	71.22	71.92	78.30	76.82	298.26	76.41	53
9	11	5	13	.342	.421	.624	270	.378	476	.667	77.59	70.86	78.03	73.48	299.95	76.48	100
5	10	7	24	.316	.410	.637	244	.347	467	.663	70.11	64.94	76.56	73.11	284.73	72.59	191
3	10	10	15	.323	.404	.611	241	.370	433	.665	69.25	69.37	70.98	73.31	282.91	72.13	210

Complete Career Statistics R

Total Career Statistics & Adjusted Career, 10 year, 5 year, and Single Year Analysis

Robinson, Jackie: *Jack Roosevelt Robinson, b. Jan 31, 1919, Cairo, GA*

Rating Category			Year	Ranked Seasons & Adjustment	G	AB	H	1B	2B	3B	HR	RUN	RBI	BB	SO	SB	
			1947		151	590	175	127	31	5	12	125	48	74	36	29	
			1948		147	574	170	112	38	8	12	108	85	57	37	22	
10 Year Total	5 Year Total		1949	1st	156	593	203	137	38	12	16	122	124	86	27	37	
			1950		144	518	170	113	39	4	14	99	81	80	24	12	
			1951		153	548	185	126	33	7	19	106	88	79	27	25	
			1952		149	510	157	118	17	3	19	104	75	106	40	24	
			1953		136	484	159	106	34	7	12	109	95	74	30	17	
			1954		124	386	120	79	22	4	15	62	59	63	20	7	
			1955		105	317	81	65	6	2	8	51	36	61	18	12	
			1956		117	357	98	71	15	2	10	61	43	60	32	12	
Career Total			1947-1956		1,382	4,877	1,518	1,054	273	54	137	947	734	740	291	197	
Career Adj. to 10,000 BO			1947-1956	1.720874	2,378	8,393	2,612	1,814	470	93	236	1,630	1,263	1,273	501	339	
Career Adj. to 10,000 AB			1947-1956	2.050441	2,834	10,000	3,113	2,161	560	111	281	1,942	1,505	1,517	597	404	
10 Year Total			1947-1956		1,382	4,877	1,518	1,054	273	54	137	947	734	740	291	197	
5 Year Total			1949-1953		738	2,653	874	600	161	33	80	540	463	425	148	115	
Best Single Year			1949		156	593	203	137	38	12	16	122	124	86	27	37	

Total Career Statistics & Adjusted Career, 10 year, 5 year, and Single Year Analysis

Robinson, Jackie

CS	HBP	SF	GDP	AVG	OBP	SLG	Total Offensive Production Statistics				TRP Rating	RPA Rating	TNB Rating	TBA Rating	TOP Composite		
							TRP	RPA	TNB	TBA					TOP	Rating	Ranking
10	9	-	5	.297	.383	.427	173	.255	354	.522	49.71	47.81	59.67	59.17	216.37	55.17	
-	7	-	7	.296	.367	.453	193	.299	346	.536	55.46	56.07	56.72	59.12	227.37	57.97	
14	8	-	22	.342	.432	.528	246	.347	430	.606	70.69	65.02	70.49	66.84	273.04	69.61	
-	5	-	11	.328	.423	.500	180	.293	356	.580	51.72	54.93	58.36	63.90	228.92	58.37	
8	9	-	10	.338	.429	.527	194	.300	394	.610	55.75	56.27	64.59	67.22	243.83	62.17	
7	14	-	16	.308	.440	.465	179	.277	374	.579	51.44	51.92	61.31	63.81	228.48	58.25	
4	7	-	12	.329	.425	.502	204	.354	337	.584	58.62	66.25	55.25	64.37	244.49	62.33	
3	7	4	13	.311	.413	.505	121	.256	269	.569	34.77	47.93	44.10	62.68	189.48	48.31	
3	3	3	8	.256	.378	.363	87	.222	188	.480	25.00	41.59	30.82	52.86	150.26	38.31	
5	3	2	9	.275	.382	.412	104	.241	217	.503	29.89	45.22	35.57	55.49	166.16	42.37	
54	72	9	113	.311	.409	.474	1,681	.289	3,265	.562	37.60	69.27	38.61	74.69	220.16	56.22	118
93	124	15	194	.311	.409	.474	2,893	.289	5,619	.562	69.27	69.27	74.69	74.69	287.91	71.98	82
111	148	18	232	.311	.409	.474	3,447	.289	6,695	.562	65.99	69.27	71.15	74.69	281.09	70.27	77
54	72	9	113	.311	.409	.474	1,681	.289	3,265	.562	57.10	65.97	65.87	70.89	259.83	66.64	105
33	43	-	71	.329	.430	.505	1,003	.314	1,891	.592	65.90	67.19	72.51	71.83	277.43	71.08	95
14	8	-	22	.342	.432	.528	246	.347	430	.606	70.69	65.02	70.49	66.84	273.04	69.61	305

Complete Career Statistics R

Total Career Statistics & Adjusted Career, 10 year, 5 year, and Single Year Analysis

Rodriguez, Alex: *Alexander Emmanuel Rodriguez, b. July 27, 1975, New York, NY*

Rating Category	Year	Ranked Seasons & Adjustment	G	AB	H	1B	2B	3B	HR	RUN	RBI	BB	SO	SB
	1994		17	54	11	11	-	-	-	4	2	3	20	3
	1995		48	142	33	20	6	2	5	15	19	6	42	4
	1996	4th	146	601	215	124	54	1	36	141	123	59	104	15
	1997		141	587	176	110	40	3	23	100	84	41	99	29
	1998	6th	161	686	213	131	35	5	42	123	124	45	121	46
	1999		129	502	143	76	25	-	42	110	111	56	109	21
	2000	3rd	148	554	175	98	34	2	41	134	132	100	121	15
	2001	1st	162	632	201	114	34	1	52	133	135	75	131	18
	2002	2nd	162	624	187	101	27	2	57	125	142	87	122	9
	2003	5th	161	607	181	98	30	6	47	124	118	87	126	17
	2004		155	601	172	110	24	2	36	112	106	80	131	28
Career Total**	1994-2004		1,430	5,590	1,707	993	309	24	381	1,121	1,096	639	1,126	205
Career Adj. to 10,000 BO**	1994-2004	1.539172	2,201	8,604	2,627	1,528	476	37	586	1,725	1,687	984	1,733	316
Career Adj. to 10,000 AB**	1994-2004	1.788909	2,558	10,000	3,054	1,776	553	43	682	2,005	1,961	1,143	2,014	367
10 Year Total**	1995-2004		1,413	5,536	1,696	982	309	24	381	1,117	1,094	636	1,106	202
5 Year Total**	1999-2003		762	2,919	887	487	150	11	239	626	638	405	609	80
Best Single Year**	2001		162	632	201	114	34	1	52	133	135	75	131	18
2nd Best Year**	2002		162	624	187	101	27	2	57	125	142	87	122	9
3rd Best Year**	2000		148	554	175	98	34	2	41	134	132	100	121	15
4th Best Year**	1996		146	601	215	124	54	1	36	141	123	59	104	15
5th Best Year**	2003		161	607	181	98	30	6	47	124	118	87	126	17
6th Best Year**	1998		161	686	213	131	35	5	42	123	124	45	121	46

Complete Career Statistics R

10 Year Total

5 Year Total

Total Career Statistics & Adjusted Career, 10 year, 5 year, and Single Year Analysis

Rodriguez, Alex

CS	HBP	SF	GDP	AVG	OBP	SLG	Total Offensive Production Statistics				TRP Rating	RPA Rating	TNB Rating	TBA Rating	TOP Composite		
							TRP	RPA	TNB	TBA					TOP	Rating	Ranking
-	-	1	-	.204	.241	.204	6	.103	17	.293	1.72	19.38	2.79	32.30	56.20	14.33	
2	-	-	-	.232	.264	.408	34	.230	66	.446	9.77	43.05	10.82	49.15	112.79	28.76	
4	4	7	15	.358	.414	.631	264	.385	453	.660	75.86	72.11	74.26	72.78	295.02	75.22	
6	5	1	14	.300	.350	.496	184	.284	360	.556	52.87	53.21	59.02	61.23	226.33	57.70	
13	10	4	12	.310	.360	.560	247	.326	472	.624	70.98	61.14	77.38	68.72	278.21	70.93	
7	5	8	12	.285	.357	.586	221	.379	369	.633	63.51	71.03	60.49	69.76	264.79	67.51	
4	7	11	10	.316	.420	.606	266	.390	454	.666	76.44	73.08	74.43	73.37	297.32	75.80	
3	16	9	17	.318	.399	.622	268	.358	499	.666	77.01	67.05	81.80	73.43	299.29	76.31	
4	10	4	14	.300	.392	.623	267	.361	491	.664	76.72	67.70	80.49	73.23	298.14	76.01	
3	15	6	16	.298	.396	.600	242	.331	480	.657	69.54	62.03	78.69	72.37	282.63	72.06	
4	10	7	18	.286	.375	.512	218	.304	422	.589	62.64	57.05	69.18	64.96	253.83	64.72	
50	82	58	128	.305	.381	.574	2,217	.341	4,083	.628	49.59	81.71	48.28	83.54	263.11	67.19	67
77	126	89	197	.305	.381	.574	3,412	.341	6,284	.628	81.71	81.71	83.54	83.54	330.49	82.62	17
89	147	104	229	.305	.381	.574	3,966	.341	7,304	.628	75.93	81.71	77.63	83.54	318.80	79.70	20
50	82	57	128	.306	.383	.577	2,211	.343	4,066	.631	75.10	78.30	82.03	79.67	315.11	80.82	22
21	53	38	69	.304	.394	.608	1,264	.363	2,293	.658	83.05	77.58	87.92	79.80	328.35	84.12	19
3	16	9	17	.318	.399	.622	268	.358	499	.666	77.01	67.05	81.80	73.43	299.29	76.31	104
4	10	4	14	.300	.392	.623	267	.361	491	.664	76.72	67.70	80.49	73.23	298.14	76.01	107
4	7	11	10	.316	.420	.606	266	.390	454	.666	76.44	73.08	74.43	73.37	297.32	75.80	112
4	4	7	15	.358	.414	.631	264	.385	453	.660	75.86	72.11	74.26	72.78	295.02	75.22	123
3	15	6	16	.298	.396	.600	242	.331	480	.657	69.54	62.03	78.69	72.37	282.63	72.06	214
13	10	4	12	.310	.360	.560	247	.326	472	.624	70.98	61.14	77.38	68.72	278.21	70.93	248

Complete Career Statistics   R

Total Career Statistics & Adjusted Career, 10 year, 5 year, and Single Year Analysis

Rose, Pete: *Peter Edward "Charlie Hustle" Rose, Sr., b. April 14, 1941, Cincinnati, OH*

Rating Category	Year	Ranked Seasons & Adjustment	G	AB	H	1B	2B	3B	HR	RUN	RBI	BB	SO	SB
	1963		157	623	170	130	25	9	6	101	41	55	72	13
	1964		136	516	139	120	13	2	4	64	34	36	51	4
5 Year Total	1965		162	670	209	152	35	11	11	117	81	69	76	8
	1966		156	654	205	146	38	5	16	97	70	37	61	4
	1967		148	585	176	124	32	8	12	86	76	56	66	11
	1968		149	626	210	152	42	6	10	94	49	56	76	3
	1969	1st	156	627	218	158	33	11	16	120	82	88	65	7
10 Year Total	1970		159	649	205	144	37	9	15	120	52	73	64	12
	1971		160	632	192	148	27	4	13	86	44	68	50	13
	1972		154	645	198	150	31	11	6	107	57	73	46	10
	1973		160	680	230	181	36	8	5	115	64	65	42	10
	1974		163	652	185	130	45	7	3	110	51	106	54	2
	1975		162	662	210	152	47	4	7	112	74	89	50	-
	1976		162	665	215	157	42	6	10	130	63	86	54	9
	1977		162	655	204	150	38	7	9	95	64	66	42	16
	1978		159	655	198	137	51	3	7	103	52	62	30	13
	1979		163	628	208	159	40	5	4	90	59	95	32	20
	1980		162	655	185	141	42	1	1	95	64	66	33	12
	1981		107	431	140	117	18	5	-	73	33	46	26	4
	1982		162	634	172	140	25	4	3	80	54	66	32	8
	1983		151	493	121	104	14	3	-	52	45	52	28	7
	1984		121	374	107	90	15	2	-	43	34	40	27	1
	1985		119	405	107	91	12	2	2	60	46	86	35	8
	1986		72	237	52	42	8	2	-	15	25	30	31	3
Career Total	1963-1986		3,562	14,053	4,256	3,215	746	135	160	2,165	1,314	1,566	1,143	198
Career Adj. to 10,000 BO	1963-1986	0.622975	2,219	8,755	2,651	2,003	465	84	100	1,349	819	976	712	123
Career Adj. to 10,000 AB	1963-1986	0.711592	2,535	10,000	3,029	2,288	531	96	114	1,541	935	1,114	813	141
10 Year Total	1969-1978		1,597	6,522	2,055	1,507	387	70	91	1,098	603	776	497	92
5 Year Total	1965-1969		771	3,162	1,018	732	180	41	65	514	358	306	344	33
Best Single Year	1969		156	627	218	158	33	11	16	120	82	88	65	7

Complete Career Statistics   R

Total Career Statistics & Adjusted Career, 10 year, 5 year, and Single Year Analysis

Rose, Pete

CS	HBP	SF	GDP	AVG	OBP	SLG	TRP	RPA	TNB	TBA	TRP Rating	RPA Rating	TNB Rating	TBA Rating	TOP	Rating	Ranking
15	5	6	8	.273	.334	.371	142	.204	289	.415	40.80	38.18	47.38	45.70	172.06	43.87	
10	2	1	6	.269	.319	.326	98	.175	200	.357	28.16	32.73	32.79	39.29	132.97	33.90	
3	8	2	10	.312	.382	.446	198	.261	381	.502	56.90	48.88	62.46	55.32	223.56	57.00	
9	1	1	12	.313	.351	.460	167	.237	334	.474	47.99	44.39	54.75	52.21	199.34	50.82	
6	3	2	9	.301	.364	.444	162	.247	324	.495	46.55	46.34	53.11	54.52	200.53	51.13	
7	4	4	11	.335	.391	.470	143	.204	350	.499	41.09	38.22	57.38	55.03	191.72	48.88	
10	5	6	13	.348	.428	.512	202	.273	411	.556	58.05	51.22	67.38	61.30	237.94	60.66	
7	2	4	7	.316	.385	.470	172	.234	385	.524	49.43	43.85	63.11	57.73	214.12	54.59	
9	3	3	9	.304	.373	.421	130	.182	341	.477	37.36	34.07	55.90	52.56	179.89	45.86	
3	7	2	7	.307	.382	.417	164	.223	356	.485	47.13	41.87	58.36	53.46	200.81	51.20	
7	6	-	14	.338	.401	.437	179	.234	371	.485	51.44	43.84	60.82	53.45	209.55	53.43	
4	5	6	9	.284	.385	.388	161	.207	362	.465	46.26	38.78	59.34	51.28	195.67	49.89	
1	11	1	13	.317	.406	.432	186	.240	385	.496	53.45	44.91	63.11	54.68	216.16	55.11	
5	6	2	17	.323	.404	.450	193	.249	395	.509	55.46	46.60	64.75	56.10	222.92	56.84	
4	5	4	9	.311	.377	.432	159	.215	366	.495	45.69	40.32	60.00	54.59	200.59	51.14	
9	3	7	8	.302	.362	.421	155	.211	345	.469	44.54	39.52	56.56	51.73	192.35	49.04	
11	2	5	18	.331	.418	.430	149	.199	376	.503	42.82	37.33	61.64	55.40	197.18	50.27	
8	6	4	13	.282	.352	.354	159	.214	308	.414	45.69	40.05	50.49	45.63	181.85	46.37	
4	3	3	8	.325	.391	.390	106	.216	217	.442	30.46	40.45	35.57	48.71	155.20	39.57	
8	7	3	12	.271	.345	.338	134	.186	287	.398	38.51	34.78	47.05	43.81	164.14	41.85	
7	2	7	11	.245	.316	.286	97	.172	195	.345	27.87	32.17	31.97	38.04	130.05	33.16	
1	3	1	11	.286	.359	.337	77	.179	169	.394	22.13	33.63	27.70	43.42	126.88	32.35	
1	4	4	10	.264	.395	.319	106	.208	226	.444	30.46	39.02	37.05	48.94	155.47	39.64	
-	4	1	2	.219	.316	.270	40	.146	101	.369	11.49	27.35	16.56	40.63	96.03	24.48	
149	107	79	247	.303	.375	.409	3,479	.217	7,474	.466	77.81	51.90	88.38	61.89	279.98	71.50	40
93	67	49	154	.303	.375	.409	2,167	.217	4,656	.466	51.90	51.90	61.89	61.89	227.58	56.89	127
106	76	56	176	.303	.375	.409	2,476	.217	5,318	.466	47.40	51.90	56.52	61.89	217.71	54.43	127
59	53	35	106	.315	.390	.438	1,701	.227	3,717	.496	57.78	51.78	74.98	62.60	247.14	63.39	116
35	21	15	55	.322	.384	.466	872	.245	1,800	.506	57.29	52.39	69.02	61.32	240.03	61.49	126
10	5	6	13	.348	.428	.512	202	.273	411	.556	58.05	51.22	67.38	61.30	237.94	60.66	374

Complete Career Statistics R

Total Career Statistics & Adjusted Career, 10 year, 5 year, and Single Year Analysis

Ruth, Babe: *George Herman "The Bambino" or "The Sultan of Swat" Ruth, b. Feb. 6, 1895, Baltimore, MD*

Rating Category	Year	Ranked Seasons & Adjustment	G	AB	H	1B	2B	3B	HR	RUN	RBI	BB	SO	SB
	1914		5	10	2	1	1	-	-	1	2	-	4	-
	1915		42	92	29	14	10	1	4	16	21	9	23	-
	1916		67	136	37	26	5	3	3	18	15	10	23	-
	1917		52	123	40	29	6	3	2	14	12	12	18	-
	1918		95	317	95	47	26	11	11	50	66	58	58	6
	1919	12th	130	432	139	64	34	12	29	103	114	101	58	7
	1920	3rd	142	458	172	73	36	9	54	158	137	150	80	14
	1921	1st	152	540	204	85	44	16	59	177	171	145	81	17
	1922		110	406	128	61	24	8	35	94	99	84	80	2
	1923	7th	152	522	205	106	45	13	41	151	131	170	93	17
	1924	9th	153	529	200	108	39	7	46	143	121	142	81	9
	1925		98	359	104	65	12	2	25	61	66	59	68	2
	1926	8th	152	495	184	102	30	5	47	139	146	144	76	11
	1927	2nd	151	540	192	95	29	8	60	158	164	137	89	7
	1928	6th	154	536	173	82	29	8	54	163	142	137	87	4
	1929	10th	135	499	172	94	26	6	46	121	154	72	60	5
	1930	4th	145	518	186	100	28	9	49	150	153	136	61	10
	1931	5th	145	534	199	119	31	3	46	149	163	128	51	5
	1932	11th	133	457	156	97	13	5	41	120	137	130	62	2
	1933		137	459	138	80	21	3	34	97	103	114	90	4
	1934		125	365	105	62	17	4	22	78	84	104	63	1
	1935		28	72	13	7	-	-	6	13	12	20	24	-
Career Total	1914-1935		2,503	8,399	2,873	1,517	506	136	714	2,174	2,213	2,062	1,330	123
Career Adj. to 10,000 BO	1914-1935	0.951928	2,383	7,995	2,735	1,444	482	129	680	2,069	2,107	1,963	1,266	117
Career Adj. to 10,000 AB	1914-1935	1.190618	2,980	10,000	3,421	1,806	602	162	850	2,588	2,635	2,455	1,584	146
10 Year Total	1920-1929		1,399	4,884	1,734	871	314	82	467	1,365	1,331	1,240	795	88
5 Year Total	1927-1931		730	2,627	922	490	143	34	255	741	776	610	348	31
5 Year Total	1920-1924		709	2,455	909	433	188	53	235	723	659	691	415	59
Best Single Year	1921		152	540	204	85	44	16	59	177	171	145	81	17
2nd Best Year	1927		151	540	192	95	29	8	60	158	164	137	89	7
3rd Best Year	1920		142	458	172	73	36	9	54	158	137	150	80	14
4th Best Year	1930		145	518	186	100	28	9	49	150	153	136	61	10
5th Best Year	1931		145	534	199	119	31	3	46	149	163	128	51	5
6th Best Year	1928		154	536	173	82	29	8	54	163	142	137	87	4
7th Best Year	1923		152	522	205	106	45	13	41	151	131	170	93	17
8th Best Year	1926		152	495	184	102	30	5	47	139	146	144	76	11
9th Best Year	1924		153	529	200	108	39	7	46	143	121	142	81	9
10th Best Year	1929		135	499	172	94	26	6	46	121	154	72	60	5
11th Best Year	1932		133	457	156	97	13	5	41	120	137	130	62	2
12th Best Year	1919		130	432	139	64	34	12	29	103	114	101	58	7

Complete Career Statistics R

10 Year Total

5 Year Total

5 Year Total

Total Career Statistics & Adjusted Career, 10 year, 5 year, and Single Year Analysis

Ruth, Babe

CS	HBP	SF	GDP	AVG	OBP	SLG	TRP	RPA	TNB	TBA	TRP Rating	RPA Rating	TNB Rating	TBA Rating	TOP	Rating	Ranking
-	-	-	-	.200	.200	.300	3	.300	3	.300	0.86	56.21	0.49	33.06	90.63	23.11	
-	-	-	-	.315	.376	.576	37	.366	62	.614	10.63	68.64	10.16	67.66	157.10	40.05	
-	-	-	-	.272	.322	.419	33	.226	67	.459	9.48	42.35	10.98	50.58	113.40	28.91	
-	-	-	-	.325	.385	.472	26	.193	70	.519	7.47	36.09	11.48	57.15	112.18	28.60	
-	2	-	-	.300	.411	.555	116	.308	242	.642	33.33	57.66	39.67	70.75	201.41	51.35	
-	6	-	-	.322	.456	.657	217	.403	398	.738	62.36	75.44	65.25	81.38	284.42	72.52	
14	3	-	-	.376	.532	.847	295	.483	541	.885	84.77	90.47	88.69	97.59	361.52	92.17	
13	4	-	-	.378	.512	.846	348	.505	610	.885	100.00	94.64	100.00	97.58	392.22	100.00	
5	1	-	-	.315	.434	.672	193	.393	355	.723	55.46	73.66	58.20	79.69	267.00	68.07	
21	4	-	-	.393	.545	.764	282	.405	569	.818	81.03	75.92	93.28	90.10	340.34	86.77	
13	4	-	-	.378	.513	.739	264	.391	533	.790	75.86	73.29	87.38	87.03	323.55	82.49	
4	2	-	-	.290	.393	.543	127	.302	254	.605	36.49	56.66	41.64	66.65	201.45	51.36	
9	3	-	-	.372	.516	.737	285	.444	514	.801	81.90	83.18	84.26	88.24	337.58	86.07	
6	-	-	-	.356	.486	.772	322	.476	555	.820	92.53	89.12	90.98	90.35	362.99	92.55	
5	3	-	-	.323	.463	.709	305	.451	519	.768	87.64	84.54	85.08	84.62	341.89	87.17	
3	3	-	-	.345	.430	.697	275	.479	425	.740	79.02	89.77	69.67	81.60	320.07	81.61	
10	1	-	-	.359	.493	.732	303	.463	516	.788	87.07	86.68	84.59	86.83	345.17	88.00	
4	-	-	-	.373	.494	.700	312	.471	503	.760	89.66	88.31	82.46	83.74	344.17	87.75	
2	2	-	-	.341	.489	.661	257	.436	434	.737	73.85	81.76	71.15	81.21	307.97	78.52	
5	2	-	-	.301	.442	.582	200	.348	382	.664	57.47	65.18	62.62	73.22	258.49	65.90	
3	2	-	-	.288	.448	.537	162	.344	300	.637	46.55	64.45	49.18	70.20	230.38	58.74	
-	-	-	2	.181	.359	.431	25	.266	51	.543	7.18	49.84	8.36	59.80	125.18	31.92	
117	42	-	2	.342	.474	.690	4,387	.418	7,903	.752	98.12	100.00	93.45	100.00	391.57	100.00	1
111	40	-	2	.342	.474	.690	4,176	.418	7,523	.752	100.00	100.00	100.00	100.00	400.00	100.00	1
139	50	-	2	.342	.474	.690	5,223	.418	9,409	.752	100.00	100.00	100.00	100.00	400.00	100.00	1
93	27	-	-	.355	.488	.740	2,696	.438	4,875	.793	91.58	99.95	98.35	100.00	389.87	100.00	1
28	7	-	-	.351	.474	.722	1,517	.468	2,518	.776	99.67	100.00	96.55	94.11	390.33	100.00	1
66	16	-	-	.370	.511	.777	1,382	.437	2,608	.825	90.80	93.46	100.00	100.00	384.27	98.45	n/r
13	4	-	-	.378	.512	.846	348	.505	610	.885	100.00	94.64	100.00	97.58	392.22	100.00	1
6	-	-	-	.356	.486	.772	322	.476	555	.820	92.53	89.12	90.98	90.35	362.99	92.55	2
14	3	-	-	.376	.532	.847	295	.483	541	.885	84.77	90.47	88.69	97.59	361.52	92.17	3
10	1	-	-	.359	.493	.732	303	.463	516	.788	87.07	86.68	84.59	86.83	345.17	88.00	12
4	-	-	-	.373	.494	.700	312	.471	503	.760	89.66	88.31	82.46	83.74	344.17	87.75	15
5	3	-	-	.323	.463	.709	305	.451	519	.768	87.64	84.54	85.08	84.62	341.89	87.17	17
21	4	-	-	.393	.545	.764	282	.405	569	.818	81.03	75.92	93.28	90.10	340.34	86.77	20
9	3	-	-	.372	.516	.737	285	.444	514	.801	81.90	83.18	84.26	88.24	337.58	86.07	22
13	4	-	-	.378	.513	.739	264	.391	533	.790	75.86	73.29	87.38	87.03	323.55	82.49	37
3	3	-	-	.345	.430	.697	275	.479	425	.740	79.02	89.77	69.67	81.60	320.07	81.61	41
2	2	-	-	.341	.489	.661	257	.436	434	.737	73.85	81.76	71.15	81.21	307.97	78.52	73
-	6	-	-	.322	.456	.657	217	.403	398	.738	62.36	75.44	65.25	81.38	284.42	72.52	194

Complete Career Statistics   R

Total Career Statistics & Adjusted Career, 10 year, 5 year, and Single Year Analysis

Schmidt, Mike: *Michael Jack Schmidt, b. Sept. 27, 1949, Dayton, OH*

Rating Category	Year	Ranked Seasons & Adjustment	G	AB	H	1B	2B	3B	HR	RUN	RBI	BB	SO	SB
	1972		13	34	7	6	-	-	1	2	3	5	15	-
	1973		132	367	72	43	11	-	18	43	52	62	136	8
	1974		162	568	160	89	28	7	36	108	116	106	138	23
	1975		158	562	140	65	34	3	38	93	95	101	180	29
	1976		160	584	153	80	31	4	38	112	107	100	149	14
	1977		154	544	149	73	27	11	38	114	101	104	122	15
10 Year Total	1978		145	513	129	79	27	2	21	93	78	91	103	19
	1979		160	541	137	63	25	4	45	109	114	120	115	9
5 Year Total	1980	1st	150	548	157	76	25	8	48	104	121	89	119	12
	1981		102	354	112	60	19	2	31	78	91	73	71	12
	1982		148	514	144	80	26	3	35	108	87	107	131	14
	1983		154	534	136	76	16	4	40	104	109	128	148	7
	1984		151	528	146	84	23	3	36	93	106	92	116	5
	1985		158	549	152	83	31	5	33	89	93	87	117	1
	1986		160	552	160	93	29	1	37	97	119	89	84	1
	1987		147	522	153	90	28	-	35	88	113	83	80	2
	1988		108	390	97	62	21	2	12	52	62	49	42	3
	1989		42	148	30	17	7	-	6	19	28	21	17	-
Career Total	1972-1989		2,404	8,352	2,234	1,219	408	59	548	1,506	1,595	1,507	1,883	174
Career Adj. to 10,000 BO	1972-1989	0.980200	2,356	8,187	2,190	1,195	400	58	537	1,476	1,563	1,477	1,846	171
Career Adj. to 10,000 AB	1972-1989	1.197318	2,878	10,000	2,675	1,460	489	71	656	1,803	1,910	1,804	2,255	208
10 Year Total	1974-1983		1,493	5,262	1,417	741	258	48	370	1,023	1,019	1,019	1,276	154
5 Year Total	1979-1983		714	2,491	686	355	111	21	199	503	522	517	584	54
Best Single Year	1980		150	548	157	76	25	8	48	104	121	89	119	12

Complete Career Statistics S

Total Career Statistics & Adjusted Career, 10 year, 5 year, and Single Year Analysis

Schmidt, Mike

CS	HBP	SF	GDP	AVG	OBP	SLG	Total Offensive Production Statistics				TRP Rating	RPA Rating	TNB Rating	TBA Rating	TOP Composite		
							TRP	RPA	TNB	TBA					TOP	Rating	Ranking
-	1	-	-	.206	.325	.294	5	.125	16	.400	1.44	23.42	2.62	44.09	71.57	18.25	
2	9	4	8	.196	.324	.373	95	.211	214	.476	27.30	39.56	35.08	52.41	154.35	39.35	
12	4	5	4	.282	.395	.546	224	.326	431	.627	64.37	61.10	70.66	69.14	265.26	67.63	
12	4	1	7	.249	.367	.523	188	.279	416	.616	54.02	52.19	68.20	67.92	242.33	61.79	
9	11	7	7	.262	.376	.524	219	.309	422	.595	62.93	57.88	69.18	65.60	255.59	65.17	
8	9	9	10	.274	.393	.574	215	.318	432	.639	61.78	59.60	70.82	70.43	262.63	66.96	
6	4	8	4	.251	.364	.435	171	.276	331	.534	49.14	51.68	54.26	58.84	213.92	54.54	
5	3	9	13	.253	.386	.564	223	.325	432	.630	64.08	60.91	70.82	69.41	265.22	67.62	
5	2	13	6	.286	.380	.624	225	.342	440	.669	64.66	64.07	72.13	73.70	274.56	70.00	
4	4	3	9	.316	.435	.644	169	.381	313	.707	48.56	71.48	51.31	77.87	249.23	63.54	
7	3	7	11	.280	.403	.547	195	.304	398	.620	56.03	56.92	65.25	68.33	246.52	62.85	
8	3	4	10	.255	.399	.524	213	.314	410	.604	61.21	58.78	67.21	66.55	253.75	64.70	
7	4	8	15	.277	.383	.536	199	.308	377	.583	57.18	57.63	61.80	64.22	240.84	61.40	
3	3	6	10	.277	.375	.532	182	.278	380	.580	52.30	52.07	62.30	63.94	230.60	58.79	
2	7	9	8	.290	.390	.547	216	.325	397	.597	62.07	60.86	65.08	65.80	253.81	64.71	
1	2	6	17	.293	.388	.548	201	.319	372	.590	57.76	59.78	60.98	65.08	243.60	62.11	
-	6	6	11	.249	.337	.405	114	.247	216	.468	32.76	46.24	35.41	51.53	165.93	42.31	
1	-	3	6	.203	.297	.372	47	.264	75	.421	13.51	49.48	12.30	46.44	121.72	31.03	
92	79	108	156	.267	.380	.527	3,101	.304	6,072	.595	69.36	72.79	71.80	79.11	293.06	74.84	24
90	77	106	153	.267	.380	.527	3,040	.304	5,952	.595	72.79	72.79	79.11	79.11	303.80	75.95	58
110	95	129	187	.267	.380	.527	3,713	.304	7,270	.595	71.08	72.79	77.26	79.11	300.25	75.06	39
76	47	66	81	.269	.388	.548	2,042	.315	4,025	.622	69.36	71.92	81.20	78.43	300.91	77.18	39
29	15	36	49	.275	.398	.576	1,025	.330	1,993	.641	67.35	70.52	76.42	77.75	292.03	74.82	65
5	2	13	6	.286	.380	.624	225	.342	440	.669	64.66	64.07	72.13	73.70	274.56	70.00	298

Complete Career Statistics S

Total Career Statistics & Adjusted Career, 10 year, 5 year, and Single Year Analysis

Sheffield, Gary: *Gary Antonian Sheffield, b. Nov. 18, 1968, Tampa, FL*

Rating Category	Year	Ranked Seasons & Adjustment	G	AB	H	1B	2B	3B	HR	RUN	RBI	BB	SO	SB
	1988		24	80	19	14	1	-	4	12	12	7	7	3
	1989		95	368	91	68	18	-	5	34	32	27	33	10
	1990		125	487	143	102	30	1	10	67	67	44	41	25
	1991		50	175	34	18	12	2	2	25	22	19	15	5
	1992		146	557	184	114	34	3	33	87	100	48	40	5
	1993		140	494	145	100	20	5	20	67	73	47	64	17
	1994		87	322	89	45	16	1	27	61	78	51	50	12
	1995		63	213	69	45	8	-	16	46	46	55	45	19
	1996	2nd	161	519	163	87	33	1	42	118	120	142	66	16
	1997		135	444	111	67	22	1	21	86	71	121	79	11
	1998		130	437	132	81	27	2	22	73	85	95	46	22
	1999		152	549	165	111	20	-	34	103	101	101	64	11
	2000		141	501	163	93	24	3	43	105	109	101	71	4
	2001		143	515	160	94	28	2	36	98	100	94	67	10
	2002		135	492	151	100	26	-	25	82	84	72	53	12
	2003	1st	155	576	190	112	37	2	39	126	132	86	55	18
	2004		154	573	166	99	30	1	36	117	121	92	83	5
Career Total**	1988-2004		2,036	7,302	2,175	1,350	386	24	415	1,307	1,353	1,202	879	205
Career Adj. to 10,000 BO	1988-2004	1.124986	2,290	8,215	2,447	1,519	434	27	467	1,470	1,522	1,352	989	231
Career Adj. to 10,000 AB	1988-2004	1.369488	2,788	10,000	2,979	1,849	529	33	568	1,790	1,853	1,646	1,204	281
10 Year Total**	1995-2004		1,369	4,819	1,470	889	255	12	314	954	969	959	629	128
5 Year Total**	2000-2004		728	2,657	830	498	145	8	179	528	546	445	329	49
Best Single Year**	2003		155	576	190	112	37	2	39	126	132	86	55	18
2nd Best Year**	1996		161	519	163	87	33	1	42	118	120	142	66	16

Complete Career Statistics S

10 Year Total

5 Year Total

Total Career Statistics & Adjusted Career, 10 year, 5 year, and Single Year Analysis

Sheffield, Gary

CS	HBP	SF	GDP	AVG	OBP	SLG	Total Offensive Production Statistics				TRP Rating	RPA Rating	TNB Rating	TBA Rating	TOP Composite		
							TRP	RPA	TNB	TBA					TOP	Rating	Ranking
1	-	1	5	.238	.295	.400	24	.258	41	.441	6.90	48.36	6.72	48.59	110.56	28.19	
6	4	3	4	.247	.303	.337	66	.163	159	.392	18.97	30.46	26.07	43.16	118.65	30.25	
10	3	9	11	.294	.350	.421	134	.242	267	.482	38.51	45.32	43.77	53.12	180.72	46.08	
5	3	5	3	.194	.277	.320	47	.229	78	.380	13.51	42.96	12.79	41.94	111.19	28.35	
6	6	7	19	.330	.385	.580	187	.294	376	.590	53.74	55.01	61.64	65.06	235.44	60.03	
5	9	7	11	.294	.361	.476	140	.246	303	.533	40.23	46.19	49.67	58.79	194.88	49.69	
6	6	5	10	.276	.380	.584	139	.353	251	.637	39.94	66.11	41.15	70.21	217.41	55.43	
4	4	2	3	.324	.467	.587	92	.332	199	.718	26.44	62.24	32.62	79.18	200.47	51.11	
9	10	6	16	.314	.465	.624	238	.343	483	.697	68.39	64.35	79.18	76.82	288.74	73.62	
7	15	2	7	.250	.424	.446	157	.267	338	.574	45.11	49.95	55.41	63.25	213.72	54.49	
7	8	9	7	.302	.428	.524	158	.284	347	.624	45.40	53.25	56.89	68.78	224.32	57.19	
5	4	9	10	.301	.407	.523	204	.303	398	.591	58.62	56.80	65.25	65.18	245.84	62.68	
6	4	6	13	.325	.438	.643	214	.342	425	.680	61.49	64.16	69.67	74.95	270.27	68.91	
4	4	5	12	.311	.417	.583	198	.314	404	.641	56.90	58.89	66.23	70.68	252.69	64.43	
2	11	4	16	.307	.404	.512	166	.279	345	.580	47.70	52.28	56.56	63.91	220.44	56.20	
4	8	8	16	.330	.419	.604	258	.372	456	.657	74.14	69.66	74.75	72.42	290.97	74.19	
6	11	8	16	.290	.393	.534	238	.340	408	.583	68.39	63.71	66.89	64.24	263.22	67.11	
93	110	96	179	.298	.400	.528	2,660	.299	5,278	.594	59.49	71.66	62.41	78.93	272.49	69.59	51
105	124	108	201	.298	.400	.528	2,992	.299	5,938	.594	71.66	71.66	78.93	78.93	301.17	75.29	62
127	151	131	245	.298	.400	.528	3,643	.299	7,228	.594	69.74	71.66	76.82	78.93	297.14	74.29	43
54	79	59	116	.305	.424	.558	1,923	.319	3,803	.630	65.32	72.70	76.72	79.55	294.29	75.48	48
22	38	31	73	.312	.414	.575	1,074	.331	2,038	.628	70.57	70.80	78.14	76.17	295.68	75.75	59
4	8	8	16	.330	.419	.604	258	.372	456	.657	74.14	69.66	74.75	72.42	290.97	74.19	140
9	10	6	16	.314	.465	.624	238	.343	483	.697	68.39	64.35	79.18	76.82	288.74	73.62	159

Complete Career Statistics S

Total Career Statistics & Adjusted Career, 10 year, 5 year, and Single Year Analysis

Simmons, Al: *Aloysius Harry Simmons (Aloys Szymanski), b. May 22, 1902, Milwaukee, WI*

Rating Category	Year	Ranked Seasons & Adjustment	G	AB	H	1B	2B	3B	HR	RUN	RBI	BB	SO	SB
	1924		152	594	183	135	31	9	8	69	102	30	60	16
	1925	5th	153	658	253	174	43	12	24	122	129	35	41	7
	1926		147	583	199	117	53	10	19	90	109	48	49	10
	1927		106	406	159	97	36	11	15	86	108	31	30	10
	1928		119	464	163	106	33	9	15	78	107	31	30	1
	1929	2nd	143	581	212	128	41	9	34	114	157	31	38	4
	1930	1st	138	554	211	118	41	16	36	152	165	39	34	9
	1931	4th	128	513	200	128	37	13	22	105	128	47	45	3
	1932	3rd	154	670	216	144	28	9	35	144	151	47	76	4
	1933		146	605	200	147	29	10	14	85	119	39	49	5
	1934		138	558	192	131	36	7	18	102	104	53	58	3
	1935		128	525	140	95	22	7	16	68	79	33	43	4
	1936		143	568	186	129	38	6	13	96	112	49	35	6
	1937		103	419	117	78	21	10	8	60	84	27	35	3
	1938		125	470	142	92	23	6	21	79	95	38	40	2
	1939		102	351	96	67	17	5	7	39	44	24	43	-
	1940		37	81	25	20	4	-	1	7	19	4	8	-
	1941		9	24	3	2	1	-	-	1	1	1	2	-
	1943		40	133	27	21	5	-	1	9	12	8	21	-
	1944		4	6	3	3	-	-	-	1	2	-	-	-
Career Total*	1924-1944		2,215	8,763	2,927	1,932	539	149	307	1,507	1,827	615	737	87
Career Adj. to 10,000 BO*	1924-1944	1.060333	2,349	9,292	3,104	2,049	572	158	326	1,598	1,937	652	781	92
Career Adj. to 10,000 AB*	1924-1944	1.141162	2,528	10,000	3,340	2,205	615	170	350	1,720	2,085	702	841	99
10 Year Total*	1925-1934		1,372	5,592	2,005	1,290	377	106	232	1,078	1,277	401	450	56
5 Year Total*	1928-1932		682	2,782	1,002	624	180	56	142	593	708	195	223	21
Best Single Year*	1930		138	554	211	118	41	16	36	152	165	39	34	9
2nd Best Year*	1929		143	581	212	128	41	9	34	114	157	31	38	4
3rd Best Year*	1932		154	670	216	144	28	9	35	144	151	47	76	4
4th Best Year*	1931		128	513	200	128	37	13	22	105	128	47	45	3
5th Best Year*	1925		153	658	253	174	43	12	24	122	129	35	41	7

Complete Career Statistics S

10 Year Total

5 Year Total

Total Career Statistics & Adjusted Career, 10 year, 5 year, and Single Year Analysis

Simmons, Al

CS	HBP	SF	GDP	AVG	OBP	SLG	Total Offensive Production Statistics				TRP Rating	RPA Rating	TNB Rating	TBA Rating	TOP Composite		
							TRP	RPA	TNB	TBA					TOP	Rating	Ranking
15	2	-	-	.308	.343	.431	171	.273	289	.462	49.14	51.19	47.38	50.88	198.58	50.63	
14	1	-	-	.384	.416	.596	251	.362	421	.607	72.13	67.77	69.02	66.86	275.77	70.31	
3	1	-	-	.341	.392	.564	199	.315	385	.609	57.18	59.00	63.11	67.14	246.44	62.83	
2	1	-	-	.392	.436	.645	194	.443	302	.689	55.75	83.00	49.51	75.99	264.24	67.37	
4	3	-	-	.351	.396	.558	185	.371	290	.582	53.16	69.61	47.54	64.18	234.49	59.79	
2	1	-	-	.365	.398	.642	271	.442	407	.664	77.87	82.84	66.72	73.18	300.61	76.64	
2	1	-	-	.381	.423	.708	317	.534	439	.739	91.09	100.00	71.97	81.45	344.51	87.84	
3	3	-	-	.390	.444	.641	233	.414	379	.673	66.95	77.55	62.13	74.19	280.83	71.60	
2	1	-	-	.322	.368	.548	295	.411	417	.581	84.77	76.99	68.36	64.01	294.13	74.99	
1	2	-	-	.331	.373	.481	204	.316	336	.520	58.62	59.17	55.08	57.33	230.20	58.69	
2	2	-	-	.344	.403	.530	206	.336	352	.574	59.20	62.97	57.70	63.29	243.16	62.00	
6	2	-	-	.267	.313	.427	147	.263	257	.459	42.24	49.19	42.13	50.58	184.14	46.95	
4	2	-	-	.327	.383	.484	208	.336	328	.530	59.77	62.97	53.77	58.40	234.91	59.89	
2	4	-	-	.279	.329	.434	144	.320	214	.476	41.38	59.96	35.08	52.41	188.84	48.15	
1	2	-	-	.302	.357	.511	174	.341	281	.551	50.00	63.93	46.07	60.73	220.72	56.27	
-	2	-	13	.274	.324	.410	83	.213	170	.436	23.85	39.88	27.87	48.04	139.64	35.60	
-	-	-	4	.309	.341	.395	26	.292	36	.404	7.47	54.74	5.90	44.58	112.69	28.73	
-	-	-	2	.125	.160	.167	2	.074	5	.185	0.57	13.88	0.82	20.41	35.68	9.10	
1	-	-	3	.203	.248	.263	21	.146	42	.292	6.03	27.33	6.89	32.15	72.39	18.46	
-	-	-	1	.500	.500	.500	3	.429	3	.429	0.86	80.31	0.49	47.23	128.89	32.86	
64	30	-	23	.334	.380	.535	3,334	.354	5,353	.568	74.57	84.65	63.30	75.45	297.97	76.09	20
68	32	-	24	.334	.380	.535	3,535	.354	5,676	.568	84.65	84.65	75.45	75.45	320.20	80.05	26
73	34	-	26	.334	.380	.535	3,805	.354	6,109	.568	72.84	84.65	64.92	75.45	297.86	74.46	41
35	16	-	-	.359	.403	.588	2,355	.392	3,728	.620	79.99	89.37	75.21	78.28	322.85	82.81	14
13	9	-	-	.360	.404	.618	1,301	.436	1,932	.647	85.48	93.17	74.08	78.45	331.18	84.85	17
2	1	-	-	.381	.423	.708	317	.534	439	.739	91.09	100.00	71.97	81.45	344.51	87.84	14
2	1	-	-	.365	.398	.642	271	.442	407	.664	77.87	82.84	66.72	73.18	300.61	76.64	98
2	1	-	-	.322	.368	.548	295	.411	417	.581	84.77	76.99	68.36	64.01	294.13	74.99	128
3	3	-	-	.390	.444	.641	233	.414	379	.673	66.95	77.55	62.13	74.19	280.83	71.60	232
14	1	-	-	.384	.416	.596	251	.362	421	.607	72.13	67.77	69.02	66.86	275.77	70.31	288

Complete Career Statistics S

Total Career Statistics & Adjusted Career, 10 year, 5 year, and Single Year Analysis

Sisler, George: *George Harold "Georgeous George" Sisler, b. Mar. 24, 1893, Manchester, OH*

Complete Career Statistics S

Rating Category	Year	Ranked Seasons & Adjustment	G	AB	H	1B	2B	3B	HR	RUN	RBI	BB	SO	SB
	1915		81	274	78	63	10	2	3	28	29	7	27	10
	1916		151	580	177	141	21	11	4	83	76	40	37	34
	1917		135	539	190	149	30	9	2	60	52	30	19	37
5 Year Total	1918		114	452	154	122	21	9	2	69	41	40	17	45
	1919		132	511	180	124	31	15	10	96	83	27	20	28
10 Year Total	1920	1st	154	631	257	171	49	18	19	137	122	46	19	42
	1921		138	582	216	148	38	18	12	125	104	34	27	35
	1922	2nd	142	586	246	178	42	18	8	134	105	49	14	51
	1924		151	636	194	148	27	10	9	94	74	31	29	19
	1925		150	649	224	176	21	15	12	100	105	27	24	11
	1926		150	613	178	138	21	12	7	78	71	30	30	12
	1927		149	614	201	156	32	8	5	87	97	24	15	27
	1928		138	540	179	144	27	4	4	72	70	31	17	11
	1929		154	629	205	155	40	8	2	67	79	33	17	6
	1930		116	431	133	108	15	7	3	54	67	23	15	7
Career Total	1915-1930		2,055	8,267	2,812	2,121	425	164	102	1,284	1,175	472	327	375
Career Adj. to 10,000 BO	1915-1930	1.138045	2,339	9,408	3,200	2,414	484	187	116	1,461	1,337	537	372	427
Career Adj. to 10,000 AB	1915-1930	1.209629	2,486	10,000	3,401	2,566	514	198	123	1,553	1,421	571	396	454
10 Year Total	1918-1927		1,280	5,274	1,850	1,361	282	123	84	920	802	308	195	270
5 Year Total	1918-1922		680	2,762	1,053	743	181	78	51	561	455	196	97	201
Best Single Year	1920		154	631	257	171	49	18	19	137	122	46	19	42
2nd Best Year	1922		142	586	246	178	42	18	8	134	105	49	14	51

Total Career Statistics & Adjusted Career, 10 year, 5 year, and Single Year Analysis

Sisler, George

CS	HBP	SF	GDP	AVG	OBP	SLG	Total Offensive Production Statistics				TRP Rating	RPA Rating	TNB Rating	TBA Rating	TOP Composite		
							TRP	RPA	TNB	TBA					TOP	Rating	Ranking
9	2	-	-	.285	.307	.369	57	.201	111	.392	16.38	37.74	18.20	43.23	115.55	29.46	
26	5	-	-	.305	.355	.400	159	.254	285	.456	45.69	47.67	46.72	50.26	190.34	48.53	
-	3	-	-	.353	.390	.453	112	.196	314	.549	32.18	36.69	51.48	60.50	180.85	46.11	
-	5	-	-	.341	.400	.440	110	.221	289	.581	31.61	41.47	47.38	64.09	184.55	47.05	
-	5	-	-	.352	.390	.530	179	.330	331	.610	51.44	61.77	54.26	67.18	234.65	59.83	
17	2	-	-	.407	.449	.632	259	.381	472	.695	74.43	71.48	77.38	76.61	299.89	76.46	
11	5	-	-	.371	.411	.560	229	.369	389	.626	65.80	69.10	63.77	69.04	267.71	68.26	
19	3	-	-	.420	.467	.594	239	.375	432	.677	68.68	70.19	70.82	74.63	284.32	72.49	
17	3	-	-	.305	.340	.421	168	.251	304	.454	48.28	46.99	49.84	50.01	195.10	49.74	
12	-	-	-	.345	.371	.479	205	.303	337	.499	58.91	56.82	55.25	54.94	225.92	57.60	
8	3	-	-	.290	.327	.398	149	.231	281	.435	42.82	43.22	46.07	47.94	180.04	45.90	
7	4	-	-	.327	.357	.430	184	.287	312	.486	52.87	53.70	51.15	53.56	211.29	53.87	
1	2	-	-	.331	.370	.419	142	.248	269	.469	40.80	46.44	44.10	51.74	183.08	46.68	
-	4	-	-	.326	.363	.424	146	.219	310	.465	41.95	41.08	50.82	51.30	185.15	47.21	
-	2	-	-	.309	.346	.397	121	.265	203	.445	34.77	49.72	33.28	49.06	166.84	42.54	
127	48	-	-	.340	.379	.468	2,459	.280	4,639	.528	55.00	67.01	54.85	70.18	247.04	63.09	88
145	55	-	-	.340	.379	.468	2,798	.280	5,279	.528	67.01	67.01	70.18	70.18	274.37	68.59	104
154	58	-	-	.340	.379	.468	2,974	.280	5,611	.528	56.95	67.01	59.64	70.18	253.77	63.44	118
91	30	-	-	.351	.390	.499	1,722	.307	3,147	.561	58.49	69.97	63.49	70.75	262.70	67.38	97
47	20	-	-	.381	.426	.559	1,016	.341	1,913	.642	66.75	72.96	73.35	77.88	290.95	74.54	68
17	2	-	-	.407	.449	.632	259	.381	472	.695	74.43	71.48	77.38	76.61	299.89	76.46	101
19	3	-	-	.420	.467	.594	239	.375	432	.677	68.68	70.19	70.82	74.63	284.32	72.49	196

Complete Career Statistics S

Total Career Statistics & Adjusted Career, 10 year, 5 year, and Single Year Analysis

Snider, Duke: *Edwin Donald "The Silver Fox" Snider, b. Sept. 19, 1926, Los Angeles, CA*

Rating Category	Year	Ranked Seasons & Adjustment	G	AB	H	1B	2B	3B	HR	RUN	RBI	BB	SO	SB
	1947	40	83	20	16	3	1	-	6	5	3	24	2	-
	1948		53	160	39	22	6	6	5	22	21	12	27	4
	1949		146	552	161	103	28	7	23	100	92	56	92	12
	1950		152	620	199	127	31	10	31	109	107	58	79	16
	1951		150	606	168	107	26	6	29	96	101	62	97	14
	1952		144	534	162	109	25	7	21	80	92	55	77	7
	1953	2nd	153	590	198	114	38	4	42	132	126	82	90	16
	1954	3rd	149	584	199	110	39	10	40	120	130	84	96	6
	1955	1st	148	538	166	84	34	6	42	126	136	104	87	9
	1956		151	542	158	80	33	2	43	112	101	99	101	3
	1957		139	508	139	67	25	7	40	91	92	77	104	3
	1958		106	327	102	72	12	3	15	45	58	32	49	2
	1959		126	370	114	78	11	2	23	59	88	58	71	1
	1960		101	235	57	25	13	5	14	38	36	46	54	1
	1961		85	233	69	42	8	3	16	35	56	29	43	1
	1962		80	158	44	25	11	3	5	28	30	36	32	2
	1963		129	354	86	61	8	3	14	44	45	56	74	-
	1964		91	167	35	24	7	-	4	16	17	22	40	-
Career Total	1947-1964		2,143	7,161	2,116	1,266	358	85	407	1,259	1,333	971	1,237	99
Career Adj. to 10,000 BO	1947-1964	1.197461	2,566	8,575	2,534	1,516	429	102	487	1,508	1,596	1,163	1,481	119
Career Adj. to 10,000 AB	1947-1964	1.396453	2,993	10,000	2,955	1,768	500	119	568	1,758	1,861	1,356	1,727	138
10 Year Total	1949-1958		1,438	5,401	1,652	973	291	62	326	1,011	1,035	709	872	88
5 Year Total	1953-1957		740	2,762	860	455	169	29	207	581	585	446	478	37
Best Single Year	1955		148	538	166	84	34	6	42	126	136	104	87	9
2nd Best Year	1953		153	590	198	114	38	4	42	132	126	82	90	16
3rd Best Year	1954		149	584	199	110	39	10	40	120	130	84	96	6

Complete Career Statistics S

10 Year Total

5 Year Total

Total Career Statistics & Adjusted Career, 10 year, 5 year, and Single Year Analysis

Snider, Duke

CS	HBP	SF	GDP	AVG	OBP	SLG	Total Offensive Production Statistics				TRP Rating	RPA Rating	TNB Rating	TBA Rating	TOP Composite		
							TRP	RPA	TNB	TBA					TOP	Rating	Ranking
1	-	-	.241	.276	.301	11	.126	31	.356	3.16	23.69	5.08	39.27	71.21		18.15	
-	-	-	4	.244	.297	.450	43	.244	88	.500	12.36	45.78	14.43	55.11	127.67	32.55	
5	4	-	8	.292	.361	.493	192	.310	339	.547	55.17	58.03	56.39	61.15	230.74	58.83	
-	-	-	9	.321	.379	.553	216	.314	417	.607	62.07	58.91	68.36	66.90	256.24	65.33	
10	-	-	23	.277	.344	.483	197	.285	359	.520	56.61	53.42	58.85	57.26	226.14	57.66	
4	-	-	17	.303	.368	.494	172	.284	322	.531	49.43	53.18	52.79	58.56	213.96	54.55	
7	3	-	10	.336	.419	.627	258	.377	464	.677	74.14	70.58	76.07	74.66	295.44	75.32	
6	4	6	12	.341	.423	.647	250	.362	466	.675	71.84	67.89	76.39	74.43	290.56	74.08	
7	1	6	9	.309	.418	.628	262	.398	445	.676	75.29	74.61	72.95	74.54	297.39	75.82	
3	1	4	16	.292	.399	.598	213	.322	424	.640	61.21	60.29	69.51	70.59	261.60	66.70	
4	1	3	17	.274	.368	.587	183	.302	375	.619	52.59	56.59	61.48	68.20	238.85	60.90	
2	1	4	11	.312	.371	.505	103	.275	198	.528	29.60	51.47	32.46	58.19	171.72	43.78	
5	-	2	8	.308	.400	.535	147	.336	252	.575	42.24	62.89	41.31	63.41	209.85	53.50	
-	1	2	7	.243	.366	.519	74	.254	170	.584	21.26	47.65	27.87	64.39	161.17	41.09	
1	1	1	6	.296	.375	.562	91	.337	161	.596	26.15	63.15	26.39	65.72	181.42	46.25	
-	2	-	5	.278	.418	.481	58	.289	116	.577	16.67	54.07	19.02	63.61	153.36	39.10	
1	1	4	2	.243	.345	.401	89	.213	198	.475	25.57	39.99	32.46	52.33	150.36	38.34	
-	-	-	2	.210	.302	.323	33	.173	76	.398	9.48	32.37	12.46	43.85	98.17	25.03	
55	21	32	166	.295	.380	.540	2,592	.310	4,901	.587	57.97	74.32	57.95	78.01	268.26	68.51	58
66	25	38	199	.295	.380	.540	3,104	.310	5,869	.587	74.32	74.32	78.01	78.01	304.67	76.17	56
77	29	45	232	.295	.380	.540	3,620	.310	6,844	.587	69.30	74.32	72.74	78.01	294.37	73.59	53
48	15	23	132	.306	.386	.564	2,046	.326	3,809	.607	69.50	74.29	76.84	76.53	297.16	76.22	43
27	10	19	64	.311	.407	.618	1,166	.353	2,174	.659	76.61	75.54	83.36	79.85	315.35	80.79	29
7	1	6	9	.309	.418	.628	262	.398	445	.676	75.29	74.61	72.95	74.54	297.39	75.82	111
7	3	-	10	.336	.419	.627	258	.377	464	.677	74.14	70.58	76.07	74.66	295.44	75.32	120
6	4	6	12	.341	.423	.647	250	.362	466	.675	71.84	67.89	76.39	74.43	290.56	74.08	147

Complete Career Statistics S

Complete Career Statistics S

Total Career Statistics & Adjusted Career, 10 year, 5 year, and Single Year Analysis

Sosa, Sammy: *Samuel Peralta Sosa, b. Nov. 12, 1968, San Pedro De Macoris, Dominican Republic*

Rating Category	Year	Ranked Seasons & Adjustment	G	AB	H	1B	2B	3B	HR	RUN	RBI	BB	SO	SB
	1989		58	183	47	35	8	-	4	27	13	11	47	7
	1990		153	532	124	73	26	10	15	72	70	33	150	32
	1991		116	316	64	43	10	1	10	39	33	14	98	13
	1992		67	262	68	51	7	2	8	41	25	19	63	15
	1993		159	598	156	93	25	5	33	92	93	38	135	36
	1994		105	426	128	80	17	6	25	59	70	25	92	22
	1995		144	564	151	95	17	3	36	89	119	58	134	34
	1996		124	498	136	73	21	2	40	84	100	34	134	18
	1997		162	642	161	90	31	4	36	90	119	45	174	22
10 Year Total / 5 Year Total	1998	2nd	159	643	198	112	20	-	66	134	158	73	171	18
	1999	3rd	162	625	180	91	24	2	63	114	141	78	171	7
	2000	4th	156	604	193	104	38	1	50	106	138	91	168	7
	2001	1st	160	577	189	86	34	5	64	146	160	116	153	-
	2002		150	556	160	90	19	2	49	122	108	103	144	2
	2003		137	517	144	82	22	-	40	99	103	62	143	-
	2004		126	478	121	65	21	-	35	69	80	56	133	-
Career Total**	1989-2004		2,138	8,021	2,220	1,263	340	43	574	1,383	1,530	856	2,110	233
Career Adj. to 10,000 BO**	1989-2004	1.089799	2,330	8,741	2,419	1,376	371	47	626	1,507	1,667	933	2,299	254
Career Adj. to 10,000 AB**	1989-2004	1.246727	2,666	10,000	2,768	1,575	424	54	716	1,724	1,907	1,067	2,631	290
10 Year Total**	1995-2004		1,480	5,704	1,633	888	247	19	479	1,053	1,226	716	1,525	108
5 Year Total**	1998-2002		787	3,005	920	483	135	10	292	622	705	461	807	34
Best Single Year**	2001		160	577	189	86	34	5	64	146	160	116	153	-
2nd Best Year**	1998		159	643	198	112	20	-	66	134	158	73	171	18
3rd Best Year**	1999		162	625	180	91	24	2	63	114	141	78	171	7
4th Best Year**	2000		156	604	193	104	38	1	50	106	138	91	168	7

Total Career Statistics & Adjusted Career, 10 year, 5 year, and Single Year Analysis

Sosa, Sammy

CS	HBP	SF	GDP	AVG	OBP	SLG	Total Offensive Production Statistics				TRP Rating	RPA Rating	TNB Rating	TBA Rating	TOP Composite		
							TRP	RPA	TNB	TBA					TOP	Rating	Ranking
5	2	2	6	.257	.303	.366	40	.196	82	.402	11.49	36.74	13.44	44.30	105.98	27.02	
16	6	6	10	.233	.282	.404	142	.242	270	.460	40.80	45.33	44.26	50.69	181.09	46.17	
6	2	1	5	.203	.240	.335	72	.213	129	.382	20.69	39.92	21.15	42.06	123.82	31.57	
7	4	2	4	.260	.317	.393	66	.227	134	.460	18.97	42.50	21.97	50.75	134.18	34.21	
11	4	1	13	.261	.309	.485	185	.283	357	.546	53.16	53.01	58.52	60.16	224.85	57.33	
13	2	4	7	.300	.339	.545	129	.278	268	.578	37.07	52.10	43.93	63.66	196.76	50.16	
7	5	2	8	.268	.340	.500	208	.327	372	.584	59.77	61.19	60.98	64.36	246.30	62.80	
5	5	4	14	.273	.323	.564	184	.332	333	.600	52.87	62.12	54.59	66.13	235.72	60.10	
12	2	5	16	.251	.300	.480	209	.294	365	.514	60.06	55.16	59.84	56.66	231.71	59.08	
9	1	5	20	.308	.377	.647	292	.394	499	.673	83.91	73.74	81.80	74.12	313.57	79.95	
8	3	6	17	.288	.367	.635	255	.350	477	.654	73.28	65.55	78.20	72.12	289.13	73.72	
4	2	8	12	.320	.406	.634	244	.340	479	.668	70.11	63.77	78.52	73.63	286.04	72.93	
2	6	12	6	.328	.437	.737	306	.427	545	.760	87.93	79.97	89.34	83.78	341.02	86.95	
-	3	4	14	.288	.399	.594	230	.338	438	.644	66.09	63.38	71.80	70.99	272.27	69.42	
1	5	5	14	.279	.358	.553	202	.335	352	.584	58.05	62.77	57.70	64.34	242.86	61.92	
-	2	3	9	.253	.332	.517	149	.272	305	.557	42.82	50.95	50.00	61.34	205.11	52.29	
106	54	70	175	.277	.348	.545	2,913	.317	5,405	.589	65.15	76.02	63.91	78.30	283.38	72.37	33
116	59	76	191	.277	.348	.545	3,175	.317	5,890	.589	76.02	76.02	78.30	78.30	308.63	77.16	48
132	67	87	218	.277	.348	.545	3,632	.317	6,739	.589	69.53	76.02	71.61	78.30	295.46	73.86	52
48	34	54	130	.286	.366	.588	2,279	.343	4,165	.627	77.41	78.29	84.02	79.17	318.89	81.79	17
23	15	35	69	.306	.397	.649	1,327	.370	2,438	.680	87.19	79.15	93.48	82.45	342.28	87.69	7
2	6	12	6	.328	.437	.737	306	.427	545	.760	87.93	79.97	89.34	83.78	341.02	86.95	18
9	1	5	20	.308	.377	.647	292	.394	499	.673	83.91	73.74	81.80	74.12	313.57	79.95	57
8	3	6	17	.288	.367	.635	255	.350	477	.654	73.28	65.55	78.20	72.12	289.13	73.72	156
4	2	8	12	.320	.406	.634	244	.340	479	.668	70.11	63.77	78.52	73.63	286.04	72.93	180

Complete Career Statistics S

Total Career Statistics & Adjusted Career, 10 year, 5 year, and Single Year Analysis

Speaker, Tris: *Tristam E. "The Grey Eagle" Speaker, b. April 4, 1888, Hubbard, TX*

Rating Category	Year	Ranked Seasons & Adjustment	G	AB	H	1B	2B	3B	HR	RUN	RBI	BB	SO	SB
	1907		7	19	3	3	-	-	-	-	1	1	-	-
	1908		31	116	26	21	2	3	-	12	9	4	-	3
	1909		143	544	168	122	26	13	7	73	77	38	-	35
	1910		141	538	183	142	20	14	7	92	65	52	-	35
	1911		141	500	167	112	34	13	8	88	70	59	-	25
	1912	2nd	153	580	222	147	53	12	10	136	90	82	-	52
	1913		141	520	190	130	35	22	3	94	71	65	22	46
	1914		158	571	193	125	46	18	4	100	90	77	25	42
	1915		150	547	176	139	25	12	-	108	69	81	14	29
	1916		151	546	211	160	41	8	2	102	79	82	20	35
	1917		142	523	184	129	42	11	2	90	60	67	14	30
	1918		127	471	150	106	33	11	-	73	61	64	9	27
	1919		134	494	146	94	38	12	2	83	63	73	12	15
	1920	3rd	150	552	214	145	50	11	8	137	107	97	13	10
	1921		132	506	183	114	52	14	3	107	75	68	12	2
	1922		131	426	161	94	48	8	11	85	71	77	11	8
	1923	1st	150	574	218	131	59	11	17	133	130	93	15	10
	1924		135	486	167	113	36	9	9	94	65	72	13	5
	1925		117	429	167	115	35	5	12	79	87	70	12	5
	1926		150	539	164	97	52	8	7	96	86	94	15	6
	1927		141	523	171	120	43	6	2	71	73	55	8	9
	1928		64	191	51	23	23	2	3	28	30	10	5	5
Career Total	1907-1928		2,789	10,195	3,515	2,382	793	223	117	1,881	1,529	1,381	220	434
Career Adj. to 10,000 BO	1907-1928	0.856238	2,388	8,729	3,010	2,040	679	191	100	1,611	1,309	1,182	188	372
Career Adj. to 10,000 AB	1907-1928	0.980873	2,736	10,000	3,448	2,336	778	219	115	1,845	1,500	1,355	216	426
10 Year Total	1916-1925		1,369	5,007	1,801	1,201	434	100	66	983	798	763	131	147
5 Year Total	1920-1924		698	2,544	943	597	245	53	48	556	448	407	64	35
Best Single Year	1923		150	574	218	131	59	11	17	133	130	93	15	10
2nd Best Year	1912		153	580	222	147	53	12	10	136	90	82	-	52
3rd Best Year	1920		150	552	214	145	50	11	8	137	107	97	13	10

Complete Career Statistics S — *10 Year Total* — *5 Year Total*

Total Career Statistics & Adjusted Career, 10 year, 5 year, and Single Year Analysis

Speaker, Tris

CS	HBP	SF	GDP	AVG	OBP	SLG	Total Offensive Production Statistics				TRP Rating	RPA Rating	TNB Rating	TBA Rating	TOP Composite		
							TRP	RPA	TNB	TBA					TOP	Rating	Ranking
-	-	-	-	.158	.200	.158	1	.050	4	.200	0.29	9.37	0.66	22.04	32.36	8.25	
-	2	-	-	.224	.262	.293	21	.172	43	.352	6.03	32.25	7.05	38.85	84.18	21.46	
-	7	-	-	.309	.362	.443	150	.255	321	.545	43.10	47.72	52.62	60.07	203.51	51.89	
-	6	-	-	.340	.404	.468	157	.263	345	.579	45.11	49.36	56.56	63.80	214.83	54.77	
-	13	-	-	.334	.418	.502	158	.276	348	.608	45.40	51.76	57.05	67.05	221.26	56.41	
-	6	-	-	.383	.464	.567	226	.338	469	.702	64.94	63.40	76.89	77.38	282.60	72.05	
-	7	-	-	.365	.443	.535	165	.279	396	.669	47.41	52.23	64.92	73.72	238.28	60.75	
29	7	-	-	.338	.423	.503	190	.290	384	.586	54.60	54.36	62.95	64.61	236.52	60.30	
25	7	-	-	.322	.416	.411	177	.279	317	.499	50.86	52.23	51.97	55.02	210.08	53.56	
27	4	-	-	.386	.470	.502	181	.286	368	.582	52.01	53.66	60.33	64.18	230.18	58.69	
-	7	-	-	.352	.432	.486	150	.251	358	.600	43.10	47.08	58.69	66.09	214.96	54.81	
-	3	-	-	.318	.403	.435	134	.249	299	.556	38.51	46.67	49.02	61.25	195.45	49.83	
-	8	-	-	.296	.395	.433	146	.254	310	.539	41.95	47.58	50.82	59.42	199.77	50.93	
13	5	-	-	.388	.483	.562	244	.373	409	.625	70.11	69.91	67.05	68.93	276.00	70.37	
4	2	-	-	.362	.439	.538	182	.316	340	.590	52.30	59.21	55.74	65.06	232.30	59.23	
3	1	-	-	.378	.474	.606	156	.310	341	.677	44.83	58.00	55.90	74.57	233.30	59.48	
9	4	-	-	.380	.469	.610	263	.392	448	.668	75.57	73.44	73.44	73.59	296.05	75.48	
7	4	-	-	.344	.432	.510	159	.283	322	.573	45.69	53.01	52.79	63.15	214.64	54.72	
2	4	-	-	.389	.479	.578	166	.330	325	.646	47.70	61.84	53.28	71.21	234.03	59.67	
1	-	-	-	.304	.408	.469	182	.288	352	.556	52.30	53.88	57.70	61.29	225.17	57.41	
8	4	-	-	.327	.395	.444	144	.247	292	.502	41.38	46.36	47.87	55.30	190.91	48.67	
1	2	-	-	.267	.310	.455	58	.286	103	.507	16.67	53.54	16.89	55.92	143.01	36.46	
129	103	-	-	.345	.428	.501	3,410	.292	6,894	.590	76.27	69.92	81.52	78.46	306.17	78.19	15
110	88	-	-	.345	.428	.501	2,920	.292	5,903	.590	69.92	69.92	78.46	78.46	296.76	74.19	72
127	101	-	-	.345	.428	.501	3,345	.292	6,762	.590	64.04	69.92	71.87	78.46	284.28	71.07	72
65	42	-	-	.360	.448	.526	1,781	.306	3,520	.606	60.50	69.88	71.01	76.42	277.80	71.25	66
36	16	-	-	.371	.460	.565	1,004	.338	1,860	.627	65.97	72.36	71.32	76.01	285.65	73.18	83
9	4	-	-	.380	.469	.610	263	.392	448	.668	75.57	73.44	73.44	73.59	296.05	75.48	118
-	6	-	-	.383	.464	.567	226	.338	469	.702	64.94	63.40	76.89	77.38	282.60	72.05	215
13	5	-	-	.388	.483	.562	244	.373	409	.625	70.11	69.91	67.05	68.93	276.00	70.37	284

Complete Career Statistics S

Complete Career Statistics S

Total Career Statistics & Adjusted Career, 10 year, 5 year, and Single Year Analysis

Stargell, Willie: *Wilver Dornel Stargell, b. March 6, 1940, Earlsboro, OK*

Rating Category	Year	Ranked Seasons & Adjustment	G	AB	H	1B	2B	3B	HR	RUN	RBI	BB	SO	SB
	1962		10	31	9	5	3	1	-	1	4	3	10	-
	1963		108	304	74	46	11	6	11	34	47	19	85	-
	1964		117	421	115	68	19	7	21	53	78	17	92	1
	1965		144	533	145	85	25	8	27	68	107	39	127	1
	1966		140	485	153	90	30	-	33	84	102	48	109	2
10 Year Total	1967		134	462	125	81	18	6	20	54	73	67	103	1
	1968		128	435	103	63	15	1	24	57	67	47	105	5
	1969		145	522	160	94	31	6	29	89	92	61	120	1
	1970		136	474	125	73	18	3	31	70	85	44	119	-
	1971	2nd	141	511	151	77	26	-	48	104	125	83	154	-
5 Year Total	1972		138	495	145	82	28	2	33	75	112	65	129	1
	1973	1st	148	522	156	66	43	3	44	106	119	80	129	-
	1974		140	508	153	87	37	4	25	90	96	87	106	-
	1975		124	461	136	80	32	2	22	71	90	58	109	-
	1976		117	428	110	67	20	3	20	54	65	50	101	2
	1977		63	186	51	26	12	-	13	29	35	31	55	-
	1978		122	390	115	67	18	2	28	60	97	50	93	3
	1979		126	424	119	68	19	-	32	60	82	47	105	-
	1980		67	202	53	31	10	1	11	28	38	26	52	-
	1981		38	60	17	13	4	-	-	2	9	5	9	-
	1982		74	73	17	10	4	-	3	6	17	10	24	-
Career Total	1962-1982		2,360	7,927	2,232	1,279	423	55	475	1,195	1,540	937	1,936	17
Career Adj. to 10,000 BO	1962-1982	1.091703	2,576	8,654	2,437	1,396	462	60	519	1,305	1,681	1,023	2,114	19
Career Adj. to 10,000 AB	1962-1982	1.261511	2,977	10,000	2,816	1,613	534	69	599	1,508	1,943	1,182	2,442	21
10 Year Total	1965-1974		1,394	4,947	1,416	798	271	33	314	797	978	621	1,201	11
5 Year Total	1971-1975		691	2,497	741	392	166	11	172	446	542	373	627	1
Best Single Year	1973		148	522	156	66	43	3	44	106	119	80	129	-
2nd Best Year	1971		141	511	151	77	26	-	48	104	125	83	154	-

Total Career Statistics & Adjusted Career, 10 year, 5 year, and Single Year Analysis

Stargell, Willie

CS	HBP	SF	GDP	AVG	OBP	SLG	Total Offensive Production Statistics				TRP Rating	RPA Rating	TNB Rating	TBA Rating	TOP Composite		
							TRP	RPA	TNB	TBA					TOP	Rating	Ranking
1	-	-	-	.290	.353	.452	5	.147	16	.471	1.44	27.56	2.62	51.87	83.48	21.28	
2	2	3	6	.243	.290	.428	81	.243	149	.446	23.28	45.44	24.43	49.17	142.31	36.28	
1	2	1	7	.273	.304	.501	131	.292	230	.513	37.64	54.79	37.70	56.58	186.72	47.61	
1	7	3	8	.272	.328	.501	175	.297	313	.531	50.29	55.58	51.31	58.47	215.65	54.98	
3	6	5	7	.315	.381	.581	186	.338	335	.608	53.45	63.25	54.92	67.01	238.63	60.84	
-	3	2	12	.271	.365	.465	127	.233	286	.524	36.49	43.59	46.89	57.73	184.70	47.09	
-	6	7	12	.237	.315	.441	124	.245	250	.493	35.63	45.83	40.98	54.35	176.79	45.07	
-	6	5	10	.307	.382	.556	181	.300	358	.593	52.01	56.15	58.69	65.33	232.18	59.20	
1	5	6	14	.264	.329	.511	155	.285	290	.534	44.54	53.49	47.54	58.86	204.43	52.12	
-	7	5	8	.295	.398	.628	229	.373	411	.669	65.80	69.89	67.38	73.78	276.84	70.58	
1	2	7	7	.293	.373	.558	187	.325	343	.595	53.74	60.83	56.23	65.63	236.43	60.28	
-	3	4	6	.299	.392	.646	225	.366	420	.683	64.66	68.55	68.85	75.27	277.33	70.71	
2	6	4	8	.301	.407	.537	186	.303	364	.594	53.45	56.86	59.67	65.45	235.42	60.02	
-	3	4	9	.295	.375	.516	161	.301	299	.559	46.26	56.39	49.02	61.60	213.27	54.37	
-	5	4	4	.257	.339	.458	119	.242	253	.515	34.20	45.41	41.48	56.79	177.88	45.35	
1	3	2	4	.274	.383	.548	64	.283	135	.597	18.39	53.06	22.13	65.84	159.42	40.65	
2	7	3	8	.295	.382	.567	157	.343	279	.609	45.11	64.23	45.74	67.14	222.23	56.66	
1	3	6	10	.281	.352	.552	142	.290	283	.578	40.80	54.30	46.39	63.65	205.15	52.31	
-	2	1	2	.262	.351	.485	66	.283	126	.541	18.97	53.08	20.66	59.60	152.30	38.83	
-	-	1	-	.283	.333	.350	11	.167	26	.394	3.16	31.23	4.26	43.42	82.07	20.92	
-	-	2	1	.233	.318	.411	23	.267	40	.465	6.61	50.11	6.56	51.26	114.54	29.20	
16	78	75	143	.282	.360	.529	2,735	.299	5,206	.568	61.17	71.50	61.56	75.55	269.77	68.90	55
17	85	82	156	.282	.360	.529	2,986	.299	5,683	.568	71.50	71.50	75.55	75.55	294.09	73.52	75
20	98	95	180	.282	.360	.529	3,450	.299	6,567	.568	66.06	71.50	69.80	75.55	282.90	70.72	74
8	51	48	92	.286	.368	.545	1,775	.308	3,370	.585	60.29	70.29	67.98	73.83	272.40	69.87	77
3	21	24	38	.297	.389	.579	988	.335	1,837	.622	64.91	71.55	70.44	75.42	282.32	72.33	86
-	3	4	6	.299	.392	.646	225	.366	420	.683	64.66	68.55	68.85	75.27	277.33	70.71	257
-	7	5	8	.295	.398	.628	229	.373	411	.669	65.80	69.89	67.38	73.78	276.84	70.58	265

Complete Career Statistics **S**

Complete Career Statistics S

Total Career Statistics & Adjusted Career, 10 year, 5 year, and Single Year Analysis

Stovey, Harry: *Harry Duffield Stovey (Stowe), b. Dec. 20, 1856, Philadelphia, PA*

Rating Category	Year	Ranked Seasons & Adjustment	G	AB	H	1B	2B	3B	HR	RUN	RBI	BB	SO	SB
	1880		83	355	94	53	21	14	6	76	28	12	46	-
	1881		75	341	92	58	25	7	2	57	30	12	23	-
	1882		84	360	104	76	13	10	5	90	26	22	34	-
	1883		94	421	128	77	31	6	14	110	66	27	-	-
	1884		104	448	146	91	22	23	10	124	83	26	-	-
	1885		112	486	153	104	27	9	13	130	75	39	-	-
10 Year Total	1886		123	489	144	98	28	11	7	115	59	64	-	68
5 Year Total	1887		124	553	198	151	31	12	4	125	77	56	-	74
	1888		130	530	152	98	25	20	9	127	65	62	-	87
	1889	1st	137	556	171	101	38	13	19	152	119	77	68	63
	1890	2nd	118	481	143	95	25	11	12	142	84	81	38	97
	1891		134	544	152	85	31	20	16	118	95	79	69	57
	1892		113	429	101	63	22	12	4	79	67	54	51	40
	1893		56	201	48	33	8	6	1	47	34	52	14	23
Career Total	1880-1893		1,487	6,194	1,826	1,183	347	174	122	1,492	908	663	343	509
Career Adj. to 10,000 BO	1880-1893	1.451800	2,159	8,992	2,651	1,717	504	253	177	2,166	1,318	963	498	739
Career Adj. to 10,000 AB	1880-1893	1.614466	2,401	10,000	2,948	1,910	560	281	197	2,409	1,466	1,070	554	822
10 Year Total	1883-1892		1,189	4,937	1,488	963	280	137	108	1,222	790	565	226	486
5 Year Total	1887-1891		643	2,664	816	530	150	76	60	664	440	355	175	378
Best Single Year	1889		137	556	171	101	38	13	19	152	119	77	68	63
2nd Best Year	1890		118	481	143	95	25	11	12	142	84	81	38	97

Total Career Statistics & Adjusted Career, 10 year, 5 year, and Single Year Analysis

Stovey, Harry

CS	HBP	SF	GDP	AVG	OBP	SLG	Total Offensive Production Statistics				TRP Rating	RPA Rating	TNB Rating	TBA Rating	TOP Composite		
							TRP	RPA	TNB	TBA					TOP	Rating	Ranking
-	-	-	-	.265	.289	.454	104	.283	173	.471	29.89	53.10	28.36	51.95	163.30	41.63	
-	-	-	-	.270	.295	.402	87	.246	149	.422	25.00	46.18	24.43	46.52	142.13	36.24	
-	-	-	-	.289	.330	.422	116	.304	174	.455	33.33	56.90	28.52	50.20	168.96	43.08	
-	-	-	-	.304	.346	.506	176	.393	240	.536	50.57	73.61	39.34	59.04	222.58	56.75	
-	4	-	-	.326	.368	.545	207	.433	274	.573	59.48	81.15	44.92	63.18	248.72	63.41	
-	4	-	-	.315	.371	.488	205	.388	280	.529	58.91	72.61	45.90	58.34	235.76	60.11	
-	1	-	-	.294	.377	.440	174	.314	348	.628	50.00	58.85	57.05	69.23	235.13	59.95	
-	7	-	-	.358	.424	.479	202	.328	402	.653	58.05	61.45	65.90	71.93	257.32	65.61	
-	3	-	-	.287	.365	.460	192	.323	396	.666	55.17	60.47	64.92	73.35	253.91	64.74	
-	1	-	-	.308	.393	.525	271	.427	433	.683	77.87	80.10	70.98	75.27	304.22	77.56	
-	5	-	-	.297	.404	.470	226	.399	409	.721	64.94	74.69	67.05	79.50	286.18	72.96	
-	2	-	-	.279	.373	.498	213	.341	409	.654	61.21	63.86	67.05	72.12	264.24	67.37	
-	4	-	-	.235	.326	.371	146	.300	257	.528	41.95	56.18	42.13	58.16	198.42	50.59	
-	-	-	-	.239	.395	.353	81	.320	146	.577	23.28	59.99	23.93	63.60	170.80	43.55	
-	31	-	-	.295	.366	.466	2,400	.348	4,090	.594	53.68	83.43	48.36	78.93	264.40	67.52	66
-	45	-	-	.295	.366	.466	3,484	.348	5,938	.594	83.43	83.43	78.93	78.93	324.73	81.18	20
-	50	-	-	.295	.366	.466	3,875	.348	6,603	.594	74.18	83.43	70.18	78.93	306.72	76.68	31
-	31	-	-	.301	.377	.479	2,012	.364	3,448	.623	68.34	82.92	69.56	78.63	299.45	76.81	40
-	18	-	-	.306	.392	.487	1,104	.364	2,049	.675	72.54	77.74	78.57	81.80	310.64	79.58	37
-	1	-	-	.308	.393	.525	271	.427	433	.683	77.87	80.10	70.98	75.27	304.22	77.56	84
-	5	-	-	.297	.404	.470	226	.399	409	.721	64.94	74.69	67.05	79.50	286.18	72.96	179

Complete Career Statistics S

Total Career Statistics & Adjusted Career, 10 year, 5 year, and Single Year Analysis

Terry, Bill: *William Harold "Memphis Bill" Terry, b. Oct. 30, 1898, Atlanta, GA*

Rating Category	Year	Ranked Seasons & Adjustment	G	AB	H	1B	2B	3B	HR	RUN	RBI	BB	SO	SB
	1923		3	7	1	1	-	-	-	1	-	2	2	-
	1924		77	163	39	25	7	2	5	26	24	17	18	1
	1925		133	489	156	108	31	6	11	75	70	42	52	4
	1926		98	225	65	43	12	5	5	26	43	22	17	3
	1927		150	580	189	124	32	13	20	101	121	46	53	1
	1928		149	568	185	121	36	11	17	100	101	64	36	7
	1929		150	607	226	168	39	5	14	103	117	48	35	10
10 Year Total / 5 Year Total	1930	1st	154	633	254	177	39	15	23	139	129	57	33	8
	1931		153	611	213	141	43	20	9	121	112	47	36	8
	1932		154	643	225	144	42	11	28	124	117	32	23	4
	1933		123	475	153	122	20	5	6	68	58	40	23	3
	1934		153	602	213	169	30	6	8	109	83	60	47	-
	1935		145	596	203	157	32	8	6	91	64	41	55	7
	1936		79	229	71	54	10	5	2	36	39	19	19	-
Career Total	1923-1936		1,721	6,428	2,193	1,554	373	112	154	1,120	1,078	537	449	56
Career Adj. to 10,000 BO	1923-1936	1.426127	2,454	9,167	3,127	2,216	532	160	220	1,597	1,537	766	640	80
Career Adj. to 10,000 AB	1923-1936	1.555694	2,677	10,000	3,412	2,418	580	174	240	1,742	1,677	835	699	87
10 Year Total	1926-1935		1,429	5,540	1,926	1,366	325	99	136	982	945	457	358	51
5 Year Total	1928-1932		760	3,062	1,103	751	199	62	91	587	576	248	163	37
Best Single Year	1930		154	633	254	177	39	15	23	139	129	57	33	8

Total Career Statistics & Adjusted Career, 10 year, 5 year, and Single Year Analysis

Terry, Bill

CS	HBP	SF	GDP	AVG	OBP	SLG	Total Offensive Production Statistics				TRP Rating	RPA Rating	TNB Rating	TBA Rating	TOP Composite		
							TRP	RPA	TNB	TBA					TOP	Rating	Ranking
-	-	-	-	.143	.333	.143	1	.111	3	.333	0.29	20.82	0.49	36.74	58.34	14.87	
1	-	-	-	.239	.311	.399	50	.278	82	.456	14.37	52.05	13.44	50.21	130.07	33.16	
5	1	-	-	.319	.374	.474	145	.273	274	.515	41.67	51.07	44.92	56.76	194.42	49.57	
-	-	-	-	.289	.352	.453	69	.279	127	.514	19.83	52.35	20.82	56.67	149.66	38.16	
-	2	-	-	.326	.377	.529	222	.354	356	.567	63.79	66.24	58.36	62.48	250.87	63.96	
-	-	-	-	.326	.394	.518	201	.318	365	.578	57.76	59.59	59.84	63.65	240.84	61.40	
-	-	-	-	.372	.418	.522	220	.336	375	.573	63.22	62.94	61.48	63.10	250.73	63.93	
-	1	-	-	.401	.452	.619	268	.388	458	.663	77.01	72.67	75.08	73.05	297.82	75.93	
-	2	-	-	.349	.397	.529	233	.353	380	.576	66.95	66.15	62.30	63.46	258.86	66.00	
-	1	-	-	.350	.382	.580	241	.357	410	.607	69.25	66.80	67.21	66.85	270.12	68.87	
-	-	-	10	.322	.375	.423	126	.240	244	.465	36.21	44.97	40.00	51.22	172.40	43.96	
-	2	-	8	.354	.414	.463	192	.286	341	.507	55.17	53.54	55.90	55.93	220.54	56.23	
-	-	-	13	.341	.383	.451	155	.238	317	.488	44.54	44.68	51.97	53.75	194.94	49.70	
-	-	-	7	.310	.363	.424	75	.294	116	.455	21.55	55.11	19.02	50.14	145.82	37.18	
6	9	-	38	.341	.393	.506	2,198	.313	3,848	.549	49.16	75.06	45.50	72.95	242.67	61.97	97
9	13	-	54	.341	.393	.506	3,135	.313	5,488	.549	75.06	75.06	72.95	72.95	296.01	74.00	73
9	14	-	59	.341	.393	.506	3,419	.313	5,986	.549	65.47	75.06	63.62	72.95	277.09	69.27	82
-	8	-	31	.348	.398	.516	1,927	.319	3,373	.559	65.46	72.80	68.05	70.51	276.81	71.00	70
-	4	-	-	.360	.409	.555	1,163	.351	1,988	.600	76.41	75.05	76.23	72.73	300.42	76.96	51
-	1	-	-	.401	.452	.619	268	.388	458	.663	77.01	72.67	75.08	73.05	297.82	75.93	109

Complete Career Statistics   T

Total Career Statistics & Adjusted Career, 10 year, 5 year, and Single Year Analysis

Thomas, Frank; *Frank Edward "The Big Hurt" Thomas, b. May 27, 1968, Columbus, GA*

Rating Category	Year	Ranked Seasons & Adjustment	G	AB	H	1B	2B	3B	HR	RUN	RBI	BB	SO	SB
	1990		60	191	63	42	11	3	7	39	31	44	54	-
	1991		158	559	178	113	31	2	32	104	109	138	112	1
	1992		160	573	185	113	46	2	24	108	115	122	88	6
	1993	5th	153	549	174	97	36	-	41	106	128	112	54	4
	1994	3rd	113	399	141	68	34	1	38	106	101	109	61	2
	1995		145	493	152	85	27	-	40	102	111	136	74	3
	1996	2nd	141	527	184	118	26	-	40	110	134	109	70	1
	1997	4th	146	530	184	114	35	-	35	110	125	109	69	1
	1998		160	585	155	89	35	2	29	109	109	110	93	7
	1999		135	486	148	97	36	-	15	74	77	87	66	3
	2000	1st	159	582	191	104	44	-	43	115	143	112	94	1
	2001		20	68	15	8	3	-	4	8	10	10	12	-
	2002		148	523	132	74	29	1	28	77	92	88	115	3
	2003		153	546	146	69	35	-	42	87	105	100	115	-
	2004		74	240	65	31	16	-	18	53	49	64	57	-
Career Total**	1990-2004		1,925	6,851	2,113	1,222	444	11	436	1,308	1,439	1,450	1,134	32
Career Adj. to 10,000 BO**	1990-2004	1.154068	2,222	7,907	2,439	1,410	512	13	503	1,510	1,661	1,673	1,309	37
Career Adj. to 10,000 AB**	1990-2004	1.459641	2,810	10,000	3,084	1,784	648	16	636	1,909	2,100	2,116	1,655	47
10 Year Total**	1991-2000		1,470	5,283	1,692	998	350	7	337	1,044	1,152	1,144	781	29
5 Year Total**	1993-1998		698	2,498	835	482	158	1	194	534	599	575	328	11
Best Single Year**	2000		159	582	191	104	44	-	43	115	143	112	94	1
2nd Best Year**	1996		141	527	184	118	26	-	40	110	134	109	70	1
3rd Best Year**	1994		113	399	141	68	34	1	38	106	101	109	61	2
4th Best Year**	1997		146	530	184	114	35	-	35	110	125	109	69	1
5th Best Year**	1993		153	549	174	97	36	-	41	106	128	112	54	4

Left margin: **Complete Career Statistics T**

Within table (vertical labels): **10 Year Total**, **5 Year Total**

Total Career Statistics & Adjusted Career, 10 year, 5 year, and Single Year Analysis

Thomas, Frank

CS	HBP	SF	GDP	AVG	OBP	SLG	Total Offensive Production Statistics				TRP Rating	RPA Rating	TNB Rating	TBA Rating	TOP Composite		
							TRP	RPA	TNB	TBA					TOP	Rating	Ranking
1	2	3	5	.330	.454	.529	70	.286	146	.596	20.11	53.54	23.93	65.68	163.27	41.63	
2	1	2	20	.318	.453	.553	213	.296	447	.621	61.21	55.43	73.28	68.42	258.34	65.87	
3	5	11	19	.323	.439	.536	223	.305	437	.599	64.08	57.24	71.64	65.98	258.94	66.02	
2	2	13	10	.317	.426	.607	234	.341	449	.655	67.24	63.92	73.61	72.14	276.90	70.60	
3	2	7	15	.353	.487	.729	207	.389	401	.754	59.48	72.91	65.74	83.07	281.21	71.70	
2	6	12	14	.308	.454	.606	213	.322	442	.669	61.21	60.38	72.46	73.70	267.75	68.26	
1	5	8	25	.349	.459	.626	244	.362	444	.659	70.11	67.84	72.79	72.60	283.34	72.24	
1	3	7	15	.347	.456	.611	235	.354	436	.657	67.53	66.32	71.48	72.37	277.69	70.80	
-	6	11	14	.265	.381	.480	218	.300	404	.556	62.64	56.27	66.23	61.33	246.47	62.84	
3	9	8	14	.305	.414	.471	151	.250	325	.538	43.39	46.77	53.28	59.21	202.64	51.67	
3	5	8	13	.328	.436	.625	258	.358	479	.665	74.14	67.15	78.52	73.32	293.13	74.74	
-	-	1	-	.221	.316	.441	18	.228	40	.506	5.17	42.69	6.56	55.80	110.23	28.10	
-	7	10	10	.252	.361	.472	169	.265	345	.541	48.56	49.64	56.56	59.60	214.35	54.65	
-	12	4	11	.267	.390	.562	192	.285	419	.623	55.17	53.46	68.69	68.62	245.94	62.70	
2	6	1	2	.271	.434	.563	102	.326	203	.649	29.31	61.06	33.28	71.48	195.13	49.75	
23	71	106	187	.308	.429	.567	2,747	.317	5,417	.625	61.44	75.91	64.05	83.10	284.51	72.66	30
27	82	122	216	.308	.429	.567	3,170	.317	6,252	.625	75.91	75.91	83.10	83.10	318.02	79.51	29
34	104	155	273	.308	.429	.567	4,010	.317	7,907	.625	76.77	75.91	84.03	83.10	319.81	79.95	15
20	44	87	159	.320	.439	.581	2,196	.327	4,264	.635	74.59	74.55	86.02	80.10	315.26	80.86	21
9	18	47	79	.334	.455	.631	1,133	.352	2,172	.675	74.44	75.31	83.28	81.86	314.90	80.67	32
3	5	8	13	.328	.436	.625	258	.358	479	.665	74.14	67.15	78.52	73.32	293.13	74.74	132
1	5	8	25	.349	.459	.626	244	.362	444	.659	70.11	67.84	72.79	72.60	283.34	72.24	206
3	2	7	15	.353	.487	.729	207	.389	401	.754	59.48	72.91	65.74	83.07	281.21	71.70	228
1	3	7	15	.347	.456	.611	235	.354	436	.657	67.53	66.32	71.48	72.37	277.69	70.80	253
2	2	13	10	.317	.426	.607	234	.341	449	.655	67.24	63.92	73.61	72.14	276.90	70.60	263

Complete Career Statistics   T

Total Career Statistics & Adjusted Career, 10 year, 5 year, and Single Year Analysis

Thome, Jim: *James Howard Thome, b. Aug. 27, 1970, Peoria, IL*

Rating Category		Year	Ranked Seasons & Adjustment	G	AB	H	1B	2B	3B	HR	RUN	RBI	BB	SO	SB
		1991		27	98	25	18	4	2	1	7	9	5	16	1
		1992		40	117	24	18	3	1	2	8	12	10	34	2
		1993		47	154	41	23	11	-	7	28	22	29	36	2
		1994		98	321	86	45	20	1	20	58	52	46	84	3
		1995		137	452	142	85	29	3	25	92	73	97	113	4
		1996	2nd	151	505	157	86	28	5	38	122	116	123	141	2
		1997		147	496	142	77	25	-	40	104	102	120	146	1
		1998		123	440	129	63	34	2	30	89	85	89	141	1
10 Year Total	5 Year Total	1999		146	494	137	75	27	2	33	101	108	127	171	-
		2000		158	557	150	79	33	1	37	106	106	118	171	1
		2001	3rd	156	526	153	77	26	1	49	101	124	111	185	-
		2002	1st	147	480	146	73	19	2	52	101	118	122	139	1
		2003	4th	159	578	154	74	30	3	47	111	131	111	182	-
		2004		143	508	139	68	28	1	42	97	105	104	144	-
Career Total**		1991-2004		1,679	5,726	1,625	861	317	24	423	1,125	1,163	1,212	1,703	18
Career Adj. to 10,000 BO**		1991-2004	1.400756	2,352	8,021	2,276	1,206	444	34	593	1,576	1,629	1,698	2,385	25
Career Adj. to 10,000 AB**		1991-2004	1.746420	2,932	10,000	2,838	1,504	554	42	739	1,965	2,031	2,117	2,974	31
10 Year Total**		1995-2004		1,467	5,036	1,449	757	279	20	393	1,024	1,068	1,122	1,533	10
5 Year Total**		1999-2003		766	2,635	740	378	135	9	218	520	587	589	848	2
Best Single Year**		2002		147	480	146	73	19	2	52	101	118	122	139	1
2nd Best Year**		1996		151	505	157	86	28	5	38	122	116	123	141	2
3rd Best Year**		2001		156	526	153	77	26	1	49	101	124	111	185	-
4th Best Year**		2003		159	578	154	74	30	3	47	111	131	111	182	-

Complete Career Statistics T

Total Career Statistics & Adjusted Career, 10 year, 5 year, and Single Year Analysis

Thome, Jim

CS	HBP	SF	GDP	AVG	OBP	SLG	Total Offensive Production Statistics				TRP Rating	RPA Rating	TNB Rating	TBA Rating	TOP Composite		
							TRP	RPA	TNB	TBA					TOP	Rating	Ranking
1	1	-	4	.255	.298	.367	16	.148	42	.389	4.60	27.76	6.89	42.86	82.10	20.93	
-	2	2	3	.205	.275	.299	20	.149	49	.366	5.75	27.97	8.03	40.30	82.05	20.92	
1	4	5	3	.266	.385	.474	50	.256	107	.549	14.37	48.05	17.54	60.48	140.43	35.80	
3	-	1	11	.268	.359	.523	110	.290	214	.565	31.61	54.39	35.08	62.23	183.31	46.74	
3	5	3	8	.314	.438	.558	165	.292	355	.628	47.41	54.72	58.20	69.25	229.58	58.53	
2	6	2	13	.311	.450	.612	238	.367	438	.675	68.39	68.72	71.80	74.38	283.29	72.23	
1	3	8	9	.286	.423	.579	206	.324	410	.645	59.20	60.69	67.21	71.05	258.15	65.82	
-	4	4	7	.293	.413	.584	174	.320	351	.645	50.00	59.93	57.54	71.11	238.59	60.83	
-	4	4	6	.277	.426	.540	209	.329	398	.627	60.06	61.67	65.25	69.08	256.06	65.28	
-	4	5	8	.269	.398	.531	212	.306	419	.605	60.92	57.41	68.69	66.73	253.75	64.70	
1	4	3	9	.291	.416	.624	225	.345	442	.677	64.66	64.56	72.46	74.60	276.28	70.44	
2	5	6	5	.304	.445	.677	219	.354	451	.730	62.93	66.40	73.93	80.43	283.70	72.33	
3	4	5	5	.266	.385	.573	242	.344	443	.630	69.54	64.50	72.62	69.45	276.12	70.40	
2	2	4	10	.274	.396	.581	202	.322	399	.635	58.05	60.27	65.41	70.02	253.75	64.70	
19	48	52	101	.284	.410	.569	2,288	.320	4,518	.633	51.17	76.74	53.42	84.12	265.46	67.79	64
27	67	73	141	.284	.410	.569	3,205	.320	6,329	.633	76.74	76.74	84.12	84.12	321.73	80.43	22
33	84	91	176	.284	.410	.569	3,996	.320	7,890	.633	76.50	76.74	83.86	84.12	321.22	80.31	13
14	41	44	80	.288	.418	.585	2,092	.331	4,106	.649	71.06	75.45	82.83	81.93	311.28	79.84	24
6	21	23	33	.281	.413	.587	1,107	.335	2,153	.652	72.73	71.71	82.55	79.08	306.08	78.42	40
2	5	6	5	.304	.445	.677	219	.354	451	.730	62.93	66.40	73.93	80.43	283.70	72.33	202
2	6	2	13	.311	.450	.612	238	.367	438	.675	68.39	68.72	71.80	74.38	283.29	72.23	208
1	4	3	9	.291	.416	.624	225	.345	442	.677	64.66	64.56	72.46	74.60	276.28	70.44	276
3	4	5	5	.266	.385	.573	242	.344	443	.630	69.54	64.50	72.62	69.45	276.12	70.40	282

Complete Career Statistics T

Total Career Statistics & Adjusted Career, 10 year, 5 year, and Single Year Analysis

Thompson, Sam; *Samuel Luther "Big Sam" Thompson, b. March 5, 1860, Danville, IN*

Rating Category	Year	Ranked Seasons & Adjustment	G	AB	H	1B	2B	3B	HR	RUN	RBI	BB	SO	SB
	1885		63	254	77	52	11	7	7	58	44	16	22	-
	1886		122	503	156	125	19	4	8	100	89	35	31	13
	1887	3rd	127	576	234	172	29	23	10	118	166	32	19	22
	1888		55	238	67	44	9	8	6	51	40	23	10	5
	1889		128	533	158	99	35	4	20	103	111	36	22	24
	1890		132	549	172	121	38	9	4	114	102	42	29	25
10 Year Total	1891		133	551	163	127	20	9	7	108	90	52	20	33
	1892		151	602	183	135	31	8	9	109	104	59	19	30
5 Year Total	1893	4th	130	583	220	162	33	14	11	130	126	50	17	18
	1894	2nd	102	458	185	117	29	26	13	115	141	40	13	29
	1895	1st	118	533	210	128	42	22	18	131	165	31	11	24
	1896		119	517	158	112	27	7	12	103	100	28	13	11
	1897		3	13	3	2	-	1	-	2	3	1	-	-
	1898		14	63	23	16	3	3	1	13	15	4	-	2
	1906		8	31	7	6	-	1	-	4	3	1	-	-
Career Total	1885-1906		1,405	6,004	2,016	1,418	326	146	126	1,259	1,299	450	226	236
Career Adj. to 10,000 BO	1885-1906	1.534448	2,156	9,213	3,093	2,176	500	224	193	1,932	1,993	691	347	362
Career Adj. to 10,000 AB	1885-1906	1.665556	2,340	10,000	3,358	2,362	543	243	210	2,097	2,164	750	376	393
10 Year Total	1887-1896		1,195	5,140	1,750	1,217	293	130	110	1,082	1,145	393	173	221
5 Year Total	1892-1896		620	2,693	956	654	162	77	63	588	636	208	73	112
Best Single Year	1895		118	533	210	128	42	22	18	131	165	31	11	24
2nd Best Year	1894		102	458	185	117	29	26	13	115	141	40	13	29
3rd Best Year	1887		127	576	234	172	29	23	10	118	166	32	19	22
4th Best Year	1893		130	583	220	162	33	14	11	130	126	50	17	18

Total Career Statistics & Adjusted Career, 10 year, 5 year, and Single Year Analysis

Thompson, Sam

CS	HBP	SF	GDP	AVG	OBP	SLG	Total Offensive Production Statistics				TRP Rating	RPA Rating	TNB Rating	TBA Rating	TOP Composite		
							TRP	RPA	TNB	TBA					TOP	Rating	Ranking
-	-	-	-	.303	.344	.484	102	.378	139	.515	29.31	70.79	22.79	56.74	179.63	45.80	
-	-	-	-	.310	.355	.412	189	.351	255	.474	54.31	65.83	41.80	52.24	214.18	54.61	
-	9	-	-	.406	.446	.589	284	.460	402	.652	81.61	86.25	65.90	71.81	305.57	77.91	
-	3	-	-	.282	.352	.462	91	.345	141	.534	26.15	64.59	23.11	58.86	172.72	44.04	
-	6	-	-	.296	.348	.490	214	.372	327	.569	61.49	69.74	53.61	62.68	247.52	63.11	
-	8	-	-	.313	.371	.437	216	.361	315	.526	62.07	67.57	51.64	57.96	239.24	61.00	
-	8	-	-	.296	.365	.403	198	.324	315	.516	56.90	60.72	51.64	56.82	226.08	57.64	
-	11	-	-	.304	.376	.427	213	.317	357	.531	61.21	59.39	58.52	58.55	237.68	60.60	
-	6	-	-	.377	.432	.539	256	.401	388	.607	73.56	75.07	63.61	66.92	279.16	71.17	
-	1	-	-	.404	.453	.666	256	.513	375	.752	73.56	96.13	61.48	82.83	314.00	80.06	
-	5	-	-	.394	.432	.657	296	.520	410	.721	85.06	97.48	67.21	79.42	329.16	83.92	
-	6	-	-	.306	.348	.455	203	.368	280	.508	58.33	69.04	45.90	56.01	229.28	58.46	
-	-	-	-	.231	.286	.385	5	.357	6	.429	1.44	66.92	0.98	47.23	116.58	29.72	
-	-	-	-	.365	.403	.556	28	.418	41	.612	8.05	78.31	6.72	67.44	160.52	40.93	
-	-	-	-	.226	.250	.290	7	.219	10	.313	2.01	40.99	1.64	34.44	79.08	20.16	
-	63	-	-	.336	.388	.502	2,558	.393	3,761	.577	57.21	93.99	44.47	76.71	272.39	69.56	52
-	97	-	-	.336	.388	.502	3,925	.393	5,771	.577	93.99	93.99	76.71	76.71	341.40	85.35	9
-	105	-	-	.336	.388	.502	4,260	.393	6,264	.577	81.57	93.99	66.57	76.71	318.84	79.71	19
-	63	-	-	.340	.394	.512	2,227	.398	3,310	.591	75.65	90.75	66.77	74.63	307.80	78.95	27
-	29	-	-	.355	.407	.543	1,224	.418	1,810	.618	80.42	89.33	69.40	74.90	314.05	80.46	33
-	5	-	-	.394	.432	.657	296	.520	410	.721	85.06	97.48	67.21	79.42	329.16	83.92	30
-	1	-	-	.404	.453	.666	256	.513	375	.752	73.56	96.13	61.48	82.83	314.00	80.06	55
-	9	-	-	.406	.446	.589	284	.460	402	.652	81.61	86.25	65.90	71.81	305.57	77.91	79
-	6	-	-	.377	.432	.539	256	.401	388	.607	73.56	75.07	63.61	66.92	279.16	71.17	245

Complete Career Statistics   T

Total Career Statistics & Adjusted Career, 10 year, 5 year, and Single Year Analysis

Traynor, Pie: *Harold Joseph Traynor; b. Nov. 11, 1899, Framingham, MA*

Rating Category	Year	Ranked Seasons & Adjustment	G	AB	H	1B	2B	3B	HR	RUN	RBI	BB	SO	SB
	1920		17	52	11	7	3	1	-	6	2	3	6	1
	1921		7	19	5	5	-	-	-	-	2	1	2	-
	1922		142	571	161	128	17	12	4	89	81	27	28	17
	1923		153	616	208	158	19	19	12	108	101	34	19	28
	1924		142	545	160	116	26	13	5	86	82	37	26	24
	1925		150	591	189	130	39	14	6	114	106	52	19	15
10 Year Total	1926		152	574	182	137	25	17	3	83	92	38	14	8
5 Year Total	1927		149	573	196	150	32	9	5	93	106	22	11	11
	1928		144	569	192	139	38	12	3	91	124	28	10	12
	1929		130	540	192	149	27	12	4	94	108	30	7	13
	1930	1st	130	497	182	140	22	11	9	90	119	48	19	7
	1931		155	615	183	129	37	15	2	81	103	54	28	6
	1932		135	513	169	130	27	10	2	74	68	32	20	6
	1933		154	624	190	156	27	6	1	85	82	35	24	5
	1934		119	444	137	104	22	10	1	62	61	21	27	3
	1935		57	204	57	43	10	3	1	24	36	10	17	2
	1937		5	12	2	2	-	-	-	3	-	-	1	-
Career Total	1920-1937		1,941	7,559	2,416	1,823	371	164	58	1,183	1,273	472	278	158
Career Adj. to 10,000 BO	1920-1937	1.233198	2,394	9,322	2,979	2,248	458	202	72	1,459	1,570	582	343	195
Career Adj. to 10,000 AB	1920-1937	1.322926	2,568	10,000	3,196	2,412	491	217	77	1,565	1,684	624	368	209
10 Year Total	1922-1931		1,447	5,691	1,845	1,376	282	134	53	929	1,022	370	181	141
5 Year Total	1927-1931		708	2,794	945	707	156	59	23	449	560	182	75	49
Best Single Year	1930		130	497	182	140	22	11	9	90	119	48	19	7

Complete Career Statistics T

Total Career Statistics & Adjusted Career, 10 year, 5 year, and Single Year Analysis

Traynor, Pie

CS	HBP	SF	GDP	AVG	OBP	SLG	TRP	RPA	TNB	TBA	TRP Rating	RPA Rating	TNB Rating	TBA Rating	TOP	Rating	Ranking
3	1	-	-	.212	.268	.308	8	.143	18	.321	2.30	26.77	2.95	35.43	67.44	17.20	
-	-	-	-	.263	.300	.263	2	.100	6	.300	0.57	18.74	0.98	33.06	53.36	13.60	
3	4	-	-	.282	.319	.375	170	.282	259	.430	48.85	52.92	42.46	47.42	191.64	48.86	
13	5	-	-	.338	.377	.489	209	.319	355	.542	60.06	59.79	58.20	59.73	237.78	60.62	
18	1	-	-	.294	.340	.417	168	.288	271	.465	48.28	54.00	44.43	51.23	197.93	50.46	
9	2	-	-	.320	.377	.464	220	.341	334	.518	63.22	63.91	54.75	57.07	238.96	60.92	
-	1	-	-	.317	.361	.436	175	.285	297	.485	50.29	53.49	48.69	53.40	205.87	52.49	
-	3	-	-	.342	.370	.455	199	.333	297	.497	57.18	62.36	48.69	54.74	222.97	56.85	
-	1	-	-	.337	.370	.462	215	.360	304	.508	61.78	67.37	49.84	56.03	235.02	59.92	
-	3	-	-	.356	.393	.472	202	.353	301	.525	58.05	66.06	49.34	57.90	231.34	58.98	
-	1	-	-	.366	.423	.509	209	.383	309	.566	60.06	71.73	50.66	62.37	244.81	62.42	
-	-	-	-	.298	.354	.416	184	.275	316	.472	52.87	51.54	51.80	52.06	208.27	53.10	
-	4	-	-	.329	.373	.433	142	.259	264	.481	40.80	48.47	43.28	53.00	185.55	47.31	
-	1	-	14	.304	.342	.372	167	.248	273	.405	47.99	46.43	44.75	44.64	183.81	46.86	
-	1	-	23	.309	.341	.410	123	.252	207	.423	35.34	47.13	33.93	46.66	163.07	41.58	
-	3	-	9	.279	.323	.373	60	.265	91	.403	17.24	49.75	14.92	44.38	126.29	32.20	
-	-	-	1	.167	.167	.167	3	.231	2	.154	0.86	43.24	0.33	16.96	61.39	15.65	
46	31	-	47	.320	.362	.435	2,456	.303	3,904	.481	54.93	72.53	46.16	64.00	237.62	60.68	98
57	38	-	58	.320	.362	.435	3,029	.303	4,814	.481	72.53	72.53	64.00	64.00	273.04	68.26	105
61	41	-	62	.320	.362	.435	3,249	.303	5,165	.481	62.20	72.53	54.89	64.00	253.61	63.40	119
43	21	-	-	.324	.368	.449	1,951	.321	3,043	.500	66.27	73.15	61.39	63.13	263.94	67.70	93
-	8	-	-	.338	.380	.461	1,009	.338	1,527	.512	66.29	72.31	58.55	62.04	259.20	66.40	120
-	1	-	-	.366	.423	.509	209	.383	309	.566	60.06	71.73	50.66	62.37	244.81	62.42	370

Complete Career Statistics T

Total Career Statistics & Adjusted Career, 10 year, 5 year, and Single Year Analysis

Trosky, Hal: *Harold Arthur Trosky (Troyavesky), Sr., b. Nov. 11, 1912, Norway, IA*

Rating Category			Year	Ranked Seasons & Adjustment	G	AB	H	1B	2B	3B	HR	RUN	RBI	BB	SO	SB
			1933		11	44	13	9	1	2	1	6	8	2	12	-
10 Year Total	5 Year Total		1934	2nd	154	625	206	117	45	9	35	117	142	58	49	2
			1935		154	632	171	105	33	7	26	84	113	46	60	1
			1936	1st	151	629	216	120	45	9	42	124	162	36	58	6
			1937		153	601	179	102	36	9	32	104	128	65	60	3
			1938		150	554	185	117	40	9	19	106	110	67	40	5
			1939		122	448	150	90	31	4	25	89	104	52	28	2
			1940		140	522	154	86	39	4	25	85	93	79	45	1
			1941		89	310	91	63	17	-	11	43	51	44	21	1
			1944		135	497	120	76	32	2	10	55	70	62	30	3
			1946		88	299	76	59	12	3	2	22	31	34	37	4
Career Total*			1933-1946		1,347	5,161	1,561	944	331	58	228	835	1,012	545	440	28
Career Adj. to 10,000 BO*			1933-1946	1.734605	2,337	8,952	2,708	1,637	574	101	395	1,448	1,755	945	763	49
Career Adj. to 10,000 AB*			1933-1946	1.937609	2,610	10,000	3,025	1,829	641	112	442	1,618	1,961	1,056	853	54
10 Year Total*			1933-1944		1,259	4,862	1,485	885	319	55	226	813	981	511	403	24
5 Year Total*			1934-1938		762	3,041	957	561	199	43	154	535	655	272	267	17
Best Single Year			1936		151	629	216	120	45	9	42	124	162	36	58	6
2nd Best Year			1934		154	625	206	117	45	9	35	117	142	58	49	2

Complete Career Statistics T

Total Career Statistics & Adjusted Career, 10 year, 5 year, and Single Year Analysis

Trosky, Hal

CS	HBP	SF	GDP	AVG	OBP	SLG	Total Offensive Production Statistics				TRP Rating	RPA Rating	TNB Rating	TBA Rating	TOP Composite		
							TRP	RPA	TNB	TBA					TOP	Rating	Ranking
-	1	-	-	.295	.340	.477	14	.298	24	.511	4.02	55.82	3.93	56.28	120.05	30.61	
2	2	-	-	.330	.388	.598	259	.378	434	.634	74.43	70.85	71.15	69.83	286.25	72.98	
2	1	-	-	.271	.321	.468	197	.290	342	.504	56.61	54.37	56.07	55.51	222.55	56.74	
5	3	-	-	.343	.382	.644	286	.428	445	.666	82.18	80.23	72.95	73.42	308.78	78.73	
1	1	-	-	.298	.367	.547	232	.348	397	.595	66.67	65.18	65.08	65.60	262.52	66.93	
1	1	-	-	.334	.407	.542	216	.347	372	.598	62.07	65.07	60.98	65.92	254.04	64.77	
3	1	-	6	.335	.405	.589	193	.381	316	.623	55.46	71.33	51.80	68.69	247.29	63.05	
2	4	-	5	.295	.392	.529	178	.292	358	.587	51.15	54.68	58.69	64.68	229.20	58.44	
2	1	-	6	.294	.383	.455	94	.260	185	.512	27.01	48.79	30.33	56.48	162.61	41.46	
2	1	-	15	.241	.327	.374	125	.217	250	.435	35.92	40.74	40.98	47.92	165.56	42.21	
3	-	-	11	.254	.330	.334	53	.154	135	.392	15.23	28.87	22.13	43.25	109.48	27.91	
23	16	-	43	.302	.371	.522	1,847	.320	3,258	.565	41.31	76.72	38.52	75.12	231.67	59.17	105
40	28	-	75	.302	.371	.522	3,204	.320	5,651	.565	76.72	76.72	75.12	75.12	303.68	75.92	59
45	31	-	83	.302	.371	.522	3,579	.320	6,313	.565	68.52	76.72	67.09	75.12	287.44	71.86	63
20	16	-	32	.305	.373	.533	1,794	.331	3,123	.576	60.94	75.47	63.00	72.69	272.09	69.79	79
11	8	-	-	.315	.372	.560	1,190	.358	1,990	.599	78.19	76.63	76.30	72.65	303.77	77.82	42
5	3	-	-	.343	.382	.644	286	.428	445	.666	82.18	80.23	72.95	73.42	308.78	78.73	71
2	2	-	-	.330	.388	.598	259	.378	434	.634	74.43	70.85	71.15	69.83	286.25	72.98	178

Complete Career Statistics T

Total Career Statistics & Adjusted Career, 10 year, 5 year, and Single Year Analysis

Vaughn, Mo: *Maurice Samuel Vaughn, b. Dec. 15, 1967, Norwalk, CT*

Rating Category		Year	Ranked Seasons & Adjustment	G	AB	H	1B	2B	3B	HR	RUN	RBI	BB	SO	SB	
10 Year Total	5 Year Total	1991		74	219	57	41	12	-	4	21	32	26	43	2	
		1992		113	355	83	52	16	2	13	42	57	47	67	3	
		1993		152	539	160	96	34	1	29	86	101	79	130	4	
		1994		111	394	122	70	25	1	26	65	82	57	112	4	
		1995		140	550	165	95	28	3	39	98	126	68	150	11	
		1996	1st	161	635	207	133	29	1	44	118	143	95	154	2	
		1997		141	527	166	107	24	-	35	91	96	86	154	2	
		1998		154	609	205	132	31	2	40	107	115	61	144	-	
		1999		139	524	147	94	20	-	33	63	108	54	127	-	
		2000		161	614	167	100	31	-	36	93	117	79	181	2	
		2002		139	487	126	82	18	-	26	67	72	59	145	-	
		2003		27	79	15	10	2	-	3	10	15	14	22	-	
Career Total		1991-2003		1,512	5,532	1,620	1,012	270	10	328	861	1,064	725	1,429	30	
Career Adj. to 10,000 BO		1991-2003	1.527884	2,310	8,452	2,475	1,546	413	15	501	1,316	1,626	1,108	2,183	46	
Career Adj. to 10,000 AB		1991-2003	1.807664	2,733	10,000	2,928	1,829	488	18	593	1,556	1,923	1,311	2,583	54	
10 Year Total		1991-2000		1,346	4,966	1,479	920	250	10	299	784	977	652	1,262	30	
5 Year Total		1994-1998		707	2,715	865	537	137	7	184	479	562	367	714	19	
Best Single Year		1996		161	635	207	133	29	1	44	118	143	95	154	2	

Complete Career Statistics V

Total Career Statistics & Adjusted Career, 10 year, 5 year, and Single Year Analysis

Vaughn, Mo

CS	HBP	SF	GDP	AVG	OBP	SLG	Total Offensive Production Statistics				TRP Rating	RPA Rating	TNB Rating	TBA Rating	TOP Composite		
							TRP	RPA	TNB	TBA					TOP	Rating	Ranking
1	2	4	7	.260	.339	.370	53	.205	110	.426	15.23	38.49	18.03	46.99	118.75	30.28	
3	3	3	8	.234	.326	.400	99	.238	192	.462	28.45	44.59	31.48	50.87	155.39	39.62	
3	8	7	14	.297	.390	.525	187	.289	371	.573	53.74	54.16	60.82	63.20	231.91	59.13	
4	10	2	7	.310	.408	.576	147	.313	294	.626	42.24	58.61	48.20	68.94	217.99	55.58	
4	14	4	17	.300	.388	.575	224	.343	405	.620	64.37	64.28	66.39	68.36	263.40	67.16	
-	14	8	17	.326	.420	.583	261	.339	481	.625	75.00	63.60	78.85	68.94	286.39	73.02	
2	12	3	10	.315	.420	.560	187	.293	393	.616	53.74	54.92	64.43	67.89	240.97	61.44	
-	8	3	13	.337	.402	.591	222	.320	429	.618	63.79	59.94	70.33	68.13	262.19	66.85	
-	11	3	11	.281	.358	.508	171	.284	331	.549	49.14	53.14	54.26	60.50	217.04	55.34	
-	14	5	14	.272	.365	.498	210	.289	401	.552	60.34	54.20	65.74	60.88	241.16	61.49	
1	10	2	15	.259	.349	.456	139	.243	290	.506	39.94	45.46	47.54	55.78	188.72	48.12	
-	2	1	2	.190	.323	.329	25	.255	42	.429	7.18	47.80	6.89	47.23	109.11	27.82	
18	108	45	135	.293	.383	.523	1,925	.294	3,739	.571	43.06	70.43	44.21	75.94	233.63	59.67	103
28	165	69	206	.293	.383	.523	2,941	.294	5,713	.571	70.43	70.43	75.94	75.94	292.73	73.18	76
33	195	81	244	.293	.383	.523	3,480	.294	6,759	.571	66.62	70.43	71.83	75.94	284.82	71.20	70
17	96	42	118	.298	.387	.533	1,761	.300	3,407	.580	59.82	68.37	68.73	73.18	270.10	69.28	85
10	58	20	64	.319	.408	.578	1,041	.323	2,002	.621	68.40	69.05	76.76	75.29	289.50	74.17	74
-	14	8	17	.326	.420	.583	261	.339	481	.625	75.00	63.60	78.85	68.94	286.39	73.02	175

Complete Career Statistics V

Total Career Statistics & Adjusted Career, 10 year, 5 year, and Single Year Analysis

Wagner, Honus: *John Peter "The Flying Dutchman" Wagner, b. Feb. 24, 1874, Chartiers, PA*

Rating Category	Year	Ranked Seasons & Adjustment	G	AB	H	1B	2B	3B	HR	RUN	RBI	BB	SO	SB
	1897		61	241	83	60	17	4	2	38	39	15	-	19
	1898		148	591	180	135	31	4	10	80	105	31	-	27
	1899		144	549	197	130	47	13	7	102	113	40	-	37
	1900		134	528	201	130	45	22	4	107	100	41	-	38
	1901		141	556	196	141	39	10	6	100	126	53	-	49
	1902		137	538	177	125	33	16	3	105	91	43	-	42
	1903		129	512	182	128	30	19	5	97	101	44	-	46
	1904		132	490	171	109	44	14	4	97	75	59	-	53
	1905		147	548	199	147	32	14	6	114	101	54	-	57
	1906		142	516	175	126	38	9	2	103	71	58	-	53
	1907		142	515	180	122	38	14	6	98	82	46	-	61
	1908	1st	151	568	201	133	39	19	10	100	109	54	-	53
	1909		137	495	168	114	39	10	5	92	100	66	-	35
	1910		150	556	178	132	34	8	4	90	81	59	47	24
	1911		130	473	158	110	23	16	9	87	89	67	34	20
	1912		145	558	181	119	35	20	7	91	102	59	38	26
	1913		114	413	124	99	18	4	3	51	56	26	40	21
	1914		150	552	139	114	15	9	1	60	50	51	51	23
	1915		156	566	155	100	32	17	6	68	78	39	64	22
	1916		123	432	124	99	15	9	1	45	39	34	36	11
	1917		74	230	61	53	7	1	-	15	24	24	17	5
Career Total	1897-1917		2,787	10,427	3,430	2,426	651	252	101	1,740	1,732	963	327	722
Career Adj. to 10,000 BO	1897-1917	0.868508	2,421	9,056	2,979	2,107	565	219	88	1,511	1,504	836	284	627
Career Adj. to 10,000 AB	1897-1917	0.959049	2,673	10,000	3,290	2,327	624	242	97	1,669	1,661	924	314	692
10 Year Total	1899-1908		1,399	5,320	1,879	1,291	385	150	53	1,023	969	492	-	489
5 Year Total	1900-1904		673	2,624	927	633	191	81	22	506	493	240	-	228
Best Single Year	1908		151	568	201	133	39	19	10	100	109	54	-	53

Note: "5 Year Total" spans years 1900–1904; "10 Year Total" spans years 1899–1908.

Total Career Statistics & Adjusted Career, 10 year, 5 year, and Single Year Analysis

Wagner, Honus

CS	HBP	SF	GDP	AVG	OBP	SLG	Total Offensive Production Statistics				TRP Rating	RPA Rating	TNB Rating	TBA Rating	TOP Composite		
							TRP	RPA	TNB	TBA					TOP	Rating	Ranking
-	1	-	-	.344	.385	.473	77	.300	149	.580	22.13	56.14	24.43	63.90	166.59	42.47	
-	6	-	-	.305	.346	.421	185	.295	313	.498	53.16	55.20	51.31	54.93	214.60	54.72	
-	11	-	-	.359	.413	.530	215	.358	379	.632	61.78	67.15	62.13	69.62	260.68	66.46	
-	8	-	-	.381	.433	.572	207	.359	389	.674	59.48	67.22	63.77	74.30	264.78	67.51	
-	6	-	-	.353	.415	.491	226	.367	381	.620	64.94	68.86	62.46	68.28	264.54	67.45	
-	14	-	-	.329	.393	.467	196	.329	350	.588	56.32	61.73	57.38	64.83	240.26	61.26	
-	7	-	-	.355	.414	.518	198	.352	362	.643	56.90	65.90	59.34	70.87	253.01	64.51	
-	4	-	-	.349	.423	.520	172	.311	371	.671	49.43	58.28	60.82	73.94	242.47	61.82	
-	7	-	-	.363	.427	.505	215	.353	395	.649	61.78	66.15	64.75	71.49	264.17	67.35	
-	10	-	-	.339	.416	.459	174	.298	358	.613	50.00	55.83	58.69	67.56	232.08	59.17	
-	5	-	-	.350	.408	.513	180	.318	376	.664	51.72	59.59	61.64	73.22	246.17	62.76	
-	5	-	-	.354	.415	.542	209	.333	420	.670	60.06	62.46	68.85	73.83	265.20	67.61	
-	3	-	-	.339	.420	.489	192	.340	346	.613	55.17	63.79	56.72	67.61	243.30	62.03	
-	5	-	-	.320	.390	.432	171	.276	328	.529	49.14	51.68	53.77	58.31	212.90	54.28	
-	6	-	-	.334	.423	.507	176	.322	333	.610	50.57	60.40	54.59	67.22	232.78	59.35	
-	6	-	-	.324	.395	.496	193	.310	368	.591	55.46	58.05	60.33	65.10	238.94	60.92	
-	5	-	-	.300	.349	.385	107	.241	211	.475	30.75	45.16	34.59	52.38	162.87	41.53	
8	2	-	-	.252	.317	.317	110	.182	243	.402	31.61	34.07	39.84	44.27	149.78	38.19	
15	4	-	-	.274	.325	.422	146	.240	289	.475	41.95	44.92	47.38	52.30	186.56	47.56	
-	8	-	-	.287	.350	.370	84	.177	213	.449	24.14	33.21	34.92	49.53	141.79	36.15	
-	1	-	-	.265	.337	.304	39	.153	100	.392	11.21	28.66	16.39	43.22	99.48	25.36	
23	124	-	-	.329	.392	.469	3,472	.302	6,674	.580	77.66	72.21	78.92	77.05	305.83	78.10	17
20	108	-	-	.329	.392	.469	3,015	.302	5,796	.580	72.21	72.21	77.05	77.05	298.51	74.63	67
22	119	-	-	.329	.392	.469	3,330	.302	6,401	.580	63.75	72.21	68.02	77.05	281.03	70.26	78
-	77	-	-	.353	.416	.512	1,992	.338	3,781	.642	67.66	77.14	76.28	81.01	302.09	77.48	37
-	39	-	-	.353	.415	.513	999	.344	1,853	.638	65.64	73.59	71.05	77.39	287.67	73.70	79
-	5	-	-	.354	.415	.542	209	.333	420	.670	60.06	62.46	68.85	73.83	265.20	67.61	333

Complete Career Statistics W

Total Career Statistics & Adjusted Career, 10 year, 5 year, and Single Year Analysis

Walker, Larry: *Larry Kenneth Robert Walker, b. Dec. 1, 1966, Maple Ridge, B.C., Canada*

Rating Category	Year	Ranked Seasons & Adjustment	G	AB	H	1B	2B	3B	HR	RUN	RBI	BB	SO	SB
	1989		20	47	8	8	-	-	-	4	4	5	13	1
	1990		133	419	101	61	18	3	19	59	51	49	112	21
	1991		137	487	141	93	30	2	16	59	64	42	102	14
	1992		143	528	159	101	31	4	23	85	93	41	97	18
10 Year Total	1993		138	490	130	79	24	5	22	85	86	80	76	29
	1994		103	395	127	62	44	2	19	76	86	47	74	15
	1995		131	494	151	79	31	5	36	96	101	49	72	16
	1996		83	272	75	35	18	4	18	58	58	20	58	18
	1997	1st	153	568	208	109	46	4	49	143	130	78	90	33
5 Year Total	1998		130	454	165	93	46	3	23	113	67	64	61	14
	1999	2nd	127	438	166	99	26	4	37	108	115	57	52	11
	2000		87	314	97	60	21	7	9	64	51	46	40	5
	2001	3rd	142	497	174	98	35	3	38	107	123	82	103	14
	2002		134	477	161	91	40	4	26	95	104	65	73	6
	2003		143	454	129	81	25	7	16	86	79	98	87	7
	2004		82	258	77	40	16	4	17	51	47	49	57	6
Career Total**	1989-2004		1,886	6,592	2,069	1,189	451	61	368	1,289	1,259	872	1,167	228
Career Adj. to 10,000 BO**	1989-2004	1.282051	2,418	8,451	2,653	1,524	578	78	472	1,653	1,614	1,118	1,496	292
Career Adj. to 10,000 AB**	1989-2004	1.516990	2,861	10,000	3,139	1,804	684	93	558	1,955	1,910	1,323	1,770	346
10 Year Total**	1993-2002		1,228	4,399	1,454	805	331	41	277	945	921	588	699	161
5 Year Total**	1997-2001		639	2,271	810	459	174	21	156	535	486	327	346	77
Best Single Year**	1997		153	568	208	109	46	4	49	143	130	78	90	33
2nd Best Year**	1999		127	438	166	99	26	4	37	108	115	57	52	11
3rd Best Year**	2001		142	497	174	98	35	3	38	107	123	82	103	14

Complete Career Statistics **W**

Total Career Statistics & Adjusted Career, 10 year, 5 year, and Single Year Analysis

Walker, Larry

CS	HBP	SF	GDP	AVG	OBP	SLG	Total Offensive Production Statistics				TRP Rating	RPA Rating	TNB Rating	TBA Rating	TOP Composite		
							TRP	RPA	TNB	TBA					TOP	Rating	Ranking
1	1	-	-	.170	.264	.170	8	.151	14	.264	2.30	28.28	2.30	29.11	61.99	15.81	
7	5	2	8	.241	.326	.434	110	.228	250	.518	31.61	42.67	40.98	57.05	172.31	43.93	
9	5	4	7	.290	.349	.458	123	.226	275	.505	35.34	42.29	45.08	55.61	178.33	45.47	
6	6	8	9	.301	.353	.506	178	.301	326	.551	51.15	56.34	53.44	60.69	221.63	56.51	
7	6	6	8	.265	.371	.469	171	.290	338	.573	49.14	54.31	55.41	63.14	222.00	56.60	
5	4	6	8	.322	.394	.587	162	.352	293	.637	46.55	65.99	48.03	70.20	230.78	58.84	
3	14	5	13	.306	.381	.607	197	.343	376	.654	56.61	64.20	61.64	72.07	254.52	64.89	
2	9	3	7	.276	.342	.570	116	.373	200	.643	33.33	69.89	32.79	70.88	206.89	52.75	
8	14	4	15	.366	.452	.720	273	.402	526	.775	78.45	75.34	86.23	85.38	325.40	82.96	
4	4	2	11	.363	.445	.630	180	.336	364	.680	51.72	63.04	59.67	74.99	249.43	63.59	
4	12	6	12	.379	.458	.710	223	.425	387	.737	64.08	79.59	63.44	81.24	288.36	73.52	
5	9	3	12	.309	.409	.506	115	.299	214	.557	33.05	56.12	35.08	61.42	185.67	47.34	
5	14	8	9	.350	.449	.662	230	.377	434	.711	66.09	70.65	71.15	78.41	286.31	73.00	
5	7	4	8	.338	.421	.602	199	.355	360	.642	57.18	66.47	59.02	70.73	253.39	64.61	
4	11	1	9	.284	.422	.476	165	.288	328	.572	47.41	53.96	53.77	63.09	218.23	55.64	
-	8	1	8	.298	.424	.589	98	.302	215	.664	28.16	56.68	35.25	73.14	193.22	49.26	
75	129	63	144	.314	.401	.568	2,548	.327	4,900	.628	56.99	78.22	57.94	83.50	276.66	70.65	45
96	165	81	185	.314	.401	.568	3,267	.327	6,282	.628	78.22	78.22	83.50	83.50	323.45	80.86	21
114	196	96	218	.314	.401	.568	3,865	.327	7,433	.628	74.00	78.22	79.00	83.50	314.73	78.68	23
48	93	47	103	.331	.416	.613	1,866	.357	3,492	.668	63.38	81.36	70.45	84.24	299.44	76.80	41
26	53	23	59	.357	.445	.658	1,021	.374	1,925	.704	67.08	79.89	73.81	85.40	306.18	78.44	39
8	14	4	15	.366	.452	.720	273	.402	526	.775	78.45	75.34	86.23	85.38	325.40	82.96	34
4	12	6	12	.379	.458	.710	223	.425	387	.737	64.08	79.59	63.44	81.24	288.36	73.52	162
5	14	8	9	.350	.449	.662	230	.377	434	.711	66.09	70.65	71.15	78.41	286.31	73.00	177

Complete Career Statistics W

Total Career Statistics & Adjusted Career, 10 year, 5 year, and Single Year Analysis

Waner, Paul: *Paul Glee "Big Poison" Waner, b. April 16, 1903, Harrah, OK*

Rating Category		Year	Ranked Seasons & Adjustment	G	AB	H	1B	2B	3B	HR	RUN	RBI	BB	SO	SB	
		1926		144	536	180	115	35	22	8	101	79	66	19	11	
	5 Year Total	1927	1st	155	623	237	168	42	18	9	114	131	60	14	5	
		1928		152	602	223	148	50	19	6	142	86	77	16	6	
		1929		151	596	200	127	43	15	15	131	100	89	24	15	
10 Year Total		1930		145	589	217	159	32	18	8	117	77	57	18	18	
		1931		150	559	180	129	35	10	6	88	70	73	21	6	
		1932		154	630	215	134	63	10	8	107	82	56	24	13	
		1933		154	618	191	130	38	16	7	101	70	60	20	3	
		1934		146	599	217	155	32	16	14	122	90	68	24	8	
		1935		139	549	176	124	29	12	11	98	78	61	22	2	
		1936		148	585	218	151	53	9	5	107	94	74	29	7	
		1937		154	619	219	178	30	9	2	94	74	63	34	4	
		1938		148	625	175	132	31	6	6	77	69	47	28	2	
		1939		125	461	151	112	30	6	3	62	45	35	18	-	
		1940		89	238	69	51	16	1	1	32	32	23	14	-	
		1941		106	329	88	74	10	2	2	45	50	55	14	1	
		1942		114	333	86	67	17	1	1	43	39	62	20	2	
		1943		82	225	70	53	16	-	1	29	26	35	9	-	
		1944		92	143	40	35	4	1	-	17	17	29	8	1	
		1945		1	-	-	-	-	-	-	-	-	1	-	-	
Career Total		1927-1945		2,549	9,459	3,152	2,242	606	191	113	1,627	1,309	1,091	376	104	
Career Adj. to 10,000 BO		1927-1945	0.933271	2,379	8,828	2,942	2,092	566	178	105	1,518	1,222	1,018	351	97	
Career Adj. to 10,000 AB		1927-1945	1.057194	2,695	10,000	3,332	2,370	641	202	119	1,720	1,384	1,153	398	110	
10 Year Total		1927-1936		1,494	5,950	2,074	1,425	417	143	89	1,127	878	675	212	83	
5 Year Total		1926-1930		747	2,946	1,057	717	202	92	46	605	473	349	91	55	
Best Single Year		1927		155	623	237	168	42	18	9	114	131	60	14	5	

Total Career Statistics & Adjusted Career, 10 year, 5 year, and Single Year Analysis

Waner, Paul

CS	HBP	SF	GDP	AVG	OBP	SLG	TRP	RPA	TNB	TBA	TRP Rating	RPA Rating	TNB Rating	TBA Rating	TOP	Rating	Ranking
-	4	-	-	.336	.413	.528	180	.297	364	.601	51.72	55.66	59.67	66.20	233.26	59.47	
-	3	-	-	.380	.437	.549	245	.357	410	.598	70.40	66.92	67.21	65.87	270.41	68.94	
-	5	-	-	.370	.446	.547	228	.333	417	.610	65.52	62.46	68.36	67.19	263.53	67.19	
-	3	-	-	.336	.424	.534	231	.336	425	.618	66.38	62.91	69.67	68.08	267.05	68.09	
-	4	-	-	.368	.428	.525	194	.298	388	.597	55.75	55.93	63.61	65.79	241.07	61.46	
-	4	-	-	.322	.404	.453	158	.248	336	.528	45.40	46.55	55.08	58.23	205.26	52.33	
-	2	-	-	.341	.397	.511	189	.275	393	.571	54.31	51.48	64.43	62.96	233.17	59.45	
-	2	-	10	.309	.372	.456	171	.248	347	.503	49.14	46.44	56.89	55.43	207.89	53.00	
-	2	-	15	.362	.429	.539	212	.310	401	.586	60.92	58.08	65.74	64.61	249.35	63.57	
-	3	-	15	.321	.392	.477	176	.280	328	.522	50.57	52.51	53.77	57.56	214.42	54.67	
-	3	-	15	.373	.446	.520	201	.297	388	.573	57.76	55.63	63.61	63.17	240.16	61.23	
-	-	-	11	.354	.413	.441	168	.242	340	.491	48.28	45.43	55.74	54.07	203.51	51.89	
-	1	-	16	.280	.331	.378	146	.212	286	.415	41.95	39.71	46.89	45.75	174.29	44.44	
-	-	-	12	.328	.375	.438	107	.211	237	.467	30.75	39.47	38.85	51.42	160.49	40.92	
-	-	-	4	.290	.352	.378	64	.242	113	.426	18.39	45.25	18.52	47.00	129.17	32.93	
-	-	-	10	.267	.372	.328	95	.241	164	.416	27.30	45.18	26.89	45.88	145.24	37.03	
-	1	-	7	.258	.376	.324	82	.203	173	.429	23.56	38.13	28.36	47.31	137.36	35.02	
1	1	-	9	.311	.406	.396	55	.204	124	.459	15.80	38.17	20.33	50.62	124.92	31.85	
-	-	-	3	.280	.401	.322	34	.194	76	.434	9.77	36.41	12.46	47.86	106.50	27.15	
-	-	-	-	.000	1.000	.000	-	.000	1	1.000	-	-	0.16	110.21	110.38	28.14	
1	38	-	127	.333	.404	.474	2,936	.274	5,711	.533	65.67	65.61	67.53	70.85	269.66	68.87	56
1	35	-	119	.333	.404	.474	2,740	.274	5,330	.533	65.61	65.61	70.85	70.85	272.92	68.23	106
1	40	-	134	.333	.404	.474	3,104	.274	6,038	.533	59.43	65.61	64.17	70.85	260.05	65.01	107
-	31	-	55	.349	.418	.512	2,005	.299	3,833	.571	68.10	68.13	77.32	72.06	285.62	73.26	57
-	19	-	-	.359	.430	.537	1,078	.325	2,004	.605	70.83	69.56	76.84	73.32	290.54	74.44	71
-	3	-	-	.380	.437	.549	245	.357	410	.598	70.40	66.92	67.21	65.87	270.41	68.94	315

Complete Career Statistics W

| Total Career Statistics & Adjusted Career, 10 year, 5 year, and Single Year Analysis |||||||||||||||

Williams, Bernie: *Bernabe Williams (Figueroa), b. Sept. 13, 1968, San Juan, Puerto Rico*

Rating Category	Year	Ranked Seasons & Adjustment	G	AB	H	1B	2B	3B	HR	RUN	RBI	BB	SO	SB
	1991		85	320	76	50	19	4	3	43	34	48	57	10
	1992		62	261	73	52	14	2	5	39	26	29	36	7
	1993		139	567	152	105	31	4	12	67	68	53	106	9
	1994		108	408	118	76	29	1	12	80	57	61	54	16
	1995		144	563	173	117	29	9	18	93	82	75	98	8
	1996		143	551	168	106	26	7	29	108	102	82	72	17
	1997		129	509	167	105	35	6	21	107	100	73	80	15
	1998		128	499	169	108	30	5	26	101	97	74	81	15
	1999		158	591	202	143	28	6	25	116	115	100	95	9
	2000	1st	141	537	165	92	37	6	30	108	121	71	84	13
	2001		146	540	166	102	38	-	26	102	94	78	67	11
	2002		154	612	204	146	37	2	19	102	102	83	98	8
	2003		119	445	117	82	19	1	15	77	64	71	61	5
	2004		148	561	147	95	29	1	22	105	70	85	96	1
Career Total**	1991-2004		1,804	6,964	2,097	1,379	401	54	263	1,248	1,132	983	1,085	144
Career Adj. to 10,000 BO**	1991-2004	1.215362	2,193	8,464	2,549	1,676	487	66	320	1,517	1,376	1,195	1,319	175
Career Adj. to 10,000 AB**	1991-2004	1.435956	2,590	10,000	3,011	1,980	576	78	378	1,792	1,626	1,412	1,558	207
10 Year Total**	1995-2004		1,410	5,408	1,678	1,096	308	43	231	1,019	947	792	832	102
5 Year Total**	1996-2000		699	2,687	871	554	156	30	131	540	535	400	412	69
Best Single Year**	2000		141	537	165	92	37	6	30	108	121	71	84	13

Left margin: Complete Career Statistics W

Total Career Statistics & Adjusted Career, 10 year, 5 year, and Single Year Analysis

Williams, Bernie

CS	HBP	SF	GDP	AVG	OBP	SLG	Total Offensive Production Statistics				TRP Rating	RPA Rating	TNB Rating	TBA Rating	TOP Composite		
							TRP	RPA	TNB	TBA					TOP	Rating	Ranking
5	1	3	4	.238	.336	.350	77	.205	166	.441	22.13	38.37	27.21	48.66	136.37	34.77	
6	1	-	5	.280	.354	.406	65	.220	137	.463	18.68	38.54	22.46	47.78	127.46	32.50	
9	4	3	17	.268	.333	.400	135	.210	284	.441	38.79	39.28	46.56	48.60	173.23	44.17	
9	3	2	11	.289	.384	.453	137	.282	256	.528	39.37	52.93	42.30	58.63	193.22	49.26	
6	5	3	12	.307	.392	.487	175	.266	356	.541	50.29	49.84	58.36	59.63	218.11	55.61	
4	-	7	15	.305	.391	.535	210	.321	390	.595	60.34	60.08	63.93	65.62	249.98	63.73	
8	1	8	10	.328	.408	.544	207	.344	358	.596	59.48	64.54	58.69	65.65	248.36	63.32	
9	1	4	19	.339	.422	.575	198	.332	368	.616	56.90	62.15	60.33	67.94	247.31	63.05	
10	1	5	11	.342	.435	.536	231	.326	417	.589	66.38	61.14	68.36	64.91	260.79	66.49	
5	5	3	15	.307	.391	.566	229	.363	388	.615	65.80	68.00	63.61	67.77	265.19	67.61	
5	6	9	15	.307	.395	.522	196	.302	372	.574	56.32	56.68	60.98	63.27	237.25	60.49	
4	3	1	19	.333	.415	.493	204	.284	392	.546	58.62	53.24	64.26	60.17	236.30	60.25	
-	3	2	21	.263	.367	.411	141	.260	262	.483	40.52	48.75	42.95	53.28	185.49	47.29	
5	2	2	19	.262	.360	.435	175	.262	327	.489	50.29	49.02	53.61	53.87	206.78	52.72	
85	36	52	193	.301	.388	.488	2,380	.289	4,473	.544	53.23	69.26	52.89	72.26	247.65	63.25	87
103	44	63	235	.301	.388	.488	2,893	.289	5,436	.544	69.26	69.26	72.26	72.26	283.05	70.76	90
122	52	75	277	.301	.388	.488	3,418	.289	6,423	.544	65.43	69.26	68.26	72.26	275.22	68.80	86
56	27	44	156	.310	.398	.511	1,966	.306	3,630	.565	66.78	69.76	73.23	71.26	281.03	72.08	63
36	8	27	70	.324	.410	.551	1,075	.337	1,921	.602	70.63	72.02	73.66	72.97	289.27	74.11	76
5	5	3	15	.307	.391	.566	229	.363	388	.615	65.80	68.00	63.61	67.77	265.19	67.61	334

Complete Career Statistics W

Total Career Statistics & Adjusted Career, 10 year, 5 year, and Single Year Analysis

Williams, Billy: *Billy Leo Williams, b. June 15, 1938, Whistler, AL*

Rating Category	Year	Ranked Seasons & Adjustment	G	AB	H	1B	2B	3B	HR	RUN	RBI	BB	SO	SB
	1959		18	33	5	4	-	1	-	-	2	1	7	-
	1960		12	47	13	9	-	2	2	4	7	5	12	-
	1961		146	529	147	95	20	7	25	75	86	45	70	6
	1962		159	618	184	132	22	8	22	94	91	70	72	9
	1963		161	612	175	105	36	9	25	87	95	68	78	7
	1964		162	645	201	127	39	2	33	100	98	59	84	10
	1965		164	645	203	124	39	6	34	115	108	65	76	10
	1966		162	648	179	122	23	5	29	100	91	69	61	6
	1967		162	634	176	115	21	12	28	92	84	68	67	6
	1968		163	642	185	117	30	8	30	91	98	48	53	4
	1969		163	642	188	124	33	10	21	103	95	59	70	3
	1970	1st	161	636	205	125	34	4	42	137	129	72	65	7
	1971		157	594	179	119	27	5	28	86	93	77	44	7
	1972		150	574	191	114	34	6	37	95	122	62	59	3
	1973		156	576	166	122	22	2	20	72	86	76	72	4
	1974		117	404	113	75	22	-	16	55	68	67	44	4
	1975		155	520	127	83	20	1	23	68	81	76	68	-
	1976		120	351	74	51	12	-	11	36	41	58	44	4
Career Total	1959-1976		2,488	9,350	2,711	1,763	434	88	426	1,410	1,475	1,045	1,046	90
Career Adj. to 10,000 BO	1959-1976	0.933620	2,323	8,729	2,531	1,646	405	82	398	1,316	1,377	976	977	84
Career Adj. to 10,000 AB	1959-1976	1.069519	2,661	10,000	2,899	1,886	464	94	456	1,508	1,578	1,118	1,119	96
10 Year Total	1963-1972		1,605	6,272	1,882	1,192	316	67	307	1,006	1,013	647	657	63
5 Year Total	1968-1972		794	3,088	948	599	158	33	158	512	537	318	291	24
Best Single Year	1970		161	636	205	125	34	4	42	137	129	72	65	7

10 Year Total · *5 Year Total*

Complete Career Statistics W

Total Career Statistics & Adjusted Career, 10 year, 5 year, and Single Year Analysis

Williams, Billy

CS	HBP	SF	GDP	AVG	OBP	SLG	Total Offensive Production Statistics				TRP Rating	RPA Rating	TNB Rating	TBA Rating	TOP Composite		
							TRP	RPA	TNB	TBA					TOP	Rating	Ranking
-	-	-	2	.152	.176	.212	2	.056	8	.222	0.57	10.41	1.31	24.49	36.79	9.38	
-	-	-	1	.277	.346	.489	11	.208	28	.528	3.16	38.89	4.59	58.23	104.87	26.74	
-	5	4	11	.278	.338	.484	161	.271	312	.525	46.26	50.79	51.15	57.89	206.09	52.54	
9	4	7	11	.298	.369	.466	185	.261	362	.510	53.16	48.82	59.34	56.19	217.52	55.46	
6	2	3	12	.286	.358	.497	182	.261	375	.538	52.30	48.93	61.48	59.30	222.00	56.60	
7	2	3	11	.312	.370	.532	198	.275	407	.565	56.90	51.53	66.72	62.30	237.45	60.54	
1	3	5	20	.315	.377	.552	223	.302	433	.587	64.08	56.62	70.98	64.66	256.35	65.36	
3	4	6	12	.276	.347	.461	191	.258	375	.507	54.89	48.43	61.48	55.93	220.72	56.27	
3	2	6	13	.278	.346	.481	176	.243	378	.523	50.57	45.61	61.97	57.62	215.78	55.01	
1	2	7	13	.288	.336	.500	189	.265	374	.525	54.31	49.74	61.31	57.89	223.26	56.92	
2	4	3	15	.293	.355	.474	198	.274	368	.509	56.90	51.32	60.33	56.10	224.64	57.27	
1	2	4	13	.322	.391	.586	266	.366	453	.623	76.44	68.56	74.26	68.68	287.94	73.41	
5	3	3	17	.301	.383	.505	179	.258	382	.550	51.44	48.33	62.62	60.67	223.06	56.87	
1	6	8	14	.333	.398	.606	217	.327	418	.630	62.36	61.24	68.52	69.38	261.50	66.67	
3	1	6	13	.288	.369	.438	158	.235	330	.491	45.40	44.06	54.10	54.12	197.68	50.40	
5	1	2	9	.280	.382	.453	123	.255	250	.518	35.34	47.72	40.98	57.05	181.09	46.17	
-	2	3	9	.244	.341	.419	149	.244	296	.485	42.82	45.77	48.52	53.48	190.59	48.59	
2	-	3	4	.211	.320	.339	77	.185	179	.430	22.13	34.68	29.34	47.42	133.58	34.06	
49	43	73	200	.290	.361	.492	2,885	.269	5,728	.535	64.53	64.50	67.73	71.08	267.84	68.40	59
46	40	68	187	.290	.361	.492	2,693	.269	5,348	.535	64.50	64.50	71.08	71.08	271.17	67.79	109
52	46	78	214	.290	.361	.492	3,086	.269	6,126	.535	59.07	64.50	65.11	71.08	259.76	64.94	109
30	30	48	140	.300	.366	.519	2,019	.283	3,963	.555	68.58	64.51	79.95	70.06	283.10	72.61	61
10	17	25	72	.307	.372	.533	1,049	.298	1,995	.567	68.92	63.73	76.50	68.72	277.86	71.19	92
1	2	4	13	.322	.391	.586	266	.366	453	.623	76.44	68.56	74.26	68.68	287.94	73.41	164

Complete Career Statistics W

Total Career Statistics & Adjusted Career, 10 year, 5 year, and Single Year Analysis

Williams, Ken: *Kenneth Roy Williams, b. June 28, 1890, Grant's Pass, OR*

Rating Category		Year	Ranked Seasons & Adjustment	G	AB	H	1B	2B	3B	HR	RUN	RBI	BB	SO	SB
		1915		71	219	53	39	10	4	-	22	16	15	20	4
		1916		10	27	3	3	-	-	-	1	1	2	5	1
		1918		2	1	-	-	-	-	-	-	1	1	-	-
10 Year Total	5 Year Total	1919		65	227	68	47	10	5	6	32	35	26	25	7
		1920		141	521	160	103	34	13	10	90	72	41	26	18
		1921	1st	146	547	190	128	31	7	24	115	117	74	42	20
		1922		153	585	194	110	34	11	39	128	155	74	31	37
		1923		147	555	198	120	37	12	29	106	91	79	32	18
		1924		114	398	129	86	21	4	18	78	84	69	17	20
		1925		102	411	136	75	31	5	25	83	105	37	14	10
		1926		108	347	97	58	15	7	17	55	74	39	23	5
		1927		131	423	136	90	23	6	17	70	74	57	30	9
		1928		133	462	140	106	25	1	8	59	67	37	15	4
		1929		74	139	48	29	14	2	3	21	21	15	7	1
Career Total*		1915-1929		1,397	4,862	1,552	994	285	77	196	860	913	566	287	154
Career Adj. to 10,000 BO*		1915-1929	1.832845	2,560	8,911	2,845	1,822	522	141	359	1,576	1,673	1,037	526	282
Career Adj. to 10,000 AB*		1915-1929	2.056767	2,873	10,000	3,192	2,044	586	158	403	1,769	1,878	1,164	590	317
10 Year Total*		1919-1928		1,240	4,476	1,448	923	261	71	193	816	874	533	255	148
5 Year Total*		1921-1925		662	2,496	847	519	154	39	135	510	552	333	136	105
Best Single Year		1922		153	585	194	110	34	11	39	128	155	74	31	37

Total Career Statistics & Adjusted Career, 10 year, 5 year, and Single Year Analysis

Williams, Ken

CS	HBP	SF	GDP	AVG	OBP	SLG	Total Offensive Production Statistics				TRP Rating	RPA Rating	TNB Rating	TBA Rating	TOP Composite		
							TRP	RPA	TNB	TBA					TOP	Rating	Ranking
3	2	-	-	.242	.297	.324	38	.161	89	.377	10.92	30.17	14.59	41.56	97.25	24.79	
-	-	-	-	.111	.172	.111	2	.069	6	.207	0.57	12.92	0.98	22.80	37.28	9.51	
-	-	-	-	.000	.500	.000	1	.500	1	.500	0.29	93.69	0.16	55.11	149.25	38.05	
-	2	-	-	.300	.376	.467	67	.263	141	.553	19.25	49.23	23.11	60.94	152.54	38.89	
8	4	-	-	.307	.362	.480	162	.286	305	.539	46.55	53.63	50.00	59.39	209.57	53.43	
17	4	-	-	.347	.429	.561	232	.371	388	.621	66.67	69.56	63.61	68.42	268.25	68.39	
20	7	-	-	.332	.413	.627	283	.425	465	.698	81.32	79.62	76.23	76.95	314.13	80.09	
17	2	-	-	.357	.439	.623	197	.310	428	.673	56.61	58.04	70.16	74.17	258.98	66.03	
11	1	-	-	.324	.425	.533	162	.346	291	.622	46.55	64.86	47.70	68.53	227.65	58.04	
5	3	-	-	.331	.390	.613	188	.417	297	.659	54.02	78.11	48.69	72.58	253.40	64.61	
4	1	-	-	.280	.354	.510	129	.333	218	.563	37.07	62.46	35.74	62.08	197.35	50.32	
7	1	-	-	.322	.403	.525	144	.299	282	.586	41.38	56.10	46.23	64.62	208.32	53.11	
9	1	-	-	.303	.356	.413	126	.252	224	.448	36.21	47.22	36.72	49.38	169.52	43.22	
5	-	-	-	.345	.409	.540	42	.273	86	.558	12.07	51.10	14.10	61.55	138.82	35.39	
106	28	-	-	.319	.393	.530	1,773	.325	3,221	.590	39.66	77.81	38.09	78.47	234.03	59.77	102
194	51	-	-	.319	.393	.530	3,250	.325	5,904	.590	77.81	77.81	78.47	78.47	312.58	78.14	41
218	58	-	-	.319	.393	.530	3,647	.325	6,625	.590	69.82	77.81	70.41	78.47	296.51	74.13	49
98	26	-	-	.324	.399	.543	1,690	.336	3,039	.604	57.40	76.54	61.31	76.16	271.41	69.61	81
70	17	-	-	.339	.421	.595	1,062	.373	1,869	.657	69.78	79.80	71.66	79.62	300.86	77.08	48
20	7	-	-	.332	.413	.627	283	.425	465	.698	81.32	79.62	76.23	76.95	314.13	80.09	54

Complete Career Statistics W

Total Career Statistics & Adjusted Career, 10 year, 5 year, and Single Year Analysis

Williams, Ted: *Theodore Samuel "The Splendid Splinter" Williams, b. Aug. 30, 1918, San Diego, CA*

Rating Category	Year	Ranked Seasons & Adjustment	G	AB	H	1B	2B	3B	HR	RUN	RBI	BB	SO	SB
	1939	5th	149	565	185	99	44	11	31	131	145	107	64	2
	1940	8th	144	561	193	113	43	14	23	134	113	96	54	4
	1941	2nd	143	456	185	112	33	3	37	135	120	147	27	2
	1942	3rd	150	522	186	111	34	5	36	141	137	145	51	3
10 Year Total / 5 Year Total	1946	4th	150	514	176	93	37	8	38	142	123	156	44	-
	1947	7th	156	528	181	100	40	9	32	125	114	162	47	-
	1948	6th	137	509	188	116	44	3	25	124	127	126	41	4
	1949	1st	155	566	194	109	39	3	43	150	159	162	48	1
	1950		89	334	106	53	24	1	28	82	97	82	21	3
	1951		148	531	169	107	28	4	30	109	126	144	45	1
	1952		6	10	4	2	-	1	1	2	3	2	2	-
	1953		37	91	37	18	6	-	13	17	34	19	10	-
	1954		117	386	133	80	23	1	29	93	89	136	32	-
	1955		98	320	114	62	21	3	28	77	83	91	24	2
	1956		136	400	138	84	28	2	24	71	82	102	39	-
	1957	9th	132	420	163	96	28	1	38	96	87	119	43	-
	1958		129	411	135	84	23	2	26	81	85	98	49	1
	1959		103	272	69	44	15	-	10	32	43	52	27	-
	1960		113	310	98	54	15	-	29	56	72	75	41	1
Career Total*	1939-1960		2,292	7,706	2,654	1,537	525	71	521	1,798	1,839	2,021	709	24
Career Adj. to 10,000 BO*	1939-1960	1.001703	2,296	7,719	2,659	1,540	526	71	522	1,801	1,842	2,024	710	24
Career Adj. to 10,000 AB*	1939-1960	1.297690	2,974	10,000	3,444	1,995	681	92	676	2,333	2,386	2,623	920	31
10 Year Total*	1939-1951		1,421	5,086	1,763	1,013	366	61	323	1,273	1,261	1,327	442	20
5 Year Total*	1942-1949		748	2,639	925	529	194	28	174	682	660	751	231	8
Best Single Year*	1949		155	566	194	109	39	3	43	150	159	162	48	1
2nd Best Year*	1941		143	456	185	112	33	3	37	135	120	147	27	2
3rd Best Year*	1942		150	522	186	111	34	5	36	141	137	145	51	3
4th Best Year*	1946		150	514	176	93	37	8	38	142	123	156	44	-
5th Best Year*	1939		149	565	185	99	44	11	31	131	145	107	64	2
6th Best Year*	1948		137	509	188	116	44	3	25	124	127	126	41	4
7th Best Year*	1947		156	528	181	100	40	9	32	125	114	162	47	-
8th Best Year*	1940		144	561	193	113	43	14	23	134	113	96	54	4
9th Best Year*	1957		132	420	163	96	28	1	38	96	87	119	43	-

Total Career Statistics & Adjusted Career, 10 year, 5 year, and Single Year Analysis

Williams, Ted

CS	HBP	SF	GDP	AVG	OBP	SLG	TRP	RPA	TNB	TBA	TRP Rating	RPA Rating	TNB Rating	TBA Rating	TOP	Rating	Ranking
1	2	-	10	.327	.436	.609	276	.404	454	.664	79.31	75.61	74.43	73.15	302.50	77.13	
4	3	-	13	.344	.442	.594	247	.367	432	.642	70.98	68.77	70.82	70.75	281.31	71.72	
4	3	-	10	.406	.553	.735	255	.414	483	.784	73.28	77.57	79.18	86.42	316.44	80.68	
2	4	-	12	.356	.499	.648	278	.407	488	.714	79.89	76.27	80.00	78.75	314.90	80.29	
-	2	-	12	.342	.497	.667	265	.387	501	.732	76.15	72.60	82.13	80.73	311.60	79.45	
1	2	-	10	.343	.499	.634	239	.340	498	.709	68.68	63.80	81.64	78.19	292.30	74.52	
-	3	-	10	.369	.497	.615	251	.387	446	.688	72.13	72.58	73.11	75.86	293.68	74.88	
1	2	-	22	.343	.490	.650	309	.411	532	.707	88.79	77.00	87.21	77.97	330.97	84.38	
-	-	-	12	.317	.452	.647	179	.418	301	.703	51.44	78.37	49.34	77.51	256.66	65.44	
1	-	-	10	.318	.464	.556	235	.343	439	.641	67.53	64.28	71.97	70.63	274.41	69.96	
-	-	-	-	.400	.500	.900	5	.417	11	.917	1.44	78.08	1.80	101.03	182.35	46.49	
1	-	-	1	.407	.509	.901	51	.459	100	.901	14.66	86.09	16.39	99.29	216.43	55.18	
-	1	3	10	.345	.513	.635	182	.340	382	.713	52.30	63.63	62.62	78.55	257.10	65.55	
-	2	4	8	.356	.496	.703	160	.376	320	.753	45.98	70.54	52.46	82.98	251.96	64.24	
-	1	-	13	.345	.479	.605	153	.297	345	.669	43.97	55.56	56.56	73.69	229.77	58.58	
1	5	2	11	.388	.526	.731	183	.329	430	.772	52.59	61.56	70.49	85.08	269.73	68.77	
-	4	4	19	.328	.458	.584	166	.310	343	.640	47.70	58.03	56.23	70.53	232.49	59.28	
-	2	5	7	.254	.372	.419	75	.222	168	.497	21.55	41.58	27.54	54.78	145.45	37.08	
1	3	2	7	.316	.451	.645	128	.322	278	.700	36.78	60.42	45.57	77.18	219.95	56.08	
17	39	20	197	.344	.482	.634	3,637	.364	6,951	.696	81.35	87.24	82.19	92.55	343.33	87.68	6
17	39	20	197	.344	.482	.634	3,643	.364	6,963	.696	87.24	87.24	92.55	92.55	359.58	89.90	3
22	51	26	256	.344	.482	.634	4,720	.364	9,020	.696	90.36	87.24	95.86	92.55	366.02	91.50	3
14	21	-	121	.347	.484	.633	2,534	.387	4,574	.698	86.07	88.16	92.27	88.04	354.54	90.94	4
4	13	-	66	.351	.496	.643	1,342	.387	2,465	.711	88.17	82.73	94.52	86.15	351.57	90.07	5
1	2	-	22	.343	.490	.650	309	.411	532	.707	88.79	77.00	87.21	77.97	330.97	84.38	29
4	3	-	10	.406	.553	.735	255	.414	483	.784	73.28	77.57	79.18	86.42	316.44	80.68	48
2	4	-	12	.356	.499	.648	278	.407	488	.714	79.89	76.27	80.00	78.75	314.90	80.29	52
-	2	-	12	.342	.497	.667	265	.387	501	.732	76.15	72.60	82.13	80.73	311.60	79.45	65
1	2	-	10	.327	.436	.609	276	.404	454	.664	79.31	75.61	74.43	73.15	302.50	77.13	88
-	3	-	10	.369	.497	.615	251	.387	446	.688	72.13	72.58	73.11	75.86	293.68	74.88	130
1	2	-	10	.343	.499	.634	239	.340	498	.709	68.68	63.80	81.64	78.19	292.30	74.52	135
4	3	-	13	.344	.442	.594	247	.367	432	.642	70.98	68.77	70.82	70.75	281.31	71.72	225
1	5	2	11	.388	.526	.731	183	.329	430	.772	52.59	61.56	70.49	85.08	269.73	68.77	322

Complete Career Statistics W

Complete Career Statistics W

Total Career Statistics & Adjusted Career, 10 year, 5 year, and Single Year Analysis

Wilson, Hack: *Lewis Robert Wilson, b. April 26, 1900, Elwood City, PA*

Rating Category	Year	Ranked Seasons & Adjustment	G	AB	H	1B	2B	3B	HR	RUN	RBI	BB	SO	SB
	1923		3	10	2	2	-	-	-	-	-	-	1	-
	1924		107	383	113	72	19	12	10	62	57	44	46	4
	1925		62	180	43	26	7	4	6	28	30	21	33	5
	1926		142	529	170	105	36	8	21	97	109	69	61	10
	1927	3rd	146	551	175	103	30	12	30	119	129	71	70	13
	1928		145	520	163	91	32	9	31	89	120	77	94	4
	1929	2nd	150	574	198	124	30	5	39	135	159	78	83	3
	1930	1st	155	585	208	111	35	6	56	146	191	105	84	3
	1931		112	395	103	64	22	4	13	66	61	63	69	1
	1932		135	481	143	78	37	5	23	77	123	51	85	2
	1933		117	360	96	72	13	2	9	41	54	52	50	7
	1934		74	192	47	36	5	-	6	24	30	43	37	-
Career Total	1923-1934		1,348	4,760	1,461	884	266	67	244	884	1,063	674	713	52
Career Adj. to 10,000 BO	1923-1934	1.828488	2,465	8,704	2,671	1,616	486	123	446	1,616	1,944	1,232	1,304	95
Career Adj. to 10,000 AB	1923-1934	2.100840	2,832	10,000	3,069	1,857	559	141	513	1,857	2,233	1,416	1,498	109
10 Year Total	1924-1933		1,271	4,558	1,412	846	261	67	238	860	1,033	631	675	52
5 Year Total	1926-1930		738	2,759	914	534	163	40	177	586	708	400	392	33
Best Single Year	1930		155	585	208	111	35	6	56	146	191	105	84	3
2nd Best Year	1929		150	574	198	124	30	5	39	135	159	78	83	3
3rd Best Year	1927		146	551	175	103	30	12	30	119	129	71	70	13

Row groupings: **10 Year Total** spans 1924–1933; **5 Year Total** spans 1926–1930.

Total Career Statistics & Adjusted Career, 10 year, 5 year, and Single Year Analysis

Wilson, Hack

CS	HBP	SF	GDP	AVG	OBP	SLG	Total Offensive Production Statistics				TRP Rating	RPA Rating	TNB Rating	TBA Rating	TOP Composite		
							TRP	RPA	TNB	TBA					TOP	Rating	Ranking
-	-	-	-	.200	.200	.200	-	.000	2	.200	-	-	0.33	22.04	22.37	5.70	
3	1	-	-	.295	.369	.486	119	.278	232	.542	34.20	51.74	38.03	59.33	183.29	46.73	
2	1	-	-	.239	.322	.422	58	.287	101	.500	16.67	53.80	16.56	55.11	142.13	36.24	
-	6	-	-	.321	.406	.539	206	.341	370	.613	59.20	63.91	60.66	67.52	251.27	64.06	
-	6	-	-	.318	.401	.579	248	.395	409	.651	71.26	74.00	67.05	71.78	284.09	72.43	
-	2	-	-	.313	.404	.588	209	.349	389	.649	60.06	65.38	63.77	71.57	260.78	66.49	
-	2	-	-	.345	.425	.618	294	.450	438	.670	84.48	84.24	71.80	73.81	314.34	80.14	
-	1	-	-	.356	.454	.723	337	.488	532	.770	96.84	91.39	87.21	84.85	360.29	91.86	
-	-	-	-	.261	.362	.435	127	.277	236	.515	36.49	51.96	38.69	56.79	183.93	46.90	
-	1	-	-	.297	.366	.538	200	.375	313	.587	57.47	70.31	51.31	64.72	243.82	62.16	
-	-	-	8	.267	.359	.389	95	.226	199	.474	27.30	42.38	32.62	52.22	154.53	39.40	
-	-	-	7	.245	.383	.365	54	.223	113	.467	15.52	41.81	18.52	51.46	127.32	32.46	
5	20	-	15	.307	.395	.545	1,947	.356	3,334	.610	43.55	85.25	39.42	81.03	249.25	63.65	85
9	37	-	27	.307	.395	.545	3,560	.356	6,096	.610	85.25	85.25	81.03	81.03	332.56	83.14	14
11	42	-	32	.307	.395	.545	4,090	.356	7,004	.610	78.31	85.25	74.44	81.03	319.03	79.76	18
5	20	-	8	.310	.396	.553	1,893	.363	3,219	.617	64.30	82.75	64.94	77.85	289.84	74.34	52
-	17	-	-	.331	.419	.612	1,294	.407	2,138	.673	85.02	87.13	81.98	81.62	335.74	86.02	11
-	1	-	-	.356	.454	.723	337	.488	532	.770	96.84	91.39	87.21	84.85	360.29	91.86	5
-	2	-	-	.345	.425	.618	294	.450	438	.670	84.48	84.24	71.80	73.81	314.34	80.14	53
-	6	-	-	.318	.401	.579	248	.395	409	.651	71.26	74.00	67.05	71.78	284.09	72.43	199

Complete Career Statistics W

Total Career Statistics & Adjusted Career, 10 year, 5 year, and Single Year Analysis

Winfield, Dave: *David Mark Winfield, b. Oct. 3, 1951, St. Paul, MN*

Rating Category	Year	Ranked Seasons & Adjustment	G	AB	H	1B	2B	3B	HR	RUN	RBI	BB	SO	SB
	1973		56	141	39	31	4	1	3	9	12	12	19	-
	1974		145	498	132	90	18	4	20	57	75	40	96	9
	1975		143	509	136	99	20	2	15	74	76	69	82	23
	1976		137	492	139	96	26	4	13	81	69	65	78	26
	1977		157	615	169	108	29	7	25	104	92	58	75	16
	1978		158	587	181	122	30	5	24	88	97	55	81	21
10 Year Total	1979	1st	159	597	184	113	27	10	34	97	118	85	71	15
	1980		162	558	154	103	25	6	20	89	87	79	83	23
	1981		105	388	114	75	25	1	13	52	68	43	41	11
5 Year Total	1982		140	539	151	82	24	8	37	84	106	45	64	5
	1983		152	598	169	103	26	8	32	99	116	58	77	15
	1984		141	567	193	136	34	4	19	106	100	53	71	6
	1985		155	633	174	108	34	6	26	105	114	52	96	19
	1986		154	565	148	88	31	5	24	90	104	77	106	6
	1987		156	575	158	108	22	1	27	83	97	76	96	5
	1988		149	559	180	116	37	2	25	96	107	69	88	9
	1990		132	475	127	83	21	2	21	70	78	52	81	-
	1991		150	568	149	90	27	4	28	75	86	56	109	7
	1992		156	583	169	107	33	3	26	92	108	82	89	2
	1993		143	547	148	98	27	2	21	72	76	45	106	2
	1994		77	294	74	46	15	3	10	35	43	31	51	2
	1995		46	115	22	15	5	-	2	11	4	14	26	1
Career Total	1973-1995		2,973	11,003	3,110	2,017	540	88	465	1,669	1,833	1,216	1,686	223
Career Adj. to 10,000 BO	1973-1995	0.790014	2,349	8,693	2,457	1,593	427	70	367	1,319	1,448	961	1,332	176
Career Adj. to 10,000 AB	1973-1995	0.908843	2,702	10,000	2,827	1,833	491	80	423	1,517	1,666	1,105	1,532	203
10 Year Total	1979-1988		1,473	5,579	1,625	1,032	285	51	257	901	1,017	637	793	114
5 Year Total	1982-1986		742	2,902	835	517	149	31	138	484	540	285	414	51
Best Single Year	1979		159	597	184	113	27	10	34	97	118	85	71	15

Total Career Statistics & Adjusted Career, 10 year, 5 year, and Single Year Analysis

Winfield, Dave

CS	HBP	SF	GDP	AVG	OBP	SLG	TRP	RPA	TNB	TBA	TRP Rating	RPA Rating	TNB Rating	TBA Rating	TOP	Rating	Ranking
-	-	1	5	.277	.331	.383	21	.132	66	.415	6.03	24.75	10.82	45.75	87.35	22.27	
7	1	5	14	.265	.318	.438	132	.237	261	.468	37.93	44.33	42.79	51.55	176.60	45.02	
4	3	7	11	.267	.354	.403	150	.250	296	.494	43.10	46.92	48.52	54.46	193.01	49.21	
7	3	5	14	.283	.366	.431	150	.259	299	.516	43.10	48.54	49.02	56.92	197.58	50.37	
7	-	5	12	.275	.335	.467	196	.284	354	.513	56.32	53.23	58.03	56.54	224.13	57.14	
9	2	5	13	.308	.367	.499	185	.279	362	.547	53.16	52.36	59.34	60.27	225.14	57.40	
9	2	2	9	.308	.395	.558	215	.309	426	.613	61.78	57.97	69.84	67.56	257.14	65.56	
7	2	4	13	.276	.365	.450	176	.268	348	.530	50.57	50.27	57.05	58.47	216.36	55.16	
1	1	7	13	.294	.360	.464	120	.265	234	.518	34.48	49.75	38.36	57.06	179.65	45.80	
3	-	8	20	.280	.331	.560	190	.310	349	.570	54.60	58.17	57.21	62.85	232.84	59.36	
6	2	6	30	.283	.345	.513	215	.310	376	.542	61.78	58.05	61.64	59.71	241.18	61.49	
4	-	6	14	.340	.393	.515	206	.322	347	.542	59.20	60.31	56.89	59.76	236.15	60.21	
7	-	4	17	.275	.328	.471	219	.310	362	.513	62.93	58.13	59.34	56.51	236.91	60.40	
5	2	6	20	.262	.349	.462	194	.290	341	.509	55.75	54.26	55.90	56.09	222.00	56.60	
6	-	3	20	.275	.358	.457	180	.267	338	.501	51.72	50.04	55.41	55.27	212.45	54.17	
4	2	1	19	.322	.398	.530	203	.312	372	.572	58.33	58.52	60.98	63.08	240.91	61.42	
1	2	7	17	.267	.338	.453	148	.268	268	.485	42.53	50.15	43.93	53.41	190.03	48.45	
2	1	6	21	.262	.326	.472	161	.247	330	.506	46.26	46.27	54.10	55.78	202.42	51.61	
3	1	3	10	.290	.377	.491	200	.295	368	.542	57.47	55.19	60.33	59.73	232.73	59.34	
3	-	2	15	.271	.325	.442	148	.243	286	.470	42.53	45.54	46.89	51.76	186.71	47.60	
1	-	2	7	.252	.321	.425	78	.234	157	.470	22.41	43.76	25.74	51.81	143.72	36.64	
-	1	-	5	.191	.285	.287	15	.111	49	.363	4.31	20.82	8.03	40.00	73.17	18.65	
96	25	95	319	.283	.353	.475	3,502	.277	6,589	.521	78.33	66.25	77.91	69.19	291.68	74.49	26
76	20	75	252	.283	.353	.475	2,767	.277	5,205	.521	66.25	66.25	69.19	69.19	270.88	67.72	110
87	23	86	290	.283	.353	.475	3,183	.277	5,988	.521	60.93	66.25	63.64	69.19	260.02	65.00	108
52	11	47	175	.291	.362	.499	1,918	.297	3,493	.542	65.15	67.82	70.47	68.34	271.78	69.71	80
25	4	30	101	.288	.349	.503	1,024	.308	1,775	.534	67.28	65.92	68.06	64.78	266.04	68.16	112
9	2	2	9	.308	.395	.558	215	.309	426	.613	61.78	57.97	69.84	67.56	257.14	65.56	358

Complete Career Statistics W

Total Career Statistics & Adjusted Career, 10 year, 5 year, and Single Year Analysis

Yastrzemski, Carl: *Carl Michael "Yaz" Yastrzemski, b. Aug, 22, 1939, Southampton, NY*

Rating Category	Year	Ranked Seasons & Adjustment	G	AB	H	1B	2B	3B	HR	RUN	RBI	BB	SO	SB
	1961		148	583	155	107	31	6	11	71	80	50	97	6
	1962		160	646	191	123	43	6	19	99	94	66	82	7
	1963		151	570	183	126	40	3	14	91	68	95	72	8
	1964		151	567	164	111	29	9	15	77	67	75	90	6
	1965		133	494	154	86	45	3	20	78	72	70	58	7
	1966		160	594	165	108	39	2	16	81	80	84	60	8
	1967	1st	161	579	189	110	31	4	44	112	121	91	69	10
	1968		157	539	162	105	32	2	23	90	74	119	90	13
	1969		162	603	154	84	28	2	40	96	111	101	91	15
	1970	2nd	161	566	186	117	29	–	40	125	102	128	66	23
	1971		148	508	129	91	21	2	15	75	70	106	60	8
	1972		125	455	120	88	18	2	12	70	68	67	44	5
	1973		152	540	160	112	25	4	19	82	95	105	58	9
	1974		148	515	155	113	25	2	15	93	79	104	48	12
	1975		149	543	146	101	30	1	14	91	60	87	67	8
	1976		155	546	146	100	23	2	21	71	102	80	67	5
	1977		150	558	165	107	27	3	28	99	102	73	40	11
	1978		144	523	145	105	21	2	17	70	81	76	44	4
	1979		147	518	140	90	28	1	21	69	87	62	46	3
	1980		105	364	100	63	21	1	15	49	50	44	38	–
	1981		91	338	83	61	14	1	7	36	53	49	28	–
	1982		131	459	126	87	22	1	16	53	72	59	50	–
	1983		119	380	101	67	24	–	10	38	56	54	29	–
Career Total	1961-1983		3,308	11,988	3,419	2,262	646	59	452	1,816	1,844	1,845	1,394	168
Career Adj. to 10,000 BO	1961-1983	0.699252	2,313	8,383	2,391	1,582	452	41	316	1,270	1,289	1,290	975	117
Career Adj. to 10,000 AB	1961-1983	0.834168	2,759	10,000	2,852	1,887	539	49	377	1,515	1,538	1,539	1,163	140
10 Year Total	1965-1974		1,507	5,393	1,574	1,014	293	23	244	902	872	975	644	110
5 Year Total	1966-1971		801	2,881	856	524	159	10	163	504	488	523	376	69
Best Single Year	1967		161	579	189	110	31	4	44	112	121	91	69	10
2nd Best Year	1970		161	566	186	117	29	–	40	125	102	128	66	23

(Rating Category column spans, left to right: 10 Year Total, 5 Year Total)

Complete Career Statistics Y

Total Career Statistics & Adjusted Career, 10 year, 5 year, and Single Year Analysis

Yastrzemski, Carl

CS	HBP	SF	GDP	AVG	OBP	SLG	Total Offensive Production Statistics				TRP Rating	RPA Rating	TNB Rating	TBA Rating	TOP Composite		
							TRP	RPA	TNB	TBA					TOP	Rating	Ranking
5	3	5	19	.266	.324	.396	151	.229	285	.432	43.39	42.87	46.72	47.59	180.58	46.04	
4	3	2	27	.296	.363	.469	193	.259	375	.504	55.46	48.61	61.48	55.55	221.10	56.37	
5	1	1	12	.321	.418	.475	159	.234	370	.545	45.69	43.88	60.66	60.06	210.28	53.61	
5	2	1	30	.289	.374	.451	144	.213	334	.495	41.38	39.97	54.75	54.54	190.64	48.61	
6	1	4	16	.312	.395	.536	150	.256	337	.576	43.10	48.05	55.25	63.49	209.89	53.51	
9	1	1	17	.278	.368	.431	161	.231	340	.488	46.26	43.28	55.74	53.76	199.05	50.75	
8	4	5	5	.326	.418	.622	233	.341	457	.668	66.95	63.83	74.92	73.64	279.34	71.22	
6	2	4	12	.301	.426	.495	164	.243	395	.584	47.13	45.46	64.75	64.40	221.74	56.53	
7	1	2	14	.255	.362	.507	207	.287	416	.577	59.48	53.80	68.20	63.59	245.07	62.48	
13	1	2	12	.329	.452	.592	227	.320	474	.669	65.23	59.99	77.70	73.68	276.61	70.52	
7	1	5	14	.254	.381	.392	145	.229	307	.484	41.67	42.86	50.33	53.37	188.22	47.99	
4	4	9	13	.264	.357	.391	138	.252	250	.456	39.66	47.19	40.98	50.28	178.11	45.41	
7	-	6	19	.296	.407	.463	177	.264	357	.533	50.86	49.50	58.52	58.73	217.62	55.48	
7	3	11	12	.301	.414	.445	172	.267	341	.529	49.43	49.97	55.90	58.27	213.56	54.45	
4	2	2	14	.269	.371	.405	151	.233	313	.483	43.39	43.66	51.31	53.24	191.60	48.85	
6	1	8	12	.267	.357	.432	173	.267	316	.488	49.71	50.10	51.80	53.83	205.45	52.38	
1	1	11	10	.296	.372	.505	201	.308	366	.560	57.76	57.68	60.00	61.77	237.21	60.48	
5	3	8	9	.277	.367	.423	151	.244	299	.483	43.39	45.71	49.02	53.24	191.35	48.79	
3	2	8	12	.270	.346	.450	156	.259	297	.493	44.83	48.56	48.69	54.37	196.45	50.09	
2	-	3	9	.275	.350	.462	99	.236	210	.500	28.45	44.17	34.43	55.11	162.15	41.34	
1	-	3	10	.246	.338	.355	89	.223	168	.420	25.57	41.69	27.54	46.29	141.10	35.97	
1	2	3	12	.275	.358	.431	125	.234	258	.482	35.92	43.78	42.30	53.15	175.15	44.65	
-	2	1	13	.266	.359	.408	94	.209	211	.469	27.01	39.14	34.59	51.68	152.42	38.86	
116	40	105	323	.285	.379	.462	3,660	.256	7,476	.523	81.86	61.28	88.40	69.49	301.03	76.88	18
81	28	73	226	.285	.379	.462	2,559	.256	5,228	.523	61.28	61.28	69.49	69.49	261.54	65.39	121
97	33	88	269	.285	.379	.462	3,053	.256	6,236	.523	58.45	61.28	66.28	69.49	255.50	63.87	117
74	18	49	134	.292	.399	.490	1,774	.270	3,674	.559	60.26	61.58	74.12	70.57	266.53	68.36	87
43	9	14	60	.297	.405	.529	992	.284	2,082	.597	65.18	60.84	79.83	72.39	278.23	71.28	90
8	4	5	5	.326	.418	.622	233	.341	457	.668	66.95	63.83	74.92	73.64	279.34	71.22	243
13	1	2	12	.329	.452	.592	227	.320	474	.669	65.23	59.99	77.70	73.68	276.61	70.52	269

Complete Career Statistics Y

Total Career Statistics & Adjusted Career, 10 year, 5 year, and Single Year Analysis

York, Rudy: *Preston Rudolph York, b. Aug. 17, 1913, Ragland, AL*

Rating Category			Year	Ranked Seasons & Adjustment	G	AB	H	1B	2B	3B	HR	RUN	RBI	BB	SO	SB
			1934		3	6	1	1	-	-	-	-	-	1	3	-
10 Year Total	5 Year Total		1937		104	375	115	59	18	3	35	72	103	41	52	3
			1938		135	463	138	76	27	2	33	85	127	92	74	1
			1939		102	329	101	64	16	1	20	66	68	41	50	5
			1940	1st	155	588	186	101	46	6	33	105	134	89	88	3
			1941		155	590	153	94	29	3	27	91	111	92	88	3
			1942		153	577	150	99	26	4	21	81	90	73	71	3
			1943		155	571	155	88	22	11	34	90	118	84	88	5
			1944		151	583	161	109	27	7	18	77	98	68	73	5
			1945		155	595	157	109	25	5	18	71	87	59	85	6
			1946		154	579	160	107	30	6	17	78	119	86	93	3
			1947		150	584	136	86	25	4	21	56	91	58	87	1
			1948		31	51	8	8	-	-	-	4	6	7	15	-
Career Total			1934-1948		1,603	5,891	1,621	1,001	291	52	277	876	1,152	791	867	38
Career Adj. to 10,000 BO			1934-1948	1.460067	2,340	8,601	2,367	1,462	425	76	404	1,279	1,682	1,155	1,266	55
Career Adj. to 10,000 AB			1934-1948	1.697505	2,721	10,000	2,752	1,699	494	88	470	1,487	1,956	1,343	1,472	65
10 Year Total			1937-1946		1,419	5,250	1,476	906	266	48	256	816	1,055	725	762	37
5 Year Total			1937-1941		651	2,345	693	394	136	15	148	419	543	355	352	15
Best Single Year			1940		155	588	186	101	46	6	33	105	134	89	88	3

* Player missed time for military service. 5 and 10 consecutive year statistics may exclude or consolidate years of military service.

** Active player. Statistics through 2004 season

TOP ranking for players with less than 70% rating is based upon comparison to listed players only.

Total Career Statistics & Adjusted Career, 10 year, 5 year, and Single Year Analysis

York, Rudy

CS	HBP	SF	GDP	AVG	OBP	SLG	Total Offensive Production Statistics				TRP Rating	RPA Rating	TNB Rating	TBA Rating	TOP Composite		
							TRP	RPA	TNB	TBA					TOP	Rating	Ranking
-	-	-	-	.167	.286	.167	-	.000	2	.286	-	-	0.33	31.49	31.82	8.11	
2	-	-	-	.307	.375	.651	175	.421	286	.688	50.29	78.83	46.89	75.77	251.77	64.19	
2	2	-	-	.298	.417	.579	212	.381	361	.648	60.92	71.32	59.18	71.43	262.85	67.02	
-	2	-	8	.307	.387	.544	134	.353	227	.597	38.51	66.08	37.21	65.84	207.63	52.94	
2	4	-	12	.316	.410	.583	239	.345	437	.631	68.68	64.62	71.64	69.50	274.44	69.97	
1	1	-	16	.259	.360	.456	202	.289	364	.521	58.05	54.15	59.67	57.39	229.26	58.45	
3	-	-	16	.260	.343	.428	171	.257	320	.480	49.14	48.11	52.46	52.96	202.66	51.67	
5	1	-	22	.271	.366	.527	208	.307	386	.569	59.77	57.49	63.28	62.75	243.28	62.03	
3	1	-	18	.276	.353	.439	175	.261	327	.488	50.29	48.94	53.61	53.79	206.63	52.68	
6	-	-	23	.264	.330	.413	158	.233	305	.451	45.40	43.73	50.00	49.65	188.79	48.13	
2	1	-	16	.276	.371	.437	197	.289	341	.500	56.61	54.13	55.90	55.11	221.74	56.54	
-	-	-	22	.233	.302	.397	147	.221	291	.438	42.24	41.48	47.70	48.30	179.73	45.82	
-	-	-	2	.157	.259	.157	10	.167	15	.250	2.87	31.23	2.46	27.55	64.12	16.35	
26	12	-	155	.275	.362	.483	2,028	.296	3,662	.535	45.36	70.90	43.30	71.07	230.64	58.90	107
38	18	-	226	.275	.362	.483	2,961	.296	5,347	.535	70.90	70.90	71.07	71.07	283.95	70.99	89
44	20	-	263	.275	.362	.483	3,443	.296	6,216	.535	65.91	70.90	66.06	71.07	273.95	68.49	88
26	12	-	131	.281	.370	.496	1,871	.306	3,354	.548	63.55	69.74	67.66	69.17	270.13	69.29	84
7	9	-	36	.296	.390	.556	962	.350	1,675	.610	63.21	74.94	64.23	73.98	276.36	70.80	96
2	4	-	12	.316	.410	.583	239	.345	437	.631	68.68	64.62	71.64	69.50	274.44	69.97	314

Complete Career Statistics Y

GLOSSARY OF BASEBALL STATISTICS

Capitalized terms are defined in this glossary. Some rules and time lines for their adoption are set forth in Chapter 4 of this book.

At-Bats: An official **At-Bat (AB)** is charged to the batter when he makes a hit or an out (including obtaining a base on an error). They are not counted for Walks, HBP, and at various times, for Sacrifice Flies (SF) or sacrifice bunts.

Base on Balls: (BB) or **Walk** awards a batter first base when the pitcher throws four balls (pitches outside the strike zone that the batter does not convert to a strike by swinging) prior to a hit or out. The number of balls for a walk was varied (see Chapter 4).

Batting Average: (BA) or **(AVG)** is calculated as base hits divided by official At-Bats.

Batting Opportunities: (BO) is the same as Plate Appearances used today for computing a player's On-Base-Percentage, but adding one Batting Opportunity for each appearance lost to the team due to hitting into a double play (GDP). It therefore includes (i) official At-Bats; (ii) Walks, HBP and SF (included in official Plate Appearances); and (iii) one additional Batting Opportunity for each time the player Grounds into a Double Play (GDP).

Caught Stealing: (CS) occurs when a runner is put out trying to steal a base or leading off from a base. This is a reduction of one base in the computation of TNB and TBA.

Games: (G) are the number of games in which a player appears as a batter, runner, fielder and/or pitcher, whether or not the player gets an official At-Bat or Plate Appearance. This number does not apply to any of the TOP statistics.

Ground-Into-Double-Play: (GDP) is the act of a batter creating two outs in a single At-Bat, usually by forcing out two runners (which need not include the batter). This results in an additional lost Batting Opportunity to the team, and is therefore included in the denominator of the TBA and RPA.

Hit-By-Pitch: (HBP) occurs when a batter receives a base for being hit by a pitch. It is included as reaching base and as a Plate Appearance for the OBP, as a base for TNB, and as a Batting Opportunity for the TBA and RPA.

Hit: or **Base Hits** are scored when a batter safely reaches first base as a result of a batted ball that touches the field (or is fair and out of the field), subject to unusual situations scored by the official scorer. Hits are scored as a **Single (IB)**, **Double (2B)**, **Triple (3B)** or **Home Run (HR)** depending upon the base at which a batter stops as a result of his own batted ball, considering all the details. All Hits are included in BA, OBP, SLG, Total Bases, TNB and TBA.

On-Base-Percentage: (OBP) is the average of a player's times attaining a base divided by his total Plate Appearances. Attaining a base includes Hits + Walks + Hit-By-Pitch (HBP) plus Sacrifice Flies (SF). Plate Appearances are defined below.

Plate Appearances: (PA) are recorded for the times a player completes a turn at the plate, and are used in the computation of a player's On-Base-Percentage (OBP). It includes all official At-Bats + Walks + HBP + SF.

Run: are scored for a batter when the batter safely reaches home plate and the run is scored for his team. Runs are included in TRP and RPA.

Run-Batted-In: (RBIs) are scored for a batter when an offensive player (whether or not the batter) safely reaches home plate as a result of the batter's action at the plate. A batter does not receive a RBI if the run scored is the result of a double play or an error that would not normally score a run. RBIs are included in TRP and RPA.

Run Production Average: (RPA)™ is an average computed by dividing the Total Run Production (TRP) of a player by his Batting Opportunities (defined above).

Sacrifices: are scored when a batter intentionally advances a runner while creating an out through a fly ball (**Sacrifice Fly (SF)**) or a bunt (**Sacrifice Bunt**). While the rule has been changed from time to time, in most statistical services (and this book) a Sacrifice Fly is not counted as an official At-Bat, but is considered a Plate Appearance or Batting Opportunity, while Sacrifice Bunts are included as official At-Bats. SF is therefore not included in the computation of BA or SLG, but is included in the OBP, TBA and RPA.

Slugging Average: (SLG) is the average bases earned by a player for each official At-Bat. It is the average of the Total Bases of a player divided by his official At-Bats.

Stolen Bases: (SB) are credited to a runner who safely advances a base without the assistance of a batting activity, wild pitch or pass ball. Certain steals are not counted when there is no attempt to stop the steal or need to do so. SBs are included in TNB and the TBA.

Strike Out: (SO) is charged to a batter when an out results from a third strike (including a dropped third strike) or a foul bunt after two strikes. More than three strikes were necessary in some early years (see Chapter 4). SOs are not included in any averages or TOP statistics.

Total Base Average: (TBA)™ is the average of the Total Net Bases (TNB) of a player divided by his Batting Opportunities (defined above).

Total Bases: (TB) is a single number combining the bases hit by a player and used for the determination of a player's Slugging Average (single =1, double =2, triple =3, and home run=4). It is a component of TNB and TBA.

Total Net Bases: (TNB)™ is a single number combining Total Bases as used for the determination of a player's Slugging Average (single =1, double =2, triple =3, and home run=4) plus the bases used for a player's On-Base-Percentage (Walks and times HBP). To these numbers are added the other bases created by a player and those reduced by the player. Total Net Bases therefore also adds a base for each Stolen Base and reduces the total for each time the player is Caught Stealing. **Total Net Bases (TNB)**™ is therefore Total Bases + Walks +HBP + SB – CS.

Total Offensive Production: (TOP)™ is a combination of the relative ratings for the four individual TOP statistics (TRP, RPA, TNB and TBA). Each player is first rated with all others for the same category and given a relative rating for that statistic based on the highest number in that category. The highest rating for a player in each category would be 100.00, and each player with a lesser statistic would be given a rating based upon his percentage of that number. If, for instance, the highest TRP for a season was 360, that player would have a 100.00 TRP rating. A player with a TRP of 270 would have a TRP rating of 75.00 (270/360). The combination of these four ratings is the TOP Composite of the player, and the TOP Rating is the TOP Composite adjusted to produce a 100.00 for the highest player and lower ratings for all others. By combining the best statistics available, statistics that cover all factors for batting prowess, the Total Offensive Production (TOP) of a player should allow each player to be judged against his peers on a fair and equal basis.

Total Offensive Production Ranking is the listing, in numeric order, of the best baseball batters based upon their relative TOP Rating for the category (single season, career, etc.).

Glossary

Total Offensive Production Rating is a rating of 100.00 and below, based upon the total of any player for all four Total Offensive Production Statistics (calculated for a season, consecutive year period or career—whether actual or adjusted) and compared to the best total for those combined statistics for that period.

Total Offensive Production Statistics are all of the four new statistics developed by this book, including **Total Run Production (TRP)**™, **Run Production Average (RPA)**™, **Total Net Bases (TNB)**™, and **Total Base Average (TBA)**™

Total Run Production: **(TRP)**™ is the total of all Runs scored by the player plus all Runs-Batted-In by the player for the period over which the statistic is determined (i.e., a season, 5 year period or career).

* Total Offensive Production (TOP)™, Total Net Bases (TNB)™, Total Run Production (TRP)™, Total Base Average (TBA)™ and Run Production Average (RPA)™ are service marks of SportStats LLC, and cannot be used without its permission. Application for registration of these marks has been filed with the U.S. Patent and Trademark Office.

PLAYER INDEX

Player Index